A
DICTIONARY
OF
CONTEMPORARY
QUOTATIONS

Also by Jonathon Green
in Pan Books
Famous Last Words

A
DICTIONARY
OF
CONTEMPORARY
QUOTATIONS

COMPILED BY
JONATHON GREEN

DAVID & CHARLES
Newton Abbot   London

British Library Cataloguing in Publication Data

Green, Jonathon
  A dictionary of contemporary quotations.
  1. Quotations, English
  I. Title
  080   PN6081

  ISBN 0–7153–8417–1

Printed in Great Britain
by Redwood Burn Ltd, Trowbridge, Wiltshire
for David & Charles (Publishers) Limited
Brunel House Newton Abbot Devon

For
LMG and SF

ACKNOWLEDGEMENTS

In collecting these entries I have been helped and encouraged by many people in many ways. To name everyone who offered their personal favourite would be impossible, but I would like to mention these in person:

In particular Susie Ford and my parents.
Also Don Atyeo, Klaus Boehm, Kyle Cathie, Michael Cohen, Nick Cole, Mick and Betsy Farren, Leslie Gardner, Rebecca John, Pearce Marchbank, Heather Page, Susan Ready, Cindy Rose, Shaie Selzer, Clare Toynbee and Vanessa Williams-Ellis.

I am also grateful for the help provided by the staffs of these libraries:

The London Library, the British Library, the Bodleian Library, the New York Public Library, Leicester University, Australia House, Camden, Kensington and Westminster Reference Libraries.

CONTENTS

INTRODUCTION

This is a collection of some seven thousand modern quotations, dating in the main from 1945 to the present day. They range over the widest possible areas of contemporary life, adding to the usually quoted worlds of politics, poetry, the theatre and writing those of science, television, film, rock 'n'roll, psychology and many more. The whole diversity, as far as possible, of modern life.

It is, of course, a book more of 'quotes', in the journalistic sense – celebrity opinions, snappy one-liners – than one of the traditional deathless 'quotation', embodied, and some might say entombed, in more venerable collections. Culled in great part from ephemeral journalism rather than the finely honed *mots*, the proverbial generalities and the popular favourites from the classics that are the staples of older dictionaries, these entries come freshly minted and as yet unsanctified by century-long use. While some of them certainly are, or will certainly grow to be quotations in the traditional sense, few so far will help addicts of the *Times* crossword.

This is hardly surprising. In an age of mass media, of instant communication, the honing process has little chance; the flood of information is simply too vigorous, too unremitting to allow so gradual a development. Yet, paradoxically, it is this same flood of information, and the mass literacy to which it caters, that make a book of strictly modern quotations, ranging outside the traditional disciplines, both necessary and feasible. The traditional dictionaries of quotations were, and remain, rooted in the tastes of a small elite of the knowledgable, whose own libraries more often than not would contain many of the volumes from which the quotations were drawn. Today's public is so much larger and its interests are correspondingly more diverse. The line between scholarly and popular cultures persists, indeed the two may be far more distant, but now the less scholarly areas can claim their own validity. For better or for worse, more people want to hear from Ernie Wise than from Wittgenstein – and they are both available here.

Thus mass culture has come to be the predominant culture and if its audience lacks the intellectual cachet of more rarified zones it is still the culture that sways more and more of the media and which has contributed massively to this collection. Its vast nature has naturally meant that the quotations gathered here are only a representative fraction of those available. It would have hardly been possible for me to read and review everything. In the end these entries are the ones that I have selected from the sources that I have chosen to research. By this token it stands as an unashamedly idiosyncratic book. From the press clippings, the magazines, the bound volumes, the books and periodicals, the interviews, slogans, film and radio scripts – I have pulled out the lines, the phrases and paragraphs which have appealed to me, and, I would hope, to the larger audience. The sources are innumerable, I have touched on only the most accessible fraction. These quotations remain my favourite lines from my preferred sources, extending my limits when and where I could. Naturally I have checked out my fellow compilers, but I trust that on the whole my ideas and researches remain the basis of this collection.

It has been suggested that in putting together a collection of modern quotes which inevitably lacks the honing process of the decades, I am creating my own *ad hoc* 'quotations'. If that is so, I would be delighted, though all credit must go to those who spoke the lines in the first place. But whether or not these entries are accorded the status of the *Oxford Dictionary of Quotations*, they all together offer something unavailable to that august volume. This dictionary is above all a verbal picture of the last three and a half decades, from a multitude of attitudes and from several thousand points of view. If, as it seems, the overall tone tends towards the pessimistic, albeit reasonably wittily, then that no doubt is a reflection of my own view and the one my tastes have led me to assemble.

Idiosyncratic or not, I *have* attempted to include all the most generally remembered quotations and the section called 'Events' includes the verbal vignettes of the last thirty-five years – the scandals, the revelations and the comments on a variety of current affairs. Similarly 'Abuse' contains the sharper put-downs of one purportedly great man or woman of their hapless peers. But for those lines honestly and best recalled by most people, the areas to pursue are those of the advertising slogans and the media catchphrases. Like the lyrics of those favourite pop songs whose releases delineated our adolescence, the great campaigns and the great comedy lines have lodged in the collective subconscious. 'Drinka Pinta Milka Day', 'Wakey-Wakey!!', 'Didn't he do well???' – the whole ghastly, irresistible gamut.

It was the massive common memory of such lines that inspired this book in the first place and I hope they are adequately represented. Along side them come the rest of the modern pop culture parade. Rock stars, film stars, radio and TV 'personalities', sportsmen and women, architects, photographers, painters, sculptors, actors, psychoanalysts, entrepreneurs and the rest. Variously they comment on the myriad aspects of the world, and occasionally on each other, both to congratulate and to condemn. And in the midst of such a welter of modernity, there are still many representatives of the more traditional areas. Scholars, writers, philosophers, critics, statesmen, politicians and generals. They are all as forthcoming as ever. I have also attempted to feature scientists, usually an under-represented group, as an articulate complement to so much 'arts' pontification.

In no sense would I propose that this dictionary be considered as 'the last word'. It is merely a collection of the latest. It is, and cannot be, either definitive or truly complete, but to me, at least, these are among its charms. The world would be even more terrifying if this were the sum of its comments. It should be, nonetheless, enjoyable, interesting and even informative. I trust that it will prove all of these.

A note on 'literature'

As will become obvious at the briefest glance, 'literature' – works of fiction – does not figure massively below. The Dictionary is essentially a non-fiction compilation. There are a number of plays and films but, justifiably or not, I found myself having to steer clear of the novel, but for a small selection of literary 'one-offs', discovered by chance rather than actively pursued. In the end I felt, alleged decline or not of the novel notwithstanding, that I was simply not equipped to make an adequate selection of quotes from thirty-five years of fiction. I regret the omission, but can only say, to paraphrase Lenny Bruce: if you can select the one-liners from *Gravity's Rainbow*, you may cast the first stone.

A note on sources, dates, etc.

The idea for this book emerged in 1974, although it did not start to take on its present shape until 1979. Thus I have been collecting quotations, at first sporadically, but with an increasingly consuming obsession, for about seven years. This means, unfortunately, that their dating and attribution is nothing if not variable. Where possible I have included the full name, occupation, source and date of my originator and his or her quotation. More often, I fear, the reader must bear with a less immaculate reference, the result either of ignorance, forgetfulness or the condition of whatever scrap of paper I was using as a filing system at the time. Where I have inserted the word 'quoted' or 'quoted in', I am citing the secondary source – most likely a magazine or newspaper – in which the quote was used without proper attribution. If the line comes from an interview, a piece of writing, or similar direct source, then it stands as it is.

The intention of this book was to limit my selections to a period after 1945. To a very great extent I have disciplined myself accordingly, even though this has meant excluding many personal, and still reasonably modern favourites. In the end I have stretched the boundary slightly. To forestall chronological criticisms I should explain: If a subject died within the period and was not in his or her dotage throughout, then I have let the occasional earlier line slip through. For instance, Jean Cocteau, thriving well into the Sixties, may well have offered some of his *mots* in prewar days. On the other hand, where a subject has been sufficiently prolific, such as Orwell, both before and after the war, I have tried to exclude the pre-1945 offerings, irrespective of quality. Like all rules, these are made to be broken and I claim no perfect consistency.

Finally, as to accuracy, I can only promise that I made no quotation up. For what the press may have done before me, I naturally cannot speak.

If you have any suggestions for quotations to be included in future editions of this book please send them to me c/o Pan Books Ltd, Cavaye Place, London, SW10 9PG.

Jonathon Green

UNIVERSE
The World

T. W. ADORNO
German academic
quoted in New York Review of Books 1971
Of the world as it exists, one cannot be
enough afraid.

PETER BEARD
American photographer
in 'Loose Talk' ed. Linda Botts 1980
The whole world is a scab. The point is
to pick it constructively.

SIR ISAIAH BERLIN
British philosopher
Sunday Times 1962
Man cannot live without seeking to de-
scribe and explain the universe.

STEWART BRAND
American environmentalist
Esquire 1970
You can't blame the baby for the
afterbirth.

ELIAS CANETTI
Bulgarian writer 1957
The Earth – a globe carelessly hurled
into the Universe to annoy the Heavens.

RAYMOND CHANDLER
American novelist
'The Simple Art of Murder' 1950
It is not a very fragrant world, but it is
the world you live in, and certain writers
with tough minds and a cool spirit of
detachment can make very interesting
and even amusing patterns out of it. It
is not funny that a man should be killed,
but it is sometimes funny that he should
be killed for so little and that his death
should be the coin of what we call
civilisation.

QUENTIN CRISP
British author
'The Naked Civil Servant' 1968
Is not the whole world a vast house of
assignation to which the filing system
has been lost?

MARY DOUGLAS
'Purity and Danger'
Where there is dirt there is system. Dirt
is the by-product of a systematic ordering and classification of matter.

GEORGES DUHAMEL
French writer
'Cecile parmi nous'
The desire for order is the only order in
the world.

ALBERT EINSTEIN
German physicist
The environment is everything that isn't
me.

Life 1950
The most incomprehensible thing about
the world is that it is comprehensible.

R. BUCKMINSTER FULLER
American engineer
quoted in 'Contemporary Architects' 1980
You can't reorder the world by talking
to it.

The most important thing about Spaceship Earth – an instruction book didn't
come with it.

EDWARD GOREY
American illustrator
Esquire 1976
The world is not what it purports to be,
but it has no other meaning.

ARLO GUTHRIE
American singer
The world has shown me what it has to
offer ... it's a nice place to visit but I
wouldn't want to live there.

ARTHUR KOESTLER
British philosopher 1978
In my twenties I regarded the universe
as an open book full of mathematical
formulae. And now I regard it as an
invisible piece of writing in which we
can now and then decipher a letter or a
word and then it's gone again.

STANLEY KUBRICK
American film director
The destruction of this planet would have no significance on a cosmic scale. To an observer in the Andromeda nebula, the sign of our extinction would be no more than a match flaring for a second in the heavens.

R. D. LAING
British psychiatrist
'The Politics of Experience' 1967
We live in a moment of history where change is so speeded up that we begin to see the present only when it is already disappearing.

JOHN LENNON &
PAUL McCARTNEY
British rock composers
'Yellow Submarine'
We all live in a yellow submarine. (Northern Songs)

CLAUDE LEVI-STRAUSS
French anthropologist
'Tristes Tropiques' 1955
The world began without man, and it will complete itself without him.

GEN. DOUGLAS MacARTHUR
American soldier 1955
There is no security on this earth, there is only opportunity.

MARSHALL McLUHAN
Canadian academic
'The Gutenberg Galaxy' 1962
The new electronic interdependence recreates the world in the image of a global village.

HENRY MILLER
American writer
'Sexus' 1949
The world is *not* to be put in order, the world *is* order incarnate. It is for us to put ourselves in unison with this order., to know what is the world order in contradistinction to the wishful thinking orders we wish to impose upon one another. The power which we long to possess, in order to establish the good, the true and the beautiful would prove to be, if we could have it, but the means of destroying one another. It is fortunate that we are powerless.

ZERO MOSTEL
American comedian
Esquire 1972
I wanted to say something about the Universe. There's God, angels, planets . . . and horseshit.

J. ROBERT OPPENHEIMER
American physicist
Look 1966
Science has, as its whole purpose, the rendering of the physical world understandable and beautiful. Without this you have only tables and statistics. The measure of our success is our ability to live with this knowledge effectively actively and eventually with delight. If we succeed we will be able to cope with our knowledge and not create despair. But this also means appreciation of the plurality of knowledge. Order is not monolithic, it is plural.

CESARE PAVESE
Italian novelist
in 'The Faber Book of Aphorisms' 1964
Every luxury must be paid for, and everything is a luxury, starting with the world.

SIR KARL POPPER
British philosopher
'Conjectures and Refutations' 1963
We do not know where or how to start our analysis of this world. There is no wisdom to tell us. Even the scientific tradition does not tell us. It only tells us where and how other people started, and where they got to.

FRANK RHODES
American academic
The qualities that scientists measure may have as little relation to the world itself as a telephone number has to its subscriber.

JULES ROMAINS
French writer
'Les hommes de bonne volonté'
The world is an enormous injustice.

KARL-HEINZ STOCKHAUSEN
German composer
Sunday Times 1973
The earth is a penal settlement. People

are brainwashed and don't know any more why they are punished. I am a postman who is bringing the mail without knowing what is in the letters.

SIMONE WEIL
French philosopher
'The Need for Roots' 1952
Death and labour are things of necessity and not of choice. The world only gives itself to Man in the form of food and warmth if Man gives himself to the world in the form of labour. But death and labour can be submitted to either in an attitude of revolt or in one of consent. They can be submitted to in their naked truth or else wrapped around with lies.

PATRICK WHITE
Australian writer
in New York Review of Books
Why is the world, which seems so near, so hard to get hold of?

HEATHCOTE WILLIAMS
British playwright
'The Immortalist' 1978
The Universe is an intelligence test.

How much do you think you're going to score by dying?

TENNESSEE WILLIAMS
American playwright
The Observer 1957
The world is a funny paper read backwards – and that way it isn't so funny.

LUDWIG WITTGENSTEIN
German philosopher
The world and life are one.

The totality of thought is a picture of the world.

The world is a totality of facts, not things.

FRANK LLOYD WRIGHT
American architect
You have to have some order in a disordered world.

FRANK ZAPPA
American rock musician
In the fight between you and the world, back the world.

Religion

WOODY ALLEN
American film star
'Getting Even' 1972
Not only is there no God, but try getting a plumber on weekends.

ANONYMOUS
quoted in Gerald Brenan 'Thoughts in a Dry Season' 1978
I do not believe in God because if he existed he would long ago have destroyed the human race for its cruelty and evil.

JEAN ANOUILH
French playwright
'The Lark' 1955
Every man thinks God is on his side.

The rich and powerful know he is.
'Becket' 1959
Saintliness is also a temptation.

BABA RAM DASS (Richard Alpert)
American philosopher
Esquire 1972
If I see one dilemma with Western man, it's that he can't accept how beautiful he is. He can't accept that he is pure light, that he's pure love, that he's pure consciousness, that he's divine.

JAMES BALDWIN
American author
'The Fire Next Time' 1963
If the concept of God has any validity or use, it can only be to make us larger, freer and more loving. If God cannot do this, it is time we got rid of Him.

IMAMU AMIRI BARAKA (LeRoi Jones)
American playwright
'Home' 1966
God has been replaced, as he has all over the West, with respectability and air conditioning.

CAPTAIN BEEFHEART
American rock star
Earth – God's golf ball.

PAUL BLANCHARD
American lawyer
Christianity is so full of fraud that any honest man should renounce the whole shebang and espouse atheism instead.

DANIEL J. BOORSTIN
American writer
The Image 1962
God is the Celebrity-Author of the World's Best-Seller. We have made God into the biggest celebrity of all, to contain our own emptiness.

JORGE LUIS BORGES
Argentine writer
'Labyrinths' 1962
To die for a religion is easier than to live it absolutely.

CHARLES P. BOYLE
American scientist
quoted in 'The Official Rules' by P. Dickson, 1978
The success of any venture will be helped by prayer, even in the wrong denomination.

GENERAL OMAR BRADLEY
American soldier 1948
We have grasped the mystery of the atom and rejected the sermon on the mount.

ANDRÉ BRETON
French artist
I have always laid down my bets against God and what little profit I made in this world is simply the winnings on this bet. Absurdly low though the stakes may have been, I am aware of having won completely. For me, the single word 'God' suggests everything that is slippery, shady, squalid, foul and grotesque.

LENNY BRUCE
American comedian
quoted in 'The Essential Lenny Bruce' ed. Cohen 1967
If you believe there is a God, a God that made your body, and yet you think that you can do anything with that body that's dirty, then the fault lies with the manufacturer.

ERIC BURDON
British rock star
You don't have to be perfect to be Christ. All you have to do is stick your neck out and say the system sucks. They'll find a way of nailing you to the cross.

ABIGAIL VAN BUREN
American agony columnist 1970
A church is a hospital for sinners, not a museum for saints.

WILLIAM S. BURROUGHS
American writer
'Writers at Work' 1967 3rd series
I think there are innumerable Gods. What we on earth call God is a little tribal God who has made an awful mess. Certain forces operating through human consciousness control events.

RICHARD BURTON
Welsh actor 1970
Jesus Christ was unquestionably Welsh.

ELIAS CANETTI
Bulgarian writer 1952
Most religions do not make men better, only warier.

JIMMY CARTER
American politician 1976
We should live our lives as though Christ was coming this afternoon.

WILLA CATHER
American writer
'On Writing' 1949
Religion and art spring from the same root and are close kin. Economics and art are strangers.

ARTHUR C. CLARKE
British science writer
It may be that our role on this planet is not to worship God, but to create him.

DR. COGGAN
British clergyman 1965
The tragedy of modern TV religion is that you have a bunch of ignorami discussing what they know little about, with the result that at the end of the programme the gormless millions know far less than they knew before.

BILLY CONNOLLY
Scottish comedian
On Christ 1975
The door opens . . . crash! And in he comes. The Big Yin. With the long dress and the casual sandals.

RICHARD, CARDINAL CUSHING
American clergyman
Saints are all right in Heaven, but they're hell on Earth.

CYRIL DEAN DARLINGTON
British biologist
'The Evolution of Man & Society' 1969
No society can . . . reach a high development without some kind of priesthood, which organises a religion designed to govern its breeding behaviour. If breeding behaviour is left solely at the discretion of a governing class that class, and with it the whole society, is liable to disintegrate.

MOSES DAVID (Berg)
leader of the Children of God, hardline Jesus-freaks in US, 1974
We have a sexy God and a sexy religion and a very sexy leader. If you don't like sex, you better get out while you can.

JUDE DOUGHERTY
American academic 1980
If religion is not based on a rational footing, then *anything* can be considered religion.

GEORGES DUHAMEL
French writer
'Le desert de Bièvres'
I respect the idea of God too much to hold him responsible for so absurd a world.

WILL & ARIEL DURANT
American historians
'The Story of Civilisation' Vol. VI 1961
The soul of a civilisation is its religion, and it dies with its faith.

FREDERICK J.
EIKERENKOETTER II 'The Reverend Ike'
American evangelist
Don't wait for pie in the sky when you die! Get yours now, with icecream on top!

ALBERT EINSTEIN
German physicist
God casts the die, not the dice.

God is subtle, but he is not bloody minded.

'Out of My Later Years' 1950
Science without religion is lame, religion without science is blind.

'Cosmic Religion'
Before God we are all equally wise – and equally foolish.

WERNER ERHARD
(John Paul Rosenberg)
est founder 1976
If the Buddha could reach four hundred million people without television, we can certainly get 40 million.

How do I know I am not the reincarnation of Jesus Christ. You wouldn't believe the feelings I have inside me.

NORMAN EVANS
American footballer
'On God's Squad'
I guarantee you Christ would be the toughest guy who ever played this game if he were alive today. I would picture him as a 6'6", 260 lb defensive tackler who would make the big plays and would be hard to keep out of the backfield. Anytime you were up against him you would know you were in for a long afternoon. He would be aggressive and a tremendous competitor.

ALEXANDER EVERETT
British prophet
'Mind Dynamics' 1969
Jesus Christ was first in this field. We are all spinoffs.

JAMES K. FEIBLEMAN
American philosopher
Understanding Philosophy 1973
A myth is a religion in which no one any longer believes.

JULES FEIFFER
American cartoonist
quoted in Lawrence J. Peter 'Peter's Quotations' 1977
Christ died for our sins. Dare we make his martyrdom meaningless by not committing them.

LORD FISHER
British clergyman
in 'The Wit of the Church' ed. M. Bateman and S. Stenning 1967
An ex-archbishop: a kind of extinct volcano, still able to erupt from time to time in a private and unofficial way.

LARRY FLYNT
American publisher
It's just as Christian to get down on your knees for sex as it is for religion.

JAMES FOX
British actor/born-again Christian 1971
It helps me to know that God is here in Australia just as much as he is in England, twelve thousand miles away.

STAN FREBERG
American comedian
Playboy 1971
Christmas has two Ss in it, and they're both $$ signs.

ERICH FROMM
American psychologist
'The Sane Society' 1955
In the 19th Century the problem was that God is dead; in the 20th Century the problem is that man is dead.

R. BUCKMINSTER FULLER
American engineer
'No More Second-hand God'
God to me, it seems / is a verb / not a noun / proper or improper.

MUHAMMAR GADDHAFI
Libyan President 1972
I am not afraid of anything. If you fear God you do not fear anything else.

GEORGE GALLUP
American pollster
I could prove God statistically.

MOHANDAS K. GANDHI
Indian leader
If God were to appear to starving people, he would not dare to appear in any other form than food.

ARCHBISHOP GARBETT
British clergyman
in 'The Wit of the Church' ed. M. Bateman and S. Stenning 1967
I can always tell when the clergy have given up any serious attempt to read or think. It becomes obvious at about the age of 45. If a man is an Anglo-Catholic he becomes a bigot. If he is an Evangelical he becomes a sentimentalist.

AL GOLDSTEIN
American pornzine publisher
Playboy 1974
If there is a God I'm sure he's jerking off to *Screw*.

LORD GRADE
British TV mogul
The Observer 1979
The Pope's got great charisma. I'd like to sign him up.

BILLY GRAHAM
American preacher 1966
I can tell you that God is alive because I talked to him this morning.

quoted in The Spectator 1980
Judgement is the dark line in the face of God.

on basing his organisation in Washington, DC 1955
I just want to lobby for God.

REV. GEOFFREY GRAY
British clergyman
in 'The Wit of the Church' ed. M. Bateman and S. Stenning 1967
People expect their priest to have the skill in sermon composition of Knox, the oratorical power of Churchill, the personal charm of a film star, the tact of Royalty, the hide of a hippo, the administrative ability of Lord Nuffield, the wisdom of Socrates and the patience of Job. Some people must often be disappointed.

JULIEN GREEN
French writer
'Journal'
Every man, at some time or another, is an evangelist without knowing it.

GRAHAM GREENE
British novelist 1967
I'm not easily inspired by religion. Interested, yes – inspired, no.

DAG HAMMARSKJOLD
Swedish diplomat
Your cravings as a human animal do not become a prayer just because it is God whom you ask to attend to them.

STEPHEN W. HAWKING
British scientist
Nature 1975
God not only plays dice. He also sometimes throws them where they cannot be seen. [cf. Einstein]

HUGH HEFNER
American publisher 1969
I think the essence of Judaic/Christian teaching is very similar to *Playboy*.

ERNEST HEMINGWAY
American writer
letter to Adriana Ivancic, quoted in The Times 1967
People who win (the Nobel Prize) always seem to have to write the Old and New Testaments to show how great they are. They forget that these were written well enough in the first place.

BISHOP HENSLEY HENSON
British clergyman
in 'The Wit of the Church' ed. M. Bateman and S. Stenning 1967
Clergy are like manure – spread thinly on the land they are very good. But put them in a heap and . . . pooh!

BOB HOPE
American comedian
Playboy 1973
The good news is that Jesus is coming back. The bad news is that he's really pissed off.

FRED HOYLE
British astronomer
Daily Mail 1974
To take an almost religious view, this earth is nothing very special. There have probably been millions of earths just like ours each producing a particular intelligent species. That is not to say that they all developed well, that they all achieved some sort of perfection. And if the planner made lots of them and some of them chose to destroy themselves, then we can only suppose that the planner is a hard and practical man.

BISHOP TREVOR HUDDLESTON
British clergyman 1952
It has been the teaching of the Church throughout the centuries that when government degenerates into tyranny, laws cease to be binding on its subjects.

HUBERT HUMPHREY
American politician 1968
If we can't trust one another how can we trust God Almighty?

ALDOUS HUXLEY
British writer
'Collected Essays'
Nobody can have the consolations of religion or philosophy unless he has first experienced their desolations.

DEAN INGE
British clergyman
interviewed shortly before his death, 1954
If I could live my life over again I don't think I would be a clergyman. I know as much about the after-life as you do. I don't even know if there is one – in the sense the church teaches.

EUGENE IONESCO
French playwright
Esquire 1974
In the name of religion, one tortures, persecutes, builds pyres. In the guise of ideologies, one massacres, tortures and kills. In the name of justice one punishes . . . in the name of love of one's country or of one's race one hates other countries, despises them, massacres them. In the name of equality and brotherhood there is suppression and torture. There is nothing in common between the means and the end, the means go far beyond the end . . . Ideologies and

religions act as alibis, they are the alibis of the means.

REV. LESLIE IRVING
British clergyman
in 'The Wit of the Church' ed. M. Bateman and S. Stenning 1967
The only way of stimulating interest is to substitute a performing elephant in place of a sermon.

HOLBROOK JACKSON
British writer
Man is a dog's ideal of what God should be.

REV. J. F. JACQUES
British clergyman
in 'The Wit of the Church' ed. M. Bateman and S. Stenning 1967
One thing is pretty obvious in these days. If the clergy went on strike, society would soon learn to live without them.

REV. ALAN JONES
British clergyman
in 'The Wit of the Church' ed. M. Bateman and S. Stenning 1967
Church-going declines, not so much because of unbelief, but because Dad has made a down-payment on the car.

C. G. JUNG
Swiss psychoanalyst
inscription on the lintel of his front door:
Whether invoked or not, God will be present.

quoted in 1975
We can never finally know. I simply believe that some part of the human Self or Soul is not subject to the laws of space and time.

JOHN F. KENNEDY
American president 1963
The supreme reality of our time is our indivisibility as children of God and the common vulnerability of this planet.

JOMO KENYATTA
Kenyan leader
quoted in Newsweek 1978
When the missionaries arrived the Africans had the land and the missionaries had the bible. They taught us to pray with our eyes closed, when we opened them, they had the land and we had the bible.

JACK KEROUAC
American novelist
quoted in Image 1973
Every night I still ask the Lord 'why' and I haven't heard a decent answer yet.

MARTIN LUTHER KING JR.
American activist
quoted in The Times 1968
I don't know what will happen now, we've got some difficult days ahead. It really doesn't matter with me now, because I've been on the mountain top. I won't mind. Like anybody I would like to live a long life. Longevity has its place. But I'm not concerned about that just now. I want to do God's will and he's allowed me to go up to the mountain, and I've looked over and I've seen the Promised Land. I may not get there with you, but I want you to know tonight that we as a people will get to the Promised Land. Well, I'm happy tonight. I'm not worried about anything. I'm not fearing any man. Mine eyes have seen the glory of the coming of the Lord!

ARTHUR KOESTLER
British philosopher
'The Ghost In The Machine' 1967
God seems to have left the receiver off the hook and time is running out.

Encounter 1970
If the creator had a purpose in equipping us with a neck, he surely meant us to stick it out.

KARL KRAUS
German artist
'Karl Kraus' by Harry Zohn
The devil is an optimist if he thinks he can make people meaner.

STANLEY KUBRICK
American film director
Playboy 1968
All the attributes assigned to God could be the characteristics of biological entities who have evolved into something so remote from man as man is remote from the primordial ooze from which he first emerged.

HAROLD LASKI
British politician
letter
Apart from theology and sex there is really nothing to talk about.

STANISLAW J. LEC
Polish poet
'Unkempt Thoughts' 1962
All Gods *were* immortal.

GYPSY ROSE LEE
American stripper 1975
God is love, but get it in writing.

ROBERT E. LEE
American playwright
in 'Contemporary Dramatists' 1977
The devil's name is Dullness.

JOHN LENNON
British songwriter
'God'
God is a concept / by which we measure our pain. (Northern Songs)

C. S. LEWIS
British author
The Gods will not speak to us face to face until we ourselves have a face.

JERRY LEE LEWIS
American rock star
Either be hot or cold. If you are luke-warm, the Lord will spew you forth from his mouth.

MARY WILSON LITTLE
American writer
Men who make no pretensions to being good on one day out of seven are called sinners.

If man is only a little lower than the angels, the angels should reform.

NGUYEN LOAN
the S. Vietnamese officer killing the Vietcong prisoner in famous 1968 photograph
Buddha will understand.

FATHER BERNARD LONERGAN S. J.
British clergyman 1970
The church always arrives on the scene a little breathless and a little late.

PEDRO ALONSO LOPEZ
'The Strangler of the Andes' S. American mass murderer
Time 1980
I strangled them so that their souls would go to heaven, and they would not suffer on earth.

DR. J. D. McCOUGHEY
Australian theologian, 1974
God is dead, but 50,000 social workers have risen to take his place.

ARCHIBALD MacLEISH
American poet
'JB' 1958
We have no choice but to be guilty God is unthinkable if we are innocent.

JOHN McLOUGHLIN
British musician
Everyone is going to the shore of attainment. If you attempt to attain the supreme goal, all lesser goals are achieved. Because I am moving along the spiritual path, all my lesser goals will be fulfilled. All my musical aspirations will be met.

ANDRE MALRAUX
French writer
'L'espoir'
Christ . . . an anarchist who succeeded. That's all.

THOMAS MANN
German writer
In every spiritual attitude, a political attitude is latent.

BOB MARLEY
Jamaican singer
Politics and church are the same thing. They keep the people in ignorance.

H. L. MENCKEN
American essayist
'Minority Report' 1956
It takes a long while for a naturally trustful person to reconcile himself to the idea that after all God will not help him.

God is the immemorial refuge of the incompetent, the helpless, the miserable. They find not only sanctuary in His arms, but also a kind of superiority, soothing to their macerated egos; He will set them above their betters.

We must respect the other fellow's religion, but only in the sense and to the extent that we respect his theory that his wife is beautiful and his children smart.

Penetrating so many secrets, we cease to believe in the unknowable. But there it sits nevertheless, calmly licking its chops.

Metaphysics is almost always an attempt to prove the incredible by an appeal to the unintelligible.

JONATHAN MILLER
British doctor and writer
'Beyond the Fringe' 1961
I'm not really a Jew, just Jew-ish, not the whole hog.

HENRI DE MONTHERLANT
French writer
'Notebooks'
Religion is the venereal disease of mankind. Politics is its cancer.

HENRY MOORE
British sculptor
Sunday Telegraph 1968
To be obsessed with some vision and to have the continuous opportunity of working towards that vision can be looked upon as God's greatest gift to anyone.

MALCOLM MUGGERIDGE
British journalist
in 'Muggeridge Through the Microphone' 1968
If on Judgement Day I was confronted with God, and I found God took Himself seriously, I would ask to go to the other place.

Esquire 1969
The only ultimate disaster that can befall us ... is to feel ourselves to be at home here on earth. As long as we are aliens we cannot forget our true homeland which is that other kingdom You proclaimed.

AXEL MUNTHE
Norwegian writer
The Gods sell all things at a fair price. There is no entrance fee to the starlit hall of night.

'The Book of San Michele'
The soul needs more space than the body.

VLADIMIR NABOKOV
Russian writer
God – the contrapuntal genius of human fate.

MOHAMMAD NAGUIB
Egyptian politician 1953
Religion is a candle inside a multi-coloured lantern. Everyone looks through a particular colour, but the candle is still there.

RANDY NEWMAN
American songwriter
God is implausible. I wouldn't lay that on my kids, though. I would let them find out for themselves.

REINHOLD NIEBUHR
American theologian
'Christian Realism & Political Problems' 1953
There is no social evil, no form of injustice, whether of the feudal or the capitalist order which has not been sanctified in some way or another by religious sentiment and thereby rendered more impervious to change.

The tendency to claim God as an ally for our partisan values and ends is ... the source of all religious fanaticism.

J. ROBERT OPPENHEIMER
American physicist
Look 1966
The use of the word 'responsibility' is almost a secular device for using a religious notion without attachment to a transcendent being.

CESARE PAVESE
Italian novelist
in 'The Faber Book of Aphorisms' 1964
Religion consists in believing that everything which happens is extraordinarily important. It can never disappear from the world, precisely for this reason.

PABLO PICASSO
Spanish artist
quoted in 'Life with Picasso' by F. Gilot and C. Lake 1964
God is really only another artist. He in-

vented the giraffe, the elephant, the cat. He has no real style. He just goes on trying other things.

RAYMOND QUENEAU
French historian
'A Model History'
Religions tend to disappear with man's good fortune.

DR. MICHAEL RAMSAY
British clergyman
in 'The Wit of the Church' ed. M. Bateman and S. Stenning 1967
I think sermons would be better if the clergy did not preach quite so many.

The supreme question is not what we make of the Eucharist, but what the Eucharist is making of us.

MORDECAI RICHLER
Canadian novelist
'Joshua Then and Now' 1980
There are ten commandments, right? Well, it's like an exam. You get eight out of ten, you're just about top of the class.

MIES VAN DER ROHE
American architect
quoted in New York Herald Tribune obituary 1969
God is in the details.

JEAN ROSTAND
French scientist
'Thoughts of a Biologist'
Kill one man and you are a murderer. Kill millions and you are a conqueror. Kill all and you are a God.

'A Biologist's Notebook'
God, that dumping ground of our dreams.

BERTRAND RUSSELL
British philosopher
So far as I can remember, there is not one word in the Gospels in praise of intelligence.

JANE RUSSELL
American film actress
Esquire 1971
God is a living doll.

GEORGE SANTAYANA
American philosopher
People who feel themselves to be exiles in this world are mightily inclined to believe themselves citizens of another.

JEAN-PAUL SARTRE
French philosopher
The Words 1964
Respectable society believed in God in order to avoid having to speak about Him.

There is no salvation anywhere.

SATYA SAI BABA
Indian guru 1975
The Lord can be addressed by any name that tastes sweet to your tongue, or pictured in any form that appeals to your sense of wonder and awe.

FLORIAN SCHNEIDER
German musician
In the past people said that God could hear everything. Today it is the tape-recorder, the new God.

ALBERT SCHWEITZER
German missionary
A man does not have to be an angel in order to be a saint.

RAMON J. SENDER
Spanish poet
'Requiem for a Spanish peasant'
Priests are people who create much work by not working.

T. W. SHALES
American journalist
New York/Washington Examiner, 1968
If Jesus wanted to make it today, I thought he'd be a rock singer, too. Maybe he'd even be James Morrison.

BISHOP FULTON J. SHEEN
American clergyman
Look 1955
An atheist is a man who has no invisible means of support.

PAUL SIMON
American singer
'Sounds of Silence'
The words of the prophets are written / On the subway walls and tenement halls. (Charing Cross Music)

ISAAC BASHEVIS SINGER
American writer
Esquire 1974
God is a writer and we are both the heroes and the readers.

PATTI SMITH
American singer and poet
When I perform I always opt for communication with God and in pursuit of communicating with God you can fall into some very dangerous territory. I have also come to realize that total communication with God is physical death.

LORD SOPER
British clergyman
As a Methodist I must look at the Prayer Book in much the same way as the pious look at a harp. They are not much involved with it at present, but hope to be much later on.

ROD STEIGER
American film star
Playboy 1969
That's all a religion is – some principle you believe in . . . man has accomplished far more miracles than the God he invented. What a tragedy it is to invent a God and then suffer to keep him King.

Esquire 1969
Complacency in the presence of miracles is like opening the door to your own tomb.

ARCHBISHOP TEMPLE
British clergyman
in 'The Wit of the Church' ed. M. Bateman and S. Stenning 1967
The church is the only co-operative society that exists for the benefit of non-members.

MOTHER TERESA OF CALCUTTA
Missionary 1980
God has not called me to be successful, he has called me to be faithful.

PAUL TILLICH
American theologian
'The Shaking of the Foundations' 1962
He who knows about depth knows about God.

PETE TOWNSHEND
British rock composer
'Tommy'
See me, feel me, touch me, heal me . . .
(Essex Music)

When you hold out an empty cup to God and demand that he fill it with wine, He fills it faster than you can ever drink.

DR. ELTON TRUEBLOOD
The world is equally shocked at hearing Christianity criticised and seeing it practised.

U.S. ARMY CHAPLAIN
with the 11th Armoured Cavalry in Vietnam, praying for a big body count . . .
Oh Lord, give us the strength to fight the bastards and the strength to fight on.

PETER USTINOV
British actor and wit
Everybody's 1957
The habit of religion is oppressive, an easy way out of personal thought.

GORE VIDAL
American writer
The Listener 1978
The idea of a good society is something you do not need a religion and eternal punishment to buttress; you need a religion if you are terrified of death.

KURT VONNEGUT JR.
American writer 1967
God lets you write, he also lets you not write.

EVELYN WAUGH
British novelist
You don't know how much nastier I would be if I hadn't become a Catholic.

SIMONE WEIL
French philosopher
in 'The Faber Book of Aphorisms' 1964
God gives Himself to men as powerful or perfect. It is for them to choose.

CEDRIC WHITMAN
American classicist 1969
Mythology is what grownups believe, folklore is what they tell children, and religion is both.

HEATHCOTE WILLIAMS
British playwright
'The Speakers' 1964
What do you think the Trinity is? James
Bond? You and your priests, you come
out here and say *This Is God* and offer
me a drop of red biddy on a dog's bis-
cuit. Your religion grew out of superstition and priestcraft because the
church is a business. With three hundred
million pounds of capital they don't believe in the Holy Ghost, they believe in
the trinity of rent, interest and profit.

TENNESSEE WILLIAMS
American playwright
'Camino Real' 1953
We're all of us guinea pigs in the lab-
oratory of God. Humanity is just a work
in progress.

D. W. WINNICOTT
British paediatrician
'On Communication' 1963
To be alive is all. It is a constant struggle
to get to the starting point and keep
there. No wonder there are those who
make a special business of existing and
who turn it into a religion.

TOM WOLFE
American journalist
'In Our Time' 1980
A cult is a religion with no political
power.

History

ALFRED ANDERESCH
German writer
'Winterspelt'
History tells how it was. A story – how
it might have been.

MICHELANGELO ANTONIONI
Italian Film Director 1975
I don't like nostalgia. I don't like to look
back, only forward.

HANNAH ARENDT
American writer
New York Review of Books 1971
The good things in history are usually of
very short duration, but afterwards have
a decisive influence over what happens
over long periods of time.

BROOKS ATKINSON
American essayist
'Once Around the Sun' 1951
In every age 'the good old days' were a
myth. No one ever thought they were
good at the time. For every age has con-
sisted of crises that seemed intolerable to
the people who lived through them.

W. H. AUDEN
British poet
Columbia Forum 1970
Tradition means giving votes to that ob-
scurest of classes, our ancestors. It is the
democracy of the dead.

RUSSELL BAKER
American writer
'The Sayings of Poor Russell' Harpers 1972
The people who are always hankering
loudest for some golden yesteryear
usually drive new cars.

GEORGE W. BALL
American statesman
Newsweek 1971
Nostalgia is a seductive liar.

MAX BEERBOHM
British author
The past is a work of art, free of irrele-
vancies and loose ends.

BERNARD BERENSON
British art historian
History is an art which must not neglect
the known facts.

YVES BONNEFOY
French writer
'L'improbable'
Understanding is the last recourse of nostalgia.

HEYWOOD BROUN
American writer
Collected Works
Posterity is as likely to be wrong as anybody else.

CHARLES BUKOWSKI
American writer
'Notes of a Dirty Old Man' 1969
We have wasted History like a bunch of drunks shooting dice back in the men's crapper of the local bar.

ALBERT CAMUS
French writer
'The Rebel' 1951
The history of man, in one sense, is the sum total of his successive rebellions.

LOUIS FERDINAND CELINE
French writer
in L'Express
History doesn't pass the dishes again.

E. M. CIORAN
French philosopher
in 'Faber Book of Aphorisms' 1964
The hour of their crime does not strike simultaneously for all nations. This explains the permanence of history.

RICHARD COBB
British historian
The Listener 1978
The frontiers between history and imagination are very little more than Chinese screens, removable at will.

JEAN COCTEAU
French writer and film director 1957
What is history after all? History is facts which become legend in the end; legends are lies which become history in the end.

NOEL COWARD
British playwright
quoted in The Observer 1973
There is nothing more old-fashioned than being up-to-date.

There's nothing more modern than nostalgia. That's why I shall always be up to date.

ROBERTSON DAVIES
Canadian writer
'A Voice from the Attic' 1960
The world is full of people whose notion of a satisfactory future is, in fact, a return to the idealised past.

CHRISTOPHER DAWSON
British historian
quoted in The Listener 1978
Happy is the people that is without a history, and thrice happy is a people without a sociology, for as long as we possess a living culture we are unconscious of it, and it is only when we are in danger of losing it or when it is already dead that we begin to realise and study it scientifically.

HUGO DEMARTINI
Czech artist 1968
quoted in 'Contemporary Artists' 1977
People are always talking about tradition, but they forget we have a tradition of a few hundred years of nonsense and stupidity, that there is a tradition of idiocy, incompetence and crudity.

WILL DURANT
American historian
Reader's Digest 1972
One of the lessons of history is that nothing is often a good thing to do and always a clever thing to say.

WILL & ARIEL DURANT
American historians
History is mostly guessing, the rest is prejudice.

LAWRENCE DURRELL
British writer
The Listener 1978
History is an endless repetition of the wrong way of living.

ABBA EBAN
Israeli politician 1970
History teaches us that men and nations behave wisely once they have exhausted all other alternatives.

LOREN EISELEY
American anthropologist
'The Firmament of Time'
Without the past the pursued future has no meaning.

ERTE (Romain de Tirtoff)
French designer
The Guardian 1975
It's a waste of time thinking hard about the past. There's nothing you can do to change it.

CLIFTON FADIMAN
American essayist
We are all citizens of history.

J. G. FARRELL
British novelist
in 'Contemporary Novelists' 1976
As a rule, people have already made up their minds what they think about the present. About the past they are more susceptible to clarity of vision.

WILLIAM FAULKNER
American novelist
No man can cause more grief than that one clinging blindly to the vices of his ancestors.

JEAN GENET
French writer
notes for play 'The Screens' 1973
Crimes of which a people is ashamed constitute its real history. The same is true of man.

PIETER GEYL
Dutch historian 1972
History is an argument without end.

'THE GO-BETWEEN'
Columbia 1971 screenplay by Harold Pinter, based on novel by L. P. Hartley
Michael Redgrave: The past is a foreign country, they do things differently there.

GUNTER GRASS
German novelist
'Der Burger und Seine Stimme' 1974
History is, to begin with at any rate, an absurd happening into which more or less gifted people attempt to introduce some perspectives.

'Dokumente zur Politischen Wirkung' 1971
History offers us no comfort. It hands out hard lessons. It makes absurd reading, mostly. Admittedly, it moves on, but progress is not the result of history. History is never-ending. We are always inside history, never outside it.

PHILIP GUEDALLA
British author
'Supers and Supermen'
History repeats itself. Historians repeat each other.

KARL-HEINZ HANSEN
W. German politician
The Listener 1978
A people not prepared to face its own history cannot manage its own future.

LILLIAN HELLMAN
American playwright
'Scoundrel Time' 1976
I do not believe in recovery. The past, with its pleasures, its rewards, its foolishness, its punishments, is there for each of us forever, and it should be.

ALDOUS HUXLEY
British writer
'Collected Essays' 1959
That men do not learn very much from the lessons of history is the most important of all the lessons that history has to teach.

EUGENE IONESCO
French playwright
'Present Past Past Present' 1971
History is pure madness – one must tell oneself that history is always wrong, whereas it is generally believed that history is always right.

'Notes and Counter-Notes'
It is the enemies of History that, in the end, make it.

MURRAY KEMPTON
American journalist
'Part of Our Time' 1955
The bearers of the myth of every decade seem to carry in their hands the axe and the spade to execute and inter the myth of the previous one.

MAX LERNER
American academic
'The Unfinished Country' 1959
Human history, if you read it right, is
the record of the attempts to tame
Father.

MARY McCARTHY
American writer
'On the Contrary' 1962
Every age has a keyhole to which its eye
is pasted.

COLIN MacINNES
Australian writer
'England, Half English' 1961
Tradition, if not constantly recreated,
can be as much a millstone as a mill-
wheel.

ALI A. MAZRUI
Asian political scientist
in The Listener 1978
A people denied history is a people deprived of dignity.

GEORGE MELLY
British musician and critic
Melody Maker 1975
What becomes nostalgic is trash. What
doesn't is meaningful. It lasts.

The Observer 1981
We all rewrite our own pasts to reinforce
our present view of ourselves.

ARTHUR MILLER
American playwright
An era can be said to end when its basic
illusions are exhausted.

HENRY MILLER
American writer
'Plexus' 1953
History is the myth, the true myth, of
man's fall made manifest in time.

HERBERT J. MULLER
American writer
'Freedom in the Western World'
It has become too easy to see that the
luckless men of the past lived by mistakes, even absurd beliefs, so we may
well fail in a decent respect for them,
and forget that historians of the future
will point out that we too lived by myths.

JAWAHARLAL NEHRU
Indian leader
You don't change the course of history
by turning the faces of portraits to the
wall.

FRANK NORMAN
British writer
'The Guntz' 1962
The great thing about the past is that
it's happened.

JOSE ORTEGA Y GASSET
Spanish philosopher
in 'The Faber Book of Aphorisms' 1964
Our age cannot be completely understood if all the others are not understood.
The song of history can only be sung as
a whole.

It is the mission of history to make our
fellow beings acceptable to us.

GAETON PICON
French writer
'L'Ecrivain et son ombre'
It is not history that makes judgements,
but judgements that make history.

FRANCIS PONGE
French writer
History – that little sewer where man
loves to wallow.

'PRIVATE EYE' 1978
British satirical magazine
History repeats itself – the first time as
tragi-comedy, the second time as bed-
room farce.

RAYMOND QUENEAU
French historian
'A Model History'
Happy nations have no history. History
is the study of mankind's misfortunes.

'QUOTE AND UNQUOTE'
*from Signature, the Diner's Club Magazine
1970*
History is always repeating itself, but
each time the price goes up.

Nostalgia is the realisation that things
weren't as unbearable as they seemed at
the time.

JULES ROMAINS
French writer
'Les hommes de bonne volonté'
History: the category of human phenom-

ena which tends to catastrophe.

CARL SANDBURG
American poet
History is a bucket of ashes.

PAUL SIMON
American singer
'Peace Like A River'
You can run lots of rules/But you know you can't outrun the history train. (Pattern Music)

LEE SIMONSON
American historian
Any event, once it has occurred, can be made to appear inevitable by a competent historian.

STEPHEN SPENDER
British poet
History is the ship carrying living memories to the future.

JAMES THURBER
American humorist
New York Herald Tribune 1961
Nostalgic reverie, like amorous fantasy, belongs in the category of escape.

JOSIP BROZ TITO
Yugoslav leader
Any movement in history which

attempts to perpetuate itself becomes reactionary.

ARNOLD TOYNBEE
British historian
Playboy 1967
It is a historian's business to make himself at home in other times and places besides his own in order to bring those times and places alive again for his contemporaries.

ALDO VAN EYCK
Dutch architect
'Contemporary Architects' 1980
History – that great gathering body of experience – is there in the mind's interior – to be used and not spilt.

BILLY WILDER
American film director
Hindsight is always 20:20

CHARLES E. WILSON
American government official
It's futile to talk too much about the past – like trying to make birth control retroactive.

CHARLES WOLF JR.
quoted in Wall Street Journal 1976
Those who don't study the past will repeat its errors; those who do study it will find other ways to err.

The Modern World

WOODY ALLEN
American film star
'Side Effects' 1981
Modern man is here defined as any person born after Nietzsche's edict that 'God is dead' but before the hit recording 'I Wanna Hold Your Hand'.

HANNAH ARENDT
American writer
'On Violence'
If you ask a member of this generation

two simple questions: 'How do you want the world to be in 50 years' and 'What do you want your life to be like five years from now?' the answers are often preceded by 'Provided there is still a world' and 'Provided I am still alive.'

BERNARD BARUCH
American financier
Coins a phrase:
We are in the midst of a cold war.

STAFFORD BEER
British writer
'Designing Freedom' 1974
Our institutions are failing because they are disobeying laws of effective organisation which their administrators do not know about, to which indeed their cultural mind is closed, because they contend that there exists and can exist, no science competent to discover those laws.

SAUL BELLOW
American writer
The Listener 1969
The hero of society is society itself.

ERIC BENTLEY
American writer
'The Dramatic Event' 1954
Ours is the age of substitutes: instead of language we have jargon; instead of principles, slogans; and, instead of genuine ideas, bright ideas.

PIERRE BOULEZ
French composer
Esquire 1969
We are living in a blotter society which absorbs everything. Avant garde movements today remind me of a bunch of couturiers – they must present their . . . collection . . . and its function is, like fashion, self-destruction, so it can be replaced with a new collection. To do this in art is to seek a very low common denominator.

BRIGID BROPHY
Irish writer
'In transit'
The thriller is the cardinal twentieth century form. All it, like the twentieth century, wants to know is: Who's Guilty?

WILLIAM S. BURROUGHS
American writer
The Guardian 1969
Modern man has lost the option of silence.

DAVID CAMPTON
British playwright
in 'Contemporary Dramatists' 1977
The chaos affecting everyone today . . . is so all-pervading that it cannot be ignored, yet so shattering that it can only be approached through comedy. Tragedy demands firm foundations; today we are dancing among the ruins.

E. M. CIORAN
French philosopher
'Syllogismes de l'amertume' 1952
To be modern is to potter about in the terminal ward.

PAUL CLAUDEL
French composer
'Conversations dans le Loir-et-Cher'
The only living society is that which is animated by inequality and injustice.

JEAN COCTEAU
French writer and film director
quoted in New York Review of Books 1971
What can one hope for of an age like ours, which does not even believe in its conjurors.

NIK COHN
British writer
'Awopbopaloobopalopbamboom' 1969
Generation to generation . . . nothing changes in Bohemia.

JUDY COLLINS
American singer 1979
Keeping up with the times is just a matter of living every day.

QUENTIN CRISP
British author
'The Naked Civil Servant' 1968
In an expanding universe, time is on the side of the outcast. Those who once inhabited the suburbs of human contempt find that without changing their address they eventually live in the metropolis.

e. e. cummings
American poet
Poems 1954
Take the socalled 'standardofliving'. What do mostpeople mean by 'living'? They dont mean living. They mean the latest and closest plural approximation to singular prenatal passivity which science, in its finite but unbounded wisdom, has succeeded in selling their wives.

ALBERT EINSTEIN
German physicist
'Out of my later years' 1950
Perfections of means and confusion of goals seem – in my opinion – to characterize our age.

MAX ERNST
French artist
Believe me, today crocodiles are no longer crocodiles.

EDGAR Z. FRIEDENBERG
American sociologist
'The Vanishing Adolescent' 1959
It takes a kind of shabby arrogance to survive in our time, and a fairly romantic nature to want to.

R. BUCKMINSTER FULLER
American engineer
quoted in Nova 1970
The world has moved from the wire to the wireless, the track to the trackless, the visible to the invisible. More and more can be done with less and less.

LORD GEORGE-BROWN
British politician
The Listener 1979
We are a miserable society in many ways, and in nothing are we so miserable as in our elevation of the word 'consensus'.

ALLEN GINSBERG
American poet
'Howl' 1956
I saw the best minds of my generation destroyed by madness, starving hysterical naked.

PAUL GOODMAN
American writer
'Growing Up Absurd' 1960
Our society cannot have it both ways: to maintain a conformist and ignoble system *and* to have skillful and spirited men to man that system.

LORD HAILSHAM
British politician
quoted in The Spectator 1980
We are living in the City of Destruction, a dying country in a dying civilisation, and across the plain there is no wicket gate offering a way of escape.

LORAINE HANSBERRY
American playwright
diary 1963
Ball points belong to their age. They make everyone write alike.

ALDOUS HUXLEY
British writer
in 'The Faber Book of Aphorisms' 1964
If it were not for the intellectual snobs who pay – in solid cash – the tribute which philistinism owes to culture, the arts would perish with their starving practitioners. Let us thank heaven for hypocrisy.

IVAN ILLICH
American philsopher
'Tools for Conviviality' 1973
In a consumer society there are inevitably two kinds of slaves: the prisoners of addiction and the prisoners of envy.

EUGENE IONESCO
French playwright
To think contrary to one's era is heroism. But to speak against it is madness.

MICK JAGGER
British rock star
Esquire 1969
Society is all wrong. All those vibrations of fear. You have to change not only the setup but the whole concept. You have to learn how to live in the moment and enjoy it.

BERTRAND DE JOUVENAL
French writer 1970
Year by year we are becoming better equipped to accomplish the things we are striving for. But what are we actually striving for?

CAROLINE KELLY
Australian anthropologist 1966
We give people a box in the suburbs, it's called a house, and every night they sit in it staring at another box, in the morning they run off to another box called an office, and at the weekends they get into another box, on wheels this time, and grope their way through endless traffic jams.

PROF. ALEXANDER KIRA
Czech academic
'The Bathroom' 1976
A society can have anything it cares enough about and is willing to pay for.

RONALD KNOX
British clergyman and writer
'Let Dons Delight'
It is so stupid of modern civilisation to have given up believing in the devil when he is the only explanation of it.

LOUIS KRONENBERGER
American critic
'Company Manners' 1954
The trouble with our age is that it is all signpost and no destination.

ROSS LOCKRIDGE
American writer
'Raintree County' 1948
The whole cockeyed civilisation is a series of pricetags hanging out for people to read each other by.

SIR BERNARD LOVELL
British astronomer
The Observer 1975
The simple belief in automatic material progress by means of scientific discovery is a tragic myth of our age.

MARY McCARTHY
American writer
'On The Contrary' 1962
It is only the middle-class people who, quite mistakenly, imagine that a lively pursuit of the latest in reading or painting will advance their status in the world.

MARSHALL McLUHAN
Canadian academic 1975
We're now living 200 years per annum. When you're moving at that clip there's no place to stand. It's like putting a Model T on the highway at 100 mph. It breaks down.

NORMAN MAILER
American writer
'Of a Fire on the Moon' 1970
The horror of the twentieth century is the size of each event and the paucity of its reverberation.

ELSA MAXWELL
American socialite
'How To Do It' 1957
We live in a cocktail culture whose unlovely symbol is the ring on the best mahogany.

ARTHUR MILLER
American playwright
'Writers at Work' 3rd series 1967
I have always felt that concentration camps . . . are the logical conclusion of contemporary life.

MALCOLM MUGGERIDGE
British journalist
Esquire 1970
Never . . . was any generation of men intent upon the pursuit of happiness more advantageously placed to attain it who yet, with seeming deliberation, took the opposite course – towards chaos, not order, towards breakdown, not stability, towards death, destruction and darkness, not life, creativity and light.

'NETWORK'
United Artists 1976 screenplay by Paddy Chayevsky
Peter Finch: We know the air is unfit to breathe and our food is unfit to eat – and we sit watching our TVs while some local newscaster tells us that today we had 15 homicides and 63 violent crimes, as if that's the way it's supposed to be. We know things are bad. Worse than bad. They're crazy. It's like everything everywhere is going crazy. So we don't go out any more. We sit in the house and slowly the world we're living in is getting smaller and all we say is 'Please, at least leave us alone in our living rooms. Let me have my toaster and my TV and my steel-belted radials and I won't say anything. Just leave us alone.'

POLY STYRENE (Marian Elliott)
British rock singer
I like to consume, because if you don't, then it consumes you.

WILHELM REICH
German psychoanalyst
'Selected Writings' 1960
All boundaries between science and religion, science and art, objective and

subjective, quantity and quality, physics and psychology, astronomy and religion, God and Ether, are irretrievably breaking down, being replaced by a conception of the basic unity, a basic common functional principle of all nature which branches out into the various kinds of human experience.

DON ROBINSON
quoted in Reader's Digest 1963
One of the weaknesses of our age is our apparent inability to distinguish our needs from our greeds.

R. D. ROSEN
American writer
'Psychobabble' New Times 1975
Psychobabble is just a way of using candor in order not to be candid. . . Confession is the new handshake.

GEORGES ROUAULT
French artist
Life 1953
One goes faster and faster. There is not even time to gasp at the moment of dying. Art in this mechanical age – should it not be considered a miracle.

KEN RUSSELL
British film director
Esquire 1973
This isn't the age of manners, it's the age of kicking people in the crotch.

CARL SANDBURG
American poet
New York Post 1960
In these times you have to be an optimist to open your eyes when you awake in the morning.

PROFESSOR WILLIAM B. SHOCKLEY
American inventor and eugenics theorist
Esquire 1973
Society must have a reason for the old forms of address not outmoded by a new means of contraception.

LOGAN PEARSALL SMITH
American essayist
in 'The Faber Book of Aphorisms' 1964
We are children of our age, but children who can never know their mother.

SUSAN SONTAG
American essayist
'Against Interpretation' 1961
The two pioneering forces of modern sensibility are Jewish moral seriousness and homosexual aestheticism and irony.

EDWARD DURELL STONE
American architect
New York Times 1964
If you look around, and you give a damn, it makes you want to commit suicide.

ALVIN TOFFLER
American academic
The Observer 1972
We are moving towards a world not merely of throwaway products but throwaway friends and marriages.

AUBERON WAUGH
British journalist
in 'In And Out: Debrett 1980/81' by Neil Mackwood 1980
Generally speaking, the best people nowadays go into journalism, the second best into business, the rubbish into politics and the shits into law.

ALFRED NORTH WHITEHEAD
British mathematician
quoted in Esquire 1969
Vigorous societies harbour a certain extravagance of objectives.

GEOFFREY WOLFF
American writer
New Times 1979
Epochs like ours take on the value of pornographic novels: Each novelty must be topped by the next, yet the body's apertures are finite, and their geography known. It's hard to be subversive in an age that retains no shared values to subvert.

Newsweek 1969
An age is best revealed by its artists of the second rank.

Progress

KINGSLEY AMIS
British author
Encounter 1960
More will mean worse.

RUSSELL BAKER
American writer
'The Sayings of Poor Russell' Harpers 1972
Usually, terrible things that are done with the excuse that progress requires them are not really progress at all, but just terrible things.

JACQUES BARZUN
American academic
'The House of Intellect' 1959
Great cultural changes begin in affectation and end in routine.

CAPTAIN BEEFHEART
American rock star
True progress is Chanel No 5 on the rocks.

BERNARD BERENSON
British art historian
Consistency requires you to be as ignorant today as you were a year ago.

JOHN BRIGHT-HOLMES
British publisher
quoted in 'The Official Rules' by P. Dickson 1978
People don't change, they only become more so.

ABIGAIL VAN BUREN
American agony columnist 1974
People who fight fire with fire usually end up with ashes.

JOHN C. BURTON
American businessman
New York Times 1972
Careful consideration is the best known defence against change.

e. e. cummings
American poet
Progress is a comfortable disease.

RENE DUBOS
American ecologist
Every decision is like murder and our march forward is over the stillborn bodies of all our possible selves that will never be.

SYDNEY J. HARRIS
American journalist
'Strictly Personal'
As the horsepower in modern automobiles steadily rises, the congestion of traffic steadily lowers the possible speed of your car. This is known as Progress.

FREDERICK HAYES
American bureaucrat
Fortune 1969
There is no way to make people like change. You can only make them feel less threatened by it.

THOR HEYERDAHL
Norwegian anthropologist
'Fatu-hiva' 1974
Progress is man's ability to complicate simplicity.

CHRISTO JAVACHEFF
American artist who wraps things 1969
It's not a very permanent world, anyway.

C. G. JUNG
Swiss psychoanalyst
'Psychological Reflections' 1953
We cannot change anything unless we accept it. Condemnation does not liberate, it oppresses.

ERNST JUNGER
quoted in 'The Rebel' by Albert Camus 1951
Evolution is far more important than living.

KENNETH KAUNDA
President of Zambia, 1965
Inability of those in power to still the voices of their own consciences is the great force leading to desired changes.

JOHN F. KENNEDY
American president
When it is not necessary to change, it is necessary not to change.

The one unchangeable certainty is that nothing is certain or unchangeable.

STANISLAW J. LEC
Polish poet
'Unkempt Thoughts' 1962
Is it progress if a cannibal uses a fork?

HENRY MILLER
American writer
'The World of Sex' 1957
Morally, spiritually, we are fettered. What have we achieved in mowing down mountain ranges, harnessing the energy of mighty rivers, or moving whole populations about like chess pieces, if we ourselves remain the same restless, miserable, frustrated creatures we were before. To call such activity progress is utter delusion.

JEAN RENOIR
French film director
'My Life & My Films' 1974
Progress is dangerous because it is based on perfect technology.

ANTOINE DE ST EXUPERY
French writer
'The Wisdom of the Sands' 1948
Man's 'progress' is but a gradual discovery that his questions have no meaning.

GEORGE A. SARTON
American scientist
'The Study of the History of Science' 1957
Definition – Science is systematized positive knowledge, or what has been taken as such at different ages and in different places. Theorem – The acquisition and systematisation of positive knowledge are the only human activities which are truly cumulative and progressive. Corollary – The history of science is the only history which can illustrate the progress of mankind. In fact, progress has no definite and unquestionable meaning in other fields than the field of science.

JAMES THURBER
American humorist
attrib.
Progress was all right. Only it went on too long.

ALVIN TOFFLER
American academic
'Future Shock'
Man has a limited biological capacity for change. When this capacity is overwhelmed, the capacity is in future shock.

HARRY S. TRUMAN
American President
Men don't change. The only thing new in the world is the history you don't know.

PAUL VEZELAY
British artist
'Contemporary Artists' 1977
Much that seems incomprehensible today may prove to be the inevitable sequence of all that immediately preceded it.

L. VON BERTALANFFY
German scientist
Scientific Monthly 1956
What is called human progress is a purely intellectual affair . . . not much development, however, is seen on the moral side. It is doubtful whether the methods of modern warfare are preferable to the big stones used for cracking the skull of the fellow-Neanderthaler. It is rather obvious that the moral standards of Laotse and Buddha were not inferior to ours.

ANDY WARHOL
American artist
'From A to B and Back Again' 1975
They always say that time changes things, but you actually have to change them yourself.

SIMONE WEIL
French philosopher
in 'The Faber Book of Aphorisms' 1964
The great mistake of . . . the Nineteenth Century was to think that by walking straight on one mounted upward into the air.

E. B. WHITE
American writer
The only sense that is common in the long run, is the sense of change, and we all instinctively avoid it.

ALFRED NORTH WHITEHEAD
British philosopher
The art of progress is to preserve order amid change and to preserve change amid order.

NORBERT WIENER
American mathematician
'The Human Use of Human Beings' 1954
The simple faith in progress is not a conviction belonging to strength, but one belonging to acquiescence and hence to weakness.

FRANK ZAPPA
American rock musician 1980
Without deviation, progress is not possible.

EBERHARD ZEIDLER
Canadian architect
'Contemporary Architects' 1980
Progress might be a circle, rather than a straight line.

The Future

DEAN ACHESON
American politician
in 'Quote and Unquote' 1979
The best thing about the future is that it only comes one day at a time.

LAUREN BACALL
American film star
But, Jesus, you can't start worrying about what's *going* to happen. You get spastic enough worrying about what's happening now.

JAMES BALDWIN
American author
Nobody Knows My Name 1961
The future is like heaven – everyone exalts it, but no one wants to go there now.

JORGE LUIS BORGES
Argentine writer
'Borges On Writing' 1974
Men who live in the present do not look forward to their fates.

ALBERT CAMUS
French writer
'The Rebel' 1951
The future is the only kind of property that the masters willingly concede to slaves.

PAUL CHAMSON
French writer
'On ne voit pas les coeurs'
One should never place confidence in the future – it doesn't deserve it.

QUENTIN CRISP
British author
'The Naked Civil Servant' 1968
I still lived in the future – a habit which is the death of happiness.

PIERRE DAC
French writer
'L'Os à nivelle'
The future is the past in preparation.

ALBERT EINSTEIN
German physicist
I never think of the future – it comes soon enough.

CLIFTON FADIMAN
American essayist
'Selected Writings' 1955
Science fiction is a kind of archaeology of the future.

ERICH FROMM
American psychologist
'The Sane Society' 1955
The danger of the past was that men became slaves. The danger of the future is that men may become robots.

J. B. S. HALDANE
British scientist
This is my prediction for the future – whatever hasn't happened will happen and no one will be safe from it.

ALDOUS HUXLEY
British writer
'Brave New World Revisited' Esquire 1956
The most distressing thing that can happen to a prophet is to be proved wrong. The next most distressing thing is to be proved right.

ARTHUR KOESTLER
British philosopher 1968
We have to live with the bugs and the bomb not for the next ten years but for the next ten thousand.

SOMERSET MAUGHAM
British writer
in Richard Hughes 'Foreign Devil' 1972
It is bad enough to know the past; it would be intolerable to know the future.

SIR MARK OLIPHANT
British scientist 1970
We are going to have to be rather clever people if we are going to escape from our own cleverness in the past.

GEORGE ORWELL
British essayist
'1984' 1948
If you want a picture of the future, imagine a boot stamping on the human face – forever. . . And remember that is forever.

POPE PAUL VI
on technology 1970
We must all take care that the forward movement does not degenerate into a headlong run. We must see to it that enthusiasm for the future does not give rise to contempt for the past.

FRANKLIN D. ROOSEVELT
American President 1945
The only limit to our realization of tomorrow will be our doubts of today.

IGOR STRAVINSKY
Russian composer
Esquire 1972
We can neither put back the clock nor slow down our forward speed, and as we are already flying pilotless, on instrument controls, it is even too late to ask where we are going.

ALVIN TOFFLER
American academic
The Observer 1972
Future shock is the disorientation that affects an individual, a corporation or a country when he or it is overwhelmed by change and the prospect of change. It is the consequence of having to make too many decisions about too many new and unfamiliar problems in too short a time. Future shock is more than a metaphor. It is a form of personal and social breakdown. We are in collision with tomorrow. Future shock has arrived.

FATHER DESMOND WILSON
Belfast community worker
The Listener 1979
It is the act of forgiveness that opens up the only possible way to think creatively about the future at all.

SIR SOLLY ZUCKERMAN
British scientist
Daily Mirror 1964
Science creates the future without knowing what the future will be. If science knew tomorrow's discovery they would make it.

MAXIMS

JANE ACE
American radio comedienne
quoted in 'The Fine Art of Hypochondria' by Goodman Ace, 1966
Time wounds all heels.

HAROLD ACTON
British man of letters
The Times 1970
The happy host makes a sad guest.

KONRAD ADENAUER
German statesman
A thick skin is a gift from God.

NELSON ALGREN
American author
'What Every Young Man Should Know'
Never eat at a place called Mom's.
Never play cards with a man named
Doc. And never lie down with a woman
who's got more troubles than you.

FRED ALLEN
American wit
If the grass is greener in the other fellow's yard, let him worry about cutting
it.

WOODY ALLEN
American film star
in 'Sleeper' 1973
I believe in sex and death – two experiences that come once in a lifetime.

ELIZABETH ARDEN
American cosmetician
quoted in Fortune 1973
Nothing that costs only a dollar is worth
having.

DUKE OF ARGYLL
British aristocrat
attrib. by Art Buchwald in 'I Chose Caviar'
As far as I am concerned there only two
kinds of people in the world. Those who
are nice to their servants and those who
aren't.

BRITISH & AMERICAN ARMY
AXIOM
*quoted in The Official Rules by P. Dickson
1978*
If it moves, salute it, if it doesn't move
pick it up and if you can't pick it up,
paint it.

EARL OF ARRAN
British journalist 1967
My father always told me that if you saw
a man in a Rolls Royce you could be
sure he was not a gentleman unless he
was the chauffeur.

RICHARD AVEDON
American photographer
Playboy 1975
Scratch the surface, and if you're really
lucky, you'll find more surface.

JEFFREY BARNARD
British journalist
The Spectator 1980
If you haven't got any socks, you can't
pull them up.

PIO BAROJA
Spanish poet
Most of us swim in the ocean of the
commonplace.

BRUCE BARTON
American advertising man
Conceit is God's gift to little men.

LORD BEAVERBROOK
Canadian press magnate
Buy old masters. They fetch a better
price than old mistresses.

SAMUEL BECKETT
Irish author
quoted in New York Review of Books 1981
You can't keep a dead mind down.

SIR THOMAS BEECHAM
British conductor
Try everything once except incest and
folk-dancing.

BRENDAN BEHAN
Irish playwright
Weekend 1968
The most important things to do in this
world are to get something to eat, some-
thing to drink and somebody to love you.

EDMUND C. BERKELEY
American editor
in 'Computers & Automation' 1969
An exception *tests* a rule, it never *proves*
it.

J. D. BERNAL
British scientist
lecture 1960
All that glisters may not be gold, but at
least it contains free electrons.

SIR HENRY BOLTE
Australian politician 1969
Litter is a disgusting way of proving your
affluence.

ERMA BOMBECK
American humorist
quoted in 'The Official Rules' by P. Dickson 1978
Never go to a doctor whose office plants have died.

EDWARD DE BONO
British writer
Think sideways!

LORD BRABAZON
British aristocrat 1955
If you cannot say what you have to say in twenty minutes, you should go away and write a book about it.

ANDRE BRETON
French artist
'Surrealism & Painting' 1972
First Commandment: Everything should be capable of being freed from its shell (from its distance, its comparative size, its physical and chemical properties). Never believe in the interior of a cave, always in the surface of an egg.

Second Commandment: Wander, the wings of augury will come and attach themselves to your shoulders.

Third Commandment: Place your desire beyond reach and you will re-create it endlessly.

Fourth Commandment (always promulgated, always valid) Beauty will be convulsive or it will not be.

Fifth Commandment: Deprive yourself. Revelation is the daughter of refusal.

Sixth Commandment: Whatever happens, never doubt. Love is always before you, Love (Seventh, and, to this day, last commandment)

DREW 'BUNDINI' BROWN
American boxing personality 1973
You don't look in the mirror to see life; you gotta look out of the window.

LENNY BRUCE
American comedian
'The Essential Lenny Bruce' ed. Cohen 1967
You can't get snot off a suede jacket.

Carnegie Hall concert
A knowledge of syphilis is not an instruction to contract it.

ARTHUR CALWELL
Australian politician 1968
It is better to be defeated on principle than to win on lies.

MARK CAMERON
American weightlifter 1976
Every man ought to get a tattoo and shave his head at least once.

ELIAS CANETTI
Bulgarian writer 1951
Only the unexpected can bring good fortune, but it must come up against much of the expected and disperse it.

DALE CARNEGIE
Self-help evangelist
The only way to get the best of an argument is to avoid it.

LOUIS-FERDINAND CELINE
French writer
'Journey to the End of the Night'
If you aren't rich, you should always look useful.

SIR WINSTON CHURCHILL
British statesman
When the eagles are silent the parrots begin to jabber.

ELDRIDGE CLEAVER
American radical
slogan 1968
You're either part of the solution or part of the problem.

JEAN COCTEAU
French writer and film director
One sits down first, one thinks afterwards.

BARRY COMMONER
American ecologist
Nothing ever goes away.

SHIRLEY CONRAN
British writer
'Superwoman'
First things first, second things never.

NOEL COWARD
British playwright
Never trust a man with short legs –
brains too near their bottoms.

DR. ALAN CRAWFORD
**IPC magazines marketing director
1970**
I persuade; you educate; they
manipulate.

QUENTIN CRISP
British writer
'How To Become A Virgin' 1981
Nothing shortens a journey so pleasantly
as an account of misfortunes at which
the hearer is permitted to laugh.

What is privacy if not for invading?

Other-cheekism is not only a way of pu-
rifying the soul, it is also part of every
weak person's survival kit.

Never keep up with the Joneses. Drag
them down to your level. It's cheaper.

DAVID CROSBY
American rock star
It can't happen here is number one on
the list of famous last words.

FATHER JOHN CULKIN S.J.
American priest
in 'McLuhan Hot and Cool' 1967
We don't know who it was discovered
water, but we're pretty sure it wasn't a
fish.

NICK 'THE GREEK' DANDALOS
American bookmaker
Remember this: the house doesn't beat
a player. It merely gives him the chance
to beat himself.

SAM DASH
American lawyer 1973
When you play a game you have to play
by the rules. Otherwise there can be no
game.

BO DIDDLEY
American musician
Don't let your mouth write no cheque
your tail can't cash.

JOAN DIDION
American writer
'On Self Respect' 1961
Self-respect . . . is a question of recog-
nising that anything worth having has
its price.

SENATOR EVERETT DIRKSEN
American politician
Don't get mad, get even.

GEORGES DUHAMEL
French writer
'Le Combat contre les ombres'.
It is always brave to say what everyone
thinks.

DWIGHT D. EISENHOWER
American president 1958
What counts is not necessarily the size
of the dog in the fight – it's the size of
the fight in the dog.

BARBARA ETTORE
Harper's Magazine 1974
Ettore's Observation: The other line
always moves faster.

BERGEN EVANS
American educator
Stoicism is the wisdom of madness and
cynicism the madness of wisdom.

FEDERICO FELLINI
Italian film director
All methods are legal.

FIRST LAW OF DEBATE
in 'Murphy's Law' by Arthur Block 1979
Never argue with a fool – people might
not know the difference.

BUD FLANAGAN
British comedian
in 'Quote and Unquote' 1970
No dog can go as fast as the money you
bet on him.

B. C. FORBES
American publisher
'Epigrams'
Patience is not only a virtue – it pays.

E. M. FORSTER
British novelist
epigraph to 'Howard's End'
Only connect.

The Observer 1951
Spoon feeding in the long run teaches us nothing but the shape of the spoon.

BETTY FRIEDAN
American feminist
'The Feminine Mystique' 1963
A mystique does not compel its own acceptance.

MILTON FRIEDMAN
American economist
Playboy 1973
One man's opportunism is another man's statesmanship.

There's no such thing as a free lunch.

R. BUCKMINSTER FULLER
American engineer
Playboy 1972
If we do more with less, our resources will be adequate to take care of everybody.

WILLIAM H. GASS
American philosopher
New York Review of Books 1971
We always ski on the higher slopes when we can.

CHARLES DE GAULLE
French statesman 1958
When everything is going badly and you are trying to make up your mind, look towards the heights, no complications there.

ANDRE GIDE
French Writer
in 'The Faber Book of Aphorisms' 1964
We wholly conquer only what we assimilate.

LILLIAN GISH
American film star
Esquire 1969
What you get is a living – what you give is a life.

SIR JAMES GOLDSMITH
British businessman
On paying top salaries on his magazine 'Now!' 1979
If you pay peanuts, you get monkeys.

RUTH GORDON
American actress
New York Post 1971
I think there is one smashing rule – never face the facts.

THE GREEN BERETS
American special troops
unofficial motto . . .
If you've got 'em by the balls, their hearts and minds will follow.

DANIEL S. GREENBERG
American science writer
Washington Post 1977
Don't ask the barber whether you need a haircut.

TREVOR GRIFFITHS
British playwright
'The Comedians'
Cough and the world coughs with you. Fart and you stand alone.

LORD HAILSHAM
British lawyer 1960
The best way I know to win an argument is to start by being in the right.

DAVID HALBERSTAM
American journalist
advice on success in politics . . .
Always stay in with the outs.

H. R. HALDEMAN
American official
Once the toothpaste is out of the tube, it's hard to get it back in.

ALEX HAMILTON
British journalist
The Listener 1978
Those who stand for nothing fall for anything.

RUSSELL HARTY
British TV chat-show host 1981
God made it a firm principle that, with one private and marginally indelicate exception everyone else's smells are more fragrant than one's own . . . cooking . . . soap . . . books.

HENRY S. HASKINS
American writer
Good behaviour is the last refuge of mediocrity.

'Meditations in Wall Street'
Study any confusion and you will find
that it is peace in an early stage.

When a thing is not worth overdoing,
leave it alone.

ROLF HOCHHUTH
German playwright
'The Representative' 1966
The man who says what he thinks is
finished, and the man who thinks what
he says is an idiot.

NODDY HOLDER
British rock musician
If you can't say it in a three minute song,
you can't say it at all.

MICK JAGGER
British rock star
It's all right letting yourself go, as long
as you can get yourself back.

LYNDON B. JOHNSON
American President
I never trust a man unless I've got his
pecker in my pocket.

Never trust a man whose eyes are too
close to his nose.

While you're saving your face, you're
losing your ass.

I've got on my watch the Golden Rule:
Do unto others as you would have them
do unto you.

JOHN JUNOR
British journalist 1979
An ounce of emotion is equal to a ton of
facts.

JANOS KADAR
Hungarian leader 1961
Whoever is not against us is with us.

ELIA KAZAN
American firm director
in 'The Understudy' 1975
Never say never.

HENRY KISSINGER
American diplomat 1976
A little uncertainty is good for everyone.

JOHN F. KENNEDY
American president
Stay out of sight and you stay out of
trouble.

Inaugural speech . . .
Let us never negotiate out of fear, but let
us never fear to negotiate.

KEN KESEY
American novelist
Take what you can use and let the rest
go by.

NIKITA KHRUSCHEV
Russian leader
If you cannot catch a bird of paradise,
better take a wet hen.

KARL KRAUS
German artist
'Karl Kraus' by Harry Zohn
It is better not to express what one
means than to express what one does not
mean.

R. D. LAING
British psychiatrist
'Massey Lectures' 1968
Rule A: Don't. Rule A1: Rule A does not
exist. Rule A2: Do not discuss the exist-
ence or non-existence of Rules A, A1 or
A2.

FRAN LEBOWITZ
American journalist
'Metropolitan Life' 1978
If you are of the opinion that the contemplation of suicide is sufficient evidence of a poetic nature, do not forget
that actions speak louder than words.

STANISLAW J. LEC
Polish poet
in 'The Faber Book of Aphorisms' 1964
Every stink that fights the ventilator
thinks it is Don Quixote.

He who has no conscience makes up by
lacking it.

MAX LERNER
American academic
'The Unfinished Country' 1959
I have a simple principle for the conduct
of life – never to resist an adequate
temptation.

DAVID LEVINE
American caricaturist
Esquire 1971
There is no such thing as a plain face.

LIBERACE
(Walter Valentino Liberace)
American pianist
quoted in The Times 1981
Too much of a good thing is simply wonderful.

ARNOLD LOBEL
American writer
'Fables' 1980
Wishes, on their way to coming true, will not be rushed.

Too much of anything often leaves one with a feeling of regret.

Without a doubt, there is such a thing as too much order.

DAVID MAHONEY
American businessman
in M. Korda 'Power in the Office' 1976
If two people agree all the time, one of them is unnecessary.

GABRIEL GARCIA MARQUEZ
Argentine writer
'El Coronel no Tiene quien le Escriba'
When you have a healthy appetite there is no such thing as bad bread.

ROBERT MORLEY
British actor and wit
The Observer 1964
Beware of the conversationalist who adds 'In other words'. He is merely starting afresh.

GEORGE NAPPER
American policeman
Time 1981
When you're up to your ass in alligators, it's hard to remember that your purpose is draining the swamp.

SATCHELL PAIGE
American baseball star
Don't look back, something might be gaining on you.

C. NORTHCOTE PARKINSON
American historian
'Inlaws and Outlaws' 1962
Expansion means complexity and com-
plexity decay.
in 'Murphy's Law' by Arthur Block, 1979
Delay is the deadliest form of denial.

DONN PEARCE
American writer
'Cool Hand Luke'
Sometimes nothing is a real cool hand.

ALFRED PERLMAN
American railroad executive
New York Times 1958
After you've done a thing the same way for two years look it over carefully. After five years look at it with suspicion and after ten years throw it away and start all over again.

HAROLD 'KIM' PHILBY
British diplomat and Russian spy
1967
To betray, you must first belong.

PRINCE PHILIP
1962
The art of being a good guest is to know when to leave.

'THE PRODUCERS'
Embassy 1968 screenplay by Mel Brooks
Zero Mostel: Leo, he who hesitates is poor.

MAGNUS PYKE
British scientist
The Listener 1963
To see is often to understand. This may be as true in science as in ordinary life.

SAM RAYBURN
American politician
maxim:
If you want to get along, go along.

ALAIN RESNAIS
French film director
An influence ceases when the person receiving it becomes aware of it.

GINGER ROGERS
American film star
in 'The Wit of Women' ed. L. and M. Cowan 1969
The only way to enjoy anything in this life is to earn it first.

MIES VAN DER ROHE
American architect
maxim:
Less is more.

quoted in National Observer obituary 1969
It is better to be good than to be original.

BILLY ROSE
American theatrical producer
New York Post 1957
Never put your money in anything that eats or needs repainting.

JOHNNY ROTTEN (John Lydon)
British rock star
Turn the other cheek too often and you get a razor through it.

TODD RUNDGREN
American rock star
Anything you can just go out and get isn't going to inspire people as much as something they have to go through a little bit of hell to have.

DAMON RUNYON
American writer
The race is not always to the swift, nor the battle to the strong, but that's the way to bet.

ROBB SAGENDORPH
American economist
Esquire 1969
Try to find something that works and stay with it.

EDWARD 'DEATH VALLEY SCOT-TY' SCOTT
American nomad
last words 1954
I've got four things to live by: don't say nothin' that will hurt anybody; don't give advice, nobody will take it anyway; don't complain; don't explain.

DAVID O. SELZNICK
American film producer
There are only two classes – first class and no class.

GEORGE BERNARD SHAW
Irish writer and playwright
'Maxims for Revolutionists'
Do not do unto others as they would they should do unto you – their tastes may not be the same.

PAUL SIMON
American singer
Song Title
One Man's Ceiling Is Another Man's Floor (Pattern Music)

WILLIE 'THE LION' SMITH
American jazz musician
Esquire 1964
It's better to duck than to hurry yourself out of this world by thinking you can roll with the punches.

NANCY SPAIN
British journalist
Only a fool would make the bed every day.

ADLAI STEVENSON
American politician
quoted 1969
One man's cliché can be another man's conviction.

STEWART'S LAW OF RETROACTION
in 'Murphy's Law Book Two' by Arthur Bloch 1980
It is easier to get forgiveness than permission.

KARL-HEINZ STOCKHAUSEN
German composer
dictum 1956
No neo-, no repetition, no variation, no development.

TOM STOPPARD
British playwright
Guardian 1973
It's better to be quotable than to be honest.

'Rosencrantz & Guildenstern are Dead' 1967
Every exit is an entry somewhere.

THEODORE STURGEON
American science fiction writer
Ninety per cent of everything is crap.

DAVID THOMAS
British rock musician 1979
If you can explain it, it's not worth doing.

HUNTER S. THOMPSON
American journalist
maxim:
When the going gets weird – the weird get going.

JAMES THURBER
American humorist
'The Thurber Carnival' 1945
He who hesitates is sometimes saved.

TINY TIM
(Herbert Buckingham Khaury)
American singer
motto:
Keep walking and keep smiling.

ROBERT TOWNSEND
American businessman
'Up The Organisation' 1970
Getting there isn't half the fun – it's all the fun.

ARNOLD TOYNBEE
British historian
'Civilisation on Trial'
Familiarity is the opiate of the imagination.

1947
No annihilation without representation.

PROF. ROBERT TRIFFIN
American academic 1974
We used to say that things will get worse before they get better; now we say they will be worse before they're still worse.

KENNETH TYNAN
British critic
review of 'Titus Andronicus' 1957
Those who devote themselves to making silk purses out of sows' ears are in duty bound to go the whole hog.

JOHN UPDIKE
American writer
The New Yorker 1975
Appealingness is inversely proportional to attainability.

Possession diminishes perception of value, immediately.

ANDY WARHOL
American artist
'From A to B & Back Again 1975
As soon as you stop wanting something you get it. I've found that to be absolutely axiomatic.

'Exposures' 1979
One's company, two's a crowd and three's a party.

'WE'RE NO ANGELS'
Paramount 1955 screenplay by Ranald Mac-Dougall based on La Cuisine des Anges, play by Albert Husson
John Baer: Sentiment has no cash value.

ALFRED NORTH WHITEHEAD
British philosopher
in 'The Faber Book of Aphorisms' 1964
Seek simplicity and distrust it.

'Necessity is the mother of invention' is a silly proverb. 'Necessity is the mother of futile dodges' is much nearer the truth.

KATHARINE WHITEHORN
British journalist
The Observer 1974
I am firm. You are obstinate. He is a pig-headed fool.

MAE WEST
American film star
Keep a diary and one day it'll keep you.

RICHARD WEST
American journalist 1975
Sooner or later, everything becomes too important for someone else to handle.

BUD WILKINSON
American college football coach 1954
The man who tried his best and failed is superior to the man who never tried.

FLIP WILSON
American comedian 1971
You can't expect to hit the jackpot if you don't put a few nickels in the machine.

Time 1972
Be sudden, be neat. Be unimpassioned. If you are serious about something, leave it out.

HAROLD WILSON
British politician 1970
One man's wage rise is another man's price increase.

FRANK LLOYD WRIGHT
American architect
quoted in New Society 1967
Keep your eye on the filling station, it is the true agent of decentralisation.

'The Future of Architecture' 1953
Less is only more where more is no good.

FRANK ZAPPA
American rock musician 1979
One of my favourite philosophical tenets is that people will agree with you only if they already agree with you. You do not change people's minds.

HUMANITY
Mankind

LOUIS ARAGON
French playwright
Man does not seem to be endowed with
an infinite capacity for wonder.

JACOBO ARBENZ
Guatemalan revolutionary,1953
Man is not just a stomach . . . above all
he hungers for dignity.

RAYMOND ARON
French academic
'Dimensions de la Conscience Historique'
Man is a reasonable being, but is
mankind.

JEAN ARP
French poet
'Dadaland'
Man declares red what he called green
the day before, and what in reality is
black. He is forever making definitive
statements on life, man and art, and he
has no more idea that a mushroom what
life, man and art actually are.

'Notes from a Diary'
I am justified in my theory that man is
a pot the handles of which fell out of his
own holes.

FERNANDO ARRABAL
Spanish playwright
The Times 1971
Man is like an iceberg – the more im-
portant part is hidden under the water.
It interests me to dive down to the most
hidden places.

ALAN AYCKBOURN
British playwright
TV Times 1976
There's an awful lot of grey in people.

GASTON BACHELARD
French scientist
'La psychanalyse du feu'
Man is a creation of desire, not of need.

KARL BARTH
Swiss theologian
Time 1954
Men have never been good, they are not
good, they never will be good.

CAPTAIN BEEFHEART
American rock star
Friends 1970
There are forty people in the world and
five of them are hamburgers.

ERIC BERNE
American psychologist
'Games people Play' 1964
To say that the bulk of social activity
consists of playing games does not
necessarily mean that it is mostly 'fun',
or that the parties are not seriously engaged in the relationship. . . The essential characteristic of human play is not
that the emotions are spurious, but that
they are regulated.

RAY BRADBURY
British science fiction writer
We are anthill men upon an anthill
world.

STEWART BRAND
American environmentalist
in the 'Whole Earth Catalogue' 1969
We are as Gods and might as well get
used to it.

BERTOLT BRECHT
German playwright
'The Messingkauf Dialogues' 1965
Man's fate has become man himself.

Man is the sum of all the social conditions of all times.

JACOB BRONOWSKI
British scientist
quoted The Listener 1979
Man is a singular creature. He has a set
of gifts which make him unique among
the animals, so that unlike them he is
not a figure in the landscape – he is the
shaper of the landscape.

ALBERT CAMUS
French writer
quoted in New York Times 1977
We are all special cases.

ELIAS CANETTI
Bulgarian writer
Mankind has collected together all the wisdom of his ancestors, and can see what a fool man is.

What is man without respect? But what has respect made of him?

'Crowds and Power'
Here, each of us is a king in a field of corpses.

RAYMOND CHANDLER
American novelist
'Casual Notes on the Mystery Novel' 1949
Show me a man or woman who cannot stand mysteries and I will show you a fool, a clever fool, perhaps, but a fool just the same.

JACQUES CHARDONNE
French writer
'Propos comme ça'
Science and time have the imagination. Man is a driveller.

MALCOLM DE CHAZAL
French writer
'Sens Plastique' 1949
Man looks to himself for what he does not find in others, and to others for what he has too much of in himself.

SIR WINSTON CHURCHILL
British statesman
Broadly speaking, human beings may be divided into three classes: those who are billed to death, those who are worried to death and those who are bored to death.

E. M. CIORAN
French philosopher
'The Fall Into Time' 1971
One is never so much a man as when one regrets being so.

PHILIP K. DICK
American science fiction writer
'The Three Stigmata of Palmer Eldritch' 1966
I mean, after all; you have to consider that we're only made out of dust. That's admittedly not much to go on and we

shouldn't forget that. But even considering, I mean it's a sort of bad beginning, we're not doing too bad. So I personally have faith that even in this lousy situation we're faced with we can make it. You get me?

LORD DUNSANY
Irish poet 1954
Humanity, let us say, is like people packed in an automobile which is travelling downhill without lights at terrific speed and driven by a four-year-old child. The signposts along the way are all marked 'Progress'.

CHARLES DYER
British playwright
'Contemporary Dramatists' 1977
Man's disease is loneliness; God's is progress.

MAX ERNST
German painter
'Writings'
Such is the vocation of man: to deliver himself from blindness.

MICK FARREN
British writer
We're all hookers. What matters is dignity.

WILLIAM FAULKNER
American novelist
Nobel Prize speech 1950
I believe that man will not merely endure. He will prevail.

FREDERICK FORSYTH
British novelist
The Observer 1974
My ideal qualities . . . strength without brutality, honesty without priggishness, courage without recklessness, humour without frivolity, humanity without sentimentality, intelligence without deviousness, sceptisism (sic) without cynicism.

KIM FOWLEY
American rock producer
The only guy who is honest is the guy who sings in the shower. Everyone else is a prostitute.

JUANA FRANCES
Spanish artist
Contemporary Artists 1977
Man is trampled by the same forces he had created.

R. BUCKMINSTER FULLER
American engineer
Playboy 1972
Man's function in the universe is to do certain sortings that need to be done in order to maintain its total integrity.

Evolution *is* man, man in his universal aspect, functioning as part of the universe.

ANDRE GIDE
French writer
'Journal'
Man is more interesting than men. It's *him*, not *them* whom God made in his image. Each is more precious than all.(cf. Stalin)

JOSEPH GOLDBERG
American grocer 1970
The grocery store is the great equalizer where mankind comes to grips with the facts of life like toilet tissue.

WITOLD GOMBROWICZ
Polish writer
quoted in 'Contemporary Artists' 1977
Man is made in such a way that he continually has to define himself and continually escape his own definitions.

ANDREW HACKER
American political scientist
in 'Malice in Blunderland' by Thomas L. Martin Jr 1973
The belief that enhanced understanding will necessarily stir a nation (or an organisation) to action is one of mankind's oldest illusions.

JOSEPH HELLER
American novelist
Some men are born mediocre, some men achieve mediocrity, and some men have mediocrity thrust upon them.

RAYNER HEPPENSTALL
British writer
'Contemporary Novelists' 1976

We are all largely fictitious, even to ourselves.

'HONDO'
Warner Bros 1953 screen play by James Edward Grant, based on short story by Louis L'Amour
John Wayne: A man ought to do what he thinks is right.

ARTHUR KOESTLER
British philosopher
'Bricks to Babel' 1981
The disastrous history of our species indicates the futility of all attempts at a diagnosis which do not take into account the possibility that *homo sapiens* is a victim of one of evolution's countless mistakes.

The Observer 1969
Man is an aberrant species, suffering from a biological malfunction, a specific disorder of behaviour which sets him apart from all other animal species, just as language science and art set him apart in a positive sense.

Man may even manage to defuse the time bomb around his neck, once he has understood the mechanisms which make it tick.

R. D. LAING
British psychiatrist
quoted in The Image 1973
Behind, above beyond and in man the war rages on. We are shattered, tattered, demented remnants of a once glorious army. . . This is no time for dignity or heroics. It has gone past all that, all that last desperate clutch. I do assure you. The dreadful has already happened.

CLAUDE LEVI-STRAUSS
French anthropologist
'World on the Wane' 1961
Man is not alone in the universe, any more than the individual is alone in the group, or any one society alone among other societies.

SALVADOR DE MADRIAGA
Spanish writer
'Morning without Noon'
Considering how bad men are, it is wonderful how well they behave.

ANDRE MALRAUX
French writer
'Antimemoires'
The truth of a man is first and foremost what he hides.

What is man? A miserable little pile of secrets.

JONATHAN MILLER
British doctor and writer
'The Body in Question' 1978
The human species is, to some extent, the result of mistakes which arrested our development and prevented us from assuming the somewhat unglamorous form of our primitive ancestors.

ALBERTO MORAVIA
Italian writer
'Man as an End' 1964
Modern man – whether in the womb of the masses, or with his workmates, or with his family, or alone – can never for one moment forget that he is living in a world in which he is a means and whose end is not his business.

DESMOND MORRIS
British anthropologist
The Naked Ape 1967
We are, to put it mildly, in a mess, and there is a strong chance that we shall have exterminated ourselves by the end of the century. Our only consolation will have to be that, as a species, we have had an exciting term of office.

There are one hundred and ninety-three living species of monkeys and apes. One hundred and ninety-two of them are covered with hair. The exception is a naked ape, self-named *Homo sapiens*.

REV. DR. EDWARD NORMAN
British academic
Reith Lecturer 1978
On the whole, people are rubbish, and they deserve to be awakened to the need to change and amend themselves not by some social factor or some force of circumstance but by conversion of their soul.

    I really do not personally feel entitled to good things in this life, to the promise of truth, to an understanding of reality, to a happy family life or whatever. All the problems of our society are caused by the false expectations of people who are led to suppose that they are entitled to these things.

JOSE ORTEGA Y GASSET
Spanish philosopher
'Aesthetic Essays' 1956
Primitive man is by definition tactile man.

GEORGE ORWELL
British essayist
'Collected Essays'
On the whole human beings want to be good, but not too good and not quite all the time.

KERRY PACKER
Australian entrepreneur 1977
There's a little bit of the whore in all of us.

ANTONIO PORCHIA
Argentine writer
'Voces' 1968
If you do not raise your eyes you will think you are the highest point.

ADAM CLAYTON POWELL
American politician
'Keep the Faith, Baby!' 1967
Human thought, like God, makes the world in its own image.

RAYMOND QUENEAU
French historian
'A Model History'
Man's usual routine is to work and to dream.

BERTRAND RUSSELL
British philosopher
'New Hopes for a Changing World' 1951
The more we realise our minuteness and our impotence in the face of cosmic forces, the more amazing becomes what human beings have achieved.

JEAN-PAUL SARTRE
French philosopher
preface to a book on Algeria by Henri Alleg
Anybody, at any time, may equally find himself victim or executioner.

Man can will nothing unless he has first understood that he must count on no one but himself; that he is alone, abandoned on earth in the midst of his infinite responsibilities, without help, with no other aim than the one he sets himself, with no other destiny than the one he forges for himself on this earth.

Situations 1947/49
Man is not the sum of what he had already, but rather the sum of what he does not yet have, of what he could have.

MURRAY SCHISGAL
American writer
Playboy 1975
To be human is to be fucked. To know that you're fucked right off the bat.

CHARLES M. SCHULZ
American cartoonist
'Go Fly a Kite, Charlie Brown' 1963
I love mankind, it's people I can't stand.

ALBERT SCHWEITZER
German missionary
on politics
Man is a clever animal who behaves like an imbecile.

ALEXANDER SOLZHENITSYN
Russian novelist
The Times 1973
There is one psychological peculiarity in the human being that strikes you: to shun even the slightest signs of trouble on the outer edge of your existence at time of well being. To yield in many situations, even important and spiritual and central ones, as long as it prolongs one's well-being and suddenly, reaching the last frontiers, then he finds himself enough firmness to support himself on the final step and give up his life, but not his principles. Because of the first quality mankind has never been able to hold on to one single attained plateau; thanks to the second quality mankind has pulled itself out of all bottomless chasms.

SUSAN SONTAG
American essayist
'Styles of Radical Will' 1969
The becoming of man is the history of the exhaustion of his possibilities.

STANLEY SYKES
British anaesthetist
in 'The Wit of Medicine' ed. L. and M. Cowan 1972
Nineteenth Century scientists actually classified man as *Homo Sapiens* – man the wise. How foolish of them. Man the clever, if you like; man the brainy, man the intellectual, but not man the wise. Wisdom is very different from cleverness.

ALLEN TATE
American critic
quoted in 'Contemporary Literary Critics' ed. Elmer Borklund 1977
Man is a creature that in the long run has got to believe in order to know, and to know in order to do.

PAUL TILLICH
American theologian
Saturday Evening Post 1958
Man transforms everything he encounters into a tool; and in doing so he himself becomes a tool. But if he asks, a tool for what, there is no answer.

ARNOLD TOYNBEE
British historian
The Observer 1963
The human race's prospects of survival were considerably better when we were defenceless against tigers than they are today when we have become defenceless against ourselves.

GENERAL HENNING VON TRESCKOW
an anti-Hitler plotter
suicide note 1945
The worth of a man is certain only if he is prepared to sacrifice his life for his convictions.

DAME REBECCA WEST
British writer
quoted in 'Rebecca West: Artist and Thinker' by Peter Wolfe
Man is a hating rather than a loving animal.

'The Court and the Castle' 1957
Humanity is never more sphinxlike than when it is expressing itself.

EDWARD WESTON
American photographer
*in 'Photographers on Photography' ed. N.
Lyons 1966*
Man is the actual medium of expression
– not the tool he elects to use as a means.

PATRICK WHITE
Australian writer
Southerly 1973
Man is like Frankenstein's monster who
periodically gets out of control.

Life

ISABELLE ADJANI
French actress
Time 1979
Life is worth being lived, but not being
discussed all the time.

SPIRO AGNEW
American politician 1969
All life is essentially the contributions
that come from compromise.

EDWARD ALBEE
American playwright
*quoted in 'Behind the Scenes' ed. Joseph F.
McCrindle*
People would rather sleep their way
through life than stay awake for it.

WOODY ALLEN
American film star
Esquire 1977
Life is a concentration camp. You're
stuck here and there's no way out and
you can only rage impotently against
your persecutors.

LOUIS ARAGON
French playwright
'Les Voyageurs de l'imperiale'
Life is a traveller who lets his suitcase
drag behind him to cover his tracks.

BROOKS ATKINSON
American essayist
'Once Around the Sun' 1951
Life is seldom as unendurable as, to
judge by the facts, it logically ought to
be.

FRANCIS BACON
British artist
Sunday Times 1975
Existance, in a way, is so banal, that you
might as well make a kind of grandeur

of it, rather than be nursed to oblivion.

JOOST BALJEU
Dutch artist
'Contemporary Artists' 1977
Contemporary life demonstrates the
tragic divorce of economics and
aesthetics.

PROFESSOR WILLIAM BARRETT
British philosopher
The Listener 1978
It is the familiar that usually eludes us
in life. What is before our nose is what
we see last.

SAMUEL BECKETT
Irish author
quoted in New York Review of Books 1971
Our life is a succession of Paradises successively denied, . . . the only true Paradise is the Paradise that has been lost.

ALAN BENNETT
British playwright
'Beyond The Fringe' 1961
Life is rather like a tin of sardines, we're
all of us looking for the key.

JACK BENNY
American comedian
Esquire 1965
Everything is habit. Everything is
rhythm.

BERNARD BERENSON
British art historian
'Notes' 1950
Life is a one-way street.

SIR ISAIAH BERLIN
British philosopher
'Personal Impressions' 1980
Life may be seen through many win-

dows, none of them necessarily clear or opaque, less or more distorting than any of the others.

J. D. BERNAL
British scientist
'The Origin of Life' 1967
Life is a partial, continuous, progressive, multiform and conditionally interactive self-realisation of the potentialities of atomic electron states.

WOLF BIERMANN
German poet
'Bilanzballade in Dreissigsten Jahr'
Life goes at such a terrific pace – A few years full of youth and grace and then you fall flat on your face before world history.

BIFF KARDZ
British series of postcards
postcard 1981
Life is a meaningless comma in the sentence of life.

BURT BLECHMAN
American writer
'Maybe' 1967
Maybe the biggest problem in life is how to spend it.

PAUL BOCUSE
French chef
The Listener 1978
Life is a practical joke.

JORGE LUIS BORGES
Argentine writer
quoted as epigraph for the Gae Aulenti exhibition at MOMA 1972
Nothing is built on stone; all is built on sand, but we must build as if the sand were stone.

MICHEL BUTOR
French writer
'Repertoire II'
Our daily life is a bad serial by which we let ourselves be bewitched.

ALBERT CAMUS
French writer
'Notebooks' 1962
Every minute of life carries with it its miraculous value, and its face of eternal youth.

JULIA CHILD
American cookery writer
Life itself is the proper binge.

CYRIL CONNOLLY
British critic
'The Unquiet Grave' 1945
Life is a maze in which we take the wrong turning before we have learnt to walk.

QUENTIN CRISP
British writer
'How To Become A Virgin' 1981
The very purpose of existence is to reconcile the glowing opinion we hold of ourselves with the appalling things that other people think about us.

'The Naked Civil Servant' 1968
Life was a funny thing that happened to me on the way to the grave.

RODNEY DANGERFIELD
American comedian
Life is just a bowl of pits.

GERALD DURRELL
British animal conservationist
The Guardian 1971
Anyone who has got any pleasure at all should try to put something back. Life is like a superlative meal and the world is like the maitre d'hotel. What I am doing is the equivalent of leaving a reasonable tip.

IAN DURY
British rock musician
The only two things that matter in life: the one is tits and the other is prison. Prison, would be solitude, frustration, study and tits would be all those things which I enjoy, starting with tits, cos I'm a red-blooded, half-cocked little chap.

ALBERT EINSTEIN
German physicist
quoted in 'Contemporary Architects' 1980
The most beautiful thing to be felt by man is the mysterious side of life. There is the cradle of Art and real Science.

WILLIAM EMPSON
British critic
quoted in Contemporary Literary Critics ed. Elmer Borklund 1977
The object of life, after all, is not to un-

derstand things, but to maintain one's defences and equilibrium and live as well as one can.

WERNER ERHARD
(John Paul Rosenberg)
founder of est
The Listener 1978
There is no secret. The secret is what is, is; and what isn't, isn't.

EDITH EVANS
British actress
The Sunday Times 1961
Life is long enough, it seems to me, but not quite broad enough. Things crowd in so thickly it takes time for experience to become clarified before it can be placed to the full service of art.

CLIFTON FADIMAN
American essayist 1960
For most men life is a search for the proper manila envelope in which to get themselves filed.

FEDERICO FELLINI
Italian film director
There is no end. There is no beginning. There is only the infinite passion of life.

ERICH FROMM
American psychologist
There is no meaning to life except the meaning man gives his life by the unfolding of his powers.

GINSBERG'S THEOREM
quoted in Arthur Bloch 'Murphy's Law' 1979
1. You can't win.
2. You can't break even.
3. You can't even quit the game.

JULIEN GREEN
French writer
'Journal'
Our life is a book that writes itself alone. We are characters in a novel who don't always understand very well what the author wants.

DAG HAMMARSKJOLD
Swedish diplomat
'Markings' 1964
Life only demands from you the strength you possess. Only one feat is possible – not to have run away.

WERNER HEISENBERG
German scientist
'Physics and Beyond' 1971
Unless you stake your life, life will not be won.

KATHARINE HEPBURN
American film star
Esquire 1967
Life is to be lived. If you have to support yourself, you had bloody well better find some way that is going to be interesting. And you don't do that by sitting around wondering about yourself.

L. RUST HILLS
American journalist
Esquire 1970
Most people's lives aren't complex – they're just complicated.

DUSTIN HOFFMAN
American film star
Playboy 1975
Life is really a game and you must treat it as a game... Life stinks, but that doesn't mean you don't enjoy it.

'THE INN OF THE SIXTH HAPPINESS'
20th Century Fox 1958 screenplay by Isabel Lennart, based on The Small Woman, book by Alan Burgess
Robert Donat: A life that is planned is a closed life... It can be endured, perhaps. It cannot be lived.

WALLACE JOHNSON
American hotelier
Esquire 1964
This life of yours is just like an empty field. Your mind doesn't care what you plant in it . . . but whatever you plant, you fertilize it, and that is what grows.

'KEY LARGO'
Warner Bros 1948 screenplay John Huston & Richard Brooks, based on play by Maxwell Anderson
Humphrey Bogart: If your head says one thing and your whole life says another, your head always loses.

NIKITA KHRUSCHEV
Russian leader
quoted in New York Times 1958
Life is short. Live it up.

MICHAEL KORDA
British writer
'Power in the Office' 1976
All life is a game of power. The object of the game is simple enough: to know what you want and get it.

TOM LEHRER
American humorist
Life is a sewer. What you take out depends on what you put into it.

JERRY LEE LEWIS
American rock star
Life is just a vapour. You breathe in and what the heck.

DAVID MADDEN
British novelist
in 'Contemporary Novelists' 1976
One's life should be a self-created contradiction of the fact that life is basically absurd.

RENE MAGRITTE
Belgian artist
quoted in New Society 1969
Life, the Universe, the Void have no value for thought when it is truly free. The only thing that has value for it is meaning, that moral concept of the impossible.

BERNARD MALAMUD
American novelist
New York Times 1979
Life is a tragedy full of joy.

ANDRE MALRAUX
French writer
'Antimemoires'
This inn without roads that we call life.

'THE MATCHMAKER'
Paramount 1958 screenplay by John Michael Hayes, based on play by Thornton Wilder
Shirley Booth: Life's never quite interesting enough, somehow. You people who come to the movies know that.

ELSA MAXWELL
American socialite
'How To Do It' 1957
Someone said that life is a party. You join after it's started and you leave before it's finished

HENRY MILLER
American writer
'The World of Sex' 1957
Life moves on, whether we act as cowards or heroes. Life has no other discipline to impose, if we would but realize it, than to accept life unquestioningly. Everything we shut our eyes to, everything we run away from, everything we deny, denigrate or despise, serves to defeat us in the end. What seems nasty, painful, evil, can become a source of beauty, joy and strength, if faced with an open mind. Every moment is a golden one for him who has the vision to recognise it as such.

'Quiet Days in Clichy' 1956
Life is constantly providing us with new funds, new resources, even when we are reduced to immobility. In life's ledger there is no such thing as frozen assets.

VAN MORRISON
British rock star
You do what you're doing and if it's going to happen it will and there's nothing you can do about it.

MALCOLM MUGGERIDGE
British journalist 1965
For myself I grow daily more convinced with a kind of inward delight amounting at times to ecstasy that the voyage of life is an episode of derisive insignificance.

LEWIS MUMFORD
American critic
'In the Name of Sanity'
Let us confess it – the human situation is always desperate.

VLADIMIR NABOKOV
Russian writer
'Commentary' in Pale Fire 1962
Human life is but a series of footnotes to a vast, obscure unfinished masterpiece.

Our existence is but a brief crack of light between two eternities of darkness.

OGDEN NASH
American poet
'The Ogden Nash Pocket Book'
In real life it only takes one to make a quarrel.

JAWAHARLAL NEHRU
Indian leader
Life is like a game of cards. The hand that is dealt you represents determinism. The way you play it is free will.

REINHOLD NIEBUHR
American theologian
'Faith and History' 1949
Life has no meaning except in terms of responsibility.

JOSE ORTEGA Y GASSET
Spanish philosopher
Partisan Review 1949
We do not live to think but, on the contrary, we think in order that we may succeed in surviving.

GEORGE ORWELL
British essayist
'Shooting an Elephant' 1950
Most people get a fair amount of fun out of their lives, but on balance life is suffering and only the very young or the very foolish imagine otherwise.

DOROTHY PARKER
American writer
Life is a glorious cycle of song/A medley of extemporania/And love is a thing that can never go wrong/And I am Marie of Rumania.

CESARE PAVESE
Italian novelist
'The Burning Brand' 1961
The art of living is the art of knowing how to believe lies.

WALKER PERCY
American writer
'Questions They Never Asked Me' Esquire 1977
As Einstein once said, ordinary life in an ordinary place on an ordinary day in the modern world is a dreary business. I mean *dreary*. People will do anything just to escape this dreariness.

ST. JOHN PERSE
French writer
Life has become an office routine and has lost the experimental contact with Nature.

'THE PICTURE OF DORIAN GRAY'
MGM 1945 screenplay by Albert Lewis, based on novel by Oscar Wilde
George Sanders: When a man says he has exhausted life, you may be sure life has exhausted him.

ANTONIO PORCHIA
Argentine writer
'Voces' 1968
One lives in the hope of becoming a memory.

ANTHONY POWELL
British novelist
New York Times 1958
Life is full of internal dramas, instantaneous and sensational, played to an audience of one.

KAREL REISZ
British film director
Daily Mail 1966
Life isn't a choice. Something comes up or it doesn't. A lot of choices choose you.

ALAIN ROBBE-GRILLET
French novelist
The Guardian 1967
Life is a game whose rules each of us invents for himself. No one knows the rules. Reality is continually unreal, but is also continually real. What we do is invent something which also exists.

ELEANOR ROOSEVELT
American First Lady
'Autobiography' 1961
Life was meant to be lived and curiosity must be kept alive. One must never, for whatever reason, turn his back on life.

TODD RUNDGREN
American rock star
So many people go through life without a direction. They just go from stop to stop. It's like they're on a bus and the only time they get off is to piss.

STANLEY J. SARNOFF
American physiologist
Time 1963
The process of living is the process of reacting to stress.

JEAN-PAUL SARTRE
French philosopher
Life begins on the other side of despair.

JOE SCHMIDT
American pro football player 1976
Life is a shit sandwich and everyday you take another bite.

BILLY SCOTT
American racing driver
If a man can fuck and drive race cars. . . Man, I mean, what else is there?

N. F. SIMPSON
British playwright
in 'Contemporary Dramatists' 1977
Life . . . a man trying to get a partially inflated rubber lilo into a suitcase slightly too small to take it even when *un*inflated.

CORNELIA OTIS SKINNER
American actress
One learns in life to keep silent and draw one's own confusions.

SUSAN SONTAG
American essayist
'Styles of Radical Will' 1969
Existence is no more than the precarious attainment of relevance in an intensely mobile flux of past, present and future.

WILLIE STARGELL
American baseball star 1976
Life is like a train. You expect delays from time to time. But not a derailment.

ROD STEIGER
American film star
Playboy 1969
It's true that tomorrow may be better – or worse. But today may not be so bad. You must appreciate the miracle that you're alive right now and forget about how, or if, you're going to live tomorrow.

Esquire 1969
We come. We go. And in between we try to understand.

TOM STOPPARD
British playwright
'Rosencrantz & Guildenstern Are Dead' 1967
Life is a gamble at terrible odds, if it was a bet you wouldn't take it.

'SUMMER OF '42'
Warner Bros 1971 Screenplay by Herman Raucher
Robert Mulligan: Life is made up of small comings and goings, and for everything that we take with us, there is something that we leave behind.

R. H. TAWNEY
British historian
The Observer 1953
What matters is the kind of life which people lead and the satisfaction they find in it. And here, I suspect, most of us think too much of problems and too little of persons.

CALVIN THOMAS
American writer
book title
Living Well Is The Best Revenge.

DYLAN THOMAS
British poet
'Under Milk Wood'
Polly Garter: Isn't life a terrible thing, thank God.

quoted in Equire 1965
We are born in other's pain and perish in our own.

PETE TOWNSHEND
British rock star
Nothing can really be better than waking up in the morning and everything is still the same as it was the day before. That's the best thing you can have in life – consistency of some kind.

KENNETH TYNAN
British critic
The Guardian 1971
All of life is more or less what the French would call *'s'imposer'* – to be able to create one's own terms for what one does.

GORE VIDAL
American writer
in 'Behind the Scenes' ed. Joseph P. McCrindle
Forcing the world to adjust to oneself has always seemed to me an honourable life work . . . that one fails in the end is irrelevant.

KURT VONNEGUT JR.
American writer
Life happens too fast for you ever to think about it. If you could just persuade people of this, but they insist on amassing information.

PETER DE VRIES
American writer
'The Vale of Laughter'
Life is a zoo in a jungle.

ANDY WARHOL
American artist
'From A to B and Back Again' 1975
Being born is like being kidnapped. And then sold into slavery.

ALAN WATTS
American philosopher
'Beat Zen, Square Zen and Zen'
If we live, we live; if we die, we die; if we suffer, we suffer; if we are terrified, we are terrified. There is no problem about it.

ALFRED NORTH WHITEHEAD
British philosopher
in 'The Faber Book of Aphorisms' 1964
Life is an offensive, directed against the repetition mechanism of the universe.

We think in generalities, but we live in detail.

'Science & the Modern World'
Human life is a flash of occasional enjoyments lighting up a mass of pain and misery, a bagatelle of transient experience.

THORNTON WILDER
American writer
The Observer 1957
Life is an unbroken succession of false situations.

HEATHCOTE WILLIAMS
British playwright
'The Speakers'
You come out of a woman and you spend the rest of your life trying to get back inside.

'The Immortalist' 1978
Life is simply an accumulation of all the forces that resist death.

KENNETH WILLIAMS
British actor
'Acid Drops' 1980
Our birth certificates should bear the warning 'Life is about dying', but like the cautionary instruction on the cigarette packet it would be just as much ignored.

TENNESSEE WILLIAMS
American playwright
Sunday Times 1974
Life is a terrifying experience, but oblivion is sadder.

'The Milk Train Doesn't Stop Here Any More' 1963
We all live in a house on fire, no fire department to call; no way out, just the upstairs window to look out of while the fire burns the house down with us trapped, locked in it.

Playboy 1973
All creative work, all life, in a sense, is a cri de coeur.

ANGUS WILSON
British writer
The Guardian 1973
The moral point is that everything is extremely complex and difficult and it mustn't be supposed that any of it can be done by rubbing a button and saying 'Abracadabra'. . . .life can be more satisfactory if people don't think there are easy answers.

Life is a serious attempt to make something of oneself and one's surroundings, but I also see it as a marvellous thing that you're put into where you get a lot of fun out of the impossibility of it all.

LUDWIG WITTGENSTEIN
German philosopher
in 'The Faber Book of Aphorisms' 1964
Physiological life is of course not 'Life'. And neither is psychological life. Life is the world.

TOM WOLFE
American journalist
The Listener 1970
The question that intrigues me: after you've met all the great threats and found that the great catastrophes of world history are not bearing down on

you, what do you do with your life? I don't think politicians are ready for this question, I don't think intellectuals are ready for it. But there are a lot of people who are instinctively ready to cross over into a really weird frontier in which more and more of life is dedicated to simply extending your own ego.

FRANK ZAPPA
American rock composer

'Brown Shoes Don't Make It'
Do you love it? Do you hate it?/There it is, the way you made it. (Frank Zappa Music)

'ZORBA THE GREEK'
20th Century Fox 1964 screenplay by Michael Cacoyannis from novel by Nikos Kazantakis
Anthony Quinn: Life is trouble. Only death is not. To be alive is to undo your belt and look for trouble.

Death

WOODY ALLEN
American film star
New York Herald Tribune 1975
The difference between sex and death is that with death you can do it alone and no one is going to make fun of you.

'Getting Even' 1972
On the plus side, death is one of the few things that can be done as easily lying down.

in E. Lax 'Woody Allen & His Comedy'
I don't want to achieve immortality through my work. I want to achieve it through not dying.

Newsweek 1975
It's not that I'm afraid to die, I just don't want to be there when it happens.

JEAN BAECHLER
French writer
'Suicides' 1980
Every suicide is a solution to a problem.

JAMES BALDWIN
American author
A TV film 1981
There is no refuge from confession except in suicide and suicide is confession.

'BANG THE DRUM SLOWLY'
Paramount 1973 screenplay by Mark Harris based on his novel
Michael Moriarty: Everybody knows everybody is dying. That's why people are as good as they are.

TALLULAH BANKHEAD
American film star
We're all paid off in the end, and the fools first.

S. N. BEHRMAN
American writer
I think immortality is an over-rated commodity.

ERIC BENTLEY
American writer
If one truly has lost hope, one would not be on hand to say so.

JORGE LUIS BORGES
Argentine writer
'Conversations with Jorge Luis Borges' ed. Richard Burgin 1973
You may win your heart's desire, but in the end you're cheated of it by death.

PIERRE BOULEZ
French composer
The Observer 1971
If you kill imagination, that is a kind of long-term suicide.

MEL BROOKS
American film director
Playboy 1975
Why do we have to die? As a kid you get nice little white shoes with white laces and a velvet suit with short pants and a nice collar and you go to college, you meet a nice girl and get married, work a few years and then you have to *die*!

What is that shit? They never wrote that in the contract!

NORMAN O. BROWN
American philosopher
There is no death by natural causes.

ANTHONY BURGESS
British writer
Playboy 1974
Death comes along like a gas bill one can't pay – and that's all one can say about it.

WILLIAM S. BURROUGHS
American writer
epigraph for Adrian Henri Poem 'Adrian Henri's Last Will & Testament' 1967
Nobody owns life, but anyone who can pick up a frying pan owns death.

ALBERT CAMUS
French writer
Neither in the hearts of men nor in the manners of society will there be a lasting peace until we outlaw death.

RENE CHAR
French writer
'La parole en archipel'
One is born amongst men; one dies, unconsoled, among the gods.

MONTGOMERY CLIFT
American film star
in 'Short Lives' by Katinka Matson 1980
Look! Look! If you look really hard at things you'll forget you're going to die.

CYRIL CONNOLLY
British critic
'The Unquiet Grave' 1945
There are many who dare not kill themselves for fear of what the neighbours will say.

LUIS MIGUEL DOMINGUIN
Spanish bullfighter 1959
Death is only a risk. The ring is the very essence of life itself.

CARL DOUGLAS
American pro football player 1972
Try not to take life too seriously. You're not going to get out of it alive anyway.

BOB DYLAN
American singer
'It's All Right Ma (I'm Only Bleeding)'
He not busy being born / Is busy dying. (M. Witmark & Sons)

ALBERT EINSTEIN
German physicist
quoted in 'The Immortalist' by Heathcote Williams 1978
The fear of death is the most unjustified of all fears, for there's no risk of accident to someone who's dead.

SUSAN ERTZ
quoted in A. Andrews 'Quotations for Speakers & Writers'
Millions long for immortality who do not know what to do with themselves on a rainy Sunday afternoon.

EDWARD GOREY
American illustrator
Esquire 1976
Now that Agatha Christie has died the one thing that keeps me from suicide is . . . how would I know who won next year's Academy Awards?

DAG HAMMARSKJOLD
Swedish diplomat
'Diaries'
In the last analysis it is our conception of death which decides our answers to all the questions that life puts to us.

'HARRY AND TONTO'
20th Century Fox 1974 screenplay by Paul Mazursky & Josh Greenfield
Art Carney: You know, you never really feel somebody suffering. You only feel their death.

WILL HAY
British comedian
this passage from the last book he was reading was carved on his gravestone 1949
For each of us there comes a moment when death takes us by the hand and says – it is time to rest, you are tired, lie down and sleep.

JOSEPH HELLER
American novelist
Playboy 1975
In a way dying is like having children – you never know what will come out.

DR. EDWARD HENDERSON
British clergyman
in 'The Wit of the Church' ed. M. Bateman and S. Stenning 1967
A great deal of money is expended on funerals and that, in itself, seems to betray a lack of confidence in the resurrection of the dead.

ERIC HOFFER
American philosopher
'The True Believer' 1951
Death has but one terror – that it has no tomorrow.

PROFESSOR SYDNEY HOOK
American academic
The fear of death has been the greatest ally of tyranny past and present.

ALFRED KAZIN
American critic
New York Review of Books 1981
Probably no one commits suicide without thinking of it much of his life.

JOHN MAYNARD KEYNES
British economist
In the long run we are all dead.

'KNOCK ON ANY DOOR'
directed by Nicholas Ray from the novel by Willard Motley
John Derek: Live fast, die young, and leave a good-looking corpse.

JOE LOUIS
American boxer 1965
Everybody wants to go to heaven, but nobody wants to die.

'LOVE STORY'
Paramount 1970 screenplay by Erich Segal from his novel
Ryan O' Neal: What can you say about a 25-year-old girl who died? That she was beautiful? And brilliant? That she loved Mozart and Bach? And the Beatles? And me?

ANDRE MALRAUX
French writer
'The Human Condition'
Only music can speak of death.

'L'espoir'
Death is not so serious. Pain is.

CHARLES MANSON
American murderer
quoted in Esquire 1971
Death is psychosomatic.

MAO ZEDONG (Mao Tse-tung)
Chinese leader
quoted in Playboy 1973
Death comes to everyone, but it varies in its significance. To die for the reactionary is as light as a feather, but to die for the revolution is heavier than Mount Tai.

JONATHAN MILLER
British doctor and writer
'The Body in Question' 1979
Mortality is not simply an avoidable accident, but a natural appointment, from which there is no hope of escape.

HENRI DE MONTHERLANT
French writer
'Notebooks'
There are two moments in life when every man is respectable – his childhood and his deathbed.

MALCOLM MUGGERIDGE
British journalist 1969
For us humans, everything is permanent – until it changes, as we are immortal until we die.

VLADIMIR NABOKOV
Russian novelist
Time 1981
Life is a great surprise. I do not see why death should not be an even greater one.

GEORGE ORWELL
British essayist
'Shooting an Elephant' 1950
One wants to stay alive, of course, but one only stays alive by virtue of the fear of death.

DOROTHY PARKER
American writer
'Writers at Work' 1st series 1958
It's not the tragedies that kiss us, it's the messes.

VERN PARTLOW
We hold these truths to be self-evident: all men could be cremated equal.

CESARE PAVESE
Italian novelist
in 'The Faber Book of Aphorisms' 1964
Many men on the point of an edifying death would be furious if they were suddenly restored to health.

JOHN PHILLIPS
American rock musician
Death is when you get sick one day and you don't get well again. Can't seem to shake it off.

SYLVIA PLATH
British poet
'Lady Lazarus'
Dying / Is an art, like everything else. / I do it exceptionally well.

FRANCIS PONGE
French writer
'Tome Premier'
A man sometimes shows in his death that he is worthy of living.

ANTONIO PORCHIA
Argentine writer
'Voces' 1968
I began my comedy as its only actor and I came to the end of it as it's only spectator.

ELEANOR ROOSEVELT
American First Lady
letter 1960
When you cease to make a contribution you begin to die.

ISAAC BASHEVIS SINGER
American writer
'The Family Moskat'
Death is the Messiah. That's the real truth.

TOM SNEVA
American motor racing star
The Guardian 1977
You have to treat death like any other part of life.

'SPARTACUS'
Universal 1960 screenplay by Dalton Trumbo based on novel by Howard Fast
Kirk Douglas: A free man dies, he loses the pleasure of life; a slave loses pain. Death is the only freedom a slave knows. That's why he's not afraid of it.

JOSEPH STALIN
Russian leader
quoted in 1958
A single death is a tragedy, a million deaths is a statistic.

TOM STOPPARD
British playwright
'Rosencrantz and Guildenstern are Dead' 1967
Eternity is a terrible thought. I mean, where's it going to end?

The bad end unhappily, the good unluckily. That's what tragedy means.

EVELYN WAUGH
British novelist
'Diaries' ed. Michael Davie 1976
We are American at puberty. We die French.

LINA WERTMULLER
Italian film director 1976
I don't think suicide is so terrible. Some rainy winter Sundays when there's a little boredom, you should always carry a gun. Not to shoot yourself, but to know exactly that you're always making a choice.

JOHN WHITING
British playwright
'John Whiting On Theatre' 1966
The tragedy of men is that they are men. And when there is food and drink, houses and clothing, peace, security and sanity for all, men will still be scared to death of death.

HEATHCOTE WILLIAMS
British playwright
'The Immortalist' 1978
Digital watches are death's dominoes.

Death comes like a thief in the night. Don't let yourself get mugged!

Immortality is the only cause you can't die for. If you can't take it with you, don't go!

TENNESSEE WILLIAMS
American playwright
'Cat on a Hot Tin Roof' 1955
Mendacity is a system that we live in. Liquor is one way out, and death's the other.

A. DICKSON WRIGHT
British surgeon
We are humble men in our profession.

We do our best. But all our efforts inevitably end up in vain. Up the chimney at Golders Green.

Famous Last Words

NANCY ASTOR
British politician
seeing all her children assembled at her bedside in her last illness 1964
Am I dying, or is this my birthday?

MAX BAER
German boxer
last words 1959
Oh God, here I go. . .

LORD BEAVERBROOK
Canadian press magnate
last public statement before his death, 1964
This is my final word. It is time for me to become an apprentice once more. I have not settled in which direction. But somewhere, sometime, soon.

MARTHA BECK
American murderess, executed 1951
Last words:
My story is a love story, but only those who are tortured by love can understand what I mean. I was pictured as a fat, unfeeling woman. True, I am fat, but if that is a crime, how many of my sex are guilty. I am not unfeeling, stupid or moronic. My last words and my last thoughts are: Let him who is without sin cast the first stone.

ANEURIN BEVAN
British politician
during his last illness 1960
I want to live because there are a few things I want to do.

JESSE BISHOP
American murderer, executed 1979
Last words:
This is just one more step down the road of life.

LEON BLUM
French Prime Minister
last words 1950
My belief is rooted in hope.

HUMPHREY BOGART
American film star
last words, attributed, 1957
I should have never switched from Scotch to Martinis.

PAUL CLAUDEL
French composer
last words 1955
Doctor, do you think it could have been the sausage?

LOU COSTELLO
American comedian
last words 1959
That was the best ice-cream soda I ever tasted.

NOEL COWARD
British playwright
last words, on going to bed 1976
Goodnight my darlings, I'll see you tomorrow.

BERNARD COY
American murderer
shot down attempting to escape from Alcatraz Prison, 1946
It don't matter; I figure I licked the Rock anyway.

BING CROSBY
American singer
last words 1977
That was a great game of golf, fellers.

JAMES DEAN
American film star
shortly before his fatal car crash, 1955
My fun days are over.

ANDREA 'WHIPS' FELDMAN
Warhol superstar
suicide by jumping through a window. Last words:
I'm going for the big time – heaven.

ERROL FLYNN
American film star
shortly before his death, 1959
I've had a hell of a lot of fun and I've enjoyed every minute of it.

GARY GILMORE
American murderer
who chose death by a firing squad, 1977. Last words to the squad:
Let's do it.

and to a priest:
Dominus vobiscum.

CHARLEY GOLDMAN
American boxing trainer
last words 1970
Only suckers get hit with right hands.

PAUL HOWE
British teenage desperado
shot by police 1979
I want to go out in a puff of smoke and take a few policemen with me!

THE SHAH OF IRAN
shortly before his death, 1980
I am fed up with living artificially. I don't want to live like Tito.

AL JOLSON
American singer
last words 1950
This is it. I'm going. I'm going.

THE REVEREND JIM JONES
founder of the 'People's Temple'
last words during the mass suicide of 913 followers, 1978
We didn't commit suicide. We committed an act of revolutionary suicide, protesting the conditions of an inhumane world.

JOHN F. KENNEDY
American president
on arriving in Dallas 1963
If someone is going to kill me, they will kill me.

MARTIN LUTHER KING JR.
American activist 1968
suggesting his own eulogy. . .
Yes, if you want to say that I was a drum major, say that I was a drum major for justice; say that I was a drum major for peace; I was a drum major for righteousness. And all of the other shallow things will not matter.

FRANZ LEHAR
Hungarian composer
last words 1948
Now I have finished with all earthly business, and high time too. Yes, yes, my dear child, now comes death.

PERCY WYNDHAM LEWIS
British artist
whose nurse asked him about the state of his bowels on his deathbed, 1957. Last words:
Mind your own business.

SIR ALFRED MacALPINE
British building tycoon
Last words:
Keep Paddy behind the big mixer.

JAMES McLAIN
American criminal
Killed by the police 1970 as he tried to shoot his way to freedom at his own trial
Take lots of pictures! We are the revolutionaries!

MALCOLM X
American radical
last words before being assassinated at a meeting, 1966
Cool it, brothers. . .

MANOLETE
Spanish matador
killed in the bullring, last words 1947
I can't feel anything in my right leg. I can't feel anything in my left leg. Doctor, are my eyes open? I can't see!

SOMERSET MAUGHAM
British writer
last words 1965
Dying is a very dull, dreary affair. My advice to you is to have nothing whatever to do with it.

H. L. MENCKEN
American essayist
composing his own epitaph; he died 1956
If, after I depart this vale, you remember me and have some thought to please my ghost. Forgive some sinner and wink your eye at some homely girl.

DRAZA MIHAJLOVIC
Yugoslav guerrilla
executed 1946, last words:
I found myself in a whirl of events and intrigues. I found destiny was merciless to me when it threw me into the most difficult whirlwinds. I wanted much, I began much – the whirlwind, the whirlwind, carried me and my work away.

AARON MITCHELL
'The Gambling Man', the last man to be executed in San Quentin, 1967. Last words:
Do you know I am going to die just like Jesus Christ did? I will die to save you guys.

ALDO MORO
Italian politician
communication shortly before his assassination 1978
Morally you are here in my place, but physically it is me.

BENITO MUSSOLINI
Italian dictator
executed 1945, last words:
But, but, Mr. Colonel. . .

NHAT CHI MAI
Vietnamese student
burnt self to death, 1967. Last poem served as a note:
I offer my body as a torch/to dissipate the dark/to waken love among men/to give peace to Vietnam.

CESARE PAVESE
Italian novelist
suicide note 1950
The thing most feared in secret always happens; all it needs is a little courage. The more the pain grows clearer and definite, the more the instinct for life reasserts itself and the thought of suicide recedes. It seemed easy when I thought of it. Weak women have done it. It needs humility, not pride. I am sickened by all this. No words. Action. I shall write no more.

MARSHALL PETAIN
French soldier
died 1951, last words:
Do not weep, do not grieve.

ST. JOHN PHILBY
British arabist
last words 1960
God, I'm bored.

PABLO PICASSO
Spanish artist
last words 1973
Drink to me.

ELVIS PRESLEY
American rock star
concluding what would be a last press conference, 1977
I hope I haven't bored you.

JAMES W. RODGERS
American criminal
executed by firing squad 1960. Asked for a last request. . .
Why yes, a bullet-proof vest!

FRANKLIN D. ROOSEVELT
American president
last words 1945
I have a terrific headache.

ETHEL ROSENBERG
Alleged atom spy
electrocuted with her husband Julius, last words, 1953
We are the first victims of American fascism!

JULIUS ROSENBERG
Alleged atom spy
executed 1953, last words:
We are innocent. That is the whole truth. To forsake this truth is to pay too high a price even for the priceless gift of life. For life thus purchased we could not live out in dignity.

DAMON RUNYON
American writer
last words 1946
You can keep the things of bronze and stone and give me one man to remember me just once a year.

GEORGE SANDERS
British film star
suicide note 1970
Dear World,
I am leaving you because I am bored. I am leaving you with your worries. Good luck.

JEAN SEBERG
American film star
suicide note 1979
I can't live any longer with my nerves.

SIR STANLEY SPENCER
British artist died 1959
Last words to a nurse who had given him an injection. . .
Beautifully done.

ADLAI STEVENSON
American politician
collapsing 1968. Last words:
I feel faint.

ERICH VON STROHEIM
(Oswald van Nordenwall)
German film director died 1957
Last words for Hollywood:
This isn't the worst. The worst is that they stole twenty-five years of my life.

'SUNSET BOULEVARD'
Paramount 1950 screenplay by Charles Brackett, Billy Wilder and D. M. Marshman Jr.
Gloria Swanson: All right, Mr. De Mille, I'm ready for my closeup.

JAMES THURBER
American humorist
last words 1961
God bless. . . God damn. . .

STEPHEN WARD
British osteopath suicide 1963
One of his ten notes:
I'm sorry to disappoint the vultures.

ETHEL WATERS
American blues singer, died 1977
A last interview. . .
I'm not afraid to die, honey. In fact, I'm kind of looking forward to it. I know the Lord has his arms wrapped around this big, fat sparrow.

H. G. WELLS
British writer, died 1946
Last words to his nurse
Go away. I'm all right.

'WHITE HEAT'
Warner Bros 1949. screenplay by Ivan Goff & Ben Roberts; based on a story by Virginia Kellogg
James Cagney: Made it Ma, top of the world!

CHARLES WHITMAN
American murderer
shot by police after he had killed 16 and wounded 30 people, 1966. He left a note before he started his rampage:
Life is not worth living.

Women

BELLA ABZUG
American politician
Nova 1972
The press either want to print your recipes, or they turn you into a blizzard and say you swear.

KINGSLEY AMIS
British author
quoted in The Listener 1978
Women are really much nicer than men

/ No wonder we like them.

ANN-MARGRET
American film star
A man who is honest with himself wants a woman to be soft and feminine, careful of what she's saying and talk like a man.

ANTONIN ARTAUD
French playwright
Evil comes from the darkness of women.

BRIGITTE BARDOT
French film star
News of the World 1973
There are no really ugly women. Every
woman is a Venus in her own way.

MARY RITTER BEARD
American historian
'Woman as a Force In History' 1946
The dogma of woman's complete historical subjection to man must be rated as
one of the most fantastic myths ever created by the human mind.

SIMONE DE BEAUVOIR
French writer
quoted in Esquire 1971
The division of the sexes is a biological
fact, not an event in history.

'The Second Sex' 1953
One is not born a woman, one becomes
one.

The Observer 1974
If any man had proved sufficiently self-
centred and commonplace to attempt
my subjugation, I should have judged
him, found him wanting and left him.
The only sort of person in whose favour
I could ever wish to surrender my au-
tonomy would be just the one who did
his utmost to prevent any such thing.

in a documentary film, 1978
A woman writer is first a writer who
consecrates her life to writing and has
no other occupations.

JEAN-PAUL BELMONDO
French film star
Women over thirty are at their best, but
men over thirty are too old to recognise
it.

ELIANA GIANINI BELOTTI
Italian feminist
'Little Girls' 1973
No woman, except for so-called 'de-
viants' seriously wishes to be male and
have a penis. But most women would
like to have the privileges and opportunities that go with it.

SUSAN BROWNMILLER
American feminist
'Against Our Will'
Rape is . . . nothing more or less than a

conscious process of intimidation by
which all men keep all women in a state
of fear.

PEARL S. BUCK
American writer
'To My Daughters, With Love' 1967
The bitterest creature under heaven is
the wife who discovers that her husband's bravery is only bravado, that his
strength is only a uniform, that his
power is but a gun in the hands of a fool.

STOKELY CARMICHAEL
American radical 1965
The only position for women in S.N.C.C.
is prone.

CHARLIE CHAPLIN
American film star
Every woman needs a man to discover
her.

COLETTE
French novelist
*in 'The Reader's Digest Treasury of Great
Quotations' 1979*
A woman who thinks she is intelligent
demands equal rights with men. A
woman who *is* intelligent does not.

CYRIL CONNOLLY
British critic
in 'The Faber Book of Aphorisms' 1964
There is no fury like a woman searching
for a new lover.

'THE COUNTRY GIRL'
*Paramount 1954 screenplay by George Seaton,
based on the play by Clifford Odets*
William Holden: There are two kinds of
women – those who pay too much attention to themselves and those who don't
pay enough.

LAWRENCE DURRELL
British writer 1973
If you really worship women they'll forgive you everything, even if your balls
are dropping off.

BOB DYLAN (né Zimmerman)
American singer
It's an honourable thing to change your
name – women do it when they're
married.

ERTE (Romain de Tirtoff)
French designer
The Guardian 1975
A resourceful woman who is almost downright plain can achieve the reputation of a beauty simply by announcing to everybody she meets that she is one.

'Things I Remember' 1975
The feminine body is essentially a malleable entity which fashion moulds in its own way.

EDNA FERBER
American writer
Reader's Digest 1954
A woman can look both moral and exciting – if she also looks as if it were quite a struggle.

EVA FIGES
British writer
quoted in 'The Descent of Women' by Elaine Morgan 1972
When modern women discovered the orgasm it was, combined with modern birth control, perhaps the biggest single nail in the coffin of male dominance.

MARILYN FRENCH
American novelist
All men are rapists and that's all they are. They rape us with their eyes, their laws and their codes.

J. K. GALBRAITH
American economist
Time 1969
The more underdeveloped the country, the more overdeveloped the women.

'Annals of an Abiding Liberal' 1980
The decisive economic contribution of women in the developed industrial society is rather simple ... It is, overwhelmingly, to make possible a continuing and more or less unlimited increase in the sale and use of consumer goods.

GERMAINE GREER
Australian feminist
Most women still need a room of their own and the only way to find it may be outside their own homes.

Playboy 1972
We've been castrated. It's all very well to let a bullock out into the field when you've already cut off his balls because you know he's not going to do anything. That's exactly what's happened to women.·

'INDISCREET'
Warner Bros 1958 screenplay by Norman Krasna, based on his play Kind Sir
Cecil Parker: There is no sincerity like a woman telling a lie.

JILL JOHNSTON
American feminist
'A Dialogue on Women's Liberation' 1971
All women are Lesbians, except those who don't know it yet.

LENA JEGER
British politician
The Observer 1955
It's a sad woman that buys her own perfume.

ELIZABETH JENKINS
British biographer
in 'The Faber Book of Aphorisms' 1964
The woman whose behaviour indicates that she will make a scene if she is told the truth asks to be deceived.

ERICA JONG
American writer
Playboy 1975
Many women have the gut feeling that their genitals are ugly. One reason women are gratified by oral-genital relations is that it is a way of a man's saying 'I like your cunt. I can eat it'.

Time 1978
Women are the only exploited group in history who have been idealised into powerlessness.

BARBARA JORDAN
American politician
New York Times 1977
Human rights apply equally to Soviet dissidents, Chilean peasants and American women.

SALLY KEMPTON
American journalist
Esquire 1970
It is hard to fight an enemy who has outposts in your head.

Men are brought up to command,

women to seduce. To admit the necessity of seduction is to admit that one has not the strength to command.

Women are the true maintenance class. Society is built upon their acquiescence and upon their small and necessary labours.

The fact is that one cannot talk in feminist terms without revealing feelings which have been traditionally regarded as neurotic.

KARL KRAUS
German artist
A woman who cannot be ugly is not beautiful.

LADIES HOME JOURNAL 1947
The average girl would rather have beauty than brains because she knows that the average man can see much better than he can think.

MOON LANDRIEU
American politician
on women's role in politics Esquire 1976
Women do the lickin' and the stickin'.

BILL LAWRENCE
American newsman
to J. F. Kennedy, on admitting women to the all-male Gridiron Club . . .
Look, Mr. President, I might sleep with them, but I'm damned if I'll eat lunch with them.

HELEN LAWRENSON
American journalist
Esquire 1971
If a woman is sufficiently ambitious, determined *and* gifted – there is practically nothing she can't do.

You have to go back to the Children's Crusade in 1212 AD to find as unfortunate and fatuous an attempt at manipulated hysteria as the Women's Liberation Movement.

FRAN LEBOWITZ
American journalist
'Metropolitan Life' 1978
Girls who put out are tramps. Girls who don't are ladies. This is however, a rather archaic use of the word. Should one of you boys happen upon a girl who doesn't put out, do not jump to the conclusion that you have found a lady. What you have probably found is a lesbian.

JOHN LENNON
British rock star
Women should be obscene and not heard.

JOHN LENNON & YOKO ONO
British rock composers
Song Title
Woman Is The Nigger of the World.

ANITA LOOS
American writer
International Herald Tribune 1973
Women are brighter than men. That's true. But it should be kept very quiet or it ruins the whole racket.

CLARE BOOTHE LUCE
American diplomat
But if God had wanted us to think with our wombs, why did He give us a brain?

in 'The Wit of Women'
A woman's best protection is a little money of her own.

They say women talk too much. If you have worked in Congress you know that the filibuster was invented by men.

MARY McCARTHY
American writer 1971
I've never met a woman that I would regard as liberated who was at all strong for Women's Lib.

ELSA MAXWELL
American socialite
More than one woman since Lot's wife has betrayed herself by looking back.

ROBIN MORGAN
American feminist
Women are not inherently passive or peaceful. We're not inherently anything but human.

'Sisterhood Is Powerful'
Woman is: finally screwing and your groin and buttocks and thighs ache like hell and you're all wet and bloody and it wasn't like a Hollywood movie at all but Jesus, at least you're not a virgin

anymore but is this what it's all about? And meanwhile he's asking 'Did you come?'

JULIA MORLEY
British organiser of 'Miss World' 1970
If it is a flesh market, you won't find finer flesh anywhere.

ALVA MYRDAL & VIOLA KLEIN
American writers
'Women's Two Roles'
The sentimental cult of domestic virtues is the cheapest method at society's disposal of keeping women quiet without seriously considering their grievances or improving their position.

OGDEN NASH
American poet
'First Families, Move Over'
A lady is known by the product she endorses.

ARISTOTLE ONASSIS
Greek millionaire
If women didn't exist all the money in the world would have no meaning.

JOE ORTON
British playwright
'Entertaining Mr. Sloane' 1964
Ed: Women are like banks, boy. Breaking and entering is a serious business.

DOLLY PARTON
American singer
I think that women have it made if they know how to go about it. A woman don't have to work, really, if she don't want to and is smart enough to make a man a good wife he's gonna take care of her.

CESARE PAVESE
Italian novelist
in 'The Faber Book of Aphorisms' 1964
Woman gives herself as a prize to the weak and as a prop to the strong, and no man ever has what he should.

PABLO PICASSO
Spanish artist
There's nothing so similar to one poodle dog as another poodle dog, and that goes for women too.

'PILLOW TALK'
Universal 1959 screenplay by Stanley Shapiro & Maurice Richlin, based on story by Russell Rouse & Clarence Greene
Thelma Ritter: If there's anything worse than a woman living alone, it's a woman saying she likes it.

SYLVIA PLATH
British poet
'Daddy'
Every woman adores a Fascist / The boot in the face, the brute / Brute heart of a brute like you.

NANCY REAGAN
wife of the politician, Ronald 1981
Woman is like a teabag – you can't tell how strong she is until you put her in hot water.

BETTY ROLLIN
American feminist
'First, you cry' 1976
Scratch most feminists and underneath there is a woman who longs to be a sex object, the difference is that is not *all* she longs to be.

HELEN ROWLAND
American journalist
When you see what some girls marry, you realize how they must hate to work for a living.

Failing to be there when a man wants her is woman's greatest sin, except to be there when he doesn't want her.

HELENA RUBINSTEIN
French cosmetician
There are no ugly women, only lazy ones.

JILL RUCKELSHAUS
American feminist
No one should have to dance backwards all their lives.

FRANCOISE SAGAN
French novelist
Daily Express 1957
Every little girl knows about love. It is only her capacity to suffer because of it that increases.

KATHIE SARACHILD
American feminist
The only problem with women is men.

DOROTHY L. SAYERS
British crime novelist
The keeping of an idle woman is a badge of superior social status.

HAZEL SCOTT
American feminist
Ms 1976
Any woman who has a great deal to offer the world is in trouble.

R. Z. SHEPPARD
American critic
reviewing 'The Bleeding Heart' by Marilyn French in Time 1980
The best-seller is the AK-47 of the Women's Liberation movement.

CORNELIA OTIS SKINNER
American actress
Women's virtue is man's greatest invention.

PATTI SMITH
American singer and poet 1977
As far as I am concerned being any gender is a drag.

SAUL STEINBERG
American artist
'Saul Steinberg' by Harold Rosenberg 1978
A beautiful woman is like a rainbow, a sunset, a moon – all stuff that should be looked at, but not painted.

STEPHEN STILLS
Canadian rock star
There are three things men can do with women: love them, suffer for them or turn them into literature.

JAMES THURBER
American humorist
A woman's place is in the wrong.

FRANCOIS TRUFFAUT
French film director
Esquire 1970
Being a woman is a profession whose only patron is God.

SOPHIE TUCKER
American singer 1953
From birth to age eighteen a girl needs good parents, from eighteen to thirty-five she needs good looks, from thirty-five to fifty-five she needs a good personality. From fifty-five on, she needs good cash.

KENNETH TYNAN
British critic 1970
A century and a half ago there were no knickers and girls read the Bible, now they wear impenetrable body stockings and read *Portnoy's Complaint*.

MAMIE VAN DOREN
American film actress
in 'Quote and Unquote' 1970
It is possible that blondes also prefer gentlemen.

VIVA
American actress
Hearing that there's no such thing as a vaginal orgasm was as good as news of the birth of Christ.

JOHN WAYNE
American film star
on liberated women
They have a right to work wherever they want to – as long as they have dinner ready when you get home.

CHARLOTTE WHITTON
quoted in Nancy McPhee 'The Book of Insults' 1978
Whatever women do they must do twice as well as men to be thought half as good. Luckily, this is not difficult.

CLOUGH WILLIAMS-ELLIS
British architect
The Observer 1946
Too many homes are built on foundations of crushed women.

DUCHESS OF WINDSOR
No woman can be too rich or too thin. (also attrib. to Truman Capote on David Susskind Show 1958)

WOMEN'S LIBERATION SLOGAN
Australia 1975
If you catch a man, throw him back.

A. DICKSON WRIGHT
British surgeon
In these days when royalties vanish, when children turn against their parents, when husbands turn on wives and uncles on nieces, one thing stands unshaken – the love of a woman for her gynaecologist.

Men

MARCEL ACHARD
French playwright
Quote 1956
Women like silent men. They think they're listening.

'THE BAD AND THE BEAUTIFUL'
MGM 1952 screenplay by Charles Schnee, based on short stories by George Bradshaw
Elaine Stewart: There are no great men, buster. There are only men.

BRIGID BROPHY
Irish writer 1968
I refuse to consign the whole male sex to the nursery, I insist on believing that some men are my equals.

MARLENE DIETRICH
German film star
The average man is more interested in a woman who is interested in him than he is in a woman with beautiful legs.

IAN DURY
British rock musician
The natural thing is to grab hold of someone and go *wallop!* That's what we've been born to, us blokes.

BETTY FRIEDAN
American feminist
Man is not the enemy here, but the fellow victim. The real enemy is women's denigration of themselves.

ZSA ZSA GABOR
Hungarian film star
Macho does not prove mucho.

GERMAINE GREER
Australian feminist
The Observer 1979
I love men like some people like good food or wine.

'The Female Eunuch' 1970
Probably the only place where a man can feel really secure is in a maximum security prison, except for the imminent threat of release.

JILL JOHNSTON
American feminist
The penis is obviously going the way of the veriform appendix.

FLORYNCE KENNEDY
American feminist 1976
If men could get pregnant, abortion would be a sacrament.

replying to a male heckler who asked 'Are you a lesbian?'
Are you my alternative?

PAUL LEAUTAUD
French writer
'Passe-Temps'
Sensible men prefer evening to morning, night to day, and mature women to young girls.

LADY LEWISHAM
British aristocrat
in 'Violets and Vinegar' ed. J. Cooper and T. Hartman 1980
Nothing is more debasing for a real man than a plastic apron.

SIR MARCUS LOANE
Australian clergyman
rejecting female ordination, 1977
As God is the head of Christ, so Christ is the head of man, so is man the head of woman.

NORMAN MAILER
American writer
Nova 1969
Women think of being a man as a gift. It is a duty. Even making love can be a

duty. A man has always got to get it up and love isn't always enough.

JAYNE MANSFIELD
American film star
Men are those creatures with two legs and eight hands.

MARCELLO MASTROIANNI
Italian film star
Playboy 1965
Modern man isn't as virile as he used to be. Instead of making things happen, he waits for things to happen to him. He goes with the current. Something . . . has led him to stop swimming upstream.

MARGARET MEAD
American anthropologist
Quote 1958
Women want mediocre men and men are working to be as mediocre as possible.

KATE MILLETT
American feminist
To each masquerading male the female is a mirror in which he beholds himself.

STIRLING MOSS
British racing driver 1963
There are two things no man will admit he can't do well: drive and make love.

MARCEL PAGNOL
French screenwriter 1954
The most difficult secret for a man to keep is his own opinion of himself.

'THE ROAD TO UTOPIA'
Paramount 1945 screenplay by Norman Panama and Melvin Frank
Bob Hope: I'll take a lemonade. In a dirty glass.

LEO ROSTEN
American writer
Saturday Review 1970
Most men do not mature, they simply grow taller.

HELEN ROWLAND
American journalist
A bachelor never quite gets over the idea that he is a thing of beauty and a boy forever.

The hardest task in a girl's life is to prove to a man that his intentions are serious.

Never trust a husband too far nor a bachelor too near.

There are only two kinds of men – the dead and the deadly.

The follies which a man most regrets in his life are those which he didn't commit when he had the opportunity.

FRANCOISE SAGAN
French novelist
I like men to behave like men – strong and childish.

CARL SANDBURG
American poet
'Incidentals'
Shame is the feeling you have when you agree with the woman who loves you that you are the man she thinks you are.

ISAAC BASHEVIS SINGER
American writer
'The Magician of Lublin'
Those who run around with women don't walk tightropes. They find it hard enough to crawl on the ground.

ROD STEIGER
American film star
Playboy 1969
There are only two superlative compliments you can receive from a woman: 'I think you're a master-chef' and 'I think you're a great lay'. The two basic drives in life.

TAKI
British gossip columnist
The Spectator 1980
It is a mark of civilised men that they defend their women.

HENRIETTA TIARKS
British socialite 1957
A gentleman is a patient wolf.

PETE TOWNSHEND
British rock composer
'Tattoo'
Me and my brother were talking to each other./About what makes a man a man./Was it brains, was it brawn, or the month you were born./We just couldn't understand. (Essex Music)

RAQUEL WELCH
American film star
quoted in Sunday Times 1980
There aren't any hard women, just soft
men.

MAE WEST
American film star
Give a man a free hand and he'll run it
all over you.

Relationships

J. R. ACKERLEY
British editor
'My Father and Myself' 1968
I was born in 1896 and my parents were
married in 1919.

JOEY ADAMS
American comedian
'Cindy and I'
The most popular labour-saving device
today is still a husband with money.

ALFRED ADLER
German analyst
*quoted in 'The Marriage Book' ed. Count Her-
mann Keyserling*
Most married couples conduct themselves as if each party were afraid that
the other one could see it was the
weaker.

WOODY ALLEN
American film star
quoted in Daily Mirror 1964
Basically my wife was immature. I'd be
at home in the bath and she'd come in
and sink my boats.

CLEVELAND AMORY
American writer
'Who Killed Society' 1960
A 'good' family is one that used to be
better.

'ANNIE HALL'
*UA 1977 screenplay by Woody Allen and Mar-
shall Brickman*
Woody Allen: A relationship I think is
. . . is like a shark. You know it has to
constantly move forward or it dies.

ANONYMOUS
*quoted in 'Penguin Modern Dictionary of Quo-
tations' by J. M. & M. J. Cohen 1980*
Marriage is an attempt to change a night
owl into a homing pigeon.

ANONYMOUS
New York Times 1948
There is one woman whom fate has des-
tined for each of us. If we miss her, we
are saved.

ANONYMOUS WOMAN
*quoted as Epigraph to 'Fear of Flying' by
Erica Jong, 1975*
Bigamy is having one husband too
many. Monogamy is the same.

ANONYMOUS WOMAN
quoted in Observer survey on marriage 1972
Marriage is the price I pay for having
hormones.

W. H. AUDEN
British poet
'The Dyer's Hand' 1962
Almost all of our relationships begin and
most of them continue as forms of mutual exploitation, a mental or physical
barter, to be terminated when one or
both parties run out of goods.

JIM BACKUS
American film star
Many a man owes his success to his first
wife, and his second wife to his success.

BRIGITTE BARDOT
French film star
News of the World 1974
In marriage you are chained, it is an

obligation; living with someone is a mutual agreement that is renegotiated and reendorsed every day.

VICKI BAUM
American writer
'And Life Goes On'
Marriage always demands the greatest understanding of the art of insincerity possible between two human beings.

SIMONE DE BEAUVOIR
French writer
'La Force de l'Age'
Harmony between two individuals is never granted — it has to be conquered indefinitely.

Marriage is traditionally the destiny offered to women by society. Most women are married or have been, or plan to be or suffer from not being.

GERALD BRENAN
British writer
'Thoughts in a Dry Season' 1978
The great thing about marriage is that it enables one to be alone without feeling loneliness.

Marriage is an arrangement by which two people start by getting the best out of each other and often end by getting the worst.

JOYCE BROTHERS
American psychologist
Good Housekeeping 1972
Marriage is not just spiritual communion and passionate embraces; marriage is also three meals a day and remembering to carry out the trash.

MARC CHAGALL
French painter
The Observer 1977
If you are human you love and doubt. The only thing there shouldn't be any doubt about is your wife. If there is, it's finished.

MALCOLM DE CHAZAL
French writer
'Sens Plastique' 1949
The family is a court of justice which never shuts down for night or day.

AGATHA CHRISTIE
British crime writer
The Observer 1955
An archaeologist is the best husband any woman can have — the older she gets the more interested he is in her.

COLETTE
French novelist
auoted in 'The Wit of Women'by L. and M. Cowan
The only really masterful noise a man ever makes in a house is the noise of his key, when he is still on the landing, fumbling for the lock.

BILLY CONNOLLY
Scottish comedian
in Duncan Campbell 'Billy Connolly, the Authorized Version'
Marriage is a wonderful invention, but then again, so is the bicycle repair kit.

CYRIL CONNOLLY
British critic
'The Unquiet Grave' 1945
The tragedy of modern marriage is that married couples no longer enjoy the support of society, although marriage, difficult at any time, requires every social sanction.

NOEL COWARD
British playwright 1956
I've sometimes thought of marrying, and then I've thought again.

QUENTIN CRISP
British writer
'How To Become A Virgin' 1981
It is explained that all relationships require a — little give and take. This is untrue. Any partnership demands that we give and give and give and at the last, as we flop into our graves exhausted, we are told that we didn't give enough.

'The Naked Civil Servant' 1968
As we all know from witnessing the consuming jealousy of husbands who are never faithful, people do not confine themselves to the emotions to which they are entitled.

The consuming desire of most human beings is deliberately to plant their whole life in the hands of some other person. For this purpose they frequently choose someone who doesn't even want the beastly thing. I would describe this method of searching for happiness as immature ... development of character consists solely in moving towards self-sufficency.

The *vie de bohème* is a way of life that has two formidable enemies – time and marriage. Even hooligans marry, though they know that marriage is but for a little while. It is alimony that is for ever ...

'DARLING'
Embassy 1965 screenplay by Frederic Raphael
Dirk Bogarde: Your idea of fidelity is not having more than one man in bed at the same time.

MICKEY DEANS
Judy Garland's last husband
after her death 1969
I don't expect anything except the bills.

PHYLLIS DILLER
American comedienne
'Phyllis Diller's Housekeeping Hints'
Never go to bed mad. Stay up and fight.

BOB DYLAN
American singer
'Absolutely 4th Street'
Yes I wish that for just one time / You could stand inside my shoes / You'd know what a drag it is / To see you. (M. Witmark & Sons)

DR. ALBERT ELLIS
American psychologist 1967
Adultery can be a more 'healthy' recreation than for example the game of Mah Jongg or watching television.

ZSA ZSA GABOR
Hungarian film star
Newsweek 1960
Husbands are like fires – they go out when unattended.

GRETA GARBO
Swedish film star
I cannot see myself as a wife – ugly word.

JAMES GARNER
American film star 1980
Marriage is a lot like the army: everyone

complains, but you'd be surprised at the large number that re-enlist.

'GIGI'
MGM 1958 screenplay by Alan Jay Lerner based on novel by Colette
Isabel Jeans: Bad table manners, my dear Gigi, have broken up more households than infidelity.

GUNTER GRASS
German novelist
I am not faithful, but I am attached.

GERMAINE GREER
Australian feminist
'The Female Eunuch' 1970
Mother is the dead heart of the family, spending father's earnings on consumer goods to enhance the environment in which he eats, sleeps and watches television.

SACHA GUITRY
French writer
'Une folie'
To be faithful, very often, is to chain up the other person.

LADY HASLUCK
wife of Australian Governor-General 1971
The worst thing about work in the house or home is that whatever you do it is destroyed, laid waste or eaten within 24 hours.

CMDR. G. H. HATHERILL
British policeman
The Observer 1954
There are only about 20 murders a year in London and not all are serious – some are just husbands killing their wives.

EDWARD HEATH
British politician 1970
Pitt the younger was a great British Prime Minister. He saved Europe from Napoleon, he was the pilot who weathered the storm. I don't know whether he'd have done it any better or quicker had he been married.

SIR SEYMOUR HICKS
British actor
The Observer 1946
A man does not buy his wife a fur coat

to keep her warm, but to keep her pleasant.

MICK JAGGER & KEITH RICHARD
British rock composers
'Sitting On A Fence'
All of my friends at school grew up and settled down / Then they mortgaged up their lives / . . . They just got married 'cos there's nothing else to do. (Essex Music)

POPE JOHN PAUL II
1980
Adultery is in your heart not only when you look with excessive sexual desire at a woman who is not your wife, but also if you look in the same manner at your wife.

MAXINE HONG KINGSTON
American writer
'The Woman Warrior' 1976
Adultery is extravagance.

IRVING KRISTOL
American academic 1979
All egalitarian revolutions, in the end, turn against the family. The family legitimizes inequality.

Ladies Home Journal
Of course a platonic relationship is possible – but only between husband and wife.

SIR EDMUND LEACH
British academic
Reith Lecture 1967
Far from being the basis of the good society, the family, with its narrow privacy and tawdry secrets, is the source of all our discontents.

EMMA LEE
Not all women give most of their waking thoughts to the problem of pleasing men. Some are married.

JOHN LENNON
British rock star 1968
I do not think marriage is the product of love.

JOHN LENNON & PAUL McCARTNEY
British rock composers

'Paperback Writer'
It's a dirty story of a dirty man / And his clinging wife doesn't understand. (Northern Songs)

OSCAR LEVANT
American pianist and composer
'Memoirs of an Amnesiac'
Marriage is a triumph of habit over hate.

CLARE BOOTHE LUCE
American diplomat
quoted in 'The Wit of Women' by L. and M. Cowan
There's nothing like a good dose of another woman to make a man appreciate his wife.

NORMAN MAILER
American writer who has had four wives, two mistresses and nine children.
1980
Alimony is the curse of the writing classes.

Nova 1969
There are four stages to a marriage. First there's the affair, then the marriage, then children and finally the fourth stage, without which you cannot know a woman, the divorce.

ANDRE MAUROIS
French writer
'Memories'
A happy marriage is a long conversation which always seems too short.

ANDRE DE MISSON
French writer
You study one another for three weeks, you love each other for three months, you fight for three years and you tolerate the situation for thirty.

NAOMI MITCHISON
British writer
The Times 1979
Being married is a value: it is bread and butter, but it may make one less able to provide the cake.

'MOULIN ROUGE'
United Artists 1952 screenplay by Anthony Veiller & John Huston based on novel by Pierre La Mure
Jose Ferrer: Marriage is like a dull meal, with the dessert at the beginning.

GEORGE JEAN NATHAN
American critic 1958
Marriage is based on the theory that when a man discovers a brand of beer exactly to his taste he should at once throw up his job and go to work in the brewery.

JACK NICHOLSON
American film star
Playboy 1972
If there is any realistic deterrent to marriage, it's the fact that you can't afford divorce.

HAROLD NICOLSON
British politician
The great secret of a successful marriage is to treat all disasters as incidents and none of the incidents as disasters.

ANTHONY PIETROPINTO
American sociologist
'Husbands and Wives' 1979
Marriages peter out or pan out.

J. B. PRIESTLEY
British writer
Marriage is like paying an endless visit in your worst clothes.

JOEY RAMONE
American rock star
Marriage is worse than dying. Why stay with *one* person for 50 years? We advise against marriage.

VIRGINIE DES RIEUX
French writer
Marriage is a lottery in which men stake their liberty and women their happiness.

HELEN ROWLAND
American journalist
It isn't tying himself to one woman that a man dreads when he thinks of marrying; it's separating himself from all the others.

When a girl marries she exchanges the attentions of many men for the inattention of one.

Before marriage a man will lie awake all night thinking about something you said; after marriage he will fall asleep before you have finished saying it.

Every man wants a woman to appeal to his better side, his nobler instincts and his higher nature, and another woman to help him forget them.

A husband is what's left of the lover once the nerve has been extracted.

One man's folly is another man's wife.

ADELA ROGERS ST. JOHN
American writer
Los Angeles Times 1974
I think every woman is entitled to a middle husband she can forget.

CHARLES M. SCHULZ
American cartoonist
'Peanuts' 1952
Big sisters are the crabgrass on the lawn of life.

CARLY SIMON
American singer
I've never bought that open marriage thing, I've never seen it work. But that doesn't mean I believe in monogamy. Sleeping with someone else doesn't necessarily constitute an infidelity . . . (what does is) having sex with someone and telling your spouse, anything you feel guilty about.

PHILIP SLATER
'The Pursuit of Loneliness' 1970
Having created a technological and social-structural juggernaut by which they are daily buffeted, men tend to use their wives as opiates to soften the impact of the forces they have set in motion against themselves.

STEVIE SMITH
British poet
If you cannot have your dear husband for a comfort and a delight, for a breadwinner and a crosspatch, for a sofa, chair or hot water bottle, one can use him as a Cross to be borne.

'A STAR IS BORN'
Warner Bros 1954 screenplay by Moss Hart, based on screenplay by Dorothy Parker, Alan Campbell and Robert Carson and original story by William A. Wellman and Robert Carson
Judy Garland: Hello everybody. This is Mrs. Norman Maine.

LADY SUMMERSKILL
British politician 1966
The so-called 'divorce reformer' can equally be called a marriage breaker.

LANA TURNER
American film star 1980
A successful man is one who makes more money than his wife can spend. A successful woman is one who can find such a man.

PETER DE VRIES
American writer
The value of marriage is not that adults produce children, but that children produce adults.

HEATHCOTE WILLIAMS
British playwright
'The Speakers' 1964
There is no family life left in England. If somebody's head gets in the way of the television set, they bash it in.

SHELLEY WINTERS
American film star
In Hollywood all marriages are happy. It's trying to live together afterwards that causes the problems.

Friends

ANONYMOUS
in New York Times 1947
It's what the guests say as they swing out of the drive that counts.

CHARLES BUKOWSKI
American writer
'Notes of a Dirty Old Man' 1969
That's what friendship means: sharing the prejudice of experience.

If you want to know who your friends are, get yourself a jail sentence.

DALE CARNEGIE
American self-help evangelist
You can make more friends in two months by becoming interested in other people than you can in two years by trying to get other people interested in you.

COLETTE
French novelist
quoted in 'The Wit of Women' by L. and M. Cowan
It is prudent to pour the oil of delicate politeness on the machinery of friendship.

MARLENE DIETRICH
German film star
It's the friends you can call up at 4am that matter.

NORMAN DOUGLAS
British author
'An Almanac'
To find a friend one must close one eye; to keep him – two.

BRUCE JAY FRIEDMAN
American writer
'Sex and the Lonely Guy' Esquire 1977
A Code of Honour – Never approach a friend's girl friend or wife with mischief as your goal. There are just too many women in the world to justify that sort of dishonourable behaviour. Unless she's *really* attractive.

JIMMY HOFFA
American labour racketeer 1957
It's always been my theory that you keep the door open to your enemies. You know all about your friends.

HEDDA HOPPER
American gossip columnist
quoted in 'The Wit of Women' by L. and M. Cowan
Having only friends would be dull anyway – like eating eggs without salt.

BARRY HUMPHRIES
Australian comedian 1965
Friendship is tested rather in the thick years of success than in the thin years of struggle.

ST. JOHN IRVINE
Irish author
London Calling 1950
When a friend dies, part of yourself dies too.

ARNOLD LOBEL
American writer
'Fables' 1980
Advice from friends is like the weather: some of it is good; some of it is bad.

HENRY MILLER
American writer
'Sexus' 1949
When one is trying to do something beyond his known powers it is useless to seek the approval of friends. Friends are at their best in moments of defeat.

'THE PICTURE OF DORIAN GRAY'
MGM 1945 screenplay by Albert Lewin based on novel by Oscar Wilde
George Sanders: I always choose my friends for their good looks and my enemies for their good intellects. Man cannot be too careful in his choice of enemies.

BERTRAND RUSSELL
British philosopher
If we were all given by magic the power to read each other's thoughts, I suppose the first effect would be to dissolve all friendships.

ANDRE SIEGFRIED
French writer
'Some Maxims'
Antipathy analyses best, but it is sympathy which understands.

LOGAN PEARSALL SMITH
American essayist
'All Trivia'
We need two kinds of acquaintances: one to complain to, while we boast to the other.

in 'The Faber Book of Aphorisms' 1964
I might give up my life for my friend, but he had better not ask me to do up a parcel.

Don't tell your friends their faults; they will cure the fault and never forgive you.

ROD STEIGER
American film star
Playboy 1969
How many of us today can actually strip our insides bare and say to somebody 'Look, I really need you'. We can say 'I love you' twenty-seven times a day, but it's not like saying 'Look, here I am, vomit and all, sick and frightened. Recognize my need and my humanity.'

JEREMY THORPE
British politician
On Prime Minister Harold Macmillan's 1962 cabinet massacre. . .
Greater love hath no man than this, that he lay down his friends for his life.

PETER USTINOV
British actor and wit
'Dear Me'
I do not believe that friends are necessarily the people you like best, they are merely the people who got there first.

ORSON WELLES
American film director
New York Times 1962
When you are down and out something always turns up – and it is usually the noses of your friends.

Love

CHER
American singer
Playboy 1975
Romance and work are great diversions to keep you from dealing with yourself.

MARGARET ANDERSON
American author
'The Fiery Fountains' 1969
In real love you want the other person's good. In romantic love you want the other person.

JEAN ANOUILH
French playwright
'Ardele' 1948
Oh, love is real enough, you will find it some day, but it has one archenemy – and that is life.

HANNAH ARENDT
American writer
in 'The Faber Book of Aphorisms' 1964
Love, in distinction from friendship, is killed, or rather extinguished, the moment it is displayed in public.

TI-GRACE ATKINSON
American feminist
Love is the victim's response to the rapist.

W. H. AUDEN
British poet
Money cannot buy/The fuel of love/but is excellent kindling.

SAMUEL BECKETT
Irish author
quoted in New York Review of Books 1971
That desert of loneliness and recrimination that men call love.

ABEL BONNARD
French writer
'Savoir Aimer'
To love is to escape through one being the mediocrity of others.

GERALD BRENAN
British writer
'Thoughts In A Dry Season' 1978
Men would like to love themselves but they usually find that they cannot. That is because they have built an ideal image of themselves which puts their real self in the shade.

NORMAN O. BROWN
American philosopher
Love without attachment is light.

RITA MAE BROWN
American writer 1970
To love without role, without power plays, is revolution.

CHARLES BUKOWSKI
American writer
'Notes of a Dirty Old Man' 1969
Love is a way with some meaning; sex is meaning enough.

When Love becomes a command, Hatred can become a pleasure.

Of course it's possible to love a human being if you don't know them too well.

DAVID BYRNE
American rock star 1979
Sometimes its a form of love just to talk to somebody that you have nothing in common with and still be fascinated by their presence.

'CAT ON A HOT TIN ROOF'
MGM 1958 screenplay by Richard Brooks and James Poe, from play by Tennessee Williams
Paul Newman: You don't know what love means. To you it's just another four-letter word.

LOUIS-FERDINAND CELINE
French writer
'Journey to the end of the Night'
Love, Arthur, is a poodle's chance of attaining the infinite, and personally I have my pride.

MAURICE CHEVALIER
French film star 1955
Many a man has fallen in love with a girl in a light so dim he would not have chosen a suit by it.

E. M. CIORAN
French philosopher
'Syllogismes de l'amertume' 1952
The art of love? It's knowing how to join the temperament of a vampire to the discretion of an anemone.

QUENTIN CRISP
British author
'The Naked Civil Servant' 1968
What better proof of love can there be than money? A ten shilling note shows incontrovertibly just how mad about you a man is.

MARLENE DIETRICH
German film star
'Marlene Dietrich's ABC' 1961
Grumbling is the death of love.

MAUREEN DUFFY
British writer
'Wounds' 1969
Love is the only effective counter to death.

BOB DYLAN
American singer
'Talking World War III Blues'
I'll let you be in my dreams,/if I can be in yours. I said that.
(M. Witmark & Sons)

PAUL ELDRIDGE
American writer
'Horns of Glass'
Jealousy would be far less tortuous if we understood that love is a passion entirely unrelated to our merits.

MAX ERNST
German artist
in 'Max Ernst' by John Russell, 1967
Love is the great enemy of Christian morality. The virtue of pride, which was once the beauty of mankind has given place to that fount of all ugliness, Christian humility. Love, as Rimbaud said, must be reinvented.

E. M. FORSTER
British novelist
'Albergo Empedocle & Other Writings' 1971
Ecstasy cannot last, but it can carve a channel for something lasting.

BETTY FRIEDAN
American feminist
'The Feminine Mystique' 1963
It is easier to live through someone else than to become complete yourself.

CLARK GABLE
American film star
It's an extra dividend when you like the girl you're in love with.

ZSA ZSA GABOR
Hungarian film star
Newsweek 1960
A man in love is incomplete until he is married. Then he is finished.

'GENTLEMEN PREFER BLONDES'
20th Century Fox 1953 screenplay by Charles Lederer, based on novel by Anita Loos
Marilyn Monroe: I always say a kiss on the hand might feel very good, but a diamond tiara lasts for ever.

ROBERT GRAVES
British poet
'Occupation: Writer'
In love as in sport, the amateur status must be strictly maintained.

'Collected Poems' 1961
Love is a universal migraine/A bright stain on the vision/Blotting out reason.

GERMAINE GREER
Australian feminist
'The Female Eunuch' 1970
Love is . . . the drug which makes sexuality palatable in popular mythology.

Love, love, love – all the wretched cant of it, masking egotism, lust, masochism, fantasy under a mythology of sentimental postures, a welter of self induced miseries and joys, blinding and masking the essential personalities in the frozen gestures of courtship, in the kissing and the dating and the desire, the compliments and the quarrels which vivify its barrenness.

JERRY HALL
American model
Interview 1978
Jealousy is the fear of losing the thing you love most. It's very normal. Suspicion is the thing that's abnormal.

BEN HECHT
American screenwriter
'Winkelberg'
Love is a hole in the heart.

ADRIAN HENRI
British poet
'Love Is. . .'
Love is a fan club with only two fans.

KATHARINE HEPBURN
American film star
Look 1958
Only the really plain people know about love. The very fascinating ones try so hard to create an impression that they soon exhaust their talents.

A sharp knife cuts the quickest and hurts the least.

**MICK JAGGER &
KEITH RICHARD
British rock composers**
'Bitch'
It must be love, it's a bitch. (Essex Music)

**ARTHUR JERSILD
American psychologist**
'Educational Psychology'
One privilege of being associated with people whom a person loves is that of being angry with them.

**FRITZ LANG
German film director**
Love has become a four letter word.

**JOHN LENNON &
PAUL McCARTNEY
British rock composers**
'I'm Looking Through You'
Why, tell me why, did you not treat me right? / Love has a nasty habit of disappearing over night. (Northern Songs)

'LOVE STORY'
Paramount 1970 screenplay by Erich Segal, from his novel
Ryan O' Neil: Love means never having to say you're sorry.

**MIGNON McLAUGHLIN
American writer**
'The Neurotic's Notebook' 1963
The head never rules the heart, but just becomes its partner in crime.

**ANNA MAGNANI
Italian film star**
quoted in 'The Egotists' by Oriana Fallaci 1963
Great passions don't exist – they are liar's fantasies. What do exist are little loves that may last for a short or longer while.

**RENE MAGRITTE
Belgian artist**
quoted in 'Magritte: The True Art of Painting' ed. H. Torczyner 1979
A man is privileged when his passion obliges him to betray his convictions to please the woman he loves.

**JACQUES MARITAIN
French philosopher**
'Reflections on America' 1958
We don't love qualities, we love a person; sometimes by reason of their defects as well as their qualities.

**W. SOMERSET MAUGHAM
British writer**
'A Writer's Notebook'
Love is only the dirty trick played on us to achieve continuation of the species.

**H. L. MENCKEN
American essayist**
Love is the triumph of imagination over intelligence.

**ASHLEY MONTAGU
British writer**
'The Natural Superiority of Women' 1954
Love, for too many men in our time, consists of sleeping with a seductive woman, one who is properly endowed with the right distribution of curves and conveniences and one upon whom a permanent lien has been acquired through the institution of marriage.

**IRIS MURDOCH
British writer 1968**
Falling out of love is very enlightening, for a short while you see the world with new eyes.

Love ... is the extremely difficult realization that something other than oneself is real.

**ANAIS NIN
French novelist**
The only abnormality is the incapacity to love.

**GEORGE ORWELL
British essayist**
'Collected Essays'
To an ordinary human being love means nothing if it does not mean loving some people more than others.

**WARNER PAGLIARA
American record business executive**
Esquire 1971
Love is universal, and love is easy to merchandise.

'THE PICTURE OF DORIAN GRAY'
MGM 1945 screenplay by Albert Lewin based on novel by Oscar Wilde
George Sanders: The only difference between a caprice and a lifelong passion is that the caprice lasts a little longer.

KATHERINE ANNE PORTER
American writer
quoted in 'Contemporary Novelists' 1976
Love is purely a creation of the human imagination . . . the most important example of how the imagination continually outruns the creature it inhabits.

ELVIS PRESLEY
American rock star
song title
I'm Left, You're Right, She's Gone.

THEODORE REIK
American psychologist
'The Psychology of Sex Relations' 1945
Love is an attempt to change a piece of a dream-world into reality.

ALAIN RESNAIS
French film director
New York Herald Tribune 1963
Love is the common denominator.

PIERRE REVERDY
French writer
'En vrac'
To love is to allow abuse.

SIGMUND ROMBERG
Hungarian composer
A love song is just a caress set to music.

ELEANOR ROOSEVELT
American First Lady
The giving of love is an education in itself.

JOHNNY ROTTEN (John Lydon)
British rock star
Love is two minutes fifty-two seconds of squishing noises. It shows your mind isn't clicking right.

MARTIN SCORSESE
American film director
You've got to love something enough to kill it.

FLORIDA SCOTT-MAXWELL
American psychologist
'The Measure of My Days' 1972
I wonder why love is so often equated with joy, when it is everything else as well – devastation, balm, obsession, granting and receiving excessive value, and losing it again. It is recognition, often, of what you are not, but might be. It sears and heals. It is beyond pity and above law. It can seem like truth.

Is there any stab as deep as wondering where and how you failed those you loved?

MR. JUSTICE SELBY
American divorce court judge 1968
Love is a wonderful thing, but as long as it is blind I will never be out of a job.

WOLFMAN JACK SMITH
American disc jockey
Love is not a matter of counting the years – it's making the years count.

WILLIE 'The Lion' SMITH
American jazz musician
Esquire 1964
Romance without finance is no good.

PHIL SPECTOR
American rock producer
Song Title
To Know, Know, Know You, Is To Love, Love, Love You.

'SWEET BIRD OF YOUTH'
MGM 1962 screenplay by Richard Brooks, based on play by Tennessee Williams
Shirley Knight: No one in love is free – or wants to be.

Paul Newman: The great difference between people in this world is not between the rich and the poor or between the good and the evil. The big difference between people are the ones who have had pleasure in love and those who haven't.

JEREMY THORPE
British politician
letter to Norman Scott 1961
Bunnies *can* and *will* go to France. Yours affectionately, Jeremy. I miss you.

JAMES THURBER
American humorist
Life 1960
Love is what you've been through with somebody.

FRANCOIS TRUFFAUT
French film director 1979
In love women are professionals, men are amateurs.

PETER USTINOV
British wit and actor
Christian Science Monitor 1958
Love is an act of endless forgiveness, a tender look which becomes a habit.

GORE VIDAL
American writer
Sunday Times 1973
I can understand companionship. I can understand bought sex in the afternoon. I cannot understand the love affair.

GENE VINCENT &
SHERIFF TEX DAVIS
American rock composers
'Be-bop-a-lula'
Be-bop-a-lula she's my baby / Be-bop-a-lula I don't mean maybe.
(Lowery Music)

MR. JUSTICE WALLINGTON
British lawyer 1957
It is not love that produces jealousy – it is selfishness.

ANDY WARHOL
American artist
'From A to B & Back Again' 1975
Fantasy love is much better than reality

love. Never doing it is very exciting. The most exciting attractions are between two opposites that never meet.

Everybody winds up kissing the wrong person goodnight.

SIMONE WEIL
French philosopher
in 'The Faber Book of Aphorisms' 1964
Belief in the existence of other human beings as such is love.

Love is not consolation, it is light.

MAE WEST
American film star
Love conquers all things except poverty and toothache.

Esquire 1968
Just a little more loving and a lot less fighting and the world would be all right.

THYRA SAMTER WINSLOW
American author
Platonic love is love from the neck up.

WOODROW WYATT
British politician
'To The Point' 1981
A man falls in love through his eyes. A woman through her ears.

FRANK ZAPPA
American rock composer
'Dirty Love'
Give me / Your dirty love / Like some tacky little pamphlet in your Daddy's bottom drawer.
(Frank Zappa Music)

Success

FRED ALLEN
American wit
'Treadmill to Oblivion' 1954
A celebrity is a person who works hard all his life to become known, then wears dark glasses to avoid being recognised.

GEORGE ALLEN
American pro football coach 1974
The achiever is the only person who is truly alive. There can be no inner satisfaction in simply driving a fine car, eating in a fine restaurant or watching a

good movie or television programme. Those who think that they're enjoying themselves doing that are half-dead and don't know it.

EDDIE ARCARO
American champion jockey 1950
Once a guy starts wearing silk pyjamas, it's hard to get up early.

CHARLES AZNAVOUR
French singer
Success is the result of a collective hallucination stimulated by the artist.

JAMES BALDWIN
American author
'Nobody Knows My Name' 1961
The real world accomplishes its seductions not by offering you opportunities to be wicked, but by offering opportunities to be good, to be active and effective, to be admired and central and apparently loved.

Harpers 1961
It is rare that one *likes* a world famous man. By the time they become world famous they rarely like themselves.

CLIVE BARNES
British critic 1980
On showbusiness awards:
The concept of artistic merit as a racehorse is obviously distasteful.

BELA BARTOK
Hungarian composer
Saturday Review 1962
Competitions are for horses, not artists.

INGRID BENGIS
American feminist
Ms 1973
The real trap of fame is its irresistibility.

IRVING BERLIN
American composer
Theatre Arts 1958
The toughest thing about success is that you've got to keep on being a success.

DR. SMILEY BLANTON
American guru
'Love or Perish' 1955
The truth is that all of us attain the greatest success and happiness possible in this life whenever we use our native capacities to their greatest extent.

DANIEL J. BOORSTIN
American writer
'The Image' 1962
A sign of a celebrity is often that his name is worth more than his services.

Being well known for their well-knowness, celebrities intensify their celebrity images simply by being well-known for relations among themselves. By a kind of symbiosis, celebrities live off each other.

BERTOLT BRECHT
German playwright
'The Messingkauf Dialogues' 1965
How I loathe moralizing! Holding a mirror up to the great! As if they didn't admire their own looks in it.

ELIAS CANETTI
Bulgarian writer
Success listens only to applause. To all else it is deaf.

HENRI CARTIER-BRESSON
French photographer
Harpers 1961
Success depends on one's general culture, on one's set of values, one's clarity of mind and vivacity. The thing to be most feared is the artificially contrived, the contrary to life.

JOHNNY CASH
American singer
Winners got scars too.

BENNETT CERF
American publisher
Esquire 1964
Fame – anyone who says he doesn't like it is crazy.

COCO CHANEL
French couturier
'Coco Chanel - Her Life, Her Secrets' by M. Haedrich 1971
That's what fame is – solitude.

Legend is the consecration of fame.

JEAN COCTEAU
French writer and film director
We must believe in luck. For how else can we explain the success of those we don't like.

quoting Eric Satie in 'Writers at Work' 3rd series 1967
The great thing is not to refuse the Legion of Honour, the great thing is not to have deserved it.

NIK COHN
British writer
'Awopbopaloobopalopbamboom' 1969
When you've made your million, when you've cut your monsters, when your peak has been passed . . . what happens next? What about the fifty years before you die?

CYRIL CONNOLLY
British critic
New York Times 1977
Those whom the Gods wish to destroy they first call promising.

SIR CHARLES CURRAN
British broadcasting executive 1975
It may be that in private moments the language at Buckingham Palace is quite similar to that of a rugby changing room.

SALVADOR DALI
Spanish artist
The thermometer of success is merely the jealousy of the malcontents.

RAY DAVIES
British rock musician
One luxury of being a successful band is that you can experiment in public sometimes.

KIRK DOUGLAS
American film star
Esquire 1970
If you become a star, *you* don't change, everyone else does.

BOB DYLAN
American singer
What's money? A man is a success if he gets up in the morning and goes to bed at night and in between does what he wants to do.

ALBERT EINSTEIN
German physicist
The Observer 1950
If A is success in life, then A equals X plus Y plus Z. Work is X, Y is play and Z is keeping your mouth shut.

Try not to become a man of success but rather try to become a man of value.

BRIAN ENO
British musician
I am interested quite much in just making music. But I'm also interested in talking about it and one of the things about the traditional rock star role is that you don't say anything. The best way to maintain your conceit is to keep your mouth shut and I'm certainly not prepared to do that. I couldn't.

ORIANA FALLACI
Italian journalist
'The Egotists' 1963
Glory is a heavy burden, a murdering poison, and to bear it is an art. And to have that art is rare.

WILLIAM FAULKNER
American novelist
'Writers at Work' 1st series 1958
Success is feminine and like a woman; if you cringe before her she will override you. So the way to treat her is to show her the back of your hand. Then maybe she will do the crawling.

ERROL FLYNN
American film star
My problem lies in reconciling my gross habits with my net income.

GENE FOWLER
American writer
What is success? It is a toy balloon among children armed with pins.

ERICH FROMM
American psychologist
'Man For Himself'
Since modern man experiences himself both as the seller and as the commodity to be sold on the market, his self-esteem depends on conditions beyond his control. If he is 'successful' he is valuable; if he is not, he is worthless.

JUDY GARLAND
American singer and film star
If I'm such a legend, then why am I so lonely? . . . let me tell you, legends are all very well if you've got somebody around who loves you . . .

GLYME'S FORMULA FOR SUCCESS
in 'Murphy's Law Book Two' by Arthur Bloch 1980
The secret of success is sincerity. Once you can fake that you've got it made.

SAM GOLDWYN
American film producer
on CBS-TV 1954
God makes the star. God gives them the talent. It's up to the producers to recognise that talent and develop it.

PETER GRANT
British rock manager
Silence makes legends.

BERNARD GRASSET
French writer
'Remarques sur l'action'
Success is often only a revenge on happiness.

GRAHAM GREENE
British novelist
Radio Times 1964
Fame is a powerful aphrodisiac

ERNESTO 'CHE' GUEVARA
Bolivian radical
'Man & Socialism In Cuba'
On Western individualism . . . It is a race of wolves. He who arrives does so only at the expense of the failure of others.

H. G. 'BLONDIE' HASLER
American yachtsman
The Observer 1968
You cannot have the success without the failures.

LAFCADIO HEARN
American writer
'Life & Letters' ed. Elizabeth Bisland
Literary success of any enduring kind is made by refusing to do what publishers want, by refusing to write what the public wants, by refusing to accept any popular standard, by refusing to write anything to order.

JOSEPH HELLER
American novelist
Playboy 1975
Success and failure are both difficult to

endure. Along with success come drugs, divorce, fornication, bullying, travel, meditation, medication, depression, neurosis and suicide. With failure comes failure.

LILLIAN HELLMAN
American playwright
The Listener 1979
Success and failure are not true opposites and they're not even in the same class; they're not even a couch and a chair.

DAVID HEMMINGS
British film star
after 'Blow Up', 1966
It's amazing, one hit picture and two-inch lifts in your shoes and you feel ten feet tall.

BILLIE HOLIDAY
American singer
'Lady Sings The Blues' 1973
I'm always making a comeback but nobody ever tells me where I've been.

BILLY IDOL
British rock singer
You have to prevent yourself from being conned so you don't con other people.

FRANK INFANTE
American rock musician 1979
When you become that popular, that successful, that big it becomes nothing more than an exhibition. It's no longer a question of how good or bad you are . . . the fact that they're actually on stage outweighs the reasons why they're actually on stage in the first place.

CHARLES IVES
American composer
asked whether he was bitter about receiving no awards . . .
No. Awards are merely the badges of mediocrity.

MICK JAGGER
British rock star
For most people the fantasy is driving around in a big car, having all the chicks you want and being able to pay for it. It always has been, still is, and always will be. Anyone who says it isn't is talking bullshit.

FRANCIS KING
British writer
The Listener 1978
Words of delight, praise and enthusiasm are like visiting-cards. The bigger the card, the less important the man; the bigger the word, the less important the emotion.

LOUIS KRONENBERGER
American critic
'Company Manners' 1954
On any morning these days whole segments of the population wake up to find themselves famous, while, to keep matters shipshape, whole contingents of celebrities wake up to find themselves forgotten.

VALERY LARBAUD
French writer
'Ce vice impuni, la lecture'
Glory is only one of the forms of human indifference.

CHRISTOPHER LASCH
American historian
'The Culture of Narcissism' 1979
Nothing succeeds like the appearance of success.

REGGIE LEACH
American pro ice hockey star 1976
Success is not the result of spontaneous combustion. You must set yourself on fire.

ANNIE LEIBOWITZ
American photographer
Most people think that entertainers see the world. But after the 26th city, especially if you're doing one-nighters, your hotel room is your world.

BERNARD LEVIN
British journalist
on Mao 1967
Whom the mad would destroy they first make Gods.

CHARLES LUCKMAN
American architect
New York Mirror 1955
Success is that old ABC – ability, breaks and courage.

MIGNON McLAUGHLIN
American writer
'The Neurotic's Notebook' 1963
Every society honours its live conformists and its dead troublemakers.

DON MCLEAN
American rock composer
Success is like a shot of heroin. It's up to you to decide whether you want to continue to put the needle in your arm.

NORMAN MAILER
American writer
on receiving National Book Award for 'Armies of the Night' 1969
Awards are a measurement of the degree to which an Establishment meets the talent which it had hindered and helped.

DEREK MARLOWE
British writer
'Soliloquy on James Dean's 45th Birthday' New York Magazine 1976
If a man can bridge the gap between life and death, if he can live after he's died, maybe then he was a great man. Immortality is the only true success.

W. SOMERSET MAUGHAM
British writer
quoted in Michael Korda 'Success' 1977
The common idea that success spoils people by making them vain, egotistic, and self complacent is erroneous – on the contrary it makes them, for the most part, humble, tolerant and kind. Failure makes people bitter and cruel.

H. L. MENCKEN
American essayist
'Minority Report' 1956
When I hear a man applauded by the mob I always feel a pang of pity for him. All he has to do to be hissed is to live long enough.

JONATHAN MILLER
British doctor and writer
The Observer 1967
After a while you find that you're on a self perpetuating treadmill of involvement with the result that your public person takes on a sort of pop art image of itself that bears very little relationship to reality.

New Statesman 1972
Fame is being known by more people than you know. It is vulnerability.

ROBERT MITCHUM
American film star
Esquire 1964
Stardom . . . it's a dull aching euphoria. You have no friends. You have disciples.

MALCOLM MUGGERIDGE
British journalist 1969
I note that, according to a recent poll, some 40% of the British population think that Alf Garnett is a real person and some 90% that I am. On this point I find myself among the 'don't knows'.

JACK NICHOLSON
American film star
The whole thing is to keep working and pretty soon they'll think you're good.

GARY NUMAN
British rock singer 1980
If you were a normal person walking down the street they wouldn't come up to you and say 'Cor, I think you're ugly'. If you're famous they think it's their right.

DENIS O'BRIEN
Australian journalist, 1968
Fame is being insulted by Groucho Marx.

JOHN OSBORNE
British playwright 1966
Financial success improves people who are good and debases people who are bad.

GRAHAM PARKER
British rock musician
When you're obscure, when you're just the average joe you don't think you should be. You want people to recognise you. And then when they do, it doesn't mean a great deal.

ANDY PARTRIDGE
British rock singer
Success is nothing but being a quote.

PABLO PICASSO
Spanish artist 1973
The tragedy of being famous is that you have to devote so much time to being famous.

IGGY POP
American rock musician
All the successes I know are really boring little cheeses. Once these guys are exposed to that dirty thing called the public they become ignorant and inhuman.

ELVIS PRESLEY
American rock star
It's very hard to live up to an image.

LUCINDA PRIOR-PALMER
British showjumper
The Guardian 1976
I mean, fame's quite fun and all that, but as soon as anything goes wrong or you make a big bog of something, everyone knows about it and that does taint it a bit.

'THE PRODUCERS'
Embassy 1968 screenplay by Mel Brooks
Zero Mostel: That's it, baby! When you got it, flaunt it! Flaunt it!

VANESSA REDGRAVE
British actress
in 'Goodbye Baby & Amen' by D. Bailey 1969
Integrity is so perishable in the summer months of success.

LOU REED
American rock star
The real thing is not something that you'd want to idolize.

JEAN RENOIR
French film director
'My Life and My Films' 1974
Is it possible to succeed without any act of betrayal?

LINDA RONSTADT
American rock singer
You have to erect a fence and say 'OK, scale this'. It's like on top of a glass mountain.

ARTUR RUBINSTEIN
Polish pianist 1974
Of course there is no formula for success,

except perhaps, an unconditional acceptance of life and what it brings.

ROSALIND RUSSELL
American film star
Success is a public affair. Failure is a private funeral.

HARRY SECOMBE
British comedian
These days a star is anyone who can hold a microphone; a superstar is someone who has shaken hands with Lew Grade; and a super-superstar is someone who has refused to shake hands with Lew Grade.

MARLENA SHAW
American singer
Philadelphia Inquirer 1977
Success means only being exposed to more people.

FRED SHERO
American pro ice hockey coach 1975
Success requires no explanation, failure presents no alibis.

There is plenty of room at the top, but not enough to sit down.

PAUL SIMON
American singer
The public hungers to see talented young people kill themselves.

JACK SOLOMONS
British boxing promoter (and ex-fishmonger) 1950
If you want to sell 'em fish, sell 'em big fish. That's the secret of success.

PHIL SPECTOR
American rock producer
You can always come back, but you've got to come back better. If you come back worse, or even the same, you're dead.

STEPHEN SPENDER
British poet
New York Review of Books 1973
In England, success is supposed to be kept within the bounds of decency ... to bring to your friends credit for knowing you, but not pushed to that extent where they might become envious.

CASEY STENGEL
American baseball manager
Ability is the art of getting credit for all the home runs someone else hits.

JOSEF VON STERNBERG
German film director
The only way to succeed is to make people hate you. That way they remember you.

ADLAI STEVENSON
American politician 1961
Flattery is all right – if you don't inhale.

STING (Gordon Sumner)
British rock star 1980
Success always necessitates a degree of ruthlessness. Given the choice of friendship or success, I'd probably choose success.

We're not in control of the forces that could make us next week's hasbeens.

TOM STOPPARD
British playwright
The Times 1972
The trouble with success is that it immediately diminishes your mental conception of what it should be.

ANTHONY STORR
British psychiatrist
'Human Aggression' 1968
It is a tragic paradox that the very qualities that have led to man's extraordinary capacity for success are also those most likely to destroy him.

BARBRA STREISAND
American singer
Life 1963
Success to me is having ten honeydew melons and eating only the top half of each one.

STUDS TERKEL
American writer
Dick Cavett TV show 1978
A celebrity is someone who is known for being known.

NICCOLO TUCCI
Italian writer
in 'Contemporary Novelists' 1976
The temptations of Success are far more

sinister than those of habit, laziness or fatigue, in fact they are the *real* tools of the Devil.

SOPHIE TUCKER
American singer
'Some of These Days' 1945
Success in show business depends on your ability to make and keep friends.

JOHN UPDIKE
American writer
Esquire 1965
The world is mocked – belittled, perforated – by the success of one's contemporaries in it. The world of deeds and wealth, which to a child appears a gaudy heaven staffed with invincibly brilliant powers, is revealed as a tattered heirloom limply descending from one generation of caretakers to another.

ANDY WARHOL
American artist
dictum 1960s
In the future everyone will be famous for fifteen minutes.

'Exposures' 1979
In fifteen minutes everybody will be famous.

'From A to B and Back Again' 1975
A good reason to be famous . . . is so you can read all the big magazines and know everybody in all the stories. Page after page, it's just all people you've met.

MUDDY WATERS
American blues singer
You can't be the best. You can just be a good 'un.

TENNESSEE WILLIAMS
American playwright
'Memoirs' 1975
High station in life is earned by the gallantry with which appalling experiences are survived with grace.

WALTER WINCHELL
American columnist
Nothing recedes like success.

Success is the reward of anyone who looks for trouble.

SHELLEY WINTERS
American film star
Sunday Express 1975
Stardom can be very destructive – particularly if you believe in it.

P. G. WODEHOUSE
British humorist
'Louder & Funnier'
Success comes to a writer, as a rule, so gradually, that it is always something of a shock to him to look back and realize the heights to which he has climbed.

STEVIE WONDER
American musician
When you begin thinking you really *are* number one . . . that's when you begin to go nowhere.

Failure

MAX BEERBOHM
British writer
'Mainly on the Air' 1946
There is much to be said for failure. It is more interesting than success.

JOHN CALE
British rock musician
A cult figure is a guy who hasn't got the musical ability to make it to the charts.

MONTGOMERY CLIFT
American film star
quoted in 'Short Lives' by Katinka Matson 1980
Failure and its accompanying misery is for the artist his most vital source of creative energy.

quoted in NY Post 1966
One tries his best to become a part of what one has to do. If you fail, you fail.

CYRIL CONNOLLY
British critic
The Unquiet Grave 1945
Doing is overrated, and success undesir-
able, but the bitterness of Failure even
more so.

MARGARET DRABBLE
British novelist
quoted in 'The Wit of Women' by L. and M.
Cowan
Nothing succeeds, they say, like success.
And certainly nothing fails like failure.

BOB DYLAN
American singer
'Love Minus Zero / No Limit'
She knows there's no success like failure
/ And that failure's no success at all.
(M. Witmark & Sons)

LESLIE FIEDLER
American critic
'Love & Death in the American Novel' 1960
The image of man in art, however magnificently portrayed – indeed, when it is
most magnificently portrayed – is the
image of a failure. There is no way
out. . .

ERROL FLYNN
American film star
quote beneath his picture in Charley O's New
York bar
Any man who has $10,000 left when he
dies is a failure.

JOE HARVEY
The Guardian 1973
Those who tell you it's tough at the top
have never been at the bottom.

IAN HUNTER
British rock singer 1979
It's good to fail now and again – you
learn a lot more out of failure than you
do out of success.

CLIVE JAMES
Australian critic
The Observer 1978
For famous people who fail to protect
themselves there seems to be no mercy.

JOHN F. KENNEDY
American president
Failure has no friends.

CLAUDE LELOUCH
French film director
The Guardian 1972
The real loser of our times is the one
who is expected to win.

GROUCHO MARX
American comedian
No one is completely unhappy at the
failure of his best friend.

ELSA MAXWELL
American socialite
Keep your talent in the dark and you'll
never be insulted.

MALCOLM MUGGERIDGE
British journalist
'Boring for England' 1966
In politics, as in womanizing, failure is
decisive. It sheds its retrospective gloom
on earlier endeavour which at the time
seemed full of promise.

'ON THE WATERFRONT'
Columbia 1954 screenplay by Budd Schulberg
from his own novel
Marlon Brando: I coulda had class! I
coulda been a contender! I coulda been
somebody! Instead of a bum which is
what I am!

'THE PRODUCERS'
Embassy 1968 screenplay by Mel Brooks
Zero Mostel: Bloom, Bloom, I'm drowning. Other men have sailed through life.
Bialystock has struck a reef. Bloom, I'm
going under. I'm being sunk by a society
that demands success when all I can offer is failure.

NICHOLAS RAY
American film director
There is no formula for success. But
there is a formula for failure, and that is
trying to please everybody.

'SWEET BIRD OF YOUTH'
MGM 1962 screenplay by Richard Brooks,
based on play by Tennessee Williams
Paul Newman: Failure is a highly con-
tagious disease.

GORE VIDAL
American writer
The 'Sexus' of Henry Miller 1965
Yet from Rousseau to Gide the true confessors have been aware that not only is life mostly failure, but that in one's failure or pettiness or wrongness exists the living drama of the self.

LOELIA
Duchess of Westminster
Anyone seen on a bus after the age of thirty has been a failure in life.

Children

ALFRED ADLER
German analyst
quoted in New York Times 1949
Whenever a child lies you will always find a severe parent. A lie would have no sense unless the truth were felt to be dangerous.

BRIAN ALDISS
British author
The Guardian 1971
When childhood dies, its corpses are called adults and they enter society, one of the politer names of hell. That is why we dread children, even if we love them. They show us the state of our decay.

MAYA ANGELOU
American writer
'I Know Why the Caged Bird Sings' 1969
Children's talent to endure stems from their ignorance of alternatives.

PRINCESS ANNE
Daily Telegraph 1981
Being pregnant is a very boring six months. I am not particularly maternal. It's an occupational hazard of being a wife.

ANONYMOUS
Spokesman for the British Boy Scouts 1971
Long trousers and all that they stand for have been accepted as inevitable in a world of change.

ALEXANDRE ARNOUX
French writer
'Etudes et Caprices'
The state of innocence contains the germs of all future sin.

NIGEL BALCHIN
British author
Sunday Express 1965
Children are cruel, ruthless, cunning and almost incredibly self-centred. Far from cementing a marriage children more frequently disrupt it. Child-rearing is on the whole an expensive and unrewarding bore, in which more has to be invested, both materially and spiritually, than ever comes out in dividends.

JAMES BALDWIN
American author
'Fifth Avenue, Uptown' Esquire 1960
Children have never been very good at listening to their elders, but they have never failed to imitate them.

SIMONE DE BEAUVOIR
French writer
'La Femme Rompue'
What is an adult? A child blown up by age.

'The Second Sex' 1953
In a sense the mystery of the incarnation is repeated in each woman. Every child who is born is a god who makes himself a man.

ROBERT BENCHLEY
American wit
There are two classes of travel — first class, and with children.

SIR ISAIAH BERLIN
British philosopher
The Listener 1978
Society moves by some degree of parricide, by which children, on the whole, kill, if not their fathers, at least the be-

liefs of their fathers and arrive at new beliefs. That is what progress is.

JOHN MASON BROWN
American essayist
New York Times 1955
Reasoning with a child is fine, if you can reach the child's reason without destroying your own.

SIR WINSTON CHURCHILL
British statesman
There is no finer investment for any community than putting milk into babies.

JUDGE TOM CLARK
American lawyer 1981
Time
Every boy, in his heart, would rather steal second base than an automobile.

JEAN COCTEAU
French writer and film director
in 'The Faber Book of Aphorisms' 1964
Children and lunatics cut the Gordian knot which the poet spends his life patiently trying to undo.

AL COHN
quoted in New York Times 1968
It's what you listen to when you're growing up that you always come back to.

COLETTE
French novelist
'Journey for Myself' 1972
To talk to a child, to fascinate him, is much more difficult than to win an electoral victory. But it is also more rewarding.

MARCELENE COX
American writer
Ladies Home Journal 1948
The illusions of childhood are necessary experiences. A child should not be denied a balloon because an adult knows that sooner or later it will burst.

MONTA CRANE
quoted in Reader's Digest 1977
There are three ways to get something done: do it yourself, hire someone, or forbid your kids to do it.

PHYLLIS DILLER
American comedienne
Cleaning your house while your kids are still growing is like shovelling the walk before it stops snowing.

NORMAN DOUGLAS
British writer
in 'The Faber Book of Aphorisms' 1964
Nobody can misunderstand a boy like his own mother.

RICHARD EDER
New York Times 1973
Childhood is the country that produces the most nostalgic, contentious and opinionated exiles.

PAUL EHRLICH
American scientist
The mother of the year should be a sterilized woman with two adopted children.

CLIFTON FADIMAN
American essayist
'Any Number Can Play' 1957
All children talk with integrity up to about the age of five, when they fall victim to the influences of the adult world and mass entertainment. It is then they begin, all unconsciously, to become plausible actors. The product of this process is known as maturity, or you and me.

FRANTZ FANON
French radical
'The Wretched of the Earth' 1961
Each generation must out of relative obscurity discover its mission, fulfill it or betray it.

IMOGENE FEY
quoted in 'Violets & Vitriol' ed. J. Cooper and T. Hartman 1980
A man finds out what is meant by a spitting image when he tries to feed cereal to his infant.

R. BUCKMINSTER FULLER
American essayist
Every child is born a genius.

'GIANT'
Warner Bros 1956 screenplay by Fred Guiol and Ivan Moffat, based on Edna Ferber novel
Elizabeth Taylor: Well, Vashti, all you

can do is raise them. You can't live their lives for them.

GERMAINE GREER
Australian feminist
'The Female Eunuch' 1970
It is known that a father is necessary, but not known how to identify him, except negatively.

ERNEST HEMINGWAY
American writer
in 'Papa Hemingway' by A. E. Hotchner 1966
To be a successful father, there's one absolute rule: when you have a kid, don't look at it for the first two years.

RANDALL JARRELL
American critic
'The Third Book of Criticism'
One of the most obvious facts about grownups to a child, is that they have forgotten what it is like to be a child.

C. G. JUNG
Swiss psychoanalyst
'Psychological Reflections' 1953
If there is anything we wish to change in the child, we should first examine it and see whether it is not something that could be better changed in ourselves.

CHINA KANTNER
Daughter of American rock star Paul and originally named 'god'
I like my name, but I want to change it to Susie though.

SALLY KEMPTON
American journalist
Esquire 1970
All children are potential victims, dependant on the world's goodwill.

Boys grow up and have to kill their fathers. Girls can be made to understand their place.

FLORYNCE KENNEDY
American feminist
Ms 1973
Being a mother is a noble status, right? Right. So why does it change when you put 'unwed' or 'welfare' in front of it?

R. D. LAING
British psychiatrist
'The Politics of Experience' 1967
From the moment of birth, when the Stone Age baby confronts the 20th century mother, the baby is subjected to these forces of violence, called love, as its mother and father, and their parents and their parents before them, have been. These forces are mainly concerned with destroying most of its potentialities.

PHILIP LARKIN
British poet
'This Be The Verse'
They fuck you up, your mum and dad / They may not mean to, but they do / They fill you up with the faults they had / And add some extra, just for you.

JEAN DE LA VARENNE
French writer
'Le Centaure de Dieu'
Childhood is a forgotten journey.

FRAN LEBOWITZ
American journalist
'Metropolitan Life' 1978
All God's children are not beautiful. Most of God's children are, in fact, barely presentable.

JOHN LENNON
British rock star
Our children will hate us too, y'know.

ART LINKLETTER
American humorist
'A Child's Garden of Misinformation'
Posterity is the patriotic name for grandchildren.

MARY McCARTHY
American writer
'On the Contrary' 1962
The only form of action open to a child is to break something or strike someone, its mother or another child; it cannot cause things to happen in the world.

SHIRLEY MacLAINE
American film star 1969
We had to analyse the whole of the motivation behind this insane need to propagate.

YUKIO MISHIMA
Japanese novelist
'Confessions of a Mask' 1972
The period of childhood is a stage on which time and space become entangled.

NANCY MITFORD
British writer
I love children. Especially when they cry – for then someone takes them away.

DESMOND MORRIS
British anthropologist
'The Naked Ape' 1967
The age of a child is inversely correlated with the size of animals it prefers.

J. B. MORTON
British humorist
'Beachcomber' 'Dictionary for Today' in Daily Express, passim
Prodigy: a child who plays the piano when he ought to be in bed.

RANDY NEWMAN
American songwriter
'Memo To My Son'
I don't know if you think much of me / But someday you'll understand / Wait till you learn to talk, baby / I'll show you how smart I am.
(Warner Bros. Music)

BRIAN O'NOLAN
Irish writer
(Myles na gCopaleen) in 'The Best of Myles' 1968
Do engine drivers, I wonder, eternally wish they were small boys.

JOE ORTON
British playwright
'Entertaining Mr. Sloane' 1964
Kath: Can he be present at the birth of his child?. . .
Ed: It's all any reasonable child can expect if the dad is present at the conception.

PABLO PICASSO
Spanish artist
Every child is an artist. The problem is how to remain an artist once he grows up.

ALICE ROSSI
American feminist
'The Feminist Papers' 1973
Sons forget what grandsons wish to remember.

PHILIP ROTH
American novelist
'Portnoy's Complaint' 1969
Enough with being a nice Jewish boy. Publicly pleasing my parents while privately pulling my *putz*. Enough!

The Jewish boy with parents alive is a fifteen-year-old boy and will remain a fifteen-year-old boy until they die.

BERTRAND RUSSELL
British philosopher
New York Times 1963
The fundamental defect of fathers is that they want their children to be a credit to them.

JEAN-PAUL SARTRE
French philosopher
'The Words' 1964
There is no good father, that is the rule. Don't lay the blame on men, but on the bond of paternity, which is rotten.

Childhood decides.

FLORIDA SCOTT-MAXWELL
American psychologist
'The Measure of My Days' 1972
No matter how old a mother is, she watches her middle-aged children for signs of improvement.

DR. SEUSS
American children's writer
in 'Bartlett's Unfamiliar Quotations' ed. L. L. Levinson
Adults are obsolete children.

IGNAZIO SILONE
Italian radical 1963
No one can ever write about anything that happened to him after he was twelve years old.

B. F. SKINNER
American behaviourist
Society attacks early when the individual is helpless.

LOGAN PEARSALL SMITH
American essayist
in 'The Faber Book of Aphorisms' 1964
What is more enchanting than the voices of young people when you can't hear what they say.

DR. BENJAMIN SPOCK
American paediatrician
'Baby & Child Care'
How to fold a diaper depends on the size of the baby and the diaper.

JOHN STEINBECK
American writer
quoted in 'To Be a Father' ed. Alvin Schwartz
Father and son are natural enemies and each is happier and more secure in keeping it that way.

PETE TOWNSHEND
British rock composer
'Substitute'
I was born with a plastic spoon in my mouth. (Essex Music)

HARRY S. TRUMAN
American President
on TV 1955
The best way to give advice to your children is to find out what they want and advise them to do it.

PETER USTINOV
British actor and wit
Sunday Times 1964
Children are a kind of confirmation of life. The only form of immortality that we can be sure of.

E. B. WHITE
American writer
'The Second Tree from the Corner' 1954
The time not to become a father is eighteen years before a war.

DUKE OF WINDSOR
Look 1957
The thing that impresses me most about America is the way parents obey their children.

D. W. WINNICOTT
British paediatrician
'On Communication' 1963
In healthy development the infant (theoretically) starts off (psychologically) without life and becomes lively simply because of being, in fact, alive.

'Through Paediatrics to Psychoanalysis' 1958
The most remarkable thing about a mother is her ability to be hurt so much by her baby and to hate so much without paying the child out, and her ability to wait for rewards that may or may not come at a later date. Perhaps she is helped by some of the nursery rhymes she sings, which her baby enjoys but fortunately does not understand? 'Rock-abye baby, on the tree top / When the wind blows the cradle will rock / When the bough breaks the cradle will fall / Down will come baby, cradle and all.'

SIR JOHN WOLFENDEN
British politician
Sunday Times 1958
Schoolmasters and parents exist to be grown out of.

WOODROW WYATT
British politician
'To The Point' 1981
We have children because we want immortality and this is the most reliable way of getting it.

DENNIS DE YOUNG
American rock musician
In England kids are disillusioned with having too little. In America they're disillusioned with having too much.

FRANK ZAPPA
American rock musician
In the old days you'd drag your old man out on the lawn and kick the shit out of each other and he'd say 'Be home by midnight' and you'd be home by midnight. Today parents daren't tell you what time to be in. They're frightened you won't come back.

If your children ever found out how lame you are, they'd kill you in your sleep.

Ageing

WOODY ALLEN
American film star
New Yorker 1974
The worst thing that could happen to anyone is getting older, it's like drawing the Ace of Spades, and everyone gets it. Though being very young isn't always great either. It can be like living in a concentration camp.

CHER
American singer
Playboy 1975
Getting married and getting old are the two things that save everybody's ass.

JOSEPH ALSOP
American journalist
I have no views. When one is retired it is sensible to refrain from having views.

LANCE ALWORTH
American pro football player
For a while you're a veteran, and then you're just old.

LOUIS ARMSTRONG
American musician
Esquire 1969
There is no such thing as 'on the way out'. As long as you are still doing something interesting and good, you're in business because you're still breathing.

BRIGITTE BARDOT
French film star
Nova 1970
It's sad to grow old, but nice to ripen.

News of the World 1974
What could be more beautiful than a dear old lady growing wise with age? Every age can be enchanting, provided you live within it.

JONAH BARRINGTON
British squash star 1969
It's not how old you are, it's how hard you work at it.

ETHEL BARRYMORE
American actress
You grow up the day you have your first real laugh at yourself.

BERNARD BARUCH
American financier
The Observer 1955
Old age is always 15 years older than I am.

SIMONE DE BEAUVOIR
French writer
'The Coming of Age' 1972
Old age is life's parody.

The role of a retired person is no longer to possess one.

'Joie de Vivre' Harpers 1972
Never, on any plane, does the aged person lapse into a 'second childhood', since childhood is, by definition a forward, upward movement.

JORGE LUIS BORGES
Argentine writer
'Conversations with Jorge Luis Borges' ed. Richard Burgin 1973
Through the years, a man peoples a space with images of provinces, kingdoms, mountains, bays, ships, islands, fishes, rooms, tools, stars, horses and people. Shortly before his death he discovers that the patient labyrinth of lines traces the image of his own face.

JULIUS BOROS
American golf star 1978
Retire? Retire to what? I already fish and play golf.

GENERAL OMAR BRADLEY
American soldier
Daily Telegraph 1959
The best service a retired general can perform is to turn in his tongue along with his unit, and mothball his opinions.

GERALD BRENAN
British writer
'Thoughts in a Dry Season' 1978
Old age takes away from us what we have inherited and gives us what we have earned.

LENNY BRUCE
American comedian
'How To Talk Dirty & Influence People' 1965
There is nothing sadder than an old hipster.

PEARL S. BUCK
American writer
'China Past and Present' 1972
Perhaps one has to be very old before one learns to be amused rather than shocked.

CHARLES BUKOWSKI
American writer
'Notes of a Dirty Old Man' 1969
Who cares about a dead battery?

The face is the first thing you throw out when the luck gets bad. The remaining decay follows in slower order.

HERB CAEN
American columnist
A man begins cutting his wisdom teeth the first time he bites off more than he can chew.

JOYCE CARY
British novelist
'Art & Reality' 1958
A man of eighty has outlived probably three new schools of painting, two of architecture and poetry, a hundred in dress.

COCO CHANEL
French couturier
on reaching sixty
Cut off my head and I am thirteen.

New York Times 1971
A woman has the age she deserves.

'Coco Chanel – Her Life, Her Secrets' by M. Haedrich 1971
Youth is something very new. Twenty years ago no one mentioned it.

Ladies Home Journal 1956
Nature gives you the face you have at twenty, but it's up to you to merit the face you have at fifty. (cf. Orwell)

Reader's Digest 1979
We are born with one face but, laughing or crying, wisely or unwisely, eventually we form our own.

MAURICE CHEVALIER
French film star
New York Times 1960
Old age isn't so bad when you consider the alternative.

SARAH CHURCHILL
British actress
The Observer 1981
As long as you can still be disappointed, you are still young.

E. M. CIORAN
French philosopher
'Syllogismes de l'amertume' 1952
In growing old one learns to barter fears against sneers.

LADY DIANA COOPER
British aristocrat
Age wins and one must learn to grow old.

Age is an ugly thing, and it goes on getting worse.

ELVIS COSTELLO
British rock musician
Watching someone you admired struggling to be inspired is the most pathetic sight imaginable.

QUENTIN CRISP
British author
'The Naked Civil Servant' 1968
The young always have the same problem – how to rebel and conform at the same time. They have now solved this by defying their parents and copying one another.

Sunday Times 1981
The joy of being older is that in one's life one can, towards the end of the run, over-act appallingly.

LORD DAWSON
British Royal doctor
in 'The Wit of Medicine' ed. L. and M. Cowan 1972
Middle aged people may be divided into three classes: those who are still young, those who have forgotten they were young, and those who were never young.

MARLENE DIETRICH
German film star born c.1901
Say I am seventy-five and let it go at that.

BOB DYLAN
American singer
'Blowin' In The Wind'
How many roads must a man walk down

/ Before you call him a man?
(M. Witmark & Sons)

'Ballad of a Thin Man'
Something is happening here / But you
don't know what it is / Do you, Mr.
Jones?
(M. Witmark & Sons)

WILLIAM FEATHER
American businessman
'The Business of Life' 1949
Setting a good example for your children
takes all the fun out of middle age.

EDNA FERBER
American writer
Being an old maid is like death by
drowning: a really delightful sensation
after you cease to struggle.

BRENDAN FRANCIS
If the pleasures that an age offers are
insipid, passionate souls will seek pain.

GLENN FREY
American rock star
The great thing about being 30 is that
there are a great deal more available
women. The young ones look younger
and the old ones don't look nearly as
old.

DOROTHY FULDHEIM
'A Thousand Friends' 1974
Youth is a disease from which we all
recover.

GRETA GARBO
Swedish film star
refusing ever again to perform, c1946
I have made enough faces.

CHARLES DE GAULLE
French statesman
Old age is a shipwreck.

GRAHAM GREENE
British novelist
'Ways of Escape'
What a mess those inexperienced years
can be! Lust and boredom and sentimentality . . . in that twilight world of
calf-love any number of girls can re-
hearse simultaneously a sentimental part
which never reaches performance.

TONY HANCOCK
British comedian
The trouble is, you're not allowed to
grow old in the world any more. We are
all moth eaten kids, really.

LESLIE HANSCOM
American journalist
Newsweek 1963
Whatever happened to Saturday night?

MARCUS LEE HANSEN
Newsweek 1977
What the son wishes to forget, the grand-
son wishes to remember. (cf Alice Rossi
p85)

HELEN HAYES
American actress
quoted in 'Showcase' by Roy Newquist
Every human being on this earth is born
with a tragedy, and it isn't original sin.
He's born with the tragedy that he has
to grow up . . . a lot of people don't have
the courage to do it.

KATHARINE HEPBURN
American filmstar
*quoted in 'The Wit of Women' by L. and M.
Cowan*
If you survive long enough, you're re-
vered – rather like an old building.

HOLBROOK JACKSON
British writer
'Ladies Home Journal' 1950
No man is ever old enough to know
better.

'Platitudes in the Making'
Don't try to convert the elderly person,
circumvent him.

MICK JAGGER
British rock star
A lot of people start to fall to bits at
thirty . . . quite honestly once you are
able to reproduce you're over the hill.
You start to go downhill at eighteen,
physically.

MICK JAGGER &
KEITH RICHARD
British rock composers
'Mother's Little Helper'
What a drag it is getting old.
(Essex Music)

POPE JOHN XXIII
quoted in Gerald Brenan 'Thoughts In a Dry Season' 1978
Men are like wine – some turn to vinegar, but the best improve with age.

REV. WILLIAM JOYCE
British clergyman
in 'The Wit of the Church' ed. M. Bateman and S. Stenning 1967
Too many young people are beginning to regard home as a filling station by day and a parking place for the night.

RAY KROC
American junk food entrepeneur;
His motto
When you're green you're growing, when you're ripe you rot.

STANISLAW J. LEC
Polish poet
'Unkempt Thoughts' 1962
Wounds heal and become scars, but scars grow with us.

JOHN LENNON &
PAUL McCARTNEY
British rock composers
'When I'm Sixty-Four'
Will you still need me / Will you still feed me / When I'm sixty-four? (Northern Songs)

MARY WILSON LITTLE
American writer
A youth with his first cigar makes himself sick – a youth with his first girl makes other people sick.

JOHN LYDON (Johnny Rotten)
British rock star 1979
I'm only twenty-two and I feel I've seen everything. It makes it very difficult sometimes.

MOMS MABLEY
American comedienne
Daily News 1975
The children had 'em, let 'em raise 'em. That's what kills so many elderly women – raising grandchildren.

COLLEEN McCULLOUGH
Australian writer 1977
The lovely thing about being 40 is that you can appreciate 25-year-old men more.

HAROLD MACMILLAN
British politician
It has been said that there is no fool like an old fool, except a young fool. But the young fool has first to grow up to be an old fool to realize what a damn fool he was when he was a young fool.

ANNA MAGNANI
Italian film star
quoted in Interview 1978 to a photographer . . .
Please don't retouch my wrinkles. It took me so long to earn them.

ANDRE MALRAUX
French writer
'Le Voie royale'
Youth is a religion from which one always ends up being converted.

MICKEY MANTLE
American baseball player
Esquire 1968
You don't want to reach a point where people think you're just hanging on.

GROUCHO MARX
American comedian 1974
Anyone can get old, all you have to do is live long enough.

Growing old is something you do if you're lucky.

W. SOMERSET MAUGHAM
British writer
1957 visiting London and failing to obtain crumpets at the Dorchester, then aged 83 . . .
When I was young one could have crumpets and muffins for tea. One cannot any more in this hard life we lead.

GOLDA MEIR
Israeli politician
Old age is like a plane flying through storm. Once you're aboard there's nothing you can do.

'MILDRED PIERCE'
Warner Bros 1945 screenplay by Ronald MacDougall, based on novel by James M Cain
Zachary Scott: As you grow older, you'll find the only things you regret are the things you didn't do.

'MR PEABODY AND THE MERMAID'
Universal, 1948 screenplay by Nunally Johnson from the novel 'Peabody's Mermaid' by Guy and Constance Jones
William Powell: Fifty – the old age of youth and the youth of old age.

RANDY NEWMAN
American songwriter
It's a hell of an ambition, wanting to be mellow. It's like wanting to be senile.

DENIS NORDEN
British humorist
The Observer 1976
Middle age is when wherever you go on holiday you pack a sweater.

GEORGE ORWELL
British essayist
Journals 1949
At 50 everyone has the face he deserves.

STEVE OWEN
American pro football coach
The older you get, the faster you ran as a kid.

IAN PAIGE
British rock musician 1979
Teenage revolution is practising at being someone.

Every teenage revolution is the same . . . the function of youth is to change laws made by old men for young men that old men would never break.

LAURENCE J. PETER
Canadian educator
'Peter's Quotations' 1977
Middle age is when anything new you feel is most likely to be a symptom.

MARY PICKFORD
American film star
1973
People remember me most as a little girl with long golden curls. I don't want them to see me as a little old lady.

V. S. PRITCHETT
British critic
'The Tale Bearers' 1980
Being young is a quest.

JEAN RENOIR
French film director
The advantage of being eighty years old is that one has had many people to love.

BRANCH RICKEY
American baseball manager
on ageing . . .
First you forget names, then you forget faces; then you forget to zip your fly, then you forget to unzip your fly.

JEAN ROSTAND
French scientist
'Thoughts of a Biologist'
To be adult is to be alone.

JERRY RUBIN
American activist c1966
Never trust anyone over thirty.

GEORGE BERNARD SHAW
Irish writer and playwright
'Stray Sayings'
Every man over forty is a scoundrel.

'SHIP OF FOOLS'
Columbia Pictures 1965. Screenplay by Abby Mann, based on novel by Katherine Anne Porter
Heinz Ruhmann: Adolescence! What is adolescence? Adolescence is a time when people worry about things there's no need to worry about.

LOGAN PEARSALL SMITH
American essayist
in 'The Faber Book of Aphorisms' 1964
To deprive elderly people of their bogeys is as brutal as snatching from babies their big stuffed bears.

It seemed so simple when one was young and new ideas were mentioned not to grow red in the face and gobble.

ROD STEIGER
American film star
Esquire 1969
Age is the elasticity of a person's intelligence and the longevity of that elasticity.

JOHN STEINBECK
American writer
It is the nature of a man as he grows older . . . to protest against change, particularly change for the better.

ADLAI STEVENSON
American politician 1952
Nothing so dates a man as to decry the younger generation.

I. F. STONE
American journalist
If you live long enough, the venerability factor creeps in: you get accused of things you never did and praised for virtues you never had.

TOM STOPPARD
British playwright
in 'Goodbye Baby & Amen' by D. Bailey 1969
I think age is a very high price to pay for maturity.

'SUNSET BOULEVARD'
Paramount 1950 screenplay Charles Brackett, Billy Wilder & D. M. Marshman Jr.
Glora Swanson: I *am* big. It's the *pictures* that got small.

LOWELL THOMAS
American broadcaster
Time 1978
After the age of eighty, everything reminds you of something else.

PAUL TILLICH
American theologian
Time 1963
The awareness of the ambiguity of one's highest acheivements, as well as one's deepest failures, is a definite symptom of maturity.

ALICE B. TOKLAS
American writer
letter 1960
Dawn comes slowly, but dusk is rapid.

PETE TOWNSHEND
British rock composer
'My Generation'
People try to put us down / Talkin' 'bout my generation / Just because we get around / Talkin' 'bout my generation / Things they do look awful c-c-cold / Talkin' 'bout my generation / Hope I die before I get old. (Essex Music)

FRANCOIS TRUFFAUT
French film director 1979
As one gets older one loses the sense of fiction. Fiction is something linked with youth. Films made in older age are generally misunderstood. They are more theoretical, less physical.

GORE VIDAL
American writer
Evening Standard 1981
For certain people, after 50, litigation takes the place of sex.

BRIAN WILSON
American rock composer
'I Get Around'
None of the guys goes steady, 'cos it wouldn't be right / To leave your best girl home on a Saturday night. (Burlington Music Ltd)

SIR HAROLD WILSON
British politician
The Observer 1981
At sixty you might come back; at seventy they think you are ga-ga.

LARRY ZOLF
Canadian politician
on Prime Minister Joe Clark 1977
No shirt is too young to be stuffed.

Fear & Loathing

ARTHUR ADAMOV
playwright
The Observer 1962
I find that realisation of the difficulty of life is so much truer and so much more tragic than to say that life is absurd.

When one has said that life is difficult that means that it is very difficult to struggle; when one has said that life is absurd, that means that one is not struggling and that it is all complacent fun.

ALFRED ADLER
German analyst
quoted in Sunday Times 1968
To be a human being is to feel oneself inferior.

WOODY ALLEN
American film star
in 'Annie Hall'
Life is divided into the horrible and the miserable.

'Side Effects' 1981
More than any other time in history, mankind faces a crossroads. One path leads to despair and utter hopelessness. The other, to total extinction. Let us pray we have the wisdom to choose correctly.

MICHELANGELO ANTONIONI
Italian film director 1967
I cannot make a horror film because nothing scares me; I cannot make a comedy because nothing amuses me except sex.

HANNAH ARENDT
American writer
in 'The Faber Book of Aphorisms' 1964
The human condition is such that pain and effort are not just symptoms which can be removed without changing life itself, they are rather the modes in which life itself, together with the necessity to which it is bound, makes itself felt. For mortals 'the easy life of the gods' would be a lifeless life.

Only one who is in pain really senses nothing but himself; pleasure does not enjoy itself, but something beside itself. Pain is the only inner sense found by introspection which can rival in independence from experienced objects the self-evident certainty of logical and arithmetical reasoning.

NEIL ARMSTRONG
American astronaut 1969
Fear is not an unknown emotion to us.

NEAL ASCHERSON
British journalist
The Observer 1966
Prod a familiar myth and it splits into unfamiliar worries.

W. H. AUDEN
British poet
quoted in 'Contemporary Literary Critics', Ed. Elmer Borklund 1977
The basic problem is man's anxiety in time; eg. his present anxiety over himself in relation to his past and his parents (Freud); his present anxiety over himself in relation to his future and his neighbours (Marx); his present anxiety over himself in relation to eternity and God (Kierkegaard).

RUSSELL BAKER
American writer
'The Sayings of Poor Russell' Harpers 1972
Misery no longer loves company. Nowadays it insists on it.

JAMES BALDWIN
American author
Nobody Knows My Name 1961
The price one pays for pursuing any profession or calling, is an intimate knowledge of its ugly side.

CHRISTIAAN BARNARD
South African transplant surgeon 1970
I am a victim of history.

PROFESSOR WILLIAM BARRETT
British philosopher
The Listener 1978
Anxiety is simply part of the condition of being human. If we were not anxious, we would never create anything.

SIMONE DE BEAUVOIR
French writer
'Tous les hommes sont mortels'
If you live long enough, you'll see that every victory turns into a defeat.

SAMUEL BECKETT
Irish writer
in 'Beckett' by A. Alvarez 1973
Suffering is the main condition of the artistic experience.

ROBERT BENCHLEY
American wit
quoted in 'Wit's End' by James R. Gaines 1977
Everyone becomes the thing they most despise.
(cf. Ray Davies)

INGMAR BERGMAN
Swedish film director
We walk in circles, so limited by our own anxieties that we can no longer distinguish between true and false, between the gangster's whim and the purest ideal.

BIFF KARDZ
British series of postcards
postcard 1981
We are all vicitms of apathy brought about by spiritual constipation.

JAMES BLISH
American writer
Rewriting Job is the humanist's favourite pastime . . . and his favourite political platform, too.

ERMA BOMBECK
American humorist
Book title
If life's a bowl of cherries, why am I in the pits?

DR. EDWARD DE BONO
British writer
The Observer 1977
Unhappiness is best defined as the difference between our talents and our expectations.

JORGE LUIS BORGES
Argentine writer
'Borges On Writing' 1974
That is what always happens: we never know whether we are victors or whether we are defeated.

BERTOLT BRECHT
German playwright
He who laughs has not yet heard the bad news.

'The Caucasian Chalk Circle' prod. 1954
Fear is the seductive power of goodness.

GERALD BRENAN
British writer
'Thoughts In A Dry Season' 1978
We confess our bad qualities to others out of fear of appearing naive or ridiculous by not being aware of them.

GEORGE BUCHANAN
British novelist
Without the skeleton at the feast, it is questionable whether the feast tastes good.

CHARLES BUKOWSKI
American writer
'Notes of a Dirty Old Man' 1969
What's the difference between a guy in the bighouse and the average guy you pass on the street? The guy in the bighouse is a Loser who has *tried*.

The reason most people are at the racetrack is that they are in agony, ey yeh, and they are so desperate that they will take a chance on further agony rather than face their present position. . .

VLADIMIR BUKOVSKY
Soviet dissident 1972
The essence of the struggle in my view is the struggle against fear.

WILLIAM S. BURROUGHS
American writer
Friends 1970
A paranoid is a man who knows a little of what's going on.

R. A. BUTLER
British politician 1971
In the animal pack, animals that show they are ill or disappointed or bitter are turned on and bitten by the other animals. I like to be a healthy animal and gallop along – my fangs embedded in my jaw, my tail waving. I wouldn't like to slink into a corner. I'm sure they'd kill me if I did.

ALBERT CAMUS
French writer
'Notebooks' 1962
If you are convinced of your despair you must either act as if you did hope after all – or kill yourself. Suffering gives no rights.

ELIAS CANETTI
Bulgarian writer
Distrust of pain is always a pain in itself.

WHITTAKER CHAMBERS
American government official
'Witness' 1952
Every man is crucified upon the cross of himself.

MAURICE CHAPELAIN
French writer
'Main Courante'
The final delusion is the belief that one
has lost all delusions.

ALEXANDER CHASE
American journalist
'Perspectives' 1966
For the unhappy man death is the com-
mutation of a sentence of life im-
prisonment.

FRANCIS P. CHISHOLM
Motive
Purposes, as understood by the pur-
poser, will be judged otherwise by
others.

E. M. CIORAN
French philosopher
'Syllogismes de l'amertume' 1952
Sadness: an appetite that no misfortune
can satisfy.

CYRIL CONNOLLY
British critic
in 'The Faber Book of Aphorisms' 1964
We fear something before we hate it. A
child who fears noises becomes a man
who hates noise.

QUENTIN CRISP
British author
'The Naked Civil Servant' 1968
It is those who, for some unknown
reason, have no idea how they will behave in a social emergency, who quite
naturally dread the world's censure.

RAY DAVIES
British rock musician
In the end you become part of every-
thing you hate, basically. (cf. Robert
Benchley)

LUIS MIGUEL DOMINGUIN
Spanish bullfighter 1971
Fear is essential. It is like a drug. Fear
makes you think you will die. For that
reason each minute has intensity. It is a
kind of purification.

BOB DYLAN
American singer
You must be vulnerable to be sensitive

to reality. And to me being vulnerable
is just another way of saying that one
has nothing more to lose. I don't have
anything but darkness to lose.

E. M. FORSTER
British novelist
The Observer 1959
One has two duties – to be worried and
not to be worried.

BRENDAN FRANCIS
Every man, through fear, mugs his aspirations a dozen times a day.

ART GARFUNKEL
American singer
Never underestimate people's ability not
to know when they're in pain.

DAVID GERROLD
American science fiction writer
in Starlog 1978
The human race never solves any of its
problems, it only outlives them.

ANDRE GIDE
French writer
In hell there is no other punishment than
to begin over and over again the tasks
left unfinished in your lifetime.

MARTHA GRAHAM
American dancer
Misery is a communicable disease.

GRAHAM GREENE
British novelist
Ways of Escape 1980
I distinguish between terror and fear.
From terror one escapes screaming, but
fear has an odd seduction. Fear and the
sense of sex are linked in secret con-
spiracy, but terror is a sickness like hate.

SYDNEY J. HARRIS
American journalist
'Strictly Personal'
Regret for the things we did can be tem-
pered by time; it is regret for the things
we did not do that is inconsolable.

HENRY S. HASKINS
American writer
'Meditations in Wall Street'
Disappointments should be cremated,
not embalmed.

ERNEST HEMINGWAY
American writer
'Men at War' 1942
Cowardice, as distinguished from panic, is almost always simply a lack of ability to suspend the functioning of the imagination.

ERIC HOFFER
American philosopher
'The Passionate State of Mind' 1954
Often the thing we pursue most passionately is but a substitute for the other thing we really want and cannot have.

Far more crucial than what we know or do not know is what we do not want to know.

in *'The Faber Book of Aphorisms' 1964*
Our greatest pretences are built up not to hide the evil and the ugly in us, but our emptiness. The hardest thing to hide is something that is not there.

To have a grievance is to have a purpose in life. A grievance can almost serve as a substitute for hope; and it not infrequently happens that those who hunger for hope give their allegiance to him who offers them a grievance.

RALF HUTTER
German rock musician
refusing a photo session
We do not pose. We have our own pictures. We are paranoid.

JOHN B. KEANE
Irish playwright
in *'Contemporary Dramatists' 1977*
The anguish of our times is the Frankenstein monster that has been created by our convenient and long silences. We reap this anguish because we have encouraged its growth by pulling the bedclothes over our heads, hoping that the ogres might go away and that dawn might purify all.

JOHN F. KENNEDY
American politician 1959
When written in Chinese, the word 'crisis' is composed of two characters – one represents danger and the other represents opportunity.

IRVING KRISTOL
American academic 1977
Being frustrated is disagreeable, but the real disasters in life begin when you get what you want.

R. D. LAING
British psychiatrist
'The Politics of Experience' 1967
We have to realise that we are as deeply afraid to live and to love as we are to die.

FRAN LEBOWITZ
American journalist
'Metropolitan Life' 1978
There is no such thing as inner peace. There is only nervousness or death. Any attempt to prove otherwise constitutes unacceptable behaviour.

STANISLAW J. LEC
Polish poet
'Unkempt Thoughts' 1962
Do not turn your back on anyone. You may be painted on one side only.

LE CORBUSIER
(Charles Edouard Jeanneret)
French architect
'When the Cathedrals Were White'
Life never stops. The torment of men will be eternal, unless the function of creating and acting and changing, living intensely through each day, be considered an eternal joy.

JOHN LENNON
British rock star 1971
Pain is what we're in most of the time. And I think the bigger the pain the more gods we need.

'I Found Out'
I seen through junkies, I been through it all / I seen religion, from Jesus to Paul / Don't let them fool you, with dope and cocaine / Can't do you no harm to feel your own pain.
(Northern Songs)

JOHN LENNON &
PAUL McCARTNEY
British rock composers
Song Title
It's Been A Hard Day's Night.
(Northern Songs)

A. J. LIEBLING
American writer
'The Press' 1975
If you just try long enough and hard enough, you can always manage to boot yourself in the posterior.

MARSHALL McLUHAN
Canadian academic
Innumerable confusions and a feeling of despair invariably emerge in periods of great technological and cultural transition.

HAROLD MACMILLAN
British politician
New York Times 1959
To be alive at all involves some risk.

RENE MAGRITTE
Belgian artist
'Le Surrealisme en Plein Soleil' 1946
We mustn't fear daylight just because it almost always illuminates a miserable world.

NORMAN MAILER
American writer
What I fear far more than selling out is wearing out.

BERNARD MALAMUD
American novelist
Nova 1967
Since all life is victimisation, all of us are victims.

CHARLES MANSON
American murderer
quoted in Esquire 1971
Paranoia is just a kind of awareness, and awareness is just a form of love.

LOUIS B. MAYER
American film producer
Look out for yourself, or they'll pee on your grave.

H. L. MENCKEN
American essayist
'A Mencken Chrestomathy' 1949
Conscience is the inner voice that warns us that someone might be looking.

DAVID MERCER
British playwright
'A Suitable Case For Treatment' 1966

Morgan: Violence has a kind of dignity in a baffled man.

IRIS MURDOCH
British writer
'Sartre: Romantic Realist' 1953
We are anxiety ridden animals. Our minds are continually active, fabricating an anxious, usually self-protective, often falsifying *veil* which partially conceals the world.

RICHARD NIXON
Former American president 1977
Some of my friends have suggested that there was a conspiracy to get me. There may have been. I don't know what the CIA had to do.

DOROTHY PARKER
American writer
Esquire 1964
If you can get through the twilight, you'll live through the night.

CESARE PAVESE
Italian novelist
in 'The Faber Book of Aphorisms' 1964
Mistakes are always initial.

ST. JOHN PERSE
French writer
The only menace is inertia.

HENRI PETIT
French writer
'Les Justes Solitudes'
To believe is to believe the bad.

JEAN RHYS
British author
Radio Times 1974
Everyone is a victim in some way, aren't they?

LORD ROTHSCHILD
British academic
Dimbleby Lecture 1978
There is no point getting into a panic about the risks of life until you have compared the risks that worry you with those that do not.

BERTRAND RUSSELL
British philosopher
quoted in 'The Faber Book of Aphorisms' 1964
Men who are unhappy, like men who

sleep badly, are always proud of the fact.

'An Outline of Intellectual Rubbish' 1950
Fear is the main source of superstition and one of the main sources of cruelty. To conquer fear is the beginning of wisdom.

FRANCOISE SAGAN
French novelist
Sunday Express 1957
We cry when we are born and what follows can only be an attentuation of this cry.

JEAN-PAUL SARTRE
French philosopher
'Saint Genet'
To the right-thinking man, to be alone and to be wrong are one and the same.

DELMORE SCHWARTZ
American writer
Paranoids have real enemies too.

ERIC SEVAREID
American newscaster 1970
The chief cause of problems is solutions.

ISAAC BASHEVIS SINGER
American writer
Esquire 1970
It is on himself that man can inflict the worst punishments.

DODIE SMITH
American writer
'I Capture the Castle' 1948
Noble deeds and hot baths are the best cures for depression.

LOGAN PEARSALL SMITH
American essayist
in 'The Faber Book of Aphorisms' 1964
Those who are contemptuous of everyone are more than anyone terrified of contempt.

STEVIE SMITH
British poet
'Selected Poems' 1964
I was much further out than you thought / And not waving but drowning.

T. V. SMITH
British rock musician
If everything went right there would be

something wrong. You have to have tension to keep alive.

SUSAN SONTAG
American essayist
'Death Kit' 1967
He who despises himself esteems himself as a great self-despiser.

DR. WILHELM STEKHEL
German psychoanalyst *'The Depths of the Soul'*
Many an attack of depression is nothing but the expression of regret at having to be virtuous.

WILLIAM STYRON
American novelist
'Writers at Work' 1st series 1958
The good writing of any age has always been the product of *someone's* neurosis, and we'd have a mighty dull literature if all the writers that came along were a bunch of happy chuckleheads.

GAY TALESE
American journalist
The real problem is what to do with the problem solvers after the problems are solved.

JAMES THURBER
American humorist
cartoon caption
Well, I'm disenchanted too. We're all disenchanted.

PAUL TILLICH
American theologian
'The Courage To Be'
One cannot remove anxiety by arguing it away.

KATHARINE WHITEHORN
British journalist
The Observer 1974
Worry. How pointless. I know the theory is that all this concern for the frustrated aged or forgotten Chinese children helps to change attitudes and to create at least an atmosphere in which something might happen – double beds in the geriatric ward or maybe chow mein on the school dinner menus – but I wonder if it doesn't work the other way round as well. Seeing so many tragedies that you can't do anything about may in the end

simply wear the nerve-ends down so that there's no shock any more. You get too used to it. You just shrug. It could be that having our withers so constantly wrung on behalf of this or that distressed group, this aspect of the national disaster this *piste* on the Gadarene slope, has much the same effect. We get so we hardly notice any of it.

HEATHCOTE WILLIAMS
British playwright
'The Speakers' 1964
Don't call me *Mister* Webster. You've got nothing on me.

TENNESSEE WILLIAMS
American playwright
The Observer 1958
Don't look forward to the day when you

stop suffering. Because when it comes you'll *know* that you're dead.
'Camino Real' 1953
We have to distrust each other. It is our only defence against betrayal.
to Rex Reed 1972
I am a paranoiac, baby, so I hope you don't make the mistake of labouring under the false impression that you are talking to a sane person.

YEVGENY YEVTUSHENKO
Russian poet 1968
He who is conceived in a cage yearns for the cage.

WARREN ZEVON
American singer 1979
It's hard to say you're happy with your balls sewn shut in your mouth.

Action

ALFRED ADLER
German analyst
It is easier to fight for one's principles than to live up to them. (cf. Adlai Stevenson)

WOODY ALLEN
American film star
Esquire 1977
The fundamental thing behind *all* motivation and all activity is the constant struggle against annihilation and against death.

MARIAN ANDERSON
American singer
New York World Telegram 1965
A person has to be busy to stay alive.

JEAN ANOUILH
French playwright
'Catch as Catch Can' 1960
Effective action is always unjust.

ANTONIN ARTAUD
French playwright
If our life lacks a constant magic it is because we choose to observe our acts

and lose ourselves in consideration of their imagined form instead of being impelled by their force.

GASTON BACHELARD
French scientist
'La Psychanalyse du feu'
The conquering of the superfluous gives greater spiritual excitement than the conquest of the necessary.

ANEURIN BEVAN
British politician 1953
We know what happens to people who stay in the middle of the road: they get run over.

ARTHUR BLOCH
American cosmologist
'Murphy's Law' 1977
Bookers Law: An ounce of application is worth a ton of abstraction.

DIETRICH BONHOEFFER
German theologian
'Letters & Papers from Prison' 1953
Action springs not from thought, but from a readiness for responsibility.

PIERRE BOULEZ
French composer
Esquire 1969
Compromise never pays. One must be intransigent. If you do something out of conviction, and you are wrong, you are wrong in an interesting way. But if you are wrong because you have compromised, all you have is a sense of failure and discouragement.

ANDRE BRETON
French artist
quoted in Esquire 1969
The simplest surrealist act would be to go out into the street, revolver in hand, and fire at random into the crowd.

ROGER CALLOIS
French writer
'L'homme et le sacré'
There are no useless efforts. Sisyphus was developing his muscles.

PRINCE CHARLES
1978
I believe in living life dangerously, and I think a lot of others do too.

ARTHUR C. CLARKE
British science writer
'Profiles of the Future' 1962
The only way to discover the limits of the possible is to go beyond them, to the impossible.

BARRY COMMONER
American conservationist
No action is without its side effects.

'DAVEY CROCKETT'
American TV character
catchphrase, c.1956
Make sure you're right, then go ahead.

DANIEL ELLSBERG
American defence expert
Esquire 1971
To act responsibly you have to take leaps without being sure.

JAMES T. EVANS
American lawyer
in 'The Official Rules' by P. Dickson 1978
Nothing worth a damn is ever done as a matter of principle. If it is worth doing,
it's done because it is worth doing. If it is not, it's done as a matter of principle.

ANDRE GIDE
French writer
'Journals'
There enters into all human action more luck than judgement.

ROBERT GRAVES
British poet
Playboy 1970
If men do nothing, they aren't good men. Good is a positive action.

HENRY S. HASKINS
American writer
'Meditations in Wall Street'
Enthusiasm finds the opportunities, and energy makes the most of them.

KATHARINE HEPBURN
American film star
Esquire 1967
What the hell – you might be right, you might be wrong . . . but don't just *avoid*.

C. G. JUNG
Swiss psychoanalyst
'Psychological Reflections' 1953
The greater the contrast, the greater is the potential. Great energy only comes from a correspondingly great tension between opposites.

JOHN F. KENNEDY
American president 1961
There are risks and costs to a programme of action. But they are far less than the long-range risks and costs of comfortable inaction.

MARTIN LUTHER KING JR.
American activist
'Strength to Love' 1963
The ultimate measure of a man is not where he stands in moments of comfort, but where he stands at times of challenge and controversy.

HENRY KISSINGER
American diplomat
Time 1978
The absence of alternatives clears the mind marvellously.

JERZY KOSINSKI
Czech writer
'The Art of the Self' 1968
The grotesque is the language of the emotions which silently provokes our actions. Hence the subversive quality of art.

MIGNON McLAUGHLIN
American writer
'The Neurotic's Notebook'
The only courage that matters is the kind that gets you from one moment to the next.

WILLIAM MENINGER
American psychiatrist
What the world needs is some 'do-give-a-damn' pills.

CLAES OLDENBURG
Danish artist
All the fun is locking horns with impossibilities.

MARIO PUZO
American novelist
Time 1978
Luck and strength go together. When you get lucky you have to have the strength to follow through. You also have to have the strength to wait for the luck.

RAYMOND QUENEAU
French historian
'Le Chiendent'
All action is deception, all thought implies error.

BERNIE RHODES
British rock manager
What is important is not where you come from but where you're going to.

LINDA RONSTADT
American rock singer
I'm a survivor ... being a survivor doesn't mean you have to made out of steel and it doesn't mean you have to be ruthless. It means you to be basically on your own side and want to win.

BERTRAND RUSSELL
British philosopher
'The Conquest of Happiness'
Nothing is so exhausting as indecision, and nothing is so futile.

WILLIE 'THE LION' SMITH
American jazz musician
Esquire 1964
It's never too late to reach your destination. You should never doubt what is in front of your eyes.

TOM WAITS
American singer
You have to keep busy. After all, a dog's never pissed on a moving car. Know what I mean.

EVELYN WAUGH
British novelist
Sunday Times, 1962
Sloth is the condition in which a man is fully aware of the proper means of his salvation but refuses to take them because the whole apparatus of salvation fills him with tedium and disgust.

Work

ANONYMOUS
quoted in The Spectator 1980
There is no such thing as graduate unemployment, only idiots with naive and inflexible ambitions.

JULES BECKER
American businessman
in 'The Official Rules' by P. Dickson, 1978
It is much harder to find a job than to keep one.

ALBERT CAMUS
French writer
New York Times 1960
A man's work is nothing but the long journey to recover, through the detours of art, the two or three simple and great images which first gained access to his heart.

BLAISE CENDRARS
French novelist
'Writers at Work' 3rd series, 1968
I never forget that work is a curse – which is why I've never made it a habit.

NOEL COWARD
British playwright
The Observer 1963
Work is much more fun than fun.

QUENTIN CRISP
British writer
'How To Become a Virgin' 1981
In England regular employment is considered . . . to be a way of winning eternal life on the principal that work tastes so nasty it must be doing you good. In America a job is an excuse for going out into the world.

JOHN DOS PASSOS
American writer
New York Times 1959
People don't choose their careers. They are engulfed by them.

BERYL DOWNING
British journalist
The Times 1980
Some are born lazy, some have idleness thrust upon them and others spend a great deal of effort creating a careless nonchalance.

PETER DRUCKER
American management expert
So much of what we call management consists in making it difficult for people to work.

Production is not the application of tools to materials, but logic to work.

CARLOS 'THE JACKAL' EVERTSZ
terrorist
The Observer
I used to try interrogation first, but sometimes it doesn't work and you have to put some physical pressure on. You have to understand – it's a job, just a job. To me it's just a way of making a living. Some people learn a trade. Well, this has been my trade.

WILLIAM FAULKNER
American novelist
'Writers at Work' 1st series 1958
One of the saddest things is that the only thing a man can do for eight hours a day, day after day, is work. You can't eat eight hours a day, nor drink for eight hours a day nor make love for eight hours.

WILLIAM FEATHER
American businessman
Ladies Home Journal 1949
We always admire the other fellow more after we have tried his job.

ANDREAS FEININGER
American photographer
'Total Picture Control' 1972
No one can do inspired work without genuine interest in his subject and understanding of its characteristics.

MALCOLM S. FORBES
American publisher
'The Sayings of Chairman Malcolm' 1978
If you have a job without aggravations, you don't have a job.

BRENDAN FRANCIS
Most people perform essentially meaningless work. When they retire that truth is borne in upon them.

ROBERT FROST
American poet
in 'Quote and Unquote' 1970
The world is full of willing people. Some willing to work, the rest willing to let them.

PAUL GALLICO
American writer
'Confessions of a Story Teller' 1961
One is always seeking the touchstone that will dissolve one's deficiencies as a person and a craftsman. And one is always bumping up against the fact that there is none except hard work, concentration and continued application.

ALLEN GINSBERG
American poet
'America' 1956
America, I'm putting my queer shoulder to the wheel.

WALTER GROPIUS
German architect
Only work which is the product of inner compulsion can have spiritual meaning.

CHRISTOPHER HAMPTON
British playwright
'The Philanthropist'
I always divide people into two groups. Those who live by what they know to be a lie, and those who live by what they believe, falsely, to be the truth.

SYDNEY J. HARRIS
American journalist
'Strictly Personal'
Few men ever drop dead from overwork, but many quietly curl up and die because of undersatisfaction.

ERNEST HEMINGWAY
American writer
'Death in the Afternoon'
The great thing is to last and get your work done, and see and hear and understand and write when there is something that you know and not before and not too damn much after.

ABBIE HOFFMAN
American radical
quoted in Harpers Magazine 1970
Work is the only dirty four-letter word in the language.

ERICH KASTNER
German author
Work is half one's life – and the other half too.

FLORYNCE KENNEDY
American feminist
Writers Digest 1974
There are very few jobs that actually require a penis or a vagina. All other jobs should be open to everybody.

GEORGE LOIS
American art director
'The Art of Advertising' 1977
If a man does not work passionately (even furiously) at being the best in the world at what he does, he fails his talent, his destiny and his God.

JOHN MOORES
British businessman
Work seven days a week and nothing can stop you.

ROBERT MORLEY
British actor and wit
Anybody who works is a fool. I don't work, I merely inflict myself on the public.

OGDEN NASH
American poet
'Will Consider Situation'
People who work sitting down get paid more than people who work standing up.

SIR HENEAGE OGILVIE
British surgeon
'No Miracles Among Friends'
The really idle man gets nowhere. The perpetually busy man does not get much further.

The examples that have been held up to us in praise of work are a little unfortunate. 'How doth the little busy bee improve each shining hour, and gather honey all the day from every opening flower'. Well, he does not. He spends most of the day in buzzing and aimless aerobatics, and gets about a fifth of the honey he would collect if he organised himself.

C. NORTHCOTE PARKINSON
American historian
The Economist 1955
It is a commonplace observation that work expands so as to fill the time available for its completion.

LAURENCE J. PETER
Canadian educator
'The Peter Principle' 1969
In a hierarchy every employee tends to rise to his level of incompetence . . . in time every post tends to be occupied by an employee who is incompetent to carry out its duties . . . Work is accomplished by those employees who have not yet reached their level of imcompetence.

PRINCE PHILIP
1966
I must confess that I am interested in leisure in the same way that a poor man is interested in money.

DR. THEODORE REIK
American psychologist
'Of Love and Lust' 1959
Work and love – these are the basics. Without them there is neurosis.

MIES VAN DER ROHE
American architect 1963
I work so hard to find out what I have to do, not what I like to do.

MIKE ROMANOFF
Hollywood restaurateur
Work is the curse of the drinking classes.

BERTRAND RUSSELL
British philosopher
'The Conquest of Happiness'
A sense of duty is useful in work but offensive in personal relations. People wish to be liked, not endured with patient resignation.

quoted in 'The Faber Book of Aphorisms' 1964
Work is of two kinds: first, altering the position of matter at or near the earth's surface relatively to other matter; second, telling other people to do so. The first kind is unpleasant and ill-paid; the second is pleasant and highly paid.

ANTHONY SAMPSON
British journalist
The Observer 1981
We are an indispensable team; *you* are overmanned; *they* are redundant.

LOGAN PEARSALL SMITH
American essayist
in 'The Faber Book of Aphorisms' 1964
The test of a vocation is the love of the drudgery it involves.

RINGO STARR
British rock star
I never work on anything. Dedication is such a weird word after all, after Albert Schweitzer and people like that. That's dedication, when you give your whole life. No one dedicates themselves to anything now.

R. H. TAWNEY
British historian
quoted in New Statesman 1960
The purpose of industry is the conquest of nature in the service of man.

quoted in The Guardian 1961
To those who clamour, as many do, 'Produce, produce!' one simple question may be addressed: 'Produce what?'

JOHNNIE TILLMON
American activist 1972
Wages are the measure of the dignity that society puts on a job.

LILY TOMLIN
American comedienne
The trouble with the rat race is that even if you win, you're still a rat.

ROBERT TOWNSEND
American businessman
'Up The Organisation' 1970
Management consultants . . . are people who borrow your watch to tell you what time it is and then walk off with it.

ARNOLD TOYNBEE
British historian
Saturday Review 1969
Anxiety and conscience are a powerful pair of dynamos. Between them, they have ensured that I shall work hard, but they cannot ensure that one shall work at anything worthwhile.

HARRY S. TRUMAN
American President 1958
Its a recession when your neighbour loses his job; its a depression when you lose yours.

ANDY WARHOL
American artist
'Exposures' 1979
Employees make the best dates. You don't have to pick them up and they're always tax deductible.

EVELYN WAUGH
British novelist
Sunday Times 1962
Most of the world's troubles seem to come from people who are too busy. If only politicians and scientists were lazier, how much happier we should all

be. The lazy man is preserved from the commission of almost all the nastier crimes and many of the motives which makes us sacrifice to toil the innocent enjoyment of leisure are amongst the most ignoble: pride, avarice, emulation, vainglory and the appetite for power over others.

ORSON WELLES
American film director 1969
Just as it is vulgar to work for the sake of money, so it is vulgar to work for posterity.

Newsweek 1967
In show business you're a fruit picker – you go where the work is.

KATHARINE WHITEHORN
British journalist
'Roundabout'
An office party is not, as is sometime supposed, the Managing Director's chance to kiss the tea-girl. It is the tea-girl's chance to kiss the Managing Director (however bizarre an ambition this may seem to anyone who has seen the Managing Director face on).

The Observer 1975
The best careers advice given to the young is 'Find out what you like doing best and get someone to pay you for doing it.'

HEATHCOTE WILLIAMS
British playwright
'The Speakers' 1964
Work is just another of man's diseases and prevention is better than cure. If you don't look for work, it won't look for you. No man is born with the urge to work, for you cannot work and think.

RAYMOND WILLIAMS
British academic
The Listener 1961
The real dividing line between the things we call work and the things we call leisure is that in leisure, however active we may be, we make our own choices and our own decisions. We feel for the time being that our life is our own.

WALTER WINCHELL
American columnist
quoted in Esquire 1968
It is silly to nurse bouquets. They seem to sour with keeping. But if the world will take even the smallest thing you can give it – even one word of slang – that's a career . . . and an epitaph.

JOHN P. YOUNG
Australian management consultant 1972
Human beings, unfortunately, tend to respond to negative incentives – such as dismissal.

Animals

CAPTAIN BEEFHEART
American rock star
You can tell by the kindness of a dog how a human should be.

ELIAS CANETTI
Bulgarian writer
'Aufzeichnungen' 1949
Is it possible that animals have less worries since they live without speech?

WALT DISNEY
American animator
in Walter Wagner 'You Must Remember This'
I love Mickey Mouse more than any woman I've ever known.

HARLAN ELLISON
American science fiction writer
'The Glass Teat' 1970
The reason men are greater than animals isn't because we can dream of the stars . . . it's because we have something they haven't. Greed.

ERICH FROMM
American psychologist
'The Sane Society' 1955
Man is the only animal that can be bored.

ROMAIN GARY
French writer
'The Roots of Heaven'
Dogs aren't enough any more. Men need elephants.

PROF. RICHARD HARRISON
British scientist 1971
Many people have equated the intelligence of the dolphin with that of man, but I am afraid that in the comparison the dolphin comes off rather badly.

WILLIAM KUNSTLER
American lawyer
Esquire 1971
A dog is like a liberal. He wants to please everybody. A cat really doesn't need to know that everybody loves him.

GEORGE ORWELL
British essayist
'Animal Farm' 1945
All animals are equal, but some are more equal than others.

JEAN-PAUL SARTRE
French philosopher
'The Words' 1964
When one loves animals and children *too much*, one loves them against human beings.

MARTHA SCOTT
quoted in 'Violets & Vitriol' ed. J. Cooper and T. Hartman, 1980
Don't make the mistake of treating your dogs like humans or they'll treat you like dogs.

KARL-HEINZ STOCKHAUSEN
German composer
Sunday Times 1973
I respond very positively to certain birds. Especially eagles; and now I know from my experiences in dreams that at some time in my past life I have been a bird of that particular kind, because I know exactly the feeling of flying and living in the body of that bird.

IGOR STRAVINSKY
Russian composer
New York Review of Books 1971
Does anyone ever look at these statues? Do they satisfy any requirements – apart from dogs'?

JAMES THURBER
American humorist
cartoon caption:
All right, have it your way – you heard a seal bark.

I have always thought of a dog lover as a dog that was in love with another dog.

RUTH WESTON
American actress 1955
A fox is a wolf who sends flowers.

ALFRED NORTH WHITEHEAD
British philosopher
in 'The Faber Book of Aphorisms' 1964
One main factor in the upward trend of animal life has been the power of wandering.

GRANT WOOD
American artist
All the good ideas I ever had came to me while I was milking a cow.

ABUSE

JAMES AGATE
British critic
on Katharine Hepburn
She has a cheekbone like a death's head allied to a manner as sinister and aggressive as crossbones.

JOSEPH & STEWART ALSOP
American journalists
syndicated column, 1953.
(Joseph) McCarthy is the only major politician in the country who can be labelled 'liar' without fear of libel.

ANONYMOUS
on Richard Nixon, quoted in 'Nixon's Head' by Arthur Woodstone 1972
Fatty ham fried in grease.

ANONYMOUS REVIEWER
on Quentin Crisp in the Times 1977
If Quentin Crisp had never existed it is unlikely that anyone would have had the nerve to invent him.

ANONYMOUS S. VIETNAMESE OFFICIAL
on the nomination of Le Duc Tho and Henry Kissinger for the Nobel Peace Prize 1973
Like nominating a whore as honorary chairman of the PTA.

JAMES T. AUBREY JR.
American president CBS-TV
On Tennessee Williams' 'Glass Menagerie', suggested for TV.
You think I'm crazy? Who wants to look at that? It's too downbeat. The girl's got a limp.

LORD BEAVERBROOK
Canadian press magnate
Churchill on top of the wave has in him the stuff of which tyrants are made.

SIR THOMAS BEECHAM
British conductor
On Herbert von Karajan:
He's a sort of musical Malcolm Sargent.

BERNARDO BERTOLUCCI
Italian film director
on Marlon Brando
An angel as a man, a monster as an actor.

'THE BEST MAN'
United Artists 1964 screenplay by Gore Vidal, based on his play
Henry Fonda: He has every characteristic of a dog except loyalty.

ANEURIN BEVAN
British politician
on Harold Wilson
All facts – no bloody ideas.

on a man who he always denied was the Labour leader, Hugh Gaitskell . . . 1954
I know that the right kind of political leader for the Labour Party is a dessicated calculating machine.

on Winston Churchill. . .
I welcome this opportunity of pricking the bloated bladder of lies with the poniard of truth.

His ear is so sensitively attuned to the bugle note of history that he is often deaf to the more raucous clamour of contemporary life.

during the Suez Crisis, 1956, ceasing his questioning of Foreign Minister Selwyn Lloyd on seeing Eden enter the House of Commons
Why should I question the monkey when I can question the organ grinder.

on Sir Anthony Eden. . .
The juvenile lead.

ERNEST BEVIN
British politician
on the relationship between Winston Churchill and Lord Beaverbrook, quoted in 'Beaverbrook' by A. J. P. Taylor 1973
He's like a man who has married a whore. He knows she's a whore, but he loves her all the same.

BLACKWELL
American designer 1968
Elizabeth Taylor looks like two small

boys fighting underneath a mink blanket.

CHARMIAN BRENT
British housewife
on her train-robber husband Ronald Biggs' escapades in Brazil, 1974
For a pregnant Brazilian girl Ron's a prime catch.

ART BUCHWALD
American humorist
on J. Edgar Hoover
A mythical person first thought up by the Reader's Digest.

WILLIAM S. BURROUGHS
American writer 1980
Nixon is a man that had the morals of a private detective.

ARTHUR CALWELL
Australian politician 1969
There are too many ratbags in the Australian Broadcasting Co.

JAMES CAMERON
British journalist
'Point of Departure' 1967
John Foster Dulles . . . a diplomatic bird of prey smelling out from afar the corpses of dead ideals.

TRUMAN CAPOTE
American writer
on Jack Kerouac's 'On The Road'
That's not writing – it's typing.

on CBS boss William S. Paley, quoted in 'The Powers That Be' by David Halberstam 1979
He looks like a man who has just swallowed an entire human being.

SIR WINSTON CHURCHILL
British statesman
berated by fellow MP Bessie Braddock
BB: Winston, you're drunk!
WSC: Bessie, you're ugly. And tomorrow morning I shall be sober.

ROY COHN
American lawyer 1950
Joe McCarthy bought communism in much the same way as other people purchase a new automobile.

HUGH CUDLIPP
British newspaper owner
'The Prerogative of the Harlot' 1980 on William Randolph Hearst. . .
Truth for him was a moving target; he never aimed for the bull and rarely pierced the outer ring.

HOWARD DIETZ
American scriptwriter
on Tallulah Bankhead
A day away from Tallulah is like a month in the country.

KEN DODD
British comedian
The Times 1965
The trouble with Freud is that he never played the Glasgow 'Empire' Saturday night.

VINCE GAIR
Australian politician
on Billy Sneddon 1974
Billy Sneddon couldn't go two rounds with a revolving door.

BARRY GOLDWATER
American politician
Hubert Humphrey talks so fast that listening to him is like trying to read Playboy magazine with your wife turning the pages.

SAM GOLDWYN
American film producer 1957
at Louis B. Mayer's funeral
The only reason so many people showed up was to make sure that he was dead.

GERMAINE GREER
Australian feminist
on Ernest Hemingway
When his cock wouldn't stand up he blew his head off. He sold himself a line of bullshit and he bought it.

BOB HAWKE
Australian trades unionist
on Malcolm Fraser, 1975
Fraser could be described as a cutlery man: he was born with a silver spoon in his mouth and he uses it to stab his colleagues in the back.

PROFESSOR SIDNEY HOOK
American academic
The next time anyone asks you 'What is Bertrand Russell's philosophy?' the correct answer is 'What year, please?'

MURRAY KEMPTON
American journalist 1966
Vice President Humphrey has no function in any game his government plays, except to lead the cheers.

NIKITA KHRUSCHEV
Russian leader
to US Labor leader Walter Reuther, 1960
You are like a nightingale. It closes its eyes when it sings and sees nothing and hears nobody but itself.

JOHN LEONARD
American critic
on Muhammad Ali, New York Times 1975
The Jackie Onassis of the sweat set.

EARL LONG
American politician
on Henry Luce, when he sued Luce Publications for libel. . .
Mr. Luce is like a man that owns a shoestore and buys all the shoes to fit himself. Then he expects other people to buy them.

ALICE ROOSEVELT LONGWORTH
American socialite
to Joseph McCarthy, who called her 'Alice'. . .
The policeman and the trashman may call me Alice. You cannot.

MARY McGRORY
American journalist 1962
Richard Nixon was like a kamikaze pilot who kept apologizing for the attack.

HAROLD MACMILLAN
British politician
on Sir Anthony Eden
He is forever poised between a cliché and an indiscretion.

on Aneurin Bevan. . .
He enjoys prophesying the imminent fall of the capitalist system and is prepared to play a part, any part, in its burial – except that of a mute.

on Harold Wilson, leader of the Opposition. Remarking on HW's much vaunted poor childhood. . .
If Harold Wilson ever went to school without any boots it was merely because he was too big for them. (also attrib. to Ivor Bulwer-Thomas, MP 1949)

Churchill was fundamentally what the English call unstable – by which they mean anybody who has that touch of genius which is inconvenient in normal times.

NORMAN MAILER
American writer
on Truman Capote 'Advertisements for Myself' 1959
At his worst Capote has less to say than any good writer I know.

'Miami and the Siege of Chicago' 1968. On Governor Lester Maddox of Georgia. . .
Governor Maddox has the face of a three month old infant who is mean and bald and wears eye-glasses.

HERMAN MANKIEWICZ
American screenwriter
on Louis B. Mayer
There, but for the grace of God, goes God.

W. SOMERSET MAUGHAM
British writer 1955
in Sunday Times referring to Kingsley Amis' 'Lucky Jim' in particular and redbricks in general. . .
They are scum.

on Winston Churchill
If you think I'm gaga, you should see Winston.

STRATTON MILLS
British politician 1969
Bernadette Devlin is Fidel Castro in a miniskirt.

DAN E. MOLDEA
American journalist
'The Hoffa Wars' 1978. On labour racketeer Jimmy Hoffa. . .
Jimmy Hoffa's most valuable contribution to the American labour movement came at the moment he stopped breathing on July 30, 1975.

LORD MONTGOMERY
British soldier
sitting for Augustus John who had been commissioned to paint his portrait. . .
Who is this chap? He drinks, he's dirty and I know there are women in the background.

KITTY MUGGERIDGE
wife of Malcolm
Now! 1981 on David Frost
Frost has risen without trace.

JACK NICHOLSON
American film star
accepting an Oscar 1976
Most of all I'd like to thank my agent of ten years ago who told me I'd never be an actor.

RICHARD NIXON
former American President
interviewed on TV by David Frost, 1977. . .
I gave them a sword. And they stuck it in and they twisted it with relish. And I guess if I'd been in their position, I'd have done the same thing.

REGINALD PAGET
British politician
attacking Sir Anthony Eden 1956
An overripe banana, yellow outside, squishy in.

defending Macmillan in the Profumo scandal . . . 1963
From Lord Hailsham we have had a virtuoso performance in the art of kicking a fallen friend in the guts. . . When self-indulgence has reduced a man to the shape of Lord Hailsham, sexual continence requires no more than a sense of the ridiculous.

DOROTHY PARKER
American writer
That woman can speak eighteen languages and she can't say no in any of them.

She tells enough white lies to ice a cake.

on Katharine Hepburn
She runs the gamut of emotions from A to B.

on hearing that Clare Boothe Luce was invariably kind to her inferiors. . .
And where does she find them?

JOE PASTERNAK
American film producer
on Judy Garland
An angel, with spurs.

S. J. PERELMAN
American humorist 1965
Working for the Marx brothers was not unlike being chained to a galley car and lashed at ten minute intervals.

OTTO PREMINGER
American film director
on Marilyn Monroe
A vacuum with nipples.

REX REED
American journalist
on Marlon Brando
Most of the time he sounds like he has a mouth full of wet toilet paper.

RICHARD ROVERE
American journalist
'Senator Joe McCarthy'. . .
This Typhoid Mary of conformity. . .

MORT SAHL
American comedian
in Penguin Book of Modern Quotations 1980 by M. J. and J. M. Cohen
On Nixon: Would you buy a second hand car from this man?

HARRISON E. SALISBURY
American journalist
valedictory for Walter Lippman 1974
Lippmann was a true muckraker, a muckraker on the global scale, a man who knew that . . . when statesmen prepare to commit genocide they come to the green baize table in striped pants and morning coats.

TELLY SAVALAS
American film actor 1975
The greatest villain that ever lived, a man worse than Hitler or Stalin. I am speaking of Sigmund Freud.

RED SKELTON
American comedian
on crowds at producer Harry Cohn's funeral, 1958
It proves what they always say: give the public what they want to see and they'll come out for it.

ADLAI STEVENSON
American politician
on John Foster Dulles foreign policy
The power of positive brinking.

I. F. STONE
American journalist 1968
It was hard to listen to Goldwater and realize that a man could be half Jewish and yet sometimes appear twice as dense as the normal gentile.

on John Foster Dulles, 1953. . .
Smooth is an inadequate word for Dulles. His prevarications are so highly polished as to be aesthetically pleasurable.

JOSEF STRAUSS
German politician
on De Gaulle 1966
He is not a genius, just a political cosmonaut, continually in orbit.

A. J. P. TAYLOR
British historian
on Sir Anthony Eden
Eden did not face the dictators; he pulled faces at them.

HUNTER S. THOMPSON
American journalist
'Fear and Loathing on the Campaign Trail' 1972. On Hubert Humphrey. . .
A treacherous, gutless old ward-heeler who should be put in a bottle and sent out with the Japanese current.

On Ed Muskie. . .
Muskie talked like a farmer with terminal cancer trying to borrow on next year's crop.

BARBARA TUCHMAN
American historian
on the 1980 Presidential candidates
God! The country that produced George Washington has got this collection of crumb-bums!

KENNETH TYNAN
British critic
on Malcolm Muggeridge 1968
Muggeridge, a garden gnome expelled from Eden, has come to rest as a gargoyle brooding over a derelict cathedral.

GORE VIDAL
American writer
on Ronald Reagan, The Observer 1981
There's a lot to be said for being *nouveau riche*, and the Reagans mean to say it all.

on Edward Kennedy, quoted in The Observer 1981
Every country should have at least one King Farouk.

on Ronald Reagan, quoted in The Observer 1981
A triumph of the embalmer's art.

VICKY
London Evening Standard cartoonist, 1958
Caption
Introducing Super-Mac.

MADELAINE VIONNET
French couturière
aged 96, 1973 on Coco Chanel. . .
She was a woman of taste, one has to admit, *but* she was a *modiste*; that is to say, she understood hats.

AUBERON WAUGH
British journalist
on Edward Heath, Private Eye 1974. . .
In any civilised country Heath would have been left hanging upside down on a petrol pump years ago.

EVELYN WAUGH
British novelist
on an operation on Randolph Churchill
It was a typical triumph of modern science to find the only part of Randolph that was not malignant and remove it.

FIELD MARSHAL LORD WAVELL
British soldier
on Winston Churchill
Winston is always expecting rabbits to come out of empty hats.

ORSON WELLES
American film director
attributed opinion of singer Donny Osmond
He has Van Gogh's ear for music.

DAME REBECCA WEST
British writer
He is every other inch a gentleman.

on Richard Crossman 1977
. . . a charming companion and a vir-

tuous conversationalist and not a selfish one. He was a wonderful hand at conducting a general conversation and could bring out the best in the shy and the alien. But he had his handicaps. The chief of these was his failure to tell the truth... He also had no sense of humour.

GARRY WILLS
American journalist
on Billy Graham New York Times 1979
Dr. Graham has, with great self-discipline, turned himself into the thinking man's Easter bunny.

HAROLD WILSON
British politician
on Harold Macmillan
The Right Hon. Gentleman has inherited the streak of charlatanry in Disraeli without his vision and the self-righteousness of Gladstone without his dedication to principle.

The Times 1981 on Anthony Wedgwood Benn...
I have always said about Tony that he immatures with age .... he was a very good Postmaster General.

on the new Tory Leader, Lord Home, 1963
After half a century of democratic advance, the whole process has ground to a halt with a 14th Earl.

LORD HOME OF THE HIRSEL
British politician
1963. Replying to Wilson's attack...
As far as the 14th Earl is concerned, I suppose Mr. Wilson, when you come to think of it, is the 14th Mr. Wilson.

MICHAEL WINNER
British film director
on producers, Sunday Times 1970
Most of them couldn't earn twopence in any other business and I wouldn't trust any of them to book me a bus from Green Park to Piccadilly. They're inept, arrogant, foolish, and totally uncaring for the artist.

HUGO YOUNG
British journalist
Sunday Times 1980...
James Callaghan, living proof that the short-term schemer and the frustrated bully can be made manifest in one man.

MIND
Ideals & Ethics

JACQUES BARZUN
American academic
'The House of Intellect' 1959
In any assembly the simplest way to stop the transacting of business and split the ranks is to appeal to a principle.

ALAN BENNETT
British playwright
'Forty Years On' 1968
Headmaster: Standards are always out of date. That's what makes them standards.

WILLIAM F. BUCKLEY JR.
American essayist
Idealism is fine, but as it approaches reality the cost becomes prohibitive.

MALCOLM DE CHAZAL
French writer
'Sens Plastique' 1949
The idealist walks on his toes, the materialist on his talons.

J. K. GALBRAITH
American economist 1968
There are times in politics when you must be on the right side and lose.

JEAN-LUC GODARD
French film director
quoted in Susan Sontag 'Styles of Radical Will' 1969
It may be true that one has to choose between ethics and aesthetics, but it is no less true that whichever one chooses, one will always find the other at the end of the road.

ALDOUS HUXLEY
British writer 1963
Idealism is the noble toga that political gentlemen drape over their will to power.

SIR ELWYN JONES
British lawyer 1966
Someone has described a technicality as a point of principle which we have forgotten.

ALLEN KLEIN
American rock music accountant
Playboy 1971
Ethics . . . every man makes his own. It's like a war. You choose your side early and from then on you're being shot at. The man you beat is likely to call you unethical. So what! You got to live with yourself. That's all.

CLARE BOOTHE LUCE
American diplomat
in 'The Book of Laws' Henry Faber 1980
No good deed will go unpunished. (also attrib. Walter Annenburg)

HAROLD NICOLSON
British politician
We are all inclined to judge ourselves by our ideals; others by their acts.

MAGNUS PYKE
British scientist
The Guardian 1974
Scientists tend to be very naive on ethical problems. At the drop of a hat scientists are addicted to one of the most dangerous modern diseases: instant wisdom.

The Listener 1962
The trouble is, that science is neutral. It allows us to achieve all the technical triumphs . . . but it gives us no guidance on how best to use these marvels when we have them.

PIERRE REVERDY
French writer
'Le livre de mon bord'
Ethics are aesthetics from within.

CARL SANDBURG
American poet
I'm an idealist: I don't know where I'm going but I'm on my way.

ARTHUR SCARGILL
British trade unionist 1974
I have never been an idealist – that implies you aren't going to achieve something.

ALBERT SCHWEITZER
German missionary
'Out of My Life & Thought'
Anyone who proposes to do good must
not expect people to roll stones out of his
way, but must accept his lot calmly if
they even roll a few more upon it.

LOGAN PEARSALL SMITH
American essayist
When they come down from their Ivory
Towers, idealists are very apt to walk
straight into the gutter.

ELVIN STACKMAN
American scientist
Life 1950
Science cannot stop while ethics catches
up.

LUDWIG WITTGENSTEIN
German philosopher
Ethics and aesthetics are one and the
same.

in 'The Faber Book of Aphorisms' 1964
Ethics does not treat of the world. Ethics
must be a condition of the world, like
logic.

Psychology

JOEY ADAMS
American comedian
'Cindy and I'
A psychiatrist is a fellow who asks you
a lot of expensive questions your wife
asks you for nothing.

WOODY ALLEN
American film star
'Getting Even' 1972
These modern analysts, they charge so
much! In my day, for five marks Freud
himself would treat you. For ten marks
he would treat you and press your pants.
For fifteen marks Freud would let *you*
treat *him* – and that included a choice of
any two vegetables.

**AMERICAN PSYCHIATRIC
ASSOCIATION**
quoted in The Listener 1978
If encounter groups were a drug they
would be completely banned from the
market.

ANONYMOUS
*quoted in 'The Wit of Medicine' ed. L. and
M. Cowan 1972*
Psychiatry – the care of the id by the
odd.

ANONYMOUS
Popular Definition

A neurotic is a man who builds a castle
in the air. A psychotic is a man who lives
in it. And a psychiatrist is the man who
collects the rent. (cf. Alan Hull)

ANTONIN ARTAUD
French playwright
in 'Selected Writings' 1976
There is in every lunatic a misunderstood genius whose idea, shining in his
head, frightened people, and for whom
delirium was the only solution to the
strangulation that life had prepared for
him.

And what is an authentic madman? It
is a man who preferred to become mad
in the socially accepted sense of the
word, rather than forfeit a certain superior idea of human honour. So society
has strangled in its asylums all those it
wanted to get rid of or protect itself from,
because they refused to become its accomplices in certain great nastinesses.
For a madman is also a man whom society did not want to hear and whom it
wanted to prevent from uttering certain
intolerable truths.

CLAUDE AVELINE
French writer
'La Double Mort de Frederic Belot'
The craziest imagination has less re-
sources than destiny.

SAMUEL BECKETT
Irish author
'Waiting for Godot' 1952
We are all born mad. Some of us remain so.

MAX BEERBOHM
British critic
quoted in 'Max' by Lord David Cecil 1964
Only the insane take themselves quite seriously.

UGO BETTI
Italian playwright
'The Fugitive' 1953
All of us are mad. If it weren't for the fact every one of us is slightly abnormal, there wouldn't be any point in giving each person a separate name.

ABIGAIL VAN BUREN
American agony columnist 1974
Psychotherapy, unlike castor oil which will work no matter how you get it down, is useless when forced on an unco-operative patient.

MARC CHAGALL
French artist
'Artists on Art' 1947
All our interior world is reality – and that perhaps more so than our apparent world.

E. M. CIORAN
French philosopher
'The Temptation to Exist' 1956
We cannot be *normal* and *alive* at the same time.

JEAN COCTEAU
French writer and film director
'Le Rappel à l'Ordre'
The extreme limits of wisdom – that's what the public calls madness.

CYRIL CONNOLLY
British critic
The Unquiet Grave 1945
In youth, the life of reason is not in itself sufficient; afterwards the life of emotion, except for short periods, becomes unbearable.

CHRISTIAN DIOR
French couturier
Colliers 1955
To manufacture emotion a man must have a working agreement with madness.

IAN DURY
British rock musician
'Screamer's Dance' 1979
It's hard to be a hero, honey, when you've had your helmet cracked.

BRENDAN FRANCIS
Many a patient, after countless sessions, has quit therapy, because he could detect no perceptible improvement in his shrink's condition.

SAM GOLDWYN
American film producer
Anyone who goes to a psychiatrist should have his head examined.

ROBERT GRAVES
British poet 1967
I don't mind how strange folk are, so long as they're clean and tidy.

GRAHAM GREENE
British writer
in A. Andrews 'Quotations for Speakers & Writers'
Sentimentality – that's what we call the sentiment we don't share.

ERNEST HEMINGWAY
American writer
letter to Adriana Ivancic, quoted in The Times 1967
All people are mixed up and it is normal, like a battle.

JULES HENRY
'Culture Against Man' 1963
Psychosis is the final outcome of all that is wrong with a culture.

HERMAN HESSE
German writer
Many persons pass for normal, and indeed for highly valuable members of society, who are incurably mad.

KAREN HORNEY
American psychologist
'Our Inner Conflicts' 1945
Fortunately analysis is not the only way to resolve inner conflicts. Life itself still remains a very effective therapist.

ALAN HULL
British rock musician
Neurotics build castles in the sky, psychotics live in them, psychiatrists collect the rent and psychopaths smash the windows.

MORTON HUNT
American psychoanalyst
New York Times 1957
Being a good psychoanalyst, in short, has the same disadvantages as being a good parent – the children desert one as they grow up.

FANNIE HURST
American novelist
quoted in *'The Wit of Women'* ed. by L. and M. Cowan
When the mind's eye turns inward, it blazes upon the dearly beloved image of oneself.

ALDOUS HUXLEY
British writer
'Themes and Variations' 1950
That we are not much sicker and much madder than we are is due exclusively to the most blessed and blessing of all natural graces, sleep.

PIERRE JANET
French psychiatrist
in *'The Wit of Medicine'* ed. L. and M. Cowan 1972
If a patient is poor he is committed to a public hospital as a 'psychotic'. If he can afford a sanitarium, the diagnosis is 'neurasthenia'. If he is wealthy enough to be in his own home under the constant watch of nurses and physicians, he is simply 'an indisposed eccentric'.

MARCEL JOUHANDEAU
French writer
'De la grandeur'
The heart has its prisons that intelligence cannot unlock.

C. G. JUNG
Swiss psychoanalyst
'Psychological Reflections' 1953
Sentimentality is a superstructure covering brutality.

JACK KEROUAC
American novelist
'On The Road' 1957
The only people for me are the mad ones, the ones who are mad to live, mad to talk, mad to be saved ... the ones who never yawn and say a commonplace thing, but burn, burn, burn, like fabulous yellow roman candles exploding like spiders across the stars.

KARL KRAUS
German artist
'Karl Kraus' by Harry Zohn
Psychoanalysis is that mental illness for which it regards itself as therapy.

LOUIS KRONENBERGER
American critic
'Company Manners' 1954
We might define an eccentric as a man who is a law unto himself, and a crank as one who, having determined what the law is, insists on laying it down for others.

R. D. LAING
British psychiatrist
'The Politics of Experience' 1967
Madness need not be all breakdown. It may also be breakthrough. It is potentially liberation and renewal as well as enslavement and existential death.

'The Self & Others'
The 'unconscious' is what we do not communicate, to ourselves or to one another.

The Listener 1978
Most psychiatrists know nothing about what I call psychiatry. Their whole practice is to stop people going through experiences they think they should not be having, to administer tranquillisers and electric shocks to anyone who is in a state of mind they do not think that person ought to be in.

'The Divided Self' 1959
Schizophrenia is a successful attempt not to adapt to pseudo-social realities.

The Guardian 1972
Doctors in all ages have made fortunes by killing their patients by means of their cures. The difference in psychiatry is that is the death of the soul.

Insanity – a perfectly rational adjustment to the insane world.

'The Politics of Experience' 1967
Society highly values its normal man. It educates children to lose themselves and to become absurd, and thus be normal. Normal men have killed perhaps 100,000,000 of their fellow normal men in the last fifty years.

'The Divided Self' 1959
The standard psychiatric patient is a function of the standard psychiatrist and of the standard mental hospital.

'The Politics of Experience' 1967
From the alienated starting point of our pseudo-sanity everything is equivocal. Our sanity is not 'true' sanity. Their madness is not 'true' madness. The madness of our patients is an artefact of the destruction wreaked on them by us and on them by themselves.

True sanity entails, in one way or another, the dissolution of the normal ego, that false self competently adjusted to our alienated social reality. The emergence of the 'inner' archetypical mediators of divine power and through the death a rebirth, and the eventual re-establishment of a new kind of ego functioning, the ego now being the servant of the divine, no longer its betrayer.

CHRISTOPHER LEHMANN-HAUPT
American critic
New York Times 1977
To be crazy is not necessarily to writhe in snake pits or converse with imaginary gods. It can sometimes be not knowing what to do in the morning.

CHRISTA LUDWIG
German singer
New York Times 1971
Psychoanalysis is like going to school about yourself.

MARSHALL McLUHAN
Canadian academic
'The Gutenberg Galaxy' 1962
Schizophrenia may be a necessary conse-

quence of literacy.

'Understanding Media' 1964
If the nineteenth century was the age of the editorial chair, ours is the age of the psychiatrist's couch.

RENE MAGRITTE
Belgian artist
statement in Walker Art Centre Catalogue, Minneapolis, Minnesota, 1962
Nobody in his right mind believes that psychoanalysis could elucidate the mystery of the universe. The very nature of the mystery annihilates curiosity. Nor has psychoanalysis anything to say about works of art that evoke the mystery of the universe. Perhaps psychoanalysis is the best subject to be treated by psychoanalysis.

NORMAN MAILER
American writer
speech 1968
Insanity consists of building major structures upon foundations which do not exist.

Cannibals & Christians 1966
Sentimentality is the emotional promiscuity of those who have no sentiment.

Playboy 1968
The obsession is a search for a useful reality.

SIR PETER MEDAWAR
British scientist
Sunday Times 1981
Common-sense psychology is all right for ordinary people, but not very helpful when it comes to helping such un-ordinary people as the neurotic and insane.

'The Hope of Progress' 1972
Considered in its entirety, psychoanalysis won't do. It is an end product, moreover, like a dinosaur or a zeppelin; no better theory can ever be erected on its ruins, which will remain for ever one of the saddest and strangest of all landmarks in the history of 20th Century thought.

ANAIS NIN
French novelist
Diaries Vol.II
An analyst does not exist in the mind of

his patient except as a figure in his own drama.

DR. FREDERICK S. PERLS
American therapist
We have to lose our minds to come to our senses.

LAURENCE J. PETER
Canadian educator
'The Peter Principle' 1977
Psychiatry enables us to correct our faults by confessing our parents' shortcomings.

PHILIP RIEFF
American sociologist
'The Triumph of the Therapeutic'
Psychoanalysis is yet another method of learning how to endure the loneliness produced by culture.

SUSAN SONTAG
American essayist
'Styles of Radical Will' 1969
It doesn't seem inaccurate to say most people in this society who aren't actively mad are, at best, reformed or potential lunatics.

MURIEL SPARK
British novelist
One should only see a psychiatrist out of boredom.

WALLACE STEVENS
American poet
'Opus Posthumous' 1957
Sentimentality is a failure of feeling.

DR. MERVYN STOCKWOOD
British clergyman
The Observer 1961
A psychiatrist is a man who goes to the Folies Bergère and looks at the audience.

ROBERT STOLLER
American psychiatrist
'Sex & Gender' 1968
My colleague Nathan Leites PhD has concluded, after a review of the literature, that the term 'identity' has little use other than as a fancy dress in which to disguise vagueness, ambiguity, tautologies, lack of clinical data and a poverty of explanation.

ANTHONY STORR
British psychiatrist
quoted in The Times 1968
An analyst is a nobody. His opportunity for self expression is minimal. If he commits himself to paper he reveals a personality and satisfies his frustrated desire to assert himself.

THOMAS SZASZ
American psychiatrist
'International Encyclopedia of the Social Sciences' 1968
We must remember that every 'mental' symptom is a veiled cry of anguish. Against what? Against oppression, or what the patient experiences as oppression. The oppressed speak in a million tongues . . .

'The Manufacture of Madness' 1973
In the past, men created witches; now they create mental patients.

EZER WEIZMAN
Israeli politician
Time 1978
Anyone who says he is not emotional is not getting what he should out of life.

WILLIAM ALLEN WHITE
American writer
Consistency is a paste jewel that only cheap men cherish.

D. W. WINNICOTT
British paediactrician
'The Maturational Process & The Facilitating Environment' 1972
In doing psychoanalysis I aim at: keeping alive, keeping well, keeping awake. I aim at being myself and behaving myself. Having begun my analysis I expect to continue with it, to survive and to endure it. I enjoy myself doing analysis and I always look forward to the end of each analysis. Analysis for analysis' sake has no meaning for me. I do analysis because that is what the patient needs to have done and to have done with. If the patient does not need analysis, then I do something else.

HEATHCOTE WILLIAMS
British playwright
'The Speakers' 1964
If you are schizophrenic you are only half way there. God is a threesome.

ELEMIRE ZOLLA
Italian writer

'The Eclipse of the Intellectuals' 1971

The sad face of madness is the only sign
to which hope can cling.

'ZORBA THE GREEK'
*20th Century Fox 1964 screenplay by Micahel
Cacoyannis, based on novel by Mikos
Kazantakis*
Anthony Quinn: A man needs a little
madness, or else . . . he never dares cut
the rope and be free.

Time

BRIAN ALDISS
British author
The Guardian 1971
Timing is all.

FAITH BALDWIN
American writer
'Face Towards the Spring' 1956
Time is a dressmaker specialising in
alteration.

AUSTEN BRIGGS
American commercial artist
Let's remind ourselves that last year's
fresh idea is today's cliché.

JOHN CAGE
American musician
All that is necessary is an empty space
of time and letting it act in its magnetic
way.

ELIAS CANETTI
Bulgarian writer 1945
In eternity everything is just beginning.

MARC CHAGALL
French artist
picture title
Time is a River without Banks.

'THE CHALK GARDEN'
*Universal 1964 screenplay by John Michael
Hayes, based on play by Enid Bagnold*
Edith Evans: 'Hurry', Maitland, is the
curse of civilisation.

CYRIL CONNOLLY
British critic
The Unquiet Grave 1945
The civilisation of one epoch becomes
the manure of the next.

ANTHONY CROSLAND
British politician
The Observer 1975
What one generation sees as a luxury,
the next sees as a necessity.

ERICH FROMM
American psychologist
'The Art of Loving' 1956
Modern man thinks he loses something
– time – when he does not do things
quickly. Yet he does not know what to
do with the time he gains – except kill
it.

DAG HAMMARSKJOLD
Swedish diplomat
'Markings' 1964
Time goes by, reputation increases,
ability declines.

BEN HECHT
American screenwriter
Time is a circus always packing up and
moving away.

LILLIAN HELLMAN
American playwright
'An Unfinished Woman' 1969
Nothing, of course, begins at the time
you think it did.

RICHARD HOFSTADTER
American academic
'Anti-Intellectualism in American Life' 1963
Yesterday's avant-garde experience is
today's chic and tomorrow's cliché.

BOB HOPE
American comedian
Playboy 1973
Timing is the essence of life.

MICK JAGGER &
KEITH RICHARD
British rock composers
'Time Waits For No One'
Time waits for no one / And it won't
wait for you. (Essex Music)

OSCAR LEVANT
American pianist and composer
So little time, so little to do.

ELISABETH LUTYENS
British composer
The Guardian 1966
You're avant-garde for twenty years,
then suddenly you're an old-fashioned
floozie.

NORMAN MAILER
American writer
'Of A Fire on the Moon' 1970
Mr Answer Man, what is the existential
equivalent of infinity? Why, insomnia,
Sandy, good old insomnia.

WILL ROGERS
American humorist
'The Autobiography of Will Rogers' 1949
Half our life is spent trying to find some-
thing to do with the time we have rushed
through life trying to save.

ROD STEIGER
American film star
Esquire 1969
Feelings sometimes make a better cal-
endar than dates.

HEATHCOTE WILLIAMS
British playwright
'The Immortalist' 1978
Don't let Father Time kick sand in your
face.

TENNESSEE WILLIAMS
American playwright
conversation:
TW: I slept through the Sixties.
Gore Vidal: You didn't miss a thing.

WILLIAM CARLOS WILLIAMS
American writer
'Selected Essays'
Time is a storm in which we are all lost.

HAROLD WILSON
British politician
A week is a long time in politics.

Boredom & Loneliness

EDWARD ALBEE
American playwright
Daily Mail 1969
Aloneness is inevitable in being human.
People cannot accept this. They should
be aware of it and use it. It heightens
your perceptions.

ANONYMOUS
in Esquire 1965
Everyone is trapped in his own rut, and
may change only through a long, unknown process.

HYLDA BAKER
British comedienne
'Quote and Unquote' 1970
Punctuality is something that if you have
it, there's often no one around to share
it with you.

CECIL BEATON
British photographer
Perhaps the world's second worst crime
is boredom. The first is being a bore.

SAMUEL BECKETT
Irish author
quoted in New York Review of Books 1971
Life ... oscillates between these two
terms: suffering, that opens a window on
the real, and is the main condition of the
artistic experience; and boredom, that
must be considered as the most tolerable, because the most durable of human
evils.

SIR THOMAS BEECHAM
British conductor
'Beecham Stories' 1978
The world is a difficult world indeed /

And people are hard to suit / And the man who plays on the violin / Is a bore to the man with a flute.

ALAN BENNETT
British playwright
'Quote and Unquote' 1970
The great advantage of being in a rut is that when one is in a rut, one knows exactly where one is.

ERIC BERNE
American psychologist
'Games People Play' 1964
The eternal problem of the human being is how to structure his waking hours.

GERALD BRENAN
British writer
'Thoughts In a Dry Season'
Everyone is a bore to someone. That is unimportant. The thing to avoid is being a bore to someone else.

CHARLES BUKOWSKI
American writer
'Notes of a Dirty Old Man' 1969
Nothing was ever promised you. You signed no contract.

WILLIAM S. BURROUGHS
American writer
What's wrong with dropping out? To me, this is the whole point: one's right to withdraw from a social environment that offers no spiritual sustenance, and to *mind one's own business*.

JOHN CAGE
American musician
'Silence' 1961
It is not irritating to be where one is. It is only irritating to think one would like to be somewhere else.

JOYCE CARY
British novelist
radio interview 1956
The most important thing about the individual is his isolation; we're all isolated in our minds; where we come in touch with other people is through our affections, our sympathies, our animosities; we don't even know ourselves well enough to tell another person exactly what we are. . .

HUGH CAVENDISH
British landowner 1975
The greatest inequality is boredom. My life is never boring, other people's are profoundly so.

CYRIL CONNOLLY
British critic
'The Unquiet Grace' 1945
We are all serving a life-sentence in the dungeon of life.

CHARLES DYER
British playwright
'Contemporary Dramatists' 1977
Outside bedtime, no one truly exists unless he is reflected through the mind of another. We exist only as others think of us. We are not real except in our own tiny minds according to our own insignificant measurement of thought. . . Such is loneliness.

With physicalities dismissed, the mind is lonelier than ever. Mind was God's accident, an unfortunate bonus. We should be more content as sparrows. . . It happens for sparrows, that is all! Anything deeper is Mind. And Mind is an excess over needs. Therefore Mind is loneliness.

BOB DYLAN
American singer
'Like A Rolling Stone'
How does it feel / To be on your own / With no direction home / Like a complete unknown / Like a rolling stone? (M. Witmark & Sons)

BRIAN ENO
British musician
Remember – the tedium is the message.

ERICH FROMM
American psychologist
'The Sane Society'
Alienation as we find it in modern society is almost total; it pervades the relationship of a man to his work, to the things he consumes, to the state, to his fellow man and to himself.

JEAN GIONO
French writer
'Le Deserteur'
Boredom is the most horrible of wolves.

JULIEN GREEN
French writer
'Journal'
Boredom is one face of death.

DAG HAMMARSKJOLD
Swedish diplomat
'Diaries'
Pray that your loneliness may spur you into finding something to live for, great enough to die for.

HENRY S. HASKINS
American writer
'Meditations in Wall Street'
Only the bravest of stay-at-homes asks the ticklish question 'Did anybody ask where I was?'

ROBERT LINDNER
American psychoanalyst
'Must You Conform' 1956
Conformity, humility, acceptance – with these coins we are to pay our fares to paradise.

'LOVE IS A MANY SPLENDORED THING'
20th Century Fox 1955 screenplay by John Patrick, based on novel A Many Splendoured Thing by Han Suyin
William Holden: A great many mistakes are made in the name of loneliness.

NORMAN MAILER
American writer
'Writers at Work' 3rd series 1967
The war between being and nothingness is the underlying illness of the twentieth century. Boredom slays more of existence than war.

LLEWELLYN MILLER
'The Encyclopedia of Etiquette' 1968
It is a sad truth that everyone is a bore to someone.

LAURENCE J. PETER
Canadian educator
'Peter's Quotations' 1977
A rut is a grave with the ends knocked out.

WILLIAM PHILLIPS
'Sense of the Present' 1967
Boredom, after all, is a form of criticism.

ELVIS PRESLEY
American rock star
I get tired of singing to the guys I beat up in motion pictures.

BERTRAND RUSSELL
British philosopher
'The Conquest of Happiness'
Boredom is a vital problem for the moralist, since at least half the sins of mankind are caused by the fear of it.

EDITH SITWELL
British poet
Everybody is somebody's bore.

EVELYN WAUGH
British novelist
'Diaries' ed. Michael Davie. entry 1962
Punctuality is the virtue of the bored.

KATHARINE WHITEHORN
British journalist
In heaven they will bore you, in hell you will bore them.

TENNESSEE WILLIAMS
American playwright
'Orpheus Descending' 1957
We're all of us sentenced to solitary confinement inside our own skins, for life.

JIMMY ZERO
American rock musician
Risk is what separates the good part of life from the tedium.

ELEMIRE ZOLLA
Italian writer
'The Eclipse of the Intellectuals' 1971
The deadly boredom of modern life demands ever new stimulants, and only this attitude of conscious duplicity, which extracts the required excitants from evil – that is, from the divorce from Nature – enables one to confront it. Hence the exaltation of evil, of the deformed, the sterile and artificial, the pleasure taken in decadence.

Optimism & Pessimism

RAYMOND ARON
French academic
'The Opium of the Intellectuals' 1957
What passes for optimism is most often the effect of an intellectual error.

W. C. BENNETT
of Trinity Ave Presbyterian Church, Durham NC
quoted in 'The Official Rules' by P. Dickson 1978
Blessed is he who expects no gratitude, for he shall not be disappointed.

JOHN BERGER
British art critic
The Guardian 1971
It seems to me that one has to take an attitude of wagering on the possibility of what we aspire to is possible. Live every wager: it is the act actually of gambling which is important, and it is only that which makes it possible to go on in good faith with oneself, to go on living.

HEYWOOD BROUN
American writer
'Pieces of Hate'
The most prolific period of pessimism comes at 21, or thereabouts, when the first attempt is made to translate dreams into reality.

PEARL S. BUCK
American writer
'To My Daughters, With Love' 1967
To eat bread without hope is still slowly to starve to death.

E. M. CIORAN
French philosopher
'Syllogismes de l'amertume' 1952
To hope is to give the lie to the future.

CYRIL CONNOLLY
British critic
'The Unquiet Grave' 1945
Optimism and self pity are the positive and negative poles of modern cowardice.

QUENTIN CRISP
British author
'The Naked Civil Servant' 1968
A pessimist is someone who, if he is in the bath, will not get out to answer the telephone.

PAUL DICKSON
American writer
Playboy 1978
Rowe's Rule: The odds are six to five that the light at the end of the tunnel is the headlight of an oncoming train.

IAN DURY
British rock musician
'This Is What We Find' 1979
The hope that springs eternal / Springs right up your behind.

GABRIEL GARCIA MARQUEZ
Argentine writer
'El Coronel no Tiene quien le Escriba'
He who awaits much can expect little.

HENRY S. HASKINS
American writer
'Meditations in Wall Street'
Hope must feel that the human breast is amazingly tolerant.

JOHN W. HAZARD
in Changing Times 1957
Gumperson's Law: The probability of anything happening is in inverse ratio to its desirability.

JONES'S LAW
in 'Murphy's Law' by Arthur Bloch 1979
The man who can smile when things go wrong has thought of someone he can blame it on.

STANISLAW J. LEC
Polish poet
'Unkempt Thoughts' 1962
When you jump for joy, beware that no one moves the ground from beneath your feet.

GOLDA MEIR
Israeli politician, 1974
Pessimism is a luxury that a Jew can never allow himself.

MURPHY'S LAW
as quoted in 'The Official Rules' by P. Dickson 1978 and passim.
If anything can go wrong, it will.

CLAUDE LEVI-STRAUSS
French anthropologist
'Mythologiques I: Le Cru et le Cuit' 1964
Each advantage gives new hope; suspended by the solution of a new difficulty, the dossier is now closed.

J. ROBERT OPPENHEIMER
American physicist
Bulletin of Atomic Scientists 1951
The optimist thinks that this is the best of all possible worlds and the pessimist knows it.

LAURENCE J. PETER
Canadian educator
'Peter's Quotations' 1977
A pessimist is a man who looks both ways when he's crossing a one-way street.

ALBERT SCHWEITZER
German missionary 1955
An optimist is a person who sees a green light everywhere, while the pessimist sees only the red stop light . . . but the truly wise person is colour-blind.

GEORGE BERNARD SHAW
Irish writer and playwright
Do you know what a pessimist is? A man who thinks everybody is as nasty as himself and hates himself for it.

H. ALLEN SMITH
American journalist
'Let the Crabgrass Grow' 1960
When there are two conflicting versions of a story, the wise course is to believe the one in which people appear at their worst.

PAUL TILLICH
American theologian
Doubt isn't the opposite of faith, it is an element of faith.

ELSA TRIOLET
French writer
'Elsa's Proverbs'
To be a prophet it's sufficient to be a pessimist.

PETER USTINOV
British actor and wit
Illustrated London News 1968
An optimist is one who knows exactly how bad a place the world can be; a pessimist is one who finds out anew every morning.

KURT VONNEGUT JR.
American writer
Playboy 1973
It strikes me as gruesome and comical that in our culture we have an expectation that a man can always solve his problems. This is so untrue that it makes me want to cry – or laugh.

WALTER WINCHELL
American columnist
Optimist: a man who gets treed by a lion, but enjoys the scenery.

FRANK ZAPPA
American rock musician 1979
I think that cynicism is a positive value. You have to be cynical. You can't not be cynical. The more people that I have encouraged to be cynical, the better job I've done.

Identity & Self

ROBERT M. ADAMS
American critic
'Nil' 1966
If we ever see how we got here, we may know a little better where we are.

CONRAD AIKEN
American poet
New York Herald Tribune 1969
Separate we come and separate we go /

And this, be it known, is all that we know.

ALAIN (Emile Chartier)
French philosopher
'Propos d'un Normand'
Who is dissatisfied with others is dissatisfied with himself. Our arrows rebound on us.

KINGSLEY AMIS
British author
Daily Express 1957
Self criticism must be my guide to action, and the first rule for its employment is that in itself it is not a virtue, only a procedure.

ANONYMOUS JAPANESE POET
Daedalus 1960
When you look into a mirror you do not see your reflection - your reflection sees you.

ANTONIN ARTAUD
French playwright
'Collected Works' 1968
Where there is a stink of shit, there is a smell of being.

A. J. AYER
British philosopher
Sunday Times 1957
There is then a simple answer to the question 'What is the purpose of our individual lives?' – they have whatever purpose we succeed in putting into them.

FAITH BALDWIN
American writer
'Harvest of Hope' 1962
Character builds slowly, but it can be torn down again with incredible swiftness.

JOHN BARTH
American author
'The End of the Road'
Everyone is necessarily the hero of his own life story.

KARL BARTH
Swiss theologian
'The Word of God and the Word of Man' 1957
Conscience is the perfect interpreter of life.

W. C. BENNETT
of the Trinity Ave Presbyterian Church, Durham NC.
quoted in 'The Official Rules' by P. Dickson, 1978
Blessed is he who has reached the point of no return, and knows it, for he shall enjoy living.

THOMAS BERNHARD
German poet
'Die Jagdgesellschaft'
Life is a torment – on the other hand we can only face up to ourselves when we're afraid.

JORGE LUIS BORGES
Argentine writer
quoted in New York Review of Books 1971
Any life, no matter how long and complex it may be, is made up of a *single moment* – the moment in which a man finds out, once and for all, who he is.

PHYLLIS BOTTOME
American spy fiction writer
quoted in 'The Wit of Women' ed. L. and M. Cowan
Nothing ever really sets human nature free, but self-control.

MEL BROOKS
American film director
Playboy 1975
You can win a conditional victory against death – it all boils down to scratching your name in the bark of a tree. I Was Here.

CHANDLER BROSSARD
American writer
in 'Contemporary Novelists' 1976
Identity is simply a kind of negotiation individuals make with other individuals to give each other the illusion of separate independence.

ALEXIS CARREL
French writer
'Reflections on Life' 1952
To accomplish our destiny it is not enough merely to guard prudently against road accidents. We must also cover before nightfall the distance assigned to each of us.

JOYCE CARY
British novelist
'Art & Reality' 1958
The most important part of man's existance, that part where he most truly lives and is aware of living, lies entirely within the domain of personal feeling.

JOHN CASSAVETES
American film director
Playboy 1971
It's bullshit when people say that ego is a bad trip. It's the *only* trip. You are who you are because of your ego; without it nothing counts.

COCO CHANEL
French couturière
'Coco Chanel – Her Life, Her Secrets' by M. Haedrich 1971
In order to be irreplaceable one must always be different.

MALCOLM DE CHAZAL
French writer
'Sens Plastique' 1949
The egotist's feelings walk in single file.

E. M. CIORAN
French philosopher
'The Fall Into Time' 1971
No one recovers from the disease of being born, a deadly wound if ever there was one.

G. NORMAN COLLIE
American educator
Education Digest 1967
Every man has one thing he can do better than anyone else and usually it is reading his own handwriting.

QUENTIN CRISP
British author
BBC2 TV 1980
You've nothing to give the world that anyone else can't give except yourself.

'The Naked Civil Servant' 1968
Even a montonously undeviating path of self-examination does not necessarily lead to a mountain of self-knowledge.

JOAN DIDION
American writer
'On Self Respect' 1961
Innocence ends when one is stripped of the delusion that one likes oneself.

BOB DYLAN
American singer
When you feel in your gut what you are and then dynamically pursue it – don't back down and don't give up – then you're going to mystify a lot of folks.

ALBERT EINSTEIN
German physicist 1955
The true value of a human being is determined primarily by the measure and sense in which he has obtained liberation from the self.

'Ideas & Opinions' 1954
The true value of a human being is determined primarily by the measure and sense in which he has attained liberation from the self.

MAX ERNST
German painter
'Writings'
Identity must be convulsive or it will not be.

BRENDAN FRANCIS
If you accept your limitations you go beyond them.

ERICH FROMM
American psychologist
'Man for Himself' 1947
Man's main task in life is to give birth to himself.

Man's main task in life is to give birth to himself, to become what he potentially is. The most important product of his effort is his own personality.

ROBERT FROST
American poet
The best things and best people rise out of their separateness. I'm against a homogenized society because I want the cream to rise.

JEAN GENET
French writer
Esquire 1968
Order, real order . . . is the freedom offered to everyone to discover and recreate himself.

ANDRE GIDE
French writer
It is better to be hated for what you are than loved for what you are not.

VALERY GISCARD D'ESTAING
French politician 1975
You must always do all that depends on you.

ARLO GUTHRIE
American singer
That's what it all comes down to; whether or not, when the time comes, you decide to jump in the pot.

DAG HAMMARSKJOLD
Swedish diplomat
'Markings' 1964
Is life so wretched? Isn't it rather your hands which are too small, your vision which is muddied. You are the one who must grow up.

HUGH HEFNER
American publisher
Esquire 1970
You reach the proper solution for yourself by analysing, again, and separating, the means and ends of not losing sight of what it is you want to accomplish.

WERNER HEISENBERG
German scientist
Esquire 1977
To the outer limits of space, man carries only the image of himself.

ERNEST HEMINGWAY
American writer
quoted in Sunday Times 1966
Every man's life ends the same way. It is only the details of how he lived and how he died that distinguish one man from another.

ERIC HOFFER
American philosopher
in 'The Faber Book of Aphorisms' 1964
Every extreme attitude is a flight from the self.

'The Ordeal of Change' 1963
Every new adjustment is a crisis in self-esteem.

RALF HUTTER
German rock musician
Individuality has been exaggerated in the 20th century. Everybody wants so much to be different. But individuality is just wishful thinking. It is a sales argument, designed to stimulate commerce . . . Germany doesn't need individuals. It doesn't want heroes. Dr Goebbels perfected the hero system. We want something more corporate. We cultivate anonymity.

MICHAEL KORDA
British writer
'Power in the Office' 1976
We live behind our faces, while they front for us.

LOUIS KRONENBERGER
American critic
'The Cart and the Horse' 1964
A great maxim of personal responsibility and mature achievement – Do It Yourself – is now the enthroned cliché for being occupied with nonessentials.

R. D. LAING
British psychiatrist
Esquire 1972
One's only task is to realise oneself.

FRANK LEAHY
American sports coach
Egotism is the anaesthetic that dulls the pain of mediocrity.

ROSS LOCKRIDGE
American writer
in 'Short Lives' by Katinka Matson 1980
We Americans make the modern error of dignifying the Individual. We do everything we can to butter him up. We give him a name . . . assure him . . . he has certain inalienable rights . . . educate him . . . let him pass on his name to his brats, and when he dies we give him a special hole in the ground and a hunk of stone with his name on it. But, after all, he's only a seed, a bloom and a withering stalk among pressing billions. Your Individual is a pretty disgusting, vain, lewd little bastard. . . By God, he has only one right guaranteed to him in Nature, and that is the right to die and stink to Heaven.

MALCOLM LOWRY
British novelist
in 'Contemporary Novelists' 1976
Whatever is given to live, you alone can live, and re-live, and re-live, until it is gasped out of you.

RENE MAGRITTE
Belgian artist
lecture quoted in 'Magritte: The True Art of Painting' ed. H. Torczyner 1979
That old question 'Who are we?' receives

a disappointing answer in the world in which we must live. Actually, we are merely the subjects of this so-called civilised world, in which intelligence, baseness, heroism and stupidity get on very well together and are alternately being pushed to the fore.

ANDRE MALRAUX
French writer
'Les Conquerants'
The one important thing in life is to see to it that you are never beaten.

HENRY MILLER
American writer
'The World of Sex' 1957
Until we lose ourselves there is no hope of finding ourselves.

VAN MORRISON
British rock star
The only thing that stands up is whether you've got it or not. The only thing that counts is if you're still around.

IRIS MURDOCH
British writer
in 'Contemporary Novelists' 1976
We are what we seem to be, transient mortal creatures subject to necessity and chance. . . Our destiny can be examined, but it cannot be justified or totally explained. We are simply here.

ANAIS NIN
French novelist
'Diary' vol V 1974
When you make a world tolerable for yourself you make a world tolerable for others.

JOSE ORTEGA Y GASSET
Spanish philosopher
Time 1955
I am I plus my circumstances.

HENRI PETIT
French writer
'Les Justes Solitudes'
One despairs of others so as not to despair too much of oneself.

POLY STYRENE (Marion Elliott)
British rock singer
quoted in The Listener 1979
Identity is the crisis which you can't see.

P. J. PROBY (James Marcus Smith)
American rock star
When you're dealing with yourself, you're alone.

TOM ROBINSON
British rock singer
You do what you can to help the things that you believe in within your own field of action. You act according to your convictions and according to your conscience and according to your sense of responsibility towards the world you live in and how you feel that dictates whether you should or shouldn't take action, get involved or don't get involved.

It comes down to how much of the thing that you have can you spread how far and with what amount of dilution. The more you spread it, the more diluted it will get, but you do get further with it. That's the balance that everyone has to figure for themselves.

LINDA RONSTADT
American rock singer
I think you should get away from competing with anything, including yourself.

You've either got to have a sense of humour, or you've got to have an attitude and a scapegoat. It helps if you have all three.

GEORGES ROUAULT
French artist
in 'Artists on Art' ed. R. Goldwater and M. Treves 1947
Anyone can revolt. It is more difficult silently to obey our own inner promptings, and to spend our lives finding sincere and fitting means of expression for our temperament and our gifts.

JEAN-PAUL SARTRE
French philosopher
introduction to 'The Wretched of the Earth' by Frantz Fanon, 1961
We only become what we are by the radical and deep-seated refusal of that which others have made of us.

'Existentialism' 1947
Man is nothing else but what he makes of himself. Such is the first principle of existentialism.

Man is free. The coward makes himself

cowardly. The hero makes himself heroic.

MAYO SMITH
American baseball manager 1956
It all boils down to what you've got to operate with and how you operate.

DR. DAVID STAFFORD-CLARK
British physician 1966
No one is born prejudiced against others, but everyone is born prejudiced in favour of himself.

DON STEELE
American disc jockey
Ego is not a four-letter word.

ROD STEIGER
American film star
Playboy 1969
You've got to think that you're something special. Otherwise how would you tolerate all the crap you have to go through.

Esquire 1969
The most important thing is to be *whatever* you are without shame.

LILY TOMLIN
American comedienne
New York Times 1976
We're all in this together – by ourselves.

PETE TOWNSHEND
British rock composer
'Substitute'
You think we look pretty good together / You think my shoes are made of leather / But I'm a substitute for another guy / I look pretty tall / But my heels are high. (Essex Music)

'The Seeker'
I'm happy when life's good / And when it's bad I cry / I got values, but I don't know how or why. (Essex Music)

GORE VIDAL
American writer
Esquire 1968
Each of us contains a private self and a public self. When the two have not met, their host tends to be average ... amiable, self-deluding and given to sudden attacks of melancholy whose origin he does not suspect. When the two selves openly disdain each other, the host is apt to be a strong-minded opportunist ... when the selves wrangle, the host is more a man of conscience than of action. When the two are in fierce and total conflict, the host is a lunatic – or a saint.

KURT VONNEGUT JR.
American writer
introduction to 'Mother Night'
We are what we pretend to be.

GEORGE WALD
American scientist
'The Origin of Optical Activity' 1957
We are the products of editing, rather than authorship.

IRVING WALLACE
American writer
'The Square Pegs' 1958
To be one's self, and unafraid whether right or wrong, is more admirable than the easy cowardice of surrender to conformity.

ALAN WATTS
American philosopher
Life 1961
Trying to define yourself is like trying to bite your own teeth.

A. J. WEBERMAN
American Dylanologist
and analyst of Bob Dylan's garbage 1971
You are what you throw away.

SIMONE WEIL
French philosopher
We do not acquire humility. There is humility in us – only we humiliate ourselves before false gods.

D. W. WINNICOTT
British paediatrician
'On Communication' 1963
I have tried to state the need we have to recognise this aspect of health: the non-communicating central self, forever immune from the reality principle, and forever silent. Here communication is not non-verbal; it is like the music of the spheres, absolutely personal. It belongs to being alive. And in health, it is out of this that communication naturally arises.

Reality

W. H. AUDEN
British poet
Esquire 1970
What one sees is a reality common to everyone, but from a unique point of view. That point of view can be interesting, even revealing, but I've never thought it would change the world.

JAMES BALDWIN
American writer
'Notes of a Native Son' 1958
People who shut their eyes to reality simply invite their own destruction. And anyone who insists on remaining in a state of innocence long after that innocence is dead, turns himself into a monster.

JORGE LUIS BORGES
Argentine writer
'Borges On Writing' 1974
Reality is not always probable, or likely.

'Conversations with Jorge Luis Borges' ed. Richard Burgin 1973
Reality favours symmetry.

JOSEPH BRODSKY
Russian academic
New York Review of Books 1981
By itself reality per se isn't worth a damn. It's perception that promotes reality to meaning.

JOYCE CARY
British novelist
'Art & Reality' 1958
The concept, the label, is perpetually hiding from us all the nature of the real . . . It is a narrow little house which becomes a prison to those who can't get out of it.

IVY COMPTON BURNETT
British author
The Guardian 1973
Real life seems to have no plots.

MARTIN ESSLIN
Austrian critic
The dignity of man lies in his ability to face reality in all its meaninglessness.

JULES FEIFFER
American cartoonist
Playboy 1971
Satire doesn't close Saturday night – as George Kaufman once said – it's *reality* closes Saturday night.

ROMAIN GARY
French writer
New York Herald Tribune 1960
Reality is not an inspiration for literature. At best, literature is an inspiration for reality.

ANDRE GIDE
French writer
In the realm of the emotions, it is impossible to separate the real from the imaginary.

J. B. S. HALDANE
British scientist
Reality is not only more fantastic than we think, but also much more fantastic than we imagine. Also reported as: The universe is not only stranger than we imagine, it is stranger than we *can* imagine.

CLIVE JAMES
Australian critic
The Observer 1977
There is no secret about why soap operas make compulsive television: they simplify life . . . in a soap opera character is destiny: everything anybody does is determined by his character. In real life we are stuck with the existentialist responsibility of remaking ourselves every morning.

ART KANE
American photographer
in 'Masters of Contemporary Photography' 1975
Reality never lives up to itself visually for me.

HENRY KISSINGER
American diplomat
'The Necessity for Choice'
The real distinction is between those who adapt their purposes to reality and

those who seek to mould reality in the light of their purposes.

MARSHALL McLUHAN
Canadian academic
'The Mechanical Bride' 1951
'Real life' often appears, at least, to be an imitation of art. Today, it is poster art.

RENE MAGRITTE
Belgian artist
quoted in 'Magritte: The True Art of Painting' ed. H. Torczyner 1979
The basic thing, whether in art or in life, is 'presence of mind'. 'Presence of mind' is unpredictable. Our so-called will does not control it. We are controlled by 'presence of mind' which reveals reality as an absolute mystery.

SEAN O'FAOLAIN
Irish writer
'The Bell'
There is only one admirable form of the imagination: the imagination that is so intense that it creates a new reality, that it makes things happen, whether it be a political thing, or a social thing or a work of art.

JANE O'REILLY
American writer
Ms 1972
Parables are un-necessary for re-organising the blatant absurdity of everyday life. Reality is lesson enough.

JOSE ORTEGA Y GASSET
Spanish philosopher
'The Dehumanisation of Art' 1948
The masses feel it is easy to flee from reality, when it is the most difficult thing in the world.

OCTAVIO PAZ
Mexican poet
'Modern European Poetry' 1966
Reality is a staircase going neither up nor down. We don't move, today is today, always is today.

PETE SHELLEY
British rock musician
In the real world you both win when you play the same game.

LORD SNOWDON
British photographer
quoted in 'Pictures on a Page' by Harold Evans 1978
It's no good saying 'Hold it' to a moment of real life.

SUSAN SONTAG
American essayist
'Photography Unlimited' New York Review of Books 1977
Reality has come to seem more and more like what we are shown by cameras.

SIMONE WEIL
French philosopher
'Gravity & Grace' 1972
Attachment is a manufacturer of illusions and whoever wants reality ought to be detached.

quoted in New York Review of Books 1981
Distance is the soul of reality.

'Gravity & Grace' 1972
A test of what is real is that it is hard and rough. Joys are found in it, not pleasure. What is pleasant belongs to dreams.

DONALD WESTLAKE
American crime novelist
quoted in 'Murder Ink', ed. Dilys Winn 1977
A realist is somebody who thinks the world is simple enough to be understood. It isn't.

Experience

MICHELANGELO ANTONIONI
Italian film director
The only thing that matters is experience. Whether you're high or sober it's all the same – it's all experience.

MAX BEERBOHM
British writer
'Mainly on the Air' 1946
Anything that is worth doing has been done frequently. Things hitherto undone should be given, I suspect, a wide berth.

DANIEL J. BOORSTIN
American writer
New York Post 1972
. . . The messiness of experience. That may be what we mean by life.

ALBERT CAMUS
French writer
'Notebooks' 1962
You cannot create experience, you must undergo it.

LOUIS-FERDINAND CELINE
French writer
'Writers at Work' 3rd series 1967
Experience is a dim lamp, which only lights the one who bears it.

DR. BROCK CHISHOLM
American physician
Ladies Home Journal 1949
Conscience is what your mother told you before you were six years old.

ALBERT EINSTEIN
German physicist
Common sense is the deposit of prejudice laid down in the mind before the age of 18.

ALDOUS HUXLEY
British writer
Reader's Digest 1956
Experience is not what happens to you. It is what you do with what happens to you.

FRANKLYN P. JONES
Experience enables you to recognise a mistake when you make it again.

KARL KRAUS
German artist
'Karl Kraus' by Harry Zohn
Experiences are savings which a miser puts aside; wisdom is an inheritance which a wastrel cannot exhaust.

EDITH MIRRIELEES
American writer
'Strong Writing' 1947
Experience shows that exceptions are as true as rules.

EDWARD R. MURROW
American broadcaster 1955
Everyone is a prisoner of his own experiences. No one can eliminate prejudices – just recognise them.

RAYMOND QUENEAU
French historian
'A Model History'
Man knows from experience that misfortune is never far away.

VITA SACKVILLE-WEST
British writer and gardener
'In Your Garden Again' 1953
I have come to the conclusion, after many years of sometimes sad experience, that you cannot come to any conclusion at all.

JOHN STEINBECK
American writer
in letter 1956
I know that no one really wants the benefit of anyone's experience which is probably why its so freely offered.

JUDITH STERN
Experience – a comb life gives you after you lose your hair.

Memory

ELIZABETH BOWEN
British novelist
Vogue 1955
The charm, one might say the genius of memory, is that it is choosy, chancy and temperamental: it rejects the edifying cathedral and indelibly photographs the small boy outside, chewing a hunk of melon in the dust.

JOSEPH BRODSKY
Russian academic
New York Review of Books 1981
If there is any substitute for love, it's memory, to memorize, then, is to restore intimacy.

ELIAS CANETTI
Bulgarian writer 1954
He who is afraid of his own memories is cowardly, really cowardly.

CYRIL CONNOLLY
British critic
in 'The Faber Book of Aphorisms' 1964
Our memories are card indexes consulted, and then put back in disorder by authorities whom we do not control.

CLIFTON FADIMAN
American essayist
'Selected Writings' 1955
A good memory is one trained to forget the trivial.

ALDOUS HUXLEY
British writer
Each man's memory is his private literature.

STANISLAW J. LEC
Polish poet
in 'The Faber Book of Aphorisms' 1964
You can close your eyes to reality but not to memories.

ANITA LOOS
American writer
'Kiss Hollywood Goodbye' 1974
Memory is more indelible than ink.

NORMAN MAILER
American writer
Playboy 1968
The surest way not to be remembered is to talk about the way you want to be.

AUSTIN O'MALLEY
Memory is a crazy woman that hoards coloured rags and throws away food.

Human Nature

HANNAH ARENDT
American writer
New Yorker 1977
Nothing and nobody exists on this planet whose very being does not presuppose a spectator. In other words, nothing that is, insofar as it appears, exists in the singular; everything that is is meant to be perceived by somebody. Not Man, but men inhabit the earth. Plurality is the law of the earth.

MARCEL ARLAND
French writer
'Antares'
We carry two or three tunes and spend our lives understanding them.

SIMONE DE BEAUVOIR
French writer
'The Second Sex' 1953
Humanity is something more than a mere species – it is a historical development.

SAUL BELLOW
American writer
There is something funny about the human condition and civilised intelligence makes fun of its own ideas.

JOHN BENSON
British academic
The Listener 1979
Any tradition which has been established for a long time must be compatible with the basic needs of human nature. Tradition provides us with the most direct access that we can have to our nature.

SIR ISAIAH BERLIN
British philosopher
'Four Essays On Liberty'
Injustice, poverty, slavery, ignorance – these may be cured by reform or revolution. But men do not live only by fighting evils. They live by positive goals, individual and collective, a vast variety of them, seldom predictable, at times incompatible.

ERIC BERNE
American psychologist
We are born princes and the civilising process makes us frogs.

THOMAS BERNHARD
German writer
'Die Ignorant und der Wahnsinninge'
We can only exist by taking our minds off the fact that we exist.

SIR JOHN BETJEMAN
British poet
The Observer 1973
I don't think life would be worth living if one were not constantly the prey of one's emotions.

JORGE LUIS BORGES
Argentine writer
'Conversations with Jorge Luis Borges' ed. Richard Burgin 1973
What you really value is what you miss, not what you have.

GEORGES BRAQUE
French artist
'Artists on Art' 1947
Nobility grows out of contained emotion.

COLM BROGAN
There is only one word for aid that is genuinely without strings and that word is blackmail.

ALBERT CAMUS
French writer
'Notebooks' 1962
He who despairs over an event is a coward, but he who holds hopes for the human condition is a fool.

JOYCE CARY
British novelist
'Art & Reality' 1958
The reality which smashes every ideologue and his system is human nature, incessantly striving towards a personal achievement in a world which is essentially free and personal.

DR. G. BROCK CHISHOLM
American physician
The only real threat to man is man himself.

E. M. CIORAN
French philosopher
'The Fall Into Time' 1971
He who has never envied the vegetable has missed the human drama.

'The Temptation to Exist' 1956
Since all life is futility, then the decision to exist must be the most irrational of all.

JEAN COCTEAU
French writer and film director
'Letters to Andre Gide' 1971
Let everyone follow his inclinations – provided he go upward.

EVAN S. CONNELL JR.
Esquire 1965
Illusion is our price and purchase. Love and fame, both are adulation.

QUENTIN CRISP
British author
'The Naked Civil Servant' 1968
Though the strongest resist the temptation, all human beings who suffer from any deficiency, real or imagined, are under compulsion to draw attention to it.

CYRIL DEAN DARLINGTON
British biologist
lecture 1960
Mankind ... will not willingly admit that its destiny can be revealed by the breeding of flies or the counting of chiasmata.

LEN DEIGHTON
British writer
The Observer 1974
I'm not much interested in the way people think, but I am very interested in the way they react and how they work the machinery that is around them.

KIRK DOUGLAS
American film star
Esquire 1970
It doesn't matter if you're a nice guy or a bastard. What matters is – you won't bend.

ROBERT FROST
American poet
Atlantic Monthly 1962
The most terrible thing is your own judgement.

J. K. GALBRAITH
American economist
'The New Industrial State' 1967
What is called a high standard of living consists, in considerable measure, in arrangements for avoiding muscular energy, increasing sensual pleasure, enhancing caloric intake beyond any conceivable nutritional requirement. Nonetheless, the belief that increased production is a worthy social goal is very nearly absolute.

WILLIE GINSBERG
American gangster
testifying on sports corruption 1956
Everyone likes hats when someone else is paying for them.

DAN GREENBURG
American writer
Esquire 1977
The rudest people are those who have neither the courage to tell the truth nor the grace to tell a convincing white lie.

DR. A. H. HALSEY
British academic
Reith Lectures 1978
Man is to be distinguished from the brutes not so much by his desire for a better life, as by the range of his conception of what that life might be, and the complexity of the language in which he is able to express that hope.

HANS WERNER HENZE
German composer 1974
The peasants in the Neapolitan Campagna have a saying: wine betrays those who betray it . . . every human being is a divinity and can only be a divinity if there are dark aspects in him as well.

KATHARINE HEPBURN
American film star
Esquire 1967
You can't change the music of your soul.

ERIC HOFFER
American philosopher
in 'The Faber Book of Aphorisms' 1964
It is always safe to assume that people are more subtle and less sensitive than they seem.

HUBERT HUMPHREY
American politician
A fellow that doesn't have any tears doesn't have any heart.

ALDOUS HUXLEY
British writer
'Collected Essays'
Too much consistency is as bad for the mind as for the body. Consistency is contrary to nature, contrary to life. The only completely consistent people are the dead.

'Themes and Variations' 1950
Most human beings have an almost infinite capacity for taking things for granted.

'INHERIT THE WIND'
UA 1960 screenplay Nathan E. Douglas & Harold Jacob Smith; based on play by Jerome Lawrence & Robert E. Lee
Gene Kelly: Darwin was wrong. Man's still an ape. His creed's still a totem pole. When he first achieved the upright position he took a look at the stars, thought they were something to eat. When he couldn't reach them he decided they were groceries belonging to a bigger creature. That's how Jehovah was born.

C. G. JUNG
Swiss psychoanalyst
'Modern Man In Search Of A Soul'
It is becoming more and more obvious that it is not starvation, nor microbes,

nor cancer but man himself who is mankind's greatest danger, because he has no adequate protection against psychic epidemics, which are infinitely more devastating in their effect than the greatest natural catastrophes.

TV interview

We need more understanding of human nature, because the only real danger that exists is man himself.

MURRAY KEMPTON
American journalist
'Part of Our Time' 1955
A man can look upon his life and accept it as good or evil; it is far, far harder for him to confess that it has been unimportant in the sum of things.

ARTHUR KOESTLER
British philosopher
The Observer 1968
If one looks with a cold eye at the mess man has made of his history, it is difficult to avoid the conclusion that he has been afflicted by some built-in mental disorder which drives him towards self-destruction. Murder within the species on an individual or collective scale, is a phenomenon unknown in the whole animal kingdom, except for man, and a few varieties of ants and rats.

LOUIS KRONENBERGER
American critic
'Company Manners' 1954
Conformity may not reign in the prosperous bourgeois suburb, but it ultimately always governs.

R. D. LAING
British psychiatrist
'The Politics of Experience' 1967
Human beings seem to have an almost unlimited capacity to deceive themselves and to deceive themselves into taking their own lies for truth.

We are all murderers and prostitutes. No matter to what culture, society, class, nation one belongs, no matter how normal, moral or mature one takes oneself to be.

JOHN McKAY
British rock musician
Everyone wants to get something more

out of their lives. To be true to themselves or whatever. It's just that some people realise it and some don't.

BUTTERFLY McQUEEN
American actress
Pittsburgh Courier 1955
We were born to improvise ourselves as human beings.

GABRIEL MARCEL
French writer
'Presence et immortalité'
To exist is to co-exist.

KARL MENINGER
American psychiatrist 1958
Unrest of spirit is a mark of life.

HENRY MILLER
American writer
'Sexus' 1949
We are all guilty of crime – the great crime of not living life to the full.

BRIAN O'NOLAN
Irish writer
(Myles na gCopaleen) in 'The Best of Myles' 1968
What is important is food, money and opportunities for scoring off one's enemies. Give a man these three things and you won't hear much squawking out of him.

HAROLD PINTER
British playwright
BBC radio interview, 1960
After all, we're all the same upside down.

GEORGES POULET
French writer
'Mesure de l'Instant'
The human being never has the time to be. He only has the time to become.

FREDERIC RAPHAEL
British writer
'Contemporary Novelists' 1976
Within the nooks and crannies of the great edifices of generalisation and judgement, the innocently guilty and the guiltily innocent scurry about carrying nuts to their families, seeking their pleasures, snapping at their enemies and providing, for those that have eyes to

see, the proof of the impossibility of final solutions to the human condition.

PIERRE REVERDY
French writer
'Le livre de mon bord'
One lives with many bad deeds on one's conscience and some good intentions in one's heart.

JOHNNY SAIN
American baseball coach
The world doesn't want to hear about the labour pains. It only wants to see the baby.

JEAN-PAUL SARTRE
French philosopher
The Words 1964
We must act out passion before we ca'. feel it.

ERIC SEVAREID
American newscaster
Reader's Digest
Human beings are not perfectible. They *are* improbable.

N. F. SIMPSON
British playwright
'A Resounding Tinkle' 1957
We are all spectators of one another, mutual witnesses of each other's discomfiture.

PHILIP SLATER
'The Pursuit of Loneliness' 1970
There is no such thing as a situation so intolerable that human beings must necessarily rise up against it. People can bear anything and the longer it exists the more placidly they will bear it.

PROFESSOR J. C. SMART
1976
A human being is a very complicated physical mechanism and nothing more.

STEPHEN SPENDER
British poet
quoted in Sunday Times 1973
It is perfectly consistent to want to be part of a way of life but to regard yourself as superior to it if it rejects you.

ROD STEIGER
American film star
Esquire 1969
That's all one should really ask of anybody – that they attempt to contribute.

JOHN STEINBECK
American writer
'The Winter of Our Discontent'
No man really knows about other human beings. The best he can do is suppose that they are like himself.

TERRY-THOMAS
British comedian
Do not assume that the other fellow has intelligence to match yours. He may have more.

ARNOLD TOYNBEE
British historian
'Cities on the Move'
The quality in human nature on which we must pin our hopes is its proven adaptability.

LIONEL TRILLING
American critic
'The Liberal Imagination' 1950
We are all ill, but even a universal sickness implies an idea of health.

PETER USTINOV
British actor and wit
The Listener 1974
That weakness in human nature which goes by the name of strength.

ALDO VAN EYCK
Dutch architect
We can discover ourselves everywhere – all places and ages – doing the same things in a different way, feeling the same differently, reacting differently to the same.

NORBERT WIENER
American mathematician
'The Human Use of Human Beings' 1954
A conscience which has been bought once will be bought twice.

D. W. WINNICOTT
British paediatrician
'The Child, the Family and the Outside World'
1964

Human beings are not animals; they are animals plus a wealth of fantasy, psyche, soul, or inner world potential or whatever you will.

Our power to think things out about human nature . . . is liable to be blocked by our fear of the full implication of what we find.

Morality

A. J. AYER
British philosopher
'Essay On Humanism'
No morality can be founded on authority, even if the authority were divine.

Sunday Times 1972
Morality is very largely founded on sympathy and affection. For that one does not require religious sanctions. Even logical positivists are capable of love.

ROBERT BOLT
British playwright
'A Man for All Seasons' 1962
Morality's *not* practical. Morality's a gesture. A complicated gesture learnt from books.

ALBERT CAMUS
French writer
Integrity needs no rules.

JACQUES CHARDONNE
French writer
'L'Amour, c'est beaucoup plus que l'amour'
Morals – the taste for what is pure and what defies the era.

GRAHAM GREENE
British novelist
'Ways of Escape' 1980
Morality comes with the sad wisdom of age. When the sense of curiosity has withered.

ERNEST HEMINGWAY
American writer
What is moral is what you feel good after.

ALDOUS HUXLEY
British writer
'The Doors of Perception'
Half at least of all morality is negative and consists in keeping out of mischief.

HENRY KISSINGER
American diplomat 1976
We must learn to distinguish morality from moralising.

GAMAL ABDEL NASSER
President of Egypt 1954
The only acceptable authority is morality, events, necessity.

LORD SHAWCROSS
British politician
The Observer 1963
The so-called new morality is too often the old immorality condoned.

ALFRED NORTH WHITEHEAD
British philosopher
Morality . . . is what the majority then and there happen to like and immorality is what they dislike.

Sin

LEO ABSE
British politician
The Spectator 1980
Adulation may be easier to relinquish than hate: now we have no heroes, but perhaps it is too painful to give up our villains.

IAN AIRD
British surgeon
in 'The Wit of Medicine' ed. L. and M. Cowan 1972
The greatest sin in the world is ignorance in motion.

ERIC AMBLER
British crime author
The Times 1970
Most people are more odious than they think. Not wicked – just odious.

SAMUEL BECKETT
Irish author
New York Herald Tribune 1964
The major sin is the sin of being born.

MARY BELL
11-year-old British murderess 1968
Murder isn't that bad. We all die sometime.

ANTHONY BURGESS
British writer
Playboy 1974
To *impose* good, whether through force or through some technique like aversion therapy, is evil. To act evilly is better than to have good imposed.

ARTHUR CAESAR
American film producer
We are not punished for our sins, but by them.

ALEXIS CARREL
French writer
'Reflections on Life' 1952
It is tempting to deny the existence of evil, since denying it obviates the need to fight it.

COLETTE
French novelist
'The South of France'
As for the authentic villain, the real thing, the absolute, the artist, one rarely meets him even once in a lifetime. The ordinary bad hat is always in part a decent fellow.

WALTER CRONKITE
American TV newscaster
Playboy 1973
Most people are good. There aren't very many really evil people. But there are an awful lot of selfish ones.

BRENDAN FRANCIS
One man's despicable evil is another man's delightful good.

WHITNEY GRISWOLD
American academic
quoted in New York Times 1963
Things have got to be wrong in order that they may be deplored.

MARTIN LUTHER KING JR.
American activist
'Strive Towards Freedom' 1958
He who passively accepts evil is as much involved in it as he who helps to perpetrate it. He who accepts evil without protesting against it is really co-operating with it.

MIGNON McLAUGHLIN
American writer
'The Neurotic's Notebook'
Many are saved from sin by being so inept at it.

PHYLLIS McGINLEY
American essayist
'The Province of the Heart' 1959
People are no longer sinful, they are only immature or underprivileged or frightened, or more particularly, sick.

VLADIMIR NABOKOV
Russian writer
'Commentary on Pale Fire' 1962
Solitude is the playfield of Satan.

J. ROBERT OPPENHEIMER
American physicist 1947
In some sort of crude sense, which no vulgarity, no humour, no overstatement can extinguish, the physicists have known sin, and this is a knowledge which they cannot lose.

MARTIN SCORSESE
American film director
'Mean Streets' 1973
You don't make up for your sins in church. You do it at home and you do it in the streets. And the rest is bullshit and you know that.

BARONESS STOCKS
British politician
We don't call it sin today – we call it self-expression.

SIMONE WEIL
French philosopher
in 'The Faber Book of Aphorisms' 1964
A hurtful act is the transference to others of the degradation which we bear in ourselves.

ANGUS WILSON
British writer
Sunday Times 1961
All the seven deadly sins are self-destroying, morbid appetites, but in their early stages at least, lust and gluttony, avarice and sloth know some gratification, while anger and pride have power, even though that power eventually destroys itself. Envy is impotent, numbed with fear, never ceasing in its appetite, and it knows no gratification, but endless self torment. It has the ugliness of a trapped rat, which gnaws its own foot in an effort to escape.

Hatred

JAMES BALDWIN
American author
'Notes of a Native Son' 1958
I imagine one of the reasons people cling to their hates so stubbornly is because they sense, once hate is gone, that they will be forced to deal with pain.

PETER BEARD
American photographer
Interview 1978
You know what they say: the sweetest word in the English language is revenge.

BERNARD BERENSON
British art historian 1957
'The Passionate Sightseer'
Life has taught me that it is not for our faults that we are disliked and even hated, but for our qualities.

DR. CHARLES BERG
American analyst
'Deep Analysis'
Love preserves life and health; discipline or training which is often merely rationalised hate, if it does not destroy them, commonly distorts their shape to fit the mould of an already mis-shapen culture.

MARK BOYLE
British artist
'Contemporary artists' 1977
The only enemy is yourself and maybe it doesn't matter too much whether you lose or win.

JACOB BRONOWSKI
British scientist
'The Face of Violence' 1954
Violence is the Sphinx by the Fireside, and she has a human face.

The wish to hurt, the momentary intoxication with pain, is the loophole through which the pervert climbs into the minds of ordinary men.

SAM BROWN
Washington Post 1977
Never offend people with style when you can offend them with substance.

CHESTER 'HOWLIN' WOLF' BURNETT
American musician
One time you let people know how much sense you got, right away they quit having anything to do with you.

TRUMAN CAPOTE
American writer
'Handcarved Coffins' 1979
Great fury, like great whiskey, requires long fermentation.

ELDRIDGE CLEAVER
American radical
'Soul on Ice' 1968
The price of hating other human beings is loving oneself less.

QUENTIN CRISP
British writer
'How To Become A Virgin' 1981
Malice is in no way redeemed by being true.

BOB ELLIS
Australian playwright 1977
An enemy is someone you haven't seen for a while.

NORA EPHRON
American journalist
Esquire 1970
How can you be angry at someone who's got your number?

H. J. EYSENCK
British sociologist
New Society 1968
What sex was to the Victorians, aggression is to us. We deplore it, sermonise over it, criticise it publicly and practise it privately. We are in favour of peace and go to war at the drop of a hat. We admonish our children when they are too aggressive, and more so when they turn the other cheek. And we certainly talk about it and write books about it.

E. M. FORSTER
British novelist
Most quarrels are inevitable at the time; incredible afterwards.

GENE FOWLER
American writer
'Skyline' 1961
Men are not against you; they are merely for themselves.

BRENDAN FRANCIS
Many a man has decided to stay alive not because of the will to live, but because of the determination not to give assorted surviving bastards the satisfaction of his death.

ATHOL FUGARD
South African playwright
The Observer 1971
We compound our suffering by victimising each other.

JEAN GENET
French writer
epigraph to 'The Blacks' 1960
What we need is hatred – from it are our ideas born.

PAUL GOODMAN
American writer
New York Review of Books 1971
Stupidity is a character defense of turned in hostility.

SACHA GUITRY
French writer
'Jusqu'à nouvel ordre'
Vanity is other people's pride.

DR. NATHAN HARE
American academic 1969
The Bible says there is a time for everything. I think this is a time for hate.

LAURENCE HARVEY
Lithuanian actor
Esquire 1968
The easiest thing in the world is malice.

ERIC HOFFER
American philosopher
'The Passionate State of Mind' 1954
Rudeness is the weak man's imitation of strength.

in 'The Faber Book of Aphorisms' 1964
You can discover what your enemy fears most by observing the means he uses to frighten you.

ALDOUS HUXLEY
British writer
'Beyond the Mexique Bay'
All enemies, except those fighting for the strictly limited food supply of a given territory, may be described as artificial enemies.

THOMAS JONES
in Wall Street Journal 1975
Friends may come and go, but enemies accumulate.

YOUSSUF KARSH
Armenian photographer
The Image 1973
Hate has no room in people who are universal in thinking.

NIKITA KHRUSCHEV
Russian leader
In a fight you don't stop to choose your cudgels.

KARL KRAUS
German artist
'Karl Kraus' by Harry Zohn
Hate must make a man productive. Otherwise one might as well love.

HAROLD MACMILLAN
British politician
quoted in The Observer 1981
There are three bodies no sensible man directly challenges: the Roman Catholic church, the Brigade of Guards and the National Union of Mineworkers.

MAURICE MERLEAU-PONTY
French philosopher
The Spectator 1964
Every opponent is a traitor, but every traitor is only an opponent.

ARTHUR MILLER
American playwright
'Incident at Vichy' 1964
Leduc: Part of knowing who we are is knowing we are not someone else. And Jew is only the name we give to that

stranger, the agony we cannot feel, the death we look at like a cold abstraction. Each man has his Jew; it is the other.

CESARE PAVESE
Italian novelist
in 'The Faber Book of Aphorisms' 1964
Hate is always a clash between our spirit and someone else's body.

SIR KARL POPPER
British philosopher
To attack a man for talking nonsense is like finding your mortal enemy drowning in a swamp and jumping in after him with a knife.

LINDA RONSTADT
American rock singer
on the pressures of public life
People look like enemies all the time, because you never know what someone's going to do.

GEORGE C. SCOTT
American film star
Esquire 1965
Never hurt a man whom you respect, nor a woman whom you do not deeply love.

H. ALLEN SMITH
American journalist 1968
living in Alpine, Texas. . .
About three other people in this town read books, and I'm the only one that writes them. Frankly these salt of the earth types make my ass want to suck a lemon.

ION TIRIAC
Rumanian tennis star 1972
Is old Rumanian proverb – 'Better your mother to weep than my mother to weep'.

VO DONG GIANG
Vietnamese politician
Time 1978
Do not fear when your enemies criticise you. Beware when they applaud.

Happiness

MICHELANGELO ANTONIONI
Italian film director
Playboy 1967
Happiness is like the bluebird of Mae-
terlinck: try to catch it and it loses its
colour. It's like trying to hold water in
your hands. The more you squeeze it the
more it runs away.

MICHAEL ARLEN
British author 1956
Any man should be happy who is
allowed the patience of his wife, the tolerance of his children and the affection
of waiters.

RUSSELL BAKER
American writer
'The Sayings of Poor Russell' Harpers 1972
In April, if the glands work properly, it
is possible to see the world as it might
be if only it were not the world.

New York Times 1967
People seem to enjoy things more when
they know a lot of other people have
been left out on the pleasure.

RUTH BENEDICT
American anthropologist
*quoted in 'An Anthropologist at Work' by M.
Mead 1951*
The trouble is not that we are never
happy – it is that happiness is so
episodical.

INGRID BERGMAN
Swedish film actress
Happiness is good health and a bad
memory.

DR. L. BINDER
in 'Quote and Unquote' 1970
Confidence is simply that quiet assured
feeling you have before you fall flat on
your face.

ELIAS CANETTI
Bulgarian writer 1951
How happy one would be in a world in
which one did not exist.

DALE CARNEGIE
American self-help evangelist
Act as if you were already happy and
that will tend to make you happy.

LOUIS-FERDINAND CELINE
French writer
'Bagatelles pour un Massacre'
The more one is hated, I find, the hap-
pier one is.

CYRIL CONNOLLY
British critic
'The Unquiet Grave' 1945
We must select the illusion which
appeals to our temperament and embrace it with passion, if we want to be
happy.

JILLY COOPER
British writer
*in 'In and Out: Debrett 1980/81' by Neil
Mackwood, 1980*
Life is happier if it is full of pretty people.

WILLIAM FEATHER
American businessman
'The Business of Life' 1949
One of the indictments of civilisation is
that happiness and intelligence are so
rarely found in the same person.

CHARLES DE GAULLE
French statesman
On the whole, women think of love and
men of gold braid or something of that
nature. Beyond that people think only of
happiness – which doesn't exist.

LILLIAN GISH
American film star
Esquire 1969
A happy life is one spent in learning,
earning and yearning.

JOYCE GRENFELL
British comedienne
The Observer 1976
There is no such thing as the pursuit of
happiness, but there is the discovery of
joy.

ELIZABETH JANE HOWARD
British writer
The Listener 1978
The capacity for pleasure is an art; and
relatively few people are good at it over
a wide range.

IRVING KRISTOL
American academic 1979
Even if we can't be happy, we must
always be cheerful.

JOHN LENNON &
PAUL McCARTNEY
British rock composers
Song Title
Happiness Is A Warm Gun.

ARNOLD LOBEL
American writer
'Fables' 1980
Satisfaction will come to those who
please themselves.

All the miles of a hard road are worth a
moment of true happiness.

LORD MANCROFT
British politician
The Observer 1966
Happy is the man with a wife to tell him
what to do and a secretary to do it.

JOHNNY MILLER
American golf star 1975
Serenity is knowing that your worst shot
is still going to be pretty good.

GEORGE ORWELL
British essayist
'Critical Essays' 1945
Men can only be happy when they do
not assume that the object of life is
happiness.

CESARE PAVESE
Italian novelist
in 'The Faber Book of Aphorisms' 1964
The only joy in the world is to begin.

CHANNING POLLOCK
Happiness is a way station between too
little and too much.

MAN RAY
French photographer
The Guardian 1969
Pleasure and the pursuit of freedom are
the guiding motives of all human
activity.

BERTRAND RUSSELL
British philosopher
New York Times 1961
If there were in the world today any
large number of people who desired their
own happiness more than they desired
the unhappiness of others, we could have
a paradise in a few years.

WILLIAM SAROYAN
American writer 1957
The greatest happiness you can have is
knowing that you do not necessarily require happiness.

RABBI HYMAN SCHACHTEL
American clergyman
'The Real Enjoyment of Living' 1954
Happiness is not having what you want,
but wanting what you have.

JAMES STEWART
American film star
The secret of a happy life is to accept
change gracefully.

LUDWIG WITTGENSTEIN
German philosopher
The world of those who are happy is
different from the world of those who are
not.

P. G. WODEHOUSE
British humorist aged 90 1971
I can detach myself from the world. If
there is a better world to detach oneself
from than the one functioning at the
moment I have yet to hear of it.

MARGUERITE YOURCENAR
French writer
'Alexis'
All happiness is innocence.

FRANK ZAPPA
American rock musician
New Musical Express 1972
Everyone has the right to be comfortable
on his own terms.

ADVERTISEMENTS

CHARLES ATLAS
(Angelo Siciliano)
American bodybuilder
advertisement for his body-building programme
You Too Can Have A Body Like Mine.

CAMAY SOAP
advertisement
You'll be a little lovelier each day, with fabulous pink Camay.

JOHN CAPLES
copywriter for Ruthruaff & Ryan
written in 1925 but used since. . .
They Laughed When I Sat Down at the Piano, But When I Started to Play. . .

COURAGE BEER
advertisement
It's what your right arm's for.

EDOUARD L. COURNAND
president of Lanvin Perfumes 1946
slogan for 'Arpège'
Promise her anything – but give her Arpège.

CUNARD STEAMSHIP LINE
slogan 1950s
Getting there is half the fun.

DE BEER CONSOLIDATED MINES
slogan 1950
A Diamond Is Forever.

JERRY DELLA FEMINA
American advertising executive
copy for 'Pretty Feet' deodorant 1969
What's the ugliest part of your body.

DOUBLE DIAMOND
advertisement
I'm only here for the beer.

DOYLE DANE & BERNBACH
American advertising agency
Avis: We Try Harder.

'EVE' CIGARETTES
advertisement 1971
The first truly feminine cigarette – almost as pretty as you are. Women have been feminine since Eve, now cigarettes are feminine. Eve, also with menthol.

TERRY LOVELOCK
British copywriter
at Collet,
Dickenson, Pearce & Partners
Heineken refreshes the parts other beers cannot reach.

HOOVER VACUUM CLEANERS
slogan
It beats as it sweeps as it cleans.

GEORGE LOIS
American art director
ad. for Cutty Sark whisky 1973 (based on their logo)
Don't give up the ship.

ad copy for Braniff Airways
When you've got it, flaunt it.

LONDON PRESS EXCHANGE
British advertising agency
Top People Read The Times.

MACKESON
beer advertisement
It looks good, it tastes good, and by golly it does you good.

JOHN MAY
British copywriter
copy for Wills
You're never alone with a Strand.

PHILIP MORRIS CIGARETTES
advertisement 1940s
Call for Philip Morris!!

'MOTOR MAGAZINE'
review copy, used by Ogilvy, Benson & Mather, American advertising agency, to advertise the Rolls Royce 1960s

At sixty miles per hour the loudest noise in this new Rolls Royce comes from the electric clock.

MUZAK CORPORATION
slogan
Music is art. Muzak the science.

NATIONAL AIRLINES
advertisements 1970s
I'm — Fly Me.

NORMAN, CRAIG & KUMMEL
American advertising agency
slogan
I dreamt I was Cleopatra in my Maidenform Bra.

OGILVY BENSON & MATHER
American advertising agency
Go To Work On An Egg.

Drinka Pinta Milka Day.

Unzipp A Banana.

PEPSODENT TOOTHPASTE
advertisement
You'll wonder where the yellow went / When you brush your teeth with Pepsodent.

QUAKER PUFFED WHEAT
advertisement
The cereal that's shot from guns!

ROSSER REEVES
American advertising executive
copy for Colgate Toothpaste c.1945
It cleans your breath while it cleans your teeth.

JERRY ROSENBERG
Discount appliance operator
Queens N.Y. TV ad campaign 1972
So what's the story, Jerry?

SANDERSON FABRICS AND WALLPAPERS
advertisement 1970s
Very — Very Sanderson.

SCHLITZ BEER
advertisement
Schlitz . . . the beer that made Milwaukee famous.

SCHWEPPES TONIC WATER
advertisement
Sccchhh . . . you know who.

SMARTIES
advertisement
WotalotIgot!

SMIRNOFF VODKA
advertisement 1970s
I was a — until I discovered Smirnoff.

STORK MARGARINE
advertisement
Can you tell Stork from butter?

BILL TAUBIN
American copywriter
for Doyle Dane & Bernbach 1959
You don't have to be Jewish to love Levy's Rye Bread.

VIRGINIA SLIMS CIGARETTES
advertisement by Leo Burnett agency
You've come a long way, Baby.

RUTH WATSON
British copywriter
at Young & Rubicam advertising agency
slogan for Heinz
Beanz Meanz Heinz.

WONDERLOAF BREAD
advertisement
Nice one, Cyril! (Latterly adopted as a soccer chant by Tottenham Hotspur fans.)

ARTS

Creativity

W. H. AUDEN
British poet
The Observer 1968
The artist is not a man of action but a maker, a fabricator of objects; to believe in the value of art is to believe that it is possible to make an object.

HORIA BERNEA
Rumanian artist
'Contemporary Artists' 1977
The artist must understand that he does not create – he materialises.

DAVID BOWIE
British rock star
I would rather retain the position of being a photo-stat machine with an image, because I think most songwriters are anyway.

The act of creating is as integral a part of life as going to the lavatory.

GERALD BRENAN
British writer
'Thoughts in a Dry Season' 1978
Imagination means letting the birds in one's head out of their cages and watching them fly up in the air.

To a writer or painter creation is the repayment of a debt. He suffers from a perpetual bad conscience until he has done this.

ERIC BURDON
British rock star
You've got to create a dream. You've got to uphold the dream. If you can't, then bugger it. Go back to the factory or go back to the desk.

JEAN COCTEAU
French writer and film director
'Writers at Work' 3rd series 1967
The work of every creator is autobiography, even if he does not know it or wish it, even if his work is 'abstract'. It is why you cannot re-do your work.

quoted in New York Review of Books 1971
Inspiration is merely expiration.

CYRIL CONNOLLY
British critic
'Previous Convictions' 1963
Art is the conscious apprehension of the unconscious ecstasy of all created things.

LOUIS DANZ
'Dynamic Dissonance'
There is nothing mysterious about originality. Nothing fantastic. Originality is merely the step beyond.

WALTER EGAN
American rock musician
A creative person needs a certain amount of insecurity to maintain that fine edge. You don't have any control over it.

MAX ERNST
German artist
quoted in The Guardian 1961
An artist is not creative. He is no more than a spectator, a witness of the creation of a picture.

MARIANNE FAITHFUL
British rock singer and actress
We're all fucked up. We've got to accept that. But it doesn't stop you operating. It doesn't stop you being creative. You can still do it.

ERNST FISCHER
German critic
'The Necessity of Art' 1963
The permanent function of art is to re-create as every individual's experience the fullness of all that he is not, the fullness of humanity at large.

BERNICE FITZGIBBON
American businesswoman
'Macy's, Gimbels and Me' 1967
Creativity varies inversely with the number of cooks involved in the broth.

PROF. CHARLES FRANKEL
American academic
Anxiety is the essential condition of intellectual and artistic creation . . . and everything that is finest in human history.

PAUL GOODMAN
American writer
'Growing Up Absurd' 1960
All men are creative, but few are artists.

CLEMENT GREENBERG
American art critic
All profoundly original work looks ugly at first.

PAULINE KAEL
American critic
'Kiss Kiss Bang Bang' 1968
Being creative is having something to sell, or knowing how to sell something, or having sold something. It has been taken over by what we used to mean by being 'wised up', knowing the tricks, the shortcuts.

ROBERT F. KENNEDY
American politician
quoted in Esquire 1969
Some men see things as they are and say why? I dream things that never were and say 'Why not?'

MARTIN LUTHER KING JR.
American activist
'Strength to Love' 1963
Human salvation lies in the hands of the creatively maladjusted.

ARTHUR KOESTLER
British philosopher
'Drinkers of Infinity' 1967
Creative activity could be described as a type of learning process where teacher and pupil are located in the same individual.

GEORGE LOIS
American art director
'The Art of Advertising' 1977
Creativity can solve almost any problem. The creative act, the defeat of habit by originality, overcomes everything.

HENRY MILLER
American writer
'Sexus' 1949
The great joy of the artist is to become aware of a higher order of things, to recognize by the compulsive and spontaneous manipulation of his own impulses the resemblance between human creation and what is called 'divine' creation.

JONATHAN MILLER
British doctor and writer
The Listener 1978
There is a particular sort of shrieking hatred which the non-creative have for the half-creative, and, equally, an exorbitant admiration that the non-creative have for the very fully-fledged creative. So, therefore, what you get from critics is the exorbitant admiration of the great, and the shrieking hatred of those who interpret the fully great.

Music & Musicians 1974
Art has nothing to do with the originator once it has left the originator's hands. The performing arts have been dogged by a sort of pedantic romanticism about the obligation we owe to the author or originator of a work. We owe him nothing at all.

LAURENCE J. PETER
Canadian educator
'Peter's Quotations' 1977
Originality is the fine art of remembering what you hear but forgetting where you heard it.

PABLO PICASSO
Spanish artist
quoted in Esquire 1968
You do something *first* and then somebody comes along and does it *pretty.*

WILLIAM PLOMER
British writer
It is the function of creative men to perceive the relations between thoughts, or things, or forms of expression that may seem utterly different, and to be able to combine them into some new forms – the power to connect the seemingly unconnected.

NORMAN PODHORETZ
American critic
Playboy 1968
Creativity represents a miraculous coming together of the uninhibited energy of the child with its apparent opposite and enemy, the sense of order imposed on . . . the disciplined adult intelligence.

COLE PORTER
American songwriter 1955
All the inspiration I ever needed was a phonecall from a producer.

MAN RAY
French photographer
'Self Portrait' 1963
A creator needs only one enthusiast to justify him.

JEAN RENOIR
French film director
Reality may be very interesting, but a work of art must be a creation.

PIERRE REVERDY
French writer
'Le livre de mon bord'
To create is to think more efficiently.

quoted in 'Surrealism & Painting' by André Breton 1972
Creation is a movement of the internal towards the external and not a movement of the external on the surface.

MIES VAN DER ROHE
American architect
The long path from material through function to creative work has only one goal – to create order out of the desperate confusion of our time.

GEORGE BERNARD SHAW
Irish writer and playwright
quoted in Daily Mail 1968
Art is kept alive not by the established trade in it, but by the desperate efforts of art-hungry individuals to create and recreate it out of nothing for its own sake.

VIKTOR SHKLOVSKY
quoted in 'On Photography' by Susan Sontag 1977
New forms in art are created by the canonisation of peripheral forms.

DMITRI SHOSTAKOVICH
Russian composer
New York Times 1959
A creative artist works on his next composition because he is not satisfied with his previous one. When he loses a critical attitude towards his own work he ceases to be an artist.

ISAAC BASHEVIS SINGER
American writer
Esquire 1974
Every creator painfully experiences the chasm between his inner vision and its ultimate expression. The chasm is never completely bridged. We all have the conviction, perhaps illusory, that we have much more to say than appears on the paper.

W. EUGENE SMITH
American photographer
Popular Photography 1958
Passion is in all great searches and is necessary to all creative endeavours.

SAUL STEINBERG
American artist
Time 1978
The life of the creative man is led, directed and controlled by boredom. Avoiding boredom is one of our most important purposes. It is also one of the most difficult . . . in the end working is good because it is the last refuge of the man who wants to be amused.

FELIX TOPOLSKI
Polish artist
at the OZ Trial, 1971
One should accept that any visual performance, if executed in earnest, is a branch of artistic creation. The assessment as to whether it is good or bad is changeable.

JOHN UPDIKE
American writer
Playboy 1968
Creativity is merely a plus name for regular activity . . . any activity becomes creative when the doer cares about doing it right, or better.

SIMONE WEIL
French philosopher
in 'The Faber Book of Aphorisms' 1964
The distance between the necessary and the good is the distance between the creature and the creator.

'Gravity & Grace' 1972
We participate in the creation of the world by de-creating ourselves.

EDWARD WESTON
American photographer
in 'Photographers on Photography' ed. N. Lyons 1966
The difference between good and bad art lies in the minds that created, rather than in the skill of hands.

ALFRED NORTH WHITEHEAD
British philosopher
in 'The Faber Book of Aphorisms' 1964
The 'silly' question is the first intimation of some totally new development.

TENNESSEE WILLIAMS
American playwright 1972
I learned that the heart of man, his body and his brain, are forged in a white-hot furnace for the purpose of conflict. That struggle for me is creation. I cannot live without it. Luxury is the wolf at the door and its fangs are the conceits and vanities germinated by success. When an artist knows this he knows where the dangers lie. Without deprivation and struggle there is no salvation, and I am just a sword cutting daisies.

The Arts

HAROLD ACTON
British man of letters
The Times 1970
The arts – to be undressed they must first be dressed.

ANSEL ADAMS
American photographer
PSA Journal 1948
Photography is but one phase of the potential of human expression; all art is the expression of one and the same thing – the relation of the spirit of man to the spirit of other men and to the world.

ROY ADZAK
British sculptor
'Contemporary Artists' 1977
Good art is not what it looks like, but what it does to us.

ALBERTI
Italian architect
quoted in 'Contemporary Architects' 1980
Arts were begot by chance and observation, nursed by use and experience, and improved and perfected by reason and study.

BRIAN ALDISS
British author
The Guardian 1971
All art is a fight against decay.

Art is one of the few things, apart from love and friendship, to be worth caring about. No matter how it is generally neglected and debased, it is a way of securing some sense of continuity in the uneven and perilous business of human life.

WOODY ALLEN
American film star
Esquire 1977
Art is the artist's false Catholicism, the fake promise of an afterlife and just as fake as heaven and hell.

AL ALVAREZ
British writer
The Listener 1971
The arts survive because artists continue to believe in the possibility of art in the teeth of everything that is anti-art.

ALAIN ARIAS-MISSON
Belgian-American painter
'Contemporary Artists' 1977
The purpose of art is not a rarified, intellectual distillate – it is *life*, intensified, brilliant life.

MARY ASTOR
American film star
You can't *make* anything *be* Art – and the minute you try it eludes you. And if you behave like an artist, you'll never be one.

BERNARD AUBERT
French artist
'Comtemporary Artists' 1977
The truth is that is incumbent upon the artist, aware of the always dehumanised state of society, to base art first of all on man.

W. H. AUDEN
British poet
Esquire 1970
In the end art is small beer. The really serious things in life are earning one's living so as not to be a parasite and loving one's neighbour.

I don't believe that art is self-expression. It is only interesting to yourself, keep it to yourself.

'Secondary Worlds' 1969
Art is impotent. The utmost an artist can hope to do for his contemporary readers is, as Dr. Johnson said, to enable them a little better to enjoy life or a little better to endure it.

AY-O (Takao Iijima)
Japanese artist
'Contemporary Artists' 1977
The Art needs the Sense of Humour.

JAMES BALDWIN
American author
New York Herald Tribune 1970
Life is more important than art, that's what makes art important.

ALFRED BARR JR.
American art critic
in Newsweek 1964
Art is not a means by which we escape from life, but a stratagem by which we conquer life's disorder.

JACQUES BARZUN
American academic
quoted in 'Murder Ink' 1977 ed. Dilys Winn
A tale charms by its ingenuity, by the plausibility with which it overcomes the suspicion that it couldn't happen. That is art.

'The House of Intellect' 1959
Art distills sensation and embodies it with enhanced meaning in memorable form – or else it is not art.

SIMONE DE BEAUVOIR
French writer
'The Mandarins'
Art is an attempt to integrate evil.

SAMUEL BECKETT
Irish author
'Marcel Proust'
Art is the apotheosis of solitude.

SAUL BELLOW
American writer
'Writers at Work' 3rd series 1967
I feel that art has something to do with the achievement of stillness in the midst of chaos. A stillness which characterises prayer, too, and the eye of the storm. I think that art has something to do with an arrest of attention in the midst of distraction.

E. C. BENTLEY
American writer
'The Life of the Drama' 1965
All art is a challenge to despair.

JOHN BERGER
British art critic
The Guardian 1971
Art has a significance only insofar as it offers an alternative to what is, an alternative which expresses the potential freedom of man in all his experiences.

'Permanent Red' 1960
We can only make sense of art if we judge it by the criterion of whether or not it helps men to claim their social rights.

LOUISE BOGAN
American poet
College English 1953
True revolutions in art restore more than they destroy.

JORGE LUIS BORGES
Argentine writer
'Conversations with Jorge Luis Borges' ed.
Richard Burgin 1973
If art is perfect, then the world is
superfluous.

GEORGES BRAQUE
French artist
'Artists on Art' 1947
In art progress does not consist in exten-
sion but in the knowledge of limits.

BERTOLT BRECHT
German playwright
All arts contribute to the greatest art of
all: *Lebenskunst* – the art of getting
through life.

CHARLES BUKOWSKI
American writer
'Notes of a Dirty Old Man' 1969
The difference between Art and Life is
that Art is more bearable.

ANTHONY BURGESS
British writer
Playboy 1974
Art never initiates. It merely takes over
what is already present in the real world
and makes an aesthetic pattern out of it,
or tries to explain it, or tries to relate it
to some other aspect of life.

'1985' 1978
Art is a vision of heaven gratuitously
given.

DON BURGY
American artist
'Contemporary Artists' 1977
Art is an open ended concept evolving
in the direction of increasing information
and away from existing information
which has been eroded by familiarity or
uselessness.

EDWARD BURRA
British artist
The Observer 1971
What a fuss art is sometimes, dearie.

WILLIAM S. BURROUGHS
American writer
*on Bryon Gysin in 'Contemporary Artists'
1977*
All art is magical in origin – music sculpture writing painting – and by magical

I mean intended to produce very definite
results. Paintings were originally formula to make what is painted happen.

ALBERT CAMUS
French writer
'Resistance, Rebellion & Death' 1960
Without freedom, no art; art lives only
on the restraint it imposes on itself, and
dies of all others.

AL CAPP
American cartoonist
Abstract art? A product of the untalented, sold by the unprincipled to the
utterly bewildered.

EUGENIO CARMI
Italian artist
'Contemporary Artists' 1977
Art is a self-respecting search for the
unknown.

LORD DAVID CECIL
British writer
quoted in 'Contemporary Literary Critics' 1977
ed. Elmer Borklund
Art is not like mathematics or philosophy. It is a subjective, sensual, highly
personal activity in which facts are the
servants of fancy and feeling, and the
artist's aim is not truth but delight.

RAYMOND CHANDLER
American novelist
'The Simple Art of Murder' 1950
In everything that can be called art there
is a quality of redemption. It may be
pure tragedy, if it is high tragedy, and
it may be pity and irony, and it may be
the raucous laughter of the strong man.
But down these mean streets a man must
go who is not himself mean, who is
neither tarnished nor afraid. The detective in this kind of story must be such a
man.

MALCOLM DE CHAZAL
French writer
'Sens Plastique' 1949
Art is nature speeded up and God
slowed down.

GIROGIO DE CHIRICO
French artist
'Artists on Art' 1947
To become truly immortal a work of art
must escape all human limits: logic and

common sense will only interfere. But once these barriers are broken, it will enter the regions of childhood vision and dream.

SIR WINSTON CHURCHILL
British statesman
Time 1953
Without tradition art is a flock of sheep without a shepherd. Without innovation it is a corpse.

JOHN CIARDI
American critic
Saturday Review
Modern art is what happens when painters stop looking at girls and persuade themselves that they have had a better idea.

JEAN COCTEAU
French writer and film director
Newsweek 1955
An artist cannot speak about his art any more than a plant can discuss horticulture.

'Writers at Work' 3rd series 1968
Art is a marriage of the conscious and the unconscious.

SUE COE
British illustrator
The Image 1973
Art must interfere with the normal commercial process. It must use the entertainment as a service for critical thought. That is the only hope. Art must aim at a radical change in modes of perception.

LOUIS DANZ
'Dynamic Dissonance'
There is a great saying that Art is all that cannot be suppressed.

'THE DARK CORNER'
20th Century Fox 1946 screenplay by Jay Dratler & Bernard C. Schoenfeld, based on story by Leo Rosten.
Clifton Webb: The enjoyment of art is the only remaining ecstasy that is neither immoral nor illegal.

DOUGLAS DAVIES
Newsweek 1975
Art stands alone and convinces society later.

JEAN DUBUFFET
French artist
Art is the most frenzied orgy a man is capable of.

'Prospectus et tous écrits suivants'
Art is a department of aberrations.

MARCEL DUCHAMP
French artist
'Wisdom' ed. James Nelson
Art is the only form of activity in which man, as man, shows himself to be a true individual who is capable of going beyond the animal state. Art is an outlet toward regions which are not ruled by time and space.

BOB DYLAN
American singer
'She Belongs To Me'
She's got everything she needs / She's an artist, she don't look back.
(M. Witmark & Sons)

Art is the perpetual motion of illusion. The highest purpose of art is to inspire. What else can you do? What else can you do for anyone but inspire them?

PIETER ENGELS
Dutch artist
'Contemporary Artists' 1977
Art is not the intellect / Art is not the emotion / Art is not something in between / Art is the outmost upper class in myself / Art is the god in my devil.

WILLIAM FAULKNER
American novelist
Art is simpler than people think because there is so little to write about. All the moving things are eternal in man's history and have been written before, and if a man writes hard enough, sincerely enough, humbly enough, and with the unalterable determination never, never to be quite satisfied with it he will repeat them because art, like poverty, takes care of its own, shares its bread.

DINO FORMAGGIO
Italian artist
quoted in 'Contemporary Artists' 1977
Art is everything that men call art.

E. M. FORSTER
British novelist
'Two Cheers for Democracy' 1951
To make us feel small in the right way
is a function of art. Men can only make
us feel small in the wrong way.

ANDRE FRANCOIS
Rumanian artist
'Contemporary Artists' 1977
Art today is a therapy or exorcism for
the artist himself. It can eventually be-
come a therapy for the public.

WOLFGANG GAFGEN
German artist
'Contemporary Artists' 1977
Art is always ultimately about reality.
Or at all events the interpretation of
what can be regarded as real.

JEAN-LUC GODARD
French film director
'La Chinoise' 1967
Art is not the reflection of reality, it is
the reality of that reflection.

Esquire 1969
We have made art into a box: this is art,
this is not. We should throw it all out.
Maybe save one example.

GUNTER GRASS
German novelist
Art is uncompromising, and life is full of
compromises.

GEORGE GROSZ
German artist
'A Little Yes & A Big No' 1946
The best thing for art is for it to be
treated as a hobby, an incidental thing.
For, after all, what do we artists, we
insignificant little ants, have to say. We,
who are nothing more than blown up
frogs? Where is our influence? Where,
our significance? Do we change the general picture in the slightest?

BEN HECHT
American screenwriter
The rule in the art world is: you cater to
the masses or you kowtow to the elite;
you can't have both.

ERNEST HELLO
American academic
'Life, Science & Art'
Art, to a certain extent and at a given
moment is a force which blows the roof
off the cave where we crouch
imprisoned.

SIR LESLIE HERRON
Australian lawyer 1966
Modern art is a cliché of the enemies of
religion and not even the sanctity of marriage is safe from the so-called
intellectuals.

ALFRED HITCHCOCK
British film director
The great art is contrivance.

DAVID HOCKNEY
British artist
'David Hockney' 1976
The truth is, the art of the past is living;
the art of the past that has died is not
around.

PETER HUTCHINSON
British artist
'Contemporary Artists' 1977
The role of an artist (is) essentially an
exploration of the self which becomes
translated into an exploration of the
world. As in most serious explorations,
there are attendant dangers and risks to
be taken. Sometimes the risks involve
the artists very existence. The risk-tak-
ing becomes addictive.

ALDOUS HUXLEY
British writer
'Essays New & Old'
The truth is that sincerity in art is not
an affair of will, of a moral choice between honesty and dishonesty. It is
mainly an affair of talent.

LINTON KWESI JOHNSON
British poet
Art in capitalist society is only available
in commodity form.

PHILIP JOHNSON
American architect
in The Observer 1964
You can't talk about art. You should do
it.

HUGH KENNER
Canadian writer
'The Stoic Comedians'
Art is the apotheosis of solitude.

PAUL KLEE
Swiss artist
'The Inward Vision' 1959
Art does not reproduce the visible, rather, it makes visible.

SEYMOUR KRIM
American writer
'Shake It For The World' 1970
Isn't that what makes artforms change – when life leaves them in the lurch?

SUSANNE K. LANGER
American educator
'Mind: An Essay On Human Feeling' 1967
Art is the objectification of feeling.

JEAN MARIE LE CLEZIO
French writer
'L'extase matérielle'
Art is without doubt the only form of progress that uses equally well the paths of truth and lies.

W. R. LETHABY
British writer
'Form in Civilisation'
Art is thoughtful workmanship.

ROY LICHTENSTEIN
American artist
Art News 1963
Art doesn't transform. It just plain forms.

HENRY LIVINGS
British playwright
in 'Contemporary Dramatists' 1977
The materials of art, observation, ritual, symbol, gesture, community, give us a chance to focus for a moment, and then go forward with fresh hope that we matter and that what we do signifies.

FRANK LLOYD
American art dealer
quoted in 'The Legacy of Mark Rothko' by Lee Seldes, 1978
If it sells, it's art.

DESMOND McCARTHY
British critic
'Theatre'
The whole of art is an appeal to a reality which is not without us, but in our minds.

MARSHALL McLUHAN
Canadian academic
'Understanding Media' 1964
I think of art, at its most significant, as ... a distant early warning system that can always be relied on to tell the old culture what is beginning to happen to it.

RENE MAGRITTE
Belgian artist
in 'Magritte' 1974
Art ... evokes the mystery without which the world would not exist.

quoted in 'Magritte: The True Art of Painting' ed. H. Torczyner 1979
There is no choice: no art without life.

Whether art is made for this or that reason makes very little difference: what counts is what it will be.

NORMAN MAILER
American writer
The Observer 1973
The final purpose of art is to intensify, even if necessary to exacerbate the moral consciousness of people.

ANDRE MALRAUX
French writer
All art is a revolt against man's fate.

'L'espoir'
You can only make art that talks to the masses when you have nothing to say to them.

'Les Voix du Silence'
What is art? That through which form becomes style.

HERBERT MARCUSE
German philosopher
quoted in New Society 1969
Art is the great refusal of the world as it is.

HENRI MATISSE
French artist
Picture Post 1949
Art should be something like a good
armchair in which to rest from physical
fatigue.

W. SOMERSET MAUGHAM
British writer
Art for art's sake makes no more sense
than gin for gin's sake.

HENRY MILLER
American writer
'The Wisdom of the Heart'
Art is only a means to life, to the life
more abundant. It merely points the way
. . . in becoming an end, it defeats itself.

JONATHAN MILLER
British doctor and writer
The Times 1973
You cannot make art by putting out
more flags.

JOAN MIRO
Spanish artist 1966
As long as art discovers something and
it is alive, it is all right

HENRY MOORE
British sculptor
The Observer 1968
Art is extra. If one was starving, one
wouldn't do art. A sculptor's art is an
expression of his religion.

ROBERT MOTHERWELL
American artist
Art is much less important than life, but
what a poor life without it.

IRIS MURDOCH
British writer
The Observer 1973
Art . . . is not a diversion or a side issue.
It is the most educational of human
activities, and a place in which the na-
ture of morality can be *seen*.

CLAES OLDENBERG
Danish artist
'Manifesto' 1961
I am for an art that is political-erotical-
mystical, that does something other than
sit on its arse in a museum. I'm for an
art that grows up, not knowing it's art
at all. An art given the chance of having
a starting point of zero. I'm for an art
that embroils itself with the everyday
crap and still comes out on top. An art
that imitates the human, that is comic
if necessary, or violent, whatever is
necessary. I am for art you can sit on,
for art you can pick your nose with or
stub your toes on, I am in favour of art
that is put on and taken off, like pants,
that develops holes, like socks, is eaten
like a piece of pie or abandoned with
great contempt like shit.

Financial Times 1970
Art is a technique of communication.
The image is the most complete tech-
nique of all communication.

JOHN OSBORNE
British playwright
The Observer 1968
The premise of art is that somebody can
do something better than you.

DOROTHY PARKER
American writer
Art is a form of catharsis.

ANN PETRY
American writer
*quoted in 'The Writers' Book' ed. H. Hull
1950*
All truly great art is propaganda.

PABLO PICASSO
Spanish artist
Quote 1958
Art is the lie that makes us realize the
truth.

*in 'Artists on Art' 1947 ed. Robert Goldwater
and Marco Treves*
Through art we express our conception
of what nature is not.

There is no abstract art. You must
always start with something.

EZRA POUND
American poet
'The Pound Era' ed. H. Kenner 1973
Art very possibly *ought* to be the supreme
achievement, the 'accomplished', but
there is the other satisfactory effect – that
of a man hurling himself at an indomi-
table chaos and yanking and hauling as

much of it as possible into some sort of order (or beauty) aware of it both as chaos and as potential.

MAX RAPHAEL
quoted in New Society 1969
All art is the undoing of the world of things.

KENNETH REXROTH
American poet
Art is the reasoned derangement of the senses.

DARRYL RHOADES
American rock musician
on Barry Manilow
To make someone go out and buy a hamburger because they heard your song on the radio, that's art.

LARRY RIVERS
American painter
'Conversations with Artists' ed. Seldon Rodman
Any art communicates what you're in the mood to receive.

KEN RUSSELL
British film director
Esquire 1973
Art is a distillation – a moment amplified, magnified.

FRANCOISE SAGAN
French writer
'Writers at Work' 1st series 1958
Art must take reality by surprise.

ARNOLD SCHOENBERG
German composer
If it is art it is not for all and if it is for all it is not art.

KURT SCHWITTERS
German artist
quoted in The Times 1968
Everything the artist spits is art.

COLIN SELF
British artist
'Contemporary Artists' 1977
Art . . . is a parasite. All the greatest art is firmly attached to and reflective of all the great religious, political, or scientific developments (or misemployment of development). Like the parasite sucker fish beneath the shark, it must travel with the shark in order to exist. Swimming on its own it becomes nothing. Art must continually mirror something outside itself to have standards.

N. F. SIMPSON
British playwright
quoted in The Observer 1962
The difficulty about art now is to give it a shape. Sometimes one feels that one is breaking faith with chaos.

PATTI SMITH
American singer and poet
The thing is, art always wins. Art will survive and I'm going to die – so I'm *not* going to give art all the best moments of my life . . . the energy I have left after my art I save for love.

SUSAN SONTAG
American essayist
'Styles of Radical Will' 1969
Art (and art-making) is a form of consciousness; the materials of art are the variety of forms of consciousness.

The history of the arts is tantamount to the discovery and formulation of a repertory of objects on which to lavish attention.

'Against Interpretation' 1961
Real art has the capacity to make us nervous. By reducing the work of art to its content, and then interpreting *that*, one tames the work of art.

The moral pleasure in art, as well as the moral service that art provides, consists in the intelligent gratification of consciousness.

ALFRED STIEGLITZ
American photographer
quoted in 'Photographers on Photography' ed. N. Lyons 1966
Art is the affirmation of life. .

LEO STEINBERG
American art critic
Modern art always projects itself into a time zone where no values are fixed. It is always born in anxiety.

1958
Whatever else it may be, all great art is about art.

STING (Gordon Sumner)
British rock star 1980
You can't simply set out to 'make art'.
You enjoy yourself first of all. I see my-
self as an entertainer because it's what
I do best. If we should happen to make
art, then it's only as a side product of
entertaining.

KARL-HEINZ STOCKHAUSEN
German composer 1973
All true art is arbitrary.

TOM STOPPARD
British playwright
Sunday Times 1974
There is a secret in Art isn't there? And
the secret consists of what the artist has
secretly and privately done. You will
tumble some, and not others. The whole
process of putting them in, albeit unconsciously gives Art that . . . texture which
sensibility tells one is valuable.

The Guardian 1973
I think art ought to involve itself in contemporary social and political history as
much as anything else but I find it deeply embarrassing when large claims are
made for such an involvement. When
because art takes notice of something important it's then claimed that art is important. It's not. We're talking about
marginalia. The tiny fraction of the
whole edifice. When Auden said his poetry didn't save one Jew from the gas
chamber, he'd said it all. I never felt

this, that art is important. That's been
my secret guilt and I think it is the secret
guilt of most artists.

IGOR STRAVINSKY
Russian composer 1970
Publicity often seems to be about all that
is left of the Arts.

ANDY WARHOL
American artist
'From A to B and Back Again' 1975
I think having land and not ruining it is
the most beautiful art that anybody
could ever want to own.

ALFRED NORTH WHITEHEAD
British philosopher
in 'The Faber Book of Aphorisms' 1964
The canons of art are merely the expression in specialized forms of the requirements for depth of experience.

CHRISTOPHER WILMARTH
British artist
'Comtemporary Artists' 1977
Art is man's attempt to communicate an
understanding of art to man.

GEOFFREY WOLFF
American writer
New Times 1979
The containment of our confusions is
what we call sanity. The resolution of
confusions, the painstaking removal of
the stew's ingredients and the remaking
of a better stew is what we call art.

The Work of Art

AL ALVAREZ
British writer
The Listener 1971
A great work of art is a kind of suicide.

ROLAND BALADI
French artist
'Contemporary Artists' 1977
By a sort of mimesis, all artworks trans-
form those who look at them.

GERALD BRENAN
British writer
'Thoughts in a Dry Season' 1978
Works of art and literature are not an
entertainment or a diversion to amuse
our leisure, but the one serious and enduring achievement of mankind – the
notches on the bank of an irrigation
channel which record the height to
which the water once rose.

LUIS BUNUEL
Spanish film director
Mystery is the essential element in every work of art.

CYRIL CONNOLLY
British critic
'The Unquiet Grave' 1945
The true work of art is one which the seventh wave of genius throws up the beach where the undertow of time cannot drag it back.

J. V. CUNNINGHAM
American critic
quoted in 'Contemporary Literary Critics' 1977 ed. Elmer Borklund
A work of art is the embodiment of an intention. To realize an intention in language is the function of a writer.

PROFESSOR PETER EVANS
British critic
'The Music of Benjamin Britten' 1979
The work of art is judged by the conviction and beauty with which it establishes long term relationships within itself.

NICHOLAS GHIKA
Greek artist
'Contemporary Artists' 1977
Every work of art is a subject metamorphosed into an object.

ANDRE GIDE
French writer
'Journals'
The work of art is an idea that one exaggerates.

in 'The Faber Book of Aphorisms' 1964
There is no work of art that is without short cuts.

There is no prejudice that the work of art does not finally overcome.

CHRISTO JAVACHEFF
American artist 1976
In the eleventh, twelfth centuries, you would not be an artist unless you were a deeply religious person. In the twentieth century this has been negated, but now we are socially aware. Any twentieth century work of art not social and political is no good.

LAJOS KASSAK
Hungarian artist
'Contemporary Artists' 1977
The father of every good work is discontent, and its mother is diligence.

LE CORBUSIER
(Charles Edouard Jeanneret)
French architect
'Contemporary Architects' 1980
I have never in my life explained a work, the work may be liked or disliked, understood or not, what difference does that make to me.

HENRI MATISSE
French artist
New York Times 1948
A work should contain its total meaning within itself and should impress it on the spectator before he even knows the subject.

FRANCOIS MORELLET
French artist
'Contemporary Artists' 1977
Works of art are like picnic areas – where one consumes what one takes there oneself.

VLADIMIR NABOKOV
Russian writer
'Strong Opinions' 1974
A work of art has no importance whatever to society. It is only important to the individual.

PABLO PICASSO
Spanish artist
in 'Artists On Art' 1947 ed. Robert Goldwater and Marco Treves
To me there is no past or future in art. If a work of art cannot live always in the present it must not be considered at all.

JEAN RENOIR
French film director
Masterpieces are made by artisans, not artists.

ALAIN RESNAIS
French film director
New York Herald Tribune 1963
A work of art causes the spectators to meet.

ALAIN ROBBE-GRILLET
French novelist
The Observer 1962
A work of art has no reference to anything outside itself.

LEO STEINBERG
American art critic
If a work of art or a new style disturbs you, then it is probably good work. If you hate it, it is probably great.

TRISTAN TZARA
French artist
Any work of art that can be understood is the work of journalism.

EVELYN WAUGH
British novelist
Letter in the Spectator (on 'Lady Chatterley's Lover') 1960, in 'The Letters of Evelyn Waugh', ed. Mark Amory 1980
A work of art is not a matter of thinking beautiful thoughts or experiencing tender emotions (though those are its raw materials) but of intelligence, skill, taste, proportion, knowledge, discipline and industry; especially discipline.

ORSON WELLES
American film director
Playboy 1967
A work of art is a conscious human effort that has to do with communication. It is that, or it is nothing.

FRANK LLOYD WRIGHT
American architect
'The Future of Architecture' 1953
Space . . . the breath of a work of art.

Music

ARI
British rock star
New Musical Express 1979
Every sound you hear is rhythm. Everything is part of the pattern. Humans are my drugs and rhythm is sex. Fucking is rhythm and so is the earth going round and every footstep and every heartbeat.

The way you go about your music is the way you go about your life.

W. H. AUDEN
British poet
'In Praise of Limestone' 1951
Music can be made anywhere, is invisible and does not smell.

quoted in Stravinsky: Chronicle of a Friendship, by Robert Craft 1972
Music is the best means we have of digesting time.

ERNEST BACON
American Composer
Notes on the Piano 1963
Singing is speech made musical, while dancing is the body made poetic.

JACQUES BARZUN
American academic
'Pleasure of Music' 1951
Music, not being made up of objects nor referring to objects, is intangible and ineffable; it can only be, as it were, inhaled by the spirit: the rest is silence.

SIR THOMAS BEECHAM
British conductor
'Beecham Stories' 1978
The function of music is to release us from the tyranny of conscious thought.

Music first and last should sound well, should allure and enchant the ear. Never mind the inner significance.

CAPTAIN BEEFHEART
American rock star
Music is all goo that you have to shape.

IRVING BERLIN
American composer
Popular music is popular because a lot of people like it.

LEONARD BERNSTEIN
American conductor
'The Unanswered Question' 1976
Music . . . can name the unnamable and communicate the unknowable.

PIERRE BOULEZ
French composer
Esquire 1969
The education of the ear is fifty years behind the education of the eye. We are still hostile to sounds that surprise us. Bad music always sounds pleasant, but good music makes you gnash your teeth.

The Observer 1975
Music cannot move forward without science.

DAVID BOWIE
British rock star
I'm not in love with music. You've got to play around with it or it gets to be a dreadful bore.

HENRY NOEL BRAILSFORD
British musicologist
On Handel's Largo
Music is neither secular nor religious. It can at best suggest the beating of the pulse, the rhythm of the blood that accompanies a given order of ideas.

ARTHUR BROWN
British rock star
Music is only sound expressing certain patterns, so to what extent is that sound architecture and to what extent theatre.

JOHN CAGE
American musician
'Empty Words' 1980
Music is work.

'Silence' 1961
When we separate music from life we get art.

Let no one imagine that in owning a record he has the music. The very practice of music is a celebration that we own nothing.

MARIA CALLAS
Italian diva
The Listener 1969
When music fails to agree to the ear, to soothe the ear and the heart and the senses, then it has missed its point.

ELIAS CANETTI
Bulgarian writer 1956
Music – the measure of mankind.

NEVILLE CARDUS
British journalist 1967
There is one great similarity between music and cricket – there are slow movements in both.

BLAISE CENDRARS
French writer
'Writers at Work' 3rd series 1967
In the beginning was not the word but the phrase, a modulation. Listen to the songs of birds!

E. M. CIORAN
French philosopher
'Syllogismes de l'amertume' 1952
Music is the refuge of souls ulcerated by happiness.

PAUL CLAUDEL
French composer
'Journal'
Music is the soul of geometry.

PAT COLLIER
British rock musician 1979
To me music's not something you sit down and write. It's something you feel, like a punch in the ear.

JOHN COLTRANE
American jazz saxophonist
in 'Jazz Is' by Nat Hentoff, 1976
If the music doesn't say it, how can the words say it *for* the music.

HUGH CORNWELL
British rock musician
Music is what you make of it. An artist reflects the environment he's in. If he's committed enough he may even want to change it.

ELVIS COSTELLO
British rock musician
Music is a matter of life and death and it doesn't matter at all.

GEORGE CRUMB
American composer
in Edition Peters Contemporary Music Catalogue 1975
Music might be defined as a system of proportions in the service of a spiritual impulse.

IAN DURY
British rock musician
Music is . . . well, I *know* it's better than working in Fords.

ROBERT FRIPP
British rock musician
Music is just a means of creating a magical state.

AMELITA GALLI-CURCI
Italian opera singer
Nobody really sings in an opera. They just make loud noises.

BENNY GREEN
British journalist
'The Reluctant Art'
A jazz musician is a juggler who uses harmonies instead of oranges.

JOSEF HOFMANN
in 'The Mystery of Music' Ed. Walter E. Koons 1977
Music is the most expensive of all noises.

RALF HUTTER
German rock musician
When you synthesise a sound it is like an acoustic autobahn.

A synthesiser is like an acoustic mirror. It can tell what kind of person you are.

ALDOUS HUXLEY
British writer
After silence, that which comes nearest to expressing the inexpressible is music.

Time 1957
Music is an ocean.

CHARLES IVES
American composer
quoted in 'Empty Words' by John Cage, 1980
What music is and is to be may be somewhere in the belief of an unknown philosopher. . . 'How can there be any bad music? All music is from heaven and if there is anything bad in it, I put it there, by my implications and limitations. Nature builds the mountains and the meadows and man puts in the fences and the labels.'

JEAN-MICHEL JARRE
French rock musician
There is a bad image about electronic music. In the minds of many people it means . . . vacuum cleaner.

Interview 1978
Music is the human treatment of sounds.

CLAUDE LEVI-STRAUSS
French anthropologist
'Mythologiques I: Le Cru et le Cuit' 1964
Music is a language by whose means messages are elaborated, that such messages can be understood by the many but sent out only by the few, and that it alone among all the languages unites the contradictory character of being at once intelligible and untranslatable – these facts make the creator of music a being like the gods and make music itself the supreme mystery of human knowledge. All other branches of knowledge stumble into it, it holds the key to their progress.

Myth and music are . . . machines for the suppression of time.

YEHUDI MENUHIN
American musician
Sunday Times 1976
Music creates order out of chaos.

Reader's Digest 1953
To play great music, you must keep your eyes on a distant star.

SIR ERNEST NEWMAN
British musicologist
Music shows us the soul of things at first hand.

ODETTA
American folk singer
in 'Loose Talk' ed. Linda Botts 1980
Music is a medicine that's pleasant to take.

AUSTIN O'MALLEY
Music is another lady that talks charmingly and says nothing.

CHARLIE PARKER
American jazz musician
in Nat Hentoff 'Hear Me Talkin' To Ya'
Music is your own experience, your
thoughts, your wisdom. If you don't live
it, it won't come out of your horn.

MAURIZIO POLLINI
Italian pianist
The music of today is a mirror of our
time, of its problems. Why is it normal
to be interested in Picasso and Joyce,
but not in Schoenberg and Stockhausen?

ROMAINA POWER
Opera singer 1974
My voice sounds like a small flute with
very little wind in it.

ELVIS PRESLEY
American rock star
I don't know anything about music. In
my line you don't have to.

LOU REED
American rock star
The music is all. People should die for
it. People are dying for everything else,
so why not the music?

NED ROREM
American musicologist
'Music from Inside Out' 1967
If music could be translated into human
speech it would no longer need to exist.

*Editions Peters Contemporary Music Cata-
logue 1975*
Music is the sole art which evokes nostalgia for the future.

GINO SEVERINI
Italian artist
quoted in 'Artists on Art' 1947
Music is but a living application of
mathematics.

WILLIE 'THE LION' SMITH
American jazz musician
Esquire 1964
What they call jazz is just the music of
people's emotions.

PHIL SPECTOR
American rock producer
Singers are instruments – they're tools
to be worked with.

ISAAC STERN
Russian violinist
Celebrity Register 1973
Music is not an acquired culture . . . it
is an active part of natural life.

1975
Unperformed music is like a cake in the
oven – not fully baked.

KARL-HEINZ STOCKHAUSEN
German composer 1973
Music is a state of being. Sometimes the
more strange it is, the more layers of
yourself you can wake up.

Evening Standard 1971
If the visual world were so full of garbage
as the acoustic world is full of acoustical
garbage, people would just protest all
the time. It just shows that most of the
people are acoustically deaf and don't
even notice the acoustic pollution of the
world. We *must* listen, as never before.

IGOR STRAVINSKY
Russian composer
'The Poetics of Music' 1947
In the pure state, music is free
speculation.

New York Times 1964
The trouble with music appreciation in
general is that people are taught to have
too much respect for music – they should
be taught to love it instead.

Esquire 1972
Music is, by its very nature, essentially
powerless to express anything at all . . .
music expresses itself.

quoted in New York Review of Books 1971
Too many pieces (of music) finish too
long after the end.

1957
To listen is an effort, and just to hear is
no merit. A duck hears also.

CECIL TAYLOR
American jazz musician
Village Voice 1975
Rhythm is the life of space of time
danced through.

BRUNO WALTER
German musician
Harpers 1961
All music is singing. The ideal is to make
the orchestra play like singers.

ANTON VON WEBERN
Polish composer
'The Path to the New Music' 1963
Music is natural law as related to the
sense of hearing.

IANNIS XENAKIS
Greek composer
New York Times 1976
The purpose of music is to draw towards

a total exaltation in which the individual
mingles, losing his consciousness in a
truth immediate.

FRANK ZAPPA
American rock musician
Most people wouldn't know good music
if it came up and bit them in the ass.

Performance

LARRY ADLER
American harmonica player 1957
Even Bach comes down to the basic
suck, blow, suck, suck, blow.

W. H. AUDEN
British poet
Time 1961
No good opera can be sensible – for
people do not sing when they are feeling
sensible.

SIR THOMAS BEECHAM
British conductor
'Beecham Stories' 1978
For a fine performance only two things
are absolutely necessary – the maximum
of virility combined with the maximum
of delicacy.

There are two golden rules for an orchestra: start together and finish together.
The public doesn't give a damn what
goes on in between.

AARON COPLAND
American conductor
Time 1978
Conducting is a real sport. You can
never guarantee what the results are
going to be so there's always an element
of chance. That's what keeps it exciting.

OTTO KLEMPERER
German conductor 1973
The important thing is that one should
let the orchestra breathe.

The art of conducting lies . . . in the
power of suggestion that the conductor
exerts, on the audience as well as on the
orchestra.

ANDRE PREVIN
American conductor 1970
The conductor is there . . . first of all for
the oversimplified reason of just being
the traffic cop, making sure everyone is
playing at the same speed and the same
volume.

ISAAC STERN
Russian violinist 1980
The profession I am in is a very simple
one and a very cruel one – there is no
way that you can create a career for
someone without talent, and no way to
stop a career of someone with talent.

WOODROW WYATT
British politician
'To The Point' 1981
Opera: it is a sham art. Large, plain,
middle-aged women galumph around
posing as pretty young girls singing to
portly, plain, middle-aged men posing as
handsome young heroes.

Composers

SIR JOHN BARBIROLLI
British conductor
quoted in 'An Encyclopedia of Quotations About Music', ed. Nat Shapiro 1978
You know why composers live so long? Because we perspire so much.

SIR THOMAS BEECHAM
British conductor
New York Times 1961
Composers should write tunes that chauffeurs and errand boys can whistle.

PABLO CASALS
Spanish musician
'Conversations with Casals' 1956
The heart of a melody can never be put down on paper.

HOWARD DIETZ
American scriptwriter 1974
Composers shouldn't think too much – it interferes with their plagiarism.

LUKAS FOSS
American composer
NY Post 1975
Composing is like making love to the future.

COLIN NEWMAN
British rock musician
Writing songs is like having a shit. It's a function, a bodily function.

SIR ERNEST NEWMAN
British musicologist
The good composer is slowly discovered, the bad composer is slowly found out.

NED ROREM
American musicologist
'The Paris Diary of Ned Rorem' 1966
Composition is notation of distortion of what composers think they've heard before. Masterpieces are marvellous misquotations.

KEN RUSSELL
British film director 1974
Composers are the nearest to doing what I'm trying to do. To express the inexpressible, or rather, to investigate it, to plumb the unplumable, the divine mystery . . . to communicate, to instruct and to entertain – that was my gig, my goal, and is still.

IGOR STRAVINSKY
Russian composer
Twentieth Century Music 1967
A good composer does not imitate – he steals.

Rock 'N' Roll

LESTER BANGS
American rock writer
'Cream'
Rock and roll at its core is merely a bunch of raving shit.

STIV BATORS
American rock musician
It's the old philosophy – if I'm too loud for you, you're too old for me.

PIERRE BOULEZ
French composer
Esquire 1969
The function of pop music is to be consumed.

D. G. BRIDSON
on disc jockeys
The wriggling ponces of the spoken word.

ARTHUR BROWN
British rock star
Groups are the working class of the leisure society.

JEAN JACQUES BURNEL
British rock musician
New Musical Express 1979
Rock 'n' roll is about cocks and jiving and the odd bloody nose . . . and about people like us talking seriously about the social order.

JOHN CALE
British rock musician
Love and all that shit isn't necessarily what rock 'n' roll's all about. What it is you pick up on the potential of a situation and expand it into something that hasn't been realised the way it is right now. If you push it far enough it'll develop into something else.

JEFFREY CONNOLLY
American rock musician
That's where rock 'n' roll is really at. Driving around in a car with the radio on.

BOB DYLAN
American singer
It's not me, it's the songs. I'm just the postman, I deliver the songs.

MAMA CASS ELLIOT
American rock musician
Probably the biggest bringdown of my life – it's so hypocritical – was being in a pop group and finding out just how much it was like everything it was supposed to be against.

MARK FARNER
American rock singer
We take the kids away from their parents and their environment, to where the only reality is the beat and the rhythm.

BOB GELDOF
Irish rock star
Rock and roll is instant coffee.

PAUL GOODMAN
American writer
New York Review of Books 1971
More happens in two bars of great music than in two minutes of rock 'n' roll.

BILL GRAHAM
American rock promoter
What we all fail to understand is that the majority of rock and roll stars are diaper people, relative to how to handle an audience.

ADRIAN HENRI
British poet
'Mrs. Albion You've Got a Lovely Daughter' in Penguin Modern Poets 10 1967
Beautiful boys with bright red guitars / In the spaces between the stars.

BILLY IDOL
British rock singer
Rock isn't art, it's the way ordinary people talk.

MICK JAGGER &
KEITH RICHARD
British rock composers
'Street Fightin' Man'
Everywhere I hear the sound of marching, charging feet, boy / 'Cos summer's here and the time is right for fighting in the street, boy / But what can a poor boy do / 'Cept sing in a rock 'n' roll band? (Essex Music)

TONY JAMES
British rock singer
It's the Catch-22 of rock 'n' roll: you can't help selling out. You have to do this to that and then other people say you've sold out.

ELTON JOHN
British rock star
Pop music is very disposable, that's the great thing about it.

It's power that runs this country. You can't change things overnight with a hit single. Rock singers getting into politics is rather stupid.

ALAN LANIER
American rock musician
Rock 'n' roll is just mindless fun, the whole fucking thing is a poetic invention, a grandchild of the whole Dada/Surrealist attitude. Rock 'n' roll thrives on negative energy. Those guys in Kiss couldn't wipe their ass by themselves.

JERRY LEIBER & MIKE STOLLER
American pop composers
'That Is Rock 'n' Roll'
You say that music's for the birds / You can't understand the words / Well, honey, if you did, you'd really blow your lid / Baby, that is rock 'n' roll.
(Tiger Music)

LITTLE RICHARD
American rock star
'Tootie Frootie' 1956
Awopbopaloobopalopbamboom!

ROGER McGUINN &
CHRIS HILLMAN
American rock composers
'So You Want To Be A Rock 'n' Roll Star'
Sell your soul to the company / Who are waiting there / To sell plastic ware / And in a week or two / If you make the charts / The girls will tear you apart. . .
(Tickson Music)

MALCOLM McLAREN
British rock manager
What most people don't realise is that the whole thing is about getting as much money as possible in as short a time as possible with as much style as possible.

JIM MORRISON
American rock star
A game is a closed field, a ring of death with, uh, sex at the centre. Performing is the only game I've got.

VAN MORRISON
British rock star
'The Great Deception'
Did you hear about the rock 'n' roll singer / Got three or four Cadillacs / Saying 'Power to the People', 'Dance to the Music' / Wants you to pat him on the back. (Web IV Music)

ANDREW LOOG OLDHAM
British rock manager
Pop music is sex and you have to hit them in the face with it.

JIMMY PAGE
British rock star
Ours is the folk music of the technological age.

CARL PERKINS
American rock musician
'Blue Suede Shoes'
Well, it's one for the money! / Two for the show! / Three to get ready! / Now, go, cat, go! (Carlin Music)

KEITH RICHARD
British rock star
You don't shoulder any responsibilities when you pick up a guitar or sing a song, because it's not a position of responsibility.

You can't take a fucking record like other people take a bible.

GENE SIMMONS
American rock star
The stage is a holy place. You do not get up there and degrade it.

FRANK SINATRA
American singer
New York Post 1957
Rock 'n' roll is the most brutal, ugly, vicious form of expression – sly, lewd, in plain fact dirty . . . rancid smelling, aphrodisiac . . . the martial music of every delinquent on the face of the earth.

MARK SMITH
British rock musician
Rock 'n' roll isn't even music really. It's a mistreating of instruments to get feelings over.

PATTI SMITH
American singer and poet
Rock 'n' roll is dream soup, what's your brand?

Rock 'n' roll is a technological art.

PHIL SPECTOR
American rock producer
Every record can be a hit if you concentrate on it enough.

It's not what I say it means, it's what that record makes you feel.

PAUL STANLEY
American rock star
Rock and roll is not meant to be criticised. If you can find someone who's willing to pay you to be a critic, then you've found a sucker.

PETE TOWNSHEND
British rock star
It really is fantastic conceit on the part of the Establishment to imagine that any particular fragment of society is ever the true subject of a rock 'n' roll song . . . the definition of rock 'n' roll lies here for me: If it screams for truth rather than help, if it commits itself with a courage that it can't be sure it really has, if it stands up and admits something is wrong but doesn't insist on blood, then its rock 'n' roll.

If you're a rock musician you don't have to put on any airs and pretend to be all grown up.

To me the success of any truly great rock song is related to the fact that people who couldn't really communicate in normal ways can quite easily communicate through the mutual enjoyment of rock music.

RICK WAKEMAN
British rock star
Classical concerts are like churches, the only people who go to them are the con-verted. Rock and roll audiences will give anything a try.

JOE WALSH
American rock musician
For the first time in history the artist is realising financial success in his lifetime.

LARRY WILLIAMS
American musician
Rock 'n' roll has no beginning and no end, for it is the very pulse of life itself.

PETER YORK
British journalist
'Style Wars' 1980
Rock and roll is the hamburger that ate the world.

FRANK ZAPPA
American rock musician
The Guardian 1968
Pop is the new politics. I think there is more truth in pop music than in most of the political statements rendered by our leaders, even when you get down to the level of really simplified pop records. I'm saying that's how bad politics is.

Film

ROBERT ALDRICH
American film director
A director is a ringmaster, a psychiatrist and a referee.

ROBERT ALTMAN
American film director
'Films & Filming' 1971
Film making is really a chance to live many lifetimes.

ALEXANDRE ASTRUC
French writer
'The New Wave'
The cinema is quite simply becoming a means of expression, just as all the other arts have been before it, and in particular painting and the novel. After having been successively a fairground attraction, an amusement analogous to boulevard theatre, or a means of preserving the images of an era, it is gradually becoming a language.

IRIS BARRY
English film theorist
The film is a machine for seeing more than meets the eye.

BERNARDO BERTOLUCCI
Italian film director 1975
Reality in front of the camera is more important than anything. It's a kind of expensive documentary. That is my technique, to use what I see there.

CLAUDE BRESSON
French film director
in 'Encountering Directors' ed. Samuels 1973
Cinema is the art of showing nothing.

ROBERT BRESSON
French film director
A film is not a spectacle, it is pre-eminently a style.

MICHAEL CAINE
British actor
Playboy 1967
Moviemaking isn't like mountain climbing. You can't plant a flag to show you've arrived when you reach the top. That's when the climb begins.

JOHN CASSAVETES
American film director
On a film set the only person less important than a director is a talent agent.

RAYMOND CHANDLER
American novelist
'Writers in Hollywood' Atlantic Monthly 1945
The making of a picture ought surely to be a rather fascinating adventure. It is not; it is an endless contention of tawdry egos, some of them powerful, almost all of them vociferous, and almost none of them capable of anything much more creative than credit-stealing and self-promotion.

CHARLES CHAPLIN
American film star
1967 on his new film 'The Countess from Hong Kong'
A millionaire falling in love with a beautiful prostitute – what better story can they have than that.

ALEXANDER CHASE
American journalist
'Perspectives' 1966
The movie actor, like the scared king of primitive tribes, is a God in captivity.

JEAN COCTEAU
French writer and film director
Esquire 1969
Cinema is death in action.

The cinema . . . that temple of sex, with its goddesses, its guardians and its victims.

Esquire 1961
A film is a petrified fountain of thought.

LEN DEIGHTON
British writer
The Observer 1974
A film's credits are not merely a list of people involved in its production, but an endorsement of the way it turned out.

MARLENE DIETRICH
German film star
The relationship between the make-up man and the film actor is one of accomplices in crime.

KIRK DOUGLAS
American film star
Films & Filming 1972
Film is a collaborative art.

JEAN EPSTEIN
French film director
There are no stories. There have never been stories. There are only situations without tail or head; without beginning, centre and end.

SAM FULLER
American film director
The film is a battleground . . . love, hate, violence, action, death – in a word, *emotion*.

WOLCOTT GIBBS
American critic
quoted in Esquire 1968
Ninety percent of the moving pictures exhibited in America are so vulgar, witless and dull that it is preposterous to write about them in any publication not intended to be read while chewing gum.

JEAN-LUC GODARD
French film director 1965
Cinema is halfway between life and art.

A film is the world in an hour and a half.

in 'Le Grand Escroc'
Cinema is the most beautiful fraud in the world.

slogan for the Dziga-Vertov Group, 1969
The problem is not to make political films, but to make films politically.

in 'Godard: Images, Sounds, Politics' by Colin McCabe 1980
You don't make a movie, the movie makes you.

The cinema is truth 24 times a second.

WILLIAM GOLDMAN
American screenwriter 1975
Screenwriting is what feminists call 'shit-work': if it's well done, it's ignored. If it's badly done, people call attention to it.

SAM GOLDWYN
American film producer
It's more than magnificent – it's mediocre.

From a polite conference comes a polite movie.

The Observer 1948
Let's have some new clichés.

I'll give you a definite maybe.

What we want is a story that starts with an earthquake and works its way up to a climax.

I can answer you in two words – Im Possible.

WERNER HERZOG
German film director
quoted in The Guardian 1978
Film is not the art of scholars but of illiterates. Film culture is not analysis but agitation of the mind.

ALFRED HITCHCOCK
British film director 1966
In films murders are always very clean. I show how difficult it is and what a messy thing it is to kill a man.

The Observer 1960
Drama is life with the dull bits cut out.

A good film is when the price of the dinner, the theatre admission and the babysitter were worth it.

The length of a film should be directly related to the endurance of the human bladder.

The cinema is not a slice of life, it's a piece of cake.

I don't care about the subject-matter, I don't care about the acting, but I do care about the pieces of film – all the technical ingredients that make the audience scream.

ST. JOHN IRVINE
Irish author
New York Mirror 1963
American motion pictures are written by the half-educated for the half-witted.

C. G. JUNG
Swiss psychoanalyst
The cinema, like the detective story, makes it possible to experience without danger, all the excitement, passion and desirousness which must be suppressed in a humanitarian ordering of society.

PAULINE KAEL
American critic
'Kiss Kiss Bang Bang' 1968
The words 'Kiss Kiss Bang Bang' which I saw on an Italian movie poster are perhaps the briefest statement imagineable of the basic appeal of movies.

What makes the movies a great popular art form is that certain artists can, at moments in their lives, reach out and unify the audience, educated and uneducated, in a shared response. The tragedy in the history of movies is that those who have this capacity are usually prevented from doing so.

Movies are so rarely great art that if we cannot appreciate great *trash* we have very little reason to be interested in them.

ALAN LADD JR.
American film producer
New York Times 1977
Can you root for the hero and heroine? Can you boo the villain? Is the action fast and furious? If these questions can be answered yes, grab the idea and get into production.

FRITZ LANG
German film director
Film is too vast a medium for self-indulgence. It's a dangerous tool and you must be responsible when you use it.

RICHARD LESTER
British film director
Film making has become a kind of hysterical pregnancy.

CLAUDIA LINNEAR
American singer
There are a lot of chicks who get laid by the director and still don't get the part.

JOSEPH LOSEY
American film director
Film is a dog: the head is commerce, the tail is art. And only rarely does the tail wag the dog.

MARSHALL McLUHAN
Canadian academic
Movies as a nonverbal form of experience are like photographs: a form of statement without syntax.

LOUIS MALLE
French film director
You see the world much better through a camera.

ROMAN POLANSKI
Polish film director
Cinema should make you forget you are sitting in a theatre.

JEAN RENOIR
French film director
The camera is a little like the surgeon's knife.

Time 1979
The saving grace of the cinema is that with a little patience and with love . . . we may arrive at that wonderfully complex creature which is called Man.

quoted in Esquire 1970
Film making all adds up to making a little contribution to the art of your times.

'My Life and My Films' 1974
A film director is not a creator, but a midwife. His business is to deliver the actor of a child that he did not know he had inside him.

WILL ROGERS
American humorist
The movies are the only business where you can go out front and applaud yourself.

'The Autobiography of Will Rogers' 1949
There is only one thing that can kill the movies – and that is education.

PIERRE SCHAEFFER
French broadcaster 1971
Cinema offers itself as a production that starts from a simulation. Radio and television seem to the confused like direct branches of reality, merely relayed by diffusion, not created by production. It is forgotten that these images are carried and multiplied in space, not as objects or authentic happenings, but as shadows, as transformations of reality fully as great as those of the cinema.

MARTIN SCORSCESE
American film director
on London Weekend Television 1981
Cinema is a matter of what is in the frame and what is out.

GILBERT SELDES
American critic
The movie is the imagination of mankind in action.

SUSAN SONTAG
American essayist
'Against Interpretation' 1961
Science fiction films are not about science, they are about disaster, one of the oldest subjects of art.

FRANCOIS TRUFFAUT
French film director
in 'The New Wave' by Peter Graham 1968
A film is a boat which is always on the point of sinking – it always tends to break up as you go along and drag you under with it.

Esquire 1970
To make a film is to improve on life, arrange it to suit oneself, it is to prolong the games of childhood, to construct something that is at once a new toy and a vase in which one can arrange, as if they were a bouquet of flowers, the ideas one feels at the moment or in a permanent way.

WALTER WANGER
American film director
Nothing is as cheap as a hit, no matter how much it costs.

ANDY WARHOL
American artist
I like making movies because its easier than painting paintings.

The camerawork is lousy, the lighting's lousy, the sound is lousy, but the people are beautiful.

ORSON WELLES
American film director
quoted in 'Tynan Left & Right' 1967
The cinema has no boundaries. It is a ribbon of dream.

The trouble with a movie these days is that it's old before it's released – it's no accident that it comes in a can.

A film is never really good unless the camera is an eye in the head of a poet.

A movie studio is the best toy a boy ever had.

The Observer 1969
A film is a dream. A dream that is vulgar, stupid, dull and shapeless; it is perhaps a nightmare. Still, at least a dream is never an illusion.

Film is a very personal thing, much more personal than the theatre, because the film is a dead thing – a ribbon of celluloid, like the paper on which one writes a poem. Theatre is a collective experience; cinema and film is the work of one single person – the director. And the camera is, therefore, much more than a recording apparatus. It is a medium via which messages reach us from another world, a world that is not ours and that brings us to the heart of a great secret. Here magic begins and you realise that a film, besides being a ribbon of celluloid, is also a ribbon of dreams.

EARL WILSON
American columnist
A movie without sex would be like a candy bar without nuts.

ELEMIRE ZOLLA
Italian writer
'The Eclipse of the Intellectuals' 1971
The eye is the window of the soul, the movies are iron shutters.

Television & Radio

SPIRO T. AGNEW
American politician 1969
On TV...
A spirit of national masochism prevails, encouraged by an effete corps of impudent snobs who characterise themselves as intellectuals.

'ALL ABOUT EVE'
20th Century Fox 1950 screenplay by Joseph L. Mankiewicz, based on 'The Wisdom of Eve' by Mary Orr
George Sanders: That's all television is, my dear. Nothing but auditions.

FRED ALLEN
American wit
Television is chewing gum for the eyes.

Television is a triumph of equipment over people, and the minds that control it are so small that you could put them in the navel of a flea and still have

enough room beside them for a network president's heart.

quoted in Esquire 1971
Imitation is the sincerest form of television.

CHER
American singer
Playboy 1975
Television is the kind of thing you pay attention to if you wish, and if you don't you go clean out your drawers.

ANONYMOUS
Sunday Times 1981
The wireless: an instrument with no strings attached.

ANONYMOUS
in 'The Filmgoers Book of Quotes' ed. L. Halliwell 1973
Television ... the bland leading the bland.

ANONYMOUS ACTOR
quoted in Manchester Guardian 1959
Television is summer stock in an iron lung.

ANONYMOUS CANADIAN TV REPORTER
Esquire 1971
Reporting the news on television is like writing with a one-ton pencil.

ANONYMOUS HIJACKER
quoted by Dr. David Hubbard, writing on hijacker psychology, quoted in Esquire 1977
Television is a whore. Any man who wants her full favours can have them in five minutes with a pistol.

JAMES T. AUBREY JR.
President CBS-TV 1961
I don't want any seamy sociological scripts. Goddamit I want happy endings. I can't communicate with the creative people. They just won't listen. The trouble with the creative people is that they don't know the people. The people out there don't want to think. I come from out there.

CLIVE BARNES
British critic
New York Times 1969
Television is the first truly democratic culture – the first culture available to everybody and entirely governed by what the people want. The most terrifying thing is what people do want.

GENE BARRY
American TV star
Esquire 1976
A year in TV is a lifetime in movies . . . it's the golden rut, a repetition exercise.

cf. Budd Schulberg 'What Makes Sammy Run?' 1941
It was right in the groove that Hollywood has been geared for, slick, swift and clever. What Kit calls the Golden Rut.

PETER BLACK
British journalist 1974
retiring after 22 years as TV critic
I began in 1952 by thinking of television as a window on the world, then as a mirror in the corner, finally as the biggest aspidistra in the world.

ROBERT BLAKE
American T.V. actor
Esquire 1976
There are maybe two or three good directors in television. The rest are atmosphere.

MARSHALL BRICKMAN
American TV talkshow producer
Esquire 1971
It's a little weird when you have the whole country watching a couple of people doing what they should be doing themselves.

HIMAN BROWN
Newsweek 1974
TV just feeds you. Radio involves you.

JOHN MASON BROWN
American essayist 1955
Some television programmes are so much chewing gum for the eyes.

ART BUCHWALD
American humorist 1959
Television has a real problem. They have no page two.

RICHARD BURTON
Welsh actor 1967
TV is an evil medium, it should never have been invented, but since we have to live with it, let us try to do something about it.

ROBERT CARSON
quoted in 'Filmgoers Book of Quotes' ed. L. Halliwell 1973
Television . . . the longest amateur night in history.

SHAUN CASSIDY
American pop and TV star
There's no way anybody's going to take you seriously if you're on a TV show.

RAYMOND CHANDLER
American novelist
letter to Charles W. Morton 1950
Television is just one more facet of that considerable segment of our society that never had any standard but the soft buck.

PADDY CHAYEFSKY
American scriptwriter
Television is democracy at its ugliest.

SIR WINSTON CHURCHILL
British statesman
on TV
A penny Punch and Judy show.

LORD CLARK
British critic 1954
Television is an avalanche of vulgarity.

The Guardian 1977
Television is a form of soliloquy.

ALAN COREN
British humourist
in 'Penguin Dictionary of Modern Quotations'
by J. M. and M. J. Cohen 1980
Television is more interesting than
people. If it were not, we should have
people standing in the corners of our
rooms.

LAURENCE C. COUGHLIN
The vast wasteland of TV is not interested in producing a better mousetrap
but in producing a worse mouse.

NOEL COWARD
British playwright
Good heavens, television is something
you appear on, you don't watch.

QUENTIN CRISP
British writer
'How To Become a Virgin' 1981
Television is a redemptive medium.

If any reader of this book is in the grip
of some habit of which he is deeply ashamed, I advise him not to give way to
it in secret but to do it on television. No
one will pass him by with averted gaze
on the other side of the street. People
will cross the road at the risk of losing
their own lives in order to say 'We saw
you on the telly'.

Books and plays are diversions about
which most of us exercise some decision,
even if our selection is based on totally
misleading publicity. The movies are in
a twilit zone. . . Television is even lower
down the scale of human choice. We
nearly always see it by default.

RICHARD CROSSMAN
British politician
Granada Lecture 1968
I do sometimes wonder whether the
people interested in politics and current
affairs cannot establish a right to be
given equal treatment with all-in wres-
tling – sixty minutes of straight outside
broadcasting would seem a lot to us.

CHARLES CURRAN
British broadcasting executive 1971
on news:
We have certain difficult problems on
television. . . It is in the nature of pictures to reflect action. It is very difficult
for them to represent thought or policy.

WILL DURANT
American historian
The finger that turns the dial rules the
air.

T. S. ELIOT
American poet
New York Post 1963
Television is a medium of entertainment
which permits millions of people to listen
to the same joke at the same time and
yet remain lonesome.

Encounter Magazine 1973
Today nobody's house is his castle – it's
a potential TV studio.

CLAY FELKER
American editor
on demise of 'Life' which claimed TV as it's
rival. . .
They were mad. You don't get steam-
rollered by TV, you get out of its way.

IAN FLEMING
British writer
quoted in 1970
The transistor radio is the modern le-
per's bell.

ANNA FORD
British TV newscaster 1979
Let's face it, there are no plain women
on television.

FRED FRIENDLY
Professor of Broadcast Journalism
at Columbia University 1967
In America television can make so

much money doing its worst, it cannot afford to do it best.

1980
The news is the one thing the networks can point to with pride. Everything else they do is crap – and they know it.

DAVID FROST
British talkshow host
'David Frost Revue' CBS-TV 1971
Television is an invention that permits you to be entertained in your living room by people you wouldn't have in your home.

J. K. GALBRAITH
American economist
'The New Industrial State' 1967
There is an insistent tendency among solemn social scientists to think of any institution which features rhymed and singing commercials, intense and lachrymose voices urging highly improbable enjoyment, caricatures of the human oesophagus in normal or impaired operation, and which hints implausibly at opportunities for antiseptic seduction as inherently trivial. This is a great mistake. The industrial system is profoundly dependant on commercial television and could not exist in its present form without it.

JEAN-LUC GODARD
French film director
Esquire 1969
Ten per cent of television is honest. We have to work in that ten per cent.

SAM GOLDWYN
American film producer
on TV
Why should people pay good money to go out and see bad films when they can stay at home and see bad television for nothing?

JACK GOULD
American critic
New York Times 1966
American TV must raise its ceiling by some method other than lowering the floor.

LORD GRADE
British TV mogul
Esquire 1976
on set of 'The Master Builder'
LG: How's the Shakespeare coming along?
Director: It's Ibsen.
LG: Oh well, it's all costume, isn't it.

DR. G. L. GRAY
American academic 1966
The television commercial is the most efficient power-packed capsule of education that appears anywhere on TV.

EDWARD GUTHMAN
quoted in 'The Official Rules' by P. Dickson, 1978. . .
Thirty seconds on the evening news is worth a front page headline in every newspaper in the world.

W. S. HAMILTON
Australian broadcasting executive 1968
There is always the danger that the TV interviewer can get to think that he is more important than the person who is being interviewed.

Sometimes we have a real job to make up our minds what the public should have, whether it's good for them and whether it's what they want.

SUSAN HARRIS
American TV scriptwriter
on her show 'Fay' whose heroine proved too independent for the NBC censors, 1977
If a woman isn't Doris Day in an organdie apron, the networks find her threatening.

ALBERT HERZOG
South African politician 1966
The vast British Empire built up over hundreds of years has been reduced to ruins largely through the influence of television.

TAHU HOLE
British TV executive 1950
The BBC does not have scoops.

RICHARD INGRAMS
British journalist
The Observer 1977
Children watch too much television not

only because indolent parents allow them to, but because the standard of most programmes is pitched at their level.

CLIVE JAMES
Australian critic
The Observer 1981
All you have to do on television is be yourself, provided, that is, that you have a self to be.

'The Crystal Bucket' 1981
Most of the blandness which experts presume to detect in television is just the thinness of overtaxed inspiration.

ERNIE KOVACS
American comedian
on television, quoted in 'The Filmgoers Book of Quotes' ed. L. Halliwell 1973
Television - a medium. So called because it is neither rare nor well-done.

FRAN LEBOWTIZ
American journalist
'Metropolitan Life' 1978
Radio news is bearable. This is due to the fact that while the news is being broadcast the disc jockey is not allowed to talk.

NORMAN LEAR
American TV executive
Playboy 1976
Television has always been a convenient whipping boy for the ills that afflict society.

JOHN LEONARD
American critic
Playboy 1976
TV is another kind of car, a windshield on the world. We climb inside, drive it, and it drives us, and we all go in the same direction, see the same thing. It is more than a mobile home, it is a mobile nation. It has become, then, our common language, our ceremony, our style, our entertainment and anxiety, our sympathetic magic, our way of celebrating, mourning, worshipping. It's flimsy glue, but for the moment it's the only thing holding America together.

A. J. LIEBLING
American writer
'The Sweet Science'
Television, if unchecked, may carry us back to a pre-tribal state of social development where the family was the largest conversational unit.

LEE LOVINGER
Quote 1967
Television is simply automated day dreaming.

QUINN MARTIN
American cop show producer
in a memo on 'The Untouchables,' quoted by Eric Barnouw 'Tube of Plenty'
I wish you would come up with a different device than running the man down with a car, as we have done this now in three different shows. I like the idea of sadism, but I hope we can come up with another approach to it.

MARGARET MEAD
American anthropologist
Time 1978
For the first time the young are seeing history being made before it is censored by their elders.

GEORGE MELLY
British musician and critic
'The Media Mob' 1980
We are all spiritualists now, and how appropriate that television should be called a medium.

LORNE MICHAELS
American TV producer
The pressure to give them less is so great in TV because the traffic will bear almost anything.

ARTHUR MILLER
American playwright
Radio: death in the afternoon and into the night.

JONATHAN MILLER
British doctor and writer
Evening Standard 1970
There are no special virtues about television, apart from the fact that it is in the home.

quoted in 'The New Priesthood', Joan Bakewell/Nicholas Garnham 1971
Television is simply a hole through which you push various communications.

MALCOLM MUGGERIDGE
British journalist
'Diaries' 1981
(There is) something inferior, cheap, horrible about television as such; it's a prism through which words pass, energies distorted, false. The exact converse of what is commonly believed – not a searcher out of truth and sincerity, but rather only lies and insincerity will register on it.

The Observer, 1969
Television is the perfect instrument – it combines seeming verisimilitude with infinite possibilities in the way of selecting and adjusting.

'The Most of Malcolm Muggeridge' 1966
Television was not meant to make human beings vacuous, but it is an emanation of their vacuity.

New Statesman 1968
Of all the inventions of our time it (TV) is likely to prove the most destructive. Whereas nuclear power can only reduce us and our world to a cinder, the camera grinds us down to spiritual dust so fine that a puff of wind scatters it, leaving nothing behind.

in 'The New Priesthood' ed. J. Bakewell & N. Garnham 1971
This medium (Television) is bound to deceive. Even if you put the truth into it, it comes out a deception.

FRANK MUIR
British humorist
The Guardian 1973
Radio and television as entertainments are fine, but they bear as much relation to the value of books as airline meals do to food.

EDWARD R. MURROW
American broadcaster
The Observer 1969
The ideal voice for radio should have no substance, no sex, no owner, and a message of importance for every housewife.

quoted in 'Prime Time – the Life of Ed. R. Murrow' by Alexander Kendrick 1969
Never sound excited. Imagine yourself at a dinner table back in the United States with the local editor, a banker and a professor talking over coffee. You try and tell what it was like, while the maid's boyfriend, a truck driver, listens from the kitchen. Try to be understood by the truck driver while not insulting the professor's intelligence.

'NETWORK'
United Artists 1976 screenplay by Paddy Chayevsky
Peter Finch: Television is not the truth. Television is a god-damned amusement park. Television is a circus, a carnival, a travelling troupe of acrobats, storytellers, dancers, singers, jugglers, sideshow freaks, lion tamers and football players. We're in the boredom-killing business.

HAROLD NICOLSON
British politician
The Observer 1947
The gift of broadcasting is, without question, the lowest human capacity to which any man could attain.

RICHARD M. NIXON
American politician 1952
No TV performance takes such careful preparation as an off the cuff talk.

DENNIS NORDEN
British humorist
in The Guardian 1969. Dictum on TV scripts:
We don't want it good – we want it Tuesday.

LAURENCE J. PETER
Canadian educator
'Peter's Quotations' 1977
An ounce of image is worth a pound of performance.

FRANCIS PONGE
French writer
'Le Grand Recueil'
Radio – all the flowing manure of the world's melody.

DENNIS POTTER
British playwright
intro. to The Nigel Barton Plays 1967
Television: the entertainment which flows like tap-water.

FREDERIC RAPHAEL
British writer
'The Language of Television' 1980
Television . . . offers a banal vision of
heaven.

LORD REITH
British broadcasting executive
quoted in BBC Official Biography 1963
Our responsibility is to carry into the
greatest number of homes everything
that is best in every department of human knowledge, endeavour and achievement and to avoid the things which are
or may be hurtful. It is occasionally in-
dicated to us that we are apparently setting out to give the public what we think
they need, not what they want. But few
people know what they want and very
few what they need. There is often no
difference. In any case it is better to over
estimate the mentality of the public than
under estimate it.

KENNETH ROBINSON
British journalist
The Listener 1978
Television is like a station bookstall.
Something we might pick up to titillate
the brain very gently ought not to be
observed with the same critical standards as something designed to feed the
mind.

NATHALIE SARRAUTE
French writer
Television has . . . lifted the manufacture
of banality out of the sphere of handi-
craft and placed it in that of a major
industry.

DANIEL SCHORR
American broadcaster
On television. . .
A nightly national seance.

Esquire 1977
Television is a medium made to order
for those with aptitudes for stage acting
and synthetic sincerity. It has encouraged the development of thespian talents
where none had been previously known
to exist.

ROD SERLING
American television producer
Drama on television must walk tiptoe

and in agony lest it offend some cereal
buyer from below the Mason Dixon
line. . . Now prejudice is alike down at
its ugly roots, and all prejudice is indeed
a universal evil. But you don't conquer
intolerance by disguising it, by clothing
it in different trappings, by slapping at
it in a wispy parable.

BISHOP FULTON J. SHEEN
American clergyman 1956
Spiritually, radio and TV are beautiful
examples of the inspired wisdom of the
ages. Radio is much like the Old Testament, inasmuch as it is the hearing of
wisdom without seeing it; TV is like the
New Testament, because in it the wisdom becomes flesh and dwells among us.

ANTHONY SMITH
British TV director
'The Shadow in the Cave' 1975
The neutrality of broadcasting . . . does
make it fearful of being the first to report
material likely to change the course of
events.

Broadcasting . . . grew up as the first
institution in history, apart from the
Church, which could deliver the whole
of a society complete to a communicator.

H. ALLEN SMITH
American journalist
'Let the Crabgrass Grow' 1960
Some performers on television appear to
be horrible people, but when you finally
get to know them in person, they turn
out to be even worse.

WOLFMAN JACK SMITH
American disc jockey
Newsweek 1973
Radio is a creative theatre of the mind.

JOHN STEVENSON
British journalist
The Listener 1978
Television is the best gauge we have of
our decay.

Time 1976
The symbiosis between audience and
show makes soap opera unique, the most
powerful entertainment on or off
television.

The soaps are like Big Macs . . . a lot of people who won't admit it eat them up.

PETER USTINOV
British wit and actor
Now! 1981
Television has prevented there being any great men any more. They're all too familiar. Part of greatness is remoteness.

Everybody's 1957
Acting on TV is like being asked by the captain to entertain the passengers while the ship goes down.

ED WARREN
American TV executive 1976
In this business the sign of creativity is to have a trenchcoat that outdoes all the others, to dress like Hemingway coming out of the tundra.

KEITH WATERHOUSE
British writer
Punch 1966
TV's power for good or evil is roughly equivalent to that of the hula-hoop.

SYLVESTER L. WEAVER
American TV executive 1954
The grand design of television is to create an aristocracy of the people, the proletariat of privilege, the Athenian masses – to make the average man the uncommon man. . . TV will make adults out of children.

ORSON WELLES
American film director
New York Herald Tribune 1956
I hate television, I hate it as much as peanuts. But I can't stop eating peanuts.

JOHN WHALE
British television producer
Esquire 1971
Television can do very little with events of which it has no foreknowledge.

THEODORE H. WHITE
American journalist
'Breach of Faith' 1976, on the launch of the East-West coaxial TV link. . .
The nation was collected as one, seeing itself in a new mirror, on a twelve-inch television tube.

BILLY WILDER
American film director
quoted in 'The Filmgoers Book of Quotes' ed. L. Halliwell 1973
Television is . . . a twenty-one inch person. I'm delighted with it, because it used to be that films were the lowest form of art. Now we've got something to look down on.

MASON WILLIAMS
American television actor
Getting an award from TV is like being kissed by someone with bad breath.

ROBIN WILLIAMS
American comedian 1979
The danger of television is repetition.

FRANK LLOYD WRIGHT
American architect
Television is chewing gum for the eyes.

ROBERT YOUNG
American actor
who starred as 'Dr. Marcus Welby' complaining when the series 'Marcus Welby MD' was dropped 1976
There are supposed to be 2,500 known diseases. We've only covered a fraction of them in 170 episodes.

The Mass Media

W. H. AUDEN
British poet
'The Dyer's Hand' 1962
What the mass media offer is not popular art, but entertainment which is intended to be consumed like food, forgotten and replaced by a new dish.

ANTHONY WEDGWOOD BENN
British politician 1969
Broadcasting is much too important to be left to the broadcasters.

DAVID BOWIE
British rock star
When you think about it, Adolf Hitler was the first pop star. It certainly wasn't his politics. He was a media pop star.

ROBERT CHRISTGAU
American rock critic
Esquire 1969
The old complaint that mass culture is designed for eleven-year-olds is of course a shameful canard. The key age has traditionally been more like fourteen.

G. RAY FUNKHOUSER
American researcher
quoted in 'The Official Rules' by P. Dickson, 1978
The quality of legislation passed to deal with a problem is inversely proportional to the volume of media clamour that brought it on.

RICHARD HOGGART
British academic
'The Uses of Literacy' 1957
Most mass entertainments are in the end . . . 'anti-life'. They are full of a corrupt brightness, of improper appeals and moral evasions . . . they tend towards a view of the world in which progress is conceived as a seeking of material possessions, equality as a moral levelling and freedom as the ground for endless irresponsible pleasure.

MARSHALL McLUHAN
Canadian academic
'Understanding Media' 1964
The medium is the message. This is merely to say that the personal and social consequences of any medium . . . result from the new scale that is introduced into our affairs by each extension of ourselves or by any new technology.

HERBERT MARCUSE
German philosopher
'One Dimensional Man' 1968
Can one really distinguish between the mass media as instruments of information and entertainment, and as agents of manipulation and indoctrination?

MALCOLM MUGGERIDGE
British journalist
Esquire 1968
The Medium is the Legend.

POPE PAUL VI
1970 on media
What a wonderful mission it is for those who place their intelligence at the service of truth and right. What a serious, a truly serious responsibility it is for those who abuse their power by supporting prejudice and dividing communities and nations, or who go so far as to turn this noble invention into an instrument of moral perversion.

KEITH RICHARD
British rock star
All you've got to do is delete the words 'punk rock' and write in 'Rolling Stones' and you've got the same press as you had fifteen years ago . . . they've made the press in England play the same old games they played with us. They puked at London Airport, we pissed in the filling station.

DAVID RIESMAN
American sociologist
The media, far from being a conspiracy to dull the political sense of the people, could be viewed as a conspiracy to disguise the extent of political indifference.

GERALDO RIVERA
American TV reporter
at the execution of Gary Gilmore 1977
Kill the Rona segment. Get rid of it. Give me air! You'll be able to hear the shots. I promise you, you'll be able to hear the shots!

I. F. STONE
American journalist
The Listener 1963
The important thing about the so-called 'communications industry' is that it is basically concerned with merchandising. News is a kind of by-product and if you want to sell things, you don't want to offend anybody.

TOM STOPPARD
British playwright
'Jumpers'

The media. It sounds like a convention of spiritualists.

DAME BARBARA WARD
British economist

Saturday Review 1961
The modern world is not given to uncritical admiration. It expects its idols to have feet of clay and can be reasonably sure that press and camera will report its exact dimensions.

The Artist

AL ALVAREZ
British writer
'The Savage God' 1971
The better the artist, the more vulnerable he seems to be.

KINGSLEY AMIS
British author
New Statesman 1975
The true artist declares himself by leaving out a lot. Even when what is left out is necessary information.

W. H. AUDEN
British poet
'The Dyer's Hand' 1962
No poet or novelist wishes he was the only one who ever lived, but most of them wish they were the only one alive, and quite a number fondly believe their wish has been granted.

FRANCIS BACON
British artist
quoted in Sunday Telegraph 1964
The job of the artist is always to deepen the mystery.

'Interviews with Francis Bacon' 1975
I want a very ordered image, but I want it to come about by chance.

JAMES BALDWIN
American author
Nobody Knows My Name 1961
All art is a kind of confession, more or less oblique. All artists, if they are to survive, are forced, at last, to tell the whole story, to vomit the anguish up.

RUDOLF BING
Director of The New York Metropolitan Opera
'5000 nights at the opera' 1972
It is so much worse to be a mediocre

artist than to be a mediocre post office clerk.

DEREK BOSHIER
British artist
'Contemporary Artists' 1977
Excluding the artists of genius that history had produced, the artist generally is not unique, he has just had the opportunity to find out ways of expressing ideas and experiences.

PIERRE BOULEZ
French composer
Esquire 1969
The problem of all great modern artists – to make a virtue of constriction.

LUIS BUNUEL
Spanish film director
quoted by Anthony Hill in 'Contemporary Artists' 1977
In any society, the artist has a responsibilty. His effectiveness is certainly limited and a painter or writer cannot change the world. But they can keep an essential margin of non-conformity alive. Thanks to them the powerful can never affirm that everyone agrees with their acts. That small difference is very important.

JOHN CAGE
American musician
'Silence' 1961
The responsibility of the artist consists in perfecting his work so that it may become attractively disinteresting.

An artist conscientiously moves in a direction which for some good reason he takes, putting one work in front of the other with the hope that he'll arrive before death overtakes him.

ALBERT CAMUS
French writer
'Resistance, Rebellion & Death' 1960
An artist may make a success or failure
of his work. He may make a success or
failure of his life. But if he can tell himself that, finally, as a result of his long
effort, he has eased or decreased the various forms of bondage weighing upon
men, then in a sense he is justified and,
to some extent, he can forgive himself.

RAYMOND CHANDLER
American novelist
letter to Helga Greene 1957
An artist cannot deny art, nor would he
want to. A lover cannot deny love. If you
believe in an ideal, you don't own it, it
owns you, and you certainly don't want
to freeze it at your own level for mercen-
ary reasons.

JEAN COCTEAU
French writer and film director
quoted in New York Review of Books 1971
An artist never leaps over steps. If he
leaps over some he loses time, for he has
to climb them all again later.

SEAN CONNERY
British film star
Playboy 1965
The main concern for an actor or writer
is not believability, but the removal of
time. When an artist can suspend time
he has succeeded.

CYRIL CONNOLLY
British critic
Conversation for an artist is a ceremony
of self-wastage.

FRANCIS FORD COPPOLA
American film director
Playboy 1975
The artist's worst fear is that he'll be
exposed as a sham. Deep down we are
living with the notion that our success is
beyond our ability.

ROBERT W. CORRIGAN
American theatre critic
The artist is the seismograph of his age.

ROBERT DELFORD-BROWN
American artist
'Contemporary Artists' 1977
The artist's primary responsibility is to

tell the truth as he sees it, not to enhance
his own self importance as an expert,
thereby perverting his responsibility as
a moral force in society.

ANDRE DERAIN
French artist
When an artist reasons, it's because he
no longer understands anything.

LAWRENCE DURRELL
British writer
'Writers at Work' 2nd series 1963
An artist is only someone unrolling and
digging out and excavating the areas
normally accessible to normal people
everywhere and exhibiting them as a sort
of scarecrow to show people what can be
done with themselves.

WILLIAM EASTLAKE
American novelist
in 'Contemporary Novelists' 1976
The artist's job is to hold the world together. What politicians cannot do with
reality, the artist does with magic.

ILYA EHRENBURG
Russian poet
Saturday Review 1967
Every master knows that the material
teaches the artist.

BRIAN ENO
British musician
The function of being an artist for me is
that it's an experimental area where I
can test out ways of thinking and operating and hopefully apply the results to
real life. The advantage of testing them
in an art context is that it doesn't matter
if you fail.

MAX ERNST
German artist
New York Herald Tribune 1963
Art lives when it moves. An artist must
not repeat himself. An artist must be
responsible, not to a party – one loses
part of one's revolt within a party – he
must be responsible to himself, his
conscience.

JAMES T. FARRELL
American novelist
Playboy 1968
It is only important that the artist be

aware of his experience and that he create original art from it . . . Art is the transcending of experience.

WILLIAM FAULKNER
American novelist
'Writers at Work' 1st series 1958
An artist is a creature driven by demons. He don't know why they choose him and he's usually too busy to wonder why.

The aim of every artist is to arrest motion, which is life, by artificial means, and hold it fixed so that a hundred years later, when a stranger looks at it, it moves again, since it is life.

JULES FEIFFER
American cartoonist
Artists can colour the sky red because they know it's blue. The rest of us, who aren't artists, must colour things the way they really are, or people might think we're stupid.

FEDERICO FELLINI
Italian film director
The artist is simply the medium between his fantasies and the rest of the world.

LYN FOULKES
American artist
'Contemporary Artists' 1977
Art is becoming (or perhaps has always been) a historical game for critics and collectors. The people don't give much of a damn for it and frankly, neither do I. The role of the artist must change. He or she must communicate more broadly . . . the masters (?) painted for kings, now the leaders of the world watch television.

ERIC GILL
British designer
The artist is not a special kind of man. Every man is a special kind of artist.

GLUCK (Hannah Gluckstein)
British artist
'Contemporary Artists' 1977
I believe that the true artist is a conduit open to any unexpected experience. There must be no preconceived ideas; variety of subject is the sign of an uninhibited spirit. All one has to do is remain faithful and undeterred to the end.

MARTHA GRAHAM
American dancer
No artist is ahead of his time. He *is* his time. It is just that others are behind the time.

GUNTER GRASS
German novelist
Sunday Times 1965
An artist is like a scrap dealer. He works with the broken stuff of history. He can ignore nothing – a little bit here, a little bit there. If he's lucky, he sells it.

PRO HART
Australian artist 1969
Like most artists, my latest paintings are my best.

DAVID HOCKNEY
British artist
'David Hockney' 1976
It is very good advice to believe only what an artist does, rather than what he says about his work.

BUDD HOPKINS
American artist
'Contemporary Artists' 1977
The artist's role is to provide possibilities of harmony, beauty and order which the viewer can construct within himself.

PHILIP JOHNSON
American architect
quoted in 'Conversations with Artists' ed. Seldon Rodman
The duty of the artist is to strain against the bonds of the existing style . . . and only this procedure makes the development of architecture possible.

PAULINE KAEL
American critic
'I Lost It at the Movies' 1965
The first prerogative of an artist in any medium is to make a fool of himself.

LAJOS KASSAK
Hungarian artist
'Contemporary Artists' 1977
The artist does not make service, he gives presents in order to get rid of his surplus goods.

WILLEM DE KOONING
American artist 1951
The attitude that nature is chaotic and the artist puts order into it is a very absurd point of view, I think. All that we can hope for is to put some order into ourselves.

LOUIS KRONENBERGER
American critic
'Company Manners' 1954
Temperament, like liberty, is important despite how many crimes are committed in its name.

AKIRA KUROSAWA
Japanese film director
The Guardian 1980
In order to find reality, each must search for his own universe, look for the details that contribute to this reality that one feels under the surface of things. To be an artist means to search, to find and look at these realities. To be an artist means never to look away.

MARIO LANZA
Italian singer 1957
Temperament is just a way of saying 'no' and we all have a right to say 'no' once in a while.

LES LEVINE
Canadian artist
'Contemporary Artists' 1977
The artist is like a hunter who must be on his toes at all times, with eyes and ears fully open to respond to the anxious signals the world sends out.

HARVEY LITTLETON
American artist
Contemporary Artists 1977
An artist gives form to his vision in material.

MARYA MANNES
American writer
'More In Anger' 1958
The world of sight is still limitless. It is the artist who limits vision to the cramped dimensions of his own ego.

HENRY MILLER
American writer
'Creative Death' in 'The Best of Henry Miller' 1960
The artist . . . he who lives only in the moment, the visionary moment of utter, far-seeing lucidity. Such clear, icy sanity that it seems like madness. By the force and power of the artist's vision the static, synthetic whole which is called the world is destroyed. The artist gives back to us a vital, singing universe, alive in all its parts.

'The Air Conditioned Nightmare' 1945
An artist is primarily one who has faith in himself. He does not respond to normal stimuli, he is neither a drudge nor a parasite. He lives to express himself and in so doing enriches the world.

JONATHAN MILLER
British doctor and writer
Radio Times 1964
The artistic community is like a great forest which simultaneously alters and depends upon the composition of the air which surrounds it.

Artists are the unacknowledged legislators of the world.

GRANDMA MOSES
American artist
A primitive artist is an amateur whose work sells.

LEWIS MUMFORD
American critic
The artist has a special task and duty – the task of reminding men of their humanity and the promise of their creativity.

CLAES OLDENBURG
Danish artist
I never saw an ugly thing in my life.

ELDER OLSON
American critic
in *'Contemporary Literary Critics'* 1977 ed. Elmer Borklund
We shall never know all about art or the values of art until all art is at an end; meanwhile artists will continue to instruct us.

WALKER PERCY
American writer
'Questions They Never Asked Me' Esquire 1977
Unlike God the artist does not start with nothing and make something of it. He starts with himself as nothing and makes something of the nothing with the things at hand. If the novelist has a secret it is not that he has a special something but that he has a special nothing.

MAN RAY
French photographer
Modern Photography 1957
Of course, there will always be those who look only at technique, who ask 'how?' while others of a more curious nature will ask 'why?'. Personally I have always preferred inspiration to information.

JEAN RENOIR
French film director
The Guardian 1961
The artist picks, perhaps, just a tiny corner of life and shows you how life really is. We are surrounded by screens. Everywhere there are screens. The artist is the one who pulls them down.

SELDON RODMAN
American critic
'Conversations with Artists'
One thing about artists is that most of them agree in thinking that nothing important can be said about art. Another is that without exception they love to talk about it.

NED ROREM
American musicologist
'Music from Inside out' 1967
An artist doesn't necessarily have deeper feelings than other people, but he can express these feelings. He is like everyone else – only more so!

ISAAC ROSENFELD
'An Age of Enormity'
It is the artist's task to fuse, to bring together the human and the animal in man, to make an imaginative synthesis of what society has dismembered.

MARK ROTHKO
American artist
The unfriendliness of society to his activity is difficult for the artist to accept. Yet this very hostility can act as a lever for true liberation.

ARTHUR SCHNITZLER
Austrian playwright
'Work & Echo'
When we speak of the artistic temperament, we are usually referring to the sum of qualities which hinder the artist in producing.

ISAAC BASHEVIS SINGER
American writer
International Herald Tribune
An artist can evoke emotions even if he distorts the natural order of things, what we call 'reality'. Artists have done this through the ages. Actually, there isn't a single work of art that is 'true to life'.

ROD STEIGER
American film star
Playboy 1969
In any art form a man's got to think secretly that he's better than anyone else – anyone who takes his talent for granted is on the way out. He's dead.

SAUL STEINBERG
American artist
'Saul Steinberg' Harold Rosenberg 1978
The tradition of the artist is to become someone else.

IGOR STRAVINSKY
Russian composer
Esquire 1972
Art postulates communion, and the artist has an imperative need to make others share the joy which he experiences himself.

'Poetics of Music'
The more constraints one imposes, the more one frees onself of the chains that shackle the spirit . . . the arbitrariness of the constraint only serves to obtain precision of execution.

DYLAN THOMAS
British poet
There is only one position for an artist anywhere: and that is, upright.

quoted in Esquire 1965
That which makes you an artist – knowledge of the actual world's deplorable sordidness, and of the invisible world's splendour.

LIONEL TRILLING
American critic
Esquire 1962
Immature artists imitate. Mature artists steal. (cf. Stravinsky, Picasso)

'The Liberal Imagination' 1950
What marks the artist is his power to shape the material of pain we all have.

JOHN UPDIKE
American writer
'Writers at Work' 4th series 1977
The artist brings something into the world that didn't exist before, and . . . he does it without destroying something else.

KEITH VAUGHAN
British artist
The prime concern of the artist is not to urge the course of events in one direction or another, but to understand what is going on, record it, and resolve the conflict in terms of his art.

GORE VIDAL
American writer
The Guardian 1970
The vanity of the artist is of a very curious nature because it is tied to death. Trying to cheat it. And all perfect nonsense, but it fills the days.

KURT VONNEGUT JR.
American writer
Playboy 1973
The canary bird in the coal mine theory of the arts: artists should be treasured as alarm systems.

EDWARD WADSWORTH
British artist
in 'Artists on Art' 1947
In his best periods, an artist does not paint what he sees, but what he knows *is*. A reality must be evoked. Not an illusion.

ANDY WARHOL
American artist
'From A to B and Back Again' 1975
An artist is somebody who produces things that people don't need to have but that he – for *some reason* – thinks it would be a good idea to give them.

EVELYN WAUGH
British novelist
'Writers at Work' 3rd series 1967
An artist must be a reactionary. He has to stand out against the tenor of the age and not go flopping along.

ORSON WELLES
American film director 1966
I passionately hate the idea of being with it, I think an artist has always to be out of step with his time.

D. W. WINNICOTT
British paediatrician
'Through Paediatrics to Psychoanalysis' 1958
For us all, as for himself, the artist is repeatedly winning brilliant battles in a war to which, however, there is no final outcome. A final outcome would be finding what is *not* true, namely, that what the world offers is identical with what the individual creates.

Painting

ANSEL ADAMS
American photographer
in 'Pictures on a Page' Harold Evans 1978
A picture is usually looked at, seldom
looked *into*.

ROBERT ALTMAN
American film director
New York Herald Tribune 1972
The problem with a film is that it has a
beginning and an end. You can look at
a painting as long as you like.

KAREL APPEL
Ducth painter
'Contemporary Artists' 1977
Painting is always a fight with yourself
and the material.

ANTONIN ARTAUD
French playwright
'Van Gogh'
Nothing has ever been painted, sculpted,
modelled, constructed or invented but to
escape in fact from Hell.

FRANCIS BACON
British artist
Sunday Times, 1975
The more you work, the more the mystery deepens of what appearance is. How
can what is called appearance be made
in another medium. And it needs a sort
of moment of magic to coagulate the colour and form that gets the equivalent of
appearance. The appearance is only riv-
eted for one moment as that appearance.
I mean appearance is like a continuously
floating thing.

JOHN BERGER
British art critic
The Observer 1963
The essence of painting is to give body
to our desires.

YRJO BLOMSTEDT
Finnish artist
'Contemporary Artists' 1977
Painting that answers questions formu-
lated beforehand is superfluous.

GEORGES BRAQUE
French artist
*quoted in 'The Painted Word' by Tom Wolfe
1975*
The painter thinks in forms and colours.
The aim is not to reconstitute an anec-
dotal fact but to constitute a pictorial
fact.

JOHN CANADAY
American art critic
Harpers 1970
The painter today has become a man
whose job it is to supply material in progressive stages for the critic's aesthetic
exercises.

MARC CHAGALL
French painter
Saturday Evening Post 1962
If the painting stands up beside a thing
man cannot make, the painting is authentic. If there is a clash between these
two, it is bad art.

THOMAS D. CHURCH
American garden designer
'Contemporary Architects' 1977
The only limit to your garden is at the
boundaries of your imagination.

SALVADOR DALI
Spanish artist
'Les cocus du vieil art moderne'
The least you can ask of a sculpture is
that it doesn't move.

MARCEL DUCHAMP
French artist
*in 'Dialogues with Duchamp' ed. Pierre Ca-
banne 1971*
I think painting dies, you understand.
After 40 or 50 years a picture dies because its freshness disappears. Sculpture
also dies. I think a picture dies after a
few years like the man who painted it.
Afterwards, it's called the history of art.

The Times 1968
Just because a man starts to paint does not mean he has to go on painting. He isn't even obliged to abandon it. I do not see the need to classify people and above all, to treat paintings as a profession.

Life 1950
Unless a picture shocks, it is nothing.

IAN DURY
British rock singer
I wonder how long it is until sculpture becomes litter?

DAN FLAVIN
American sculptor 1966
The contents of any hardware store could supply enough exhibition material to satisfy the season's needs of the most prosperous commercial gallery.

WINIFRED GAUL
German painter
'Contemporary Artists' 1977
Every painter who seriously dedicates himself to painting recognises as time goes on that painting is not the chosen vehicle for making the dreams of childhood come true, for novel discoveries or inventions, or for changing society.

JEAN-LUC GODARD
French film director
in 'Godard: Images, Sounds, Politics' by Colin McCabe 1980
A picture is life and life is a picture.

ALAN GREEN
British artist
'Contemporary Artists' 1977
Paints and Painting are a vehicle – the means used to make a permanent section of time 'my time'. Every drawing and painting is an attempt to make a kind of transportable reality.

JOSEF HERMAN
British painter
'Contemporary Artists' 1977
Painting, like all the other arts, has a way of realising what is meaningfully human, and a power of reaching, even expanding, our inner life. In this is its significance and in this its service.

EDWARD HOPPER
American artist
'Artists on Art' 1947
Painting is a record of emotion.

quoted in 'The Quotable Quotes' compiled by Alec Lewis 1980
If you could say it in words there would be no reason to paint.

ALDOUS HUXLEY
British writer
'Collected Essays'
Every good painter invents a new way of painting.

RANDALL JARRELL
American critic
quoted in 'Pop Art' Lucy Lippard 1966
The Medium is half life and half art, and competes with both life and art. It spoils its audience for both, spoils both for its audience.

AUGUSTUS JOHN
British artist
The Observer 1950
It isn't enough to have the eyes of a gazelle; you also need the claws of a cat in order to capture your bird alive and play with it before you eat it and join its life to yours. That is the mystery of painting.

MIKE McINNERNEY
British illustrator
The Image 1973
A picture is magic. It's reducing the world to pure, timeless moments. You have to work to see it and only then is it worth it. What it comes down to is that you're alone, and it always comes back to that in the end, because you're the only person you can measure your life by. Every artist has his own voice and in the end it's their own voice that they have to listen to and please.

RENE MAGRITTE
Belgian artist
Letter 1960
A truly poetic canvas is an awakened dream.

quoted in 'Magritte: The True Art of Painting' ed. H. Torczyner 1979
Painting is one of the activities – it is bound up in the series of activities – that seems to change almost nothing in life, the same habits are always recurring. . .

HENRI MATISSE
French artist
A painter has really no serious enemies like his bad paintings.

Picture Post 1949
A drawing must bring to life the space which surrounds it.

JONATHAN MILLER
British doctor and writer
The Listener 1971
An oil painting is the residue of a very complicated negotiation between an actual person and a series of actual materials, during which the artist walked up to his canvas, blobbed bits of stuff on it, stepped back to see how it looked, went back to it again. He had a relation to the canvas of man as smearer. Then he stepped back from the canvas and had a relationship to it as a replica of reality and what he leaves behind is a history of this dual relationship.

HENRY MOORE
British sculptor
Time 1978
A sculpture is like a person and you must treat it like one. You must put it in its best environment.

PAUL NOUGE
French critic
'Histoire de ne pas Rire' 1956
We question pictures, before listening to them, we question them at random. And we are astonished when the reply we had expected is not forthcoming.

PABLO PICASSO
Spanish artist
quoted in Gerald Brenan 'Thoughts in a Dry Season' 1978
Everyone wants to understand painting. Why don't they try to understand the singing of birds? People love the night, a flower, everything that surrounds them without trying to understand them. But painting – that they *must* understand.

quoted in Jean Cocteau 'Journals'
Painting is a blind man's profession. He paints not what he sees but what he feels, what he tells himself about what he has seen.

NBC–TV 1957
To draw, you must close your eyes and sing.

quoted in 'Life with Picasso' by F. Gilot and C. Lake 1964
Painting is not an aesthetic operation: it is a form of magic designed as a mediator between this strange hostile world and us, a way of seizing the power by giving form to our terrors as well as our desires.

For me, a painting is a dramatic action in the course of which reality finds itself split apart. For me that dramatic action takes precedence over all other considerations.

JACKSON POLLOCK
American artist
Painting is a state of being . . . painting is self-discovery. Every good artist paints what he is.

1950
It's just like a bed of flowers. You don't have to tear your hair out over what it means.

ROBERT RAUSCHENBERG
American artist
in 'Pop Art' by Lucy Lippard 1966
Painting relates both to art and life. Neither can be made. I try to act in that gap between the two.

JAMES ROSENQUIST
American artist
On his peers. . .
We were united by a certain focus. We'd looked for dreams and values that could come from a culture in which everything seemed to be immediately obsolete.

MARK ROTHKO
American artist
to Michelangelo Antonioni
Your pictures are like my paintings – about nothing, with precision.

quoted in The Observer 1961
A picture lives by companionship.

GEORGES ROUALT
French artist
Look 1958
Painting is a way to forget life. It is a cry in the night. A strangled laugh.

Life 1953
The painter who loves his art is a king in his realm. Be it Lilliput and he a Lilliputian. From a kitchen maid he makes a fairy queen and from a noble lady a brothel keeper if he wishes, and if he sees, because he is clairvoyant. He has a window to life and to all that the past conceals from the living.

GINO SEVERINI
Italian artist
quoted in 'Artists on Art' 1947
Philosophers and aestheticians may offer elegant and profound definitions of art and beauty but for the painter they are summed up in this phrase – to create a harmony.

SAUL STEINBERG
American artist
'Saul Steinberg' by Harold Rosenberg 1978
When I admire a scene in the country I look for a signature in the lower right hand corner.

Drawing is a way of reasoning on paper.

Time 1978
Doodling is the brooding of the hand.

MARVIN TORFFIELD
American light sculptor
Esquire 1969
Paintings on walls and sculpture on pedestals are limited as forms. Art should be something you can move in, mess around with.

LUDWIG WITTGENSTEIN
German philosopher
A picture is a model of reality.

FRANK LLOYD WRIGHT
American architect
Saturday Evening Post 1961
Pictures deface walls oftener than they decorate them.

Actors

DANA ANDREWS
American film star
All people are half actors.

BRIGITTE BARDOT
French film star
quoted in 'The Wit of Women' ed. by L. and M. Cowan
A good actress lasts, but sex appeal does not.

ETHEL BARRYMORE
American actress
quoted in G. J. Nathan's 'The Theatre in the Fifties' 1953
For an actress to be a success she must have the face of Venus, the brains of Minerva, the grace of Terpsichore, the memory of Macaulay, the figure of Juno and the hide of a rhinoceros.

CANDICE BERGEN
American actress
quoted in 'Goodbye Baby & Amen' by D. Bailey 1969
I can't think of anything grimmer than being an ageing actress – God! it's worse than being an ageing homosexual.

ERNEST BORGNINE
American film star
Acting is a matter of calculated instinct.

MARLON BRANDO
American film star
Acting is the expression of a neurotic impulse.

The Observer 1956
An actor's a guy who if you ain't talkin' about him, ain't listening.

An actor is at most a poet and at least an entertainer.

TRUMAN CAPOTE
American writer
The better the actor the more stupid he is.

JACK CARSON
quoted in 'The Wit of the Theatre' ed. R. May 1969
A fan club is a group of people who tell an actor he is not alone in the way he feels about himself.

BETTE DAVIS
American film star
quoted in 'The Wit of Women' ed. by L. and M. Cowan
A good ham is an actor who enjoys giving pleasure to people.

The real actor – like any real artist – has a direct line to the collective heart.

KIRK DOUGLAS
American film star
Esquire 1970
Acting is like prizefighting. The downtown gyms are smelly, but that's where the champions are.

HENRY FONDA
American film star
The best actors do not let the wheels show. This is the hardest kind of acting and it works only if you look as if you are not acting at all.

JANE FONDA
American film star
Acting is hell: you spend all your time trying to do what they put people in asylums for.

JOHN FORD
American film director
Actors are crap.

CLARK GABLE
American film star
Talent is the least important thing a performer needs, but humility is the one thing he must have.

RUTH GORDON
American actress
Esquire 1967
You never learn to act. By the time you learn to act you're too old to do it.

GRAHAM GREENE
British novelist
For an actor success is simply delayed failure.

GENE HACKMAN
American film star
Seventy five per cent of being successful as an actor is pure luck – the rest is just endurance.

SIR CEDRIC HARDWICKE
British actor
Theatre Arts 1958
Good actors are good because of the things they can tell us without talking. When they are talking they are the slaves of the dramatist. It is what they can show the audience when they are not talking that reveals the fine actor.

HELEN HAYES
American actress
'On Reflection' 1968
Actors cannot choose the manner in which they are born – consequently it is the one gesture in their lives completely devoid of self-consciousness.

KATHARINE HEPBURN
American film star
Life's what's important. Walking, houses, family. Birth and pain and joy. Acting's just waiting for a custard pie. That's all.

Esquire 1967
Great performing is total simplicity, in any field, the capacity to get to the essence of it, to eliminate all the frills and all the foibles.

What acting means is that you've got to get out of your own skin.

ALFRED HITCHCOCK
British film director
The best screen actor is that man who can do nothing extremely well.

JOHN HUSTON
American film director 1967
There's nothing duller than a respectable actor. Actors should be rogues, mountebanks and strolling players.

GLENDA JACKSON
British actress 1976
External rewards don't touch the continuing fascination and struggle of acting. It stays interesting because it makes increasing demands on you which you feel less and less able to fulfill.

AMANDA LEAR
British singer
Interview 1978
An actress must know a little more about life than how to look good on a headsheet. An actress must know how to suffer.

JOAN LITTLEWOOD
British theatre director
Esquire 1964
Actors should still be called comedians – wit and inventiveness are the attributes they most need.

WALTER MATTHAU
American actor 1979
I think the whole business of being an actor and being part of entertainment, whether it be TV shows or stage shows or movies, is noble. You learn about everything, and you're involved in something. You know what it is – it's acting. Look at the doctors and the lawyers. *They* think they're real people.

Acting in films is . . . retirement acting – you just give an exhibition of your former skills.

HELEN MIRREN
British actress 1970
Acting is such an un-natural thing to do.

J. B. MORTON
British humorist
'Beachcomber' 'Dictionary for Today' in Daily Express, passim
Galaxy: five or six actresses.

PAUL NEWMAN
American film star
Acting is a question of absorbing other people's personalities and adding some of your own experience.

JACK NICHOLSON
American film star
TV interview 1980
You say 'Let's get it done real' but acting is just one version of the unreal after another.

CARROLL O'CONNOR
American actor
Playboy 1973
The greatest satisfaction for an actor is to be needed.

LORD OLIVIER
British actor
The Observer 1979
Acting great parts devours you.

Time 1978
Acting is a masochistic form of exhibitionism. It is not quite the occupation of an adult.

Acting is just one big bag of tricks.

JEAN RENOIR
French film director
Time 1979
To be a star and play yourself all the time is to be a beautiful doll imitating yourself.

SIR RALPH RICHARDSON
British actor
The Observer 1947
The art of acting consists in keeping people from coughing.

GEORGE SANDERS
British film star
An actor is not quite a human being – but then, who is?

The important thing for a star is to have an interesting face. He doesn't have to move it around very much. Editing and camerawork can always produce the desired illusion that a performance is being given.

Acting is like roller skating – once you know how to do it, it is neither stimulating nor exciting.

RICHARD SCHICKEL
American film critic
A movie star is not an artist, he is an art object.

GEORGE C. SCOTT
American film star
Esquire 1965
Acting . . . that attempt to find universality, reality and truth in a world of pretending.

PETER SELLERS
British film star
I have the feeling that the film character enters my body as if I were a kind of medium. It's a little frightening.

SIMONE SIGNORET
French film actress
The body of an actor is like a well in which experiences are stored, then tapped when needed.

DONALD SUTHERLAND
American film star 1979
Actors are not really people. They have fragments of emotion which sometimes explode in a way that is different from most people.

SPENCER TRACY
American film star
Acting is not an *important* job in the scheme of things. Plumbing is.

ORSON WELLES
American film director 1956
Every actor in his heart believes every-
thing bad that's printed about him.

JOHN WHITING
British playwright
'John Whiting on Theatre' 1966
Very good actors never seem to talk
about their art. Very bad ones never
stop.

MICHAEL WILDING
British actor
You can pick out the actors by the glazed
look that comes into their eyes when the
conversation   wanders   away   from
themselves.

NICOL WILLIAMSON
British actor
Now! 1981
Actors act too much.

SHELLEY WINTERS
American actress
Saturday Evening Post 1962
Acting is like painting pictures on bath-
room tissues. Ten minutes later you
throw them away and they are gone.

Theatre

GEORGE ABBOTT
American theatrical producer
Saturday Evening Post 1955
Very few plays are any good and *no* first
plays are any good. If there's any form
of writing that takes experience, it's
stage writing. You've got to tell your
story without description, without getting inside the characters, without jumping from place to place or from time to
time, without psychological explanations. It's very hard.

JAMES AGATE
British critic
Theatre director . . . a person engaged
by the management to conceal the fact
that the players cannot act.

EDWARD ALBEE
American playwright
Sunday Times 1964
What every playwright would like to do
is make the theatre into his own face.

ANTONIN ARTAUD
French playwright
Letter 1948
The theatre is in reality the genesis of
creation. It will be done.

'Le Théâtre et la Science' 1947
The true theatre has always seemed to
me as the exercise of a terrible and dangerous act / in which, moreover, the idea
of theatre and performance is eliminated
just as / that of all science, all religion
and all art. . .

'Aliener l'Acteur' 1947
The theatre is the state / the place / the
point / where you can get hold of man's
anatomy and through it heal and dominate life.

'Collected Works' 1968
The theatre, like the plague, is a crisis
which is resolved either in death or in
the return to complete health.

HOWARD BARKER
British playwright
in 'Contemporary Dramatists' 1977
The stage is the last remaining arena for the free assault of our society. It is the sump to which our poisons and our malices, our despairs and terrors drain. It is not a place for reconciliation or relief. It is not a dark place rumbling with laughter or a padded private place for the touching of hands, but a granite crucible in which conflict and collision strike dangerous, disconcerting sparks. It is a world on high gas.

Nothing is unacceptable on stage except the breakdown of communication. Nothing is incredible or unlikely. It is the world which is incredible and unlikely and it is the business of the theatre to show the agony we experience in failing to come to terms with that. . . . To write for the theatre is to begin a process of definition of the world.

JEAN-LOUIS BARRAULT
French theatrical producer
'Nouvelle Reflexions sur le Théâtre'
The theatre is the first serum that man invented to protect himself from the sickness of despair.

BRIDGET BOLAND
Irish playwright
'Contemporary Dramatists' 1977
In the end every play is saying 'Belief is dangerous'.

BERTOLT BRECHT
German playwright
'The Messingkauf Dialogues' 1965
A theatre that can't be laughed in is a theatre to be laughed at.

PETER BROOK
British theatre director
The Observer 1970
The theatre should be necessary – like a bank or a grocer's shop. It should provide something that people can't get anywhere else.

RONALD DUNCAN
British playwright
'Collected Plays' 1971
Any dramatist finds that his plays fall into two categories: those for which he had some hopes but which went wrong either in the writing or in the production; and those for which he had none, and surprised him by achieving public approval.

T. S. ELIOT
American poet
New York Post 1963
A play should give you something to think about. When I see a play and understand it the first time, then I know it can't be much good.

MARIO FRATTI
Italian playwright
'Contemporary Dramatists' 1977
Only action is life. Theatre is and must be action. Accordingly, theatre is life. . . Theatre is a window open on the life of our fellow creatures – a window open on their secret, intimate behaviour. Let's watch in silence from that window.

WOLCOTT GIBBS
American critic
'More In Sorrow' 1958
Generally speaking, the American theatre is the aspirin of the middle classes.

JEAN GIRAUDOUX
French playwright 1958
The stage play is a trial, not a deed of violence. The soul is opened, like the combination of a safe, by means of a word. You don't require an acetylene torch.

MOSS HART
American playwright
on stage writing in 'Contemporary Dramatists' 1977
One begins with two people on a stage and one of them had better say something pretty damn quick!

LILLIAN HELLMAN
American playwright
'Pentimento' 1974
It is best in the theatre to act with confidence, no matter how little right you have to it.

BERNARD LEVIN
British journalist
Daily Express 1960
I see the theatre as a beleaguered city, infested not by hostile troops, but by the impersonal, creeping jungle. The test of any new production, therefore, is it helping to push back the jungle and extend the city's frontier, or is it by carelessness or treachery letting another patch or strangling green encroach upon the walls?

MICHAEL McCLURE
American poet and dramatist
in 'Contemporary Dramatists' 1977
Theatre is an organism of poetry – weeping and laughing, and crying and smiling and performing superhuman acts – on a shelf in space and lit with lights.

SIOBHAN McKENNA
Irish actress 1966
You can do what you like in Shakespeare because people don't understand half of it anyway. But you can't in an Irish play because it really means what it says.

ARTHUR MILLER
American playwright
Harper's 1958
The structure of a play is always the story of how the birds came home to roost.

JONATHAN MILLER
British doctor and writer
The Listener 1978
Compared to a novel, a play is simply a string of sentences which are ascribed to people who have not necessarily been described.

FRANK MOORHOUSE
Australian journalist
The Bulletin 1973
The Green Room is a pacifying cage where the circus animals, even those with natural hostility, prowl together in temporary truce.

PETER O'TOOLE
Irish actor
Playboy 1965
I think it is time there was an innovation to protect the author and the actor and the public from the vagaries of the director. Given a good play and a good team and a decent set you could put a blue-arsed baboon in the stalls and get what is known as a production.

ALAN PLATER
British playwright
The Listener 1979
The real test of a theatrical form is whether it will stand laughter, and test itself to destruction.

TERENCE RATTIGAN
British playwright
Time 1977
My forte is the play that says absolutely nothing, except possibly that human beings are strange creatures and worth putting on the stage, where they can be laughed at or cried over, as our pleasure takes us.

TONY RICHARDSON
British director 1966
I think the theatre is a wonderful holdiay but life is too short for holidays.

JEAN-PAUL SARTRE
French philosopher
The Observer 1961
The theatre is not concerned with reality, it is only concerned with truth. The cinema on the other hand seeks a reality which may contain moments of truth.

ROBERT SHERWOOD
American playwright 1955
The duty of dramatists is to express their times and guide the public through the complexities of these times.

BARRIE STAVIS
American playwright
'Contemporary Dramatists' 1977
Every playwright is responsible not only for what man is, but for what man can be.

TOM STOPPARD
British playwright
quoted in The Times 1970
All new plays are old plays.

HOWARD TAUBMAN
American journalist
New York Times 1964
It is the destiny of the theatre nearly everywhere and in every period to struggle even when it is flourishing.

KENNETH TYNAN
British critic
'Tynan on Theatre' 1964
The greatest plays are those which convince us that men can occasionally speak like angels.

1958
In most schools drama is taught as a suspiciously amusing branch of literature: we would gain much if it were taught as an offshoot of sociology.

'Pausing on the Stairs' 1957
Show me a congenital eavesdropper with the instincts of a Peeping Tom and I will show you the makings of a dramatist.

New York Herald Tribune 1957
A good many inconveniences attend playgoing in any large city, but the greatest of them is usually the play itself.

'Pausing on the Stairs' 1957
Would you know the shortest way to good playwriting? Pause on the stairs.

Time & Tide 1964
Writing a play is the most difficult thing a writer can do with a pen.

'Tynan Right & Left' 1967
If a play does anything – either tragically or comically, satirically or farcically – to explain to me why I am alive, it is a good play. If it seems unaware that such questions exist, I tend to suspect that it is a bad one.

PETER USTINOV
British actor and wit
Time & Tide
Glamour in the theatre is usually twenty chorus girls in a line all doing the same thing. It is assumed that twenty women are more glamorous than one.

GORE VIDAL
American writer
New York Times 1956
A talent for drama is not a talent for writing, but is an ability to articulate human relationships.

THORNTON WILDER
American writer
'Writers at Work' 1st series 1958
We live in what is, but we find a thousand ways not to face it. Great theatre strengthens our faculty to face it.

A dramatist is one who, from his earliest years, has found that sheer gazing at the shocks and counter-shocks among people is quite sufficiently engrossing without having to encase it in comment.

LORD WILLIS
British screenwriter 1968
If you show everything (in theatre) you are left with only the sex act to show on stage and that is impossible – at least it is for a long run.

Dance

SIR FREDERIC ASHTON
British choreographer
Nova 1975
Young dancers are like leaves – blow on them and they move.

GEORGE BALANCHINE
American choreographer
Saturday Evening Post 1965
I am a choreographer. A choreographer is a poet. I do not create. God creates. I assemble. And I will steal from everywhere to do it.

The Observer 1952
Ballets are like butterflies – the new butterfly would be ashamed of the last one.

The Guardian 1963
To make good ballet you must love beautiful women. Ballet is a woman's world in which man only participates as an honoured guest.

COMMANDER CODY
American rock musician
You gotta bop till you drop.

JEAN DUBUFFET
French artist
'Prospectus et tous écrits suivants'
Dancing is the last word in life . . . in dancing one draws nearer to oneself.

MARTHA GRAHAM
American dancer
It is not important that you should know what a dance means. It is only important that you should be stirred. If you can write the story of your dance it is a literary thing, but it is not dancing.

SIR ROBERT HELPMAN
Australian choreographer
The trouble with nude dancing is that not everything stops when the music does.

1969
Aren't all ballets sexy? I think they should be. I can think of nothing more kinky than a prince chasing a swan around all night.

Evening Gazette 1963
Ballet is like football. I don't understand a footballer's technique but I can see when he's playing brilliantly. People don't like the ballet because they think they don't understand it. Actually they do. It's the most primitive form of appeal.

AGNES DE MILLE
American dancer 1954
A good education is usually harmful to a dancer. A good calf is better than a good head.

Photography

BERENICE ABBOTT
American photographer
'Universal Photo Almanac' 1951
A photograph is not a painting, a poem, a symphony, a dance. It is not just a pretty picture . . . It is, or should be, a significant document, a penetrating statement, which can be described in a very simple term – selectivity.

Infinity 1951
Living photography builds up, does not tear down. It proclaims the dignity of man. Living photography is positive in its approach. It sings a song of life – not death.

'The World of Atget' 1964
The photographer's punctilio is his recognition of now – to see it so clearly that he looks through it to the past and senses the future . . . the photographer is the contemporary being par excellence; through his eyes the now becomes past.

in 'Pictures on a Page' Harold Evans 1978
I have yet to see a fine photograph which is not a good document.

ANSEL ADAMS
American photographer
'Portfolio One' 1948
To photograph truthfully and effectively is to see beneath the surfaces and record the qualities of nature and humanity which live or are latent in all things.

'Photographers on Photography' ed. N. Lyons 1966
A great photograph is a full expression of what one fears about what is being photographed in the deepest sense, and is thereby a true expression of what one feels about life in its entirety.

JAMES AGEE
American critic
It is a peculiar part of the good photographer's adventure to know where luck is most likely to lie in the stream, to hook it and to bring it in without unfair play, and without too much subduing it.

ANONYMOUS
in The Observer 1957
Photography is an art trying to escape from the machine.

DIANE ARBUS
American photographer
quoted in 'On Photography' by Susan Sontag 1977
The camera is a kind of license.

JOHN BERGER
British art critic
The Observer 1963
Photography intercepts reality as it exists.

GEORGES BRASSAI
French photographer
in Amateur Photographer 1969
There are many photographs which are full of life, but which are confusing and difficult to remember. It is the force of an image which matters.

HENRY CALLAHAN
American photographer
Minicam Photography 1946
Photography is an adventure.

Newsweek 1976
A photographer is able to capture a moment that people cannot always see.

HENRI CARTIER-BRESSON
French photographer
'The World of Henri Cartier-Bresson' 1968
The camera is to some extent a sort of notebook for recording sketches made in time and space, but it is also an admirable instrument for seizing upon life as it presents itself. Without the participation of intuition, sensibility and understanding, photography is nothing.

The Observer 1957
Photography is like fencing. You must keep your distance, wait, and then *thrust*.

Daily Telegraph 1970
To me, photography is the simultaneous recognition, in a fraction of a second, of the significance of an event, as well as the precise organisation of forms which give that event its proper expression.

Our job is to view events with a clinical eye, but not to distort them by means of tricks while shooting or in the darkroom.

Pictures should never be posed. They are 'revealed' so must be accepted as they are. Left alone.

A photograph is made on the spot and at once. You have no right to use tricks or play around with reality. The time element is the key to photography. One must seize the moment before it passes. The fleeting gesture, the evanescent smile.

The Observer 1968
Taking pictures is like a love affair – if someone else is there watching you can't do anything. I try not only to melt physically, but also emotionally and intellectually into the back landscape. A good fisherman does not stir up the water before he starts to fish.

The Observer 1963
Photography is a way of drawing. The camera is a means of looking from a mechanical and optic point of view in order to obtain the truth. Photography has not the right to change or distort in any way the real image. It is necessary to grasp the immediate future, the sudden gesture, the impossible smile. We are passive informants of a world which moves. Our unique moment of creation is the one twenty-fifth of a second when we press the button.

'The World of Henri Cartier-Bresson' 1968
Photography is an instantaneous operation, both sensory and intellectual expression of the world in visual terms, and also a perpetual quest and interrogation. It is at one and the same time the recognition of a fact in a fraction of a second and the rigorous arrangement of the forms visually perceived which give to that fact expression and significance.

'The Decisive Moment' 1952
Photographers deal in things which are continually vanishing and when they have vanished there is no contrivance on earth which can make them come back again . . . our task is to perceive reality, almost simultaneously recording it in the sketchbook which is our camera.

JUSTUS DAHINDEN
Swiss architect
'Contemporary Architects' 1980
It is not the camera that counts, it is the eye.

TERENCE DONOVAN
British photographer
in H. Evans 'Pictures on a Page' 1978
A seven bath developer is no substitute for thought.

HAROLD EVANS
British journalist
'Pictures on a Page' 1978
The camera cannot lie. But it can be an accessory to untruth.

HELMUT GERNSHEIM
German photographer
Creative Photography 1962
Photography is the only 'language' understood in all parts of the world and bridging all nations and cultures. It links the family of man.

JEAN-LUC GODARD
French film director
in 'Godard: Images, Sounds, Politics' by Colin McCabe 1980
The camera is communication in a solid state.

EMMET GOWIN
quoted in 'On Photography' by Susan Sontag 1977
Photography is a tool for dealing with things everybody knows about but isn't attending to.

WILSON HICKS
American photojournalist
'Words & Pictures' 1952
People are inclined to think of the photographer as a gross fellow, with a press card in the band of his battered 'newspaperman's hat' and a big cigar in his big mouth, who drives nice folks to distraction by his bedevilling insistence on 'just one more' and embarrasses them with his near-simian behaviour.

DOROTHEA LANGE
American photographer
Aperture 1952
It is in the nature of the camera to deal with what *is* – we urge that those who use the camera retire from what *might be*.

Bad as it is, the world is full of potentially good photographs. But to be good, photographs have to be full of the world.

MOMA catalogue notes 1966
While there is perhaps a province in which the photograph can tell us nothing more than what we see with our own eyes, there is another in which it proves to us how little our eyes permit us to see.

STEFAN LORANT
Hungarian picture editor
in 'Pictures on a Page' by Harold Evans 1978
The camera should be like the notebook of a trained reporter, to record events as they happen, without trying to stop them to make a picture.

CLARENCE JOHN LOUGHLIN
American photographer
quoted in 'On Photography' by Susan Sontag 1977
The creative photographer sets free the *human contents* of objects, and imparts humanity to the inhuman world around him.

DON McCULLIN
British photographer
'The Destruction Business' 1971
What's the point of getting killed if you've got the wrong exposure.

MARSHALL McLUHAN
Canadian academic
quoted in The Image 1974
The photograph is a brothel without walls.
quoted by H. Evans 'Pictures on a Page' 1978
It is one of the peculiar characteristics of the photograph that it isolates single moments in time.

MALCOLM MUGGERIDGE
British journalist
The Observer 1968
One's image is an inescapable pre-occupation. The camera, far more than even nuclear weapons is the destructive force of our time. The great falsifier. It has replaced the written and spoken word and captured the whole field of art and literature.

MAN RAY
French photographer
quoted in 'Photographers on Photography' ed. N. Lyons 1966
Open confidences are being made every day, and it remains for the eye to train itself to see them without prejudice or restraint.

AARON SISKIND
American photographer
Minicam Photography 1945
Photographically speaking, there is no compromise with reality.

HENRY HOLMES SMITH
American photographer
'Three Photographers' 1961
Photography is the most rigorously logical of man's methods of making images.

SUSAN SONTAG
American essayist
'On Photography' 1977
Photographs really are experience captured, and the camera is the ideal arm of consciousness in its acquisitive mood.

The most grandiose result of the photographic enterprise is to give us the sense that we can hold the whole world in our heads – as an anthology of images.

Today, everything exists to end in a photograph.

Life is not about significant details, illuminated in a flash, fixed for ever. Photographs are.

The camera makes everyone a tourist in other people's reality, and eventually in one's own.

EDWARD STEICHEN
American photographer
Esquire 1969
The real mission of photography is explaining man to himself.

JOSEPH STRICK
American film director
Sunday Times 1963
All camera work is a form of voyeurism.

JOHN SZARKOWSKI
American critic
quoted in 'On Photography' by Susan Sontag 1977
Photography is a system of visual editing
. . . Like chess or writing, it is a matter of choosing from among given possibilities, but in the case of photography the number of possibilities is not finite but infinite.

JERRY N. UELSMAN
quoted in 'On Photography' by Susan Sontag 1977
The camera is a fluid way of encountering that other reality.

GORE VIDAL
American writer
New Statesman 1978
Photography is the 'art form' of the untalented.

ANDY WARHOL
American artist
'Exposures' 1979
My idea of a good picture is one that is in focus, one of a famous person doing something unfamous. It's being in the right place at the wrong time.

EDWARD WESTON
American photographer
quoted in Harold Evans 'Pictures on a Page' 1978
To consult rules of composition before making a picture is a little like consulting the law of gravitation before going for a walk.

in 'Photographers on Photography' ed. N. Lyons 1966
The photographer's power lies in his ability to recreate his subjects in terms of its basic reality, and present this recreation in such a form that the spectator feels he is seeing not just a symbol for the object, but the thing itself, revealed for the first time.

Critics

ROBERT MARTIN ADAMS
American literary critic
quoted in 'Contemporary Literary Critics' 1977 ed. Elmer Borklund
It is only through the vigilant, the militant use of our critical faculties that we can confer any real benefit on the authors whom we love.

BRIAN ALDISS
British author
The Guardian 1971
I believe that critics who presume to dictate to writers or writers who set themselves up as lodestones are enemies of art since if they have any effect at all it is to deflect the aim of true writers.

NELSON ALGREN
American author
'Writers at Work' 1st series
The avocation of assessing the failures of better men can be turned into a comfortable livelihood, providing you back it up with PhD.

'ALL ABOUT EVE'
20th Century Fox 1950 screenplay by Joseph L. Mankiewicz based on 'The Wisdom of Eve' by Mary Orr
George Sanders: My native habitat is the theatre. I toil not, neither do I spin. I am a critic and a commentator. I am essential to the theatre – as ants to a picnic, as the boll weevil to a cotton field.

WALTER ALLEN
British novelist
quoted in 'Contemporary Literary Critics', ed. Elmer Borklund 1977
The reviewer's job is to read a novel, find out what the author has set out to do, estimate how far he has succeeded, decide whether his intentions were worthwhile, and report his conclusions to his readers.

W. H. AUDEN
British poet
'Writers at Work' 4th series 1977
Writing reviews can be fun, but I don't think the practice is very good for the character.

WHITNEY BALLIETT
American writer
'Dinosaurs in the Morning' 1962
A critic is a bundle of biases held loosely together by a sense of taste.

SIR THOMAS BEECHAM
British conductor
'Beecham Stories' 1978
Criticism of the arts ... taken by and large, ends in a display of suburban omniscience which sees no further than into the next-door garden.

BRENDAN BEHAN
Irish playwright
Critics are like eunuchs in a harem: they know how it's done, they've seen it done every day, but they're unable to do it themselves.

JIM BISHOP
American journalist
New York Journal-American 1957
A good writer is not *per se* a good book critic. No more than a good drunk is automatically a good bartender.

R. P. BLACKMUR
American critic
'Language as Gesture' 1952
Criticism, I take it, is the formal discourse of an amateur.

PETER BOGDANOVICH
American film director
The criterion for judging whether a picture is successful or not is time.

JORGE LUIS BORGES
Argentine writer
'June 1968'
To arrange a library is to practise / in a quiet and modest way / the art of criticism.

JOHN MASON BROWN
American essayist
To many people dramatic criticism must be like trying to tattoo soap bubbles.

ALBERT CAMUS
French writer
Those who write clearly have readers; those who write obscurely have commentators.

RAYMOND CHANDLER
American novelist
letter to Frederick L. Allen 1948
Great critics, of whom there are piteously few, build a home for the truth.

SIR WINSTON CHURCHILL
British statesman
Criticism may not be agreeable, but it is necessary. It fulfils the same function as pain in the human body. It calls attention to an unhealthy state of things.

HAROLD CLURMAN
American theatre critic
I disapprove of much but I enjoy everything.

JEAN COCTEAU
French writer and film critic
'Writers at Work' 3rd series 1967
Appreciation of art is a moral erection, otherwise mere dilettantism.

SUE COE
British illustrator
The Image 1973
The ultimate criticism of art is the integration and application of conventional aesthetic definitions toward a silk screen of a car crash in green.

WOLCOTT GIBBS
American critic
quoted in Esquire 1968 on film criticism. . .
The whole absurdity of . . . trying to write for the information of my friends about something that was plainly designed for the entertainment of their cooks.

CHRISTOPHER HAMPTON
British playwright
Sunday Times 1977
Asking a working writer what he thinks about critics is like asking a lamp-post what it thinks about dogs.

DUSTIN HOFFMAN
American film star
Playboy 1975
A good review from the critics is just another stay of execution.

EUGENE IONESCO
French playwright 1966
Mediocrity is more dangerous in a critic than in a writer.

GLENDA JACKSON
British actress 1975
Cinema criticism in the main is a total waste of everybody's time.

RANDALL JARRELL
American critic
There is something fundamentally wrong about critics: what's good is good without our saying so.

ERIC JULBER
American lawyer
Esquire 1969
In judging a man's worth, you should disregard his opinions. People's opinions are the least important thing about them.

PAULINE KAEL
American critic
Newsweek 1973
In the arts the critic is the only independant source of information. The rest is advertising.

ALFRED KAZIN
American critic
quoted in 'Contemporary Literary Critics', ed. Elmer Borklund 1977
No critic who is any good sets out deliberately to enlighten someone else; he writes to put his own ideas in order.

HILTON KRAMER
quoted in Marilyn Bender 'The Beautiful People' 1967
The more minimal the art the more maximum the explanation.

JOHN LEONARD
American critic
Playboy 1976
In writing about television you are really writing about everything. TV is like the sea we swim in. The trouble is that, like fish, we would be the last ones to notice that we were wet, or ask questions about the nature of wetness.

LIBERACE (Walter Valentino Liberace)
American pianist
rebutting adverse criticisms, 1954
What you said hurt me very much. I cried all the way to the bank.

MARSHALL McLUHAN
Canadian academic
'The Mechanical Bride' 1951
It is critical vision alone which can mitigate the unimpeded operation of the automatic.

JOHN MADDOX
British director of the Nuffield Foundation
The Listener 1979
Criticism is . . . always a kind of compliment.

FRANCOIS MAURIAC
French writer
'Second Thoughts' 1961
A good critic is the sorcerer who makes some hidden spring gush forth unexpectedly under our feet.

HENRY MILLER
American writer
'Sexus' 1949
Honest criticism means nothing: what one wants is unrestrained passion, fire for fire.

VLADIMIR NABOKOV
Russian writer
'Writers at Work' 4th series 1977
Criticism can be instructive in the sense that it gives readers, including the author of the book, some information about the critic's intelligence, or honesty, or both.

GEORGE JEAN NATHAN
American critic
'The World of George Jean Nathan' 1952
Impersonal criticism . . . is like an impersonal fist-fight, or an impersonal marriage; and just as successful.

FELIX PAPPALARDI
American rock musician
Criticism and critics, they're full of shit. If they weren't, they'd be out playing and they wouldn't have time to criticise anybody.

CHANNING POLLOCK
A critic is a legless man who teaches running.

MAN RAY
French photographer
'Self Portrait' 1963
It would be a great help if the word 'serious' could be eliminated from the vocabulary. It must have been invented by critics not too sure of themselves, condemning all of the most exciting and profound works that have been produced through the ages.

ADOLF RUPP
American college basketball coach 1958
The road to anywhere is filled with many pitfalls, and it takes a man of character and determination not to fall into them. . . Whenever you get your head above the average, someone will be there to take a poke at you . . . to sit by and worry about criticism which often comes from the misinformed or from those incapable of passing judgement on an individual or a problem is a waste of time.

GEORGE BERNARD SHAW
Irish writer and playwright
New York Times 1950
A drama critic is a man who leaves no turn unstoned.

IRWIN SHAW
American writer 1977
TV exposure has done wonders for my

book sales, but it has a strange effect on the critics.

JEAN SIBELIUS
Finnish composer
Pay no attention to what the critics say: no statue has ever been put up to a critic.

JOHN SIMON
American critic
on 'Jonathan Livingstone Seagull' Esquire 1974
Seagulls, as the film stresses, subsist on garbage, and, I guess, you are what you eat.

JOHN STEINBECK
American writer
'Writers at Work' 4th series 1977
Time is the only critic without ambition.

GEORGE STEINER
British academic
'Tolstoy or Dostoevsky: an essay in the old criticism' 1959
Literary criticism should arise out of a debt of love.

KENNETH TYNAN
British critic
New York Times 1966
A critic is a man who knows the way but can't drive the car.

'Tynan Left & Right' 1967
Drama criticism ... a self-knowing account of the way in which one's conciousness has been modified during an evening in the theatre; and the greater the self-knowledge, the better the critic. At any level, criticism must be accurate reportage of what has taken place outside you; at the highest level, it is also accurate reportage of what has taken place within you.

A good drama critic is one who perceives what is happening in the theatre of his time. A great drama critic also perceives what is *not* happening.

JOHN UPDIKE
American writer
'Writers at Work' 4th series 1977
Everything is infinitely fine, and any opinion is somehow coarser than the texture of the real thing.

JOHN WAIN
British writer
quoting Anatole France in 'Contemporary Literary Critics' ed. Elmer Borklund 1977
Criticism records the adventures of one's soul among masterpieces.

AUBERON WAUGH
British journalist
Esquire 1968
Impressions are two for a penny, but opinions are definitely precious, to be prized like jewels and defended; taken out of hiding from time to time, then polished and put back.

JERRY WEINTRAUB
American film producer 1975
All that bullshit with the New York critics is just cocktail party talk. I've become a multi-millionaire with things that Rex Reed hated.

REED WHITTEMORE
American critic
in New Republic 1971
Judgement in literature is impugned to the extent that it is exercised.

BILLY WILDER
American film director
What critics call 'dirty' in our movies, they call 'lusty' in foreign films.

P. G. WODEHOUSE
British humorist
New York Mirror 1955
Has anyone ever seen a dramatic critic in the daytime. Of course not. They come out after dark, up to no good.

Audience

ALVIN AILEY
American dance choreographer
1975
I think the people come to the theatre to look at themselves. I try to hold up the mirror.

WOODY ALLEN
American film star
Sunday Times 1970
Audiences have a way of holding your personal life against you if it doesn't match their own experience.

AL ALVAREZ
British writer
'The Savage God' 1971
The ultimate justification of the high-brow arts . . . they survive morally by becoming, in one way or another, an imitation of death in which their audience can share. To achieve this the artist, in his role of scapegoat, finds himself testing out his own death and vulnerability for and on himself.

KINGSLEY AMIS
British author
Sunday Times 1973
All amateurs must be philistines part of the time.

ROBERT ANDERSON
American dramatist
'Contemporary Dramatists' 1977
Each reader or spectator is a new collaborator, and he will, in a sense, write his own play and arrive at his own meanings, based on his own experience of life.

ALBEN W. BARKLEY
The best audience is intelligent, well-educated, and a little drunk.

E. C. BENTLEY
American writer
'The Life of the Drama' 1965
If you wish to attract an audience's attention, be violent; if you wish to hold it, be violent again . . . the psychology is sound and each man is a human being – a specimen of human psychology – before he is a scholar and a gentleman.

JOHN BERGER
British art critic
Daily Worker 1963
Philistinism means impatience with art. Impatience in both senses of the word – for it is over-hasty and aggressive. The philistine in the man protests that he is not going to be taken in before he himself has taken the work of art in.

SHELLEY BERMAN
American comedian
Daily Express 1961
Give the people what they want is good advice for grocery clerks, but lousy for performers.

GARY BERTINI
Israeli conductor
after an audience slowhandclapped a modern work, 1969
I find it very healthy if an audience reacts in any way.

HUMPHREY BOGART
American film star
The only thing you owe the public is a good performance.

quoted in Esquire 1964
When the heavy, full of crime and bitterness, grabs his wounds and talks about death and taxes in a husky voice, the audience is his and his alone.

PIERRE BOULEZ
French composer
The Observer 1971
In my opinion, it is a generalisation to speak of concert audiences. There is no one audience. There are as many audiences as there are programmes. Each one has a right to its own taste.

ANGIE BOWIE
British rock personality
Fans are smart. They bang on cars and try to get in to see you. What could be more wonderful? I don't understand how anyone could *not* think about the fans. They're the ones who make it worthwhile. You don't make records for record company executives, you make them for people.

LENNY BRUCE
American comedian
The whole motivation for any performer 'Look at me, Ma.'

CHARLES BUKOWSKI
American writer
'Notes of a Dirty Old Man' 1969
The public takes from a writer, or a writing, what it needs, and lets the remainder go. But what they take is usually what they need least and what they let go is what they need most.

ROBERT CALVERT
British rock musician
In a completely dead town it is quite a responsibility to provide an exciting and colourful two hours. That is why rock music is so popular, because it's the *only* way, short of forming terrorist cells or something, that you can actually find a sort of collective excitement without causing anyone any harm. It's a release from everyday banality, isn't it?

EDDIE CANTOR
American singer
It takes twenty years to make an overnight success.

AL CAPP
American cartoonist 1954
The public is like a piano. You have to know what keys to poke.

DICK CAVETT
American TV talkshow host
Playboy 1971
As long as people will accept crap, it will be financially profitable to dispense it.

MAURICE CHEVALIER
French film star
Holiday 1956
An artist carries on through his life a mysterious, uninterrupted conversation with his public.

LORD CLARK
British critic
on resigning as Chairman of ITA, 1957
It surprises me how many ladies and gentlemen with broken hearts, howling into the microphone like amorous cats, the public will swallow.

MONTGOMERY CLIFT
American film star
in 'Montgomery Clift' by Patricia Bosworth 1979
If you have a goal – and you're busy growing – you're safe. It's only when you start to believe of yourself what the general public believes that you start losing the courage to risk outward failure. That is the biggest pitfall.

JEAN COCTEAU
French writer and film director
'Le Potomak'
What the public criticises in you, cultivate it. It is you.

in 'The Faber Book of Aphorisms' 1964
What the public like best is fruit that is overripe.

NIK COHN
British writer
New Times 1975
Just like any other mob, most of the movie going public, most of the time, live one step away from imbecility, ready to be gulled by the first piece of plausable trash that's thrown at them. And the only possible use of the critic is to make some stand against that tide.

PETER COOK
British comedian 1974
Actors and athletes have always had a great affinity for one another. Actors, athletes and crooks. Criminals get along famously with people in our business. I think it is because they recognise us as fellow thieves. As entertainers we're also in the business of stealing the public's money. We are paid so disproportionately.

BOB DYLAN
American singer
I just have thoughts in my head and I write them. I'm not trying to lead any causes for anyone else.

ROBERT FROST
American poet
Hell is a half-filled auditorium.

quoted in Esquire 1973
The trouble with the idolators is that no matter how much they disappoint you, they always go away feeling you've disappointed them.

JUDY GARLAND
American singer and film star
All you have to do is never cheat and work your best and work your hardest and they'll respond to you.

WILLIE GAVIN
media planner for President Nixon 1968
quoted in J. McGinnis 'The Selling of the President' 1969
What you leave unsaid becomes what the audience brings to it. Lead 'em to the brink of the idea, but don't push across the brink. It's not the words, but the silences where the votes lie.

BOB GELDOF
Irish rock star
I want this thing that the whole gig becomes a psychic communion between the band and the audience, where the band becomes all but irrelevancy except that they are a band. The whole rock 'n' roll thing on stage is a catharsis, a purgative of all frustrations. It's like going to confession when I was ten years old. The weight of wanking would lift from my brain as I told the priest I'd masturbated X times. At gigs it's the same thing.

HENRY GILMER
American politician 1948
Look over your shoulder now and then to be sure that someone's following you.

MOSES HADAS
American actor
Performing Arts 1969
The larger and more indiscriminate the audience, the greater the need to safeguard and purify standards of quality and taste.

RICHARD HAMILTON
British artist 1971
A work of art does not exist without its audience.

KATHARINE HEPBURN
American film star
If you give audiences a chance they'll do half your acting for you.

HAROLD HOBSON
British critic
Sunday Times 1969
It really is not necessary, in the cause of love and brotherhood, to spit in the audience's face, stamp on its feet, shine bright lights into its eyeballs and sprinkle sweat onto it from the performers' armpits.

IAN HUNTER
British rock singer
Punish an audience – they love it.

JOHN IRVING
American author
New Times 1979
People with limited imaginations find it hard to imagine that anyone else has an imagination. Therefore they must think that everything they read in some way happened.

MICK JAGGER &
KEITH RICHARD
British rock composers
'It's Only Rock 'n' Roll'
If I could stick my knife in my heart / Suicide right on stage / Would it be enough for your teenage heart / Would it help to ease the pain? (Essex Music)

CLIVE JAMES
Australian critic
The Observer 1980
A TV programme can never be worse than its viewers; for the more stupid it is, the more stupid they are to watch it.

DAVID JOHANSEN
American rock singer
The most important thing in the world is to dig yourself and if you can't do that why the hell parade yourself around in front of an audience.

MARVIN KITMAN
American writer
'You Can't Judge a Book by its Cover' 1970
If it moves, the public will watch it.

ANDRE KOSTELANTZ
Russian musician, specialising in the 'pop' classics
Criticism is upsetting, but if what I do expands the meaning of music in terms of attendance, that's all that really matters.

BURT LANCASTER
American film star
Once the public decides what you are, you might as well give up trying to be anything else.

FRITZ LANG
German film director
The moment an audience starts to itch around you have lost them.

ELENORE LESTER
American journalist
Esquire 1969
For an avant-garde to exist there must be an audience which, by its rigidity, challenges the artist to paint another way.

JOHN LYDON (Johnny Rotten)
British rock star
New Musical Express 1979
Most of you out there are better than us, but you're too fucking lazy!

FREDDIE MERCURY
British pop musician
People want art. They want showbiz. They want to see you rush off in your limousine.

ROBERT MONTGOMERY
American film star
Applause . . . enjoy it, but never quite believe it.

JIM MORRISON
American rock star
There's this theory about the nature of tragedy, that Aristotle didn't mean catharsis for the audience, but a purgation of emotion for the actors themselves. The audience is just a witness to the event taking place onstage.

I'm beginning to think that it's easier to scare people than to make them laugh.

VLADIMIR NABOKOV
Russian writer
'Strong Opinions' 1974
I don't think the artist should bother about his audience. His best audience is the person he sees in his shaving mirror every morning. I think that the audience an artist imagines, when he imagines that kind of thing, is a room filled with people wearing his own mask.

STEVE PAUL
American rock entrepreneur
It's not enough to make good music – you've got to make people like it.

DAVID PEEL
American rock musician
No rock musician has ever paid to see an audience, why should an audience pay to see a rock musician?

KEITH RICHARD
British rock star
For all the control you have over an audience, it doesn't mean you can control the murders . . . you can't make someone's knife disappear just by looking at him, you can't be God, you can't ever pretend to play at being God.

TOM ROBINSON
British rock singer
Kids pay £1.50 to see you, £4 for an album, 80p for a single, £2 for a T-shirt . . . if you can't give them a three p. tuppeny-halfpenny badge, write back to all their letters personally even if they forgot the SAE, if you can't do that, what's it all about then? If you can make people feel you care about them, that makes them care about you. It makes perfect financial sense.

LINDA RONSTADT
American rock singer
Your attitude to your audience should be that they're a bunch of non-believers and you're the only person that could convince them.

TODD RUNDGREN
American rock star
People who have memorised your songs – how can you not love them?

RAT SCABIES
British rock musician 1979
No one goes on stage unless they want to show off. Look at me, I'm up here, you're down there, and I'm cleverer than you 'cos you paid to see me do this!

ARTUR SCHNABEL
Austrian pianist
explaining why he never played encores in 'The Musical Life' by Irving Kolodin, 1958
Applause is a receipt, not a bill.

GEORGE C. SCOTT
American film star 1975
The only real teacher of acting is the audience.

JOHNNY SHINES
American musician
It makes no difference how good you are. If you're not exposed to the public enough, then you're dead.

CARLY SIMON
American singer
Performing is a very odd thing to do, as unnatural as flying or taking an ocean voyage, and you *can* take certain drugs for that . . . people find themselves in my songs. Performing wouldn't be so bad if everyone in the audience could come up onstage and I could kiss them beforehand. As it is, it's like making love without any preliminary kissing.

BRUCE SPRINGSTEEN
American rock star
in 'Loose Talk,' ed. Linda Botts 1980
The whole idea is to deliver what money can't buy.

ELAINE STRITCH
American actress
quoted in 'How To Become A Virgin' by Quentin Crisp 1981
Don't bother with 'audience control'. Just get 'em to like you.

JAMES TAYLOR
American singer
If you feel like singing along – don't.

PETE TOWNSHEND
British rock star
Let's face it, you can't worship a guy for destroying an instrument in the name of rock.

Audiences are very much like the kids in Tommy's Holiday Camp: they want something without working for it.

JERRY WEXLER
American record business executive
New Musical Express 1979
A lot of us executives are walking around physically ill – needing to pretend that we're creating something artistically worthy . . . But since we're all capitalist enterprises, we have to capture the lowest common denominator. What's wrong is that we have to cater to the rancid, infantile, pubescent tastes of the public.

JAH WOBBLE
British rock musician 1980
Talking about 'giving the kids what they want' is meaningless. They want what they can get, what's advertised. We're not saying take anything.

SCIENCE
Art & Science

OLLE BAERTLING
Swedish artist
'Contemporary Artists' 1977
Art is research into the unknown, adding a little to the fund built up by earlier generations. This is the task of the artist.

CLAUDE BERNARD
French writer
Art is I, science is we.

GEORGES BRAQUE
French artist
'Pensées sur l'Art'
Art upsets, science reassures.

GERALD BRENAN
British writer
'Thoughts in a Dry Season' 1978
Art organises the visual world for the emotions as science does for the intellect.

JEAN COCTEAU
French writer and film director
'Le Rappel à l'Ordre'
Art is science in the flesh.

WALTER GROPIUS
German architect
speech to RIBA 1956
The reunification of art and science, without which there cannot be any true culture.

WERNER HEISENBERG
German scientist
quoted in Sunday Times 1967
No artist should be indifferent to the progress of scientific research.

ARTHUR KOESTLER
British philosopher
'Insight & Outlook' 1949
Artists treat facts as stimuli for the imagination, while scientists use their imagination to co-ordinate facts.

KARL KRAUS
German artist
Science is spectrum analysis. Art is photosynthesis.

J. ROBERT OPPENHEIMER
American physicist
quoted in 'Contemporary Architects' 1980
Scientists and artists perpetually live on the edge of mystery, being always surrounded by it.

GINO SEVERINI
Italian artist
quoted in 'Artists on Art' 1947
Art is nothing but humanised science.

C. P. SNOW
British writer
title of the Rede Lecture, 1959
The Two Cultures.

PAUL STRAND
American photographer
Photography Journal 1963
The true artist, like the true scientist, is a researcher using materials and techniques to dig into the truth and meaning of the world in which he himself lives; and what he creates, or better perhaps, brings back, are the objective results of his explorations. The measure of his talent, of his genius, if you will, is the richness he finds in such a life's voyage of discovery, and the effectiveness with which he is able to embody it through his chosen medium.

Science Is

J. D. BERNAL
British scientist
'The Origin of Life' 1967
It is characteristic of science that the full explanations are often seized in their essence by the percipient scientist long in advance of any possible proof.

BERTOLT BRECHT
Germany playwright
'Galileo'
Science knows only one commandment - contribute to science.

JACOB BRONOWSKI
British scientist
'Science & Human Values' 1956
Man masters nature not by force but by understanding. That is why science has succeeded where magic failed. because it has looked for no spell to cast on nature.
'The Ascent of Man' 1975
That is the essence of science: ask an impertinent question and you are on the way to a pertinent answer.
'Science & Human Values' 1956
Science has nothing to be ashamed of, even in the ruins of Nagasaki.
in Encounter 1971
No science is immune to the infection of politics and the corruption of power.

NORMAN O. BROWN
American philosopher
address to Phi Beta Kappa graduates at Columbia University, 1960
This is what is meant by the so-called scientific method: so-called science is the attempt to democratize knowledge, the attempt to substitute method for insight, mediocrity for genius and by getting a standard operating procedure.

EMIL BRUNNER
'Christianity and Civilisation' pt.2
Science knows what it is. It does not know what it ought to be. . . Science in our day claims more room in the totality of human life than it is entitled to.

JOHN BURROUGHS
Science has done more for the development of Western civilisation in one hundred years than Christianity did in eighteen hundred.

NOAM CHOMSKY
American philosopher
The Listener 1978
As soon as questions of will or decision arise, human science is at a loss.

MORRIS COHEN
American scientist
Science is a flickering light in our darkness, but it is the only one we have and woe to him who would put it out.

ALBERT EINSTEIN
German physicist
One thing I have learned in a long life – that all our science, measured against reality, is primitive and childlike – and yet it is the most precious thing we have.
'Out Of My Later Years' 1950
The whole of science is nothing more than a refinement of everyday thinking.

Science is the attempt to make the chaotic diversity of our sense-experience correspond to a logically uniform system of thought.

LORD FISHER
British clergyman
The Observer 1950
The only thing that science has done for man in the last hundred years is to create for him fresh moral problems.

LORD FLOREY
British scientist 1966
As a broad principle, science has been too successful in observing human life.

MAX GLUCKMAN
American writer
'Politics, Law & Ritual' 1965
A science is any discipline in which the fool of this generation can go beyond the point reached by the genius of the last generation.

J. B. S. HALDANE
British scientist
quoted in 'Acid Drops' by Kenneth Williams
You can analyse a glass of water and you're left with a lot of chemical components, but nothing you can drink.

JOSEPH WOOD KRUTCH
American essayist
'The Measure of Man' 1954
Though many have tried, no one has ever yet explained away the decisive fact that science, which can do so much, cannot decide what it ought to do.

FRAN LEBOWITZ
American journalist
'Metropolitan Life' 1978
Science is not a pretty thing. It is unpleasantly proportioned, outlandishly attired and often over-eager. What then is the appeal of science? What accounts for its popularity? And who give it its start?

PIERRE LECOMTE DE NOUY
'Man and His Destiny'
The point of science is to foresee, and not, as has often been said, to understand.

AGNES MEYER
American social worker
'Education for a New Morality' 1957
From the Nineteenth Century view of science as a God, the Twentieth Century has begun to see it as a devil. It behooves us now to understand that science is neither one nor the other.

J. ROBERT OPPENHEIMER
American physicist
Look 1966
Science is not everything, but science is very beautiful.

DEREK PRICE
British scientist 1964
Science is not just the fruit of the tree of knowledge, it is the tree itself.

DON K. PRICE
American academic
'Government & Science' 1954
Science . . . cannot exist on the basis of a treaty of strict non aggression with the rest of society; from either side, there is no defensible frontier.

PRINCE PHILIP
1966
Don't talk to me about mathematics – I've come to the conclusion that I've learnt to live without it.

MAGNUS PYKE
British scientist
The Listener 1962
Science is an exercise of the human brain to grasp the principles by which the universe works and to write them down, if possible, in crisp, precise, mathematical terms.

Science gives us knowledge of our environment. It sets the scene in which we act.

BERTRAND RUSSELL
British philosopher
What science cannot tell us, mankind cannot know.

GLENN T. SEABORG
American scientist 1964
Science is inherently neither a potential for good nor for evil. It is a potential to be harnessed by man to do his bidding.

Scientists

S. Y. AGNON
Israeli author
The Observer 1966
Along come the scientists and make the words of our fathers into folklore.

LUIS ALVAREZ
Scientist
quoted in D. S. Greenberg, 'The Politics of Pure Science' 1967
There is no democracy in physics. We

can't say that some second rate guy has as much right to opinion as Fermi.

ISAAC ASIMOV
American author
in Fantasy & Science Fiction 1977
When the lay public rallies round to an idea that is denounced by distinguished but elderly scientists, and supports that idea with great fervour and emotion, the distinguished but elderly scientists are then, after all, right.

W. H. AUDEN
British poet
'The Dyer's Hand' 1948
How happy the lot of the mathematician. He is judged solely by his peers, and the standard is so high that no colleague can ever win a reputation he does not deserve.

'The Dyer's Hand & Other Essays' 1962
When I find myself in the company of scientists, I feel like a shabby curate who has strayed by mistake into a drawing room full of dukes.

HENRY ALBERT BENT
British scientist
'The Second Law' 1965
Hell must be isothermal, for otherwise the resident engineers and physical chemists, (of which there must be some), could set up a heat engine to run a refrigerator to cool off a portion of their surroundings to any desired temperature.

SIR WINSTON CHURCHILL
British statesman
Scientists should be on tap but not on top.

ARTHUR C. CLARKE
American science writer
'Profiles of the Future' 1962
Scientists of over fifty are good for nothing except board meetings and should at all costs be kept out of the laboratory.

'Profiles of the Future' 1973
When a distinguished but elderly scientist states that something is possible, he is almost certainly right. When he states that something is impossible, he is very probably wrong.

JAMES B. CONANT
American scientist
letter in New York Times 1945
There is only one proved way of assisting the advancement of pure science – that of picking men of genius, backing them heavily, and leaving them to direct themselves.

DR. GERALD M. EDELMAN
American scientist
The scientist . . . is at the moving edge of what's happening.

E. J. HOBSBAWM
British historian
in New York Review of Books 1970
There is not much that even the most socially responsible scientists can do as individuals, or even as a group, about the social consequences of their activities.

ARTHUR KOESTLER
British philosopher
'The Roots of Coincidence' 1972
Scientists . . . peeping toms at the keyhole of eternity.

JOHN LEONARD
American critic
New York Times 1978
Scientists have reduced the number of calamities we may blame on God.

ALAN L. MACKAY
British scientist
in Science World 1969
How can we have any new ideas or fresh outlooks when ninety percent of all the scientists who have ever lived have not yet died?

JOSE ORTEGA Y GASSET
Spanish philosopher
'Complete Works' 1958
Contemporary science, with its system and methods, can put blockheads to good use.

HANS SELYE
American doctor
Newsweek 1958
The true scientist never loses the faculty of amazement. It is the essence of his being.

C. P. SNOW
British writer
The Rede Lecture 1959
Scientists . . . I should say that naturally
they had the future in their bones.

SIR HENRY TIZARD
British scientist
*quoted in C. P. Snow 'A Postscript to Science
& Government' 1962*
The secret of science is to ask the right
question, and it is the choice of problem
more than anything else that marks the
man of genius in the scientific world.

WERNHER VON BRAUN
German scientist
Daily Mirror 1968
The moral dilemma of a scientist who
makes rockets doesn't exist. You might
as well say that a man who makes aero-
planes has a dilemma. They're basically
a means of transportation – but you can
stick a bomb in the nose and drop it on
someone's head. A rocket isn't any
different.

NORBERT WIENER
American mathematician
'The Human Use of Human Beings' 1954
The independent scientist who is worth
the slightest consideration as a scientist
has a consecration that comes entirely
from within himself: a vocation which
demands the possibility of supreme
self-sacrifice.

LORD WILMOT
British politician 1946
What I like about scientists is that they
are a team, that one doesn't need to
know their names.

FRANK LLOYD WRIGHT
American architect
The Star 1959
The scientist has marched in and taken
the place of the poet. But one day somebody will find the solution to the problems of the world and remember, it will
be a poet, not a scientist.

Research

RUSSELL LINCOLN ACKOFF
American scientist
*'Decision Making in National Science Policy'
1968*
Common sense . . . has the very curious
property of being more correct retro-
spectively than prospectively. It seems
to me that one of the principal criteria
to be applied to successful science is that
its results are almost always obvious re-
trospectively; unfortunately they seldom
are prospectively. Common sense provides a kind of ultimate validation after
science has completed its work; it seldom
anticipates what science is going to
discover.

POUL ANDERSON
American science fiction writer
in New Scientist 1969
I have yet to see any problem, however
complicated, which, when you looked at
it in the right way, did not become more
complicated.

RUSSELL BAKER
American writer
New York Times 1968
Inanimate objects are classified scientifically into three major categories – those
that don't work, those that break down
and those that get lost.

MARSTON BATES
Quote 1967
Research is the process of going up alleys
to see if they are blind.

PATRICK BLACKETT
British scientist
A first rate laboratory is one in which
mediocre scientists can produce out-
standing work.

**SIR FRANK MACFARLANE
BURNET**
British physician
The Lancet 1966
There is virtually nothing that has come

from molecular biology that can be of any value to human living in the conventional sense of what is good, and quite tremendous possibilities of evil, again in the conventional sense.

CARSON'S CONSOLATION
quoted in 'The Official Rules' by P. Dickson 1978
No experiment is ever a complete failure. It can always be used as a bad example.

ERWIN CHARGAFF
American scientist
quoted in Science 1971
What counts . . . in science is to be not so much the first as the last.

JAMES B. CONANT
American scientist
'Science & Common Sense' 1951
The stumbling way in which even the ablest of scientists in every generation have had to fight through thickets of erroneous observations, misleading generalisations, inadequate formulations and unconscious prejudice is rarely appreciated by those who obtain their scientific knowledge from textbooks.

ALBERT EINSTEIN
German physicist
The process of scientific discovery is, in effect, a continual flight from wonder.

in 'Education & Ecstasy' by George B. Leonard
It is nothing short of a miracle that the modern methods of instruction have not yet entirely strangled the holy curiosity of enquiry . . . it is a very grave mistake to think that the enjoyment of seeing and searching can be promoted by means of coercion and a sense of duty.

HAROLD FABER
American journalist
The Book of Laws 1980
Young's Law: All great discoveries are made by mistake.

FINAGLE'S FIRST LAW
in 'Murphy's Law' by Arthur Bloch 1979
If an experiment works, something has gone wrong.
Fingale's Fourth Law: Once a job is fouled up, anything done to improve it only makes it worse.

SIR ALEXANDER FLEMING
British bacteriologist
quoted in People's Almanac Vol 2 1978
One sometimes finds what one is not looking for.

BRENDAN FRANCIS
The best way to escape from a problem is to solve it.

SIR CYRIL HINSHELWOOD
British scientist 1965
What many scientists are really after is the adventure of discovery itself.

JOHN F. KENNEDY
American president 1963
Scientists alone can establish the objectives of their research, but society, in extending support to science, must take account of its own needs.

KONRAD LORENZ
Austrian anthropologist
'On Aggression'
It is a good morning exercise for a research scientist to discard a pet hypothesis every day before breakfast. It keeps him young.

SIR PETER MEDAWAR
British scientist
'Advice to a Young Scientist' 1979
Scientific enquiry is an enormous potentation of common sense.

'The Art of the Soluble' 1967
If politics is the art of the possible, research is surely the art of the soluble . . . Good scientists study the most important problems they think they can solve. It is, after all, their professional business to solve problems, not merely to grapple with them.

MURPHY'S LAW OF RESEARCH
in 'Murphy's Law' by Arthur Bloch 1979
Enough research will tend to support your theory.

EDMUND MUSKIE
American politician 1971
It's pretty hard to be against cancer research.

KEITH J. PENDRED
American scientist
Bulletin of the Atomic Scientists 1963
Successful research impedes further successful research.

PROFESSOR WILLIAM B. SHOCKLEY
American inventor and eugenics theorist
Esquire 1973
If you have a bright idea and you do the right kind of experiment, you may get pretty decisive results pretty soon.

GEORGES SIMENON
French crime novelist
Daily Telegraph 1967
Inventions are made by intuition, not intelligence.

IGOR STRAVINSKY
Russian composer
'Conversations with Igor Stravinsky'
The very people who have done the breaking through are themselves often the first to try to put a scab on their achievement.

ALBERT SZENT-GYORGYI
American scientist
'Perspectives in Biology & Medicine' 1971
Research means going out into the unknown with the hope of finding something new to bring home. If you know what you are going to do, or even to find there, then it is not research at all, then it is only a kind of honourable occupation.

in 'The Scientist Speculates' 1962
Discovery consists of seeing what everybody has seen and thinking what nobody has thought.

WERNHER VON BRAUN
German scientist
in 'The Faber Book of Aphorisms' 1964
Basic research is when I'm doing what I don't know I'm doing.

NORBERT WIENER
American mathematician
'The Human Use of Human Beings' 1954
Scientific discovery consists in the interpretation for our own convenience of a system of existence which has been made with no eye to our convenience at all.

Facts & Theories

GASTON BACHELARD
French scientist
'Le nouvel esprit scientifique'
A scientific observation is always a committed observation; it confirms or denies one's preoccupations; one's first ideas, one's plan of observation; it shows by demonstration; it structures the phenomena; it transcends what is close at hand; it reconstructs the real after having reconstructed its representation.

'La formation de l'esprit scientifique'
The *scientific* experience . . . is an experience which contradicts the *communal* experience.

SIR WILLIAM BRAGG
British scientist
quoted in A. Koestler & J. R. Smithies 'Beyond Reductionism' 1968
The important thing in science is not so much to obtain new facts as to discover new ways of thinking about them.

FELIX COHEN
Generally, the theories we believe we call facts and the facts we disbelieve we call theories.

SIR ANTHONY EDEN
British politician
speech 1945
Every succeeding scientific discovery

makes greater nonsense of the old-time conceptions of sovereignty.

MANFRED EIGEN
German scientist
'The Physicist's Conception of Nature' ed. Jagdish Mehra 1973
A theory has only the alternative of being right or wrong. A model has a third possibility – it may be right, but irrelevant.

ALBERT EINSTEIN
German physicist
Life 1950
The grand aim of all science is to cover the greatest number of empirical facts by logical deduction from the smallest number of hypotheses or deductions.

HAROLD FABER
American journalist
'The Book of Laws' 1980
Leontief's Law: New scientific knowledge is like wine in the wedding at Cana: it cannot be used up; the same idea can serve many users simultaneously; and as the number of customers increases, no one need be getting less of it because the others are getting more.

SIR RICHARD GREGORY
British scientist
Science is not to be regarded merely as a storehouse of facts to be used for material purposes, but as one of the great human endeavours to be ranked with the arts and religion as the guide and expression of man's fearless quest for truth.

CHRISTOPHER HAMPTON
British playwright
'The Philanthropist'
You know very well that unless you're a scientist, it's much more important for a theory to be shapely than for it to be true.

HENRY S. HASKINS
American writer
'Meditations in Wall Street'
All solid facts were originally mist.

ALDOUS HUXLEY
British writer
'Time Must Have a Stop' 1945
Facts are ventriloquist's dummies. Sitting on a wise man's knee they may be made to utter words of wisdom; elsewhere they say nothing, or talk nonsense.

SIR JAMES JEANS
British scientist
'The Mysterious Universe'
Science should leave off making pronouncements; the river of knowledge has too often turned back on itself.

ALEKSANDER ISAACOVICH KITAIGORODSKI
Russian scientist 1975
A first rate theory predicts, a second rate theory forbids and a third rate theory explains after the event.

ARTHUR KOESTLER
British philosopher
'The Act of Creation' 1964
Creativity in science could be described as the act of putting two and two together to make five.

address to the PEN Club 1976
The progress of science is strewn, like an ancient desert trail, with the bleached skeletons of discarded theories which once seemed to possess eternal life.

KONRAD LORENZ
Austrian anthropologist
Truth in science can be defined as the working hypothesis best suited to open the way to the next better one.

MARY McCARTHY
American writer
On the Contrary 1962
In science, all facts, however trivial or banal, enjoy democratic equality.

MANN'S LAW
in 'Murphy's Law Book Two' by Arthur Bloch 1980
If a scientist uncovers a publishable fact, it will become central to his theory.

J. M. MARTIN
British businessman
Industry Week
No matter what occurs, there's always someone who beleives it happened according to his pet theory.

SIR PETER MEDAWAR
British scientist
'Advice to a Young Scientist' 1979
I cannot give any scientist of any age better advice than this: the intensity of a conviction that a hypothesis is true has no bearing over whether it is true or not.

JONATHAN MILLER
British doctor and writer
'The Body in Question' 1979
Since finding out what something is is largely a matter of discovering what it is like, the most impressive contribution to the growth of intelligibility has been made by the application of suggestive metaphors.

SIR KARL POPPER
British philosopher
'The Logic of Scientific Discovery' 1959
Science is not a system of certain, or well-established statements, nor is it a system which steadily advances towards a state of finality . . . like Bacon we might describe our own contemporary science . . . as consisting of 'anticipations, rash and premature', and as 'prejudices'.

'Problems of Scientific Revolution' 1975
In order that a new theory should constitute a discovery or a step forward it should conflict with its predecessor . . . it should contradict its predecessor; it should overthrow it. In this sense, progress in science – or at least striking progress – is always revolutionary.

MAGNUS PYKE
British scientist
The Listener 1963
Science is a way of thinking, but it can only advance on a basis of technique.

The Listener 1961
The essential genius of the scientific mode of thinking stops at nothing, accepts no authority or convention, but moves on as the logic of the facts leads it.

BERTRAND RUSSELL
British philosopher
quoted in 'The Faber Book of Aphorisms' 1964
A fact, in science, is not a mere fact, but an instance.

FREDERICK SOMMER
American photographer
in 'Photographers on Photography' ed. N. Lyons 1966
Fact is only fact when we have taken it's spiritual measure.

ALFRED NORTH WHITEHEAD
British philosopher
The aims of scientific thought are to see the general in the particular and the eternal in the transitory.

JEROME WIESNER
New Yorker 1963
Some problems are just too complicated for rational, logical solutions. They admit of insights, not answers.

DOUGLAS YATES
British scientist
No scientific theory achieves public acceptance until it has been thoroughly discredited.

Technology

BRIAN ALDISS
British author
The Guardian 1969 on space flight
The feat represents immense acheivement for the neotenic ape, species homo sapiens. But behind this lie two old attributes of the ape – tribalism and inquisitiveness.

ANTI-POLLUTION
Slogan 1970
I shot an arrow in the air – and it stuck.

REV. WILLIAM VERE AWDREY
British creator of 'Thomas the Tank Engine' books 1979
A steam engine has always got character. It's the most human of all man-made machines.

LINCOLN BARNETT
American writer
Life 1950
The quick harvest of applied science is the usable process, the medicine, the machine. The shy fruit of pure science is understanding.

ROLAND BARTHES
French academic
Mythologies 1957
Cars today are almost the exact equivalent of the great Gothic cathedrals . . . the supreme creation of an era, conceived with passion by unknown artists, and consumed in image if not in usage by a whole population which appropriates them as a purely magical object.

BERNARD BARUCH
American financier 1954
There are no such things as incurables. There are only things for which man has not found a cure.

STAFFORD BEER
British scientist
'Brain of the Firm' 1972
If it works, it's out of date.

BERKELEY UNIVERSITY
Protest Slogan c.1966
I am just a computer card – do not spindle, fold, tear or mutilate.

GERRIT A. BLAAUW
Computer engineer
quoted in 'The Official Rules' by P. Dickson 1978
Established technology tends to persist in the face of new technology.

HERBERT BLOCK
American political cartoonist
If it's good, they'll stop making it.

BERTOLT BRECHT
German playwright
'The Messingkauf Dialogues' 1965
The more we can squeeze out of nature by inventions and discoveries and improved organisation of labour, the more uncertain our existence seems to be. It's not we who lord it over things, it seems, but things which lord it over us.

SIR WINSTON CHURCHILL
British statesman 1949
Science bestowed immense new powers on man and at the same time created conditions which were largely beyond his comprehension and still more beyond his control.

The Stone Age may return on the gleaming wings of science.

ARTHUR C. CLARKE
British science writer
'Profiles of the Future' 1962
Any sufficiently advanced technology is indistinguishable from magic.

PETER COOK
British architect 1960
The prepackaged frozen lunch is more important than Palladio. It is an expression of human requirement and the symbol of one efficient interpretation of that requirement that optimises the available technology and economy.

PETER DRUCKER
American management expert
quoted in Jeremy Tunstall 'The Advertising Man' 1964
Innovation is the new conservatism.

PAUL EHRLICH
American scientist
The Saturday Review 1971
The first rule of intelligent tinkering is to save all the parts.

The Farmers Almanac 1978
To err is human but to really foul things up requires a computer.

JEAN FOURASTIE
French writer
'Le Grand Espoir du XXème Siècle'
The machine leads man to specialising in the human being.

BRENDAN FRANCIS
A pedestrian ought to be legally allowed to toss at least one hand grenade at a motorist every day.

MAX FRISCH
Architect
quoted in Playboy 1970
Technology is just a way of organising the universe so that man doesn't have to experience it.

ERICH FROMM
American psychologist
'The Sane Society' 1955
We live in a world of things, and our only connection with them is that we know how to manipulate or to consume them.

DENNIS GABOR
British physicist
'Innovations: Scientific, Technological and Social' 1970
The most important and urgent problems of technology today are no longer the satisfaction of primary needs or of archetypal wishes, but the reparation of the evils and damages wrought by the technology of yesterday.

PIERRE GALLOIS
French scientist
quoted in Reader's Digest
If you put tomfoolery into a computer, nothing comes out but tomfoolery. But this tomfoolery, having passed through a very expensive machine, is somehow ennobled and no one dares criticise it.

JOHN GLENN
American astronaut 1972
I suppose the one quality in an astronaut more powerful than any other is curiosity. They have to get some place nobody's ever been before.

MICHAEL HARRINGTON
American writer
'The Other America' 1962
If there is technological advance without social advance, there is, almost automatically, an increase in human misery.

WERNER HEISENBERG
German scientist
Science clears the fields on which technology can build.

ALDOUS HUXLEY
British writer
'Tomorrow and Tomorrow and Tomorrow'
1956
Applied Science is a conjuror, whose bottomless hat yields impartially the softest of Angora rabbits and the most petrifying of Medusas.

Technological progress has merely provided us with more efficient means for going backwards.

CLIVE JAMES
Australian critic
The Observer 1976
It is only when they go wrong that machines remind you how powerful they are.

KARL JASPERS
The beginning of modern science is also the beginning of calamity.

JOHN F. KENNEDY
American politician 1959
I am sorry to say that there is too much point to the wisecrack that life is extinct on other planets because their scientists were more advanced than ours.

NIKITA KHRUSHCHEV
Russian leader
What scientists have in their briefcases is terrifying.

MARTIN LUTHER KING JR.
American activist
'Strength to Love' 1963
The means by which we live have outdistanced the ends for which we live. Our scientific power has outrun our spiritual power. We have guided missiles and misguided men.

JOSEPH WOOD KRUTCH
American essayist
'The Twelve Seasons' 1949
Electronic calculators can solve problems which the man who made them cannot solve; but no government subsidized commission of engineers and physicists could create a worm.

DOROTHEA LANGE
American photographer
Aperture 1952
Ours is a time of the machine, and ours
is a need to know that the machine can
be put to creative human effort. If not,
the machine can destroy us.

CHARLES A. LINDBERG
American airman
The tragedy of scientific man is that he
has found no way to guide his discoveries
to a constructive end. He has devised no
weapon so terrible that he has not used
it. He has guarded none so carefully that
his enemies have not eventually obtained
it and turned it against him. His security
today and tomorrow seems to depend on
building weapons which will destroy him
tomorrow.

SIR PATRICK LINSTEAD
British scientist
The Observer 1965
It is a distinction between science and
technology that technology must always
be useful, whereas science need not be.

ARCHIBALD MacLEISH
American poet
'The Reader's Adviser' 1969
The loyalty of science is not to humanity,
but to truth – it's own truth. The law of
science is not the law of the good – what
humanity thinks of as good – meaning
moral, decent and humane, but the law
of the possible. What it is *possible* for
science to know, science must know.
What it is possible for technology to do,
technology will have done . . . Regardless, regardless of anything.

MARSHALL McLUHAN
Canadian academic
'Understanding Media' 1964
The car has become an article of dress
without which we feel uncertain, unclad
and incomplete.

quoted in The Listener 1971
If it works it's obsolete.

JAMES MAGARY
Computers can figure out all kinds of
problems, except the things in the world
that just don't add up.

MARYA MANNES
American writer
'More in Anger' 1958
People on horses look better than they
are, people in cars look worse than they
are.

MARTIN MAYER
American writer
Esquire 1969
Like sex drives, card tricks and the
weather, computers tend to be discussed
in terms of results rather than processes,
which makes them rather scary.

J. B. MORTON
British humorist
*'Beachcomber' 'Dictionary for Today' in Daily
Express, passim*
Pedestrian: anyone who is knocked down
by a motor-car.

MARCEL PAGNOL
French writer
'Critique des critiques' 1949
One has to look out for engineers – they
begin with sewing machines and end up
with the atomic bomb.

LORD CHIEF JUSTICE PARKER
British lawyer
The Observer 1961
The motor car is as much an instrument
of lawlessness as the jemmy.

PETER PATERSON
American politician
The Observer 1972
The era of low cost energy is almost
dead. Popeye has run out of cheap
spinach.

LAURENCE J. PETER
Canadian educator
'The Peter Principle'
Competence, like truth, beauty and con-
tact lenses, is in the eye of the beholder.

PABLO PICASSO
Spanish artist
*quoted in 'Life with Picasso' by F. Gilot &
C. Lake 1964*
Every positive value has its price in negative terms. And you never see anything very great which is not, at the same
time, horrible in some respect. The genius of Einstein leads to Hiroshima.

GEORGES POMPIDOU
French politician
Sunday Telegraph 1968
There are three roads to ruin – women, gambling and technicians. The most pleasant is with women, the quickest is with gambling, but the surest is with technicians.

J. B. PRIESTLEY
British writer
'Thoughts in the Wilderness' 1957
Sometimes you might think that the machines we worship make all the chief appointments, promoting the human beings who seem closest to them.

GILBERT RYLE
British astronomer
'The Concept of Mind' 1949
The Ghost in the Machine.

SHAW'S PRINCIPLE
in 'Murphy's Law' by Arthur Bloch 1979
Build a system that even a fool can use, and only a fool will want to use it.

PETER USTINOV
British actor and wit
Illustrated London News 1968
We used to have lots of questions to which there were no answers. Now, with the computer, there are lots of answers to which we haven't thought up the questions.

ANDY WARHOL
American artist
Machines have less problems. I'd like to be a machine.

'From A to B and Back Again' 1975
Telling me not to bring my tape recorder is like telling a normal person to leave his wife alone.

LORD ZUCKERMAN
British scientist
Sunday Times 1973
We live as we live because of the decisions, however explicit or however undefined, that were taken yesterday about which technological developments to encourage to satisfy man's enduring urge for an ever better life.

Nature

ROBERT ARDREY
American writer
'The Social Contract'
The tragedy and magnificence of Homo Sapiens together rise from the same smokey truth that we alone among the animal species refuse to acknowledge natural law.

J. D. BERNAL
British scientist
'The Origin of Life' 1967
In fact, we will have to give up taking things for granted, even the apparently simple things. We have to learn to understand nature, and not merely to observe it and endure what it imposes on us. Stupidity, from being an amiable individual defect, has become a social crime.

NIELS BOHR
Danish scientist
in The Times 1957
Any development of the knowledge of the rules of nature which may help to give greater command of the powers of nature holds the hope of improving the living conditions of mankind; but also holds dangers which put our entire civilisation to a serious test. The responsibility, however, that these dangers are defeated in the right way, rests not only upon the scientist but must be shared by all circles of every nation.

BERTOLT BRECHT
German playwright
'The Messingkauf Dialogues' 1965
Beauty in nature is a quality which gives the human senses a chance to be skilful.

BRIGID BROPHY
Irish writer
'The Burglar' 1967
The one consistently natural thing is to try by intelligence and imagination to improve on nature.

LORD CLARK
British critic
in 'The Faber Book of Aphorisms' 1964
It is chiefly through the instinct to kill that man achieves intimacy with the life of nature.

PAUL CLAUDEL
French composer
'Journal'
Nature is only an immense ruin.

WILL DURANT
American historian
New York Daily News 1970
Nature has never read the Declaration of Independence. It continues to make us unequal.

SIR RONALD FISHER
British scientist
Natural selection is a mechanism for generating an exceedingly high degree of improbability.

WERNER HEISENBERG
German scientist
'Physics and Philosophy' 1959
Natural science does not simply describe and explain nature; it is part of the interplay between nature and ourselves; it describes nature as exposed to our method of questioning.

MAGNUS PYKE
British scientist
The Guardian 1974
Science teaches those who immerse themselves in it to know the workings of God in Nature, but the practice of science does more than this. As the depth of their understanding grows, its students cannot fail to learn the interdependence of all creation. This is even more than the brotherhood of man, this is the harmony of all nature. Furthermore, those who devote themselves to science, thereby learn humility.

JONATHAN RABAN
British writer
Nothing shames the human more persistently and eloquently than nature.

THEODORE ROSZAK
'Where the Wasteland Ends' 1972
Nature composes some of her loveliest poems for the microscope and telescope.

LIONEL TIGER & ROBIN FOX
British anthropologists
'The Imperial Animal' 1971
In the eyes of Nature we are just another species in trouble.

H. G. WELLS
British writer
'Mind at the End of Its Tether' 1946
Adapt or perish, now as ever, is Nature's inexorable imperative.

Armageddon

THE BRITISH ARMY JOURNAL
1949
The best defence against the atom bomb is not to be there when it goes off.

MICHELANGELO ANTONIONI
Italian film director
Who is a hero under the atom bomb? Or who is not one?

BURT BLECHMAN
American writer
'Maybe' 1967
Armageddon is frightening only to those who fear progress.

GENERAL OMAR BRADLEY
American soldier
The Observer 1952
The way to win an atomic war is to make certain it never starts.

WILLIAM S. BURROUGHS
American writer
'The Naked Lunch' 1959
The Planet drifts to random insect doom.

BENNETT CERF
American publisher
The Atomic Age is here to stay – but are we?

ALBERT EINSTEIN
German physicist
The Observer 1952
The discovery of the nuclear chain re-action need not bring about the destruc-tion of mankind any more than did the discovery of matches.

asked by the Press what would happen in the event of a nuclear war:
Alas, we will no longer be able to listen to the music of Mozart.

EUGENE McCARTHY
American politician 1968
We have a three-to-one advantage over the Russians, which I understand means we have the potential to kill all the Rus-sians twice and they have the potential to kill us one and a quarter times.

MAO ZEDONG (Mao Tse-tung)
Chinese leader
The atom bomb is a paper tiger. . . Ter-rible to look at but not so strong as it seems.

MALCOLM MUGGERIDGE
British journalist 1969
The Bomb was to remain throughout the decade unbanned and unwanted, but like old soldiers, refusing to fade away.

QUENTIN REYNOLDS
British writer
in 'Quote & Unquote' 1970
The scientists split the atom; now the atom is splitting us.

SUSAN SONTAG
American essayist
'Styles of Radical Will' 1969
Cogito ergo boom.

ADLAI STEVENSON
American politician 1952
There is no evil in the atom – only in men's souls.

HARRY S. TRUMAN
American President 1945
The atomic bomb is another powerful weapon in the arsenal of righteousness.

PETER USTINOV
British actor and wit
on post-nuclear boltholes Now! 1981
The least safe place will be Australia: as lots of things will land there by mistake.

DEFINITIONS

ROBERT ALTMAN
American film director
The Observer 1981
What's a cult? It just means not enough people to make a minority.

CLEVELAND AMORY
American writer
on NBC-TV 1961
The opera is like a husband with a foreign title – expensive to support, hard to understand and therefore a supreme social challenge.

ANONYMOUS
The twist is a perpendicular expression of a horizontal desire.

ANONYMOUS
quoted in 'The Wit of Medicine' ed. L. & M. Cowan 1972
There's no fun in medicine, but there's a lot of medicine in fun.

A drug is a substance that when injected into a guinea pig produces a scientific paper.

ANONYMOUS
in 'The Harvest of a Quiet Eye' by Alan L. Mackay 1977
A metallurgist is an expert who can look at a platinum blonde and tell whether she is virgin metal or a common ore.

SIR THOMAS BEECHAM
British conductor
'Beecham Stories' 1978
The bagpipes sound exactly the same when you have finished learning them as when you start.

The upright piano is a musical growth found adhering to the walls of most semi-detached houses in the provinces.

The harpsichord sounds like two skeletons copulating on a corrugated tin roof.

The organ – a mechanical box of whistles.

ANEURIN BEVAN
British politician
quoted 1981
Trade unions are islands of anarchy in a sea of chaos.

JUDY BIRMINGHAM
British archaeologist 1968
Archaeology is very much concerned with garbage.

NIELS BOHR
Danish scientist
An expert is a man who has made all the mistakes which can be made, in a very narrow field.

GEORGES BRAQUE
French artist
Perspective is a ghastly mistake which it has taken four centuries to redress.

BRIGID BROPHY
Irish writer
'In Transit'
An airport is a free-range womb.

MARTIN BUBER
Israeli theologian
'Pointing the Way' 1957
Play is the exultation of the possible.

DR. DAVID BUTLER
British psephologist
The Observer 1969
The function of the expert is not to be more right than other people, but to be wrong for more sophisticated reasons.

JOHN CAGE
American musician
'Silence' 1961
An error is simply a failure to adjust immediately from a preconception to an actuality.

LANGSTON COLEMAN
American pro football player 1965
Luck is what you have left after you give one hundred per cent.

NOEL COWARD
British playwright
The Observer 1969
The best kind of showbiz is making your point.

PERCY CUDLIPP
British journalist 1949
Nagging is constructive criticism too frequently repeated.

CHARLES P. CURTIS
American lawyer
'A Commonplace Book' 1957
Fraud is the homage that force pays to reason.

MARCEL DUCHAMP
French artist
'Art News' 1969
Gravity is a form of condescension or politeness.

DOUGLAS DUNN
British poet
The Listener 1977
A dilettante is a product of where wealth and literature meet.

BOB DYLAN
American singer
Folk singing is just a bunch of fat people.

DR. LUDWIG ERHARD
East German politician
The Observer 1958
A compromise is the art of dividing a cake in such a way that everyone believes he has the biggest piece.

HENRY FORD I
American entrepreneur 1953
A bore is a fellow who opens his mouth and puts his feats in it.

ED GARDNER
American radio comedian
Opera is when a guy gets stabbed in the back and instead of bleeding, he sings.

ARNOLD H. GLASGOW
American academic
Reader's Digest 1966
Inflation might be called prosperity with high blood pressure.

Reader's Digest 1974
Efficiency is intelligent laziness.

WALTER GROPIUS
German architect
quoted in 'Contemporary Architects' 1980
Specialists are people who always repeat the same mistakes.

CALOUSTE GULBENKIAN
Armenian millionaire
Oilmen are like cats: you can never tell from the sound of them whether they are fighting or making love.

Oil friendships are greasy.

SYDNEY J. HARRIS
American journalist
'On the Contrary' 1962
A cynic is not merely one who reads bitter lessons from the past; he is one who is prematurely disappointed in the future.

ROBERT HEINLEIN
American science fiction author
Time Enough for Love: the Further Adventures of Lazarus Long 1972
An elephant – a mouse built to government specifications.

WERNER HEISENBERG
German scientist
'Physics & Beyond' 1971
An expert is someone who knows some of the worst mistakes that can be made in his subject and how to avoid them.

BENNY HILL
British comedian
The Observer 1977
That's what show business is – sincere insincerity.

OSCAR LEVANT
American pianist and composer
Coronet 1958
Epigram – a wisecrack that played Carnegie Hall.

CLAUDE LEVI-STRAUSS
French anthropologist
'Tristes Tropiques' 1955
Social life consists in destroying that which gives life its flavour.

MIGNON McLAUGHLIN
American writer
'The Neurotic's Notebook' 1963
It's innocence when it charms us, ignorance when it doesn't.

NORMAN MAILER
American writer
'Advertisements for Myself' 1959
Hip is the sophistication of the wise primitive in a giant jungle.

ELSA MAXWELL
American socialite
'How To Do It' 1957
Anatomise the character of a successful hostess and the knife will lay bare the fact that she owes her position to one of three things: she is liked, or she is feared, or she is important.

ROLLO MAY
British scientist
'Existence' 1958
Existentialism, in short, is the endeavour to understand man by cutting below the cleavage between subject and object which has bedevilled Western thought and science since shortly after the Renaissance.

GITA MEHTA
Indian writer
'Karma Cola' 1980
There is that difference between being kicked in the teeth and reading a description of being kicked in the teeth. Some call it existential.

KATE MILLETT
American feminist 1975
Isn't privacy about keeping taboos in their place.

NANCY MITFORD
British writer
quoted in 'The Wit of Women' ed. L. and M. Cowan 1969
An aristocracy in a republic is like a chicken whose head has been cut off. It may run about in a lovely way, but in fact it's dead.

J. B. MORTON
British humorist
'Morton's Folly'
Rush Hour: That hour when the traffic is almost at a standstill.

MALCOLM MUGGERIDGE
British journalist
New Statesman 1955
The probability is, I suppose, that the Monarchy has become a kind of ersatz religion. Chesterton once remarked that when people ceased to believe in God they do not believe in nothing, but in anything.

VLADIMIR NABOKOV
Russian writer
New York Times 1977
Prophecy is the wit of a fool.

LEFTY ROSENTHAL
American professional gambler 1973
The difference between an amateur and a professional is the difference between a general practitioner and a heart specialist. The only similarity is that they're both called doctors.

LAURENCE J. PETER
Canadian educator
'Peter's Quotations' 1977
A bore is a fellow talking who can change the subject back to his topic of conversation faster than you can change it back to yours.

BERTRAND RUSSELL
British philosopher
quoted in 'The Faber Book of Aphorisms' 1964
Mathematics is the only science where one never knows what one is talking about nor whether what is said is true.

ALBERT SCHWEITZER
German missionary
Humanitarianism consists in never sacrificing a human being for a purpose.

FRED SHERO
American ice hockey coach 1975
An oak tree is just a nut that held its ground.

A. I. SILVERMAN
British doctor
quoted in 'The Wit of Medicine' ed. L. and M. Cowan 1972
Medicine is like advice – easy to give, hard to take.

ADMIRAL VICTOR SMITH
Australian sailor 1973
A task force is a force which is organised
to carry out a certain task.

WILLIE 'THE LION' SMITH
American jazz musician
Esquire 1964
Loud people are like a bad drink of whis-
key – either you fight them or join them.
Either way it's a bad idea.

AUGUSTUS OWSLEY STANLEY
American LSD manufacturer
supreme
Chemistry is applied theology.

ADLAI STEVENSON
American politician
An independent is the guy who wants to
take the politics out of politics.

JACK TANNER
British trade unionist 1954
The shop steward is a little like an egg.
If you keep him in hot water long enough
he gets hard-boiled.

DR. EDITH SUMMERSKILL
British politician
The Observer 1960
Nagging is the repetition of unpalatable
truths.

E. S. TURNER
British writer
in 'Quote and Unquote' 1970
Sociology: the study of people who do
not need to be studied by people who
do.

MAX WALL
British comedian
The Listener 1978
Show business is like sex. When it's won-
derful, it's wonderful. But when it isn't
very good, it's still all right.

WEINBERG'S COROLLARY
in 'Murphy's Law' by Arthur Bloch 1979
An expert is a person who avoids the
small errors while sweeping on to the
grand fallacy.

KATHARINE WHITEHORN
British journalist
The Observer 1973
They should stop calling it 'Social Se-
curity'. It's as secure as a cardboard raft.

HEATHCOTE WILLIAMS
British playwright
'The Speakers' 1964
A bohemian is a person who works to
live but does not live to work. A bohemian is an imitation beatnik. A hundred
per cent beatnik is only an imitation
gypsy.

CHARLES E. WILSON
American government official
An expert is a mechanic away from
home.

FRANK LLOYD WRIGHT
American architect
quoted in Manchester Guardian 1959
The interior decorator is simply an inferior desecrator of the work of an artist.

quoted in Daily Express 1959
An expert is a man who has stopped
thinking. Why should he think? He is an
expert.

WORDS
Journalism

FRED ALLEN
American wit
To a newspaperman a human being is an item with skin wrapped around it.

BROOKS ATKINSON
American essayist
'Once Around the Sun' 1951
The evil that men do lives on the front pages of greedy newspapers, but the good is oft interred apathetically inside.

LORD BEAVERBROOK
Canadian press magnate
advice to aspirant journalist
Why don't you start a vendetta against someone? *That's* the way to get people reading your columns.

To E. J. Robertson, his manager . . .
I don't care whether you make money. All I want to see, Mr. Robertson, is a great newspaper strong in reserves.

ALAN BENNETT
British playwright
The Observer 1967
Accuracy isn't a virtue, it is a duty. That applies to entertainment and to journalism, and to why both of them are so bad.

BEN BRADLEE
American journalist
News is the first rough draft of history.
(cf. Philip Graham)

DONALD BROOK
Australian art expert
Sydney Morning Herald 1969
The paradigm Time magazine portrait is obsessively delineated, pore by pore, by a medical illustrator with the delusions of imagination that he exhibits by choosing symbolic attributes of the subject and distributing them like a secular halo.

WILLIAM S. BURROUGHS
American writer
The Guardian 1969
The idea that events have to be written before they happen has a great deal of basis. This is what newspapers are about.

Sunday Times 1970
There is a type of writing that causes people to commit crime – and that's the type of writing that's done every day in the newspapers. One story about a hijacker breeds a thousand. It's sensationalism. It's more the exposure than the quality of writing. People know a work of fiction is make-believe. People don't commit murders after reading Agatha Christie. People do commit murder after reading about murder in the paper. Similar murders.

JAMES CAMERON
British journalist
The Listener 1979
The press can only be a mirror – albeit a distorting mirror, according to its politics or the smallness of its purpose – but it rarely lies because it dare not.

ZECHARIAH CHAFFEE JR.
'The Press Under Pressure' 1948
The press is a sort of wild animal in our midst – restless, gigantic, always seeking new ways to use its strength . . . the sovereign press for the most part acknowledges accountability to no one except to its owners and publishers.

SIR WINSTON CHURCHILL
British statesman
The Press is easier squashed than squared.

ALEXANDER COCKBURN
British journalist
1974
The First Law of Journalism: To confirm existing prejudice, rather than contradict it.

JOHN CROSBY
American journalist 1966
Viewing with dismay the conditions in somebody else's backyard is a great speciality of the *New York Times*.

HUGH CUDLIPP
British newspaper owner
'The Prerogative of the Harlot' 1980
The ritual and mystique of proprietorship preclude intimacy with journalists on the payroll; metaphorically, they are expected to use the tradesman's entrance.

R. DAVIDSON
executive of Time Magazine
We report the world as we see it intelligently and thoughtfully, from a moderately conservative point of view. Though, mind you, we've often been quite liberal – in the 1930s we suggested that Negroes weren't really being treated as equal.

BOB DYLAN
American singer
If I don't talk to the press I'm a hermit. If I do talk to the press I'm trying to manipulate – I can't win.

HAROLD EVANS
British journalist
Sunday Times 1981
A headline is not an act of journalism, it is an act of marketing.

No intelligence system, no bureaucracy, can offer the information provided by competitive reporting; the cleverest agents of the police state are inferior to the plodding reporter of democracy.

ORIANA FALLACI
Italian writer 1976
Journalism combines adventure with culture.

ERROL FLYNN
American film star
It isn't what they say about you, it's what they whisper.

B. C. FORBES
American publisher
'Epigrams'
You can leave a will directing how to handle your money, but not your reputation. The public will attend to that.

GENE FOWLER
American writer
'Skyline' 1961
News is history shot on the wing. The huntsmen from the Fourth Estate seek to bag only the peacock or the eagle of the swifting day.

OTTO FRIEDRICH
American editor
on Herb Lubalin, whose art work on 'Eros' magazine had helped send its editor to jail, 1970
An art director who can get his own editor sentenced to prison may be said to have achieved the highest goal to which an art director can aspire.

WOLCOTT GIBBS
American critic
'More In Sorrow' 1958 satirising 'Timespeak', house style of Time Magazine:
Backward ran sentences until reeled the mind.

SIR JAMES GOLDSMITH
British businessman
Time 1978
Gossip columnists are diseases, like 'flu. Everyone is subject to them.

PHILIP GRAHAM
American publisher
on taking over 'Newsweek', he wanted the magazine to be . . .
The first rough draft of history.
(cf. Ben Bradlee)

JAMES C. HAGERTY
President Eisenhower's press secretary
after losing his temper with Art Buchwald
If you lose your temper at a newspaper columnist, he'll get rich, or famous, or both.

KATHARINE HEPBURN
American film star 1954
I don't care what is written about me so long as it isn't true.

JOHN HERSEY
American writer
Time 1950
Journalism allows its readers to witness

history; fiction gives its readers an opportunity to live it.

WILSON HICKS
American photo-journalist
'Words & Pictures' 1952
The basic unit of photo-journalism is one picture with words.

HOLLYWOOD MAGAZINE
Indian movie fanzine 1981
Start the New Year with scandal – We'll give you all the shoddy details.

HEDDA HOPPER
American gossip columnist
Nobody's interested in sweetness and light.

'INHERIT THE WIND'
UA 1960 screenplay by Nathan E. Douglas and Harold Jacob Smith; based on the play by Jerome Lawrence and Robert E. Lee
Gene Kelly: It's the duty of a newspaper to comfort the afflicted and to flick the comfortable.

MICK JAGGER
British rock star
As long as my picture is on the front page I don't care what they say about me on page 96.

It's really difficult to get out of gossip columns once you've got in.

LYNDON B. JOHNSON
American President
Reporters are puppets. They simply respond to the pull of the most powerful strings.

GARSON KANIN
American film-maker
quoted in 'Fanfare' by Richard Maney
No one ever won an interview.

EMERY KELEN
American journalist
The interview is an intimate conversation between journalist and politician wherein the journalist seeks to take advantage of the garrulity of the policician and the politician of the credulity of the journalist.

The press conference is the politicians'

way of being informative without actually saying anything.

MURRAY KEMPTON
American journalist
New York Review of Books 1971
One attraction of journalism as a job is that it opens doors to young men with no inherited claim for admittance.

FRANK KENT
American journalist 1977
The only way a reporter should look at a politician is down.

ALEXANDER KING
American writer
'Rich Man, Poor Man, Freud and Fruit'
To the majority of (newspapermen) a woman is either somebody's mother or a whore.

SUZY KNICKERBOCKER
American journalist 1966
As I keep repeating to anyone who will listen. There is no such thing as a secret.

ERWIN KNOLL
American editor
Everything you read in the newspapers is absolutely true except for the rare story of which you happen to have first-hand knowledge.

LOUIS KRONENBERGER
American critic
'The Cart and the Horse' 1964
It is the gossip columnist's business to write about what is none of his business.

STANISLAW J. LEC
Polish poet
in 'The Faber Book of Aphorisms' 1964
When gossip grows old it becomes myth.

MAX LERNER
American academic
'Actions and Passions' 1949
A politician wouldn't dream of being allowed to call a columnist the things a columnist is allowed to call a politician.

A. J. LIEBLING
American writer
The New Yorker 1956
People everywhere confuse what they read in newspapers with news.

WALTER LIPPMANN
American journalist
quoted in New York Times 1974
There can be no higher law in journalism than to tell the truth and to shame the devil . . . Remain detached from the great.

ALICE ROOSEVELT LONGWORTH
American socialite
If you can't say anything good about someone, sit right here by me.

ARTHUR McEWEN
American journalist
in Daniel Boorstin 'The Image'
News is anything that makes a reader say 'Gee Whiz!' News is whatever a good editor chooses to print.

MARSHALL McLUHAN
Canadian academic
'Understanding Media' 1964
Take off the dateline and one day's paper is the same as the next.

in Tom Wolfe 'The New Life Out There' 1965
People don't actually *read* newspapers. They get into them every morning like a hot bath.

NORMAN MAILER
American writer
'The Presidential Papers' 1964
Writing for a newspaper is like running a revolutionary war. You go into battle not when you are ready, but when action offers itself.

Once a newspaper touches a story, the facts are lost forever – even to the protagonists.

MARTIN MAYER
American writer
Esquire 1972
News is by definition a construct of what happened yesterday. Yesterday's newspaper is used to wrap fish and yesterday's broadcast does not exist at all.

YEHUDI MENUHIN
American musician 1970
Whenever I see a newspaper I think of the poor trees. As trees they provide beauty shade and shelter but as paper all they provide is rubbish.

ARTHUR MILLER
American playwright
The Observer 1961
A good newspaper is a nation talking to itself.

ROBERT MORLEY
British actor and wit 1967
The thing about being interviewed is that everyone expects you to have something to say.

RUPERT MURDOCH
Australian publisher
justifying pinups in his papers, 1969
We have to compete with newspapers which have double-page spreads on pubic hairs.

EDWARD R. MURROW
American broadcaster 1955
A reporter is always concerned with tomorrow. There's nothing tangible of yesterday. All I can say I've done is agitate the air ten or fifteen minutes and then boom – it's gone.

RICHARD NIXON
former American president
You know very well that whether you are on page one or page thirty depends on whether they fear you. It is just as simple as that.

DREW PEARSON
American journalist
I operate by sense of smell. If something smells wrong I go to work.

DAN RATHER
American TV reporter
Advice to politicians . . .
In dealing with the Press, do yourself a favour. Stick with one of three responses: (a) I know and I can tell you; (b) I know and I can't tell you; (c) I don't know.

JAMES RESTON
American journalist
'Sketches in the Sand' 1967
A newspaper column, like a fish, should be consumed when fresh, otherwise it is not only indigestible, but unspeakable.

Wall Street Journal 1963
If it's far away, it's news, but if it's close to home, it's sociology.

CARL ROWAN
American journalist
The New Yorker 1963
There aren't any embarassing questions
– only embarassing answers.

WILLIAM SAFIRE
American speechwriter
New York Times 1973
News expands to fill the time and space
allotted to its coverage.

RICHARD B. SALANT
American TV executive
Esquire 1969
Government plans and programmes,
even government leaders, are expenda-
ble. A free press and the truth can never
be.

FRANK SINATRA
American singer 1974
The broads who work in the press are
the hookers of the press. I might offer
them a buck and a half. I'm not sure.

ADLAI STEVENSON
American politician
An editor is one who separates the wheat
from the chaff and prints the chaff.

Accuracy to a newspaper is what virtue
is to a lady, but a newspaper can always
print a retraction.

I. F. STONE
American journalist
The Listener 1967
A good journalist should be a kind of
cross between Galahad and William
Randolph Hearst.

ARTHUR HAYS SULZBERGER
American publisher 1956
The vital measure of a newspaper is not
its size, but its spirit – that is, its responsibility to report the news, fully, accurately and fairly.

HERBERT BAYARD SWOPE
American journalist 1958
The First Duty of a newspaper is to be
Accurate. If it be Accurate, it follows
that it is Fair.

A. J. P. TAYLOR
British historian
New York Review of Books 1972
When spies discover something it can
usually be found in the newspapers as
well.

HARFORD THOMAS
British journalist
The Guardian 1981
News has a short shelf-life.

LORD THOMSON
Canadian publisher
The Observer 1959
It is part of the social mission of every
great newspaper to provide a refuge and
a home for the largest possible number
of salaried eccentrics.

NICHOLAS TOMALIN
British journalist
'Stop The Press, I Want To Get On'
The only qualities for real success in
journalism are ratlike cunning, a plau-
sible manner and a little literary ability.
The capacity to steal other people's ideas
and phrases . . . is also invaluable.

WELLS TWOMBLY
American sportswriter 1974
I took a journalism course once. They
told me if I put everything in a certain
order I would be a journalist.

GORE VIDAL
American writer
Nova 1969
The aim of so much journalism is to
exploit the moral prejudices of the
reader, to say nothing of those of the
proprietor.

EARL WARREN
American lawyer
The sports page records people's
accomplishments, the front page usually
records nothing but man's failures.

AUBERON WAUGH
British journalist
Private Eye 1977
The secret is to take no interest in what
people say is happening, and disbelieve
everything you read in the newspapers.

JANN WENNER
editor of Rolling Stone
on his success-launching 'Groupie' issue 1967
Print a famous foreskin and the world will beat a path to your door.

DAME REBECCA WEST
British writer
New York Herald Tribune 1956
Journalism – an ability to meet the challenge of filling the space.

GEOFFREY WOLFF
American writer
New Times 1975
Prophecy is journalism's occupational malady.

FRANK ZAPPA
American rock musician
Most rock journalism is people who can't write interviewing people who can't talk for people who can't read.

Books

ROBERT MARTIN ADAMS
American literary critic
quoted in 'Contemporary Literary Critics' 1977 ed. Elmer Borklund
Literature by its very nature is committed to questioning yesterday's assumptions and today's commonplaces . . . one prime aim of scholarship is to promote uncertainty.

ERIC AMBLER
British crime author
Daily Express 1961
Every story has suspense, take Jane Austen. You want to read on, so you turn the page. That's suspense.

The Times 1974
The thriller is an extension of the fairy tale. It is melodrama so embellished as to create the illusion that the story being told, however unlikely, could be true.

W. H. AUDEN
British poet
'The Dyer's Hand' 1962
Some books are undeservedly forgotten; none are undeservedly remembered.

JOHN FRANKLIN BARDIN
American crime author
in '20th Century Crime & Mystery Writers' 1980
A novel is a detector of mined experience.

ROLAND BARTHES
French academic
New York Times 1978
Literature is the question minus the answer.

'Mythologies' 1957
All of literature is a space in which a variety of writings, none of them original, blend and crash.

DAVID BEATY
British novelist
'Contemporary Novelists' 1976
Every novel is an attempt to capture time, to weave something solid out of air. The author knows it is an impossible task – that is why he keeps on trying.

DANIEL J. BOORSTIN
American writer
'The Image' 1962
A best seller was a book which somehow sold well simply because it was selling well.

JORGE LUIS BORGES
Argentine writer
quoted in New York Review of Books 1971
I have always come to life after coming to books.

'Borges On Writing' 1974
Literature is not a mere juggling of words; what matters is what is left un-

said or what may be read between the lines.

BERTOLT BRECHT
German playwright
testifying to the House UnAmerican Activities Committee 1947
Literature has the right and the duty to give to the public the ideas of the time.

GERALD BRENAN
British writer
'Thoughts in a Dry Season' 1978
The only test of a work of literature is that it shall please other ages than its own.

GEORGE BUCHANAN
British novelist
'Contemporary Novelists' 1976
The novel is an event in consciousness. Our aim isn't to copy actuality, but to modify and recreate our sense of it. The novelist is inviting the reader to watch a performance in his own brain.

ANTHONY BURGESS
British writer
New York Times 1977
Literature is recognizable through its capacity to evoke more than it says.

New York Times Book Review 1966
The possession of a book becomes a substitute for reading it.

'Writers at Work' 4th series 1977
Literature thrives on taboos, just as all art thrives on technical difficulties.

Any book has behind it all the other books that have been written.

ELIAS CANETTI
Bulgarian writer 1960
Pleasures rot away without books.

1949
The many meanings in reading – the letters are all like termites and have their own secret state.

RAYMOND CHANDLER
American novelist
quoted in 'Raymond Chandler Speaking' 1962
When a book, any sort of book, reaches a certain intensity of artistic performance it becomes literature.

JEAN COCTEAU
French writer and film director
'Le Potomak'
The greatest masterpiece in literature is only a dictionary out of order.

RICHARD CONDON
American novelist
in 'Contemporary Novelists' 1976
A writer may call himself an artist but he cannot sit down and consciously create art. What is art is not likely to be decided for decades or longer after the work has been produced – and then is often redecided – so we must not think badly if we regard literature as entertainment rather than as transcendent enlightenment... Any designation of any author's work as art ... is merely the kiss of a wish.

CLIFTON FADIMAN
American essayist
'Any Number Can Play' 1957
When you read a classic you do not see in the book more than you did before. You see more in *you* than there was before.

WILLIAM FEATHER
American businessman
'The Business of Life' 1949
Finishing a good book is like leaving a good friend.

E. M. FORSTER
British novelist
in 'Contemporary Literary Critics' ed. Elmer Borklund 1977
Human beings have their great chance in the novel.

DAVID GARNETT
British writer
in 'Contemporary Novelists' 1976
The object of the novel, as of all works of art, is to enlarge experience, not to convey facts.

ERNEST HEMINGWAY
American writer
quoted in Carlos Baker 'Hemingway: The Writer as an Artist' 1952
All good books are alike in that they are truer than if they really happened and after you are finished reading one you

will find that all that happened to you and afterwards it belongs to you. . . If you can get so that you can give that to people, then you are a writer.

in 'Papa Hemingway' by A. E. Hotchner 1966
All good books have one thing in common – they are truer than if they had really happened, and after you've read one of them you will feel that all that happened, happened to you and that it belongs to you forever. . .

KATHARINE HEPBURN
American film star
Esquire 1967
A book is only your point of view.

GRAHAM HOUGH
British literary critic
'Image & Experience' 1964
Literature is the total dream of man.

HOLBROOK JACKSON
British writer
'Southward Ho! & Other Essays'
In a way, all profoundly interesting literature is in the nature of gossip.

ARTHUR KOESTLER
British philosopher
The Observer 1973
What . . . is the aim of literature and art if not to imbue the world with feeling and meaning, to broaden and deepen our understanding of ourselves and of the things around us.

PHILIP LARKIN
British poet 1977
Many (modern novels) have a beginning, a muddle, and an end.

LEONARD LOUIS LEVINSON
American anthologist
Books – what they make a movie out of for television.

ANDRE MAUROIS
French writer
New York Times 1963
In literature as in love, we are astonished at what is chosen by others.

HENRY MILLER
American writer
'The Books in My Life' 1952
To the writer, a book is something to be

lived through, an experience, not a plan to be executed in accordance with laws and specifications.

ALBERTO MORAVIA
Italian writer
The Observer 1979
The ratio of literacy to illiteracy is constant, but nowadays the illiterates can read.

IRIS MURDOCH
British writer
The Listener 1978
Literature could be said to be a sort of disciplined technique for arousing certain emotions.

VLADIMIR NABOKOV
Russian writer
lecturing at Cornell University, 1958
The truth is that the great novels are fairy tales. . . Literature was born on the day when a boy came crying 'Wolf, wolf!' and there was no wolf behind him.

Style and structure are the essence of a book; great ideas are hogwash.

'Writers at Work' 4th series 1977
There is only one school (of literature) – that of talent.

GRACE PALEY
American writer
Ms 1974
Literature, fiction, poetry, whatever, makes justice in the world. That's why it almost always has to be on the side of the underdog.

WALKER PERCY
American writer
'Questions They Never Asked Me' Esquire 1977
A good novel is possible only after one has given up and let go.

EZRA POUND
American poet
Properly we should read for power. Man reading should be man intensely alive. The book should be a ball of light in one's hand.

'The ABC of Reading'
Literature is news that *stays* news.

V. S. PRITCHETT
British critic
'The Living Novel and Later Appreciations'
1964
The principle of procrastinated rape is said to be the ruling one in all the great bestsellers.

'Books in General'
The detective novel is the art for art's sake of yawning Philistinism.

RAYMOND QUENEAU
French historian
'A Model History'
True stories deal with hunger, imaginary ones with love.

FREDERIC RAPHAEL
British writer
'Contemporary Novelists' 1976
Truth may be stranger than fiction, but fiction is truer.

PAUL RAYMOND
British magazine publisher
who does not read, 1975
Reading could destroy my instinct for what is popular.

ALAIN ROBBE-GRILLET
French novelist
The Guardian 1967
The novel or film is not a truth that the author is putting to the audience. It is a sort of question which the author is putting to the world. Not only does he not know the answer, sometimes he doesn't even know what the question is. It is through the novel or the film that he formulates the question, discovers what it is.

BERTRAND RUSSELL
British philosopher
'The Conquest of Happiness'
There are two motives for reading a book: one, that you enjoy it; the other, that you can boast about it.

FRANCOISE SAGAN
French novelist
'Writers at Work' 1st series 1958
The illusion of art is to make one believe that great literature is very close to life, but the exact opposite is true. Life is amorphous, literature is formal.

JEAN-PAUL SARTRE
French philosopher
'Situations' 1947/49
The world could get along very well without literature; it could get along even better without man.

JOHN SIMON
American critic
New York Times 1967
The literary sensibility is geared to the timeless – that is, to the now only as an avenue by which all time can be reached.

LOGAN PEARSALL SMITH
American essayist
A best seller is the gilded tomb of a mediocre talent.

SUSAN SONTAG
American essayist
Time 1978
Books are . . . funny little portable pieces of thought.

EVELYN WAUGH
British novelist
letter to Nancy Mitford 1950, in 'The Letters of Evelyn Waugh' ed. Mark Amory 1980
The only way modern books are readable is by reading between the lines.

letter to Ann Fleming 1960, in 'The Letters of Evelyn Waugh' ed. Mark Amory 1980
Literature is simply the appropriate use of language.

ALFRED NORTH WHITEHEAD
British philosopher
in 'The Faber Book of Aphorisms' 1964
The art of literature, vocal or written, is to adjust the language so that it embodies what it indicates.

THORNTON WILDER
American writer
Time 1953
Literature is the orchestration of platitudes.

ANGUS WILSON
British writer
'Writers at Work' 1st series 1958
All fiction is for me a kind of magic and trickery – a confidence trick, trying to make people believe something is true that isn't.

Writers

ISAAC ASIMOV
American writer
'Contemporary Novelists' 1976
If there is a category of human being for whom his work ought to speak for itself, it is the writer.

SIMONE DE BEAUVOIR
French writer
'The Second Sex' 1953
The original writer, as long as he isn't dead, is always scandalous.

JORGE LUIS BORGES
Argentine writer
'Conversations with Jorge Luis Borges' ed. *Richard Burgin* 1973
The opinions of an author are wrought by the superficial accidents of circumstance.

PHYLLIS BOTTOME
American spy author
quoted in 'Who's Who In Spy Fiction', *McCormick,* 1977
If a writer is true to his characters they will give him his plot. Observations must play second fiddle to integrity.

GERALD BRENAN
British writer
'Thoughts in a Dry Season' 1978
It is by sitting down to write every morning that one becomes a writer. Those who do not do this remain amateurs.

MEL BROOKS
American film director
Playboy 1975
Every human being has hundreds of separate people living under his skin. The talent of a writer is his ability to give them their separate names, identities, personalities and have them relate to other characters living within him.

CHARLES BUKOWSKI
American writer
'Notes of a Dirty Old Man' 1969
There is only one place to write and that is *alone* at a typewriter. The writer who has to go *into* the streets is a writer who does not know the streets . . . *when you*

leave your typewriter you leave your machine gun and the rats come pouring through.

ANTHONY BURGESS
British writer
Playboy 1974
There is usually something wrong with writers the young like.

ERSKINE CALDWELL
American novelist
Atlantic Monthly 1958
I think you must remember that the writer is a simple-minded person to begin with and go on that basis. He's not a great mind, he's not a great thinker, he's not a great philosopher, he's a story teller.

ALBERT CAMUS
French writer
'The Rebel' 1951
The writer's function is now without arduous duties. By definition he cannot serve today those who make history. He must serve those who are subject to it.

BLAISE CENDRARS
French writer
'Writers at Work' 3rd series 1967
A writer should work in his cell. Turn the back. Writing is a view of the spirit . . . Humanity lives in its fiction.

In truth, writers live alongside, on the margin of life and of humanity. That's why they're very great or very small.

RAYMOND CHANDLER
American novelist
letter to Hamish Hamilton 1950
Writers . . . live over-strained lives in which far too much humanity is sacrificed to far too little art.

IRWIN S. COBB
American writer
A good storyteller is a person who has a good memory and hopes the other people haven't.

CYRIL CONNOLLY
British critic
quoted in 'Tynan Right & Left' 1967
The true function of a writer is to pro-

duce a masterpiece; no other task is of any consequence.

A writer has to construct his shell, like the caddis worm, from the debris of the past.

MALCOLM COWLEY
American critic
Esquire 1977
No complete son of a bitch ever wrote a good sentence.

QUENTIN CRISP
British author
'The Naked Civil Servant' 1968
There are three reasons for becoming a writer: the first is that you need the money; the second, that you have something to say that you think the world should know; the third is that you can't think what to do with the long winter evenings.

TIMOTHY J. CULVER
American detective fiction writer
quoted in 'Murder Ink' 1977 ed. Dilys Winn
The difference between a hack and a writer is that the hack puts down on paper things he doesn't believe.

NIGEL DENNIS
British writer
New York Review of Books 1971
It is usually a mistake to confuse the author's point of view with the form he has discovered for it. When the second is admirable, we give him the Nobel Prize for the first.

JOAN DIDION
American writer
'Slouching Towards Bethlehem' 1968
That is one last thing to remember: *writers are always selling somebody out.*

GEORGES DUHAMEL
French writer
'Le Notaire du Havre'
The novelist is the historian of the present. The historian is the novelist of the past.

WILLIAM FAULKNER
American novelist
It is the writer's privilege to help man endure by lifting his heart.

If a writer has to rob his mother he will not hesitate – the 'Ode on a Grecian Urn' is worth any number of old ladies.
quoted in obituary 1962
A writer is congenitally unable to tell the truth and that is why we call what he writes fiction.

EDNA FERBER
American writer
quoted in 'Violets and Vitriol' ed. J. Cooper and T. Hartman 1980
Life cannot defeat a writer who is in love with writing – for life itself is a writer's lover until death.

JOHN FORD
American Film director
Esquire 1964
There is no such thing as a good script.

E. M. FORSTER
British novelist
'Gide and George'
Creative writers are always greater than the causes they represent.

BRENDAN FRANCIS
What an author likes to write most is his signature on the back of a cheque.

ROBERT FROST
American poet 1960
No tears in the writer, no tears in the reader.

BRIAN GARFIELD
American crime writer
in 'Murder Ink' 1977 ed. Dilys Winn
Fan mail to a writer is like applause to an actor.

WILLIAM GERHARDIE
British writer 1970
The writer is a two-way channel, who must humbly offer the use of his voice to the life ever-lasting.

ALLEN GINSBERG
American poet 1967
I am articulating as accurately as possible in language a graph of the activity of my conscience.

'Writers at Work' 3rd series 1967
There should be no distinction between

what we write down and what we really know.

RUMER GODDEN
British author
New York Times 1963
For a dyed-in-the-wool author nothing is so dead as a book once it is written . . . she is rather like a cat whose kittens have grown up.

GRAHAM GREENE
British novelist 1980
I didn't invent the world I write about – it's all true.

'In Search of Character' 1961
The novel is an unknown man and I have to find him.

JEAN GRENIER
French writer
'Albert Camus'
Writing is putting one's obsessions in order.

LILLIAN HELLMAN
American playwright
'Writers at Work' 3rd series 1967
The writer's intention hasn't anything to do with what he achieves. The intent to earn money or the intent to be famous or the intent to be great doesn't matter in the end. Just what comes out.

ERNEST HEMINGWAY
American writer
'Men at War'
A writer should be of as great probity and honesty as a priest of God. He is either honest or not, as a woman is either chaste or not, and after one piece of dishonest writing he is never the same again.

Nobel Prize Speech 1954
The writer must write what he has to say, not speak it.

The most essential gift for a good writer is a built-in, shock-proof shit detector.

quoted in Carlos Baker 'Hemingway: The Writer as an Artist' 1952
A writer's problem does not change. It is always how to write truly and having found out what is true to project it in such a way that it becomes part of the experience of the person who reads it.

This Week 1959
People who write fiction, if they had not taken it up, might have become very successful liars.

JOHN IRVING
American author
New Times 1979
A writer uses what experience he or she has. It's the translating, though, that makes the difference.

GLORIA KATZ
American scriptwriter
New Times 1975
How can you write anything topical when it takes three years to make it.

ARTHUR KOESTLER
British philosopher
New York Times Book Review 1951
A writer's ambition should be to trade a hundred contemporary readers for ten readers in ten years' time and one reader in a hundred years' time.

F. R. LEAVIS
British critic
'The Great Tradition'
Great writers are significant in terms of the human awareness they promote.

JOHN LENNON &
PAUL McCARTNEY
British rock composers
'Paperback Writer'
I can make it longer if you like the style / I can change it round / and I want to be a paperback writer. (Northern Songs)

C. DAY LEWIS
British poet
Daily Telegraph 1967
To interview a writer is like interviewing a haunted house. The characters he invented flitting between me and the creator. They are substantial things, in a sense more real than the man who gave them life. Good novelists are seldom striking 'personalities' – their life is diffused and drained out through their creations.

BERNARD MALAMUD
American novelist
The Scotsman 1967
It is essential for a man engaged in creative work to live . . . simply. A writer must be a spectator, looking at everything with a highly critical eye. His environment, the ideals of society, his own life.

DAPHNE DU MAURIER
British novelist
quoted in 'The Wit of Women' ed. L. and M. Cowan 1969
Writers should be read – but neither seen nor heard.

EDNA ST. VINCENT MILLAY
American poet
A person who publishes a book appears wilfully in public with his pants down.

FERENC MOLNAR
Hungarian playwright
Asked how he became a writer . . .
In the same way that a woman becomes a prostitute. First I did it to please myself, then I did it to please my friends, and finally I did it for money.

ALBERTO MORAVIA
Italian writer
Time 1978
People expect from a writer what they once expected from a priest. They want spiritual and moral guidance, one of the greatest needs in our modern world.

VLADIMIR NABOKOV
Russian writer
'Writers at Work' 4th series 1977
Derivative writers seem versatile because they imitate many others, past and present. Artistic originality has only itself to copy.

V. S. NAIPAUL
West Indian writer
'Steinbeck in Monterey' 1970
A writer is in the end not his books, but his myth – and that myth is in the keeping of others.

ANAIS NIN
French novelist
'Diary' vol.V 1974
The role of the writer is not to say what

we can all say, but what we are unable to say.

JOHN O'HARA
American writer
Esquire 1969
That's what a writer is – an ordinary guy who happens to write well.

GEORGE ORWELL
British essayist
'Collected Essays'
When one says that a writer is fashionable, one practically always means that he is admired by people under thirty.

BORIS PASTERNAK
Russian novelist
The Observer 1959
The writer is the Faust of modern society, the only surviving individualist in a mass age. To his orthodox contemporaries he seems a semi-madman.

CHARLES POORE
American writer
New York Times 1962
An essayist is a lucky person who has found a way to discourse without being interrupted.

V. S. PRITCHETT
British critic
'The Tale Bearers' 1980. On H. Rider Haggard . . .
Like many popular best sellers he was a very sad and solemn man who took himself too seriously and his art not seriously enough.

FREDERIC RAPHAEL
British writer
in 'Contemporary Novelists' 1976
The novelist is, above all, the historian of conscience.

LEO ROSTEN
American writer
'Contemporary Novelists' 1976
The only reason for being a professional writer is that you just can't help it.

WILLIAM SAROYAN
American writer
quoted in 'Comtemporary Dramatists' 1977
The most solid advice to a writer is this,

I think: try to learn to breathe deeply, really to taste food when you eat, and when you sleep, really to sleep. Try as much as possible to be wholly alive, with all your might, and when you laugh, laugh like hell, and when you get angry, get good and angry. Try to be alive. You will be dead soon enough.

GEORGES SIMENON
French crime novelist
Playboy 1968
The essential condition to become a creator in the artistic domain, particularly in the novel, is to be able to enter into the skin of people.

ISAAC BASHEVIS SINGER
American writer
Esquire 1972
The most important quality by which literary talent can be recognised . . . is the inclination and the power of a man to go his own way . . . to avoid the pitfall of becoming a literary fellow traveller.

Time 1978
A writer, like a woman, never knows why people like him or why people dislike him. We never know.

JOSEPH STALIN
Russian leader
The writer is the engineer of the human soul.

JOHN STEINBECK
American writer
'Writers at Work' 4th series 1977
A good writer always works at the impossible.

'In Awe of Words' The Exonian (Exeter School, USA)
To finish is sadness to a writer – a little death. He puts the last word down and it is done. But is isn't really done. The story goes on and leaves the writer behind, for no story is ever done.

quoted in 'The Intricate Music' by Thomas Kiernan, 1980
I've thought a lot about why I set out to write. Although I didn't know it at the time I think I can say now that one of the big reasons was this: I instinctively recognised in writing an opportunity to transcend some of my personal failings

– things about myself I didn't particularly like and wanted to change but didn't know how.

TOM STOPPARD
British playwright
The Guardian 1973
I write fiction because it's a way of making statements I can disown. I write plays because dialogue is the most respectable way of contradicting myself.

ROBERT TRAVER
American writer
in 'Contemporary Novelists' 1976
A writer judging his own work is like a deceived husband – he is frequently the last person to appreciate the true state of affairs.

KENNETH TYNAN
British critic
Esquire 1968
Ever since the birth of literature all good writers have done our imagining for us. The measure of their talent has immemorially been their ability to make us see the world through their eyes.

GORE VIDAL
American writer
'Novelists & Critics of the 1940s' 1953
Writers, after all, are valuable in spite of their neuroses, obsessions, and rebellions and not because of them. It is a poor period indeed which must assess its men of letters in terms of their opposition to society.

Time 1978
Each writer is born with a repertory company in his head and . . . as you get older, you become more skilful in casting them.

'Two Sisters'
Only writers know how they use the 'real' in their fictions. And no writer has yet been willing or able to explain how he does it.

KURT VONNEGUT JR.
American writer
Playboy 1973
Writers can treat their mental illnesses every day.

Writers are specialised cells in the social organism. They are evolutionary cells. Mankind is trying to become something else, it's experimenting with new ideas all the time. And writers are a means of introducing new ideas into society and also as a means of responding symbolically to life.

ANGUS WILSON
British writer
'Contemporary Novelists' 1976
The novelist must be his own most harsh critic and also his own most loving admirer – and about both he must say nothing.

P. G. WODEHOUSE
British humorist
'Louder & Funnier'
Every author really wants to have letters printed in the papers. Unable to make the grade, he drops down a rung of the ladder and writes novels.

Writing

J. R. ACKERLEY
British literary figure
'The Ackerley Letters' ed. Neville Braybrooke 1975
If one is not scandalous it is difficult to write at all.

EDWARD ALBEE
American playwright
Evening Standard 1970
The act of writing is an act of optimism. You would not take the trouble to do it if you felt that it didn't matter.

MARTHA ALBRAND
American crime author
'Twentieth Century Crime & Mystery Authors' ed. J. Reilly 1980
All writing is a process of elimination.

WOODY ALLEN
American film star
The Listener 1978
Writing is more than anything else, because nothing can go wrong that can hurt you if you're just locked in at home.

KINGSLEY AMIS
British author
Radio Times 1971
If you can't annoy somebody, there's little point in writing.

'Contemporary Novelists' 1976
Anything a novelist (or other artist) says about his own work should be regarded with suspicion . . . as Christopher Isherwood (in effect) once remarked – no writer is aware of more than about two-thirds of what he is actually doing and saying.

JANE ARDEN
British dramatist
in 'Contemporary Dramatists' 1977
Reading can be as paralysing an act (even absorbing so-called erudite works) as Bingo, if the information does not re-create the being and radicalize the behaviour. There are no such things as creative writers – some people have better radio sets for tuning in to the only creation. The world needs healers, not 'artists'.

FERNANDO ARRABAL
Spanish playwright
The Times 1971
The writer's procedure is very much like that of a man who sets a chess problem. There is confusion and there are chess pieces. He doesn't know what he is going to do, and suddenly there is a spark. A problem has been invented.

ANTONIN ARTAUD
French playwright
'Selected Writings' 1976
All writing is garbage. People who come out of nowhere to try to put into words any part of what goes on in their minds are pigs.

BROOKS ATKINSON
American essayist
'Once Around the Sun' 1951
Writing is an artificial activity. It is a lonely and private substitute for conversation.

ALAN AYCKBOURN
British playwright
TV Times 1976
As a writer one is allowed to have conversations with oneself. What is considered sane in writers is made for the rest of the human race.

ENID BAGNOLD
British writer
foreword to 'Serena Blandish' 1946
Writing is a condition of grinding anxiety. It is an operation in which the footwork, the balance, the knowledge of sun and shade, the alteration of slush and crust, the selection of surface at high speed is a matter of exquisite fineness. When you are without judgement and hallucinations look like the truth! When experience (which trails behind) and imagination (which runs in front) will only combine by a miracle! When the whole thing is an ambidexterity of memory and creation – of the front and back of the brain – a lethargy of inward dipping and a tiptoe of poise, while the lasso is whirling for the words! It is a gamble, a toss-up, an unsure benevolence of God!

Success, to give pleasure, must be on the move . . . writing is like love: all that is past is ashes: and the thread snaps on every book that is done.

BERYL BAINBRIDGE
British author
'Contemporary Novelists' 1976
Once the grammar has been learnt (writing) is simply talking on paper and in time learning what not to say.

MARGARET C. BANNING
American novelist
The Writer 1960
Fiction is not a dream. Nor is it guess work. It is imagining based on facts, and the facts must be accurate or the imagining will not stand up.

JACQUES BARZUN
American academic
'Simple & Direct' 1977
Writing is a social act – whoever claims his neighbour's attention by writing is duty bound to take trouble – and in any case, what is life for, unless to do at least some things right?

DAVID ROYSTER BATES
American writer
in Pearl Magazine, University of Texas 1976
If a novelist has only one story, it should be a Very Important Story, and each time he tells it, it should be exceedingly better than the last.

SIMONE DE BEAUVOIR
French writer
'La Force de l'Age'
Writing is a metier . . . that one learns by writing.

SAUL BELLOW
American writer
Sunday Times 1966
The writer has sunk from the curer of souls, which was his proper business in the 19th Century, to the level of the etiquette page in the paper, advice to the lovelorn – something of that nature.

JORGE LUIS BORGES
Argentine writer
Writers at Work 4th series 1977
If a writer disbelieves what he is writing, then he can hardly expect his reader to believe it.

'Borges On Writing' 1974
A writer needs loneliness, and he gets his share of it. He needs love, and he gets shared and also unshared love. He needs friendship. In fact, he needs the universe. To be a writer is, in a sense, to be a day-dreamer – to be living a kind of double life.

'Conversations with Jorge Luis Borges' ed. Richard Burgin 1973
A writer should have another lifetime to see if he is appreciated.

The Listener 1978
What a writer wants to do is not what he does.

JIMMY BRESLIN
American writer
The number one reason why any professional writer writes is to pay the bills. This isn't the Lawn Tennis Association – where you play just for the thrill of it.

MEL BROOKS
American film director
Playboy 1975
Writing is simply one thought after another dying on the one before.

BRIGID BROPHY
Irish writer
The Listener 1963
It is not in writing about sex, it is sheerly in *writing* that honesty proves an insufficient policy. It is all very well to be so literally mindedly honest that you disdain to learn the skill necessary to make the artistic effect, but then your honest course is not to write.

WILLIAM S. BURROUGHS
American writer
Sunday Telegraph 1964
Writing's an important way of living.

MICHEL BUTOR
French writer
'Entretiens avec Georges Charbonnier'
Every word written is a victory against death.

TRUMAN CAPOTE
American writer
in 'Loose Talk' ed. Linda Botts 1980
Finishing a book is just like you took a child out in the yard and shot it.

on working on two books at once 1979
It's a bit like, I suppose, being married and having an affair on the side – the affair is almost always more exciting.

'Writers at Work' 1st series 1958
Writing has laws of perspective, of light and shade, just as painting does, or music. If you are born knowing them, fine. If not, learn them. Then rearrange the rules to suit yourself.

RAYMOND CHANDLER
American novelist
letter to Helga Greene 1957
To accept a mediocre form and make

something like literature out of it is in itself rather an accomplishment.
'A Qualified Farewell' in 'Notebooks of Raymond Chandler' 1977
Technique alone is never enough. You have to have passion. Technique alone is just an embroidered potholder.

AGATHA CHRISTIE
British crime writer 1955
The best time for planning a book is when you're doing the dishes.

SIR WINSTON CHURCHILL
British statesman
Writing a book is an adventure. To begin with it is a toy and an amusement. Then it becomes a mistress, then it becomes a master, then it becomes a tyrant. The last phase is that just as you are about to be reconciled to your servitude, you kill the monster and fling him about to the public.

JEAN COCTEAU
French writer and film director
'Writers at Work' 3rd series, 1967
This sickness, to express oneself. What is it?

MONICA DICKENS
British novelist
in 'Contemporary Novelists' 1976
Writing is a cop-out. An excuse to live perpetually in fantasy land, where you can create, direct and watch the products of your own head. Very selfish.

J. P. DONLEAVY
American writer 1968
Writing is turning one's worst moments into money.

JOHN DOS PASSOS
American writer
'Writers at Work' 4th series 1977
That's one thing to be said about writing – There is a great sense of relief in a fat volume.

WILLIAM FAULKNER
American novelist
Esquire 1964
When my horse is running good, I don't stop to give him sugar.

JULES FEIFFER
American cartoonist
'Ackroyd'
Writing, I explained, was mainly an attempt to out-argue one's past; to present events in such a light that battles lost in life were either won on paper or held to a draw.

Good swiping is an art in itself.

E. M. FORSTER
British novelist
quoted in The Observer 1958
Expansion, that is the idea the novelist must cling to, not completion, not rounding off, but opening out.

JOHN FOWLES
British novelist
interview Sunday Times 1977
There are many reasons why novelists write – but they all have one thing in common: a need to create an alternative world.

DICK FRANCIS
British crime writer
The Observer 1979
When you're writing, that's when you're lonely. I suppose that gets into the characters you're writing about. There are hours and hours of silence.

MAVIS GALLANT
Canadian author
'Contemporary Novelists' 1976
The beginning is easy; what happens next is much harder.

EDWARD GOREY
American illustrator
Esquire 1976
Mystery in writing is not in what you say but in how you say it, and I do, no matter what you might think, I do consider this the best of all possible worlds. I do think that things turn out for the best in the end.

ERNEST HEMINGWAY
American writer
letter to book critic Charles Poore quoted in The Times 1972
There is no rule on how to write. Sometimes it comes easily and perfectly; sometimes it's like drilling rock and then blasting it out with charges.

JAMES JONES
American novelist
'Writers at Work' 3rd series 1967
The quality which makes a man want to write and be read is essentially a desire for self exposure and is masochistic. Like one of those guys who has a compulsion to take his thing out and show it on the street.

ERICA JONG
American writer
Playboy 1975
In the cosmic scheme of things what matters . . . can you write something that people will still be reading to each other one hundred years from now; can you really love people, care about people and give yourself to them. These are the things that matter. The rest is total delusion.

quoted in 'The Craft of Poetry' ed. William Packard
Writing is one of the few professions left where you take all the responsibility for what you do. It's really dangerous and ultimately destroys you as a writer if you start thinking about responses to your work or what your audience needs.

JOHN LEONARD
American critic
Esquire 1975
It's a crazy business, anyway, writing, locking yourself in a room and inventing conversations, no way for a grownup to behave. Then your book is published, the sun comes up, as usual, and the sun goes down, as usual, and the world is in no way altered, and it must be someone's fault.

NORMAN MAILER
American writer
Nova 1969
Every writer thinks he is capable of anything. Scratch a Faulkner or a Hemingway and you'll find a man who thinks he can run the world.

H. L. MENCKEN
American essayist
quoted in Esquire 1965
There are no dull subjects. There are only dull writers.

HENRY MILLER
American writer
Playboy 1968
Writing, like life itself, is a voyage of discovery.

DOROTHY PARKER
American writer
If you're going to write, don't pretend to write down. It's going to be the best you can do, and it's the fact that it's the best you can do that kills you.

FRANCOISE SAGAN
French novelist
Sunday Express 1957
Writing is just having a sheet of paper, a pen and not a shadow of an idea of what you're going to say.

WILLIAM SAROYAN
American writer
You write a hit the same way you write a flop.

GEORGES SIMENON
French crime novelist
'Writers at Work' 1st series 1958
Writing is not a profession but a vocation of unhappiness. I don't think an artist can ever be happy.

JOHN STEINBECK
American writer
'Writers at Work' 4th series 1977
Writing is a very silly business at best. There is a certain ridiculousness about putting down a picture of life. . . Oh, it's a real horse's ass business. The mountain labours and groans and strains and the tiniest of rodents come out.

The craft or art of writing is the clumsy attempt to find symbols for the wordlessness. In utter loneliness a writer tries to explain the inexplicable.

Newsweek 1962
The profession of book writing makes horse racing seem like a solid, stable, business.

PAUL THEROUX
American writer
Time 1978
Writing . . . is practically the only activity a person can do that is not competitive.

CHERYL TIEGS
American model
on receiving $70,000 for putting her name to a book she did not wholly write
The problem with writing is that there's not much money in it.

LIONEL TRILLING
American critic
'The Liberal Imagination' 1950
Literature is the human activity that takes the fullest and most precise account of variousness, possibility, complexity and difficulty.

KENNETH TYNAN
British critic
The Times 1975
All forms of life are essentially games, played by oneself according to different sets of rules. Even writing, after all, is a contest to see how many meaningful words you can get into an enclosed white space by the rules of Fowler's *English Usage*.

JOHN UPDIKE
American writer 1974
Writing doesn't require drive. It's like saying a chicken has to have drive to lay an egg.

EVELYN WAUGH
British novelist
'Writers at Work' 3rd series 1967
I regard writing not as investigation of character but as an exercise in the use of language, and with this I am obsessed. I have no technical psychological interest. It is drama, speech and events that interest me.

ELIE WIESEL
Israeli writer
One written sentence is worth 800 hours of film.

TENNESSEE WILLIAMS
American playwright
Esquire 1969
All you have to do is close your eyes and wait for the symbols.

Language

ANTONIN ARTAUD
French playwright
'Ci-gît'
All true language is incomprehensible.

BURT BACHARACH
American composer
'Quote and Unquote' 1970
A synonym is a word you use when you can't spell the word you first thought of.

JACQUES BARZUN
American academic
'Simple & Direct' 1977
Communication is most complete when it proceeds from the smallest number of words, and indeed of syllables.

GERARD BAUER
French writer
'Notebooks'
The voice is a second face.

SAMUEL BECKETT
Irish author
quoted in New York Times 1974
Words are all we have.

New York Herald Tribune 1964
Every word is like an unnecessary stain on silence and nothingness.

ANDRE BRETON
French artist
'Les Pas Perdus'
Words have finished flirting. Now they are making love.

PEARL S. BUCK
American writer
in 'The Writers' Book' ed. H. Hull 1950
Self-expression must pass into communication for its fulfillment.

WILLIAM S. BURROUGHS
American writer
'Writers at Work' 3rd series 1967
Words are . . . awkward instruments and they will be laid aside eventually, probably sooner than we think.

JAMES CALLAGHAN
British politician
speech 1976
A lie can be half way around the world before the truth has got its boots on.

ALBERT CAMUS
French writer
'The Fall'
You know what charm is: a way of getting the answer yes without having asked any clear question.

ELIAS CANETTI
Bulgarian writer
Every language has its own silences.

FIDEL CASTRO
Cuban leader
Playboy 1967
A lie is simply the wilful invention of facts that do not exist.

JEAN COCTEAU
French writer and director
in 'The Faber Book of Aphorisms' 1964
Tact consists in knowing how far to go in going too far.

Daily Herald 1964
Bon mots are perhaps best described as the words other people wish they had said.

SAM ERVIN
American lawyer
at Watergate Hearings 1973
When two men communicate with each other by word of mouth, there is a twofold hazard in that communication.

BERGEN EVANS
American educator
Lying is an indispensable part of making life tolerable.

EDITH EVANS
British actress
The Times 1973
Most of the things said about everybody are untrue.

CLIFTON FADIMAN
American essayist
'Any number can play' 1957
We prefer to believe that the absence of inverted commas guarantees the originality of a thought, whereas it may be merely that the utterer has forgotten its source.

B. C. FORBES
American publisher
Forbes 1969
Information means money.

BRENDAN FRANCIS
A quotation in a speech, article or book is like a rifle in the hands of an infantryman. It speaks with authority.

MAX FRISCH
Swiss playwright
'Andorra'
Lying is a leech that has sucked truth dry.

JOHN KENNETH GALBRAITH
American economist
Anyone who says he isn't going to resign, four times, definitely will.

PAUL GOODMAN
American writer
New York Review of Books 1971
Speaking is a committment not only to a human relationship with the one spoken to, but also . . . to the existence of the thing spoken about.

JERRY HALL
American model
Interview 1978
Why would anybody lie? The truth is always more colourful.

LILLIAN HELLMAN
American playwright
'Toys In The Attic' 1972
Everybody talks too much, too many words, and gets them out of order.

ERNEST HEMINGWAY
American writer
letter to Adriana Ivancic, quoted in The Times 1967
The best ammunition against lies is the truth, there is no ammunition against gossip. It is like a fog and the clear wind blows it away and the sun burns it off.

BOB HOPE
American comedian
Playboy 1973
The only time to believe any kind of rating is when it shows you at the top.

CONSTANCE JONES
'The Ten Years' Agreement'
What are compliments? They are things you say to people when you don't know what else to say.

JAMES JONES
American novelist
'Writers at Work' 3rd series 1967
Conversation is more often likely to be an attempt at deliberate evasion, deliberate confusion, rather than communication. We're all cheats and liars, really.

R. D. LAING
British psychiatrist
'The Bird of Paradise' 1967
There is really nothing more to say when we come back to that beginning of all beginnings that is nothing at all. Only when you begin to lose that Alpha and Omega do you want to start to talk and write and then there is no end to it. Words, words, words. At best and most they are perhaps in memoriam, evocations, conjurations, incantations, emanations, shimmering, iridescent flares in the sky of darkness, a just still feasible tact, indiscretions, perhaps forgiveable . . . City lights at night, from the air, receding like these words, atoms each containing its own world and every other world. Each a fuse to set you off . . . If I could turn you on, if I could drive you out of your wretched mind. If I could tell you I would let you know.

AMANDA LEAR
British singer
Interview 1978
I hate to spread rumours – but what else can one do with them?

JOHN LEONARD
American critic
Esquire 1969
Brutalize language and you brutalize the sensations and insights it is supposed to approximate.

New York Times Book Review 1969
Co-opt is baby talk for corrupt.

CLAUDE LEVI-STRAUSS
French anthropologist
'Tristes Tropiques' 1955
What man says, language says; and what language says, society says.

'La Pensée Sauvage' 1962
Language is human reason, which has its internal logic of which man knows nothing.

MARSHALL McLUHAN
Canadian academic
Language is a form of organised stutter.

BERNARD MALAMUD
American novelist
The Guardian 1972
Words are like water – the assumption being that it moves in any direction.

MARCEL MARCEAU
French mime
Reader's Digest 1958
Do not the most moving moments of our lives find us without words?

BOB MARLEY
Jamaican singer
Music is one family but the word is the thing. Words can teach the children something. It is something really serious, not entertainment. You entertain people who are satisfied. Hungry people cannot be entertained, or people who are afraid. You can't entertain a man who has no food.

ANDRE MAUROIS
French writer
'The Art of Living'
Information is not culture. In the mind of a truly educated man, facts are organised, and they make up a living world in the image of the world of reality.

GITA MEHTA
Indian writer
'Karma Cola' 1980
The art of dialing has replaced the art of dialogue. When the person on the other end of the receiver doesn't understand the conversation, then drop the hard part, beam out the essence, and describe the resulting homogeneity as successful correspondence and cultural exchange.

WILLY MUELLER-BRITTNAU
Swiss artist
'Contemporary Artists' 1977
What can be explained with words is only the waves, the foam on the surface, but art has its place underneath the waves, in the silent depth of the unspeakable.

ROBERT OPPENHEIMER
American physicist
Time 1948
The best way to send information is to wrap it up in a person.

HAROLD PINTER
British playwright
quoted in 'Up Against the Fourth Wall' by John Lahr
One way of looking at speech is to say it is a constant stratagem to cover nakedness.

quoted in 'The Theatre of the Absurd', by Martin Esslin 1962
I feel that instead of any inability to communicate there is a deliberate evasion of communication. Communication itself between people is so frightening that rather than do that there is a continual cross-talk, a continual talking about other things, rather than what is at the root of their relationship.

quoted in 'Anger & After' by John Russell Taylor
The more acute the experience, the less articulate its expression.

RAYMOND QUENEAU
French historian
'A Model History'
Complaints of suffering are the origins of language.

SIR RALPH RICHARDSON
British actor
attributed
The most precious things in speech are pauses.

NED ROREM
American musicologist
'The Final Diary' 1974
Speech is man's most confused and egocentric expression; his most orderly and magnanimous utterance is song.

CARL SANDBURG
American poet
New York Times 1959
Slang is a language that rolls up its sleeves, spits on its hands and goes to work.

GEORGE SANTAYANA
American philosopher
Eloquence is a republican art as conversation is a democratic one.

JEAN-PAUL SARTRE
French philosopher
Words are loaded pistols.

ROGER SCRUTON
British writer
'The Meaning of Conservatism' 1980
Leisure transforms argument into conversation.

ISAAC BASHEVIS SINGER
American writer
BBC-TV 1980
Yiddish is sick – but in our history between being sick and dying is a long, long way.

ROD STEIGER
American film star
Esquire 1969
Communication without purpose is artistic masturbation.

GERTRUDE STEIN
American writer
essay 1946
Everybody gets so much information all day long that they lose their common sense.

GEORGE STEINER
British academic
'After Babel' 1975
Language is the main instrument of man's refusal to accept the world as it is.

DR. ANDRIES TEURNICHT
South African politician 1980
The word 'change' has become a political catchword for Communist propaganda.

LILY TOMLIN
American comedienne
quoted as 'Mary Jean' in Rolling Stone 1974
If you can't be direct, why be?

TUPAMAROS
Uraguayan guerillas
Slogan
Words divide us, action unites us.

TRISTAN TZARA
French artist
quoted in Esquire 1969
Thought is made in the mouth.

'L'homme approximatif'
The open breach in the hearts of our enemies – words!

GORE VIDAL
American writer
quoted in 'Contemporary Novelists' 1976
Is there any word in English quite so useful, so hopeful, so truly pregnant as 'yet'?

Esquire 1970
What is there to *say*, finally, except that pain is bad and pleasure good, life all, death nothing.

EVELYN WAUGH
British novelist
quoted in 'The State of the Language' 1979 ed.
Leonard Michaels and Christopher Ricks
Words have basic inalienable meanings, departure from which is either conscious metaphor or inexcusable vulgarity.

New York Times 1950
Words should be an intense pleasure just as leather should be to a shoemaker.

MINOR WHITE
American photographer
Magazine of Art 1952
If we had no words, perhaps we could understand each other better. The burden is ours, however.

KENNETH WILLIAMS
British actor
'Acid Drops' 1980
The nicest thing about quotes is that they give us a nodding acquaintance with the originator which is often socially impressive.

D. W. WINNICOTT
British paediatrician
'On Communication' 1963
Although healthy persons communicate and enjoy communicating, the other fact

is equally true: that each individual is an isolate, permanently non-communicating, permanently unknown, in fact, unfound.

LUDWIG WITTGENSTEIN
German philosopher
That which mirrors itself in language, language cannot represent.

Whereof one cannot speak, thereof must one be silent.

The limits of my language means the limits of my world.

What can be said can be said clearly, and what we cannot talk about we must consign to silence.

Everything that can be said can be said clearly.

Censorship

AL ALVAREZ
British writer 1968
Real pornography is movies starring Doris Day or using pictures of big breasted girls to illustrate stories on lung cancer.

ANONYMOUS AMERICAN LAWYER
Obscenity is whatever gives a judge an erection.

MICHELANGELO ANTONIONI
Italian film director
Playboy 1967
There can be no censorship better than one's own conscience.

AUSTRALIAN BROADCASTING COMPANY
annual report, 1969
Thought, to some people, is subversive.

JAMES BALDWIN
American author
Nobody Knows My Name 1961
Nobody is more dangerous than he who imagines himself pure in heart; for his purity, by definition, is unassailable.

BERNARDO BERTOLUCCI
Italian film director
Pornography is not in the hands of the child who discovers his sexuality by masturbating, but in the hands of the adult who slaps him.

ANEURIN BEVAN
British politician
Righteous people terrify me . . . virtue is its own punishment.

LADY BIRDWOOD
British moralist
after seeing 'Oh Calcutta' 1970
How long is the British taxpayer through the arts council, going to finance its own moral collapse.

SIR HENRY BOLTE
Australian politician
upholding censorship 1970
If you're going to permit them to see and read everything, you've got to permit them to do everything.

REV. EARL BRILL
American clergyman 1966
Playboy magazine is simply the house magazine of the fundamentalists of sexiosity. It shouts so loud that you wonder whether it believes itself.

VAN WYCK BROOKS
American essayist
'From A Writer's Notebook' 1958
Earnest people are often people who habitually look on the serious side of things that have no serious side.

LENNY BRUCE
American comedian
'The Essential Lenny Bruce' ed. Cohen 1967
If you can take the hot lead enema, then you cast the first stone.

'How To Talk Dirty and Influence People'
1965
Your kid is better off watching a stag movie than 'King of Kings' . . . I just don't want my kid to kill Christ when he comes back. Tell me about a stag movie where someone got killed in the end, or slapped in the mouth or heard any Communist propaganda.

ANITA BRYANT
American anti-gay campaigner 1977
As a mother, I know that homosexuals cannot biologically reproduce children; therefore, they must recruit our children.

FRANK BUCHMAN
American religious leader
Thank God for Adolf Hitler, who built a front-line defence against the anti-Christ of Communism.

AL CAPP
American cartoonist
Esquire 1970
Anyone who can walk to the welfare office can walk to work.

ALEX CAREY
Australian psychoanalyst
It was long accepted by the missionaries that morality was inversely proportional to the amount of clothing people wore.

ANGELA CARTER
British feminist
quoting Melville on 'Moby Dick' 1979 about her own book 'The Sadeian Woman'
I have written a very wicked book and I feel pure as a lamb.

DICK CAVETT
American TV talkshow host
Playboy 1971
Censorship feeds the dirty mind more than the four-letter word itself would.

NOEL COWARD
British playwright 1972
I don't think pornography is very harmful, but it is terribly, terribly boring.

The Observer 1971
If one wants to see people naked one doesn't go to the theatre, one goes to a Turkish bath.

QUENTIN CRISP
British author
'The Naked Civil Servant' 1968
Decency . . . must be an even more exhausting state to maintain than its opposite. Those who succeed seem to need a stupefying amount of sleep.

Tolerance is the result not of enlightenment, but of boredom.

ROBERTSON DAVIES
Canadian writer
'The Table Talk of Samuel Marchbanks' 1949
I have never heard of anyone who was really literate or who ever really loved books who wanted to suppress any of them. Censors only read a book with great difficulty, moving their lips as they puzzle out each syllable, when somebody tells them that the book is unfit to read.

LORD DIPLOCK
British lawyer 1971
Censorship is about stopping people reading or seeing what we do not want to read or see ourselves.

MAURICE EDELMAN
British politician 1966
I dislike censorship. Like an appendix it is useless when inert and dangerous when active.

RUSTAN FEROZE
British gynaecologist 1970
Abortion is a smutty thing under any circumstances, legal or illegal.

ROBERT FRASER
Australian art dealer
in 'Goodbye Baby & Amen' by David Bailey 1969
The only censorship which is permissible is one of quality. I don't think art has ever been able to inflame anything.

ERICH FROMM
American psychologist
Moral indignation . . . permits envy or hate to be acted out under the guise of virtue.

JAMES M. GILLIS
'This Is Our Day'
Whom the Gods would make bigots, they first deprive of humour.

PAUL GOODMAN
American writer
'Growing Up Absurd' 1960
When there is official censorship it is a sign that speech is serious. When there is none, it is pretty certain that the official spokesmen have all the loudspeakers.

BILLY GRAHAM
American preacher
1974
I think when a person has been found guilty of rape he should be castrated. That would stop him pretty quick.

backing censorship 1970
It is appalling that naked women cannot be kept out of the nation's living room.

1966
To read the papers and the magazines you would think we were almost worshipping the female bosom.

GRAHAM GREENE
British novelist 1981
Heresy is only another word for freedom of thought.

MERVYN GRIFFITHS-JONES
British prosecuting counsel
at Lady Chatterly trial, 1960
The word fuck appears thirty times, the word cunt fourteen times. The word balls thirteen times, shit six times, arse and piss three times apiece.

You may think one of the ways in which you can test this book is to ask yourself the question: would you approve of your own son and daughter, because girls can read as well as boys, reading this book? Is it a book you could have lying in your own house? Is it a book you would wish your wife or your servant to read?

HENRY S. HASKINS
American writer
'Meditations in Wall Street'
A stiff attitude is one of the attributes of rigor mortis.

Do not offer advice which has not been seasoned by your own performance.

ARTHUR KOESTLER
British philosopher
'The Heel of Achilles' 1974
Yesterday's daring metaphors are to-day's clichés. Yesterday's obscenities are today's banalities.

GERSHON LEGMAN
American academic
Murder is a crime. Describing murder is not. Sex is not a crime. Describing sex is.

JOSEPH LEWIS
American film director
The burning of an author's books, imprisonment for opinion's sake, has always been the tribute than an ignorant age pays to the genius of its times.

LINDA LOVELACE
former American porno star
Now! 1981
I would like to see all people who read pornography or have anything to do with it put in a mental hospital for observation so we could find out what we have done to them.

CLARE BOOTHE LUCE
American diplomat
Censorship, like charity, should begin at home, but unlike charity, it should end there.

MARSHALL McLUHAN
Canadian academic
quoted by Frank Moorhouse 'Days of Wine and Rage' 1980
Obscenity is linguistic violence on the frontier of reality.

HENRY MAYER 1966
The best way to get rid of pornography is not censorship but to give every schoolchild four of the most pornographic books ever written.

PAUL MAZURSKY
American writer
Esquire 1976
We've really come full circle. We're like the ancient Roman with the Colosseum. If we didn't have dirty magazines we'd have to kill for entertainment.

JONATHAN MILLER
British doctor and writer
The Guardian 1967
Censorship is nothing more than a legal corollary of public modesty.

MALCOLM MUGGERIDGE
British journalist 1970
It is even possible, quite often, to spot
women on the Pill from a certain dead-
ness about their flesh, lustiness about
their eyes and lifelessness in their
movements.

MARCEL OPHULS
French film director
The Listener 1978
Puritanism . . . helps us enjoy our misery
while we are inflicting it on others.

SIR CYRIL OSBORNE
British politician
on homosexual reform measures 1966
I am rather tired of democracy being
made safe for the pimps and prostitutes,
the spivs and the pansies and now the
queers.

LAURENCE J. PETER
Canadian educator
'Peter's Quotations' 1977
A censor is a man who knows more than
he thinks you ought to.

CHARLES REMBAR
American writer
'The End of Obscenity' 1968
Pornography is in the groin of the
beholder.

MICHAEL RUBINSTEIN
British lawyer 1978
Censorship is the ultimate blasphemy.

BERTRAND RUSSELL
British philosopher
'Selected Papers'
Men fear thought as they fear nothing
else on earth – more than ruin, more
even than death.

The infliction of cruelty with a good conscience is a delight to moralists – that is
why they invented hell.

Look 1954
Obscenity is whatever happens to shock
some elderly and ignorant magistrate.

VITTORIO DE SICA
Italian film producer
The Observer 1961
Moral indignation is in most cases 2%
moral, 48% indignation and 50% envy.

GLORIA STEINEM
American feminist
A woman reading *Playboy* feels a little
like a Jew reading a Nazi manual.

ALBIE THOMS
Australian film director
*after bulk of audience walked out of his film
'Martinetti'*
I am not offended. If more people
walked out of shows you would not need
to have a censor.

HERMINIO TRAVESIAS
American media censor
I don't like to be called a censor because
that just means saying no. I like to say
– let's find a better way of doing it.

JOHN TREVELYAN
British Film censor 1960
We are paid to have dirty minds.

KENNETH TYNAN
British critic
Esquire 1968
The liberal (on pornography) . . . is like
the man who loathes whorehouses in
practice, but doesn't mind defending
them in principle, provided they are designed by Mies van der Rohe and staffed
by social workers in Balenciaga dresses.

breaking a taboo on BBC-TV 1965
I doubt if there are any rational people
to whom the word 'fuck' would be particularly diabolical, revolting, or totally
forbidden.

MAE WEST
American film star
Playboy 1971
I believe in censorship. After all, I made
a fortune out of it.

I *invented* censorship.

EDMUND WHITE
American writer
New York Times 1979
Someone once remarked that in adolescence pornography is a substitute for
sex, whereas in adulthood sex is a substitute for pornography.

MARY WHITEHOUSE
British censor 1979
Countless, countless, *countless* people in this country would never have known of oral sex if it had not been forced into their consciousness by the media, and many, many, many people will find this distasteful.

Wit

'ALL ABOUT EVE'
20th Century Fox 1950 screenplay by Joseph Mankiewicz, based on story by Mary Orr, 'The Wisdom of Eve'
Bette Davis: Fasten your seatbelts, its going to be a bumpy night.

WOODY ALLEN
American film star
Daily Mail 1964
I cheated in the final of my metaphysics examination: I looked into the soul of the boy sitting next to me.

JIMMY BRESLIN
American writer
The professional arsonist builds vacant lots for money.

WILLIAM F. BUCKLEY
American essayist
asked what his first action would be if he won his race for being Mayor of New York City
Demand a recount.

GEORGE BURNS
American comedian
Too bad all the people who know how to run the country are busy driving taxi cabs and cutting hair.

asked why he made no movies between 'Honolulu', 1939 and 'The Sunshine Boys' 1975
My agent was afraid of overexposure.

SIR BILLY BUTLIN
British holiday camp pioneer 1968
It's funny but I spent half my life trying to get enough to eat and the other half trying to get my weight down.

MORTIMER CAPLAN
American tax official
Time 1963
There is one difference between a tax collector and a taxidermist – the taxidermist leaves the hide.

JOHN CHIENE
British surgeon
quoted in 'The Wit of Medicine' ed. L. and M. Cowan 1972
How often do we hear that the operation was successful but the patient died of something else.

BRIAN CLOSE
British cricketer
asked what would have happened if, as a very close fielder, 'it had hit you right in the centre of the forehead?'
It would have been caught at point instead of second slip.

LORD COHEN OF BIRKENHEAD
British physician
quoted in 'The Wit of Medicine' ed. L. and M. Cowan 1972
A good health educator does not frighten people to death. He frightens them to life.

CATHERINE COOKSON
British novelist 1974
The way I look at it I cast my bread upon the waters and I got a baker's shop back.

JUDITH CRIST
American film critic
leaving halfway through an especially cloying screening . . .
My family has a history of diabetes.

BETTE DAVIS
American film star
on a passing starlet:
There goes the good time that was had by all.

ALFRED HITCHCOCK
British film director
I have a perfect cure for a sore throat –
cut it.

SIR GEORGE JESSEL
English politician
1949
The human brain starts working the
moment you are born and never stops
until you stand up to speak in public.

POPE JOHN XXIII
asked how many people worked in the Vatican
About half.

FRAN LEBOWITZ
American journalist
'Metropolitan Life' 1978
The three questions of greatest concern
are – 1. Is it attractive? 2. Is it amusing?
3. Does it know its place?

Interview 1978
The telephone is a good way to talk to
people without having to offer them a
drink.

STANISLAW J. LEC
Polish poet
At the beginning there was the Word, at
the end just the Cliché.

SHIRLEY MACLAINE
American film star
I've made so many movies playing a
hooker that they don't pay me in the
regular way any more. They leave it on
the dresser.

HAROLD MACMILLAN
British politician 1960
*after watching Khrushchev pound his shoe at
the United Nations*
I'd like that translated if I may.

*watching crowds cheering Russian cosmonaut
Yuri Gagarin, first man into space, who had
been preceded by a dog, 'Little Laika', who
had died there 1959*
It would have been twice as bad if they'd
sent the dog.

GROUCHO MARX
American comedian 1969
When they said that tickets for 'Hair'
were $10 apiece I went into my bath-
room, took off my clothes and looked in
the mirror for ten minutes and said 'It
isn't worth it'.

Please accept my resignation. I don't
care to belong to any club that will have
me as a member.

GEORGE MEANY
American trade unionist
CBS-TV 1954
Anyone who has any doubts about the
ingenuity or the resourcefulness of a
plumber never got a bill from one.

J. B. MORTON
British humorist
*'Beachcomber', quoted in 'The Works of J. B.
Morton' 1974*
That Bourne from which no Hollings-
worth returns.

Every decent man carries a pencil behind his ear to write down the price of
fish.

ZERO MOSTEL
American comedian
answering Congressional investigators, 1955
Q: You are . . . known by 'Zero' as a
nickname?
ZM: Yes sir, after my financial standing
in the community – sir.

RALPH NADER
American consumer advocate
Obviously the answer to oil-spills is to
paper-train the tankers.

JOE NAMATH
American football star
*asked whether he preferred Astroturf to grass
. . .*
I don't know, I never smoked Astroturf.

MAUREEN O'HARA
America film star
*after being robbed of £50,000 worth of jewels
1970*
It never happened this way in the movies, I always won.

DOROTHY PARKER
American writer
*telegram to a friend after a much publicised
pregnancy*
Dear Mary, we all knew you had it in
you.

RINGO STARR
British rock star
Q: Why do you wear all those rings on your fingers?
A: Because I can't get them through my nose.

JAMES THURBER
American humorist
cartoon caption
That's my first wife up there. And this is the present Mrs. Harris.

Life 1960
Let the meek inherit the earth – they have it coming to them. (cf. Getty)

Comedy

FRED ALLEN
American wit
All that the comedian has to show for his years of work and aggravation is the echo of forgotten laughter.

Hanging is too good for a man who makes puns. He should be drawn and quoted.

ALAN AYCKBOURN
British playwright
'The Norman Conquests'
Few women care to be laughed at and men not at all, except for large sums of money.

quoted in 'Penguin Dictionary of Modern Quotations' 1980
Comedy is tragedy interrupted.

RONNIE BARKER
British comedian
'Sauce'
The marvellous thing about a joke with a double meaning is that it can only mean one thing.

SAUL BELLOW
American author
Sunday Times 1975
Low seriousness, you understand, is high seriousness that's failed.

ALAN BENNETT
British playwright
The Observer 1967
It sounds pretty pretentious saying this in relation to what I do, ephemeral sort of comedy, but I don't think you should be called upon to explain what you do. I don't think one should even *want* to explain, because if too much of this sort of talking and explaining goes on, in the end it effectively screens what was originally being talked about and it becomes the sum of all the boring old rubbish that's ever been said. It's why satire became dust and ashes in the mouth of anybody with any sense.

MILTON BERLE
American comedian
The Times 1970
The great comedian is the guy who's not afraid of silence . . . jokes are nothing, you can read them in magazines. It's the playing of it. It's deep. What you are.

KENNETH BIRD
British humorist 1954
Humour is falling downstairs if you do it while in the act of warning your wife not to.

JAMES BRIDIE
British doctor and playwright
'Bridie's Alphabet'
Laughter is, like assassination, one of the few remaining weapons of a sane democracy. The enemies of mankind have this in common with human beings – that they dislike being laughed at.

LENNY BRUCE
American comedian
The only honest art form is laughter. You can't fake it. Try to fake three

laughs in an hour, they'll take you away man. You can't.

Today's comedian has a cross to bear that he built himself. Today's comic is not doing an act. The audience assumes he's telling the truth. What's truth today may be a damn lie next week.

SID CAESAR
American comedian
The trouble with telling a good story is that it invariably reminds the other fellow of a dull one.

Esquire 1972
The best thing about humour is that it shows people that they're not alone.

CAROL CHANNING
American actress
Laughter is much more important than applause. Applause is almost a duty. Laughter is a reward.

CHARLIE CHAPLIN
American film star 1972
I am not interested in laughter – I just made a living from it.

NOEL COWARD
British playwright
in 'Reader's Digest Treasury of Quotations' 1979
Wit ought to be a glorious treat, like caviar. Never spread it about like marmalade.

JULES FEIFFER
American cartoonist
Playboy 1971
Satire is creating a logical argument that, followed to its basic end, is absurd . . . logically extending a premise to its totally insane conclusion, thus forcing onto an audience certain unwelcome awarenesses.

MARTY FELDMAN
British comedian
The Times 1969
Comedy, like sodomy, is an unnatural act.

ROMAIN GARY
French writer
'Promise at Dawn' 1961
Humour is an affirmation of dignity, a declaration of man's superiority to all that befalls him.

LANGSTON HUGHES
American writer
Humour is laughing at what you haven't got when you ought to have it.

EUGENE IONESCO
French playwright
'Le Démystification par l'humeur noir'
If we recognise what is atrocious and laugh at it, we can master the atrocious.

GEORGE S. KAUFMAN
American playwright
quoted in 'George S. Kaufman and his Friends' by Scott Meredith 1974
Satire is what closes Saturday night.

BUSTER KEATON
American film comedian
A comedian does funny things; a good comedian does things funny.

ARTHUR KOESTLER
British philosopher
quoted in 'Take My Word For It' by Frank Muir & Denis Norden 1978
The pun is two strings of thought tied with an acoustic knot.

in 'Encyclopedia Brittanica' 1974
Humour, in all its many-splendoured varieties, can be simply defined as a type of stimulation which tends to elicit the laughter reflex.

The Observer 1965
A joke is a kind of *coitus interruptus* between reason and emotion.

JACK KROLL
Newsweek 1976
Laughter is an orgasm triggered by the intercouse of reason with unreason.

JERRY LEWIS
American comedian
Newsweek 1972
Comedy is a man in trouble.

JACK LUDWIG
American writer
in 'Contemporary Novelists' 1976
Satire is a grappling hook thrown up the high wall of the everyday wall.

PETER McARTHUR
A satirist is a man who discovers unpleasant things about himself and then says them about other people.

FRANK MARCUS
British writer
'Transatlantic Review' 1966
Comedy is the very last alternative to despair. The greater the menace, the more potent and important the function of comedy.

BILL MAULDIN
American cartoonist
Time 1961
Humour is really laughing off a hurt. Grinning at misery.

ELSA MAXWELL
American socialite
quoting her father's last words on American TV, 1958
Laugh at yourself first, before anyone else can.

GITA MEHTA
Indian writer
'Karma Cola' 1980
You can't always count on your sense of the ridiculous when everyone around you is laughing too.

JONATHAN MILLER
British doctor and writer
The Observer 1965
Jokes are verbal mementoes of the communal experience and form a vast underground network of slightly stunted folklore through which people can make some attempt to communciate with each other, dramatise or satirise the world which they share when they are not quite on speaking terms. Jokes always flourish along the edges of moral ambiguity.

Jokes are a way of giving the amateur a chance in the game. They are like portable handpumps with simplified controls which can be used by almost anyone to give a basic yield of laughing gas, as long as the elementary instructions are observed.

Humour is vague, runaway stuff that hisses around the fissures and crevices of the mind, like some sort of loose physic gas, more valuable than oil, much harder to get and we are always prospecting for it.

SPIKE MILLIGAN
British comedian 1968
I am a disciplined comedian, of course I take direction. From God, that is.

I'm walking backwards for Christmas . . . across the Irish Sea.

MALCOLM MUGGERIDGE
British journalist
'Tread Softly For You Tread on My Jokes' 1966
Humour is practically the only thing about which the English are utterly serious.

GEORGE JEAN NATHAN
American critic
The test of a real comedian is whether you laugh at him before he opens his mouth.

LORD OLIVIER
British actor
A comedian is closer to humanity than a tragedian. He learns not to take himself seriously.

DOROTHY PARKER
American writer
'Writers at Work' 1st series 1958
Wit has truth in it, wisecracking is merely calisthenics with words.

ALAN PLATER
British playwright
in 'Contemporary Dramatists' 1977
If an idea is important enough it is worth laughing at.

HENRI POURRAT
French writer
'Gaspard des Montagnes'
Life without jokes is like a road without inns.

J. B. PRIESTLEY
British writer
'George Meredith'
Comedy, we say, is society protecting itself – with a smile.

KAREL REISZ
British film director
Daily Mail 1966
If you can't laugh at a madman for his madness, or a Jew for his Jewishness, you deny these people their humanity. The moment you express what you think you ought to feel, you start to say phoney things. If you demand sympathy for a man by simply showing him as a problem, you reduce him to a beetle in a bottle.

NED ROREM
American musicologist
The Listener 1978
Humour . . . the ability to see three sides of one coin.

PHILIP ROTH
American novelist
'Reading myself and others' 1975
Satire is moral outrage transformed into comic art.

GENE SIMMONS
American rock star
When you start making fun of yourself, when you start not taking yourself seriously, when you do sarcastic kind of stuff, you wind up cutting your own fucking throat.

GEORGE STEINER
British academic
Bronowski Memorial Lecturer 1978
Jokes and anecdotes are the radioactive tracers in human history. By their light, we can make out cardinal moments in the pulse and growth of feeling.

JAMES THURBER
American humorist
'Lanterns and Lances' 1961
The only rules comedy can tolerate are those of taste, and the only limitations those of libel.

New York Post 1960
Humour is emotional chaos remembered in tranquillity.

PETER USTINOV
British actor and wit
Comedy is simply a funny way of being serious.

The Observer 1955
Laughter would be bereaved if snobbery died.

KURT VONNEGUT JR.
American writer
Playboy 1973
Laughter or crying is what a human being does when there's nothing else he can do.

Poetry

T. W. ADORNO
German academic
quoted in 'Contemporary Literary Critics' ed. Elmer Borklund 1977
No more poetry after Auschwitz.

MULK RAJ ANAND
Indian novelist
quoted in 'Contemporary Novelists' 1976
The highest aim of poetry and art is to integrate the individual into inner growth and outer adjustment. The broken bundle of mirrors of the human personality in our time can only become the enchanted mirror if the sensibility is touched in its utmost pain and sheer pleasure and tenderest moments.

W. H. AUDEN
British poet 1971
In poetry you have a form looking for a subject and a subject looking for a form. When they come together successfully you have a poem.

'The Dyer's Hand' 1962
It is a sad fact about our culture that a poet can earn much more money writing or talking about his art than he can by practising it.

The Observer 1971
As a poet there is only one political duty – and that is to defend one's language from corruption. When it is corrupted

people lose faith in what they hear and this leads to violence.

New York Times 1960
A poet is, before anything else, a person who is passionately in love with language.

Poetry is the only art people haven't yet learned to consume like soup.

F. W. BATESON
British critic
quoted in 'Contemporary Literary Critics', 1977 ed. Elmer Borklund
Poetry is . . . the point of maximum consciousness, the synthesis of a particular social order, in which that society achieves its most significant self-expression, and ultimately its historical meaning.

SIR JOHN BETJEMAN
British poet 1974
Too many people in the modern world view poetry as a luxury, not a necessity, like petrol.

MAXWELL BODENHEIM
American poet
Poetry is the impish attempt to paint the colour of the wind.

JORGE LUIS BORGES
Argentine writer
A famous poet is a discoverer, rather than an inventor.

GERALD BRENAN
British writer
'Thoughts in a Dry Season' 1978
Poetry is the result of a struggle in the poet's mind between something he wants to say and the medium in which he is trying to say it.

GWENDOLYN BROOKS
American poet
Augusta Chronicle 1976
Poetry is life distilled.

JEAN COCTEAU
French writer and film director
'Journal d'un inconnu'
Poetry is a religion without hope.

in 'The Faber Book of Aphorisms' 1964
Take a commonplace, clean it and polish it, light it so that it produces the same effect of youth and freshness and originality and spontaneity as it did originally, and you have done a poet's job.

The poet is a liar who always speaks the truth.

CYRIL CONNOLLY
British critic
quoted in 'The Making of a Poem' by Stephen Spender
Most people do not believe in anything very much and our greatest poetry is given to us by those that do.

e. e. cummings
American poet
I did not decide to become a poet – I was always writing poetry.

YULIY DANIEL
Soviet dissident
'Prison Poems'
We are doomed to remember everything and to tell others.

BOB DYLAN
American singer
Everyone admires the poet, no matter if he's a lumberjack, or a football player or a car thief. If he's a poet he'll be admired, and respected.

T. S. ELIOT
American poet
Poetry is not an assertion of truth, but the making of that truth more real to us.

PAUL ENGLE
American poet
New York Times 1957
Poetry is ordinary language raised to the nth degree.

ROBERT FROST
American poet
explaining why he did not write free verse at Harvard
I don't like playing tennis with the net down.

New York Times 1955
Writing a poem is discovering.

quoted in Esquire 1969
Poetry is what gets lost in translation.

Vogue 1963
Poetry is a way of taking life by the throat.

Esquire 1965
Poetry is the renewal of words, setting them free, and that's what a poet is doing: loosening the words.

CHRISTOPHER FRY
British playwright
Time 1950
Poetry is the language in which man explores his own amazement.

ROBERT GRAVES
British poet
Esquire 1970
One performs autopsies only on corpses. The idea of lecturing on a living poet is all wrong. You can't get an objective idea – the man's still a menace.

BBC-TV 1962
There's no money in poetry, but then there's no poetry in money either.

Playboy 1970
Poetry can't be planned or discovered. It forces itself on you. It comes like the tense headache before a thunderstorm, which is followed by an uncontrollable violence of feeling, and the air is ionized.

'Writers at Work' 4th series 1977
Of course, a perfect poem is impossible. Once it had been written, the world would end.

Poets don't have an 'audience'. They're talking to a single person all the time.

'Horizon' 1946
To be a poet is a condition rather than a profession.

quoted in 'Contemporary Literary Critics' ed. Elmer Borklund 1977
Poetry . . . is a form of psychotherapy.

JUAN RAMON JIMENEZ
Spanish poet
'Selected Writings' 1957
Literature is a state of culture, poetry is a state of grace.

LINTON KWESI JOHNSON
British poet 1980
Poetry is basically entertainment, it's no substitute for political speech.

DENISE LEVERTOV
Russian poet
The poem has a social effect of some kind whether or not the poet wills that it have. It has kinetic force, it sets in motion . . . elements in the reader that otherwise would be stagnant.

ARCHIBALD MacLEISH
American poet
'Ars Poetica'
A poem should not mean / But be.

VLADIMIR NABOKOV
Russian writer
Poetry . . . the mysteries of the irrational perceived through rational words.

JOSE ORTEGA Y GASSET
Spanish philosopher
Partisan Review 1949
Poetry is adolescence fermented, and thus preserved.

ANDRE PIEYRA DE MANDIARGUES
French writer
'L'Age de Craie'
Poetry, like art, is inseparable from wonder.

KATHERINE ANNE PORTER
American writer 1974
No man can be explained by his personal history, least of all a poet.

SALVATORE QUASIMODO
Italian poet
New York Times 1960
Poetry is the revelation of a feeling that the poet believes to be interior and personal which the reader recognises as his own.

CARL SANDBURG
American poet
'Complete Poems' 1950
Poetry is the opening and closing of a door, leaving those who look through to guess about what is seen during a moment.

Poetry is the synthesis of hyacinths and biscuits.

NATHALIE SARRAUTE
French writer
Tel Quel
Poetry is what makes the invisible appear.

EDITH SITWELL
British poet
Life 1963
Poetry is the deification of reality.

STEPHEN SPENDER
British poet
New York Times 1961
Great poetry is always written by somebody straining to go beyond what he can do.

ROD STEIGER
American film star
Playboy 1969
Anyone who's gifted is really a poet at heart and no true poet would ever write the same poem over and over.

WALLACE STEVENS
American poet
'Opus Posthumous' 1957
The poet is the priest of the invisible.

TONY STUBBING
British artist
quoting Chinese proverb in 'Contemporary Artists' 1977
A picture is a voiceless poem; a poem is a vocal picture.

DYLAN THOMAS
British poet 1952
Poetry is what in a poem makes you laugh, cry, prickle, be silent, makes your toenails twinkle, makes you want to do this or that or nothing, makes you know that you are alone in the unknown world, that your bliss and suffering is forever shared and forever all your own.

'Quite Early One Morning' 1960
A good poem is a contribution to reality. The world is never the same once a good poem has been added to it. A good poem helps to change the shape and significance of the universe, helps to extend everyone's knowledge of himself and the world around him.

JOHN WAIN
British writer 1976
Poetry is to prose as dancing is to walking.

YEVGENY YEVTUSHENKO
Russian poet
Playboy 1972
Poets have to learn karate, these days.

Poetry must reflect the whole range of the human voice, shouts, whispers, conversation, moans, even silence. Only then will it reflect the whole range of life for a vast audience.

Scholarship

RICHARD ADAMS
British author
Radio Times 1974

I was brought up to despise your English Literateur. He's a scholastic bobbysoxer.

ALAIN (Emile Chartier)
French philosopher

There are only two kinds of scholars - those who love ideas and those who hate them.

KINGSLEY AMIS
British author
'Socialism & the Intellectuals' 1957
By his station in society a member of the intelligentsia really has no political interests to defend, except the very general one (the one he most forgets) of not finding himself bossed around by a totalitarian government.

ANONYMOUS
quoted in Arthur Koestler 'Bricks To Babel' 1981
A good terminology is half the game.

ANTONIN ARTAUD
French playwright
We must wash literature off ourselves.
We want to be men first of all. To be
human.

W. H. AUDEN
British poet
*Notes On Intellectuals from 'Collected Shorter
Poems 1927/57' 1966*
To the man-in-the-street, who, I'm sorry
to say / Is a keen observer of life, / The
word *intellectual* suggests right away / A
man who's untrue to his wife.

SIR THOMAS BEECHAM
British conductor
A musicologist is a man who can read
music but cannot hear it.

SAUL BELLOW
American writer
A great deal of intelligence can be invested in ignorance when the need for
illusion is deep.

ALEC BOURNE
British gynaecologist
'A Doctor's Creed'
It is possible to store the mind with a
million facts and still be entirely
uneducated.

KAY BOYLE
British writer
in 'Contemporary Novelists' 1976
The decision to speak out is the vocation
and the life long peril by which the intellectual must live.

GERALD BRENAN
British writer
'Thoughts in a Dry Season'
Intellectuals are people who believe that
ideas are of more importance than values; that is to say, their own ideas and
other people's values.

ALBERT CAMUS
French writer
'Notebooks' 1962
An intellectual is someone whose mind
watches itself.

ALEXIS CARREL
French writer
'Reflections on Life' 1952
The atmosphere of libraries, lecture
rooms and laboratories is dangerous to
those who shut themselves up in them
for too long. It separates us from reality
like a fog.

RENE CHAR
French writer
*quoted in Susan Sontag 'Styles of Radical
Will' 1969*
No bird has the heart to sing in a thicket
of questions.

JOHN COOPER CLARKE
British poet 1978
It's probably a very good thing to maintain a mistrust of intellectuals. You can
hear intellectuals all of the time, condoning some of the worst barbarities.

JEROME COHEN
American lawyer
Time 1971
What really matters is the name you suc-
ceed in imposing on the facts, not the
facts themselves.

ARTHUR DANTO
American philosopher
'Analytic Philosophy of Knowledge' 1968
When I transfer my knowledge I teach,
when I transfer my beliefs I indoctrinate.

HOWARD DEVOTO
British rock musician
To me an intellectual is someone who
keeps the accounts. I don't deal in messages, except the ones that come under
the category of love letters or telegrams.
And I don't deal in effects, the art rock
trap. I deal in ideas and the effect of
ideas.

J. FRANK DOBIE
'A Texan in England' 1945
The average PhD. thesis is nothing but
the transference of bones from one graveyard to another.

ALBERT EINSTEIN
German physicist
'Out of My Later Years' 1950
We should take care not to make the

intellect our god; it has, of course, powerful muscles, but no personality.

It is the supreme art of the teacher to awaken joy in creative expression and knowledge.

BERGEN EVANS
American educator
College professor – someone who talks in other people's sleep.

LEON-PAUL FARGUE
French writer
'Sous la lampe'
Don't make classical quotations – that's digging up your grandmother in front of your mistress.

FEDERICO FELLINI
Italian film director
in 'Encountering Directors' by Charles Samuels 1973
Everything that seeks to clear up an obscure process is totally academic. You only invent categories. I do things and then forget them.

HOMER FERGUSON
American politician 1954
An egghead is one who stands firmly on both feet is mid air on both sides of an issue.

MILTON FRIEDMAN
American economist
Playboy 1973
I believe it would be very hard to find any examples of mislabelling that can approach what is practised by those of us who write for the public at large. We're the worst advertisers of the lot. We screech about how important our products are, how good they are, how they'll cure every ill, and yet some of us complain when businessmen do the same thing.

A. BARTLETT GIAMETTI
American academic
Time 1978
The university must be a tributary to a larger society, not a sanctuary from it.

DR. A. H. HALSEY
British academic
Reith Lecturer 1978. The Listener 1978
There is always some sort of tendency

for intellectuals to create a paradise somewhere else.

HENRY S. HASKINS
American writer
'Meditations in Wall Street'
Academic questions are interlopers in a world where so few of the real ones have been answered.

LILLIAN HELLMAN
American playwright
'An Unfinished Woman' 1969
Intellectuals can tell themselves anything, sell themselves any bill of goods, which is why they were so often patsies for the ruling classes. . .

ERNEST HEMINGWAY
American writer
letter to Adriana Ivancic quoted in The Times 1967
What do intellectuals know? Only to write about each other. The intellectuals never know the names . . . you always have to come along and rebuild the language because the Academy destroys it.

RANDALL JARRELL
American critic
I think that one possible definition of our modern culture is that it is one in which nine-tenths of our intellectuals can't read any poetry.

JOHN MAYNARD KEYNES
British economist
The avoidance of taxes is the only intellectual pursuit that still carries any reward.

STANLEY KUBRICK
American film director
If you can talk brilliantly about a problem, it can create the consoling illusion that it has been mastered.

FRANCES LANAHAN
American writer
Esquire 1965
People who live entirely by the fertility of their imaginations are fascinating, brilliant and often charming. But they should be sat next to at dinner parties, not lived with.

PAUL LEAUTAUD
French writer
'Théâtre de Maurice Broissard'
Intelligence? Simply a question of organic chemistry, nothing more. One is no more responsible for being intelligent as for being stupid.

ANDRE MALRAUX
French writer
Intellectuals are like women – they go for the military.

ERNEST MAY
quoted in Wall Street Journal 1973
A university is a place where men of principle outnumber men of honour.

VLADIMIR NABOKOV
Russian writer
'Writers at Work' 4th series 1977
My method of teaching precluded genuine contact with my students. At best they regurgitated a few bits of my brain during examinations.

ROBERT OPPENHEIMER
American physicist
Time 1948
Scholarship is less than sense, therefore seek intelligence.

ROBERT B. PARKER
American crime writer
in 'Murder Ink' ed. Dilys Winn 1977
14 years in the professor dodge has taught me that one can argue ingeniously on behalf of any theory, applied to any piece of literature. This is rarely harmful because normally no one reads such essays.

JAMES PERKINS
American educator
in Newsweek 1970
The university is simply the canary in the coalmine. It is the most sensitive barometer of social change.

PHILIP RIEFF
American sociologist
New York Herald Tribune 1961
Scholarship is polite argument.

JEAN ROSTAND
French scientist
'A Biologist's Notebook'
Certitude is servitude.

GILBERT RYLE
British philosopher
'The Concept of Mind' 1970
The sorts of things that I can find out about myself are the same as the sorts of things that I can find out about other people and the methods of finding them out are much the same.

DR. JULIUS SCOTT
American academic
Atlanta Chronicle 1977
The true scholar is a responsible human being.

GEORGE BERNARD SHAW
Irish writer and playwright
Great Communities are built by men who sign with a mark; they are wrecked by men who write Latin verses.

ISRAEL SHENKER
American writer
New York Times 1971
Intellectuals, like fish, often move in schools following a leader.

SAUL STEINBERG
American artist
'Saul Steinberg' by Harold Rosenberg 1978
Every explanation is an over-explanation.

DAVID STOREY
British writer
'Arnold Middleton' 1959
Everything has to be defined. Yet how can you define anything except by its limitations?

LIONEL TRILLING
American critic
'The Liberal Imagination' 1950
This is the great vice of academicism – that it is concerned with ideas rather than with thinking.

FRANK LLOYD WRIGHT
American architect
Daily Telegraph 1957
I hate intellectuals. They are from the top down. I am from the bottom up.

Biography

KATHERINE ANTHONY
American writer
'Writing Biography' 1950
To the biographer, all lives bar none are dramatic constructions.

QUENTIN CRISP
British author
'The Naked Civil Servant' 1968
Autobiography is an obituary in serial form with the last instalment missing.

PHILIP GUEDALLA
British writer
Autobiography is an unrivalled vehicle for telling the truth about other people.

DONAL HENAHAN
New York Times 1977
Next to the writer of real estate advertisements, the autobiographer is the most suspect of prose artists.

ROGER JELLINEK
American publisher
New York Times Book Review 1969
The purpose of Presidential Office is not power, or leadership of the Western World, but reminiscence, best-selling reminiscence.

DESMOND MacCARTHY
British critic
A biographer is an artist upon oath.

MALCOLM MUGGERIDGE
British journalist
Esquire 1970
The best biographers are, generally speaking, the most foolish.

JOSE ORTEGA Y GASSET
Spanish philosopher
Partisan Review 1949
Every life is, more or less, a ruin among whose debris we have to discover what the person ought to have been.

Daily Telegraph 1962
Every life is more or less a ruin among whose debris we have to discover what the person ought to have been. The matter of the greatest interest is not the man's struggle with the world, but his struggle with his vocation.

CESARE PAVESE
Italian novelist
in 'The Faber Book of Aphorisms' 1964
To pass judgement on people or on characters in a book is to make silhouettes of them.

HESKETH PEARSON
British biographer
'Dickens'
A man's character never changes radically from youth to old age. What happens is that circumstances bring out characteristics which had not been obvious to the superficial observer.

MARECHAL PETAIN
French soldier 1946
To write one's memoirs is to speak ill of everybody except oneself.

WILL ROGERS
American humorist
'The Autobiography of Will Rogers' 1949
When you put down the good things you ought to have done, and leave out the bad ones you did do – that's Memoirs.

EVELYN WAUGH
British novelist
'A Little Learning' 1964
Only when one has lost all curiosity about the future has one reached the age to write an autobiography.

DAME REBECCA WEST
British writer
Vogue 1952
Just how difficult it is to write biography can be reckoned by anybody who sits down and considers just how many people know the real truth about his or her love affairs.

EVENTS

PAUL ANKA
American songwriter
explaining why he gave 'My Way' to Frank Sinatra
I didn't want to find a horse's head in my bed.

NEIL ARMSTRONG
American astronaut
reported in 'Nature' 1974 on landing on the Moon, 1969:
One small step for man, one big step for mankind.
The official version became: That's one small step for a man, one giant leap for mankind.

AMERICAN ARMY
announcement in code of the Atomic Bomb Test
Babies Satisfactorily Born

ANTHONY WEDGWOOD BENN
British politician
New York Times 1962
The House of Lords is the British Outer Mongolia for retired politicians.

ARTHUR BREMER
American criminal
after his attempt to assassinate George Wallace failed, 1972
Today I am a trillionth part of history.

LORD BROOKEBOROUGH
British politician 1970
If it weren't for these troubles, Ireland would be a very happy place.

BILLY CARTER
Brother of President Jimmy Carter
facing Jewish critics of his pro-Libyan lobbying 1979
There's a helluva lot more Arabs than Jews – they can kiss my ass!

boosting his 'Billy Beer' 1977
There are more beer drinkers in America than there are born-again Baptists.

FIDEL CASTRO
Cuban leader 1953
On trial for his attack on Batista's Moncada barracks
History will absolve me!

SIR WINSTON CHURCHILL
British statesman
to Franklin Roosevelt who hoped to see the Yalta conference last only 5/6 days . . . 1945
I do not see any other way of realizing our hopes about World Organization in five or six days. Even the Almighty took seven.

on Clement Attlee
Mr Attlee is a very modest man. But then he has much to be modest about.

1946
From Stettin in the Baltic to Trieste in the Adriatic an Iron Curtain has descended across the continent.

on the ascetic Stafford Cripps . . .
There, but for the grace of God, goes God.

on Clement Attlee, Prime Minister, 1945
He is a sheep in sheep's clothing.

BARRY CREYTON
Australian actor 1968
'Swinging London' swings like it has been hung.

JOHN DEAN
adviser to President Nixon 1973
There is a cancer within, close to the Presidency, that is growing.

SIR ALEC DOUGLAS HOME
British politician 1964
There are two problems in my life. The political ones are insoluble and the economic ones are incomprehensible.

BOB DYLAN
American singer
Albert Hall, London 1966, introducing The Band
It used to be like that, now it goes like this.

SIR ANTHONY EDEN
British politician 1953
The Free World is not just a fortress, it is also a Promised Land.

on the Suez Crisis, 1956
We are not at war with Egypt. We are in an armed conflict.

LADY CLARISSA EDEN
on the Suez Crisis, 1956
During the last few weeks I have felt that the Suez Canal was flowing through my drawing room.

DANIEL ELLSBERG
American defence expert 1971
on his leaking of the 'Pentagon Papers' . . .
I think I have done a good job as a citizen.

BRIAN EPSTEIN
British record shop owner, seeing the Beatles 1961
I want to manage those four boys. It wouldn't take me more than two half days a week.

KING FAROUK
Egyptian monarch
on his being deposed 1952
There will soon be only five kings left: the Kings of England, Diamonds, Hearts, Spades and Clubs.

MICHAEL FOOT
British politician 1967
The House of Lords is the only club in the world where the proprietor pays for the drinks.

GERALD FORD
American politician, 1973
I'm a Ford, not a Lincoln.

YURI GAGARIN
Russian cosmonaut 1961
One's legs, one's arms, they weigh nothing. Objects just float in the cabin and I didn't just sit in my chair, I hung in space.

CHARLES DE GAULLE
French statesman
explaining why he had refused to act against Jean Paul Sartre, despite the philosopher's urging of French troops to desert in Algeria, 1960
One does not arrest Voltaire.

'THE GODFATHER'
Paramount 1972 screenplay by Mario Puzo and Francis Ford Coppola, from novel by Mario Puzo
Al Pacino: My father made him an offer he couldn't refuse.

BARRY GOLDWATER
American politician 1964
Extremism in the defence of liberty is no vice . . . moderation in the pursuit of justice is no virtue.

LILLIAN HELLMAN
American playwright
letter to the House Un-American Activities Committee 1952
. . . I cannot and will not cut my cloth to fit this year's fashions, even though I long ago came to the conclusion that I was not a political person and could have no comfortable place in any political group.

DOUGLAS JAY
British politician
'The Socialist Case' 1947
For in the case of nutrition and health, just as in the case of education, the gentleman in Whitehall really does know better what is good for people than the people know themselves.

LYNDON B. JOHNSON
American President 1964
So I ask you tonight to join me and march along the road . . . that leads to the Great Society, where no child will go unfed . . . where every human being has dignity and every worker has a job; where education is blind to colour and employment is unaware of race . . .

A Great Society . . . a place where the meaning of a man's life matches the marvels of man's labour.

ALLAN KAPROW
American art critic
Art News (NY) May 1961 Coins word for new artistic event . . . in title of piece:
'Happenings' In the New York Scene.

CRAIG KARPEL
American journalist
feature title in Esquire 1970
Das Hip Kapital.

CHRISTINE KEELER
leading figure in Britain's 'Profumo Affair' 1963
I'm on the gravy train with a second class ticket.

JOHN F. KENNEDY
American president
visiting Berlin, 1963
All free men, wherever they may live, are citizens of Berlin. And therefore, as a free man, I take pride in the words 'Ich bin ein Berliner'.

accepting Democratic presidential nomination 1960
We stand today on the edge of a new frontier – the frontier of the 1960s.

NIKITA KHRUSCHEV
Russian premier
describing Stalinism to the 20th Party Congress, 1956
The cult of personality.

replying to those who wondered if the USSR might abandon Communism, 1955
Those who wait for that must wait until a shrimp learns to whistle.

LABOUR PARTY
slogan 1970, on poster caricaturing Tory leaders . . .
Yesterday's Men.

GENERAL CURTIS LeMAY
American soldier 1967
Tell the Vietnamese they've got to draw in their horns and stop aggression or we're going to bomb them back to the Stone Age.

JOHN LENNON
British rock star
to the audience at the Royal Variety Performance 1963
Those of you in the cheaper seats clap your hands. Those of you in the more expensive ones rattle your jewellery.

G. GORDON LIDDY
American secret service operative
on Watergate 1974
It was just basic politics.

JOSEPH McCARTHY
American politician
launching his 'witch-hunting' campaign 1950
I have here in my hand a list of two hundred and five, a list of names that were known to the Secretary of State as being members of the Communist Party who are nevertheless still working and shaping the policy in the State Department.

PAUL McCARTNEY
British rock star
discounting rumours of a Beatles' reunion, 1977
You can't reheat a soufflé.

HAROLD MACMILLAN
British politician
speech to South African Parliament 1960
The wind of change is blowing through the continent. Whether we like it or not, this growth of national consciousness is a political fact. We must all accept it as a fact.

referring to recent resignations by Treasury Ministers, as he parted for a Commonwealth Tour, 1958 . . .
I thought the best thing to do was to settle up these little local difficulties and then turn to the wider vision of the Commonwealth.

HERBERT MORRISON
British politician
on Britain's 'Festival of Britain' 1951
The people giving themselves a pat on the back.

MALCOLM MUGGERIDGE
British journalist
on the Kennedy years 1969
Great was it at that time to be alive, but to be given an executive post or embassy was very heaven.

RUPERT MURDOCH
Australian publisher 1969
Christine Keeler is part of the history of this country.

EDWARD R. MURROW
American broadcaster
concluding CBS-TV's 'See It Now' special on McCarthy 1954
We will not walk in fear of one another, we will not be driven by fear into an age

of unreason. If we dig deep in our history and our doctrine, and remember that we are not descended from fearful men, not from men who feared to write, to speak, to associate and to defend causes which were for the moment unpopular . . .

RICHARD NEVILLE
Australian journalist
on his release after the 'OZ Obscenity Trial' 1971
I just want to go and be obscene in private with my friends.

VIVIAN NICHOLSON
British pools winner 1961
I'm going to spend, spend, spend!

RICHARD NIXON
American politician
1978
Watergate was worse than a crime – it was a blunder.

'The Checkers Speech' 1952
I should say this: Pat doesn't have a mink coat, but she does have a respectable Republican cloth coat . . . One other thing I should probably tell you, because if I don't they'll be saying this about me too. We did get something, a gift, after the election . . . a little cocker spaniel in a crate, all the way from Texas. And our little girl Trisha, the six-year-old, named it Checkers. And you know, the kids love that dog and I just want to say this right now, that regardless of what they say about it, we're gonna keep it!

'Variety' American show business magazine, on Nixon's 'Checkers' speech, echoing two contemporary soap opera titles . . .
Just Plain Dick
Dick's Other Income

ROSA PARKS
black passenger who refused to leave a 'Whites Only' seat on a Montgomery, Alabama, bus 1955
My only concern was to get home after a hard day's work.

JAMES EARL RAY
alleged assassin of Martin Luther King Jr.
before his sentence 1968
I'm not the only one in on this.

ANNE, COUNTESS OF ROSSE
Mother of Lord Snowdon
attrib. and quoted in 'Violets & Vinegar' compiled by Jilly Cooper and Tom Hartman 1980
To old crone sitting on mound of pig-dung in a turf cabin complaining about her leaky roof . . . My dear, don't change a thing; it's simply *you.*

DEAN RUSK
American diplomat
on the Cuba Crisis 1962
We're eyeball to eyeball – and the other fellow just blinked.

SIR HARTLEY SHAWCROSS
British politician 1946
on Labour's repeal of Tory acts controlling the Unions
We are the masters at the moment – and not only for the moment, but for a very long time to come.

NEIL SHEEHAN
American journalist
in Vietnam watching a US general disembark to view the war at Tan Son Nhut airbase . . .
Ah, look, another foolish Westerner come to lose his reputation to Ho Chi Minh.

IAN SMITH
Rhodesian politician 1978
Don't forget that we have been killing each other here for years.

JOHN SNAGGE
BBC commentator
watching the 1954 University Boat Race . . .
It's Oxford! No, it's Cambridge! I can't see . . . it's Oxford! . . . no . . . well, one of them must be winning!

RON STEELE
Kent State University student
under fire from U.S. National Guard 1970
My God! My God! They're killing us!

MARGARET THATCHER
British politician
defending her increasingly unpopular policies, 1980
The lady's not for turning.

LORD THOMSON OF FLEET
Canadian publisher
quoted in 'Roy Thomson of Fleet Street' by Russell Braddon, on launching independent TV companies . . .
It's just like having a licence to print your own money.

THE LONDON TIMES
heading of the first leader on the Profumo Affair, 1963 . . .
It Is A Moral Issue.

DALTON TRUMBO
American screenwriter
on the McCarthy witch-hunts . . .
It will do no good to search for villains or heroes or saints or devils, because there were none; there were only victims.

R. J. D. TURNBULL
Australian politician 1970
The United Nations is a temple to Parkinson's Law – where inefficiency and extravagance worship at its shrines and hypocrisy at its altars.

KENNETH TYNAN
British critic
on the Common Market, 1975
I do not see the E.E.C. as a great love affair. It is more like nine middle aged couples with failing marriages meeting at a Brussels hotel for a group grope.

WILLIAM WHITELAW
British politician
proposing new treatment for young offenders, 1979
A short, sharp, shock.

CHARLES E. WILSON
American businessman
reluctantly selling his shares on appointment to a government post 1953
I thought what was good for the country was good for General Motors, and vice versa.

HAROLD WILSON
British politician
justifying his alleged slagheap speculation 1974
If you buy land on which is a slagheap 120 feet high and it costs £100,000 to remove it, that is not speculation but land reclamation.

1970
If the Tories get in in five years no one will be able to afford to buy an egg.

LANGDON WINNER
American journalist
Rolling Stone
The closest western civilisation has come to unity since the Congress of Vienna in 1815 was the week that the Sergeant Pepper album was released.

POLITICS

Politics Is

KINGSLEY AMIS
British author
'Socialism & the Intellectuals' 1957
Politics is a thing that only the unsophisticated can really go for.

EUGENE W. BAER
quoted in 'The Official Rules' by P. Dickson 1978...
What's good politics is bad economics; what's bad politics is good economics; what's good economics is bad politics; what's bad economics is good politics.

NORMAN BERRY
British advertising executive
Sunday Times 1963
In the end all political advertising is 'switch-selling' – the process whereby you rouse the consumer's interest with one product, then sell him an inferior model. They promise you the bloody earth and you wind up paying more in purchase tax.

ANEURIN BEVAN
British politician
I have never regarded politics as the arena of morals. It is the arena of interests.

VERA BRITTAIN
British radical
'The Rebel Passion' 1964
Politics are usually the executive expression of human immaturity.

JERRY BROWN
Governor of California
On his entry into the Presidential race, 1976
Because I really couldn't think of a good reason not to. A little vagueness goes a long way in this business.

1978
People will tear each other apart if given half a chance. Politics is a jungle and it's getting worse. People want a dictator these days, a man on a white horse. They're looking for a man on a white horse to ride in and tell them what to do. A politician can do anything as long as he manipulates the right symbols.

JOHN MASON BROWN
American essayist 1956
Nowhere are prejudices more mistaken for truth, passion for reason, and invective for documentation than in politics. That is a realm, peopled only by villains or heroes, in which everything is black or white and grey is a forbidden colour.

R. A. BUTLER
British politician
Politics is the art of the possible.

ALBERT CAMUS
French writer
'Notebooks' 1962
Politics and the fate of mankind are shaped by men without ideals and without greatness. Men who have greatness within them don't go in for politics.

SIR WINSTON CHURCHILL
British statesman
Politics are very much like war. We may even have to use poison gas at times.

ELY CULBERTSON
American bridge champion
'Must We Fight Russia?' 1946
Power politics is the diplomatic name for the law of the jungle.

FRED DALEY
Australian politician 1978
Politics is a funny game. One day you're a rooster, the next you're a feather duster.

WYCH FOWLER
American politician
quoted in The Listener 1978
What politics is really about is a lot of mirrors and blue smoke. People have power when other people think they

have power. If they don't think that, then you're an empty vessel.

BRENDAN FRANCIS
Politicians, like prostitutes, are held in contempt. But what man does not run to them when he needs their services.

MALCOLM FRASER
Australian politician 1977
Self-criticism is luxury all politicians should indulge in, but it is best done in private.

R. BUCKMINSTER FULLER
American engineer
The end move in politics is always to pick up a gun.

Playboy 1972
Politics is an accessory after the fact.

J. K. GALBRAITH
American economist
Nothing is so admirable in politics as a short memory.

1969
Politics is not the art of the possible. It consists in choosing between the disastrous and the unpalatable.

QUINTIN HOGG (Lord Hailsham)
British lawyer 1966
The moment politics becomes dull democracy is in danger.

PROFESSOR STANLEY HOFFMAN
American academic 1980
Fine goals matter less than the right strategy.

LORD HORDER
British Royal physician
'The Little Genius'
Politicians come and go, but medicine goes on forever. The first is ephemeral. The last is eternal.

MRS. DUDLEY IRWIN
Wife of Australian politician 1970
Political life is a blackboard jungle of nervous tension, cut throat artistry, questionable morality and no place for a considerate man.

JAMES JONES
American novelist
'Writers at Work' 3rd series 1967
To me politics is like one of those annoying and potentially dangerous, but generally just painful, chronic diseases that you just have to put up with all your life if you happen to have contracted it. Politics is like having diabetes.

BARBARA JORDAN
American politician
Ebony 1975
If you're going to play the game properly, you'd better know every rule.

MURRAY KEMPTON
American journalist
Politics is property.

JOHN LEONARD
American critic
Esquire 1969
Politics is a form of astrology – and money is its sign.

EUGENE McCARTHY
American politician 1968
Being in politics is like being a football coach. You have to be smart enough to understand the game and dumb enough to think it's important.

NORMAN MAILER
American writer
'Presidential Papers' 1964
Politics has its virtues, all too many of them – it would not rank with baseball as a topic of conversation if it did not satisfy a good many things – but one can suspect that its secret appeal is close to nicotine.

'Miami & The Siege of Chicago' 1968
Politics is the hard dealing of hard men over properties; their strength is in dealing and their virility.

'St. George & the Godfather' 1972
Politics is not an art of principles but of timing. The principles are few and soft enough to curve to political winds. The fundamental action of politics is to gain the most one can from a favourable situation and pay off as little as possible whenever necessity forces an unpopular line.

MAO ZEDONG (Mao Tse-tung)
Chinese leader
'Quotations from Chairman Mao' 1966
Political power grows out of the barrel of a gun.

'Quotations from Chairman Mao' 1966
Politics is war without bloodshed while war is politics with bloodshed.

ROBERT MITCHUM
American film star 1976
I didn't bother to vote. I'm an anarchist anyway, I don't think it makes any difference who has his duke in the till.

HENRI DE MONTHERLANT
French writer
'Notebooks'
Politics is the art of helping oneself to people.

GEORGE JEAN NATHAN
American critic 1954
Politics is the diversion of trivial men who, when they succeed at it, become important in the eyes of more trivial men.

REINHOLD NIEBUHR
American theologian
The sad duty of politics is to establish justice in a sinful world.

The whole art of politics consists in directing rationally the irrationalities of men.

GEORGE ORWELL
British essayist 1946
We shall get nowhere until we start by recognising that political behaviour is largely non-rational, that the world is suffering from some kind of mental disease which must be diagnosed before it can be cured.

CHRISTABEL PANKHURST
British feminist
'Unshackled' 1959
Never lose your temper with the Press or the public is a major rule of political life.

RONALD REAGAN
American politician 1979
I used to say that politics was the second

oldest profession, and I have come to know that it bears a gross similarity to the first.

JAMES RESTON
American journalist 1968
All politics are based on the indifference of the majority.

ALAIN ROBBE-GRILLET
French novelist
New Statesman 1961
Politics always demands recognition of established meanings and facts. Historical facts, moral facts. Art is more modest, or more ambitious – nothing is known in advance.

JOHN P. ROCHE
American journalist
Albany Times-Union 1976
In politics, a straight line is the shortest distance to disaster.

WILLIAM V. SHANNON
American journalist 1968
Experience suggests that the first rule of politics is never to say never. The ingenious human capacity for manoeuvre and compromise may make acceptable tomorrow what seems outrageous or impossible today.

PAUL SIMONON
British rock musician
It's not politics – it's just the difference between right and wrong.

I. F. STONE
American journalist
'Who Are the Democrats?' 1968
The two party system is like this magic black and white squares which look like a staircase at one moment and a checkerboard the next.

LORD TREND
British civil servant 1975
As I learnt very early on in my life in Whitehall, the acid test of any political question is: What is the alternative?

GORE VIDAL
American writer
Esquire 1970
Politics . . . the grim jockeying for pos-

ition, the ceaseless trading, the deliberate use of words not for communication but to screen intention. In short, a splendidly exciting game for those who play it. . . No *good* men? No, nor bad either, at least not often. Just men at play, with us as counters to be moved about.

FRANK ZAPPA
American rock musician
Politics is a valid concept but what we have to do is not really politics . . . it's a popularity contest. It has nothing to do with politics. What it is is mass merchandising.

Politicians

DEAN ACHESON
American statesman
1970
The first requirement of a statesman is that he be dull. This is not always easy to achieve.

RUSSELL BAKER
American writer
'The Sayings of Poor Russell' Harpers 1972
The dirty work at political conventions is almost always done in the grim hours between midnight and dawn. Hangmen and politicians work best when the human spirit is at its lowest ebb.

DAVID BRODER
American journalist
in Washington Post 1973. . .
Anybody that wants the presidency so much that he'll spend two years organising and campaigning for it is not to be trusted with the office.

JOHN CONNALLY
American politician 1971
When you're out of office, you can be a statesman.

MIKE CURB
American record business executive
I think people should go into public office for a term or two then get back into their businesses and live under the laws that they passed.

YEHEZKEL DROR
Israeli policy analyst
in RAND Corp paper 1970
While human capacities to shape the environment, society and human beings are rapidly increasing, policymaking capabilities to use these capacities remain the same.

T. S. ELIOT
American poet
'The Cocktail Party' 1949
Half the harm that is done in this world / Is due to people who want to feel important.

CHARLES DE GAULLE
French statesman
1967
The true statesman is the one who is willing to take risks.

1969
In order to become the master, the politician poses as the servant.

1962
Since a politician never believes what he says, he is surprised when others believe him.

SIR HUGH GREENE
British media executive
replying to Harold Wilson's complaints vs the BBC 1968
Politicians are professionals, they should like a bit of fast bowling to show off their strokes.

RICHARD HARRIS
American journalist 1968
Probably the most distinctive characteristic of the successful politician is selective cowardice.

EDWARD HEATH
British politician 1973
If politicians lived on praise and thanks, they'd be forced into some other line of business.

LORD HORDER
British royal physician
'The Little Genius'
Who knows how much turns on whether a Prime Minister's pipe is clean or foul, or whether the head of the Foreign Office has had enough sleep.

NIKITA KHRUSCHEV
Russian leader 1960
Politicians are the same all over. They promise to build a bridge even where there is no river.

WALTER LIPPMANN
American journalist
'The Public Philosophy' 1955
Successful democratic politicians are insecure and intimidated men. They advance politically only as they placate, appease, bribe, seduce, bamboozle or otherwise manage to manipulate the demanding and threatening elements in their constituencies.

ROBERT LOWELL
American poet
The elect, the elected, they arrive shiny as dimes and leave soft and disheveled.

NORMAN MAILER
American writer
'Miami & the Siege of Chicago' 1968
It is next to useless to interview a politician. . . To surprise a skilful politician is approximately equal in difficulty to hitting a professional boxer with a barroom hook.

H. L. MENCKEN
American essayist 1955
A good politician is quite as unthinkable as an honest burglar.

HENRY MILLER
American writer
'Writers at Work' 2nd series 1963
One has to be a lowbrow, a bit of a murderer, to be a politician, ready and willing to see people sacrificed, slaughtered, for the sake of an idea, whether a good one or a bad one.

SPIKE MILLIGAN
British comedian 1968
Render any politician down and there's enough fat to fry an egg.

MALCOLM MUGGERIDGE
British journalist
Esquire 1961
Old politicians, like old actors, revive in the limelight.

GEORGES POMPIDOU
French politician
The Observer 1973
A statesman is a politician who places himself at the service of the nation. A politician is a statesman who places the nation at his service.

BERTRAND RUSSELL
British philosopher
'New Hopes for a Changing World' 1951
Our great democracies still tend to think that a stupid man is more likely to be honest than a clever man and our politicians take advantage of this prejudice by pretending to be even more stupid than nature made them.

SAM SHAFFER
American journalist
Newsweek 1971
The effectiveness of a politician varies in inverse proportion to his commitment to principle.

MARGARET CHASE SMITH
American politician
'Declaration of Conscience' 1972
Before you can become a statesman you first have to get elected. And to get elected you have to be a politician, pledging support for what the voters want.

THE LONDON TIMES
1967
High politics are unsuitable for ordinary men. Great Prime Ministers Winston Churchill and William Pitt were sociable drinkers, Lloyd George and Palmerston could not be trusted with women, Chatham, perhaps greatest of all, was actually mad.

HARRY S. TRUMAN
American President 1958
A politician is a man who understands government and it takes a politician to run a government. A statesman is a politician who's been dead ten or fifteen years.

GORE VIDAL
American writer 1961
The politician must have that instinctive sense of occasion which is also the actor's art. To the right challenge he must have the right response. He is, in the purest sense, an opportunist.

PETER DE VRIES
American writer
A politician is a man who can be verbose in fewer words than anyone else.

ANDY WARHOL
American artist
'Exposures' 1979
When you've been shot, once is enough. That's why I don't like to get too close to politicians.

Leaders

IDI AMIN
President of Uganda 1976
In any country there must be people who have to die. They are the sacrifices any nation has to make to achieve law and order.

JEAN-BEDEL BOKASSA
Emperor of the Central African Republic
watching his troops beat three convicts to death, 1972
It's tough, but that's life.

MEL BROOKS
American film director
'2,000 Year Old Man'
If Presidents don't do it to their wives, they do it to the country.

FRED BUCY
executive of Texas Instruments Inc
quoted in 'The Official Rules' by P. Dickson 1978
Nothing is ever accomplished by a reasonable man.

ANTHONY BURGESS
British writer
'Writers at Work' 4th series 1977
The US Presidency is a Tudor monarchy plus telephones.

ALBERT EINSTEIN
German physicist
'Ideas and Opinions' 1954
In the case of political, and even of religious, leaders, it is often very doubtful whether they have done more good or harm.

DAVID FRYE
American satirist 1973
Being President is never having to say that you're sorry.

CHARLES DE GAULLE
French statesman
on Algeria, quoted 1969
In politics it is necessary either to betray one's country or the electorate. I prefer to betray the electorate.

Greatness is a road leading towards the unknown.

The perfection preached in the Gospels never yet built up an Empire. Every man of action has a strong dose of optimism, pride, hardness and cunning. But all these things will be forgiven him, indeed they will be regarded as high qualities, if he can make of them the means to achieve great ends.

1967
One cannot govern with 'buts'.

AVERELL HARRIMAN
American statesman 1970
Anyone who wants to be President should have his head examined.

SIR EDMUND HILLARY
New Zealand mountaineer 1970
You don't have to be intellectually bright to be a competent leader.

IVAN ILLICH
American philosopher
New York Review of Books 1971
Leadership does not depend on being right.

LYNDON B. JOHNSON
American President 1964
Extremism in the pursuit of the Presidency is an unpardonable vice. Moderation in the affairs of the nation is the highest virtue.

C. G. JUNG
Austrian psychoanalyst
The Guardian 1976
The true leader is always led.

HERMAN KAHN
American political analyst
Authority is not power – that's coercion. Authority is not knowledge – that's persuasion or seduction. Authority is simply that the author has the right to make a statement and to be heard.

KEN KESEY
American novelist
quoted in Esquire 1970
You don't lead by pointing and telling people some place to go. You lead by going to that place and making a case.

HENRY KISSINGER
American diplomat
interviewed by Oriana Fallaci 1970
Intelligence is not all that important in the exercise of power and is often, in point of fact, useless. Just as a leader doesn't need intelligence, a man in my job doesn't need too much of it either.

ROBERT LINDNER
American psychoanalyst
'Must You Conform?' 1956
It is a characteristic of all movements and crusades that the psychopathic element rises to the top.

DOROTHY PARKER
American writer
'Salome's Dancing Lesson'
Scratch a king and find a fool.

CLARENCE B. RANDALL
American management expert
'Making Good in Management' 1964
The leader must know, must know that he knows, and must be able to make it abundantly clear to those around him that he knows.

I. F. STONE
American journalist
on Stalin's death, 1953
Every great leader is the reflection of the people he leads and Stalin in this sense was Russia.

ROBERT TOWNSEND
American businessman
'Up The Organisation' 1970
True leadership must be for the benefit of the followers, not the enrichment of the leaders.

JOHN UPDIKE
American writer
Time 1980
A leader is one who, out of madness or goodness, volunteers to take upon himself the woe of a people. There are few men so foolish, hence the erratic quality of leadership in the world.

Heroes

BROOKS ATKINSON
American essayist
'Once Around The Sun' 1951
We need supermen to rule us – the job
is so vast and the need for wise judgement is so urgent. But, alas, there are no
supermen.

J. D. BERNAL
British scientist
'Science in History' 1954
The greater a man, the more he is soaked
in the atmosphere of his time; only thus
can he get a wide enough grasp of it to
be able to change substantially the pattern of knowledge and action.

DIETRICH BONHOEFFER
German theologian
Letters and Papers from Prison 1953
It is the characteristic excellence of the
strong man that he can bring momen-
tous issues to the fore and make a decision about them. The weak are always
forced to decide between alternatives
they have not chosen themselves.

BERTOLT BRECHT
German playwright
'Galileo'
Unhappy the land that needs heroes.

SIR DENIS BROGAN
British historian
We all invent ourselves as we go along,
and a great man's myths about himself
merely tend to stick better than most.

MEL BROOKS
American film director
Playboy 1975
Any man's greatness is a tribute to the
nobility of mankind.

FIDEL CASTRO
Cuban leader
Playboy 1967
By transforming men into symbols the
people manifest a greater gratitude: they
attribute to the individual what is not
deserved by him alone but by many.

LOUIS-FERDINAND CELINE
French writer
'Bagatelles pour un Massacre'
The cult of heroes is the cult of luck.

PAUL CLAUDEL
French composer
'Journal'
People are only heroes when they cannot
do anything else.

QUENTIN CRISP
British writer
'How To Become A Virgin' 1981
To be a man of destiny is to arrive at a
point in history when the only gift you
have to offer has suddenly become
relevant.

NIGEL DENNIS
British writer
'Boys & Girls Come Out To Play'
Most acts of assent require far more
courage than most acts of protest, since
courage is clearly a readiness to risk
self-humiliation.

TAWFIQ AL-HAKIM
Egyptian writer
'Return of Consciousness', on Nasser . . .
Men need heroes in order to transcend
the limitations and disappointment they
experience in their everyday lives . . . but
the *creation* of heroes depends upon the
compliance of history, the coming together of special events and situations,
with unusual men, . . . who take hold of
these circumstances, force them upon
their own actions and personalities, and
transform them along the lines of their
own dreams.

ERNEST HEMINGWAY
American writer
*quoted in 'Portrait of Hemingway' by Lillian
Ross*
As you get older it is harder to have
heroes, but it is sort of necessary.

MURRAY KEMPTON
American journalist
The true heroes are those who die for
causes they cannot quite take seriously.

KEN KESEY
American novelist
The trouble with superheroes is what to do between phone booths.

HENRY MILLER
American writer
'The Air Conditioned Nightmare' 1945
The world goes on because a few men in every generation believe in it utterly, accept it unquestioningly, underwrite it with their lives.

'The Books In My Life' 1952
The ordinary man is involved in action. The hero acts. An immense difference.

EDDIE RICKENBACKER
American air fighter ace
in New York Post Obituary 1973
From hero to zero is about the average hero's fate.

New York Times 1963
Courage is doing what you're afraid to do. There can be no courage unless you're scared.

WILL ROGERS
American humorist
Being a hero is about the shortest lived profession on earth.

GEORGES SIMENON
French crime novelist
Daily Telegraph 1967
I don't believe in heroes, heroic deeds are chance. The hero is the person who has the courage to make a good thing of his whole life.

TOM JONES
UA 1963 screenplay by John Osborne based on novel by Henry Fielding
Heroes, whatever high ideas we may have of them, are mortal, not divine. We are all as God made us and many of us are much worse.

ANGUS WILSON
British writer
'Writers at Work' 1st series
The opportunities for heroism are limited in this world: the most people can do is sometimes not to be as weak as they've been at other times.

Government

BERNARD BERENSON
British art historian
Governments last as long as the under-taxed can defend themselves against the over-taxed.

LORD BEVERIDGE
British politician
The State is, or can be, master of money; But in a free society it is master of very little else.

LEON BLUM
French politician 1945
No government can remain stable in an unstable society and an unstable world.

BEN CHIFFLEY
Australian politician 1949
The most government can do is make plans to assist the people.

CHARLES FRANKEL
American academic
'High On Foggy Bottom' 1969. . .
Whatever happens in government could have happened differently and it usually would have been better if it had.

MILTON FRIEDMAN
American economist 1980
Governments never learn. Only people learn.

J. K. GALBRAITH
American economist
Esquire 1972
If it is dangerous to suppose that the government is always right, it will sooner or later be awkward for public administration if most people suppose that it is always wrong.

BARRY GOLDWATER
American politician
Speech 1964
A government that is big enough to give you all you want is big enough to take it all away.

1974
A government big enough to give you everything you want is a government big enough to take from you everything you have.

BEN HEINMAN
American businessman 1980
Capitalism makes mistakes, like oilspills, but they are compartmentalised, and hence limited. When a government makes a mistake, it's a big one – like the Post Office, or Vietnam.

JOHN F. KENNEDY
American president 1960
No government is better than the men who compose it.

**JOHN LENNON &
PAUL McCARTNEY**
British rock composers
'Taxman'
If you drive a car I'll tax the street / If you try to sit, I'll tax the seat.
(Northern Songs)

WALTER LIPPMANN
American journalist
'The Public Philosophy' 1955
Popular government has not yet been proved to guarantee always and everywhere, good government.

W. L. MACKENZIE-KING
Canadian politician
Government in the last analysis is organised opinion. Where there is little or no public opinion, there is likely to be bad government, which sooner or later becomes autocratic government.

HAROLD MACMILLAN
British politician 1974
Running a country is like playing the organ. You have to use all the stops, pull out one, pull back the other. It is not like playing the penny whistle.

STEPHEN MILLER
American writer
Commentary 1977
The more government tampers with the daily lives of its citizens, the less authority it ends up having.

G. NICCOL
Australian politician 1965
A plague on any government so obdurate as not to listen to doubt.

MICHAEL OAKESHOTT
British philosopher
quoted in Esquire 1979
The function of government is to tend the arrangements of society.

DREW PEARSON
American writer
Government is only as good as the men in it.

RONALD REAGAN
American politician
Saturday Evening Post 1965
Government is like a baby. An alimentary canal with a big appetite at one end and no sense of responsibility at the other.

1976
Today if you invent a better mousetrap, the government comes along with a better mouse.

1973
Government is a referee, and it shouldn't try to be a player in the game.

Governments tend not to solve problems, only rearrange them.

LORD REITH
British broadcasting executive 1966
For me the most effective kind of organisation was despotism tempered by assassination. I was never a dictator, because I could always be sacked.

JAMES RESTON
American journalist
A government is the only known vessel that leaks from the top.

BERTRAND RUSSELL
British philosopher
'Unpopular Essays' 1950
There is no nonsense so arrant that it cannot be made the creed of the vast majority by adequate governmental action.

I am persuaded that there is absolutely no limit to the absurdities that can, by government action, come to be generally believed.

LORD SOPER
British clergyman
The Listener 1978
The House of Lords has a value . . . it is good evidence of life after death.

ADLAI STEVENSON
American politician 1952
Tyranny is the normal pattern of government. It is only by intense thought, by great effort, by burning idealism and unlimited sacrifice that freedom has prevailed as a system of government.

I. F. STONE
American journalist 1959
Every government is a device by which a few control the actions of many . . . on both sides at the moment complex human societies depend for the final decisions of war and peace on a group of elderly men any sensible plant personnel manager, whether under capitalism or Communism, would hesitate to hire.

ROBERT STRAUSS
American official
Time 1978
Everybody in government is just like a bunch of ants on a log floating down the river. Each one thinks he is guiding the log, but it is really just going with the flow.

R. H. TAWNEY
British historian
The Guardian 1953
Governments, like individuals, should beware when all men speak well of them.

HARRY S. TRUMAN
American president 1959
Whenever you have an efficient government you have a dictatorship.

GORE VIDAL
American writer
'Homage to Daniel Shays' 1972
To govern is to choose how the revenue raised from taxes is spent.

TOM WICKER
American journalist 1968
Government expands to absorb revenues and then some.

Bureaucracy

DEAN ACHESON
American statesman
A memorandum is written not to inform the reader but to protect the writer.

RICHARD ADAMS
British author
Radio Times 1974
The worst thing that can be said about a civil servant is that he is emotional.

FRED ALLEN
American wit
A conference is a gathering of important people who singly can do nothing, but together can decide that nothing can be done.

ANONYMOUS
quoted in 'The Wit of the Civil Service' ed. E. Inglis 1973
A civil servant is a faceless mortal riding like a flea on the back of the dog, Legislation.

MILTON BERLE
American comedian 1954
A committee is a group that keeps the minutes and loses hours.

JAMES H. BOREN
American bureaucrat
quoted in 'The Official Rules' by P. Dickson 1972
When in doubt, mumble; when in trouble, delegate; when in charge, ponder.

JERRY BROWN
Governor of California 1973...
Too often I find that the volume of paper expands to fill the available briefcases.

SIR BARNETT COCKS
British scientist
quoted in New Scientist 1973
A committee is a cul de sac down which ideas are lured and then quietly strangled.

WILLIAM CONNOR
British journalist
Daily Mail
Civil servants – men who write minutes, make professional assessments, who are never attacked face to face, who dwell in the Sargasso Sea of the Civil Service and who love the seaweed that conceals them.

J. K. GALBRAITH
American economist
'Ambassador's Journal' 1969
Meetings are indispensable when you don't want to do anything.

Harpers 1970
A bureaucracy is a continuing congregation of people who must act more or less as one.

RICHARD N. GOODWIN
American politician
'The American Condition' 1974
Bureaucratic function is sustained by fear of failure as the church was once supported by the fear of damnation.

JO GRIMOND
British politician
Bureaucracy is the antithesis of democracy.

RICHARD HARKNESS
New York Herald Tribune 1960
What is a committee? A group of the unwilling, picked from the unfit, to do the unnecessary.

JOSEPH HELLER
American novelist
It is the anonymous 'they', the enigmatic 'they' who are in charge. Who is 'they'? I don't know. Nobody knows. Not even 'they' themselves.

ROBERT HELLER
American writer
'The Great Executive Dream' 1972
The first myth of management is that it exists. The second myth of management is that success equals skill.

DOUGLAS HOUGHTON
British politician
in 'The Wit of the Civil Service' 1973
Civil servants, like Americans, want to be loved. But one cannot love bureaucratic power. Only submit to it, fear it or hate it. Civil servants are the 'they' in our society.

LANE KIRKLAND
American trade unionist 1974
The usefulness of a meeting is in inverse proportion to the attendance.

SUZANNAH LESSARD
American journalist
Washington Monthly 1971
The civil servant is not to consider the purpose of what he does, nor even to engage in any activity resembling an expression of political commitment, lest he think about the purposes to which he daily contributes his talents. Awareness of and responsibility for the use of one's work is not only the first principle of integrity, but a basic requisite for a healthy integrated attitude towards what one does with oneself.

EUGENE McCARTHY
American politician
Time 1979
An efficient bureaucracy is the greatest threat to liberty.

GEORGE McGOVERN
American politician 1960
The longer the title, the less important the job.

ERNEST MARPLES
British politician
in 'The Wit of the Civil Service'
You don't need brains to be Minister of Transport because the civil servants have them.

RALPH NADER
American consumer advocate
'The Spoiled System'
The speed of exit of a civil servant is directly proportional to the quality of his service.

GEORGE JEAN NATHAN
American critic
Bad officials are elected by good citizens who do not vote.

PRINCE PHILIP
1967
If you really want to get your teeth into the biggest rice pudding of all, I suggest you take a look at the duties of government and its administrative structure.

JACK ROBERTSON
American electronics writer
quoted in 'The Official Rules' by P. Dickson 1978
The more directives you issue to solve a problem the worse it gets.

ANTHONY SAMPSON
British journalist
'The Anatomy of Britain'
Running a civil service department is like playing an organ – you can do almost anything with it. . . . A minister can ring a bell, ask for a report on anything, and get it.

NEVILLE SHUTE
British writer
A politician or a civil servant is still to me an arrogant fool until he is proved otherwise.

ADLAI STEVENSON
American politician
Your public servants serve you right.

LOUIS THIESS
American local government official
New York Times 1971
Working with the government is sometimes like spinning your wheels in the sand.

'TRIBUNE'
British socialist newspaper
Whitehall is the only thoroughfare in the country with a farce playing at both ends.

GORE VIDAL
American writer
'Sex, Death & Money' 1968
There is something about a bureaucrat that does not like a poem.

WERNHER VON BRAUN
German rocket engineer 1950s
We can lick gravity, but sometimes the paperwork is overwhelming.

WARREN'S RULE
in 'Murphy's Law Book Two' by Arthur Bloch 1980
To spot the expert, pick the one who predicts the job will take the longest and cost the most.

DWIGHT WALDO
American writer
in 'Elements of Public Administration' 1946
One man's red tape is another man's system.

HUW WHELDON
British broadcaster 1970
Not a month goes by when we don't have long governmental fingers dabbling in our programmes but you have to put a hammer down on them.

CHARLES E. WILSON
American government official 1952
No inanimate thing will move from one place to another without a piece of paper that goes along telling someone where to move it.

VICTOR YANNACONE
American sportsman
Sports Illustrated 1969
Civilisation declines in relation to the increase in bureaucracy.

Voting

BERNARD BARUCH
American financier
quoted in 'Meyer Berger's New York' 1960
Vote for the man who promises least –
he'll be the least disappointing.

SIMONE DE BEAUVOIR
French writer 1973
The ballot box is a most inadequate
mechanism of change.

EDGAR Z. FRIEDENBURG
American sociologist
'R. D. Laing' 1973
To vote, then, may make the voter feel
as if he has accepted some meaningless
badge from an authority he dare not admit he loathes.

BERNARD LEVIN
British journalist
Daily Mail 1964
Ask a man which way he is going to
vote, and he will probably tell you. Ask
him, however, why, and vagueness is all.

H. L. MENCKEN
American essayist
'Minority Report' 1956
Voting is simply a way of determining
which side is the stronger without put-
ting it to the test of fighting.

GEORGE F. WILL
Newsweek 1976
Voters do not decide issues. They decide
who will decide issues.

The Masses

DON AITKIN
Australian political scientist 1969
Whatever politicians, activists and ma-
nipulators propose, it is the phlegmatic,
indifferent, ingrained electorate which
disposes.

AL ALVAREZ
British writer
The Listener 1971
Mass democracy, mass morality and the
mass media thrive independently of the
individual, who joins them only at the
cost of at least a partial perversion of his
instinct and insights. He pays for his
social ease with what used to be called
his soul, his discriminations, his unique-
ness, his psychic energy, his self.

NIGEL BALCHIN
British author
Daily Express 1949
The industrial worker is a soldier who
never fights a battle. He must maintain
discipline, he must parade, he must do
fatigues, but the big emotional moment,
which gives it all point and colour, never
comes.

BRENDAN BEHAN
Irish playwright
Weekend 1968
The ordinariness of people is what is
often extraordinary.

GEORGES BIDAULT
French politician
The Observer 1962
The weak have one weapon – the errors
of those who think they are strong.

BERTOLT BRECHT
German playwright
'Caucasian Chalk Circle' 1945
Those who have had no share in the
good fortunes of the mighty / Often have
a share in their misfortunes.

FIDEL CASTRO
Cuban leader 1970
Power . . . is the simple indestructible
will of the people. That is really power.

COCO CHANEL
French couturier
*'Coco Chanel – Her Life, Her Secrets' by M.
Haedrich 1971*
Silence is the cruelty of the provincial.

ALEXANDER CHASE
American journalist
'Perspectives' 1966
People, like sheep, tend to follow a leader
– occasionally in the right direction.

STEWART COPELAND
British rock star 1979
Street credibility is full of shit. It's something journalists invented to pass the
time of day. Anyone who claims to have
street credibility is lying through his
teeth.

FRANK CREAN
Australian politician 1978
The man in the street doesn't care who
the government is once the election is
over – it's just somebody to criticise.

MAX EASTMAN
American writer
quoted in 'As the Poet Says' compiled by Ben-
jamin Musser
There is truth in the high opinion that
insofar as a man conforms, he ceases to
exist.

EDGAR Z. FRIEDENBERG
American sociologist 1966
Not only do most people accept violence
if it is perpetuated by legitimate authority, they also regard violence against certain kinds of people as inherently
legitimate, no matter who commits it.

WALTER GROPIUS
German architect
speech at Columbia University 1961
It is one thing to make an individual
conform, and another altogether to make
him keep his identity within a group of
equals while he is trying to find the common ground with them.

PHILIP HOWARD
British journalist
The Times 1981
Most history is a record of the triumphs,
disasters and follies of top people. The
black hole in it is the way of life of mute,
inglorious men and women who made
no nuisance of themselves in the world.

ALDOUS HUXLEY
British writer
'Brave New World Revisited' Esquire 1956
Hunger and self-government are incompatible . . . the under-nourished majority
will always be ruled, from above, by the
well-fed few.

MICK JAGGER
British rock star
Esquire 1969
People are so brainwashed by the rules
that they don't know what really
matters.

C. G. JUNG
Swiss psychoanalyst
'Psychological Reflections' 1953
Man in the crowd is unconsciously
lowered to an inferior moral and intellectual level, to that level which is always
there, below the threshold of consciousness, ready to break forth as soon as it
is stimulated through the formation of a
crowd.

REV. A. S. KENDALL
British clergyman
in 'The Wit of the Church' ed. M. Bateman
and S. Stenning 1967
From motives of habit or prejudice or
economic advantage, or perhaps even laziness, some people would give blind
support to a political party and would
vote for it even if the Devil himself were
the candidate.

JOHN F. KENNEDY
American president 1961
Conformity is the jailer of freedom and
the enemy of growth.

ROBERT LINDNER
American psychoanalyst
'Must You Conform' 1956
In the crowd, herd or gang, it is the mass
mind that operates – which is to say, a
mind without subtlety, a mind without
compassion, a mind, finally, uncivilized.

WALTER LIPPMANN
American journalist
quoted in 'The Book of Laws' Henry Faber
1980
When all think alike, then no one is
thinking.

HERBERT MARCUSE
German philosopher
quoted in Daily Telegraph 1972
The general will is always wrong. Wrong inasmuch as it objectively counteracts the possible transformation of society into more humane ways of life. In the dynamic of corporate capitalism, the fight for democracy thus tends to assume anti-democratic forms.

MALCOLM MUGGERIDGE
British journalist
News Chronicle 1958
This welfare state is like a kind of zoo which keeps the inmates in ease and comfort but makes them unfit for life in their natural habitat. Mangey and bleary-eyed they grumble and growl as they walk up and down in their cages, waiting for slabs of welfare to be thrown to them at mealtimes.

JOSE ORTEGA Y GASSET
Spanish philosopher
'The Revolt of the Masses' 1959
The mass believes that it has the right to impose and to give force of law to notions born in the café.

PRINCE PHILIP
visiting Paraguay 1962
It is a pleasant change to be in a country that isn't ruled by its own people.

MILTON RAKOVE
American academic
Virginia Quarterly Review 1965
A citizen is influenced by principle in direct proportion to his distance from the political situation.

ELEANOR ROOSEVELT
American First Lady
Catholic Digest 1960
No one can make you feel inferior without your consent.

S. A. RUDIN
Canadian psychologist
New Republic 1961
In a crisis that forces a choice to be made among alternative courses of action, most people will choose the worst one possible.

BERTRAND RUSSELL
British philosopher
attr.
The average man's opinions are much less foolish than they would be if he thought for himself.

ANDRE SIEGFRIED
French writer
'Inédit'
A well-governed people are generally a people who do not think much.

ADLAI STEVENSON
American politician 1952
Government cannot be stronger or more tough-minded than its people. It cannot be more inflexibly committed to the task than they. It cannot be wiser than the people.

GORE VIDAL
American writer
The genius of our ruling class is that it has kept a majority of the people from ever questioning the inequity of a system where most people drudge along paying heavy taxes for which they get nothing in return.

RAYMOND WILLIAMS
British academic
'Culture & Society' 1958
There are in fact no masses, there are only ways of seeing people as masses. In an urban industrial society there are many opportunities for such ways of seeing. The point is not to reiterate the objective conditions, but to consider personally and collectively what these have done to our thinking. The fact is, surely, that a way of seeing other people which has become characteristic of our kind of society, has been capitalised for the purposes of political or cultural exploitation. What we see, neutrally, is other people. Many others. People unknown to us.

Democracy

CLEMENT ATTLEE
former British Prime Minister 1962
Democracy means government by discussion, but it is only effective if you can stop people talking.

JAMES BALDWIN
American writer
'Open Letter to Angela Davis' New York Review of Books 1971
Democracy does not mean the coercion of all into a deadly, and finally wicked, mediocrity. But the best liberty for all to aspire to the best that is in him, or that ever has been.

WYNN CATLIN
Democracy is the art of saying 'Nice doggie' until you can find a rock.

SIR WINSTON CHURCHILL
British statesman 1947
It has been said that democracy is the worst form of government except all those other forms that have been tried from time to time.

ALAN COREN
British humorist
Daily Mail 1975
Democracy consists of choosing your dictators, after they've told you what you think it is you want to hear.

JAMES DALE DAVIDSON
exec. dir. of US National Taxpayers Union
quoted in 'The Official Rules' by P. Dickson 1978
Democracy is that form of government where everybody gets what the majority deserves.

ELIZABETH DREW
American journalist
Washington Journal 1975
Democracy, like any noncoercive relationship, rests on a shared understanding of limits.

'A FOREIGN AFFAIR'
Paramount 1948 screenplay Charles Brackett, Billy Wilder & Richard L Breen based on story by David Shaw
Michael Raffeto: If you give a hungry man a loaf of bread, that's democracy. If you leave the wrapper on, it's imperialism.

GUNTER GRASS
German novelist
The Observer 1965
The job of a citizen is to keep his mouth open.

PROFESSOR SIDNEY HOOK
American academic
'Philosophy and Public Policy' 1980
Democracy is like love in this: it cannot be brought to life by others in command.

HUBERT HUMPHREY
American politician 1965
The right to be heard does not automatically include the right to be taken seriously.

ROBERT M. HUTCHINS
American academic
Democracy . . . is the only form of government that is founded on the dignity of man, not the dignity of some men, of rich men, of educated men, or of white men, but of all men. Its sanction is not the sanction of force, but the sanction of human nature.

KARL KRAUS
German artist
'Karl Kraus' by Harry Zohn
When there were no human rights, the exceptional individual had them. That was inhuman. Then equality was created by taking the human rights away from the exceptional individual.

WALTER LIPPMANN
American journalist
A democratic society might be defined as one . . . in which the majority is always prepared to put down a revolutionary minority.

The principle of majority rule . . . is the pacific substitute for civil war.

H. L. MENCKEN
American essayist
Democracy is the art of running the circus from the monkey cage.

Democracy is a form of religion. It is the worship of jackals by jackasses.

'Minority Report' 1956
Under democracy, one party always devotes its chief energies to trying to prove that the other party is unfit to rule – and both commonly succeed, and are right.

RALPH NADER
American consumer advocate
What we have now is democracy without citizens. No one's on the public's side. All the buyers are on the corporation's side. And the bureaucrats in the Administration don't think the government belongs to the people.

Information is the currency of democracy.

OGDEN NASH
American poet
'Vive le Postmaster General'
Democrats are to the manna born.

JOSEPH NEEDHAM
British scientist
'The Grand Titration' 1969
Democracy might therefore almost in a sense be termed that practice of which science is the theory.

JAWAHARLAL NEHRU
Indian leader 1961
Democracy is good. I say this because other systems are worse.

REINHOLD NIEBUHR
American theologian
Man's capacity for justice makes democracy possible, but man's inclination to injustice makes democracy necessary.

Democracy is finding proximate solutions to insoluble problems.

LAURENCE J. PETER
Canadian educator
'Peter's Quotations' 1977
Democracy is a process by which the people are free to choose the man who will get the blame.

AUGUSTE PINOCHET
Dictator of Chile
Sometimes democracy must be bathed in blood.

RUSSELL PROWSE
Australian bank manager 1975
The term democratic socialist makes as much sense as pregnant virginity.

SNELL PUTNEY
American writer
'The Conquest of Society' 1972
If the people of a democracy are allowed to do so, they will vote away the freedoms which are essential to that democracy.

CHARLES MERRILL SMITH
American author
In a democracy you can be respected though poor, but don't count on it.

ADLAI STEVENSON
American politician 1952
Self-criticism is the secret weapon of democracy, and candour and confession are good for the political soul.

TOM STOPPARD
British playwright
'Jumpers'
It's not the voting that's democracy, it's the counting.

R. H. TAWNEY
British historian
quoted in New Statesman 1960
Equality of opportunity is not the absence of violent contrasts in income and condition, but equal opportunities of becoming unequal.

'THE TEAHOUSE OF THE AUGUST MOON'
MGM 1956 screenplay by John Patrick, based on his play
Glenn Ford: Democracy is a system of self-determination. It's the, it's the right to make the wrong choice.

'THE THIRD MAN'
written by Graham Greene and Orson Welles 1949
Orson Welles: In Switzerland they had brotherly love, five hundred years of

democracy and peace and what did they produce? The cuckoo clock!

PETER USTINOV
British actor and wit
Nova 1968
American democracy is the inalienable right to sit on your own front porch, in your pyjamas, drinking a can of beer and shouting out 'Where else is this possible?' Which doesn't seem to me to be freedom, really.

E. B. WHITE
American writer
Democracy is the recurrent suspicion that more than half the people are right more than half the time.

'One Man's Meat'
The duty of a democracy is to know then what it knows now.

Freedom

AMERICAN CIVIL LIBERTIES
UNION 1955
Liberty is always unfinished business.

CLAUDE AVELINE
French writer
'Avec Toi-même'
To be free is . . . the interior certainty that every man is responsible for humanity, and not just before it.

JAMES BALDWIN
American author
'Nobody Knows My Name' 1961
Freedom is not something that anybody can be given. Freedom is something people take, and people are as free as they want to be.

ROLAND BARTHES
French academic
Mythologies 1957
When man proclaims his primal freedom . . . his subordination is least disputable.

SIR ISAIAH BERLIN
British philosopher
'Two Concepts of Liberty'
Liberty is liberty – not equality or fairness or justice or human happiness or a quiet conscience.

LORD BOYD-ORR
British politician 1955
If people have to choose between freedom and sandwiches they will take sandwiches.

ANDRE BRETON
French artist
quoted in 'The Autobiography of Surrealism'
by Marcel Jean, 1981
It would be wrong for man to allow himself to be intimidated by a few monstrous historical failures: he is still free to *believe* in his freedom.

ALBERT CAMUS
French writer
'The Rebel' 1951
Absolute freedom mocks at justice. Absolute justice denies freedom.

ELIAS CANETTI
Bulgarian writer
The wind is the only thing in civilisation to enjoy freedom.

MALCOLM DE CHAZAL
French writer
'Sens Plastique' 1949
The freedom to be oneself is the highest form of justice towards others.

GEORGE CLINTON
American rock musician
Free your mind and your ass will follow.

LORD DEVLIN
British lawyer
in his report on Fleet Street, 1967
Diversity of opinion is the essence of freedom.

ALBERT EINSTEIN
German physicist
'Out of my later years' 1950
By freedom I understand social conditions of such a kind that the expression of opinions and assertions about general and particular matters of knowledge will not involve dangers or serious disadvantages for him who expresses them.

FEDERICO FELLINI
Italian film director
Freedom, especially a woman's freedom, is a conquest to be made, not a gift to be received. It isn't granted. It must be taken.

ROBERT FROST
American poet
Esquire 1965
The moments of freedom, they can't be given to you. You have to take them.

If society fits you comfortably enough, you call it freedom.

ATHOL FUGARD
South African playwright
The Guardian 1971
How real a concept is freedom? You start to function when coming to terms with a set of limitations.

MOHANDAS K. GANDHI
Indian leader 1959
Freedom is not worth having if it does not connote the freedom to err.

PIERRE GAXOTTE
French writer
'Themes and Variations'
Liberty is not at the beginning, but at the end. Liberty is the fruit of good order.

ERIC HOFFER
American philosopher
in 'The Faber Book of Aphorisms' 1964
The basic test of freedom is perhaps less in what we are free to do than in what we are free not to do.

'The Passionate State of Mind' 1954
When people are free to do as they please, they usually imitate each other.

ALFRED KAZIN
American critic
Esquire 1967
Freedom speaks only for freedom. Political superstition claims to speak for the world at large. No one and nothing can do that and be authentic.

JOHN F. KENNEDY
American president 1963
Freedom is indivisible and when one man is enslaved, all are not free.

1961
It is one of the ironies of our time that the techniques of a harsh and repressive system should be able to instill discipline and ardour in its servants – while the blessings of liberty have too often stood for privilege, materialism and a life of ease.

MICHAEL KUSTOW
British arts administrator
The Listener 1970
Increased awareness is the first step to freedom. A people that denies the arts is an unfree people.

ANTHONY LEJEUNE
British journalist
'Freedom and the Politicians'
Countries cannot become free. Countries cannot be oppressed. Only men can be free or not free.

MALCOLM X
American radical
'Malcolm X Speaks' 1965
Nobody can give you freedom. Nobody can give you equality or justice or anything. If you're a man, you take it.

You can't separate peace from freedom because no one can be at peace unless he has his freedom.

H. L. MENCKEN
American essayist
'Minority Report' 1956
What men value in this world is not rights, but privileges.

Most people want security in this world, not liberty.

MARIA MONTESSORI
Italian educator
'The Montessori Method'
Discipline must come through liberty. . .
We do not consider an individual disciplined when he has been rendered as artificially silent as a mute and as immovable as a paralytic. He is an individual *annihilated*, not *disciplined*.

ZERO MOSTEL
American comedian
New York Times 1965
The freedom of any society varies proportionately with the volume of its laughter.

GEORGE ORWELL
British essayist 1945
Liberty is the right to tell people what they do not want to hear.

ALAN PATON
South African writer 1967
To give up the task of reforming society is to give up one's responsibility as a free man.

DON PLATT
There is no tyranny so despotic as that of public opinion among a free people.

TOM ROBINSON
British rock singer
Freedom is indivisible. You can't have it at the expense of someone else. Either there's oppression or there isn't.

JEAN-PAUL SARTRE
French philosopher
The Observer 1970
As soon as man apprehends himself as free and wishes to use his freedom, his activity is play.

HUGH SCANLON
British trade unionist
The Observer 1977
Liberty is conforming to the majority.

ADLAI STEVENSON
American politician
A hungry man is not a free man.

GRAHAM SUTHERLAND
British artist
The Observer 1974
I don't think anyone is free – one creates one's own prison.

LECH WALESA
Polish trade unionist
interviewed by Oriana Fallaci 1981
Freedom is a food which must be carefully administered when people are too hungry for it.

SIMONE WEIL
French philosopher
'The Need for Roots' 1952
Liberty, taking the word in its concrete sense, consists in the ability to choose.

RAYMOND WILLIAMS
British academic
'Culture & Society' 1958
The practical liberty of thought and expression is a natural right and a common necessity. The growth of understanding is so difficult that none of us can arrogate to himself or to an institution or a class the right to determine its channels of advance. Any educational system will reflect the content of a society. Any emphasis or exploration will follow from an emphasis of common need. Yet no system and no emphasis can be adequate if they fail to allow for real flexibility, for real alternative courses. To deny these practical liberties is to burn the common seed.

TENNESSEE WILLIAMS
American playwright
To be free is to have achieved your life.

Liberals

ANONYMOUS
quoted in The Listener 1978
White liberals – they can't feel ashamed without telling us all about it. They escape from embarrassment into causes.

**IMAMU AMIRI BARAKA
(LeRoi Jones)
American playwright 1966**
A rich man told me recently that a liberal is a man who tells other people what to do with their money.

**LEONARD BERNSTEIN
American conductor 1966**
It is a Hamlet-like torture to be truly liberal.

**MALCOLM BRADBURY
British writer**
The Listener 1962
In a sense, the modern artist is the liberal who can't believe in himself, the man who, as Robert Frost has put it, can't take his own side in a quarrel, and whose search into anarchy is a confession of his only strong intolerance – an intolerance of himself and his role. It is with this in mind that the tragedy of our times is the spectacle of the liberal trapped in a world to which liberalism no longer offers a solution.

**LENNY BRUCE
American comedian**
The liberals can understand everything but people who don't understand them.

**FRANTZ FANON
French radical**
'The Wretched of the Earth' 1961
Every onlooker is either a coward or a traitor.

**MICHAEL FRAYN
British writer**
The Observer 1965
To be absolutely honest, what I feel really bad about is that I don't feel worse. That's the intellectual liberal's problem in a nutshell.

**ROBERT FROST
American poet**
A liberal is a man too broadminded to take his own side in a quarrel.

**BARRY GOLDWATER
American politician**
speech 1964
The big trouble with the so-called liberal today is that he doesn't understand simplicity . . . those who do not have courage want complicated answers.

**DICK GREGORY
American radical comedian**
Hell hath no fury like a Liberal scorned.

**LILLIAN HELLMAN
American playwright**
Since when do you have to agree with people to defend them from injustice?

**ERIC HOFFER
American philosopher**
'The True Believer' 1951
When hopes and dreams are loose in the streets, it is well for the timid to lock the doors, shutter the windows and lie low until the wrath has passed.

**MURRAY KEMPTON
American journalist**
'America Comes of Middle Age' 1963
Moderation, after all, is only the belief that you will be a better man tomorrow than you were yesterday.

**NORMAN MAILER
American writer**
quoted in Daily Telegraph 1971
The private terror of the liberal spirit is invariably suicide, not murder.

**GEORGE ORWELL
British essayist**
Liberal – a power worshipper without power.

WILLIS PLAYER
San Diego Tribune
A liberal is a person whose interests aren't at stake at the moment.

DON PRICE
American academic
It's easier to be a liberal a long way from home.

VINCENT PRICE
American film star
Esquire 1964
There's nothing worse than a rich liberal.

LIONEL TRILLING
American critic
'The Liberal Imagination' 1950
We who are liberal and progressive know that the poor are our equals in every sense except that of being equal to us.

WOODROW WYATT
British politician
The Observer 1966
You don't have to wear a hair shirt to be a socialist.

Revolution

SAUL ALINSKY
American radical
New York Times 1971
In any fight with the Establishment, you can count on it for at least one glorious gaffe that will bring renewed life to your languishing cause.

ANONYMOUS RIOTER 1967
Man, we've got instant urban renewal.

HANNAH ARENDT
American writer
in 'The Faber Book of Aphorisms' 1964
It is far easier to act under conditions of tyranny than to think.

'On Revolution' 1963
Wars and revolutions ... have outlived all their ideological justifications ... no cause is left but the most ancient of all, the one, in fact, that from the very beginning of our history, has determined the very existence of politics – the cause of freedom against tyranny.

New York Review of Books 1971
Revolutionaries do not make revolutions. The revolutionaries are those who know when power is lying in the street and when they can pick it up. Armed uprising by itself has never yet led to a revolution.

PEARL BAILEY
American singer
'Pearl's Kitchen' 1973
Hungry people cannot be good at learn-

ing or producing anything, except perhaps violence.

JAMES BALDWIN
American writer
'Open Letter to Angela Davis' New York Review of Books 1971
The will of the people ... has always been at the mercy of an ignorance not merely phenomenal, but sacred, and sacredly cultivated.

The Guardian 1970
What people in power never understand what people out of power are determined to do. What the people out of power are determined to do is first of all to survive you to withstand you and if they have to, to kill you. And they have the advantage, because they have nothing to lose.

PIERO BASSETTI
Italian political economist 1980
A system will not die unless it is pushed aside by something else.

DANIEL BERRIGAN
American radical
New York Review of Books 1971
A revolution is interesting insofar as it avoids like the plague the plague it promised to heal.

DANIEL J. BOORSTIN
American writer
Esquire 1968
Radicalism ... involves a commitment to the interdependence of men, and to

the sharing of their concerns, which the radical feels with an especially urgent, personal intensity.

When the true radical criticizes society he demands that society justifies itself according to some new measure of meaning.

What makes a radical radical is not that he discomfits others, but *how* he does it.

BERTOLT BRECHT
German playwright
Change the world – it can do with it!

'The Messingkauf Dialogues' 1965
The world is out of joint, certainly, and it will take powerful movements to manipulate it back again.

'The Good Person of Szechuan'
You can only help one of your luckless brothers / By trampling down a dozen others.

ELAINE BROWN
American radical
on Mao's successful revolution vs. her own problems as Black Panther leader
Mao Zedong didn't have to deal with people who were watching seven hours of television every day.

CHARLES BUKOWSKI
American writer
'Notes of a Dirty Old Man' 1969
Before you kill something make sure you have something better to replace it with; something better than political opportunist slamming hate horseshit in the public park.

JACOB BURCKHARDT
Terrorism is essentially the rage of literati in its last stage.

WILLIAM S. BURROUGHS
American writer
in 'Loose Talk' ed. Linda Botts 1980
The revolution will come from ignoring the others out of existence.

ALBERT CAMUS
French writer
'Resistance Rebellion & Death' 1960
The maximum danger implies the maximum hope.

'Notebooks' 1962
The revolution as myth is the definitive revolution.

'The Rebel' 1951
The slave begins by demanding justice and ends up wanting to wear a crown. He must dominate in his turn.

All modern revolutions have ended in a reinforcement of the power of the State.

'Resistance, Rebellion & Death' 1960
Censorship and oppression prove that the word is enough to make the tyrant tremble, but only if the word is backed up by sacrifice. For only the word fed by blood and heart can unite men, whereas the silence of tyrannies separates them.

'The Rebel' 1951
What is a rebel? A man who says no.

Every revolutionary ends up either by becoming an oppressor or a heretic.

STOKELEY CARMICHAEL
American radical 1966
Violence is as American as cherry pie.

THOMAS NIXON CARVER
American writer
The New Republic 1970
The trouble with radicals is that they only read radical literature, and the trouble with conservatives is that they don't read anything.

JERRY CASALE
American rock musician
Rebellion is outmoded. You fuck around with the corporate structure and you'll get killed.

FIDEL CASTRO
Cuban leader
New York Times 1959
It does not matter how small you are if you have faith and a plan of action.

1967
Whoever hesitates while waiting for ideas to triumph among the masses before initiating revolutionary action will never be a revolutionary. Humanity will, of course, change. Human society will, of course, continue to develop – in spite of men and the errors of men. But that is not a revolutionary attitude.

LUIS CERNUDA
Spanish poet
'La Visita de Dios'
Revolution, like a phoenix, is always re-born – rising like a flame from the bodies of the wretched.

ELDRIDGE CLEAVER
American radical 1980
The most revolutionary statement in history is 'Love thine enemy'.

DANIEL COHN-BENDIT
German radical
Esquire 1968
Stop us? Slap at water!

The moment you have a plan you cease to be a revolutionary.

FRANCOIS DUVALIER
President of Haiti
'Papa Doc' 1964
Revolutions are not made with literature. Revolutions equal gunfire.

BOB DYLAN
American singer
When you don't like your situation you either leave it or else you overthrow it. You just can't sit around and whine about it. People just get aware of your voice, they don't really get aware of you.

ALBERT EINSTEIN
German physicist
'Cosmic Religion'
An empty stomach is not a good political adviser.

FRANTZ FANON
French radical
The native is an oppressed person whose permanent dream is to become the persecutor.

'The Wretched of the Earth' 1961
Violence alone, violence committed by the people, violence organised and educated by its leaders, makes it possible for the masses to understand social truths and gives the key to them.

JIM FOURATT
American radical
Esquire 1970
Every revolution's got to have its gun runners.

BRENDAN FRANCIS
Rights are something other people grant after you've fought tooth and nail for them.

MOHANDAS K. GANDHI
Indian leader
'Non Violence in Peace and War' 1948
The moment the slave resolves that he will no longer be a slave, his fetters fall. He frees himself and shows the way to others. Freedom and slavery are mental states.

BOB GELDOF
Irish rock star
I think all revolutions are meaningless – especially those led by CBS and EMI.

JEAN-LUC GODARD
French film director
Cahiers Du Cinéma no.300 1979
On whom does repression depend – on us. On whom does liberation depend – on us.

GUNTER GRASS
German novelist
'Der Burger und Seine Stimme' 1974
Changes become possible because of changes and release changes, which again makes possible further changes. So every reform that looks at itself in isolation will fail from a lack of insight into its own consequences.

GERMAINE GREER
Australian feminist
'The Female Eunuch' 1970
The consequences of militancy do not disappear when the need for militancy is over.

ERNESTO 'CHE' GUEVARA
Bolivian radical 1953
The question is one of fighting the causes and not just being satisfied with getting rid of the effects.

The true revolutionary is guided by feelings of great love.

In a Revolution one wins or dies.

BILL HARRIS
American radical 1976
Revolutions need direction and exem-

plary leadership, but not heroes. Heroes subvert the fact that change comes about by lots of people taking action.

TOM HAYDEN
American radical
'The Port Huron Statement' 1965
We are people of this generation, bred in at least modest comfort, housed now in universities, looking uncomfortably to the world we inherit.

LILLIAN HELLMAN
American playwright
The Listener 1979
Rebels seldom make good revolutionaries, because organised action, even union with other people, is not possible for them.

KATHARINE HEPBURN
American film star 1969
Young people are digging a hole they'll never get out of.

ERIC HOFFER
American philosopher
in 'The Faber Book of Aphorisms' 1964
Those who are engrossed in the rapid realization of an extravagant hope tend to view facts as something base and unclean. Facts are counter-revolutionary,

ABBIE HOFFMAN
American radical
The first duty of a revolutionary is to get away with it.

CHARLES ISSAWI
American designer
in Columbia Forum 1970
Most people do not go to the dentist until they have a toothache. Most societies do not reform abuses until the victims begin to make life uncomfortable to others.

LYNDON B. JOHNSON
American president 1960
No member of our generation who wasn't a Communist or a dropout in the thirties is worth a damn.

JANOS KADAR
Hungarian leader
The advantage of a working class back-
ground is that I do not make the mistake of thinking every worker is a revolutionary.

DR KENNETH KAUNDA
Zambian leader
The Observer 1962
The moment you have protected an individual you have protected society.

MURRAY KEMPTON
American journalist
'Part of Our Time' 1955
A revolution requires of its leaders a record of unbroken infallibility. If they do not possess it they are expected to invent it.

ROBERT F. KENNEDY
American politician
'The Pursuit of Justice' 1964
What is objectionable, what is dangerous about extremists is not that they are extreme, but that they are intolerant. The evil is not what they say about their cause, but what they say about their opponents.

The Observer 1964
One fifth of the people are against everything all the time.

NIKITA KHRUSCHEV
Russian leader 1964
If we should promise people nothing better than only revolution, they would scratch theirs heads and say 'Isn't it better to have good goulash?'

MARTIN LUTHER KING JR.
American activist
Injustice anywhere is a threat to justice everywhere.

1968
Riots are the voices of the unheard.

WALTER LAQUEUR
American writer
'Terrorism' 1977
Terrorism . . . propaganda by deed.

STANISLAW J. LEC
Polish poet
in 'The Faber Book of Aphorisms' 1964
Burning stakes do not lighten the darkness.

JOHN LEONARD
American critic
Esquire 1969
Revolutions don't eat their young. They eat their old.

DENIS McSHANE
British trade unionist 1978
Industrial action is merely the continuation of negotiations by other means.

RENE MAGRITTE
Belgian artist
'Le Soleil Noir' 1952
Revolt against the world of today signifies the refusal to participate willingly in activities dominated by hoodlums and imbeciles. It likewise signifies the will to act against this world and to seek ways of changing it.

NORMAN MAILER
American writer
'St. George and the Godfather' 1972
Bombs are fireworks to the sleepy.

NELSON MANDELA
South African radical
in court 1962
Government violence can do only one thing – and that is to breed counter-violence.

MAO ZEDONG (Mao Tse-tung)
Chinese leader
'Quotations from Chairman Mao' 1966
A revolution is not a dinner party, or writing an essay, or painting a picture, or doing embroidery, it cannot be so refined . . . a revolution is an insurrection, an act of violence by which one class overthrows another.

HERBERT MARCUSE
German philosopher
The Listener 1978
Not every problem someone has with his girlfriend is necessarily due to the capitalist mode of production.

CARLOS MARIGHELLA
Brazilian author
in 'Minimanual of the Urban Guerilla'
The urban guerilla's reason for existence, the basic action in which he survives and acts is to shoot.

BOB MARLEY
Jamaican singer
How many rivers do we have to cross, before we get to meet the boss?

MARGARET MEAD
American anthropologist
Redbook 1961
In almost any society, I think, the quality of the nonconformists is likely to be just as good as, and no better than that of the conformists.

TAYLOR MEADE
American actor
Undermine the entire structure of society by leaving the pay toilet door ajar so the next person can get in free.

MARK MEDOFF
American playwright
in 'Contemporary Dramatists' 1977
The gun is the ambience of our society.

H. L. MENCKEN
American essayist
'Minority Report' 1956
The urge to save humanity is almost only a false-front for the urge to rule.

JIM MORRISON
American rock composer
'When The Music's Over'
The old get old / The young get younger / They got the guns / But we got the numbers. (Nipper Music)

RICHARD NEVILLE
Australian journalist 1970
Dropouts are simply anticipating future economic trends.

HUEY P. NEWTON
American radical
Esquire 1973
The reformer is an opportunist who will make it better now, but will also build an obstacle against future development. The revolutionist may appear the same, but he won't do anything to put up blocks or obstacles to future levels of development.

REV. DR. EDWARD NORMAN
British academic
Reith Lecturer 1978
It is likely that all political change ulti-

mately derives from the agitation of elites.

All political action and social action these days is merely clearing the streets for the tanks.

GEORGE ORWELL
British essayist
'Inside the Whale' 1950
So much of left wing thought is a kind of playing with fire by people who don't even know that fire is hot.

Most revolutionaries are potential Tories, because they imagine that everything can be put right by altering the shape of society; once that change is effected – as it sometimes is – they see no need for any other.

JOHN OSBORNE
British playwright
'Look Back In Anger' 1956
Jimmy Porter: There aren't any good, brave causes left. If the big bang does come, and we all get killed off, it won't be in aid of the old-fashioned grand design. It'll just be for the Brave New-nothing-very-much-thank-you. About as pointless and inglorious as stepping in front of a bus.

ALAN PATON
South African writer 1976
If you are a murderer or a rapist you will still have the protection of the rule of law. But if you are a political danger to rulers, you will have none.

ALAN PLATER
British playwright
The Listener 1979
That must be the aim of all true subversion: in the end you must be prepared to subvert yourself.

'QUO VADIS'
MGM 1951 screenplay by John Lee Mahin, S. N. Behrman, Sonya Levien, based on novel by Henryk Sienkiewicz
Peter Ustinov: No mob ever wants justice. They want vengeance.

JEAN RENOIR
French film director
The Guardian 1967
During a revolution it is not the revolu-

tionaries who win, it is the reactionaries who lose.

JAMES RESTON
American journalist
We cover revolution better than we cover evolution.

TOM ROBINSON
British rock singer
There's such a danger with the Left generally – and people involved in sexual politics in particular – that the things they attack are on their own side.

WILL ROGERS
American humorist
quoted in 'One Man's America' by Alistair Cooke
One revolution is just like one cocktail: It just gets you organised for the next.

DEAN RUSK
American diplomat
New York Times 1966
One third of the people of the world are asleep at any given moment. The other two thirds are awake and probably stirring up trouble somewhere.

ED SADLOWSKI
American union official
quoted in 'American Dreams Lost and Found' by Studs Terkel 1980
Once you stop singing, the revolution's over.

JEAN-PAUL SARTRE
French philosopher
Communist violence is no more than the childhood disease of a new era.

MARIO SAVIO
American radical 1964
There's a time when the operation of the machine becomes so odious, makes you so sick at heart, that you can't take part . . . and you've got to put your bodies upon the gears and upon the wheels and you've got to make it stop.

BOBBY SEALE
American radical
You can jail a revolutionary, but you cannot jail the revolution.

IGNAZIO SILONE
Italian radical
'Why I Became a Socialist' 1949
One earthquake achieves what the law promises but does not in practice maintain – the equality of all men.

DAVID SMITH
British sculptor 1962
Revolutionary action is never lost. Something comes out of it finally.

I. F. STONE
American journalist
'Polemics and Prophecies' 1971
All idols must be overthrown; all sacred dogmas exposed to criticism; the windows thrown open; the cobwebs swept away!

PRESIDENT SUKARNO
of Indonesia
Esquire 1965
The act of guiding a revolution is to find inspiration in everything you see.

NORMAN THOMAS
American socialist
If you want a symbolic gesture don't burn the flag, wash it.

PETE TOWNSHEND
British rock composer
'Won't Get Fooled Again'
See the new boss / Same as the old boss. (Essex Music)

TRUONG CHINH
N. Vietnamese politician 1969
It is absolutely necessary for the People's Democratic Dictatorship to use violence against those who refuse to submit to reform. Therefore we must pay continuous attention to consolidating the repressive apparatus of the People's Democratic State.

TUPAMAROS
Uruguayan guerillas
slogan
Everybody dances, or nobody dances.

KENNETH TYNAN
British critic
in 'Goodbye Baby & Amen' by D. Bailey 1969
The moment you *cease* to have a plan, you cease to be a revolution – you are a rabble.

SIMONE WEIL
French philosopher
in 'The Faber Book of Aphorisms' 1964
Whoever takes up the sword shall perish by the sword. And whoever does not take up the sword (or lets it go) shall perish on the cross.

'THE WILD ONE'
American film
1951
Q: What are you rebelling against, Johnny?
Marlon Brando: What have you got?

RAYMOND WILLIAMS
British academic
The Listener 1963
Some generations reform their beliefs. Others reform their society.

SHIRLEY WILLIAMS
British politician 1977
The saddest illusion of revolutionary socialists is that revolution itself will transform the nature of human beings.

Brotherhood

MUHAMMAD ALI
World heavyweight boxing champion
Time 1978
Service to others is the rent you pay for your room here on earth.

WOODY ALLEN
American film star
'Without Feathers'
The lion and the calf shall lie down together, but the calf won't get much sleep.

KINGSLEY AMIS
British author
Sunday Telegraph 1967
You cannot *decide* to have brotherhood. If you decide to enforce it you will before long find yourself trying to enforce something very different, and much worse than mere absence of brotherhood. All you can reasonably work for is keeping things going plus as much improvement as they will stand – an injustice righted here, an opportunity extended there.

MARLON BRANDO
American film star
If we are not our brother's keeper, let us at least not be his executioner.

JOHN CAGE
American musician
'Empty Words' 1980
More than anything else we need communion with everyone. Struggles for power have noting to do with communion. Communion extends beyond borders. It is with one's enemies also.

JIMMY CARTER
American politician
To deal with individual human needs at the small everyday level can actually be noble sometimes.

ELDRIDGE CLEAVER
American radical
'Soul on Ice' 1968
Too much agreement kills a chat.

GEORGES DUHAMEL
French writer
'Le Desert de Bievres'
Man is incapable of living alone. And he is also incapable of living in society.

GENE FOWLER
American writer
New York Mirror 1954
Never thank anybody for anything, except a drink of water in the desert – and then make it brief.

GERMAINE GREER
Australian feminist
'The Female Eunuch' 1970
The brotherhood of man will only become a reality when the consciousness of alien beings corrects man's myopia.

ALDOUS HUXLEY
British writer
'The Doors of Perception'
To see ourselves as others see us is a most salutary gift. Hardly less important is the capacity to see others as they see themselves.

GEORGE JACKSON
American radical 1970
Patience has its limits. Take it too far and it's cowardice.

HELEN KELLER
American essayist
quoted in The Image 73
How I wish that all men would take sunrise for their slogan and leave the shadow of sunset behind.

R. D. LAING
British psychiatrist
'The Politics of Experience' 1967
The brotherhood of man is evoked by particular men according to their circumstances. But it seldom extends to all men. In the name of our freedom and our brotherhood we are prepared to blow up the other half of the world and to be blown up in turn.

JOHN LENNON &
PAUL McCARTNEY
British rock composers
'I am the Walrus'
I am he / As you are he / As you are me / And we are all together.
(Northern Songs)

MAX LERNER
American academic
'Actions and Passions' 1949
Either men will learn to live like brothers or they will die like beasts.

MIGNON McLAUGHLIN
American writer
'The Neurotic's Notebook'
No one really listens to anyone else, and if you try it for a while you'll see why.

HENRY MILLER
American writer
'Ecce Homo' 1967
Until man learns to accept his fellow man with all his faults, as well as his

virtues, there can be no peace, no joy, no real understanding.

ERIC SEVAREID
American newscaster
'Not So Wild A Dream'
Brotherhood is not so wild a dream as those who profit by postponing it, pretend.

BARBARA WALTERS
American TV reporter
'How To Talk With Practically Anybody About Practically Anything' 1970

The origin of a modern party is anthropological: humans meet and share food to lower the hostility between them and indicate friendship.

The Right

TOM ANDERSON
American right-winger
urging attacks on liberalism 1975
Silence is not golden, it's yellow.

EMMANUEL BERL
French writer
'Mort de la Morale Bourgeoise'
The bourgeoisie believes it has the same relationship to the proletariat as the soul to the body.

MARCEL BREUER
Hungarian architect
The Observer 1972
You cannot control by merely forbidding. Life is not always nice or always beautiful, but it is always strong.

WILLIAM F. BUCKLEY JR.
American essayist
Playboy 1970
Conservatism is the politics of reality.

WHITTAKER CHAMBERS
American government official
New York Times 1973
The central shortcoming of conservatives is failure to retrieve their wounded.

J. K. GALBRAITH
American economist
The modern conservative is engaged in one of man's oldest exercises in moral philosophy: that is, the search for a superior moral justification for selfishness.

SIR JAMES GOLDSMITH
British businessman
The Listener 1979
Tolerance is a tremendous virtue, but the immediate neighbours of tolerance are apathy and weakness.

S. I. HAYAKAWA
American academic and politician 1967
When you've got a problem with swine, you've got to call in the pigs.

JIM JACQUET
Australian politician 1970
Certainly the film 'Easy Rider' serves the cause of communist subversion.

ERIC JULBER
American lawyer
Esquire 1969
A man becomes a conservative at that moment in his life when he suddenly realises he has something to conserve.

BLAS PINAR
Spanish politician
head of Francoesque 'Fuerza Neuva' 1980
We are not a violent party. Every time you see someone carrying a bicycle chain, it does not mean that he is a member of Fuerza Neuva. Perhaps it could be a bicycle chain manufacturer on his way home. The fact is that there are occasions that demand violence in legitimate self-defence.

CLINTON ROSSITER
Conservatism is the worship of dead revolutions.

BILLY SNEDDON
Australian politician
Organisers of the anti-Vietnam moratorium are political bikies, pack-raping democracy.

STROM THURMOND
American politician 1972
It is true, of course, that a great many of them unwilling to be drafted are conscientious objectors . . . but a great many impressed us as just downright cowards! It is clear that we are faced with the same kind of anarchism that softened up Tsarist Russia for the Bolsheviks!

Power

DEAN ACHESON
American statesman 1950
Prestige . . . the shadow cast by power.

1953
To leave positions of great responsibility and authority is to die a little.

PATRICK ANDERSON
Australian novelist
quoted in Michael Korda 'Power in the Office' 1976
Power is like a woman you want to stay in bed with forever.

HANNAH ARENDT
American writer
in 'The Faber Book of Aphorisms' 1964
The will to power . . . far from being a characteristic of the strong, is, like envy and greed, among the vices of the weak, and possibly their most dangerous one. Power corrupts indeed when the weak band together in order to ruin the strong, but not before.

RUSSELL BAKER
American writer
'The Sayings of Poor Russell' Harpers 1972
People who have the power to make things happen don't do the things that people do, so they don't know what needs to happen.

CHRISTOPHER BOOKER
British journalist
Now! 1981
The fashionable drawing rooms of London have always been happy to welcome outsiders – if only on their own, albeit undemanding terms. That is to say, artists, so long as they are not too talented, men of humble birth, so long as they have since amassed several million pounds, and socialists, so long as they are Tories.

MARTIN BUBER
Israeli philosopher 1950
Power abdicates only under stress of counter-power.

JESSE CARR
American union boss 1976
Being powerful is like being a lady. If you have to tell people you are, you ain't.

FIDEL CASTRO
Cuban leader 1966
We hope that in the future few if any men will have the authority which we the creators of this revolution have had, because its dangerous for men to have so much authority.

GREGORY CORSO
American poet
'Power'
Standing on a street corner waiting for no one is Power.

JOHN FAIRCHILD
American publisher
motto:
Influence those who influence others.

ROBERT FROST
American poet
quoted in Harper's 1970
The strong are saying nothing until they see.

DAVID GARTH
American political advertising
specialist 1978
The perception of power *is* power.

LILLIAN GISH
American film star
Esquire 1969
Power without responsibility creates havoc.

SAM GOLDWYN
American film producer
A producer shouldn't get ulcers, he should give them.

ERIC HOFFER
American philosopher
'The Passionate State of Mind' 1954
Power corrupts the few, while weakness corrupts the many.

in 'The Faber Book of Aphorisms' 1964
Everything seems possible when we are absolutely helpless or absolutely powerful – and both states stimulate our credulity.

DEAN WILLIAM INGE
British clergyman
in 'The Wit and Wisdom of Dean Inge' ed. Marchant
A man may build himself a throne of bayonets, but he cannot sit on it.

ERICH KASTNER
German author
'Das Ohnmächtige Zwiegespräch'
The only people who attain power are those who crave it.

ALFRED KAZIN
American critic
quoted in M. Korda 'Power in the Office' 1976
Only power can get people into a position where they may be noble.

HENRY KISSINGER
American diplomat
The illegal we do immediately, the unconstitutional takes a little longer.

Power is the ultimate aphrodisiac.

MICHAEL KORDA
British writer
'Power in the Office' 1976
People rise to a level of power just one step beneath that which would make them feel secure.

R. D. LAING
British psychiatrist
'Reason and Violence' 1964
The acceptance of power is the interiorisation of the powerlessness to refuse it.

ARNOLD LOBEL
American writer
'Fables' 1980
It is the high and mighty who have the longest distance to fall.

HENRY R. LUCE
American publisher
turning down the suggestion of a mural on the new Time building, despite a reference to the Sistine chapel ceiling. . .
That was good for the Pope's business. What good is a mural going to do for mine?

I want good editors with independant minds. I like to see independant thinking. If it's going the wrong way I'll straighten them out fast enough.

asked whether Time was genuinely a news magazine, not a Luce propaganda sheet. . .
Well, I invented the idea, so I guess I can call it anything I like.

VICTOR MATTHEWS
British businessman and publisher 1978
By and large the editors will have complete freedom, as long as they agree with the policy I have laid down. (cf. Luce)

HANS J. MORGENTHAU
American academic
Man is born to seek power – yet his actual condition makes him a slave to the power of others.

JIM MORRISON
American rock star
When you make your peace with authority, you become authority.

MALCOLM MUGGERIDGE
British journalist
There is nothing on earth less edifying or more ludicrous than the spectacle of the ruling class on the run.

Esquire 1968
A ruling class on the run is capable of every folly and displays a remarkable perversity in markedly preferring its enemies to its friends.

RALPH NADER
American consumer advocate
New York Times 1971
I have a theory of power: that if it's going to be responsible it has to have something to lose.

JOE ORTON
British playwright
'Loot' 1966
McLeavy: My duty is clear.
Truscott: Only the authorities can decide when your duty is clear. Wild guesses by persons like yourself can only cause confusion.

GEORGE ORWELL
British essayist
'1984' 1948
Big Brother Is Watching You.

Power is not a means, it is an end. One does not establish a dictatorship in order to safeguard a revolution; one makes the revolution in order to establish the dictatorship.

ALAN PATON
South African writer
Saturday Review 1967
When men are ruled by fear, they strive to prevent the very changes that will abate it.

AUGUSTE PINOCHET
Dictator of Chile 1980
What people do not understand with words, they understand with action.

ENOCH POWELL
British politician
In the last analysis, all power rests on opinion.

GEORGE M. REEDY
American politician
in 'The Imperial Presidency' by Arthur Schlesinger 1973
Isolation from reality is inseparable from the exercise of power.

RUDE PRAVO
Czech party newspaper
quoted in The Listener 1979
Those who lie on the rails of history must expect to have their legs chopped off.

JEAN-PAUL SARTRE
French philosopher
The Observer 1961
No one is born with a desire either to seek power or to shun it. It's a man's history that makes him move one way or the other. And even then, he is seldom quite sure.

SATYA SAI BABA
Indian guru 1975
Character makes life immortal. It survives even death. Some say knowledge is power, but this is not true. Character is power.

I. F. STONE
American journalist 1962
The nation state system that enables one or two men to decide life or death for the planet is the common enemy – not Russians or Americans, capitalists or Communists. The rest is delusion.

GEORGE SZELL
American conductor
Esquire 1971
Authority is more important than popularity.

GORE VIDAL
American writer
'Creation' 1981
Women are always attracted to power. I do not think there could ever be a conqueror so bloody that most women would not willingly lie with him in the hope of bearing a son who would be every bit as ferocious as the father.

Esquire 1970
People who obtain power do so because it delights them for its own sake and for no other reason.

A. H. WEILER
New York Times 1968
Nothing is impossible for the man who doesn't have to do it himself.

GEN. WILLIAM WESTMORELAND
American soldier
Command is getting people to go the way you want them to go – enthusiastically.

WILLIAM ALLEN WHITE
American writer
Peace without justice is tyranny.

HAROLD WILSON
British politician
quoted in Michael Korda 'Power in the Office' 1976
The only limits of power are the bounds of belief.

WALTER WINCHELL
American columnist
Dictatorship: a place where public opinion can't even be expressed privately.

Law

AMERICAN ARMY
Motto over entrance to Fort Dix stockade
Obedience to the law is freedom.

ROLAND BARTHES
French academic
Mythologies 1957
The Law is always prepared to lend you a spare brain in order to condemn you without remorse and . . . it depicts you as you should be, not as you are.

SYBILLE BEDFORD
British writer
Esquire 1965
To compress, to shape, to label the erratic sequences of life is the perennial function of the judges.

EDWARD BOND
British playwright
preface to 'Lear'
An unjust society causes and defines crimes; and an aggressive social structure which is unjust and must create aggresive social disruption, receives the moral sanction of being 'law and order'. Law and order is one of the steps taken to maintain injustice.

DR. JACOB BRONOWSKI
British scientist
quoted in 'American Dreams Lost and Found' by S. Terkel 1980
Justice has become a biological necessity in man.

LENNY BRUCE
American comedian
In the Halls of Justice the only justice is in the halls.

WARREN E. BURGER
Chief Justice of the American Supreme Court 1972
Civility is to the courtroom what antisepsis is to the hospital.

WILLIAM S. BURROUGHS
American writer
'Writers at Work' 3rd series 1967
Once the law starts asking questions, there's no stopping them.

The Guardian 1969
Police and so forth only exist insofar as they can demonstrate their authority. They say they're here to preserve order, but in fact they'd go absolutely mad if all the criminals of the world went on strike for a month. They'd be on their knees begging for a crime. That's the only existence they have.

WILLIAM SLOANE COFFIN
American clergyman
Playboy 1968
No man ever has the right to break the law; but . . . on occasion every man has the *duty* to break the law – when the law begins to dominate rather than serve men.

JERRY DELLA FEMINA
American advertising executive
Oui 1981
Anyone can end up a lawyer if he fucks up enough.

LORD DENNING
British lawyer
The Observer 1979
I would rather search for justice than for certainty.

'DETECTIVE STORY'
Paramount 1951 screenplay Philip Yordan and Robert Wyler; based on the play by Sidney Kingsley
Kirk Douglas: What do you get in place of a conscience. Don't answer, I know: a lawyer.

LORD DEVLIN
British lawyer 1976
In general the law that was made before 1914 is useful only to the remaining institutions of the nineteenth century.

RICHARD DU CANN QC
British lawyer
The Listener 1979
A lot of people make the terrible mistake of believing that a criminal trial is an investigation into the truth. It is not. It is an investigation into the truth insofar as the evidence will permit one to investigate the truth.

The accusatorial system . . . may be a civilised kind of warfare.

ALBERT EINSTEIN
German physicist
'Ideas and Opinions' 1954
Nothing is more destructive of respect for the government and the law of the land than passing laws which cannot be enforced.

LORD FISHER
British clergyman
The long and distressing controversy over capital punishment is very unfair to anyone meditating murder.

ROBERT FROST
American poet
A jury consists of twelve persons chosen to decide who has the better lawyer.

MOHANDAS K. GANDHI
Indian leader
That action alone is just which does not harm either party to a dispute.

JEAN GIRAUDOUX
French playwright
No poet ever interpreted nature as freely as a lawyer interprets truth.

LORD CHIEF JUSTICE GODDARD
British lawyer
The Observer 1955
No one has ever yet been able to find a way of depriving a British jury of its privilege of returning a perverse verdict.

LORD HAILSHAM
British lawyer 1975
Mercy is not what every criminal is entitled to. What he is entitled to is justice.

JUDGE LEARNED HAND
American lawyer
Time 1958
The aim of law is the maximum gratification of the nervous system of man.

LILLIAN HELLMAN
American playwright
Nobody outside of a baby carriage or a judge's chamber can believe in an unprejudiced point of view.

MR. HILLS
Australian politician 1970
It is worth recalling that law and order was a favourite catch cry of Hitler's Germany.

JUDGE JULIUS J. HOFFMAN
American lawyer
at The Chicago Eight trial, 1969
Let's have no talk of constitutional rights in this courtroom – the constitution sits up here with me.

J. EDGAR HOOVER
American law enforcer
Justice is incidental to law and order.

RICHARD INGRAMS
British journalist
The Guardian 1977
When lawyers talk about the law, the normal human being begins to think about something else.

'INHERIT THE WIND'

UA 1960 screenplay Nathan E. Douglas & Harold Jacob Smith, based on play by Jerome Lawrence & Robert E. Lee

Spencer Tracy: I say that you cannot administer a wicked law impartially. You can only destroy. You can only punish. I warn you that a wicked law, like cholera, destroys everyone it touches – its upholders as well as its defiers.

GRAYSON KIRK
American academic 1968

There are times when order must be maintained because order must be maintained.

STANISLAW J. LEC
Polish poet

in 'The Faber Book of Aphorisms' 1964

The dispensing of injustice is always in the right hands.

JUDGE H. C. LEON
British lawyer

The Observer 1975

I think a judge should be looked on rather as a sphinx than as a person – you shouldn't be able to imagine a judge having a bath.

JOHN C. LILLY
American biologist

in 'Murphy's Law' by Arthur Bloch 1979

All laws are simulations of reality.

HERBERT MARCUSE
German philosopher

Law and order are always and everywhere the law and order which protect the established hierarchy.

SIR ROBERT MARK
British policeman 1974

My objection to retaining the death penalty is that it hardens liberal opposition against badly needed reforms of the system of criminal justice.

There must be justice for the accuser as well as for the accused.

GROUCHO MARX
American comedian 1954

There is one way to find out if a man is honest – ask him. If he says 'Yes', you know he is crooked.

BILL MAULDIN
American cartoonist

in 'Loose Talk' ed. Linda Botts 1980

Law and order is like patriotism. Anyone who comes on strong about patriotism has got something to hide, it never fails. They always turn out to be a crook or an asshole or a traitor or something.

JUDGE ELLEN MORPHONIOS
American lawyer 1978

I have a saying – there's no justice in the law.

JOHN MORTIMER
British lawyer and playwright

'Voyage Round My Father'

No brilliance is required in the law. Just common sense and relatively clean fingernails.

J. B. MORTON
British humorist

'Beachcomber' 'Dictionary For Today' Daily Express passim

Clue: what the police find when they fail to arrest a criminal.

LAURA NADER
American writer

'No Access To Law' 1981

The law is a business whose outlook is shared by its major clients.

'THE ONION FIELD'

Avco Embassy 1979 screenplay by Joseph Wambaugh, based on his book.

Franklyn Seale: Guilty is what the man says when your luck runs out.

JOSE ORTEGA Y GASSET
Spanish philosopher

in 'The Faber Book of Aphorisms' 1964

Law is born from despair of human nature.

ROSCOE POUND
American lawyer

Christian Science Monitor 1963

Law is experience developed by reason and applied continually to further experience.

BERTRAND RUSSELL
British philosopher

'Unpopular Essays' 1950

Government can easily exist without

laws, but law cannot exist without government.

LORD SALMON
British lawyer
on penal reform in Lords debate
We accept . . . that it is better that ten guilty men should go free than one innocent man be found guilty. In my view these are the pillars of freedom without which individual liberty would wither and die.

DIANE B. SCHULDER
American lawyer
quoted in 'Sisterhood is Powerful' ed. Robin Morgan 1970
Law is a reflection and a source of prejudice. It both enforces and suggests forms of bias.

GLORIA STEINEM
American feminist
in 'Open Secrets' by Barbralee Diamonstein
Law and justice are not always the same. When they aren't, destroying the law may be the first step towards changing it.

RT. HON. SIR MELFORD STEVENSON
British judge
The Listener 1979
Starting off (a trial) with a completely open mind is a terribly dangerous thing to do.

ROBERT TOWNSEND
American businessman
'Up the Organisation' 1970
Lawyers take to politics like bears take to honey.

GORE VIDAL
American writer 1975
To the right wing 'law and order' is often just a code phrase, meaning 'get the nig-

gers'. To the left wing it often means political oppression.

SIMONE WEIL
French philosopher
in 'The Faber Book of Aphorisms' 1964
Justice: to be ever ready to admit that another person is something quite different from what we read when he is there or when we think about him. Or, rather, to read in him that he is certainly something different, perhaps something completely different, from what we read in him. Every being cries out to be read differently.

MAE WEST
American film star
'Every Day's a Holiday'
It ain't no sin if you crack a few laws now and then, just so long as you don't break any.

LADY WOOTON
British politician 1974
I don't think everyone can be cured by kindness, it would be surprising if I did after 44 years in magistrates' courts. What I do think is that nobody can be educated by being beaten, which is a different proposition.

VICTOR YANNACONE
American sportsman
Sports Illustrated 1969
Litigation is like a club, it's got to be used or it becomes a deadweight.

YEVGENY YEVTUSHENKO
Russian poet
'A Precocious Autobiography' 1963
Justice is like a train that's nearly always late.

S. C. YUTER
American scientist
Bulletin of the Atomic Scientists, 1969
Law is the backbone which keeps man erect.

Police

UGO BETTI
Italian writer
'The Inquiry'
A vague uneasiness: the police. It's like when you suddenly understand you have to undress in front of the doctor.

RICHARD DALEY
Mayor of Chicago 1968
Get the thing straight once and for all: the policeman isn't there to create disorder. The policeman is there to preserve disorder.

ANGELA DAVIS
American radical 1971
If they come for me in the morning, they will come for you at night.

MICHAEL HARRINGTON
American writer
'The Other America' 1962
For the middle class the police protect property, give directions and help old ladies. For the urban poor the police are those who arrest you.

ALFRED HITCHCOCK
British film director
I'm not *against* the police; I'm just afraid of them.

MURRAY KEMPTON
American journalist
New York Review of Books 1971
Given free play, the best policemen act badly more often than not, which is why they are given free play on any large scale only when their employers discern some social utility in their acting badly.

ROBERT F. KENNEDY
American politician 1964
Every society gets the kind of criminal it deserves. What is equally true is that every community gets the kind of law enforcement it insists on.

JOE ORTON
British playwright
'Loot' 1966
Fay: The British police force used to be run by men of integrity.
Trustcott: That is a mistake which has been rectified.

COLONEL PIENAAR
South African police commander
On Sharpeville Massacre, 1960
I do not know how many we shot. . . It all started when hordes of natives surrounded the police station. If they do these things, they must learn their lesson the hard way.

HAROLD PRESCOTT
British policeman 1971
I believe wickedness exists. There is sin. There is good and there is bad. You get the rogue in the litter . . . they want my foot on their necks.

POLICE COMMISSIONER WHITROD
Australian policeman 1974
The police force does not seem to attract intelligent people in times of full employment.

LOREN ZIMMERMAN
American policeman
on killing in self-defence Time 1981
I would rather be judged by twelve than carried by six.

Propaganda

JAMES BALDWIN
American author
'Fifth Ave, Uptown' Esquire 1960
It is a terrible, an inexorable law, that one cannot deny the humanity of another without diminishing one's own.

ANTHONY WEDGWOOD BENN
British politician 1966
It is tempting to deny, but if you deny you confirm what you won't deny, and by confirming and denying you have announced before you have decided.

SIR ISAIAH BERLIN
British philosopher
quoted in The Times 1981
When a man speaks of the need for realism one may be sure that this is always the prelude to some bloody deed.

'THE BEST MAN'
United Artists 1964 screenplay by Gore Vidal based on his play
Lee Tracy: It's par for the course, trying to fool the people, but it's downright dangerous when you start fooling yourself.

R. P. BLACKMUR
American critic
'Language as Gesture' 1952
Myths . . . gossip grown old.

CHARLES BOHLEN
quoted in New York Post 1969
What's public is propaganda, what's secret is serious.

PAUL CHAMBERS
British businessman 1961
Exhortation of other people to do something is the last resort of politicians who are at a loss to know what to do themselves.

LUCIEN CONEIN
CIA operative
Adventurer, Esquire 1976
You learn not to get attached to one side in the Agency. You take both sides.

F. M. CORNFORD
New Statesman 1978
Propaganda is that branch of the art of lying which consists in nearly deceiving your friends without quite deceiving your enemies.

ELIZABETH DREW
American writer
'Poetry: A Modern Guide to its Understanding and Enjoyment' 1959
Propaganda . . . is a seeding of the self in the consciousness of others.

ABBA EBAN
Israeli politician
Propaganda is the art of persuading others of what one does not believe oneself.

DWIGHT D. EISENHOWER
American President
to aide Jim Hagerty, asked for his position on Formosa. . .
Don't worry Jim, if that question comes up, I'll just confuse them.

JACQUES ELLUL
French writer
Propaganda begins when dialogue ends.

HAROLD EVANS
British journalist
The Sunday Times 1970
Manipulation is persuading people to make up their minds while withholding some of the facts from them.

GENERAL EVREN
Military ruler of Turkey
The Observer 1981
We have not closed down our parties – just suspended their activities.

JANET FRAME
New Zealand writer
'Faces in the Water' 1961
'For your own good' is a persuasive argument that will eventually make man agree to his own destruction.

TIM GARTON-ASH
British journalist
The Spectator 1980
The ideal act of propaganda . . . is to identify one's cause with values which are unquestioned. One such value is truth. Most politicians lie in its name.

JEAN-LUC GODARD
French film director
'British Sounds' 1969
If a million prints are made of a Marxist-Leninist film it becomes 'Gone With the Wind'.

DAVID HALBERSTAM
American journalist 1974
On politicians and the media. . .
Those who control a great deal are obsessed by the few things they do not control, particularly if these things, like television reporters, bear constant reminder that you do not control all that you think you do.

SYDNEY J. HARRIS
American journalist
You may be sure that when a man begins to call himself a realist he is preparing to do something that he is secretly ashamed of doing.

KARL GUNTHER VON HASE
W. German diplomat 1967
Communiques are like bikinis – what they reveal is alluring, but the essential points remain hidden.

HENRY S. HASKINS
American writer
'Meditations in Wall Street'
Deceiving someone for his own good is a responsibility which should be shouldered only by the gods.

BEN HECHT
American screenwriter
Evening Standard 1947
When I am writing propaganda I know exactly what to do. I just talk. Arouse and excite the reader and make him fighting mad. Propaganda is like falling in love with yourself and the veiled wonders of your own brain.

ERIC JULBER
American lawyer
Esquire 1969
One should be suspicious of 'love' as a political slogan. A government which purports to 'love' its citizens invariably desires all the prerogatives of a lover: to share the loved one's thoughts and to keep him in bondage.

MURRAY KEMPTON
American journalist
'America Comes of Middle Age' 1963
It is a function of government to invent philosophies to explain the demands of its own convenience.

JOHN F. KENNEDY
American president 1962
The great enemy of truth is very often not the lie – deliberate, contrived and dishonest – but the myth – persistent, persuasive and unrealistic.

JOHN KIFNER
New York Times 1969
Any official denial is de facto a confirmation.

ARTHUR KOESTLER
British philosopher
'Bricks to Babel' 1981
Wars are not fought for territory, but for words. Man's deadliest weapon is language. He is as susceptible to being hypnotised by slogans as he is to infectious diseases. And when there is an epidemic, the group-mind takes over.

LIN YUTANG
Chinese writer
Society can only exist on the basis that there is some amount of polished lying and that no one says exactly what he thinks.

WALTER LIPPMANN
American journalist 1967
In order to avoid the embarrassment of calling a spade a spade, newspapermen have agreed to talk about the credibility gap. This is a polite euphemism for deception.

1966
We must remember that in time of war what is said on the enemies' side of the front is always propaganda and what is said on our side of the front is truth and righteousness, the cause of humanity and a crusade for peace. Is it necessary for us at the height of our power to stoop to such self deceiving nonsense?

quoted in 'The Laugh's On Me' by Bennett Cerf
Propaganda is that branch of lying which often deceives your friends without ever deceiving your enemies.

'The Public Philosophy' 1955
When distant and unfamiliar and complex things are communicated to great masses of people, the truth suffers a considerable and often a radical distortion.

The complex is made over into the simple, the hypothetical into the dogmatic, and the relative into an absolute.

ARNOLD LOBEL
American writer
'Fables' 1980
Nothing is harder to resist than a bit of flattery.

When the need is strong, there are those who will believe anything.

GEORGE LOIS
American art director
'The Art of Advertising' 1977
Look at it this way: if there's something wrong with selling a political candidate, there's something wrong with selling a bar of soap.

EUGENE McCARTHY
American politician 1968
It is dangerous for a national candidate to say things that people might remember.

IAN McLEOD
British politician
A politician's pronouncements have a news value in direct relation to his prospects of power.

LORD MANCROFT
British politician
Reader's Digest 1967
A speech is like a love affair. Any fool can start it, but to end it requires considerable skill.

MAO ZEDONG (Mao Tse-tung)
Chinese leader 1957
Let a hundred flowers blossom and let one hundred schools of thought contend.

RON NESSEN
American government spokesman 1977
Some statements you make in public . . . are reported as . . . an unnamed source. . . Nobody believes the official spokesman . . . but everybody trusts an unidentified source.

FRITZ NOLTING
American ambassador to S. Vietnam 1962
complaining of press to reporter David Halberstam. . .
Mr. Halberstam, you're always looking for the hole in the doughnut.

GEORGE ORWELL
British essayist
'1984' 1948
Who controls the past controls the future. Who controls the present controls the past.

War is Peace
Hatred is Love
Freedom is Slavery

'Politics and the English Language' 1950
In our time, political speech and writing are largely the defence of the indefensible.

Political language . . . is designed to make lies sound truthful and murder respectable and to give an appearance of solidity to pure wind.

GRAHAM PERKIN
Australian journalist
Melbourne Age 1974
It is expecting too much for any politician to be sincerely interested in the free flow of information.

THE PRESIDENTIAL TRANSCRIPTS
of the Nixon White House. . .
Expletive deleted (passim).

JEAN-PAUL SARTRE
French philosopher
If you begin by saying 'Thou shalt not lie', there is no longer any possibility of political action.

LORD SNOW
British writer
Esquire 1971
There have been many crimes committed in the name of duty and obedience – many more than in the name of dissent.

ALEXANDER SOLZHENITSYN
Russian novelist 1974
In our country the lie has become not

just a moral category, but a pillar of the state.

I. F. STONE
American journalist
Every government is run by liars and nothing they say should be believed.

MARGARET THATCHER
British politician 1976
You don't tell deliberate lies; but sometimes you have to be evasive.

JAMES THURBER
American humorist
The Thurber Carnival 1945
You can fool too many of the people too much of the time.

HARRY S. TRUMAN
American president
If you can't convince them, confuse them.

SIMONE WEIL
French philosopher
Unless protected by an armour of lies, man cannot endure might without suffering a blow in the depth of his soul.

GOUGH WHITLAM
Australian politician 1970
Quite small and ineffectual demonstrations can be made to look like the beginnings of a revolution if the cameraman is in the right place at the right time.

WOODROW WYATT
British politician
Sunday Times 1973
Pride is a powerful element in the desire to try to speak the political truth at all times. But compromise is unavoidable in trying to create and conform to a common approach. Politicians who wish to succeed must be prepared to dissemble, at times to lie. All deceit is bad. In politics some deceit or moral dishonesty is the oil without which the machinery would not work.

YEVGENY YEVTUSHENKO
Russian poet
Playboy 1972 On propaganda. . .
If you work only in charcoal, your paintings can begin to resemble posters.

Diplomats

JOSEPH ALSOP
American journalist
The Observer 1952
Gratitude, like love, is never a dependable international emotion.

CHOU EN LAI
Chinese politician 1954
All diplomacy is a continuation of war by other means.

SIR WINSTON CHURCHILL
British statesman 1954
An appeaser is one who feeds a crocodile – hoping that it will eat him last.

JOHN FOSTER DULLES
American statesman
Life 1956
If you are scared to go to the brink you are lost.

WILL & ARIEL DURANT
American historians
One function of diplomacy is to dress realism in morality.

FERGUSON'S PRECEPT
in 'Murphy's Law Book Two' by Arthur Bloch 1980
A crisis is when you can't say 'Let's forget the whole thing'.

CHARLES DE GAULLE
French statesman 1963
Treaties are like roses and young girls – they last while they last.

DAG HAMMARSKJOLD
Swedish diplomat
It is not the Soviet Union or indeed any of the other big powers who need the United Nations for their protection. It is all the others.

HENRY KISSINGER
American diplomat
New York Times 1973
Diplomacy ... the art of restraining power.

KARL KRAUS
German artist
'Karl Kraus' by Harry Zohn
Diplomacy is a game in which the nations are checkmated.

IRVING KRISTOL
American academic 1967
The very definition of a great power is that not only its actions but the cases in which it declines to act have major consequences.

TRYGVE LIE
Secretary General of the United Nations
A real diplomat is one who can cut his neighbour's throat without having his neighbour notice it.

ART LINKLETTER
American humorist
Diplomacy: the art of jumping into troubled waters without making a splash.

KEN LOEFFLER
American college basketball coach 1956
Most of the international trouble today is due to the handshake without meaning.

HAROLD MACMILLAN
British politician 1958
echoing Churchill's 'Talking jaw to jaw is better than going to war' of 1954 ...
Jaw-jaw is better than war-war.

MALCOLM MUGGERIDGE
British journalist 1967
Spies, like whores and journalists, are usually of a slothful disposition.

ANWAR SADAT
President of Egypt
on his trip to Israel 1977
The barrier of distrust that has been between us during the last thirty years has been broken down in thirty-five hours. Amazing! Really!

JOSEPH STALIN
Russian leader
Sincere diplomacy is no more possible than dry water or wooden iron.

CASKIE STINNETT
American writer
'Out of the Red' 1960
A diplomat is a person who can tell you to go to hell in such a way that you actually look forward to the trip.

TOMI UNGERER
Danish cartoonist
The Observer 1981
One has to cultivate a certain amount of hypocrisy to be a peace-loving human being.

War

ROBERT ALTMAN
American film director
The Times 1971
You don't change people's ideas through rhetoric but by altering their way of looking at things. You will only get rid of war when you get rid of the pageantry surrounding it.

ANONYMOUS VIET CONG SOLDIER
It is the duty of our generation to die for our country.

ROBERT ARDREY
American writer
Human war has been the most successful of our cultural traditions.

HANNAH ARENDT
American writer
New York Review of Books 1971
War has . . . become a luxury which only
the small nations can afford.

W. H. AUDEN
British poet
'Epigraph'
Let us honour if we can / The vertical
man / Though we value none / But the
horizontal one.

JACQUES AUDIBERTI
French writer
'La Poupée'
Whether they are for the government or
for the government's enemies, arms
always come from the same suppliers.
Arms have a political allegiance of their
own.

JOAN BAEZ
American singer 1974
Peace might sell, but who's buying?

Non-violence is a flop. The only bigger
flop is violence.

DR. MARTIN BAX
British medical writer 1966
We need to stop treating soldiers and
ex-soldiers as heroes. Medals should be
given for cowardice in the field, not
valour.

ROGER A. BEAUMONT and
BERNARD J. JAMES
'Horizon' 1971
In war, victory goes to those armies
whose leaders' uniforms are least
impressive.

ERNEST BEVIN
British politician 1945
There has never been a war yet which,
if the facts had been put calmly before
the ordinary folk, could not have been
prevented. The common man is the
greatest protection against war.

GENERAL OMAR BRADLEY
American soldier 1950
In war there is no second prize for the
runner-up.

BERTOLT BRECHT
German playwright
On the wall in chalk is written / 'They
want war' / He who wrote it has already
fallen.

MEL BROOKS
American film director
The Listener 1978
Usually, when a lot of men get together,
it's called war.

LIEUT. WILLIAM CALLEY
American soldier
at court martial for the My Lai Massacre 1971
There was never any word as to who the
enemy was.

CAPTAIN LYNN A. CARLSON
American airman
*visiting cards dropped from his helicopter gun-
ship after attacks in Vietnam, 1968 . . .*
Congratulations. You have been killed
through courtesy of the 361st. Yours
truly, Pink Panther 20. *(On the reverse)*
Call us for death and destruction night
and day.

FIDEL CASTRO
Cuban leader
Bullets, like wine, come in vintages.

CENOTAPH
in Hiroshima
Rest in peace. The mistake shall not be
repeated.

FRANK CHURCH
American politician
Esquire 1969
Violence begets violence; incessant war-
fare becomes, at last, the accepted com-
panion of normalcy.

SIR WINSTON CHURCHILL
British statesman
In war you don't have to be nice, you
only have to be right.

1952
A prisoner of war is a man who tries to
kill you and fails, and then asks you not
to kill him.

REGIS DEBRAY
French radical
quoted in New York Review of Books 1971
The tragedy is that we do not kill ob-

jects, numbers, abstract or interchangeable instruments, but precisely, on both sides, irreplaceable individuals, essentially innocent, unique.

LEN DEIGHTON
British author
'Fighter' 1977
The history of warfare over the past couple of centuries can be thought in terms of soldiers lowering themselves closer and closer to the ground and then deeper and deeper into it.

EVERETT DIRKSEN
American politician
The oil can is mightier than the sword.

NICK DOWNIE
British TV war cameraman
Sunday Times 1980
The best way to convince man that war is not an exciting adventure is to kill half his friends, drop a bomb on his family's house, and relieve him of a limb or two. A less drastic but quite effective form of education is to show events like these on colour television.

ALBERT EINSTEIN
German physicist
That a man can take pleasure in marching in fours to the strains of a band is enough to make me despise him.

DWIGHT D. EISENHOWER
American president
We are going to have peace even if we have to fight for it.

In the final choice a soldier's pack is not so heavy as a prisoner's chains.

Esquire 1964
The proper target of mankind is man.

ADMIRAL FISHER
British sailor
quoted in Esquire 1964
The essence of war is violence. Moderation in war is imbecility.

JEAN FOLLAIN
French writer
'Appareil de la terre'
Arms are adult toys.

R. BUCKMINSTER FULLER
American engineer
The New Yorker 1966
Either war is obsolete, or men are.

MOHANDAS K. GANDHI
Indian leader
'Non-Violence in Peace and War' 1948
What difference does it make to the dead, the orphans and the homeless, whether the mad destruction is wrought under the name of totalitarianism or the holy name of liberty and democracy?

Non-violence is not a garment to be put on and off at will. Its seat is in the heart and it must be an inseparable part of our very being.

GENERAL VO NGUYEN GIAP
North Vietnamese soldier
Newsweek 1973
Peace is a continuation of war by other means.

ARTHUR GOLDBERG
American diplomat 1969
I am surprised nothing has been made of the fact that astronaut Neil Armstrong carried no sidearms when he landed on the moon.

DR. I. J. GOOD
'The Scientist Speculates'
When I hear the word 'gun' I reach for my culture.

JOHN GORTON
Australian politician
on his country's fruitless involvement in Vietnam 1971
I don't think we will have acheived our objectives, but it was fair enough for us to have attempted them.

'THE GREEN BERETS'
Warner Bros 1968 screenplay by James Lee Barrett, based on novel by Robin Moore
John Wayne: Out here (Vietnam) due process is a bullet.

GEORGE GROSZ
German artist
quoted in 'Ecce Homo' 1967
War freed many an individual from the environment he hated and the slavery of his everyday routine. This is one of the psychological causes and enigmas of war.

GENERAL BRUCE C. HALLOWAY
American soldier 1969
Deterrence is our primary mission, and peace is our profession. We have a mixed force of bombers and missiles to carry out this mission.

JOSEPH HELLER
American novelist
Playboy 1975
Wars are still initiated by a certain type of professional soldier whose ambition it is to act out fantasy scenes from war movies; and they're still fought by very young people who have no more exciting life to lead.

MICHAEL HERR
American journalist
on working in Vietnam Esquire 1970
Vietnam was what we had instead of happy childhoods.

LIEUTENANT GENERAL LEWIS B. HERSHEY
American soldier
Esquire 1969
I've lived under situations where any decent man declared war first. And I've lived under situations where you don't declare war. We've been flexible enough to kill people without declaring war.

HIPPIE SLOGAN
Make love not war.

E. J. HOBSBAWN
British historian
The Observer 1968
War has been the most convenient pseudo-solution for the problems of 20th century capitalism. It provides the incentives to modernisation and technological revolution which the market and the pursuit of profit do only fitfully and by accident, it makes the unthinkable (such as votes for women and the abolition of unemployment) not merely thinkable but practicable, in the field of policy and administration as well as mass murder. What is equally important, it can recreate communities of men and give a temporary sense to their lives by uniting them against foreigners and outsiders. This is an achievement beyond the power of private enterprise, whose characteristic is that it tends to do precisely the opposite, when left to itself.

HO CHI MINH
North Vietnamese leader 1954
Military action without politics is like a tree without a root.

PAUL HOFFMAN
American war correspondent
leaving the Congo 1961
The time to leave this place is when all white people begin to look alike.

QUINTIN HOGG (Lord Hailsham)
British lawyer 1967
You would not end wars by stopping children playing at soldiers, although you would probably stop children playing at soldiers if you prevented wars.

BOB HOPE
American comedian 1967
Sure, Vietnam's a dirty war. I've never heard of a clean one.

LYNDON B. JOHNSON
American President 1965
The guns and the bombs, the rockets and the warships, are all symbols of human failure. They are necessary symbols. They protect what we cherish. But they are witness to human folly.

GENERAL WILHELM KEITEL
Nazi general
at the Nuremburg Tribunal 1945
Oh, you know, one became such a blackguard.

JOHN F. KENNEDY
American president 1961
Only when our arms are sufficient beyond doubt can we be certain without doubt that they will never be employed.

Mankind must put an end to war or war will put an end to mankind.

election address 1960
It is an unfortunate fact that we can secure peace only by preparing for war.

ARTHUR KOESTLER
British philosopher
'Janus: A Summing Up' 1978
The most persistent sound reverberating through man's history is the beating of war drums.

HAROLD LASKI
British politician 1945
We live under a system by which the many are exploited by the few, and war is the ultimate sanction of that exploitation.

STANISLAW J. LEC
Polish poet
in 'The Faber Book of Aphorisms' 1964
In a war of ideas it is people who get killed.

CAPTAIN ROBERT LEWIS
pilot of the 'Enola Gay'
after dropping the first atomic bomb on Hiroshima, 1945
My God, what have we done?

DAVID LOW
British cartoonist 1946
I have never met anybody who wasn't against war. Even Hitler and Mussolini were, according to themselves.

GENERAL DOUGLAS MacARTHUR
American soldier 1951
In war there is no substitute for victory.

'COUNTRY' JOE MacDONALD
American rock musician
'Feel-like-I'm-fixin'-to-die-Rag'
Be the first one on your block / To have your boy come home in a box.
(April Music)

ANDRE MALRAUX
French writer
'L'espoir'
There are just wars; there are no just armies.

MAO ZEDONG (Mao Tse-tung)
Chinese leader 1948
The people are like water and the army is like fish.

'Quotations of Chairman Mao' 1966
In order to get rid of the gun, it is necessary to take up the gun.

BOB MARLEY
Jamaican singer
It is better to win the peace and to lose the war.

BILL MAULDIN
American cartoonist
in 'Loose Talk' ed. Linda Botts 1980
'Peace' is when nobody's shooting. A 'just peace' is when our side gets what it wants.

SPIKE MILLIGAN
British comedian
The army works like this: if a man dies when you hang him, keep hanging him until he gets used to it.

MALCOLM MUGGERIDGE
British journalist
Esquire 1970
Wars are a kind of collective spree or binge and whatever pacifists and others may say, they are on the whole popular, at any rate when they begin.

ABRAHAM MUSTE
American pacifist
There is no way to peace. Peace is the way.

BRIGADIER-GENERAL ROBIN OLDS
American fighter ace
on SAM-7 missiles Playboy 1973
You may not have time to be frightened, but my God, they've got your attention . . . one or two seconds off, you've had the schnitzel.

PROF. CHARLES OSGOOD
American academic 1966
An opponent can be bombed into surrender or even into non-existence, but he cannot be bombed into honest negotiations.

SAM PECKINPAH
American film director
Playboy 1972
True pacifism is the finest form of manliness. But if a man comes up to you and cuts your hand off, you don't offer him the other one. Not if you want to go on playing the piano, you don't.

SIR GEORGE PORTER
British chemist
The Observer 1973
If sunbeams were weapons of war we would have had solar energy long ago.

ENOCH POWELL
British politician 1967
History is littered with wars which everybody knew would never happen.

A man's nation is the nation for which he will fight.

JEAN FRANCOIS REVEL
French writer
'Without Marx or Jesus' 1971
Foreign policy is an imitation of war by other means.

WILL ROGERS
American humorist
'The Autobiography of Will Rogers' 1949
You can't say civilisation don't advance . . . for in every war they kill you a new way.

You take the diplomacy out of war and the thing would fall flat immediately.

BERTRAND RUSSELL
British philosopher
'Unpopular Essays' 1950
People who are vigorous and brutal often find war enjoyable, provided that it is a victorious war and that there is not too much interference with rape and plunder. This is a great help in persuading people that wars are righteous.

JEAN-PAUL SARTRE
French philosopher
'Le Diable et le bon Dieu' 1951
When the rich make war it's the poor that die.

ARTHUR SCHLESINGER JR.
American academic
All wars are popular for the first thirty days.

ALEXANDER SOLZHENITSYN
Russian novelist
The Times 1973
It seems to me that it is fully proved that only the inflexibility of the human soul which firmly puts itself on the front line against attacking violence and with readiness to sacrifice and death declares 'Not one step further'. Only this inflexibility of the soul is the real defence of personal peace, of universal peace and of all mankind.

CARDINAL SPELLMAN
American clergyman 1967
Total victory in Vietnam means peace.

ROD STEIGER
American film star
Esquire 1969
Military organisations take your soul out of you and put their tradition in.

ADLAI STEVENSON
American politician 1965
Most wars break out on the confused and disputed boundaries of changing power systems.

I. F. STONE
American journalist
quoted in Esquire 1969
The assumption is that war is a kind of game on which nations embark after consulting a computer to see who would come out ahead.

MARGARET THATCHER
British politician 1978
Fear is no basis for foreign policy.

BARBARA TUCHMAN
American historian
'The Guns of August' 1962
War is the unfolding of miscalculations.

US ARMY MAJOR
quoted by the Associated Press, referring to the town of Ben Tre, Vietnam, 1968
It became necessary to destroy the town to save it.

USAF MANUAL
'Fundamentals of Aerospace Weapons Systems' defines Military Target:
Any person, thing, idea, entity or location selected for destruction, inactivation, or rendering non-usable with weapons which will reduce or destroy the will or ability of the enemy to resist.

PETER USTINOV
British actor and wit
Illustrated London News 1968
Generals are fascinating cases of arrested development – after all, at five we all of us wanted to be generals.

VIETNAM WAR SLOGAN
Though I walk through the Valley of the Shadow of Death, I will fear no evil – 'cos I'm the meanest mother in the valley.

CAPTAIN JOHN WADDELL
American marine
New York Times 1972
I don't think anyone here thinks about blowing in and dropping bombs and killing a person. You don't hear the bombs. It's very abstract.

MICHAEL WALZER
British writer
'Just & Unjust Wars' 1978
War is always judged first with reference to the reason states have for fighting, secondly with reference to the means they adopt.

DAME REBECCA WEST
British writer
Before a war military science seems a real science, like astronomy. But after a war it seems more like astrology.

GENERAL WILLIAM WESTMORELAND
American soldier
McCall's 1966
War is fear cloaked in courage.

E. B. WHITE
American writer
'The Points of my Compass' 1963
Disarmament is a mirage. I don't mean it is indistinct or delusive, I mean it isn't there. Every ship, every plane could be scrapped. Every stockpile destroyed, every soldier mustered out. And if the original reason for holding arms was still present the world would not have been disarmed. Arms would simply be in a momentary state of suspension, preparatory to new and greater arms.

HEATHCOTE WILLIAMS
British playwright
'The Immortalist' 1978
You should make peace soon, otherwise you're going to have to accept some very punitive terms.

GARY WILLS
American journalist
New York Times 1975
Only the winners decide what were war crimes.

SIR SOLLY ZUCKERMAN
British scientist
The Lee-Knowles Lecture 1965
An arms race is a race with no finishing post. There is no absolute goal. There is no ultimate military weapon.

CATCH-PHRASES

STEVE ALLEN
American television compere
catch-phrase on 'What's My Line' 1950s
Is it bigger than a breadbox?

ARTHUR ASKEY
British comedian
catch-phrase
Ay thang yew!

Hello playmates.

HYLDA BAKER
British comedienne
catch-phrase
She knows, y'know.

EDDIE BRABEN
TV scriptwriter
running gag for 'Morecombe & Wise' shows 1970s passim
What do you think of the show so far?
Rubbish!

BERNARD BRESSLAW
British TV actor
catch-phrase in Granada TV 'Army Game' 1957/62
I only arsked. . .

BRITISH BROADCASTING CORPORATION
'Tonight' programme. Nightly signing off 1957–65:
And the next Tonight is tomorrow night.
Good night.

DREW 'BUNDINI' BROWN
American boxing personality
catch-phrase for Muhammad Ali
Float like a butterfly, sting like a bee!

BUGS BUNNY
Warner Brothers cartoon character
catch-phrase:
What's up doc?

GEORGE BURNS & GRACIE ALLEN
American TV stars 1950s
catch-phrase of the 'Burns & Allen Show'
Burns: Say good night, Gracie.
Allen: Goodnight, Gracie. (cf. Rowan & Martin)

BILLY BUTLIN
British holiday camp pioneer
Holiday Camp Slogan
Holidays with pay! Holidays with play!
A week's holiday for a week's wage.

MAX BYGRAVES
British comedian
in 'Educating Archie' radio show 1950s
Good idea, son!

I wanna tell you a story. . .
(but used far more by impersonator Mike Yarwood)

COMMANDER A. B. CAMPBELL
British radio personality
on BBC 'Brains Trust' 1940s
When I was in Patagonia. . .

JUDY CARNE
British comedienne
on 'Rowan & Martin's Laugh-In' 1960s
Sock it to me!

JIMMY CLITHEROE
British radio comedian
'The Clitheroe Kid' 1950s
Don't some mother's 'ave 'em?

PETER COOK
British comedian
catch-phrase in 'Not Only . . . But Also. . .' BBC-TV
Yer actual. . .

TOMMY COOPER
British comedian
catch-phrase. . .
Just like that!

BILLY COTTON
British bandleader
on 'Billy Cotton's Band Show' BBC radio 1949/69
Wakey-wakeeeyyy!!!

WALTER CRONKITE
CBS newscaster
signoff. . .
That's the way it is.

CHARLES DEDERICH
founder of Synanon anti-heroin
centres
Slogan c.1969:
Today is the first day of the rest of your life.

KEN DODD
British comedian
catch-phrase
How tickled I am!   ·

'DRAGNET'
American TV show 1950s and 1960s
Jack Webb (as Sgt. Joe Friday): The facts, all we want is the facts. . .

CHARLIE DRAKE
British comedian
catch-phrase:
Hello my darlings. . .

JIMMY DURANTE
American comedian
catch-phrase:
Goodnight Mrs. Calabash, wherever you are.
(allegedly an affectionate name for his late wife)

JIMMY EDWARDS
British comedian
catch-phrase in 'Take It From Here!' BBC Radio Show 1948
Black mark, Bentley!
(to Dick Bentley)

BRUCE FORSYTH
British comedian
catch-phrase:
Nice to see you, to see you (audience) nice!

'The Generation Game' 1973 catch-phrase:
Didn't he do well???!!!

DAVID FROST
British talkshow host passim
Hello, good evening, and welcome.

'That Was The Week That Was' catch-phrase c.1963
Seriously though, he's doing a grand job!

ALLEN FUNT
American TV personality
catch-phrase on 'Candid Camera':
Smile! You're on Candid Camera.

RAY GALTON & ALAN SIMPSON
British scriptwriters
catch-phrase for 'Steptoe & Son' TV series 1960s
You *dirty* old man!

BAMBER GASCOIGNE
British TV personality
catch-phrase on panel-game 'University Challenge' 1960s onwards
Here's your starter for ten. . .

BARRY GOLDWATER
American poltiician
slogan 1964 Presidential campaign. . .
In your heart you know he's right.

JOYCE GRENFELL
British comedienne
passim in 'Nursery School' sketches
George, don't do that!

FREDDIE GRISEWOOD
British radio personality
in 'In Town Tonight' (early radio quasi-chat show)
Carry on, London!

NORMAN HACKFORTH
'Mystery Voice' on BBC radio
'Twenty Questions'
And the next object is. . .

BILL HALEY
American rock singer
'Rock Around the Clock' song title, once popularised by Princess Margaret
See you later alligator
In a while crocodile!

HUGH HEFNER
American publisher
Motto over the door of his Playboy Mansion in Chicago:
If you don't swing, don't ring.

LENNY HENRY
British comedian
On ITV's 'Tiswas' 1974–81
OooooooKaaaayyyyyy!!!

CONRAD HILTON
International hotelier
slogan and book title, 1957
Be My Guest.

ITMA
British radio show
catch-phrase c.1945 Jack Train as Colonel Chinstrap...
I don't mind if I do.

Don't forget the diver!

1939/49
After you Claude ... no, after you, Cecil!
(spoken originally by Jack Train and Horace Percival)

ARTE JOHNSON
American comedian
catch-phrase on American TV show 'Rowan & Martin's Laugh-In' 1960s
Verrry interresting ... but stupid!

PROF. C. E. M. JOAD
British academic
on BBC 'Brains Trust' (in answer to listener's question 'Are thoughts things or about things)
It all depends what you mean by 'thing'.

JULIA LANG
British broadcaster
narrator of BBC Radio's 'Listen With Mother' 1950s
Are you sitting comfortably? Then I'll begin.

'THE LONE RANGER'
American TV series 1950s
Hi'yo Silver! (his horse).

PIGMEAT MARKHAM
American musician
catch-phrase 1969
Here come de judge!

MERRIE MELODIES
(Warner Bros cartoons)
passim final title
That's All Folks!

MAX MILLER
British comedian
catch-phrase, c.1945
You've gotta admit it lady, I do have a go...

BOB MONKHOUSE
British comedian
compere of 'The Golden Shot' TV show, 1960s
Bernie, the bolt!
(instructing the man who set up key apparatus for the contestants)

'MONTY PYTHON'S FLYING CIRCUS'
1969 BBC-TV show
And now for something completely different!

ERIC MORECOMBE
British comedian
catch-phrase referring to his partner Ernie Wise's alleged hair piece...
You can't see the join.

EDWARD R. MURROW
American broadcaster
signing off shows
Good night and good luck.

ROGER MUSGRAVE
British advertising copywriter
slogan for Rowntrees confectioners
Don't forget the fruit gums mum.

'THE NAKED CITY'
American TV show, 1950s. Epilogue...
There are eight million stories in the Naked City. This has been one of them.

TERRY NATION
Scriptwriter for 'Dr Who' series on BBC-TV
catch-phrase for 'The Daleks'
Exterminate! Exterminate!

ALFRED E. NEUMAN
Fictional guru of 'Mad' magazine
catch-phrase
What, Me Worry?

JANICE NICHOLLS
British television personality
'Thank Your Lucky Stars' British TV show, 1960s catch-phrase:
I'll give it foive! (also 'I like the backing').

HUGH PADDICK
British radio personality
to Kenneth Williams in 'Round the Horne' BBC radio show 1950 catch-phrase
Hello, I'm Julian, and this is my friend, Sandy.

BOB PEARSON
British comedian
as 'Mrs Hoskin' in 'Ray's A Laugh' BBC radio show. catch-phrase
It was agony, Ivy!

WILFRED PICKLES
British comedian
on 'Have A Go' BBC radio show. Catch-prases:
What's on the table, Mabel?
Give him (or her) the money, Mabel.

catch-phrase, usually asked of any single woman irrespective of age
Are yer courtin'?

AL READ
British comedian
catch-phrase:
Give over!

'READY STEADY GO'
British TV show
slogan c.1965
The weekend begins here!!

BERYL REID
British comedienne
in BBC radio show 'Educating Archie' 1950s. Catch-phrase:
Jolly hockey sticks!

DAN ROWAN & DICK MARTIN
American TV stars 1960s
Catch-phrase from the 'Rowan and Maritn Laugh-In'
Rowan: Say goodnight Dick.
Martin: Goodnight Dick.
(cf. Burns & Allen)

TELLY SAVALAS
American film actor
as Kojak, American TV show c.1970 catch-phrase:
Who loves ya, baby?

JIMMY SAVILE
British disc jockey
catch-phrase
How about that then, guys and gals?

'77 SUNSET STRIP'
American TV show 1950s
catch-phrase:
Kookie, lend me your comb.

BRITISH SOCCER CHANT 1960s
Nice one Cyril / Nice one son! /Nice one, Cyril, / Let's 'ave another one!

Georgie Best / Superstar / Walks like a woman / And he wears a bra!

'STAR TREK'
American TV series, 1960s
These are the voyages of the starship Enterprise . . . to boldly go where no man has gone before. . .

DOROTHY SUMMERS
British comedienne
as Mrs Mopp in ITMA, BBC radio show c. 1948 catch-phrase:
Can I do you now sir?

SUPERMAN
American radio and TV show 1950s
Faster than a speeding bullet! More powerful than a locomotive! Able to leap tall buildings at a single bound! Look! Up in the sky! It's a bird! It's a plane! It's Superman! Yes, it's Superman! Strange visitor from another planet, who came to earth with powers and abilities far beyond those of mortal men. Super-man! Who can change the course of mighty rivers, bend steel with his bare hands, and who – disguised as Clark Kent, mild-mannered reporter for a great metropolitan newspaper – fights a never ending battle for truth, justice and the American way!

LILY TOMLIN
American comedienne
as 'Ernestine' on 'Rowan & Martin's Laugh-In', American TV show 1960s catch-phrase:
Is this the party to whom I am speaking?

'THE TONIGHT SHOW'
American TV chat-show
introducing it's host Johnny Carson. . .
Here's Johnny!!!

'2001'
written as movie by Arthur C. Clarke & Stanley Kubrick
Open the pod door, Hal!

NORMAN VAUGHAN
British television personality
on British TV show 'Sunday Night At the London Palladium' 1960s catch-phrase
Swinging. . . Dodgy. . .

JACK WARNER
British actor
as Sgt George Dixon in BBC TV 'Dixon of Dock Green' catch-phrases
Evening all!. . . (start of show)

Mind how you go! (end of show)
also: If you're on your bike at night,
wear white.

JUNE WHITFIELD
British actress
to Dick Bentley in 'Take It From Here' BBC
radio show 1950s catch-phrase:
Oh Ron . . . yes, Eth.

KENNETH WILLIAMS
British actor
catch-phrase in BBC radio show 'Hancock's
Half Hour' 1950s
No, stop messin' about. . .

catch-phrase as Arthur Fallowfield in British
radio show 1950s 'Beyond Our Ken'
I think the answer lies in the soil.

WALTER WINCHELL
American columnist
catch-phrase on his radio show 1940s, 1950s
Good evening Mr. and Mrs. America
and all the ships at sea. Let's go to press.

HENNY YOUNGMAN
American comic
passim tag line
Take my wife – please!

BODY

Sex

PHILIP ADAMS
Australian TV critic 1968
Homosexuality is funny, provided it's on the telly; off the telly homosexuals are only fit for being punched up.

JONATHAN AITKEN
British journalist
'Confessions' in News of the World 1979
I have to find a girl attractive or its like trying to start a car without an ignition key.

WOODY ALLEN
American film star
refusing to attend Oscar ceremony 1978
I am not interested in an inanimate statue of a little bald man, I like something with long, blonde curls.

Evening Standard 1965
Sex is like having dinner: sometimes you joke about the dishes, sometimes you take the meal seriously.

New York Herald Tribune 1975
Bisexuality immediately doubles your chances for a date on Saturday night.

Love is the answer, but while you are waiting for the answer, sex raises some pretty good questions.

MAYA ANGELOU
American writer
'I Know Why the Caged Bird Sings' 1969
Most plain girls are virtuous because of the scarcity of opportunity to be otherwise.

'ANNIE HALL'
UA 1977 screenplay by Woody Allen and Marshall Brickman
Hey, don't knock masturbation. It's sex with someone I love.

ANONYMOUS
Head of a Woman's college quoted in The Listener 1979
Always remember: after ten o'clock a man becomes a beast.

ANONYMOUS
Environmental Health Officer quoted in New Statesman 1980
The proliferation of massage establishments in London in the last few years appears to indicate a dramatic increase in muscular disorders amongst the male population.

FERNANDO ARRABAL
Spanish playwright
If it is not erotic, it is not interesting.

RICHARD AVEDON
American photographer
Playboy 1975
He sleeps fastest who sleeps alone.

TALLULAH BANKHEAD
American film star
It's the good girls who keep the diaries; the bad girls never have have the time.

EDWARD BARKER
British cartoonist
1981 badge slogan:
Self-abuse is the devil's telephone booth.

SIR THOMAS BEECHAM
British conductor
'Beecham Stories' 1978
No woman is worth the loss of a night's sleep.

SAUL BELLOW
American novelist
All a writer has to do to get a woman is to say he's a writer. It's an aphrodisiac.

TONIA BERG
British singer 1971
Sex is like money – very nice to have but vulgar to talk about.

CHARLOTTE BINGHAM
British writer
quoted in 'The Wit of Women' ed. L. and M. Cowan
A twenty-five year old virgin is like the man who was set upon by thieves – everyone passes by.

LOUISE BROOKS
American film star
in 'Show People' by Kenneth Tynan 1980
Most beautiful but dumb girls think they are smart and get away with it, because other people, on the whole, aren't much smarter.

LENNY BRUCE
American comedian
quoted in 'The Essential Lenny Bruce' ed. Cohen, 1967
Man, we're all the same cats, we're all the same *schmuck* – Johnson, me, you, every *putz* has got that one chick, he's yelling like a real dum-dum: 'Please touch it once. Touch it once, touch it once!'

ANITA BRYANT
American anti-gay campaigner 1977
If homosexuality were the normal way God would have made Adam and Bruce.

CHARLES BUKOWSKI
American writer
'Notes of a Dirty Old Man' 1969
Sex is interesting, but it's not totally important. I mean its not even as important (physically) as excretion. A man can go seventy years without a piece of ass, but he can die in a week without a bowel movement.

Sexual intercourse is kicking death in the ass while singing.

WILLIAM S. BURROUGHS
American writer
The Guardian 1969
In a society where people get more or less what they want sexually, it is much more difficult to motivate them in an industrialised context, to make them buy refrigerators and cars.

TRUMAN CAPOTE
American writer
The good thing about masturbation is that you don't have to dress up for it.

'CARNAL KNOWLEDGE'
directed by Mike Nichols 1971
Jonathan: You know it. When you think of what he's got to dip into, any guy with a conscience has a right to turn soft. Am I right, Louise?

JIMMY CARTER
American politician
Playboy 1976
I've looked on a lot of women with lust. I've committed adultery in my heart many times. This is something God recognizes I will do – and I have done it – and God forgives me for it.

JOHN COOPER CLARKE
British poet 1978
He makes love like a footballer. He dribbles before he shoots.

ALEX COMFORT
British sexologist
Male sexual response is far brisker and more automatic. It is triggered easily by things – like putting a quarter in a vending machine.

New York Times 1978
An erection at will is the moral equivalent of a valid credit card.

'The Joy of Sex' 1972
There are only two guidelines in good sex: 'Don't do anything you don't really enjoy' and 'Find out your partner's needs and don't balk them if you can help it'.

Sex ought to be a wholly satisfying link between two affectionate people from which they emerge unanxious, rewarded and ready for more.

CYRIL CONNOLLY
British critic
in 'The Faber Book of Aphorisms' 1964
There is sanctuary in reading, sanctuary in formal society, in the company of old friends, and in the giving of officious help to strangers, but there is no sanctuary in one bed from the memory of another.

DAVID CORT
American writer
'Social Astonishments' 1963
Sex is the great amateur art. The professional, male or female, is frowned upon. He or she misses the whole point and spoils the show.

QUENTIN CRISP
British writer
'How To Become A Virgin' 1981
As a test of the closeness of your rela-

tionship with the world, sex could never be a patch on being murdered. (That's when someone really does risk his life for you).

Sexual freedom has become more important than identity. Indeed, it has superseded it. The modern philosophy states 'I ejaculate, therefore I am'.

'The Naked Civil Servant' 1968
Homosexuals have time for everybody . . . every detail of lives of real people, however mundane it may be, seems romantic to them.

Sex is the last refuge of the miserable.

SALVADOR DALI
Spanish artist
'Diary of a Genius' 1966
Physiological expenditure is a superficial way of self expression. People who incline towards physical love accomplish nothing at all.

JOHN DAVENPORT &
EDDIE COOLEY
American songwriters
'Fever'
Chicks were born to give you fever / Fahrenheit or Centigrade.
(Carlin Music)

DIANA DORS
British actress
The Observer 1970
Funny really. When you look at the things that go on these days my story reads like Noddy.

KIRK DOUGLAS
American film star
Virtue is not photogenic.

IAN DURY
British rock musician
Sex is about as important as a cheese sandwich. But a cheese sandwich, if you ain't got one to put in your belly, is extremely important.

JULES FEIFFER
American cartoonist
in 'Loose Talk' ed. Linda Botts 1980
The big mistake that men make is that when they turn 13 or 14 and all of a sudden they've reached puberty, they believe that they like women. Actually, you're just horny. It doesn't mean you like women any more at 21 than you did at 10.

BRENDAN FRANCIS
The big difference between sex for money and sex for free is that sex for money usually costs a lot less.

PENELOPE GILLIATT
British author
quoted in 'The Wit of Women' ed. L. and M. Cowan
Sunday should be abolished – except between consenting adults in private.

AL GOLDSTEIN
American pornzine publisher
Playboy 1974
There will always be a market for sideshows.

ROBERT GRAVES
British poet
Playboy 1970
Because of its secret nature, you should not talk or write about sex. You can have love talk with the person you're in love with – that's a different matter. But any talk of sex with others is anti-human.

SCREAMIN' JAY HAWKINS
American rock singer
Don't forget, the penis is mightier than the sword.

SIR ROBERT HELPMAN
Australian choreographer
The Observer 1970
I think you can be contemporary without taking off your clothes.

DAVID 'SCAR' HODO
Member of American rock group
'Village People'
We didn't go for a gay concept when we put the show together. We went for a totally male, masculine celebration – that men can get up there and feel their tits and do bumps and grinds and still remain men. Narcissism is a good thing. Everyone does it, I don't care what they say. Everyone gets off on mirror-tripping.

BOB HOPE
American comedian
'Quote and Unquote' 1970
People who throw kisses are hopelessly lazy.

ALDOUS HUXLEY
British writer
quoted in Sunday Times 1973
The Kama Sutra is the Mrs. Beeton of sex.

Chastity – the most unnatural of the sexual perversions.

ERIC IDLE
British comedian
in 'Monty Python's Flying Circus' TV show 1969
Wink, wink, nudge, nudge, say no more, know what I mean . . .

MICK JAGGER &
KEITH RICHARD
British rock composers
'The Spider & The Fly'
She was common, flirty / She looked about thirty / I would have run away but I was on my own / She told me later, she's a machine operator / She said she liked the way I held the microphone. (Essex Music)

JILL JOHNSTON
American feminist
'Lesbian Nation' 1973
Bisexuality is not so much a copout as a fearful compromise.

KARL KRAUS
German artist
'Karl Kraus' by Harry Zohn
A woman occasionally is quite a serviceable substitute for masturbation. It takes an abundance of imagination, to be sure.

KRIS KRISTOFFERSON
American singer and film star
What's so fucking wrong with being a sex symbol?

PAUL LEAUTAUD
French writer
'Propos d'un jour'
The advantage of being celibate is that when one sees a pretty girl one need not grieve over having an ugly one back home.

HEDY LAMARR
American film star
Any girl can be glamorous; all you have to do is stand still and look stupid.

PHILIP LARKIN
British poet
'Annus Mirabilis'
Sexual intercourse began / In Nineteen Sixty-Three / (which was rather late for me) – / Between the end of the Chatterley Ban / And the Beatles' first LP.

HELEN LAWRENSON
American journalist
Esquire 1977
Whatever else can be said about sex, it cannot be called a dignified performance.

As for that topsy turvy tangle known as soixante-neuf, personally I have always felt it to be madly confusing, like trying to pat your head and rub your stomach at the same time.

LIVERPOOL STIPENDIARY
MAGISTRATE
1978, on being told oral sex is widely practised in Britain . . .
If this is really so, I'm glad I do not have long to live.

GINA LOLLOBRIGIDA
Italian film star
The Observer 1956
Glamour is when a man knows a woman is a woman.

ANITA LOOS
American writer
The Guardian 1974
When the movies started delivering messages they lost their charisma. Now the messages are being replaced by porno. Between the two, porno is better.

New York Herald Tribune 1974
If we have to kiss Hollywood goodbye, it may be with one of those tender, old-fashioned, seven-second kisses as exchanged between two people of the opposite sex with all their clothes on.

International Herald Tribune 1973
On a plane you can pick up more and better people than on any other public conveyance since the stagecoach.

SOPHIA LOREN
Italian film star
Sex appeal is 50% what you've got and
50% what people think you've got.

VICTOR LOWNES
London Playboy club boss
*in 'In and Out: Debrett 1980–81' by Neil
Mackwood 1980*
What is a promiscuous person – it's
usually someone who is getting more sex
than you are.

CLARE BOOTHE LUCE
American diplomat
*quoted in 'The Wit of Women' ed. L. and M.
Cowan*
Nature abhors a virgin – a frozen asset.

NORMAN MAILER
American writer
Playboy 1968
Sex is not only a divine and beautiful
activity: it's a murderous activity. People
kill each other in bed. Some of the greatest crimes ever committed were committed in bed. And no weapons were used.

LEE MARVIN
American film star
Esquire 1970
The only way to resolve a situation with
a girl is to jump on her and things will
work out.

GROUCHO MARX
American comedian
A man is only as old as the woman he
feels.

in 'Quote & Unquote' 1970
Anyone who says he can see through
women is missing a lot.

Whoever named it necking was a poor
judge of anatomy.

WALTER MATTHAU
American film star
Esquire 1968
The first girl you go to bed with is *always*
pretty.

MARILYN MONROE
American film star
A sex symbol becomes a thing, I hate
being a thing.

DESMOND MORRIS
British anthropologist
quoted in Playboy 1974
Voyeurism is a healthy, non-participa-
tory sexual activity – the world *should*
look at the world.

BERYL MORTIMER
British film sound effects specialist
on dubbing sex scenes, 1979
What we don't get up to with bits of
tripe and liver and bowls of spaghetti
isn't worth getting up to.

MALCOLM MUGGERIDGE
British journalist
'The Most of Malcolm Muggeridge' 1966
The orgasm has replaced the Cross as
the focus of longing and the image of
fulfillment.

BARRY NORMAN
British critic
The Listener 1978
Perhaps at 14 every boy should be in
love with some ideal woman to put on
a pedestal and worship. As he grows up,
of course, he will put her on a pedestal
the better to view her legs.

EDNA O'BRIEN
Irish writer
*in 'Goodbye Baby & Amen' by D. Bailey
1969*
Permissiveness is simply removing the
dust sheets from our follies.

CLIFFORD ODETS
American playwright
Sex – the poor man's polo.

JACKIE ONASSIS
International socialite
*attrib. by Gore Vidal and quoted as such by
Peter York in 'Style Wars' 1980*
Sex is a bad thing because it rumples the
clothes.

PABLO PICASSO
Spanish artist
*in answer to Jean Leymarie's question on the
difference between art and eroticism . . . quoted
in 'Contemporary Artists' 1977*
There is no difference.

'PILLOW TALK'
Universal 1959 screenplay by Stanley Shapiro & Maurice Richlin; based on story by Russell Rouse and Clarence Greene
Doris Day: (to Rock Hudson): Mr. Allen, this may come as a shock to you, but there are some men who don't end every sentence with a proposition.

RICHARD PRYOR
American comedian
from his 1980 film 'Richard Pryor in Concert'
I like making love myself and I can make love for about *three minutes*. Three minutes of serious fucking and I need eight hours sleep, and a bowl of Wheaties.

PAUL RAYMOND (Geoffrey Quinn)
British magazine publisher 1970
Let's say, I think a man is more likely to make love to his wife after coming to the Revuebar than on any other night of the year.

WILHELM REICH
German psychoanalyst
The sexual drive is nothing but the motor memory of previously remembered pleasure.

JACK RICHARDSON
American writer
Harpers Magazine 1970
Nothing so splinters the self as a bed shared with an unknown body.

LINDA RONSTADT
American rock singer
I keep saying I wish I had as much in bed as I get in the newspapers. I'd be real busy.

PHILIP ROTH
American novelist
'Portnoy's Complaint' 1969
Amazing! Astonishing! Still can't get over the fantastic idea that when you are looking at a girl, you are looking at somebody who is guaranteed to have on her – a cunt! *They all have cunts!* Right under their dresses! Cunts – for fucking!

SHEL SILVERSTEIN
American cartoonist and songwriter
to applicant for job at Playboy, quoted in New Times 1975
You don't want to work here. After all, how many ways are there to say 'big tits'.

SUSAN SONTAG
American essayist
'Against Interpretation' 1961
There are some elements of life, above all sexual pleasure, about which it isn't necessary to have a position.

'Styles of Radical Will' 1969
Sexuality is something, like nuclear energy, which may prove amenable to domestication, through scruple, but then again may not.

SALLY STANFORD
American madame
'The Lady of the House' 1966
No man can be held throughout the day by what happens throughout the night.

STELLA STEVENS
American film star 1968
I think naked people are very nice. Posing in the nude is perhaps the best way of reaching people.

ELIZABETH TAYLOR
British film star 1969
Sex, treated properly, can be one of the most gorgeous things in the world.

LILY TOMLIN
American comedienne
There will be sex after death, we just won't be able to feel it.

JOHN TREVELYAN
British film censor 1970
resigning . . .
I've got nothing against sex, it's a marvellous human activity, but it was watching others do it all the time that got me down.

KENNETH TYNAN
British critic
Esquire 1968 On pornography . . .
Just as old habits die hard, old hards die habits.

The Guardian 1975
When a man and woman of unorthodox tastes make love the man could be said to be introducing his foible into her quirk.

JOHN UPDIKE
American writer
'Writers at Work' 4th series 1977
Let's take coitus out of the closet and off the altar and put it in the continuum of human behaviour.

CHERRY VANILLA
American groupie
Never do with your hands what you could do better with your mouth.

GORE VIDAL
American writer
'Norman Mailer's Self-Advertisements' 1960
Sex is. There is nothing more to be done about it. Sex builds no roads, writes no novels and sex certainly gives no meaning to anything in life but itself.

quoted in Nova 1969, from an appearance on the David Frost TV show
I'm all for bringing back the birch, but only between consenting adults.

asked whether his first sexual experience had been hetero- or homosexual . . .
I was too polite to ask.

Homosexuals as well as heterosexuals have emotional hangups. Though that usually comes to an abrupt end – when the boy asks for more money.

ANDY WARHOL
American artist
'From A to B and Back Again' 1975
Two people kissing always look like fish.

KEN WEAVER
American rock singer
'Nothing'
I've got plenty of nothing / And nothing's plenty for me / I got my hand / I got my dick / I got my fantasy.

LINA WERTMULLER
Italian film director 1976
I do not think that the solution to man's solitude is a line of men masturbating and a line of women masturbating.

MAE WEST
American film star
Sex is an emotion in motion.

EDMUND WHITE
American writer 1979
There is no middle class sexual style for men. What would it be based on? Golfing? Discussing stock options? Attending church? Downing highballs?

MARY WHITEHOUSE
British censor 1973
Sex is important, but by no means the only important thing in life.

TENNESSEE WILLIAMS
American playwright
replying to David Frost who asked him on national TV 'Are you a homosexual?'
I cover the waterfront.

VICTORIA WOOD
British playwright
'Talent' 1979
I thought *coq au vin* was love in a lorry.

FRANK ZAPPA
American rock musician
I think pop music has done more for oral intercourse than anything else that ever happened and vice versa.

SIR SOLLY ZUCKERMAN
British scientist
writing on 'Sex' in Chambers Encylopedia
Semen maketh man . . . sex merely expresses the totality of differences between male and female.

Health

BRIAN ALDISS
British author
The Guardian 1969
We are a divided species – head running ahead of heart. It is no surprise that

coronary thrombosis is the characteristic death of our time. The heart literally chokes up on the impossibility of keeping up.

RITCHIE ALLEN
American baseball player 1972
Your body is just like a bar of soap. It gradually wears down, from repeated use.

W. H. AUDEN
British poet
'The Dyer's Hand' 1962
The ear tends to be lazy, craves the familiar and is shocked by the unexpected. The eye, on the other hand, tends to be impatient, craves the novel and is bored by repetition.

ENID BAGNOLD
British writer
in 'Contemporary Novelists' 1976
Inside the brain there's a kind of instrument, never quite learnt and most *un*fully played. . .

JACOB BRONOWSKI
British scientist
'The Ascent of Man' 1975
The hand is the cutting edge of the mind.

CHARLES BUKOWSKI
American writer
'Notes of a Dirty Old Man' 1969
The ass is the face of the soul of sex.

IAN DURY
British rock musician
The human leg is a source of delight – it carries your weight and governs your height.

ROBERT FROST
American poet
The brain is a wonderful organ. It starts working the moment you get up in the morning and does not stop until you get into the office.

ARNOLD H. GLASGOW
American academic
Reader's Digest
Your body is the baggage you must carry through life. The more excess baggage, the shorter the trip.

MARTHA GRAHAM
American dancer 1979
The body never lies.

JOAN JETT
American rock singer
Girls got balls. They're just a little higher up, that's all.

TOM LANDRY
American professional football coach
sign posted in locker room of his Dallas Cowboys 1973
Will power. Intellect tires, the Will never. The brain needs sleep, the Will none. The whole body is nothing but objectified Will. The whole nervous system constitutes the antennae of the Will. Every act of the body is nothing but the act of Will objectified.

JONATHAN MILLER
British doctor and writer
'The Body in Question' 1979
We contain an internal world which is just as active and complicated as the one we live in. It is an interior of which we are largely unaware, and one to which we have no personal access. We cannot be tourists in our own insides.

JOAN MIRO
Spanish artist
Time 1980
The sex organ has a poetic power, like a comet.

ROBERT MORLEY
British actor and wit 1967
Firstly, I am a fat man.

JINABHAI NAVIK
Veteran Indian jogger 1980
If you want to live, you must walk. If you want to live long, you must run.

SUSIE ORBACH
American writer
book title 1977
Fat is a feminist issue.

GRACE PALEY
American writer
in 'Contemporary Novelists' 1976
All that is really necessary for survival of the fittest, it seems, is an interest in life, good, bad or peculiar.

SIR MALCOLM SARGENT
British conductor
I spend up to six hours a day waving my arms about and if everyone else did the same thing they would stay much healthier.

'SPARTACUS'
Universal 1960 screenplay by Dalton Trumbo, based on novel by Howard Fast
Charles Laughton: Corpulence makes a man reasonable, pleasant and phlegmatic. Have you noticed that the nastiest of talents are invariably thin?

ELIZABETH TAYLOR
British film star 1966
I try to keep a healthy body, that's all there is to it.

'VIVA ZAPATA!'
20th Century Fox 1952. screenplay John Steinbeck
Marlon Brando: A starved body has a skinny soul.

RAQUEL WELCH
American film star 1980
I'm a late bloomer. My mind and my experience have caught up to my body.

LUDWIG WITTGENSTEIN
German philosopher
'Philosophical Investigations' 1953
The human body is the best picture of the human soul.

MARTHA ZIMMERMAN
American air hostess
quoted in Wall Street Journal 1977
If God had meant us to travel tourist class he would have made us narrower.

Beauty

LUIS CERNUDA
Spanish poet
'Las Ruinas'
Everything beautiful has its moment and then passes away.

BERNARD CORNFELD
British businessman
Daily Telegraph 1974
A beautiful woman with a brain is like a beautiful woman with a club foot.

ANDRE COURREGES
French couturier
quoted in Metropolitan Museum of Modern Art Bulletin 1967
A woman is truly beautiful only when she is naked and she knows it.

CHRISTIAN DIOR
French couturier
Ladies Home Journal 1956
Zest is the secret of all beauty. There is no beauty that is attractive without zest.

JOSEPH ESHERICK
American architect
'Contemporary Architects' 1980
Beauty is a consequential thing, a by-product of solving problems correctly. It is unreal as the goal.

G. H. HARDY
British mathematician
'A Mathematician's Apology'
Beauty is the first test; there is no permanent place in the world for ugly mathematics.

JEAN KERR
American writer
'The Snake Has All The Lines' 1960
I'm tired of all this nonsense about beauty being only skin-deep. That's deep enough. What do you want – an adorable pancreas?

SOPHIA LOREN
Italian film star 1978
Beauty is how you feel inside and it reflects in your eyes. It is not something physical.

SUZY PARKER
American model 1955
I thank God for high cheekbones every time I look in the mirror in the morning.

'THE ROMAN SPRING OF MRS. STONE'
Warner Bros 1961. screenplay Gavin Lambert, from novel by Tennessee Williams
Vivian Leigh: People who are very beautiful make their own laws.

SOFU TESHIGAHARA
Japanese flower artist
Time 1978
There are many beautiful things, but the silent beauty of a flower surpasses them all.

DYLAN THOMAS
British poet
quoted in Esquire 1965
True beauty ... lies in that which is undestroyable, and logically therefore in very little.

EVELYN WAUGH
British novelist
The Observer 1962
Manners are especially the need of the plain. The pretty can get away with anything.

SIMONE WEIL
French philosopher
'Gravity & Grace' 1972
Beauty is a fruit which we look at without trying to seize it.

FRANK LLOYD WRIGHT
American architect
'The Future of Architecture' 1953
The inappropriate cannot be beautiful.

PETER YORK
British journalist
London Collection Magazine 1978
If beauty isn't genius it usually signals at least a high level of animal cunning.

Sport

ROGER BANNISTER
British athlete 1956
Running has given me a glimpse of the greatest freedom that a man can ever know, because it results in the simultaneous liberation of both body and mind.

FILBERT BAYI
Kenyan athlete 1975
World records are like shirts. Anyone can have one if he works for it.

HENRY BLAHA
American sportsman 1972
Rugby is a beastly game played by gentlemen; soccer is a gentleman's game played by beasts; football is a beastly game played by beasts.

DANNY BLANCHFLOWER
Irish soccer star 1968
Sport is a wonderfully democratic thing, one of the few honourable battlefields left. It is a conflict between good and bad, winning and losing, praise and criticism. Its true values should be treasured and protected ... they belong to the people.

JIMMY BRESLIN
American novelist and ex-sportswriter 1973
Football is a game designed to keep coal miners off the streets.

JEAN-MARIE BROHM
French gym coach 1975
Sport is an armoured apparatus for coercion, an instrument of bourgeois hegemony in a Gramscian sense, dominated by a phallocratic and fascistoid idea of virility. It is mechanisation of the body conceived as a robot, ruled by the principle of productivity.

AVERY BRUNDAGE
President of I.O.C. 1972
The Olympic Movement is a twentieth century religion. Where there is no injustice of caste, of race, of family, of wealth.

JIMMY CANNON
American sportswriter
quoted in 'No Cheering in the Pressbox' ed. Jerome Holtzman 1973
Fishing, with me, has always been an excuse to drink in the daytime.

on his job
We work in the toy department.

'CHAMPION'
UA 1949 screenplay Carl Foreman, based on the short story by Ring Lander
Paul Stewart on boxing: This is the only sport in the world where two guys get paid for doing something they'd be arrested for if they got drunk and did it for nothing.

BRIAN CLOUGH
British soccer manager
Advice on dealing with the media, 1978
Say nowt, win it, then talk your head off.

MARCEL DUCHAMP
French artist
'Art News' 1969
Chess can be described as the movement of pieces eating one another.

MICKEY DUFF
British boxing matchmaker
The Guardian 1972
A lot of boxing promoters couldn't match the cheeks of their own backside.

ALAN DUNDES
American psychiatrist
Claiming that US football was actually a gay ritual, 1978
The game is a way of allowing us to have physical contact with other men. . . . The truth hurts, and I think I've struck a nerve. Face it, there's got to be more to football than a nice way to spend Saturday afternoon. 80,000 people don't turn out for Roller Derby.

BOBBY FISCHER
American chess star
International Herald Tribune 1973
Chess is like life: the point of chess is that it represents a total kind of warfare. A sandbox, where an axiomatic landscape is firmly limited between two points. Chess is limited warfare; life, at least potentially, is total war.

GEORGE FOREMAN
American heavyweight boxing champion
The Guardian 1976
Boxing is sort of like jazz. The better it is the fewer people can understand it.

GEORGE FRAZIER IV
American pro footballer
Esquire 1968
The art of being a successful football coach seems to owe more to the axiom that nice guys finish last than to the theory that contented cows give better milk.

JANE FREDERICK
American pentathlon champion 1977
Professional sports . . . what else in life gives you an absolute measurement of where you stand and how much you've progressed.

PENELOPE GILLIAT
British critic
The Guardian 1974
The only word never used to describe what happens in football is 'kick'. The ball is always 'volleyed' or 'struck' or 'driven'. 'Kick' only happens when players do it to each other.

MIKE HAWTHORN
British racing driver 1953
Driving a racing car is like painting a picture. Anyone can doodle with a pencil. There are plenty of people who can turn out a reasonably recognisable sketch. But the real artists are few and far between. They are born, not made. Driving a racing car is just as much an art, it is not a knack that can be acquired. Either you have it or you have not.

BOB HOPE
American comedian
If you watch a game it's fun. If you play it, it's recreation. If you work at it, it's golf.

ALDOUS HUXLEY
British writer
'Ends & Means'
Like every other instrument man has invented, sport can be used for good and evil purposes. Used badly it can encourage personal vanity and group vanity, greedy desire for victory and even hatred for rivals, an intolerant esprit de corps and contempt for people who are beyond an arbitrarily selected pale.

REGGIE JACKSON
American sportsman
'Baseball Illustrated' 1975
Fans don't boo nobodies.

BEN JIPCHO
Kenyan runner
The Guardian 1975
Running for money doesn't make you run fast. It makes you run first.

PROF. ERNST JOKL
American academic
The Observer 1970
Boxing is not a sport, it is a criminal activity.

BRUCE KIDD
Canadian runner
We should stop preaching about sport's moral values. Sport, after all, isn't Lent, it's a pleasure of the flesh.

BILLY JEAN KING
American tennis star 1972
The word is always that amateurs play sport for the love of it. Listen, professionals love it just as much, probably more so. We put our lives on the line for sport.

SONNY LISTON
American boxing champion 1961
A boxing match is like a cowboy movie. There's got to be good guys and there's got to be bad guys. That's what the people pay for, to see the bad guys get beat.

VINCE LOMBARDI
American pro football coach
Nobody is hurt. Hurt is in the mind. If you can walk, you can run.

RENE MAHEU
Director General of UNESCO
Sport is an order of chivalry, a code of ethics and aesthetics, recruiting its members from all classes and all peoples. Sport is a truce: in an era of antagonisms and conflicts it is the respite of the gods in which fair competition ends in respect and friendship. Sport is education, the truest kind of education, that of character. Sport is culture because it creates beauty and, above all, for those who have the least opportunity to feast on it.

JOHN MARKS
British bullfight critic
Bullfighting is not a cruel sport, but a cruel method of achieving plastic beauty.

RODNEY MARSH
British soccer star 1971
All a manager has to do is keep eleven players happy – the eleven in the reserves. The first team are happy because they're the first team.

RICHARD MEADE
British showjumper 1972
In sport you either get tremendous fulfilment or tremendous disappointment. Nothing else in life is so cut and dried.

RINUS MICHELS
Spanish soccer coach
The Guardian 1973
Football is business. And business is business.

ROBERT MORLEY
British actor and wit 1965
The ball is man's most disastrous invention, not excluding the wheel.

There is only one kind of game worthy of human time, thought and esteem – and that is a game of chance.

J. B. MORTON
British humorist
'Beachcomber' 'Dictionary for today' Daily Express passim
Bombshell: the exclusion of a cricketer from a team.

STIRLING MOSS
British racing driver 1963
One cannot really enjoy speed to the absolute limit if there's a destination involved.

ANDREW MULLIGAN
British journalist 1965
Sport is an exportable commodity, like language and cuisine.

RANDY NEUMANN
American boxer 1975
Boxing is the best and most individual lifestyle you can have in society without being a criminal.

JOHN OAKSEY
British racing commentator
The Guardian 1971
There are, they say, fools, bloody fools, and men who remount in a steeplechase.

JOSE ORTEGA Y GASSET
Spanish philosopher
'Meditations on Hunting' 1947
One does not hunt in order to kill; on the contrary, one kills in order to have hunted.

GEORGE ORWELL
British essayist
'The Sporting Spirit' 1945
Serious sport has nothing to do with fair play. It is bound up with hatred, jealousy, boastfulness, disregard of all rules and sadistic pleasure in witnessing violence: in other words it is war minus the shooting.

KERRY PACKER
Australian entrepreneur
on the Australian Cricket Board, 1977
If they don't co-operate, they'll walk straight into a meat mangle.

WILLIE PEP
American boxer
The Guardian 1974
For ageing boxers, first your legs go. Then your reflexes go, then your friends go.

STEPHEN POTTER
British humorist
book title 1947
The Theory & Practice of Gamesmanship or, the Art of Winning Games without Actually Cheating.

MAN RAY
French photographer
quoted in The Times 1968
Chess is a game where the most intense mental activity leaves no traces.

JOHN 'BEANS' REARDON
American baseball umpire 1980
If the Pope was an umpire he'd still have trouble with the Catholics.

DON REVIE
British soccer manager
The Guardian 1976
Professionalism, if you like, is not having sex on Thursdays or Fridays.

BILL SHANKLY
British soccer manager 1973
Some people think football is a matter of life and death. I don't like that attitude. I can assure them it is much more serious than that.

FRANK SHORTER
American runner
The Guardian 1976
Running a marathon is just like reading a good book. After a while you're just not conscious of the physical act of reading.

LORD SNOW
British writer
The Guardian 1971
Try explaining cricket to an intelligent foreigner. It is far harder than explaining Chomsky's generational grammar.

TEOFILO STEVENSON
Cuban boxer
This isn't a career for me. It's a game.

JACKIE STEWART
British racing driver 1972
In my sport the quick are too often listed among the dead.

PETER STOREY
British soccer player 1973
The Sugar Plum Fairy could play cen-
treforward if it weren't for people like
me.

ANTHONY STORR
British psychiatrist
BBC-TV 1973
Sport is imposing order on what was
chaos.

JACK TATUM
American pro football player
'They Call Me Assassin' 1980
I do believe that my best hits border on
felonious assault.

JEFF THOMSON
Australian cricketer 1977
It won't take much work to get me psy-
ched up to hating anyone.

FRED TRUMAN
British cricketer 1980
Fast bowling isn't hard work, it's horse
work.

BILL VEECK
American sports entrepreneur 1976
Baseball is an island of surety in a
changing world.

VIRGINIA WADE
British tennis star 1974
Tennis is a fine balance between deter-
mination and tiredness.

YEVGENY YEVTUSHENKO
Russian poet
True sport is always a duel: a duel with
nature, with one's own fear, with one's
own fatigue, a duel in which body and
mind are strengthened.

Winning

GEORGE ALLEN
US pro football coach
Winning can be defined as the science of
being totally prepared.

Esquire 1968
Ability is not all there is – a good athlete
is not always a winning athlete.

DAVID BROOME
British showjumper 1971
To win is everything. To be second is
even worse than being secondary.

LEO DUROCHER
American baseball manager 1946
There's Mellot. Take a good look at him.
A nicer sort of guy never put a pair of
shoes on. Fine fellow, but he didn't come
to win, that's the answer. Nice guys finish last.

1950
Show me a good loser in professional
sports and I'll show you an idiot. Show
me a good sportsman and I'll show you
a player I'm looking to trade.

WOODY HAYES
American college football coach 1974
Without winners there wouldn't be any
god-damned civilisation.

BERNARD HUNT
British journalist
The Guardian 1973
Winning is a drug. Once you have ex-
perienced it you cannot do without it.

PUNCH IMLACH
American hockey star 1979
quoted in 'Hockey is a Battle' by Scott Young
Any team that loses its aggressiveness is
dead . . . you'd be playing with guys that
had broken wrists or ribs . . . you know
a guy has a broken wrist – you hammer
in there a few times and you don't have
much trouble with him for the rest of the
night. It's nothing personal, I do it
myself.

REGGIE JACKSON
American sports star
Time 1981
The will to win is worthless if you don't
get paid for it.

PHIL KEITH-ROACH
English university rugby player 1971
You can feel just empty after losing. Life just seems to stop in a void until you surface and get it in perspective. It's all over so quickly.

JOSEPH P. KENNEDY
American entrepeneur
We don't want any losers around. In this family we want winners.

VINCE LOMBARDI
American pro football coach 1965
Winning is not everything. It's the only thing.

BILL MUSSELMAN
American basketball coach 1972
Defeat is worse than death, because you have to live with defeat.

JOE NAMATH
American pro football star
When you win, nothing hurts.

VIRGINIA WADE
British tennis star 1968
Winners aren't popular. Losers often are.

Drink & Drugs

MRS. ROBIN ASKIN
wife of the Premier of New South Wales 1971
I'll probably get quite a panning for saying this but I believe that drugs are part of a Communist subversive plot.

NANCY ASTOR
British politician
in Reader's Digest 1960
One reason I don't drink is that I want to know when I'm having a good time.

HUMPHREY BOGART
American film star
quoted in Esquire 1964
Q: Were you drunk at four a.m.?
Bogart: Isn't everybody.

The trouble with the world is that everybody in it is three drinks behind.

WILLIAM S. BURROUGHS
American writer
Daily Telegraph 1964, on drug pushing:
1. Never give anything away for nothing.
2. Never give any more than you have to (always catch the buyer hungry and always make him wait).
3. Always take back everything if you possibly can.

'The Naked Lunch'
Home is the heroin, home from the sea.

The Guardian 1969
Any opiate is absolutely contra-indicated for a creative person, because it makes you less aware of what's happening around and inside you. That's the point of a pain-killer, to make you forget that your leg's been cut off. The writer is supposed to be more aware.

TRUMAN CAPOTE
American writer 1977
I'm an alcoholic, a genuine alcoholic. Not just a fake phoney alcoholic, I'm a real alcoholic.

'THE CHALK GARDEN'
Universal 1964 screenplay by John Michael Hayes, based on play by Enid Bagnold
Felix Aymer: Alcohol in the middle of the day is exciting when you're thirty, but disastrous at seventy.

JOHN CIARDI
American critic
Saturday Review 1966
There is nothing wrong with sobriety in moderation.

JEAN COCTEAU
French writer and film director
'Opium'
Everything one does in life, even love, occurs in an express train racing towards death. To smoke opium is to get out of the train while it is still moving. It is to concern oneself with something other than life, with death.

'COME FILL THE CUP'
Warner Bros. 1951. screenplay by Ivan Goff & Ben Roberts, based on novel by Harlan Ware
James Cagney: A lush can always find a reason if he's thirsty. Listen. If he's happy, he takes a couple of shots to celebrate his happiness. Sad, he needs them to drown his sorrow. Low, to pick him up, excited, to calm him down. Sick, for his health and healthy, it can't hurt him . . . a lush just can't lose.

EDDIE CONDON
American jazzman
quoted in 'Jam Session' ed. Ralph Gleason
For a bad hangover take the juice of two quarts of whiskey.

JOSEPH DARGENT
French vintner 1955
No government could survive without champagne. Champagne in the throats of our diplomatic people is like oil in the wheels of an engine.

'EASY RIDER'
by Peter Fonda and Dennis Hopper 1969
Peter Fonda: We blew it.

CLIFTON FADIMAN
American essayist
'Selected Writings' 1955
Liquor is not a necessity. It is a means of momentarily side-stepping necessity.

WILLIAM FAULKNER
American novelist
There's no such thing as bad whiskey. Some whiskeys just happen to be better than others. But a man shouldn't fool with booze until he's fifty; then he's a damn fool if he doesn't.

GRAHAM GREENE
British novelist
'Ways of Escape'
The smell of opium is more agreeable than the smell of success.

GEORGE HARRISON
British rock star
'It's All Too Much'
Show me that I'm everywhere / And get me home for tea.
(Northern Songs)

'JAMES BOND'
Ian Fleming's super spy in the film: 'Goldfinger', 1964
A martini – shaken, not stirred.

COUNCILLOR MORRIS JONES
British local government official
defeating a proposal to ban smoking for the first hour of council meetings 1979
If we're going to let this happen we might as well sit back and let the Russians take over.

EARTHA KITT
American singer 1970
People these days are thinking less and drinking more.

JOHN LENNON &
PAUL McCARTNEY
British rock composers
song title
Lucy In The Sky With Diamonds.

OSCAR LEVANT
American pianist and composer 1950
I don't drink. I don't like it. It makes me feel good.

MARGERY LOWRY
editor of 'Malcolm Lowry: Psalms & Songs' 1975
You cannot trust the ones who are too careful. As writers or drinkers. Old Goethe cannot have been so good a man as Keats or Chatterton. Or Rimbaud. The ones that burn.

DON McNEILL
The junkie is, at once, a tribute to the survival instincts and a testament to the self destructive nature of man.

NORMAN MAILER
American writer
Playboy 1968
Drugs are a spiritual form of gambling.

HERMAN MANKIEWICZ
American screenwriter
after vomiting at the table of stuffy producer Arthur Hornblow
It's all right Arthur, the white wine came up with the fish.

DEAN MARTIN
American film star
You're not drunk if you can lie on the floor without holding on.

GROUCHO MARX
American comedian
I was T.T. until prohibition.

OGDEN NASH
American poet
'Reflections on Ice-Breaking'
Candy is dandy / But liquor is quicker.

GEORGE JEAN NATHAN
American critic
quoted beneath his picture in Charlie O's bar, New York City
I only drink to make other people seem more interesting.

JACK NICHOLSON
American film star 1976
The only reason that cocaine is such a rage today is that people are too dumb and lazy to get themselves together to roll a joint.

ANAIS NIN
French novelist
'Diaries' Vol. IV 1971
Something is always born of excess: great art was born of great terrors, great loneliness, great inhibitions, instabilities and it always balances them.

LOU REED
American rock star
'Heroin'
Heroin / It's my life / And it's my wife (Sunbury Music)

KARYL ROOSEVELT
New York Times 1975
Drunks are rarely amusing unless they know some good songs and lose a lot at poker.

BISHOP SHEVILL
Australian clergyman 1970
The 'stubbie' is one of the most malevolent inventions of the decade.

TOOTS SHOR
American innkeeper
Anybody that can't get drunk by midnight ain't trying.

GRACE SLICK
American rock star
'White Rabbit'
One pill makes you larger / And one pill makes you small / But the ones that mother gives you / Don't do anything at all. (Copper Penny Music)

CHARLES MERRILL SMITH
American writer
'Instant Status' 1972
The cocktail party – a device for paying off obligations to people you don't want to invite to dinner.

LORD SOPER
British clergyman
I don't think alcohol is the Devil in solution, but it causes a great deal of misery. It is no use saying that it's all right in moderation. Shall we have arsenic in moderation and murder in moderation? Wine is the juice of the grape gone bad.

DYLAN THOMAS
British poet
An alcoholic is someone you don't like who drinks as much as you do.

JAMES THURBER
American humorist
'Thurber Country'
Some American writers who have known each other for years have never met in the daytime or when both were sober.

TOM WAITS
American singer 1979
I don't have a drink problem except when I can't get one.

FRANK ZAPPA
American rock musician
I can't understand why anybody would want to devote their life to a cause like dope. It's the most boring pastime I can think of. It ranks a close second to television.

Food

POLLY ADLER
American madame
'A House is not a Home' 1953
Too many cooks spoil the brothel.

JAMES BEARD
American food writer
quote beneath his picture in Charlie O's bar, New York
A gourmet who thinks of calories is like a tart who looks at her watch.

PAUL BOCUSE
French chef
The Listener 1978
For art, there is no future, it's the living moment, then it's dead. That's wonderful. Cuisine is like a fireworks display, nothing remains. It is *une fête*, rapid, ephemeral.

MICHEL BOURDIN
French chef
Time 1978
Cooking is a way of giving and of making yourself desirable.

MEL BROOKS
American film director
Playboy 1975
Where you eat is sacred.

The egg cream is psychologically the opposite of circumcision – it *pleasurably* reaffirms your Jewishness.

ALAIN CHAPEL
French restaurateur
Time 1978
Cooking is an act of love.

MALCOLM DE CHAZAL
French writer
'Sens Plastique' 1949
A voracious sense of smell leans forward on its nostrils like a glutton eating with his elbows on the table.

Women eat when they talk, men talk when they eat.

JULIA CHILD
American cookery writer 1973
Remember you're all alone in the kitchen, and no one can see you.

CYRIL CONNOLLY
British critic
'The Unquiet Grave' 1945
Imprisoned in every fat man a thin one is wildly signalling to be let out.
(cf. Orwell 'Coming Up For Air' 1939 – Has it ever struck you that there is a thin man inside every fat man, just as they say there is a statue inside every block of stone.)

Obesity is a mental state, a disease brought on by boredom and disappointment.

SHIRLEY CONRAN
British author of 'Superwoman'
Life is too short to stuff a mushroom.

NOEL COWARD
British playwright
The Observer 1969
Exercise is the most awful illusion. The secret is a lot of aspirin and marrons glacés.

CLIFTON FADIMAN
American essayist
'Any Number Can Play' 1957
Cheese – milk's leap towards immortality.

GAIL GREENE
American food critic 1979
Great food is like great sex – the more

you have the more you want.

eating calves' liver with sauté mushrooms:
I've always wondered what it would be like to eat a baby. I think it would taste like this.

NUBAR GULBENKIAN
Armenian millionaire
The Observer 1965
The best number for a dinner party is two – myself and a damn good head waiter.

JOHN GUNTHER
American journalist
in Newsweek 1970
All happiness depends on a leisurely breakfast.

PHILIP W. HABERMAN JR.
American writer
Vogue 1961
A gourmet is just a glutton with brains.

ALFRED HITCHCOCK
British film director
Time 1978
Conversation is the enemy of good wine and food.

LORD HORDER
British royal physician
'The Little Genius'
Our bodies are not puritanical. The pleasant habits of eating and drinking were never meant to be subject to a chemical equation.

HARRIET VAN HORNE
American columnist
Vogue 1956
Cooking is like love – it should be entered into with abandon, or not at all.

SIR ROBERT HUTCHINSON
British surgeon
quoted 'The Wit of Medicine' ed. L. and M. Cowan 1972
Vegetarianism is harmless enough, though it is apt to fill a man with wind and self-righteousness.

CHARLES JAMES
American couturier
Esquire 1964
We are all intrinsically drawn towards our nourishment.

JACK LALANNE
American fitness merchandiser
claiming that he must never die, 1980
It would wreck my image. I can't even afford to have a fat dog.

ARNOLD LOBEL
American writer
'Fables' 1980
All's well that ends with a good meal.

W. SOMERSET MAUGHAM
British writer
'A Writer's Notebook'
At a dinner party one should eat wisely but not too well, and talk well, but not too wisely.

CHRISTIAN MILLAU
French gourmet 1980
All in all, a chef who knows his trade will produce a good meal, and one who does not will serve a bad one.

ROBERT MORLEY
British actor and wit
No man is lonely while eating spaghetti.

ANTON MOSIMANN
French chef
Now! 1981
All the best cooking is simple. There is really nothing new in it. I have 4,000 cookbooks dating back to 1503 and everything that is in *nouvelle cuisine* was there 200 years ago.

'THE ODD COUPLE'
Paramount 1968 screenplay by Neil Simon from his play
Walter Matthau: I've got brown sandwiches and green sandwiches . . . it's either very new cheese or very old meat.

DAVID OGILVY
British advertising executive
Confessions of an Advertising Man 1963
M. Bourgignon, our *chef saucier*, told me that by the time a cook is forty he is either dead or crazy.

LAURENCE J. PETER
Canadian educator
The noblest of all dogs is the hot-dog: it feeds the hand that bites it.

MARIO PUZO
American novelist
Time 1978
More pasta and less panache.

MAGNUS PYKE
British scientist
The Observer 1975
We are wealthy and wasteful but this can't go on. If we don't eat dog biscuits, we could end up eating our dog instead.

1978
Meat is a status dish in which the sizzle counts for more than the intrinsic nutritional worth.

HELEN ROWLAND
American journalist
Ever since Eve started it all by offering Adam the apple, woman's punishment has been to have to supply a man with food and then suffer the consequences when it disagrees with him.

'A Guide to Men'
There is a vast difference between the savage and the civilised man, but it is never apparent to their wives until after breakfast.

BERTRAND RUSSELL
British philosopher
Undoubtedly the desire for food has been and still is one of the main causes of great political events.

GAIL SHEEHY
American journalist
When men reach their sixties and retire they go to pieces. Women just go right on cooking.

JAMES THURBER
American humorist
quoted beneath his picture in Charlie O's bar in New York City
Seeing isn't believing, it's eating that's believing.

STROM THURMOND
American politician
Sunday Times 1972
My father ate wholewheat bread and drank no coffee. I was very fortunate to have parents of such good habits. And such good intellectual attainments. They used nice verbiage.

Fashion

BRIAN ALDISS
British author
The Guardian 1971
Everything new comes in for its share of damnation. Who among the 'responsible' ever said a good word for Hollywood when it was flourishing, or for Keats when he was above ground? Who bought a Van Gogh when he was around and needed the cash?

HARDY AMIES
British couturier
1972 on his trade
We dress rich ladies.

I want gloves to do for men's hands what the Chelsea boot did for the foot.

Australia already has a national dress for men: shorts with long stockings, the wrong shoes, a short sleeved knitted shirt, a pullover and very often a tie. It's unmistakable anywhere in the world.

PIERRE BALMAIN
French couturier
The Observer 1955
The trick of wearing mink is to look as though you were wearing a cloth coat. The trick of wearing a cloth coat is to look as though you are wearing mink.

ALAN BENNETT
British playwright
'Forty Years On' 1968
But then all women dress like their mothers, that is their tragedy. No man ever does. That is his.

MALCOLM BRADBURY
British writer
in 'In & Out: Debrett 1980–81' by Neil Mackwood
Never despise fashion. It's what we have instead of a God.

MICHEL BUTOR
French writer
'Une histoire extraordinaire'
Dandyism, the modern form of stoicism, is finally a religion whose only sacrament is suicide.

DALE CARNEGIE
American self-help evangelist
The expression a woman wears on her face is more important than the clothes she wears on her back.

JOHN CAVANAGH
British couturier
on no-bra fashions 1969
I consider it is better to be trussed up than flopping about, but I suppose it depends on the individual.

COCO CHANEL
French couturière 1967
Wearing her skirt half way up the thigh does not give a woman the advantage.

'Coco Chanel – Her Life, Her Secrets' by M. Haedrich 1971
Fashion is architecture – it is a matter of proportions.

Life 1957
Fashion is made to become unfashionable.

JEAN COCTEAU
French writer and film director
Harper's Bazaar
Fashion must be beautiful first and ugly afterwards. Art must be ugly first then beautiful afterwards.

N.Y. World Telegram 1960
Art produces ugly things which frequently become beautiful with time. Fashion, on the other hand, produces beautiful things which always become ugly in time.

ANDRE COURREGES
French couturier 1971
My collections are like a race circuit: they are testing a new product.

NOEL COWARD
British playwright 1966
I have not felt it necessary to be with it. I am all for staying in my place.

JOHN CROSBY
American writer, 1969
T-shirts are the going form of immortality.

LILY DACHE
American couturière
Woman's Home Companion 1955
Glamour is what makes a man ask for your telephone number. But it is also what makes a woman ask for the name of your dressmaker.

SALVADOR DALI
Spanish artist
quoted in 'In & Out: Debrett 1980–81' by Neil Mackwood 1980
The perfect woman must be haughty, but not too beautiful . . . she must be a slave to her clothes and her jewels.

RAY DAVIES
British rock musician
'Dedicated Follower of Fashion'
One week he's in polka-dots, the next week he's in stripes / 'Cos he's a dedicated follower of fashion. (Carlin Music)

CHRISTIAN DIOR
French couturier
Collier's 1955
My dream is to save (women) from nature.

When I opened my couture house I decided to dress only the most fashionable women from the first ranks of society.

J. R. DOUBE
Australian couturier 1972
I have called the priest type costume 'Ave' after Ave Maria; the other is 'Cardinale' after Claudia Cardinale, the actress.

JACQUES ESTOREL
French couturier 1970
For other designers fashion is drama, tragedy. For me it is a toy.

BRENDAN FRANCIS
What a man enjoys most about a woman's clothes are his fantasies of how she would look without them.

HALSTON (Roy Halston Frowick)
American couturier
Esquire 1975
You're as good as the people you dress, and you live by your record.

On China:
I think it's something when you can dress a whole nation in one thing.

SYDNEY J. HARRIS
American journalist
'Strictly Personal'
Almost every man looks more so in a belted trench-coat.

NORMAN HARTNELL
British couturier 1968
If I were a woman I wouldn't give a tinker's cuss for fashion's lordly dictates if they were unflattering to me.

SIR ROBERT HELPMANN
Australian choreographer 1970
You might as well be with it, even if you're a bit past it.

MARGAUX HEMINGWAY
American model 1976
I am totally a people person.

CALVIN KLEIN
American couturier
New York Times 1977
The best thing is to look natural, but it takes make-up to look natural.

JAMES LAVER
British fashion expert 1966
New clothes are always the cads – they have to push their way up.

The same dress is indecent ten years before its time, daring one year before its time, chic, being defined as contemporary seductiveness, in its time, dowdy three years after its time, hideous twenty years after its time, amusing thirty years after it time, romantic 100 years after its time and beautiful 150 years after its time.

JOHN LENNON &
PAUL McCARTNEY
British rock composers
'Eleanor Rigby'
Wearing a face that she keeps in a jar by the door. (Northern Songs)

LIN YUTANG
Chinese writer
Ladies Home Journal 1945
All women's dresses, in every age and country, are merely variations on the eternal struggle between the admitted desire to dress and unadmitted desire to undress.

SOPHIA LOREN
Italian film star 1966
Today a man can see practically the whole woman at a single glance. It's swallowing a meal at one mouthful.

LOUISE NEVELSON
American photographer
Metropolitan Museum of Art Bulletin 1967
Being 'well-dressed' is not a question of having expensive clothes or the 'right' clothes. I don't care if you're wearing rags, but they must suit you.

BARNETT NEWMAN
American artist
Women's clothes are painting and men's clothes are sculpture.

N. PARKER
Australian psychiatrist 1969
Gentlemen who wear moustaches are generally obsessive, psychopathic, impotent or have some other sexual problem.

MARY QUANT
British fashion designer
A woman is as young as her knee.

In the Seventies we shall move towards exposure and body cosmetics and certainly pubic hair, which we can now view on the cinema and stage, will become a fashion emphasis, although not necessarily blatant.

RON RANDALL
Australian actor
The Bulletin
People are going in for a more intelligent

look – beards and moustaches can give this.

CHARLES REVSON
American businessman
quoted in 'Fire & Ice' by A. Tobias
In the factory we make cosmetics; in the store we sell hope.

ELEANOR ROOSEVELT
American First Lady
on being American First Lady, New York Herald Tribune 1960
You will feel that you are no longer clothing yourself; you are dressing a public monument.

FRANCOISE SAGAN
French novelist
The Observer 1969
A dress has no meaning unless it makes a man want to take it off.

EUGENIA SHEPPARD
New York Herald Tribune
To call a fashion wearable is the kiss of death. No new fashion worth its salt is ever wearable.

EDITH SITWELL
British poet
'Why I Look As I Do'
Why not be oneself? That is the whole secret of a successful appearance. If one is a greyhound, why try to look like a Pekingese?

JOHN TAYLOR
British fashion journalist 1966
The man who wants to show what sex he is shouldn't wear clothes.

HUNTER S. THOMPSON
American journalist
Esquire 1971
We use clothes politically – they are our finest way of mocking power and authority.

PAUL VANCE & LEE POCKRISS
American pop composers
Song title 1960
Itsy Bitsy Teenie Weenie, Yellow Polka Dot Bikini.

DIANA VREELAND
American fashion journalist
quoted in Esquire 1965
You know, don't you, that the Bikini is only the most important thing since the Atom Bomb.

I've never thought of fashion as being anything but young, because when it is old, it's a compromise. Then it's no longer fashion, it's merchandise.

SHELLEY WINTERS
American film star
Sunday Times 1971
Plunging necklines attract more attention and cost less money.

Sleep

GEORGE ALLEN
American pro football coach
Leisure time is that five or six hours when you sleep at night.

W. H. AUDEN
British poet
New York Review of Books 1971
The trouble with dreams, of course, is that other people's are so boring.

BIFF KARDZ
British series of postcards
postcard 1981
The dream is a harsh taskmaster leading us to the stars but leaving us in the gutter of reality.

JOSEPH CAMPBELL
Time 1972
Myths are public dreams, dreams are private myths.

EDWARD DAHLBERG
American writer
New York Times 1967
The people who think they are happy should rummage through their dreams.

WILLIAM DEMENT
American psychiatrist
Newsweek 1959
Dreaming permits each and every one of us to be quietly and safely insane every night of our lives.

ERICH FROMM
American psychologist
'Man for Himself'
Sleep is often the only occasion in which man cannot silence his conscience; but the tragedy of it is that when we do hear our conscience speak in sleep, we cannot act, and that, when able to act, we forget what we knew in our dream.

BARBARA GRIZZUTI HARRISON
American writer
Ms 1973
Fantasies are more than substitutes for unpleasant realities, they are also dress rehearsals. All acts performed in the world begin in the imagination.

HENRY S. HASKINS
American writer
'Meditations in Wall Street'
Daydreams are the gaseous decomposition of true purpose.

FRAN LEBOWITZ
American journalist
'Metropolitan Life' 1978
I love sleep because it is both pleasant and safe to use. . . Sleep is death without the responsibility.

RENE MAGRITTE
Belgian artist
letter 1967
If the dream is a translation of waking life, waking life is also a translation of the dream.

LOGAN PEARSALL SMITH
American essayist
in 'The Faber Book of Aphorisms' 1964
How many of our daydreams would darken into nightmares were there any danger of their coming true.

BRAINS
Genius & Talent

WOODY ALLEN
American film star
quoted in 'Loose Talk' ed. Linda Botts 1980
The truth is, there have never been very many remarkable people around at any one time. Most are always leaning on the guy next to them – asking him what to do.

JEAN ANOUILH
French playwright
New York Times 1960
Talent is like a tap, while it is open one must write. Inspiration is a farce the poets have invented to give themselves importance.

NANCY ASTOR
British politician
quoted in 'The Wit of Women' ed. L. and M. Cowan 1969
It isn't the common man who is important. It is the uncommon man.

W. H. AUDEN
British poet
'The Dyer's Hand' 1962
The supreme masters have one trait in common with the childish scribbling mass, the vulgar curiosity of a police-court reporter.

It takes little talent to see what lies under one's nose, a good deal of it to know in which way to point that organ.

foreword to 'Markings' by Dag Hammarskjold
Geniuses are the luckiest of mortals because what they must do is the same as what they most want to do.

JAMES BALDWIN
American author
'Notes of a Native Son' 1958
Any writer, I suppose, feels that the world into which he was born is nothing less than a conspiracy against the cultivation of his talent – which attitude certainly has a great deal to support it. On the other hand, it is only because the world looks on his talent with such a frightening indifference that the artist is compelled to make his talent important.

BERNARD BERENSON
British art historian
'The Decline of Art'
We define genius as the capacity for productive reaction against one's training.

JOHN BERGER
British art critic
'A Painter of Our Times'
The genius bears the full weight of what is common and exists hundreds and thousands of times over.

GERALD BRENAN
British writer
'Thoughts In A Dry Season' 1978
Wisdom means keeping a sense of the fallibility of all our views and opinions, and of the uncertainty and instability of the things we most count on.

TRUMAN CAPOTE
American writer
'Music For Chameleons' 1980
When God hands you a gift, he also hands you a whip; and the whip is intended solely for self-flagellation.

Playboy 1968
Talent, and genius as well, is like a grain of pearl sand shifting about in the creative mind. A valued tormentor.

ALEXANDER CHASE
American journalist
Perspectives 1966
The banalities of a great man pass for wit.

LORD CLARK
British critic
in 'The Faber Book of Aphorisms' 1964
True perfection is achieved only by those who are prepared to destroy it. It is a by-product of greatness.

JEAN COCTEAU
French writer and film director
quoted in New York Review of Books 1971
Genius, like electricity, is not to be analysed.

RICHARD CRUTCHFIELD
American psychoanalyst
Think 1962
The truly independent person – in whom creative thinking is at its best – is someone who can accept society without denying himself.

LOUIS DANZ
'Dynamic Dissonance'
Genius must.

BOB DYLAN
American singer
I believe that instinct is what makes a genius a genius.

PIERRE EMMANUEL
(Noel Mathieu)
French writer
'Baudelaire'
Genius is that superior alchemy that changes the vices of nature into the elements of destiny.

PAUL ENGLE
American poet
'Poems in Praise' 1959
Wisdom is knowing when you can't be wise.

MAX ERNST
German painter
New York Times 1964
In simple, there are always great painters, there are always followers. Prefaces aren't necessary – the great temperament is born to execute great things.

MARTIN ESSLIN
Austrian critic
'The Theatre of the Absurd' 1961
It is a sign of real genius that it remains unspoilt by success.

FELIX FRANKFURTER
American lawyer
'Felix Frankfurter Reminisces' 1960
Anybody who is any good is different from anybody else.

R. BUCKMINSTER FULLER
American engineer
The Guardian 1970
It is my conviction from having watched a great many babies grow up that all of humanity is born a genius but then becomes de-geniused very rapidly by unfavourable circumstances and by the frustration of their extraordinary built-in capabilities. Everyone is specialised now. We couldn't be getting ourselves into worse trouble since we also learnt that biological species became extinct because they overspecialised. So, overspecialisation is the way to extinction. And society's all tied with specialisation. If nature had wanted you to be a specialist she'd have had you born with one eye with a microscope fastened to it.

ANDRE GIDE
French writer
'Les Nourritures Terrestres'
The wise man is astonished by anything.

JEAN-LUC GODARD
French film director
Esquire 1969
The important thing to know is how to distinguish who might have genius and who hasn't got it; to try, if one can, to define genius, or to explain it. There aren't many who try.

PAUL GOODMAN
American writer
Few great men could pass Personnel.

ROBERT GRAVES
British poet
'Difficult Questions, Easy Answers' 1972
Genius not only diagnoses the situation but supplies the answer.

ERNEST HELLO
American academic
'Life, Science & Art'
A great man who succeeded in being what little men desired him to be would have only one drawback – that of being like them.

L. P. HICKOK
American journalist
Genius is the highest type of reason, talent the highest type of understanding.

JOHN IRVING
American author
New Times 1979
Nobody is so clever that he knows what
he is doing all the time.

ELTON JOHN
British rock star
If you've got a mind-shattering talent,
you want a million dollars for it.

ERICA JONG
American writer
Ms 1972
Everyone has talent. What is rare is the
courage to follow the talent to the dark
place where it leads.

YOUSSUF KARSH
Armenian photographer
Time 1978
Great men are often lonely. But that
same loneliness is part of their ability to
create. Character, like a photograph, develops in darkness.

ARTHUR KOESTLER
British philosopher
The principle mark of genius is not perfection but originality, the opening of
new frontiers.

STANISLAW J. LEC
Polish poet
in 'The Faber Book of Aphorisms' 1964
The man who is a genius and doesn't
know it probably isn't.

CLAUDE LEVI-STRAUSS
French anthropologist
'Mythologiques I: Le Cru et Le Cuit' 1964
The wise man doesn't give the right an-
swers, he poses the right questions.

SIR ARCHIBALD McINDOE
British surgeon
*quoted in 'The Wit of Medicine' ed. L. and
M. Cowan 1972*
Skill is fine and genius is splendid, but
the right contacts are more valuable
than either.

NORMAN MAILER
American writer
'Writers at Work' 3rd series 1967
Nearly everything in the scheme of
things works to dull a first rate talent.

MARILYN MONROE
American film star
quoted in 'The First Ms Reader' 1972
A career is born in public, talent in
private.

JOSE ORTEGA Y GASSET
Spanish philosopher
*quoted in John W. Aldridge 'After the Lost
Generation' 1951*
Talent is but a subjective disposition
that is brought to bear upon certain material. The material is independent of
literary gifts; and when it is lacking, genius and talent are of no avail.

CESARE PAVESE
Italian novelist
in 'The Faber Book of Aphorisms' 1964
To be a genius is to achieve complete
possession of one's own experience,
body, rhythm and memories.

V. S. PRITCHETT
British critic
'The Mythmakers' 1979
Genius is a spiritual greed.

PATTI SMITH
American singer and poet
You take a chance when you put your
stakes on somebody else, like a horse
race it often pays, but sooner or later
you're gonna be left standing in the rain.
Genius is meant to peak and pull out or
be wiped out permanently.

JOHN STEINBECK
American writer
Genius is a little boy chasing a butterfly
up a mountain.

R. H. TAWNEY
British historian
'Equality'
Clever men are impressed in their differ-
ences from their fellows. Wise men are
conscious of their resemblance to them.

HUGH TREVOR-ROPER
British historian
'Men and Events'
The function of genius is not to give new
answers, but to pose new questions –
which time and mediocrity can solve.

FRANCOIS TRUFFAUT
French film director
Esquire 1970
We must doubt our talent; we must not doubt our inspiration.

NINETTE DE VALOIS
British dancer
Time 1960
You cannot create genius. All you can do is nurture it.

GORE VIDAL
American writer
London Weekend Television 1981
Wisdom is deepest platitude.

Having no talent is no longer enough.

WILLIAM CARLOS WILLIAMS
American writer
'Writers at Work' 3rd series 1967
What can any of us do with his talent but try to develop his vision, so that through frequent failures we may learn better what we have missed in the past.

BRIAN WILSON
American rock composer
I don't think I'm a genius. I believe the word genius only applies to people who can do things that other people can't do.

Education

ANONYMOUS
quoted in Hans Gaffron 'Resistance to Knowledge' 1970
An education enables you to earn more than an educator.

W. H. AUDEN
British poet
quoted in Daily Telegraph 1966
The aim of education is to induce the largest amount of neurosis that the individual can bear without cracking.

DESMOND BAGLEY
British writer
The Guardian 1972
The world is full of young men coming down from the universities with the world's greatest novel that no one wants to read. If a man is a fool, you don't train him out of being a fool by sending him to university. You merely turn him into a trained fool, ten times more dangerous.

JACQUES BARZUN
American academic
'Teacher in America'
The young man who is not a radical about something is a pretty poor risk for education.

DEREK BOK
American academic 1978
If you think education is expensive, try ignorance.

ERMA BOMBECK
American humorist 1978
Any college that would take your son he should be too proud to go to.

LORD BOOTHBY
British politician 1973
No one who had any sense has ever liked school.

JACOB BRONOWSKI
British scientist
'The Ascent of Man' 1975
It is important that students bring a certain ragamuffin barefoot irreverence to their studies; they are not here to worship what is known, but to question it.

JOHN MASON BROWN
American essayist
Publishers Weekly 1958
. . . the best purpose of education: not to be frightened by the best, but to treat it as part of daily life.

PAUL CHAMBERS
British chairman of ICI
The Observer 1964
Life at a university, with its intellectual and inconclusive discussions at a post-graduate level is on the whole a bad training for the real world. Only men of very strong character surmount this handicap.

LORD CLARK
British critic 1974
All intellectuals complain about their schooldays. This is ridiculous. The things that happen to them are nothing compared to the initiation rites of the Australian aboriginal and Indonesian people, nothing at all.

QUENTIN CRISP
British writer
'How To Become A Virgin' 1981
Education is a mistake. Cluttering one's skull with facts about any subject other than oneself I hold to be a waste of time . . . Being well-informed is but a stone's throw from being boring and stones will be thrown.

NORMAN DOUGLAS
British author
'How About Europe'
Education is a state controlled manufactory of echoes.

WILL DURANT
American historian
quoted in National Enquirer 1980
Education is a progressive discovery of our own ignorance.

ROBERT FROST
American poet
Reader's Digest 1960
Education is the ability to listen to almost anything without losing your temper or your self-confidence.

Quote 1961
Education doesn't change life much. It just lifts trouble to a higher plane of regard . . . College is a refuge from hasty judgement.

CARDINAL HEENAN
British clergyman
quoted in 'The Wit of the Church' ed. M. Bateman and S. Stenning 1967
Two A-levels and you're an intellectual today.

H. W. E. HIGGINS
Australian public schoolboy 1969
If a boy knows some fellows from state schools, he doesn't look down on them. He treats them as normal. Perhaps in groups he looks down on them, but not individually.

IVAN ILLICH
American philosopher
New York Review of Books 1971
School removes things from everyday life by labelling them educational tools.

Schools are designed on the assumption that there is a secret to everything in life; that the quality of life depends on knowing that secret, that secrets can be known only in orderly succession; and that only teachers can properly reveal those secrets.

School . . . is the major component of the system of consumer production which is becoming more complex and specialised and bureaucratized. School is necessary to produce the habits and expectations of the managed consumer society.

CHARLES F. KETTERING
The difference between intelligence and education is this: intelligence will make you a good living.

KARL KRAUS
German artist
'Karl Kraus' by Harry Zohn
Stupidity is an elemental force for which no earthquake is a match.

WANDA LANDOWSKA
Polish musician 1950
The most beautiful thing in the world is, precisely, the conjunction of learning and inspiration. Oh, the passion for research and the joy of discovery!

ROBERT MORLEY
British actor and wit
Show me a man who has enjoyed his

schooldays and I'll show you a bully and a bore.

MALCOLM MUGGERIDGE
British journalist
The Observer 1966
Education, the great mumbo jumbo and fraud of the age purports to equip us to live and is prescribed as a universal remedy for everything from juvenile delinquency to premature senility. For the most part it only serves to enlarge stupidity, inflate conceit, enhance credulity and put those subjected to it at the mercy of brain-washers with printing presses, radio and television at their disposal.

Chronicles of Wasted Time Vol 1, 1978
Public schoolboys, whatever their particular school . . . had a language of their own . . . ways and attitudes which they took for granted but which were foreign to me: for instance their acceptance of sodomy as more or less normal behaviour.

PROFESSOR NEIL
Australian academic 1968
Any education worthy of the name is bound to be dangerous.

LAURENCE J. PETER
Canadian educator
'Peter's Quotations' 1977
Education is a method whereby one acquires a higher grade of prejudices.

NATHAN PUSEY
American academic
Time 1954
The true business of liberal education is greatness.

RAYMOND QUENEAU
French historian
'Présentation de l'Encyclopédie'
Learning to learn is to know how to navigate in a forest of facts, ideas and theories, a proliferation of constantly changing items of knowledge . . . to know what to ignore, but at the same time not rejecting innovation and research.

R. A. READ
Australian educationalist 1968
Education is the only human enterprise based on the confident anticipation of failure.

PETE SEEGER
American singer
in 'Loose Talk' ed. Linda Botts 1980
Do you know the difference between education and experience? Education is when you read the fine print; Experience is what you get when you don't.

AARON SISKIND
American photographer
Minicam Photography 1945
As the saying goes – we see in terms of our education. We look at the world and see what we have learned to believe in there. We have been conditioned to expect.

B. F. SKINNER
American behaviourist
New Scientist 1964
Education is what survives when what has been learnt has been forgotten.

LILLIAN SMITH
American writer
Redbook 1969
Education is a private matter between the person and the world of knowledge and experience, and has little to do with school or college.

JOSEPH STALIN
Russian leader
quoted 1953
Education is a weapon, whose effects depend on who holds it in his hands and at whom it is aimed.

GLORIA STEINEM
American feminist
New York Times 1971
The first problem for all of us, men and women, is not to learn, but to unlearn.

R. H. TAWNEY
British historian
quoted in New Statesman 1960
British education is neither venerable like a college nor popular like a public house. It is merely indispensable, like a pillar box.

PETER USTINOV
British actor and wit
Time & Tide
British education is probably the best in the world if you can survive it. If you can't there is nothing left for you but the diplomatic corps.

ALFRED NORTH WHITEHEAD
British philosopher
'The Aims of Education'
In the conditions of modern life the rule is absolute – the race which does not value trained intelligence is doomed.

Philosophy

GEORGE ABBOTT
American theatrical producer
Daily Mail 1965
The great temptation is to have an alibi.

CONRAD AIKEN
American poet
New York Herald Tribune 1969
There are no final solutions. Things may have no meaning. We have to face that possibility all the time. Everything is, in a sense, reversible.

EDWARD ALBEE
American playwright
'Zoo Story'
I have learned that neither kindness or cruelty by themselves, or independent of each other, create any effect beyond themselves.

BROOKS ATKINSON
American essayist
'Once Around the Sun' 1951
The most fatal illusion is the settled point of view. Since life is growth and motion, a fixed point of view kills anybody who has one.

W. H. AUDEN
British poet
Esquire 1970
There is a great deal of difference in believing something still, and believing it again.

A. J. AYER
British philosopher
Sunday Times 1962
Why should you mind being wrong if someone can show you that you are?

FRANCIS BACON
British artist
The Observer 1967
Anything that exists is a violent thing. The existence of the rose is violence.

JAMES BALDWIN
American author
'Nobody Knows My Name' 1962
Be careful what you set your heart upon – for it will surely be yours.

SAMUEL BECKETT
Irish author
quoted in 'Beckett' by A. Alvarez 1973
Habit is a compromise, effected between the individual and his environment, or, between the individual and his own organic eccentricities, the guarantee of a dull inviolability, the lightning conductor of his existence. Habit is the ballast that chains the dog to his vomit. Breathing is habit, Life is habit.

MAX BEERBOHM
British author
Good sense about trivialities is better than nonsense about things that matter.

GERALD BRENAN
British writer
'Thoughts In A Dry Season' 1978
The things we are best acquainted with are often the things we lack. This is because we have spent so much time thinking of them.

HELEN GURLEY BROWN
American journalist
Esquire 1970
Self help . . . that is my whole credo.

You cannot sit around like a cupcake asking other people to eat you up and discover your great sweetness and charm. You've got to make yourself more cupcakeable all the time, so that you're a better cupcake to be gobbled up.

MARTIN BUBER
Israeli philosopher
in 'The Faber Book of Aphorisms' 1964
Genuine responsibility exists only where there is real responding.

CHARLES BUKOWSKI
American writer
'Notes of a Dirty Old Man' 1969
Fun and danger hardly put margarine on the toast or fed the cat. You give up toast and end up eating the cat.

It all begins and ends with the mailbox, and when they find a way to remove mailboxes, much of our suffering will end.

JAMES CAAN
American film star
Playboy 1976
Sometimes it seems like that is the choice – either kick ass or kiss ass.

ALBERT CAMUS
French writer
'The Rebel' 1951
The climax of every tragedy lies in the deafness of its heroes.

'The Fall' 1956
Somebody has to have the last word. If not, every argument could be opposed by another and we'd never have done with it.

LUIS CERNUDA
Spanish poet
'No Decia Palabras'
Desire is a question to which no one has an answer.

RAY CHARLES
American singer
My voice is like a house I'm keeping up. You know, you don't just build a house and do nothing else to it. You're always washing the windows, painting, adding a room.

E. M. CIORAN
French philosopher
'The Fall Into Time' 1971
All that shimmers on the surface of the world, all that we call interesting, is the fruit of inebriation and ignorance.

SIR KENNETH CLARK
British critic
'Civilisation – A Personal View' 1970
I believe that order is better than chaos, creation better than destruction. I prefer gentleness to violence, forgiveness to vendetta. . . I think knowledge is preferable to ignorance and I am sure that human sympathy is more valuable than ideology. . . I believe in courtesy, the ritual by which we avoid hurting other people's feelings by satisfying our own egos. And I think we should remember we are part of a great whole, which for convenience we call nature. All living things are our brothers and sisters. Above all I believe in the God-given genius of certain individuals, and I value a society that makes their existence possible.

COLETTE
French novelist
last words 1954
To reach completion is to return to one's starting point. My instinctive bent which delights in curves and spheres and circles.

BOB DYLAN
American singer
I just try to understand that tomorrow is another day.

WERNER ERHARD
(John Paul Rosenberg)
founder of est 1970
What I recognised is that you can't put it together. It's already together and what you have to do is experience it being together.

FIRESIGN THEATRE
American satirists
Album Title 1970
How Can You Be In Two Places At Once When You're Not Anywhere At All?

ERICH FROMM
American psychologist
'Man For Himself'
Understanding a person does not mean condoning; it only means that one does not accuse him as if one were God or a judge placed above him.

ROBERT FROST
American poet
'The Constant Symbol' 1946
Strongly spent is synonymous with kept.

ANDRE GIDE
French writer
'Pretexts'
Complete possession is proved only by giving. All you are unable to give possesses you.

MARTHA GRAHAM
American dancer
The gesture is the thing truly expressive of the individual – as we think, so we will act.

GERMAINE GREER
Australian feminist
Playboy 1972
Pigs may like honey, but that doesn't stop it being sweet.

ROLF HOCHHUTH
German playwright
'The Representative' 1966
If your house is on fire the first thing to do is put it out. You can argue about who started it later.

ALDOUS HUXLEY
British writer
'Letters of Aldous Huxley' 1971
Every ceiling, when reached, becomes a floor, upon which one walks as a matter of course and prescriptive right.

MICK JAGGER
British rock star
I don't continually question my reason to live. It's just a state of being. The real question is what you're doing with the living you're doing, and what you want to do with that living.

MICK JAGGER &
KEITH RICHARD
British rock composers

'You Can't Always Get What You Want'
You can't always get what you want / But if you try sometimes / You might find / You get what you need.
(Essex Music)

LYNDON B. JOHNSON
American president
Doing what's right isn't the problem. It's knowing what's right.

JAN KOTT
Dutch historian
Fate is non-awareness.

JACQUES LACAN
French psychoanalyst
'The Insistence of the Letter in the Unconscious' 1957
The discourse of the unconscious is structured like a language.

STANISLAW J. LEC
Polish poet
in 'The Faber Book of Aphorisms' 1964
Some like to understand what they believe in. Others like to believe in what they understand.

LITTLE RICHARD
American rock star
It's not the size of the ship, it's the size of the waves.

ROGER MARTIN DU GARD
French writer
'Letters to André Gide'
Thought only starts with doubt.

ANDRE MAUROIS
French writer
'Climats'
Our wishes and our destiny are almost always opposed to each other.

HENRY MILLER
American writer
'The World of Sex' 1957
All that matters is that the miraculous becomes the norm.

'Big Sur & the Oranges of Hieronymus Bosch' 1956
If we are always arriving and departing, it is also true that we are eternally anchored. One's destination is never a

place but rather a new way of looking at things.

HUEY P. NEWTON
American radical 1973
I am a student of the universe and never really the master. Once you think you can't lose an argument, once you think you can't be corrected, then you're a fool.

TED NUGENT
American rock musician
I don't think about deep things. If you can't take a bite out of it it doesn't exist.

FLOYD PATTERSON
American boxer 1972
You aim at the impossible to get the unusual.

SAM PECKINPAH
American film director
Playboy 1972
All I want is to enter my home justified.

GEORGES POULET
French writer
'Le Distance Intérieure'
To understand is almost the opposite of existing.

MAN RAY
French photographer
quoted in 'Photographers on Photography' ed. N. Lyons 1966
An effort impelled by desire must also have an automatic or subconscious energy to aid its realisation.

SATYA SAI BABA
Indian guru 1975
Man's many desires are like the small metal coins he carries about in his pocket. The more he has the more they weight him down.

VITTORIO DE SICA
Italian film producer
There is always an excuse, even for the criminal.

ALDO VAN EYCK
Dutch architect
Switch on the stars before the fuses go.

JOHN WAYNE
American film star
Playboy 1971
Tomorrow is the most important thing in life. Comes in to us at midnight very clean. It's perfect when it arrives and it puts itself in our hands and hopes we've learnt something from yesterday.

ORSON WELLES
American film director
Playboy 1967
We are made out of oppositions; we live between two poles . . . you don't reconcile the poles, you just recognise them.

SHIRLEY WILLIAMS
British politician 1974
There are hazards in anything one does, but there are greater hazards in doing nothing.

LUDWIG WITTGENSTEIN
German philosopher
Everything that can be thought at all can be thought clearly. Everything that can be said at all can be said clearly. But not everything that can be thought can be said.

Thought

HANNAH ARENDT
American writer
in 'The Faber Book of Aphorisms' 1964
Ideas, as distinguished from events, are never unprecedented.

A. J. AYER
British philosopher
The Guardian 1963
Philosophers are intellectual trouble-makers. They are reluctant to take

things at their face-value. They set out to disturb complacency. Ignorance is not altogether bliss, and in the field of learning, as in politics, it is only because some people are prepared to make trouble that anything of importance ever gets done.

The Listener 1978
The right method of philosophy is to wait till somebody says something metaphysical, then show him that it is nonsense.

SIR ISAIAH BERLIN
British philosopher
Sunday Times 1962
The goal of philosophy is always the same – to assist men to understand themselves and thus operate in the open and not wildly, in the dark.

The Listener 1978
Philosophers are adults who persist in asking childish questions.

MAX BORN
German scientist
'Autobiography'
I am now convinced that theoretical physics is actual philosophy.

Intellect distinguishes between the possible and the impossible; reason distinguishes between the sensible and the senseless. Even the possible can be senseless.

ALBERT CAMUS
French writer
There is only one truly philosophical problem – and that is suicide.

ELIAS CANETTI
Bulgarian writer
Argument is the hereditary misfortune of thought.

RAYMOND CHANDLER
American novelist
letter to Charles W. Morton 1947
Ideas are poison. The more you reason the less you create.

E. M. CIORAN
French philosopher
in 'The Faber Book of Aphorisms' 1964
A philosophical fashion catches on like a gastronomical fashion – one can no

more refute an idea than a sauce.
'The Temptation to Exist' 1956
The only free mind is one that, pure of all intimacy with beings or objects, plies its own vacuity.
'Syllogismes de l'amertume' 1952
The history of ideas is the history of the grudges of solitary men.

RENE DAUMAL
French philosopher
'A Night of Serious Drinking' 1980
The philosopher is the cartographer of human life.

EVERETT DIRKSEN
American politician
nominating Barry Goldwater for the Presidency, 1964 . . .
There is no force so powerful as an idea whose time has come.

GOSTA CARL HENRIK EHRENSVARD
Danish scientist
'Man on Another World' 1965
Consciousness will always be one degree above comprehensibility.

WALTER ELLIOT
Lord High Commisioner of the Church of Scotland 1957
Force is not to be used to its uttermost. Nor is thought to be pushed to its logical conclusion.

MAX ERNST
German painter
quoted in New York Times 1964
All good ideas arrive by chance.

WILLIAM FEATHER
American businessman
'The Business of Life' 1949
An idea isn't worth much until a man is found who has the energy and ability to make it work.

MICHEL FOUCAULT
French writer
'Les mots et les choses' 1966
All modern thought is penetrated by the law of thinking of the unthought of.

ROBERT FROST
American poet
An idea is a feat of association.

J. K. GALBRAITH
American economist
Sunday Times 1970
There is nothing so futile as having the right ideas and getting no attention.

'The Affluent Society' 1958
It is a far, far better thing to have a firm anchor in nonsense than to put out on the troubled seas of thought.

JOHN W. GARDNER
American writer
Forbes 1977
The society which scorns excellence in plumbing because it is a humble activity and tolerates shoddiness in philosophy because it is an exalted activity will have neither good plumbing nor good philosophy. Neither its pipes nor its theories will hold water.

THOMAS FAVILL GLADWIN
American anthropologist 1970
No style of thinking will survive which cannot produce a usable product when survival is at stake.

PETER GOLDMARK
American inventor
An inventive idea without development is quite useless.

GUNTER GRASS
German novelist
'Speak Out' 1969
Reason stands helpless in a world of increasing adjustment.

SYDNEY J. HARRIS
American journalist
'Leaving the Surface' 1968
Any philosophy that can be put 'in a nutshell' belongs there.

EUGENE IONESCO
French playwright
It isn't what people think that is important, but the reason they think what they think.

HOLBROOK JACKSON
British writer
'Platitudes in the Making'
As soon as an idea is accepted it is time to reject it.

MURRAY KEMPTON
American journalist
'Part of Our Time' 1955
To say that an idea is fashionable is to say, I think, that it has been adulterated to a point where it is hardly an idea at all.

ARTHUR KOESTLER
British philosopher
The Observer 1965
All coherent thinking is playing a game, with a fixed set of axioms and rules, whether we are aware of them or not.

JOSEPH WOOD KRUTCH
American essayist
Logic is the art of going wrong with confidence.

STANISLAW J. LEC
Polish poet
'Unkempt Thoughts' 1962
Many tried to create the philosopher's stone by petrifying thoughts.

CLAUDE LEVI-STRAUSS
French anthropologist
'World on the Wane' 1961
To promote private preoccupations to the rank of philosophical problems is dangerous and may end in a kind of shop-girl's philosophy.

C. S. LEWIS
British writer
'Miracles' 1947
If any thought is valid, an external, self-existent reason must exist and must be the source of my own imperfect and intermittent rationality.

GEORGE LOIS
American art director
'The Art of Advertising' 1977
An idea which is six years ahead of its time is a bad idea.

MATZ'S MAXIM
in 'Murphy's Law Book Two' by Arthur Bloch 1980
A conclusion is the place where you got tired of thinking.

MAURICE MERLEAU-PONTY
French philosopher
'Eloge de la philosophie'
Philosophy is not an illusion. It is the algebra of history.

LEONARD MICHAELS
New York Times 1971
Reasons are whores.

JONATHAN MILLER
British doctor and writer
Plays & Players 1970
Ideas are the real substance of human life. Ideas guide our actions and even control our movements. It is just as well to put them in order first and then to display their anatomy.

HENRY MOORE
British sculptor
There's a right size for every idea.

STIRLING MOSS
British racing driver 1961
It is necessary to relax your muscles when you can. Relaxing your brain is fatal.

IRIS MURDOCH
British writer
The Listener 1978
Philosophy . . . means looking at things which one takes for granted and suddenly seeing that they are very odd indeed.

KATHERINE NOTT
British writer
in 'Contemporary Novelists' 1976
If philosophy interferes with life, give up philosophy.

ROBERT M. PIRSIG
American author
in 'Loose Talk' ed. Linda Botts 1980
In the Far East the master is considered a living Buddha, but in Minneapolis they wonder why he doesn't have a job.

ROBERT RAUSCHENBERG
American artist
The Guardian 1965
Thinking is our greatest sport.

BRANCH RICKEY
American baseball manager 1950
He that will not reason is a bigot. He that cannot reason is a fool. And he that dares not reason is a slave.

JOHN RUSSELL
British critic
New York Times 1979
An idea is the most exciting thing there is.

PROFESSOR WILLIAM B. SHOCKLEY
American inventor and eugenics theorist
Esquire 1973
The half baked ideas of people are better than the ideas of half baked people.

T. V. SMITH
British rock musician
You can think and still be a positive force.

SAUL STEINBERG
American artist
'Cogito' Drawings caption
I think, therefore Descartes is.

IGOR STRAVINSKY
Russian composer
To be deprived of art and left alone with philosophy is close to hell.

ARCHBISHOP TEMPLE
British clergyman
in 'The Wit of the Church' ed. M. Bateman and S. Stenning 1967
Philosophers rule the world – five hundred years after they are dead.

KENNETH TYNAN
British critic
Sunday Times 1975
I hate people who are wise *during* the event.

KURT VONNEGUT JR.
American writer
Playboy 1973
Thinking doesn't seem to help very much. The human brain is too high powered to have many practical uses in this particular universe.

EVELYN WAUGH
British novelist
letter to John Betjeman in 'The Letters of Evelyn Waugh' ed. Mark Amory 1980
Logic is simply the architecture of human reason.

ALFRED NORTH WHITEHEAD
British philosopher
'An Introduction to Mathematics' 1948
It is a safe rule to apply that, when a mathematical or philsophical author writes with a misty profundity, he is talking nonsense.

HEATHCOTE WILLIAMS
British playwright
'The Speakers' 1964
Reason is an emotion for the sexless.

COLIN WILSON
British writer
'Declaration' 1958
If an idea cannot be expressed in terms of people, it is a sure sign it is irrelevant to the real problems of life.

Sunday Express 1970
Ideas are what matter. Living in itself strikes me as a bloody bore.

LUDWIG WITTGENSTEIN
German philosopher
Philosophy is not a theory but an activity.

Philosophy is language idling.

quoted in Esquire 1970
Philosophy simply puts everything before us and neither explains nor deduces anything. Since everything lies open to view, there is nothing to explain. For what is hidden, for example, is of no interest to us.

FRANK LLOYD WRIGHT
American architect
'The Future of Architecture' 1953
An idea is salvation by imagination.

ELEMIRE ZOLLA
Italian writer
'The Eclipse of the Intellectuals' 1971
Stupidity consists in wanting to come to a conclusion.

Knowledge

ARTHUR ADAMOV
Playwright
The Observer 1962
The only thing to know is how to use your neuroses.

EDWARD DE BONO
British writer
Nova 1969
Perhaps there is no valid distinction between being clever and being well-informed. The two are so often confused as to be indistinguishable. In many situations information is so great a part of effectiveness that without information a really clever person cannot get started. With information a much less clever person can get very far.

Kova 1968
The trouble is that clever people are not

clever enough and stupid people are not stupid enough. It is not always easy to distinguish between the two. Intelligence is something that is better recognised than defined.

JACOB BRONOWSKI
British scientist
'The Ascent of Man' 1975
Human knowledge is personal and responsible, an unending adventure at the edge of uncertainty.

CHARLES BUKOWSKI
American writer
'Notes of a Dirty Old Man' 1969
Knowledge without follow-through is worse than no knowledge at all. Because if you're guessing and it doesn't work, you can just say 'shit, the gods are against me'. But if you *know* and don't

do, you've got attics and dark halls in your mind to walk up and down in and wander about.

Knowledge is knowing as little as possible.

WILLIAM S. BURROUGHS
American writer
'Writers at Work' 3rd series
Anything that can be done chemically can be done in other ways – that is, if we have sufficient knowledge of the processes involved.

ELIAS CANETTI
Bulgarian writer 1945
All knowledge has a touch of the puritanical – it provides words with a moral.

JOYCE CARY
British novelist
'Art & Reality' 1958
It is the tragedy of the world that no one knows what he doesn't know; and the less a man knows, the more sure he is that he knows everything.

LORD DAVID CECIL
British critic
The first step to knowledge is to know that we are ignorant.

CLAUDE CHABROL
French film director
Foolishness is infinitely more fascinating than intelligence, infinitely more profound. Intelligence has limits, while foolishness has none.

SIR WINSTON CHURCHILL
British statesman
It is a good thing for an uneducated man to read books of quotations.

NOEL COWARD
Playwright
'Present Indicative'
My body has certainly wandered a good deal, but I have an uneasy suspicion that my mind has not wandered enough.

QUENTIN CRISP
British author
'The Naked Civil Servant' 1968
To know all is not to forgive all. It is to despise everybody.

ALBERT EINSTEIN
German physicist
Imagination is more important than knowledge.

HANEEF A. FATMI & R. W. YOUNG
American scientists
in Nature 1970
Intelligence is that faculty of mind, by which order is perceived in a situation previously considered disordered.

ENRICO FERMI
Italian physicist
It is no good to try to stop knowledge going forward. Ignorance is never better than knowledge.

Whatever Nature has in store for mankind, unpleasant as it may be, men must accept, for ignorance is never better than knowledge.

LORD FISHER
British clergyman
quoted in 'The Wit of the Church' ed. M. Bateman and S. Stenning 1967
The world would be a much happier place if people did not know so much. The world is full of people suffering from acute indigestion – unable to digest the knowledge given to them.

SIR THEODORE FOX
British medical journalist 1965
We shall have to learn to refrain from doing things merely because we know how to do them.

J. K. GALBRAITH
American economist
'The Affluent Society' 1958
The enemy of conventional wisdom is not ideas but the march of events.

WALTER GROPIUS
German architect
The Observer 1956
The human mind is like an umbrella – it functions best when open.

HENRY S. HASKINS
American writer
'Meditations in Wall Street'
Conclusions are usually consolidated guesses.

JACQUETTA HAWKES
British archaeologist
New Statesman 1957
The only inequalities that matter begin in the mind. It is not income levels, but differences in mental equipment that keep people apart, breed feelings of inferiority.

ALDOUS HUXLEY
British writer
There is no virtue in not knowing what can be known.

CLIVE JAMES
Australian critic
The Observer 1977
Stupidity is mainly just a lack of capacity to take things in.

C. G. JUNG
Swiss psychoanalyst
'Memories, Dreams and Reflections' 1962
Man's task is to become conscious of the contents that press upwards from the unconscious. . . As far as we can discern, the sole purpose of human existence is to kindle a light in the darkness of mere being.

ARTHUR KOESTLER
British philosopher
'Bricks to Babel' 1981
Understand all – forgive yourself nothing.

Sunday Times 1965
Our perceptions of the world are corrected by our knowledge.

LUCIEN LEFEBVRE
French writer
'Combats pour l'histoire'
To understand is to complicate.

ARNOLD LOBEL
American writer
'Fables' 1980
Knowledge will not always take the place of simple observation.

WALTER MONDALE
American politician 1978
If you are sure you understand everything that is going on, you are hopelessly confused.

EDWARD R. MURROW
American broadcaster
on Vietnam
Anyone who isn't confused really doesn't understand the situation.

BERTRAND RUSSELL
British philosopher
quoted in The Listener 1964
What men really want is not knowledge but certainty.

ALBERT SCHWEITZER
German mathematician
quoted in The Listener 1962
Today thought gets no help from science. Scientific knowledge may be allied with an entirely unreflecting view of the universe. Our age has discovered how to divorce knowledge from thought, with the result that we have indeed a science that is free, but hardly any science left which reflects.

GLORIA STEINEM
American feminist
quoted in Writers Digest 1974
Intelligence at the service of poor instinct is really dangerous.

ADLAI STEVENSON
American politician 1952
If we value the pursuit of knowledge, we must be free to follow wherever that search may lead us. The free mind is no barking dog, to be tethered on a ten-foot chain.

ALBERT SZENT-GYORGYI
American scientist
Science 1964
Knowledge is a sacred cow, and my problem will be how we can milk her while keeping clear of her horns.

GORE VIDAL
American writer
New York Times 1978
The brain that doesn't feed itself, eats itself.

ORSON WELLES
American film director
Playboy 1967
What a normal, intelligent person can't learn – if he's genuinely alive and honestly curious – isn't really worth learning.

DAME REBECCA WEST
British writer
quoted in 'Rebecca West: Artist and Thinker'
by Peter Wolfe
Man does not want to know. When he knows very little he plays with the possibilities of knowledge, but when he finds that the pieces he has been putting together are going to spell out the answer he is frightened and he throws them in every direction; and another civilisation falls.

RAYMOND WILLIAMS
British academic
'Culture & Society' 1958
The human crisis is always a crisis of understanding. What we genuinely understand we can do.

YEVGENY YEVTUSHENKO
Russian poet
Playboy 1972
Curiosity enriches us, but it also destroys concentration.

FRANK ZAPPA
American rock musician
The Guardian 1968
It gets harder the more you know. Because the more you find out the uglier everything seems.

Truth

EDWARD ALBEE
American playwright
'The Death of Bessie Smith' 1959
I am sick of the disparity between things as they are and as they should be. I'm tired. I'm tired of the truth and I'm tired of lying about the truth.

W. H. AUDEN
British poet
Esquire 1970
You must learn to choose the truth before aesthetic preferences.

C. E. AYRES
'Science, the False Messiah'
A little inaccuracy saves a world of explanation.

SAUL BELLOW
American writer
'Writers at Work' 3rd series 1967
There may be some truths which are, after all, our friends in the universe.

JOHN BERGER
British art critic
The Observer 1963
The truth is that work becomes great only by virtue of the experience. The effect it has on those who experience it. Art is something that happens to people.

NIELS BOHR
Danish scientist
The opposite of a correct statement is a false statement. But the opposite of a profound truth may well be another profound truth.

. . . two sorts of truth: trivialities, where opposites are obviously absurd, and profound truths, recognised by the fact that the opposite is also a profound truth.

GEORGES BRAQUE
French painter
'Le Jour et la Nuit'
It is always necessary to have two ideas – the one to destroy the other.

'Pensées sur l'Art'
The truth exists, only fictions are invented.

JACOB BRONOWSKI
British scientist
The Listener 1952
For most of us the truth is no longer a

part of our minds; it has become a special product for experts.

'The Ascent of Man' 1975
There is no absolute knowledge . . . all information is imperfect. We have to treat it with humility.

LENNY BRUCE
American comedian
The what should be never did exist, but people keep trying to live up to it. There is no 'what should be', there is only what is.

RICHARD H. BUBE
American physicist
Time 1973
One of the most pernicious falsehoods ever to be almost universally accepted is that the scientific method is the only reasonable way to truth.

EDWARD BURRA
British painter
The Guardian 1973
Truth lies in a pit, at the bottom of a well.

ELIAS CANETTI
Bulgarian writer
Do not believe those that always speak the truth.

LOUIS-FERDINAND CELINE
French writer
'Semmelweis'
In the history of time life is just one ecstasy. The truth is death.

SIR WINSTON CHURCHILL
British statesman
in 'Murphy's Law' by Arthur Bloch 1979
Man will occasionally stumble over the truth, but most of the time he will pick himself up and continue on.

CYRIL CONNOLLY
British critic
'The Unquiet Grave' 1945
Truth is a river that is always splitting up into arms that reunite. Islanded between the arms the inhabitants argue for a lifetime as to which is the main river.

WALTER CRONKITE
American TV newscaster
Playboy 1973
In seeking truth you have to get both sides of a story.

DR. A. POWELL DAVIES 1959
The world is too dangerous for anything but the truth; too small for anything but brotherhood.

MICHEL DEGUY
French writer
'Fragment du cadastre'
The truth found in a work of art is the universal truth of a unique object.

DENG XIAOPING
Chinese leader
maxim, 1979
Practice is the only norm for verifying truth.

GEORGES DUHAMEL
French writer
'Le Notaire du Havre'
Error is the rule. Truth is an accident of error.

ALBERT EINSTEIN
German physicist
Whoever undertakes to set himself up as a judge in the field of truth and knowledge is shipwrecked by the laughter of the Gods.

PAUL ELDRIDGE
American writer
'Horn of Glass'
The nearest approach to immortality for any truth is by its becoming a platitude.

FINAGLE'S CREED
in 'The Official Rules' by Paul Dickson 1978
Science is truth; don't be misled by facts.

GERALD FORD
American president 1976
Truth means not having to guess what a candidate means.
1973
Truth is the glue that holds governments together. Compromise is the oil that makes governments go.

MOHANDAS K. GANDHI
Indian leader
'Non-Violence in Peace & War' 1948
Truth never damages a cause that is just.

ANDRE GIDE
French writer
'So Be It' 1959
Believe those who are seeking the truth; doubt those who find it.

JEAN-LUC GODARD
French film director
'Deux Ou Trois Choses . . .'
One should speak as if one were quoting the truth.

CLIVE JAMES
Australian critic
The Observer 1978
Decency means nothing if it is not vulgarised. Nor can the truth be passed on without being simplified.

KARL JASPERS
philosopher
quoted in New York Review of Books 1971
The man who will not act except in total righteousness achieves nothing. He does not enter the path of progress and he is not true because he is not real . . . the man who seeks to be true must run the risk of being mistaken, of putting himself in the wrong.

JOHN F. KENNEDY
American president 1963
We must never forget that art is not a form of propaganda, it is a form of truth.

DOROTHEA LANGE
American photographer
in 'Photographers on Photography' ed. N. Lyons 1966
On my darkroom door for many years I had posted the words of Francis Bacon: The contemplation of things as they are, without substitution or imposture, without error or confusion, is in itself a nobler thing than a whole harvest of invention.

PAUL LEAUTAUD
French writer
'Passe-Temps'
Is there anything more provoking than those honest folk who won't stop talking about their honesty? Look at the rogues, who keep quiet about their roguery.

PERCY WYNDHAM LEWIS
British artist
'Rude Assignment' 1950
Wherever there is objective truth, there is satire.

JOHN C. LILLY
American biologist
In the province of the mind, what one believes to be true either is true or becomes true.

MARY McCARTHY
American writer
The New Yorker 1958
There are no new truths, but only truths that have not been recognised by those who have perceived them without noticing.

RUTH McKENNEY
American writer
Man has no nobler function than to defend the truth.

NORMAN MAILER
American writer
'Writers at Work' 3rd series 1967
One may not have written it well enough for others to know, but you're in love with truth when you discover it at the point of a pencil. That, in and by itself, is one of the few rare pleasures in life.

HERBERT MARCUSE
German philosopher
The Listener 1978
In art, literature and music insights and truths are expressed which cannot be communicated in ordinary language and that with these truths, often an entirely new dimension is opened, which is either repressed or tabooed in reality: namely, the image of human existence and of nature no longer confined within the norms of the repressive reality principle, but really striving for their fulfilment and gratification, even at the price of death and catastrophe.

FRANCOIS MAURIAC
French writer
'Bloc-Notes'
The artist is a liar, but art is the truth.

DR. KARL MENINGER
American pyschiatrist
'A Psychiatrist's World' 1959
One of the most untruthful things possible . . . is a collection of facts, because they can be made to appear so many different ways.

MALCOLM MUGGERIDGE
British journalist
The Observer 1968
About money and sex is it impossible to be truthful ever, one's ego is too involved.

REV. DR. EDWARD NORMAN
British academic
Reith Lecturer 1978
Fortunately, truth does not cease just because people give up believing it.

LORD OLIVIER
British actor
The difference between the actual truth and the illusion of truth is what you are about to learn. You will not finish learning it until you are dead.

MAX PLANCK
German physicist
'Autobiography' 1949
A new scientific truth does not triumph by convincing its opponents and making them see the light, but rather because its opponents eventually die, and a new generation grows up that is familiar with it.

RICHARD PRYOR
American comedian 1979
I think the truth keeps you alive and young in your heart and your mind, where it counts.

PIERS PAUL READ
British author
The Observer 1981
Truth is always duller than fiction.

JEAN-PAUL SARTRE
French philosopher
'The Words' 1964
Like all dreamers I confuse disenchantment with truth.

GEORGES SCHEHADE
French writer
'La soirée des proverbes'
Truth has many faces. A lie has only one.

ALBERT SCHWEITZER
German missionary
Nobel Prize speech 1952
Truth has no special time of its own. It's hour is now – always.

GEORGE C. SCOTT
American film actor
Esquire 1965
If truth is beauty, then it is also simplicity. It is an absence of pretence.

'SEPARATE TABLES'
UA 1958 screenplay by Terence Rattigan & John Gay, based on play by Terence Rattigan
Burt Lancaster: People who hate the light usually hate the truth.

LOGAN PEARSALL SMITH
American essayist
in 'The Faber Book of Aphorisms' 1964
How awful to reflect that what people say of us is true!

WILLIE 'THE LION' SMITH
American jazz musician
Esquire 1964
The truth is delight.

SUSAN SONTAG
American essayist
'On Photography' 1977
Humankind lingers unregenerately in Plato's cave, still revelling, it's age-old habit, in mere images of the truth.

'Against Interpretation' 1961
The truth is balance, but the opposite of truth, which is unbalance, may not be a lie.

GEORGE STEINER
British academic
Bronowski Lecture 1978
Truth matters more than man . . . It is more interesting than he, even when, perhaps especially when, it puts in question his own survival.

TOM STOPPARD
British playwright
The Guardian 1973
A truth is always a compound of two half-truths, and you can never reach it, because there is always something more to say.

'SUDDENLY, LAST SUMMER'
Columbia 1959 screenplay by Gore Vidal and Tennessee Williams, based on the play by Tennessee Williams
Katharine Hepburn: Sebastian said 'Truth is the bottom of a bottomless well.

HAN SUYIN
American writer
Truth, like surgery, may hurt, but it cures.

LEO SZILARD
British scientist
quoted in Science 1972
Don't lie if you don't have to.

ANGELA THIRKELL
British writer
quoted in 'The Wit of Women' ed. L. and M. Cowan 1969
If one cannot invent a really convincing lie, it is often better to stick to the truth.

B. TRAVEN
Mexican writer
If you do not wish to be lied to, do not ask questions. If there were no questions, there would be no lies.

HARRY S. TRUMAN
American president 1956
I never gave them hell. I just tell the truth and they think it's hell.

JESSAMYN WEST
American writer
in Reader's Digest 1973
Fiction reveals truths that reality obscures.

ALFRED NORTH WHITEHEAD
British philosopher
in 'The Faber Book of Aphorisms' 1964
Apart from blunt truth, our lives sink decadently amid the perfume of hints and suggestions.

FRANK LLOYD WRIGHT
American architect
The Listener 1950
The young sentimentalist in love with truth – is there any more tragic figure on earth, in any generation.

The truth is more important than the facts.

motto quoted in The Listener 1950
Truth against the world.

ANDREW WYETH
American artist 1974
If you don't back up your dreams with truth you have a very round-shouldered art.

Style & Civilisation

HARDY AMIES
British couturier 1966
It is not pansy to be elegant, just as it is not elegant to be pansy.

ERIC ASHBY
British writer
'Technology and the Academics' 1958
The path to culture should be through

a man's specialism not by-passing it.

BILL BATTIE
American college football coach 1976
Class is: when they run you out of town, to look like you're leading the parade.

CECIL BEATON
British photographer
New York Times 1959
What is elegance? Soap and water!

SHELLEY BERMAN
American comedian
The Sun 1969
Taste is a beautiful word for those who wish to keep themselves safe. To be suddenly reminded of their humanity is very upsetting to them.

MALCOLM BRADBURY
British novelist
The Listener 1962
In the general loss of shared values, culture becomes a way of coping with world by defining it in detail.

BERTOLT BRECHT
German playwright
'The Messingkauf Dialogues' 1965
There are times when you have to choose between being human and having good taste.

MEL BROOKS
American film director
Bad taste is simply saying the truth before it should be said.

WALTER BUNNING
Australian architect 1969
Design means a good deal more than a man with long hair and sports jacket with leather patches on the sleeves teaching people how to be artistic.

EDNA WOOLMAN CHASE
American fashion journalist
'Always In Vogue' 1954
Fashion can be bought. Style one must possess.

LORD CLARK
British critic
Sunday Times
The fact that a man of genius in a moment of exuberance and ebullience can produce something which is not frightened of asserting itself, not frightened of striking a loud note, that is not in itself a condemnation of good taste.

JEAN COCTEAU
French writer and film director
'Le secret professionel'
Style is a simple way of saying complicated things.

CYRIL CONNOLLY
British critic
'The Unquiet Grave' 1945
The civilised are those who get more out of life than the uncivilised, and for this the uncivilised have not forgiven them.

in 'The Faber Book of Aphorisms' 1964
Vulgarity is the garlic in the salad of taste.

NOEL COWARD
British playwright
on style, in an ad for Gillette
A candy-striped Jeep, Jane Austen, Cassius Clay, the Times before it changed, Danny LaRue, Charleston in South Carolina, Monsieur de Givenchy, a zebra but not a zebra crossing, evading boredom, Gertrude Lawrence, the Paris Opera House, white, a seagull, a Brixham trawler, Margot Fonteyn, any Cole Porter song, English pageantry, Marlene's voice, and Lingfield has a tiny bit.

QUENTIN CRISP
British writer
'How To Become A Virgin' 1981
Culture ... television programmes so boring that they cannot be classed as entertainment.

WILL & ARIEL DURANT
American historians
Civilisation is a stream with banks. The stream is sometimes filled with blood from people killing, stealing, shouting and doing things historians usually record; while on the banks, unnoticed, people build homes, make love, raise children, sing songs, write poetry and even whittle statues. The story of civilisation is the story of what happened on the banks. Historians are pessimists because they ignore the banks for the river.

CHARLES EAMES
American designer
The Observer 1975
Every time I lay a table I am designing something.

BRIAN ENO
British musician
The function of culture is to teach you new ways of dealing with the world.

ERNST FISCHER
German critic
'The Necessity of Art' 1963
Form is social experience solidified.

MICHAEL FISH
London designer
I don't care about taste. I think taste is a word like love – it should be forgotten for fifty years. I don't even know what it means. Actually, I always think I am very vulgar. Revolutionaries have to be.

PRUDENCE GLYNN
British journalist
The Times 1980
Style is something other people have. The merest inkling that you yourself may be in possession of the commodity is enough to ensure that you are not, for style, like the Victoria Cross, is an accolade which must be bestowed by the recognition of a third party.

WALTER GROPIUS
German architect
'New Architecture & the Bauhaus' 1965
Artistic design is neither an artistic nor a material affair, but simply an integral part of the stuff of life.

SIR ROBERT HELPMAN
Australian choreographer 1974
Culture is a word that applies to cheap pearls.

ERNEST HEMINGWAY
American writer
'Writers at Work' 2nd series 1963
I might say that what amateurs call a style is usually only the unavoidable awkwardness in first trying to make something that has not heretofore been made.

MARGOT HENTOFF
American journalist
New York Herald Tribune 1971
Pop culture is, perhaps most of all, a culture of accessible fantasy.

DAVID HICKS
British interior designer 1969
Bad taste is specifically gladioli, cut glass flower bowls, two tone motor cars and dollies to hide telephones. Good taste is, frankly, what I think is good taste.

ALFRED HITCHCOCK
British film director
Style is self-plagiarism.

ALDOUS HUXLEY
British writer
'Collected Essays'
Every civilisation is, among other things, an arrangement for domesticating the passions and setting them to do useful work.

STANLEY E. HYMAN
New York Times 1968
The wider any culture is spread the thinner it gets.

PAULINE KAEL
American critic
'I Lost It At The Movies' 1965
One of the surest signs of the Philistine is his reverence for the superior tastes of those who put him down.

JACK KEROUAC
American novelist
'Writers at Work' 4th series 1977
Like Joyce I say. . . Don't bother me with politics, the only thing that interests me is style.

LISA KIRK
American comedienne
New York Journal American 1954
A gossip is one who talks to you about others; a bore is one who talks to you about himself; and a brilliant conversationalist is one who talks to you about yourself.

WILLEM DE KOONING
American artist
Sunday Times 1968
Content is a glimpse of something, an encounter, like a flash, tiny, very tiny, content.

FRAN LEBOWITZ
American journalist
'Metropolitan Life' 1978
Nothing succeeds like address.

LES LEVINE
Canadian artist
Studio International 1975
Good taste at this time in a technological democracy ends up to be nothing more than taste prejudice. If all that art does is create good or bad taste, then it has failed completely.

C. S. LEWIS
British writer
quoted in Time 1978
All that is not eternal is eternally out of date.

GEORGE LOIS
American art director
'The Art of Advertising' 1977
Most designs are not understood by most people. Most designers forget that their work must talk to human beings.

DWIGHT MacDONALD
American critic
Diogenes 1953
There seems to be a Gresham's Law in cultural as well as monetary circulation: bad stuff drives out the good, it is more easily understood and enjoyed.

MARSHAL McLUHAN
Canadian academic
A culture is an order of sensory preferences.

NORMAN MAILER
American writer
'Cannibals and Christians' 1966
Form, in general, is the record of a war.

ANDRE MALRAUX
French writer
Culture is the sum of all forms of art, of love and of thought, which, in the course of centuries, have enabled man to be less enslaved.

ANDRE MAUROIS
French writer
'The Art of Writing' 1960
Style is the hallmark of a temperament stamped upon the material at hand.

New York Times 1968
Our civilisation, which is a civilisation of machines, can teach man everything except how to be a man.

GEORGE MELLY
British musician and critic
'Revolt Into Style' 1970
Pop culture is for the most part non-reflective, non-didactic, dedicated only to pleasure. It changes constantly because it is sensitive to change, indeed it could be said that it is sensitive to nothing else. Its principle faculty is to catch the spirit of its time and translate this spirit into objects or music or fashion or behaviour. It could be said to offer a comic strip which compresses and caricatures the social and economic forces at work within out society. It draws no conclusions. It makes no comments. It admits to neither past nor future, not even its own.

MALCOLM MUGGERIDGE
British journalist
Good taste and humour are a contradiction in terms, like a chaste whore.

'Chronicles of Wasted Time' vol. 1 1978
There is no surer way of preserving the worst aspects of bourgeois style than liquidating the bourgeoisie. Whatever else Stalin may, or may not, have done, he assuredly made Russia safe for the Forsyte Saga.

BARNETT NEWMAN
American artist
New York Times Book Review 1968
Aesthetics is for the artist like ornithology is for the birds.

JOSE ORTEGA Y GASSET
Spanish philosopher
in 'The Faber Book of Aphorisms' 1964
Civilisation is nothing else but the attempt to reduce force to being the last resort.

JOE ORTON
British playwright
quoted in 'Behind The Scenes' ed. Joseph P. McCrindle
The kind of people who always go on about whether a thing is in good taste, invariably have bad taste.

GEORGE ORWELL
British essayist
'Collected Essays'
One of the effects of safe and civilised life is an immense oversensitiveness which makes all the primary emotions seem somewhat disgusting. Generosity is as painful as meanness, gratitude as hateful as ingratitude.

BERNIE OZER
Interview 1978
Chic is a personal style that comes off with integrity.

AUGUSTE PERRET
French designer
in New Society 1967
Style is a word that has no plural.

PABLO PICASSO
Spanish artist
Quote 1957
Ah, good taste – what a dreadful thing. Taste is the enemy of creativeness.

HERBERT READ
British critic
'Autobiographies'
At a certain moment the individual is carried beyond his rational self onto another ethical plane where his actions are judged by new standards. The impulse which moves him to irrational action I have called the sense of glory.

JONATHAN RICHMAN
American rock singer
New Musical Express 1979
To me, sophistication and gaol have a lot in common.

PHILIP RIEFF
American sociologist
'Freud, the Mind of the Moralist' 1960
To prevent the expression of everything: that is the irreducible function of culture.

MIES VAN DER ROHE
American architect
in Sunday Times 1971
Form is not the aim of our work, only the result.

EDITH SITWELL
British poet
New York Times 1962
Good taste is the worse vice ever invented.

'Taken Care Of' 1965
Vulgarity is, in reality, nothing but a modern chic, part descendant of the goddess Dullness.

CARMEL SNOW
American fashion journalist
'The World of Carmel Snow' 1962
Elegance is good taste, *plus* a dash of daring.

SUSAN SONTAG
American essayist
'Against Interpretation' 1961
Camp is a vision of the world in terms of style, but a particular style. It is love of the exaggerated.

JOHN SPARROW
British academic
The Listener 1979
Hypocrisy ... the pretences, the false appearances that are kept up by decent people for reasons of mutual consideration and forbearance – remains, as it always has been, a cement that holds together civilised society.

Of course, in a sense, civilisation is a sophisticated even, if you like, hypocritical construction, for the self-control on which it is based is self-interest. We forbear in hope of mutual forbearance. We do unto others what we hope they will do unto us. But it is a salutary hypocrisy. It makes possible the continuance of civilised life, it is the cement of civilised society.

WILLIAM G. SUMNER
quoted in 'Social Darwinism in American Thought' by R. Hofstadter
If we do not like the survival of the fittest, we have only one alternative, and that is the survival of the unfittest. The former is the law of civilisation, and the latter is the law of anti-civilisation.

ERNEST TOCH
Musicologist
Form is the balance between tension and relaxation.

ALVIN TOFFLER
American academic
'The Culture Consumers' 1964
The Law of Raspberry Jam – The wider any culture is spread, the thinner it gets.

ARNOLD TOYNBEE
British historian
We are in the first age since the dawn of civilisation in which people have dared to think it practicable to make the benefits of civilisation available to the whole human race.

'Civilisation on Trial'
Civilisation is a movement, not a condition. A voyage and not a harbour.

To be able to fill leisure intelligently is the last product of civilisation.

PETER USTINOV
British actor and wit
Time & Tide
The avant garde are rushing up a cul-de-sac and by the time they get back to the main road everyone will have gone past them.

GORE VIDAL
American writer
Daily Express 1973
Style is knowing who you are, what you want to say, and not giving a damn.

DIANA VREELAND
American fashion journalist
Newsweek 1962
The only real elegance is in the mind. If you've got that, the rest really follows from it.

ANDY WARHOL
American artist
I don't believe in style. I want to be a machine.

JACK WATERMAN
British broadcaster
The Listener 1978
As for bad taste, it is arguably like bad breath – better than no breath at all.

AUBERON WAUGH
British journalist
Esquire 1968
All that is left for the civilised man is to laugh at the absurdity of the human condition.

EVELYN WAUGH
British novelist
letter to Robin Campbell 1945 in 'The Letters of Evelyn Waugh' ed. Mark Amory 1980
Aesthetic value is often the by-product of the artist striving to do something else.

SIMONE WEIL
French philosopher
'The Need for Roots' 1952
Culture is an instrument wielded by professors to manufacture professors, who when their turn comes, will manufacture professors.

MAE WEST
American film star
Playboy 1971
Camp is the kind of comedy where they imitate me. (cf. Sontag)

ALFRED NORTH WHITEHEAD
British philosopher
The major advances in civilisation are processes that all but wreck the societies in which they occur.

Civilisation advances by extending the number of important operations which we can perform without thinking of them.

TOM WOLFE
American journalist
The Guardian 1966
Every style recorded in art history is the result of the same thing: a lot of attention to form plus the money to make monuments to it.

FRANK LLOYD WRIGHT
American architect
Sunday Times 1957
Taste is always a matter of ignorance. You taste because you don't know and if you like the taste of the old, you like the old; if you like the taste of the new, you like the new.

EGO

RICHARD ADAMS
British author 1974
I enjoy contradicting prevailing opinion.

MUHAMMAD ALI
world heavyweight boxing champion
making his third trip to the White House, 1980
If there is a black man to be President, they might just run me. I'm getting used to this place.

CHARLES ATLAS (Angelo Siciliano)
American bodybuilder
recalling reactions to his lying on a bed of nails eating a banana as three spectators stood on his chest . . .
Women used to faint when I did that. They couldn't stand watching a beautiful body like mine being abused.

RICHARD AVEDON
American photographer
Everything in my pictures is controlled – even the accidents.

TALLULAH BANKHEAD
American film star
The only thing I regret about my past is the length of it. If I had to live my life again, I'd make the same mistakes, only sooner.

The Observer 1957
I'm as pure as the driven slush.

SIR JOHN BARBIROLLI
British conductor
quoted in Neville Cardus biography
At a rehearsal I let the orchestra play as they like, at the concert I make them play as *I* like.

STANLEY BAXTER
British comic 1974
I'm the best known anonymity in the business.

SIR THOMAS BEECHAM
British conductor 1961
I am not the greatest conductor in this country. On the other hand I am better than any damned foreigner.

I have always been noted for my instability. I am a very, very low brow.

HONOR BLACKMAN
British actress 1971
Men who are insecure about their masculinity often challenge me to fights.

JEAN-BEDEL BOKASSA
President of the Central African Republic 1972
I am everywhere and nowhere. I see nothing, yet I see all. I listen to nothing and I hear everything. Miracles enter my body. Such is the role of a Head of State.

PRINCE CARLOS DE BOURBON
claimant to the Spanish throne 1978
The Communists have not renounced their past, the Socialists have not renounced their past and I do not feel that I have to renounce mine.

DAVID BOWIE
British rock star
I'm an instant star – just add water & stir.

quoting Victor Mature on acting
I've got two looks – my left face and my right face. Which do you want?

MICHAEL CAINE
British actor
Playboy 1967
I'm a sort of boy-next-door. If that boy has a good scriptwriter.

AL CAPONE
American gangster
I've been accused of every death except the casualty list of the World War.

CHARLIE CHAPLIN
American film star
'My Autobiography'
All I need to make a comedy is a park, a policeman and a pretty girl.

AGATHA CHRISTIE
British crime writer
on herself in G. C. Ramsey 'Agatha Christie Mistress of Mystery'
A sausage machine, a perfect sausage machine.

quoted in Esquire 1976
I would write books even if they were only read by my husband.

SIR WINSTON CHURCHILL
British statesman
accused of altering his opinions 1952
My views are a harmonious process which keeps them in relation to the current movement of events.

MARC CONNOLLY
American playwright
interviewed as a survivor of the 'Algonquin Round Table' 1978
Do you think that conversation is as witty now as it was? . . . Mine is.

LADY DIANA COOPER
English socialite
International Herald Tribune 1981
I was known as a great beauty because I had a knack for attracting publicity. I was always falling through a skylight or holding a camel wearing evening dress.

NOEL COWARD
British playwright 1972
I am an enormously talented man, after all it's no use pretending that I am not and I was bound to succeed.

QUENTIN CRISP
British writer
'How To Become a Virgin' 1981
Wherever I am on this earth, I am, and always shall be, only a resident alien.

SALVADOR DALI
Spanish artist
'The American' 1956
There is only one difference between me and a madman. I am not mad.

'Diary of a Genius' 1966
I do not take drugs, I am drugs.

BETTE DAVIS
American film star 1980
There's only one of us in each country.

CHARLES DEDERICH
American founder of Synanon anti-heroin clinic
I am not bound by the rules. I make them.

LEN DEIGHTON
British writer
The Observer 1974
I like to be able to listen to conversations without people turning round to look at me over their shoulders. I want to be the man behind you in the fish shop.

MARLENE DIETRICH
German film star
The legs aren't so beautiful, I just know what to do with them.

LAWRENCE DURRELL
British writer 1973
My problem is intense vanity and narcissism. I've always had such a good physique and such intense charm that its difficult to be true to myself.

FRANCOIS 'Papa Doc' DUVALIER
President of Haiti, 1964 . . .
Great citizens who lead their countries with firmness and with all the necessary savagery know what they are doing. Duvalier . . . knew what he was doing.

BOB DYLAN
American singer
My life is the street where I walk.

I just don't hear anyone else making the music I'm making in my head, so I'll have to do it myself.

I didn't create Bob Dylan. Bob Dylan has always been here – always was. When I was a child there was Bob Dylan. And before I was born there was Bob Dylan. I play the role because maybe I'm best equipped to do it.

MICHAEL FISH
British designer
quoted in 'Today There Are No Gentlemen' by Nik Cohn 1971
I have tried to break down the frontiers of man. Do I care about the masses? Jesus Christ had only twelve disciples and one of them was Doubting Thomas.

SIR ALEXANDER FLEMING
British scientist
quoted in 'The Wit of Medecine' ed. L. and M. Cowan 1972
I can only assume that God wanted penicillin, and that was his reason for creating Alexander Fleming.

JOHN FORD
American film director
To be quite blunt, I make pictures for money, to pay the rent. There are some great artists in this business. I am not one of them.

R. BUCKMINSTER FULLER
American engineer
'Operating Manual for Spaceship Earth' 1969
I am a passenger on the spaceship, Earth.

INDIRA GANDHI
Indian politician
on her father, Nehru
My father was a statesman, I am a political woman. My father was a saint. I am not.

LORD GEORGE-BROWN
British politician 1974
Most British statesmen have either drunk too much or womanised too much. I never fell into the second category.

SIR JOHN GIELGUD
British actor
failing to jump on a moving bus in less exalted days
Stop, stop! You're killing a genius!

JEAN-LUC GODARD
French film director
Esquire 1969
My aesthetic is the aesthetic of the sniper on the roof.

SAM GOLDWYN
American film producer
I always was an independent, even when I had partners.

BETTY GRABLE
American pinup girl
I'm strictly an enlisted man's girl.

LORD GRADE
British TV mogul 1979
The Observer 1975
All my shows are great. Some of them are bad. But they're all great.

I have the taste of the ordinary person throughout the world. What I like the majority likes.

VIRGINIA GRAHAM
American TV talkshow host
Esquire 1971
I am a living soap opera!

CARY GRANT
American film star
I improve on misquotation.

GERMAINE GREER
Australian feminist
If I had a cock for a day I would get myself pregnant.

D. W. GRIFFITH
American film director
quoted in 'The Honeycomb' Adela Rogers St. Johns
I made them *see*, didn't I . . . I changed everything. Remember how small the world was before I came along. I made them see it both ways in time as well as in space . . . I brought it all to life. I moved the whole world onto a twenty foot screen.

TY HARDIN
American film actor 1968
I'm really a very humble man. Not a day goes by that I don't thank God for my looks, my stature and my talent.

HUGH HEFNER
American publisher
Playboy 1974
I feel like a kid in the world's biggest candy store.

JIMMY HOFFA
American labour racketeer
quoted by J. Didion in 'On Keeping a Notebook' 1966
I may have my faults, but being wrong ain't one of them.

Esquire 1975
An ego is just imagination. And if a man doesn't have imagination he'll be working for somebody else for the rest of his life.

ROCK HUDSON
American film actor 1970
I can't play a loser – I don't look like one.

My greatest ambition is to become a greater actor.

CLIVE JENKINS
British trade unionist
Entry under 'Hobbies' in 'Who's Who' . . .
Organising the middle classes.

HENRY KISSINGER
American diplomat
The longer I am out of office, the more
infallible I appear to myself.

interviewed by Oriana Fallaci 1970
I've always acted alone. Americans
admire that enormously. Americans
admire the cowboy leading the caravan
alone astride his horse, the cowboy entering a village or city alone on his horse.

ARTHUR KOESTLER
British philosopher 1978
I daydream that I'm a faithhealer.

RONALD KRAY
British criminal
*quoted in 'The Profession of Violence' by J.
Pearson*
I'm a genius. I'm like Hitler. He was a
genius and he was mad. It's always been
like that. Every genius is mad.

NGUYEN CAO KY
South Vietnamese leader 1965
People ask me who my heroes are. I have
only one – Hitler. I admire Hitler because he pulled his country together
when it was in a terrible state in the
early Thirties. But the situation here is
so desperate now that one man would
not be enough. We need four or five Hit-
lers in Vietnam . . . I want to infuse in
our youth the same fanaticism, the same
dedication, the same fighting spirit as
Hitler infused in his people.

GYPSY ROSE LEE
American stripper 1966
I'm a bit of a prude myself.

JOANNA LUMLEY
British actress 1979
Sex symbol? I am non-toxic, safe. Girls
write to me asking for photographs to
send to their boyfriends.

NORMAN MAILER
American writer 1979
I'm an old piece of cheese – camembert
running at the edges. There's not a single idea you would really offer yourself
up for any longer.

JAYNE MANSFIELD
American film star 1967
I will do anything to initiate world
peace.

MAO ZEDONG (Mao Tse-tung)
Chinese leader
I am alone with the masses.

MELINA MERCOURI
Greek actress
*on the Colonels, who took away her citizenship
for attacking them 1967*
I was born Greek and I shall die Greek.
They were born fascists and they will die
fascists.

GRACE METALIOUS
American author
quoted in Esquire 1971
If I'm a lousy writer, then a hell of a lot
of people have got lousy taste.

MICHAEL X
British activist
I have no need to play the ego game
because I am the Best Known Black
Man in this entire country.

VLADIMIR NABOKOV
Russian writer
'Writers at Work' 4th series 1977
Lolita is famous, not I. I am an obscure,
doubly obscure, novelist with an un-
pronounceable name.

My loathings are simple: stupidity,
oppression, crime cruelty, soft music.
And my pleasures are the most intense
known to man: writing and butterfly
hunting.

BARNETT NEWMAN
American artist 1951
I busted geometry.

EDNA O'BRIEN
Irish author
I'm a tuning fork, tense and twanging
all the time.

JOHN OSBORNE
British playwright
The Observer 1975
I never deliberately set out to shock, but when people don't walk out of my plays I think there is something wrong.

PABLO PICASSO
Spanish artist
My paintings are the sum of destructions.

I paint objects as I think them, not as I see them.

I do not seek, I find.

I am only a public entertainer who has understood his time.

HAROLD PINTER
British playwright
'Writers at Work' 3rd series 1967
I have nothing to say about myself directly. I wouldn't know where to begin. Particularly since I often look at myself in the mirror and say 'Who the hell's that'.

MARY QUANT
British fashion designer 1972
I think I was born never wanting to grow up.

SATAYAJIT RAY
Indian film director 1968
I do not seek to compete with Doris Day.

JEAN RENOIR
French film director
Time 1979
God has not made me a hero – and I find it highly convenient to send actors to suffer in my place.

HANS RICHTER
German conductor
to incompetent second flute at Covent Garden
. . .
Your damned nonsense can I stand twice or once, but sometimes always, by God, never!

RICHARD RODGERS
American composer
When the lyrics are right it's easier for me to write a tune than to bend over and tie my shoelaces.

MORT SAHL
American comedian
on self
I'm the intellectual voice of the era (the 1950s) – which is a good measure of the era.

DR. JONAS SALK
American scientist
asked why his life has been dedicated to research
Time 1954
Why did Mozart compose music?

MALCOLM SARGENT
British conductor 1967
I don't enjoy being Malcolm Sargent.

JEAN-PAUL SARTRE
French philosopher
If the Communists are right, then I am the loneliest madman alive; if they are wrong, then there is no hope for the world.

JIMMY SAVILE
British disc jockey 1972
I'm just a change from shooting and starving and air crashes.

ARTUR SCHNABEL
German pianist
Chicago Daily News 1958
The notes I handle no better than many pianists. But the pauses between the notes – ah, that is where the art resides!

PETER SELLERS
British film star
Time 1980
There used to be a me, but I had it surgically removed.

ISAAC BASHEVIS SINGER
American writer 1980
In all my writing I tell the story of my life, over and over again.

VICTOR SILVESTER
British bandleader 1975
I suppose I've a natural sense of rhythm.

LORD SNOW
British novelist
I'm a fairly clever chap and can put my hand to things.

RINGO STARR
British rock star
on the Beatles' eternal popularity
I think the main point of the situation is that those pieces of plastic that we did are still some of the finest pieces of plastic around.

DONALD OGDEN STEWART
American screenwriter 1975
Just say that I was shot in the ass with luck.

BARBRA STREISAND
American actress
in 'Goodbye Baby & Amen' by D. Bailey 1969
I wanted to be Scarlett O'Hara and not Vivien Leigh.

ELIZABETH TAYLOR
British film star 1977
I know I'm vulgar.

ROD TAYLOR
Australian film star 1968
I'm a lover, not a fighter.

MARGARET TRUDEAU
wife of politician Pierre
I can't be a rose in any man's lapel.

TWIGGY (Leslie Hornsby)
British model
on her emaciated body
It's not what you'd call a *figure*, is it?

JOHN WAYNE
American film star 1975
I couldn't hit a wall with a sixgun, but I can twirl one. It looks good.

RAQUEL WELCH
American film star
The Observer 1979
Being a sex symbol was rather like being a convict.

MAE WEST
American film star
I'm a fast-moving girl that likes them slow.

Playboy 1971
I never loved another person the way I loved myself.

'The Wit and Wisdom of Mae West' 1967
I used to be snow white . . . but I drifted.

Playboy 1971
I'm never dirty. I'm interesting without being vulgar. I just . . . suggest.

EDY WILLIAMS
American film star 1973
I just look in the mirror and I say 'God, it's really fantastic, the Lord really gave me something'. So why on earth should I cover any of it up.

TENNESSEE WILLIAMS
American playwright 1973
You know, *Life* magazine said I was through as a writer in 1969. I'm happy to see that *Life* has folded and I'm going as strong as ever.

There's two things keep me going – swimming and my sense of humour.

NICOL WILLIAMSON
British actor
after entertaining at the Nixon White House 1972
The mome rath isn't born that could outgrabe me.

MICHAEL WINNER
British film director 1969
I can't stand vulgar publicity.

The team effort is a lot of people doing what I say.

SHELLEY WINTERS
American film star
Saturday Evening Post 1952
I have bursts of being a lady, but it doesn't last long.

I'm the modern intelligent, independent-type woman. In other words, a girl who can't get a man.

A. DICKSON WRIGHT
British surgeon
I am just a cutter-out of inconsidered trifles.

FRANK LLOYD WRIGHT
American architect
quoted in Today 1961
Give me the luxuries of life and I will willingly do without the necessities.

Early in life I had to choose between honest arrogance and hypocritical humility. I chose honest arrogance and have seen no occasion to change.

FRANK ZAPPA
American rock musician
We make a special art in an environment hostile to dreamers.

PROFESSIONS
Business

CHARLES F. ABBOTT
Business without profit is not business any more than a pickle is a candy.

ELIZABETH ARDEN
American cosmetician 1966
The cosmetics industry is the nastiest business in the world.

DR. ALI AHMED ATTIGA
Saudi Arabian delegate to OPEC, 1974
A fair price for oil is whatever you can get plus ten per cent.

IRVING AZOFF
American rock group manager
Sure I lie, but it's more like . . . tinting. It's all just negotiating theatrics.

Why should I tell the truth if it makes us look like schmucks in comparison to a liar. I lie only to correct the perspective. What are you supposed to do? Go to eight thousand people in entertainment and say 'Be honest'. There are more important causes in the world. I didn't write the rules, I just live by them.

It comes down to the old music business tactic that the guy that yells loudest is right. It's not my fault I have to yell loudest.

JAMES BLISH
American writer
Credit . . . is the only enduring testimonial to man's confidence in man.

NEIL BOGART
President of Casablanca Records
If you hype something and it succeeds, you're a genius – it wasn't a hype. If you hype it and it fails, then it's just a hype.

RICHARD H. BRIEN
American educator
in Educational Record 1970
At some time in the life cycle of virtually every organization, its ability to succeed in spite of itself runs out.

NORMAN O. BROWN
American philosopher
The dynamics of capitalism is postponement of enjoyment to the constantly postponed future.

SIR MONTAGUE BURTON
British tailor
A business must have a conscience as well as a counting house.

CHARLES CLORE
British business-man
The Observer 1974
The fact that a business is large, efficient and profitable does not mean it takes advantage of the public.

PAUL DICKSON
American writer
Playboy 1978
A businessman needs three umbrellas – one to leave at the office, one to leave at home and one to leave on the train.

PETER DRUCKER
American management expert
Business has only two functions – marketing and innovation.

The modern corporation is a political institution; its purpose is the creation of legitimate power in the industrial sphere.

BOB EZRIN
American rock producer
The key to building a superstar is to keep their mouth shut. To reveal an artist to the people can be to destroy him. It isn't to anyone's advantage to see the truth.

CLIFTON FADIMAN
American essayist
'Enter, conversing'
Experience teaches you that the man who lookes you straight in the eye, particularly if he adds a firm handshake, is hiding something.

B. C. FORBES
American publisher
in Forbes 1974
If you don't drive your business you will
be driven out of business.

HENRY FORD I
American entrepreneur
Let a man start out in life to build something better and sell it cheaper than it
has been built or sold before, let him
have that determination and the money
will roll in.

J. K. GALBRAITH
American economist
'Annals of an Abiding Liberal' 1980
The salary of the chief executive of the
large corporation is not a market award
for achievement. It is frequently in the
nature of a warm personal gesture by the
individual to himself.

MOHANDAS K. GANDHI
Indian leader
'Non-Violence in Peace and War' 1948
It is difficult but not impossible to conduct strictly honest business. What is
true is that honesty is incompatible with
the amassing of a large fortune.

SAM GOLDWYN
American film producer
A verbal contract isn't worth the paper
it's written on.

LORD GRADE
British TV mogul
in The Observer 1962
Q: What's two and two?
Grade: Buying or selling?

quoted in Sunday Times 1979
The trouble with this business is that the
stars keep ninety per cent of my money.

JON HARTMAN
American rock executive
A manager doesn't trust the artist. He's
always afraid the artist is going to blow
it. That's why he's the manager.

F. A. HAYEK
Czech economist
The Listener 1978
The pursuit of gain is the only way in
which men can serve the needs of others
whom they do not know.

LEVON HELM
American rock musician
The music industry's gotten so it's like
Vietnam. A lot of guys making a lot of
money, some guys getting cut up, and in
five years ain't much of it even going to
be worth a pinch of shit.

ABBIE HOFFMAN
American radical 1971
The counter culture has been co-opted
by Warner Bros.

JACK HURLEY
American boxing manager, 1961
Every young man should have a hobby.
Learning how to handle money is the
best one.

LANE KIRKLAND
American trade unionist
on working with capitalists, 1980
The only way to convert the heathen is
to travel into the jungle.

SPENCER KLAW
American writer
Fortune 1963
If the package doesn't say 'New' these
days, it better say 'Seven Cents Off'.

EVEL KNIEVEL
American stuntman 1976
Promoters are just guys with two pieces
of bread looking for a piece of cheese.

IRVING KRISTOL
American academic 1979
Wages and price controls are a military
solution to an economic problem.

Capitalism is based on private property,
where normal economic activity consists
of commercial transactions between consenting adults.

GEORGE LOIS
American art director
'The Art of Advertising' 1977
The business world worships mediocrity.
Officially we revere free enterprise, in-
itiative and individuality. Unofficially
we fear it.

J. B. MORTON
British humorist
'Beachcomber' in 'Dictionary for Today' Daily Express passim
Economy: cutting down other people's wages.

LEN MURRAY
British trade unionist 1980
In the first place, trade unions are about individuals, and the right of a man to answer back to his boss.

COL. TOM PARKER
American rock manager
When I first knew Elvis he had a million dollars worth of talent. Now he has a million dollars.

WILLIAM LYON PHELPS
National Observer 1969
The value of anything is not what you get paid for it, nor what it cost to produce, but what you can get for it at an auction.

'THE PRODUCERS'
Embassy 1968 screenplay by Mel Brooks
Gene Wilder: It's simply a matter of creative accounting.

CHARLES REVSON
American businessman
I don't meet competition, I crush it.

ROBERT RICE
American writer
'The Business of Crime' 1956
Crime is a logical extension of the sort of behaviour that is often considered perfectly respectable in legitimate business.

ANWAR SADAT
President of Egypt 1978
On the West's 'Oil Crisis'. . .
Those who invented the law of supply and demand have no right to complain when this law works against their interest.

DAVID SARNOFF
American businessman
quoted in Esquire 1964
Competition brings out the best in products and the worst in people.

FRANK SINATRA
American singer 1977
Hell hath no fury like a hustler with a literary agent.

BILL VEECK
American sports entrepreneur 1965
A good hustler's thoughts should be long, long thoughts. He's thinking not for the day but for the year, the decade.

A hustler is a man who will talk you into giving him a free ride and make it seem as if he is doing you a great favour.

The only promotion rules I can think of are that a sense of shame is to be avoided at all costs and there is never any reason for a hustler to be less cunning than more virtuous men. Oh yes, . . . whenever you think you've got something really great, add ten per cent more.

GORE VIDAL
American writer
Esquire 1968
It is a paradox of the acquisitive society in which we now live, that although private morals are regulated by law, the entrepreneur is allowed considerable freedom to use and abuse the public in order to make money.

HENRY C. WALLICH
American businessman
Newsweek 1967
Profits are part of the mechanism by which society decides what it wants to see produced.

SY WEINTRAUB
American film entrepreneur
Sunday Times 1965
You've got to go into a dying business, other wise you only get six per cent of the profits. This way, if the gamble comes off, you get it all.

ROBERT WOODRUFF
Chief executive of Coca-Cola company
on his product
It's a religion as well as a business.

ANDREW YOUNG
American politician 1976
Nothing is illegal if 100 businessmen decide to do it.

ELEMIRE ZOLLA
Italian writer
'The Eclipse of the Intellectuals' 1971
The good luck that comes to us in our relations with the industrial world is always the good luck of the gambler – not the glory of the warrior or the reward of the cultivator.

Money

RICHARD ADAMS
British author
Daily Mail 1974
Money is useful to keep the dogs at bay and the water out.

W. H. AUDEN
British poet
One cannot walk though a mass-production factory and not feel that one is in Hell.

MAURICE BARING
British writer
quoted by Dorothy Parker in 'Writers at Work' 1st series 1958
If you would know what the Lord God thinks of money, you have only to look at those to whom he gives it.

JOHN BENTLEY
British entrepreneur 1973
Making money is fun, but it's pointless if you don't use the power it brings.

ROBERT BLACKWELL &
JOHN MARASCALCO
American songwriters
'Rip It Up'
Well, it's Saturday night and I just got paid / Fool about my money, don't try to save. (Venice Music)

ALBERT R. 'CUBBY' BROCCOLI
American film producer 1979
I don't commit any capital, I just make it.

MICHAEL CAINE
British actor 1966
Poor people always lean forward when they speak because they want people to listen to them. Rich people can sit back.

GODFREY CAMBRIDGE
American comedian
Esquire 1964
Middle income: that means, if you steal, you can pay the rent.

ALEXANDER CHASE
American journalist
'Perspectives' 1966
The rich man may never get into heaven, but the pauper is already serving his term in hell.

JOHN CIARDI
American critic
Saturday Review
Gentility is what is left over from rich ancestors after the money is gone.

QUENTIN CRISP
British writer
'How To Become A Virgin' 1981
It is always possible for anyone to judge the financial status of his host by the distance of the table tops and chair seats from the floor. The higher the income bracket, the lower the furniture.

FATHER JAMES CURTIN
British clergyman, winner of £214,000 on pools 1970
How can gambling be wrong when you win this much?

ROGER DALTREY
British rock star
If I wanted to get anything out of this business it was never to have to go back and work in a factory again. But one thing I've learned is that money never buys you out of being working class. The middle classes never let you forget where you've come from.

OLGA DETERDING
Dutch heiress 1966
Money is only corrupting to people who have not been corrupted or who have not learnt to make good use of it.

JOSEPH DONOHUE
quoted in 'The Official Rules' by P. Dickson 1978
What's worth doing is worth doing for money.

BOB DYLAN
American singer
'It's All Right Ma (I'm Only Bleeding)'
While money doesn't talk, it swears / Obscenity, who really cares / Propaganda, all is phoney
(M. Witmark & Sons)

FREDERICK J. EIKERENKOET-TER II 'Reverend Ike'
American evangelist
Money is God in action.

FRANTZ FANON
French radical
Wealth is not the fruit of labour but the result of organized protected robbery. Rich people are no longer respectable people, they are nothing more than flesh-eating animals, jackals and vultures which wallow in the people's blood.

'Black Skin, White Masks' 1952
All forms of exploitation are identical because all of them are applied against the same 'object' – man.

WILLIAM FEATHER
American businessman
'The Business of Life' 1949
A budget tells us what we can't afford, but it doesn't keep us from buying it.

EDGAR R. FIEDLER
American economist
quoted in 'The Official Rules' by P. Dickson 1978
Once economists were asked 'If you're so smart, why ain't you rich?' Today they're asked 'Now you've proved you ain't so smart, how come you got so rich?'

GEORGE FOREMAN
Heavyweight champion of the world 1973
Money wasn't that important. Money doesn't help you sleep. Money doesn't help your mother be well, money doesn't make your brother stay interested in his studies, money don't help an argument when nobody knows what they're arguing about. Money don't help nothing. Money is only good when you've got something else to do with it. A man can lose everything, family, all your dreams, and still have a pocketful of money.

BRENDAN FRANCIS
True, you can't take it with you, but then, that's not the place where it comes in handy.

MARY FRANCIS
wife of crime writer Dick Francis 1972
Really, the ones who aren't amiable in life are the people who haven't got, not the ones who have. There's an awful lot of jealousy. People only resent wealth because they haven't got it. Why should one resent what other people have?

MILTON FRIEDMAN
American economist
Playboy 1973
What kind of society isn't structured on greed? The problem of social organisation is how to set up an arrangement under which greed will do the least harm; capitalism is that kind of a system.

1974
Inflation is one form of taxation that can be imposed without legislation.

ROBERT FROST
American poet
A bank is a place where they lend you an umbrella in fair weather and ask for it back when it begins to rain.

J. K. GALBRAITH
American economist
'The Affluent Society' 1958
Wealth has never been a sufficient source of honour in itself. It must be advertised, and the normal medium is obtrusively expensive goods.

The greater the wealth, the thicker will be the dirt. This indubitably describes a tendency of our time.

Saturday Evening Post 1968
In economics, the majority is always wrong.

People of privilege will always risk their complete destruction rather than surrender any material part of their advantage.

Time 1961
One of the greatest pieces of economic wisdom is to know what you do not know.

GEORGE GALE
British journalist
The Spectator 1980
As the worth of money crumbles, so does the worthiness of men. Inflation undoubtedly corrupts.

J. PAUL GETTY
American financier
The meek shall inherit the earth, but *not* its mineral rights.

Money is like manure. You have to spread it around or it smells. (cf. Clint Murchison.)

If you can count your money you don't have a billion dollars.

LORD GRADE
British TV mogul
Esquire 1976
If I see something I like, I buy it; then I try to sell it.

SACHA GUITRY
French writer
'Le Scandale de Monte Carlo'
The important thing in life is not to have money, but that others have it.

LAING HANCOCK
Australian millionaire 1977
The best way to help the poor is not to become one of them.

BOB HOPE
American comedian 1959
A bank is a place that will lend you money if you can prove that you don't need it.

on Bing Crosby
Bing doesn't pay income tax any more. He just asks the government what they need.

IVAN ILLICH
American philosopher
'Deschooling Society' 1971
Man must choose whether to be rich in things or in the freedom to use them.

'Towards a History of Needs' 1978
As people become apt pupils in learning how to need, the ability to shape wants from experienced satisfaction becomes a rare competence of the very rich or the seriously undersupplied.

GERALD WHITE JOHNSON
'American Freedom and the Press' 1958
In all the world there is nothing more timorous than $1,000,000, except $10,000,000. In revolutionary times the rich are always the people who are the most afraid.

SIR KEITH JOSEPH
British politician
'Equality' 1979
Envy is capable of serving the valuable social function of making the rich moderate their habits for fear of arousing it. It is because of the existence of envy that one does not drive Rolls Royces through the slums of Naples.

WALTER KANE
It is tragic that Howard Hughes had to die to prove that he was alive.

JOHN F. KENNEDY
American president
If a free society cannot help the many who are poor, it cannot help the few who are rich.

AGA KHAN III
Muslim leader
'Memoirs'
There is a great deal of truth in Andrew Carnegie's remark 'The man who dies rich dies disgraced'. I should add, the man who lives rich, lives disgraced.

MARTIN LUTHER KING JR.
American activist
'Strength to Love' 1963
Philanthropy is commendable, but it must not cause the philanthropist to over-look the circumstances of economic injustice which make philanthropy necessary.

JOHN LEONARD
American critic
New York Times
The rich are different from you and me because they have more credit.

MIGNON McLAUGHLIN
American writer
'The Neurotics Notebook' 1963
We'd all like a reputation for generosity and we'd all like to buy it cheap.

BARRY MANN / CYNTHIA WEILL / JERRY LEIBER / MIKE STOLLER
American songwriters
'On Broadway'
But when you're walking down that street / And you ain't got enough to eat / The glitter all rubs off / And you're no where / On Broadway (Columbia-Screen Gems Music)

CAROL MATTHAU
wife of film star Walter
Esquire 1968
'Rich enough' is only when you have 'No, thank you' money.

EUGENE MAYER
American publisher
quoted in 'The Powers That be' by D. Halberstam, 1979. Complaining that his wife had cut down the servants to just three . . .
You know I can't stand camping out.

Explaining to his staff the need for wage cuts

You should realize that I have made no addition to my collection of French Impressionists since I bought the *Washington Post*.

JOHNNY MILLER
American golf star 1975
The dollars aren't important – once you have them.

CLINT MURCHISON
American millionarie
Time 1971
Money is like manure. If your spread it around it does a lot of good, but if you pile it up in one place it stinks like hell.

RUPERT MURDOCH
Australian publisher
The buck stops with the guy who signs the cheques.

RICHARD NEY
American writer 1974
Money is a sixth sense which makes it possible for us to enjoy the other five.

ARTHUR OKUN
American economist
Society can transport money from rich to poor only in a leaky bucket.

ARISTOTLE ONASSIS
Greek millionaire
quoted in Esquire 1969
After a certain point money is meaningless. It ceases to be the goal. The game is what counts.

JACKIE ONASSIS
International socialite 1971
You know everyone talks about how rich I am. I'm not really that rich. I have a few thousand in my current account, some savings, a few stocks and bonds . . . of course there are a lot of things I can charge to Olympic Airways. Except for my personal possessions, I have exactly $5,200 in the bank. I just charge everything to Olympic Airways.
on being accused of a $30,000 annual clothes bill . . .
I couldn't spend that much unless I wore sable underwear.

DOROTHY PARKER
British writer
The two most beautiful words in the English language are 'Cheque Enclosed'.

C. NORTHCOTE PARKINSON
American historian
'Inlaws and Outlaws' 1962
Expenditure rises to meet income.

HESKETH PEARSON
British biographer
'The Marrying Americans' 1961
There is no stronger craving in the world than that of the rich for titles, except that of the titled for riches.

TOM PETTY
American rock star
The more you get, the more you get.

MICHAEL PHILIPS
American economist
The Seven Laws of Money 1974
Money will come when you are doing the right thing.

J. B. PRIESTLEY
British writer
'I Have Been Here Before'
It's not really worth much – being rich – too much money seems to take the taste and colour out of things. It oughtn't to do, but it does, damn it!

MARIO PUZO
American novelist
Esquire 1976
Not having to worry about money is almost like not having to worry about dying.

NADKISHORE RAM
Indian millionaire 1979
A million today doesn't go very far.

AYN RAND
American writer
Wealth is the product of man's capacity to think.

TONY RANDALL
American film actor
quoted in Playboy 1974
Compassion is a luxury of the affluent.

RONALD REAGAN
American politician
The taxpayer, that's someone who works for the federal government but doesn't have to take a civil service examination.

JACK RICHARDSON
American writer
Esquire 1965
Wherever dice are thrown or cards are

shuffled the Dark Ages get another turn on this planet.

JOHNNY ROTTEN (John Lydon)
British rock star
You can get money if you want it. You can get whatever you want. It's called effort. It doesn't take much – just a lot of guts, in which the majority of the general public seem to be lacking.

GEORGE SANDERS
British film star
What can you say about bills? Curse them if you will, but pay them you must.

JEAN-PAUL SARTRE
French philosopher
'The Words' 1964
The poor don't know that their function in life is to exercise our generosity.

FRANK SEDGEMAN
Australian tennis player 1966
Nobody *gives* you any money in this life.

PETER SELLERS
British film star
After starring in the film of Terry Southern's 'Magic Christian'
People will swim through shit if you put a few bob in it.

NEIL SIMON
American playwright
Newsweek 1970
Money brings some happiness. But after a certain point it just brings more money.

LOGAN PEARSALL SMITH
American essayist
in 'The Faber Book of Aphorisms' 1964
There are few sorrows, however poignant, in which a good income is of no avail.

To suppose, as we all suppose, that we could be rich and not behave the way the rich behave, is like supposing that we could drink all day and stay sober.

LORD SNOW
British writer
The Observer 1977
Money is not so important as a pat on the head.

LIONEL STANDER
American actor
Playboy 1967
Anyone who lives within his means suffers from a lack of imagination.

ROD STEWART
British rock star
What am I supposed to do with the money I earn? Give it back?

TOM STOPPARD
British playwright 1974
I have always treated money as the stuff with which one purchases time.

JACQUELINE SUSANN
American writer
Money is applause.

ELIZABETH TAYLOR
British film star
on being given the Krupp Diamond by Richard Burton 1968
I have a lust for diamonds, almost like a disease.

MARGARET THATCHER
British politician
quoted in The Spectator 1980
No one would remember the Good Samaritan if he only had good intentions. He had money as well.

Never in the history of human credit has so much been owed.

RAVI TIKKOO
Indian millionaire
after buying house for £500,000 1973
I cannot spend days haggling, I saw it, I liked it and I bought it.

letter to The Times, 1975
Why do they call it a floating pound when all it does is sink?

DALTON TRUMBO
American screenwriter
Never steal more than you actually need, for the possession of surplus money leads to extravagance, foppish attire, frivolous thought.

SOPHIE TUCKER
American actress
I have been poor and I have been rich. Rich is better.

ANDY WARHOL
American artist
'From A to B and Back Again' 1975
Cheques aren't money.

What we're all looking for is someone who doesn't live there, just pays for it.

DARRELL WINFIELD
'The Marlboro Man' 1977
The richest man on earth is a cowboy in town.

GEORGE WOODS
American banker 1966
A banker without money is like a doctor without pills.

Crime

EARL OF ARRAN
British journalist
New York Times 1962
It's not the people in prison who worry me. It's the people who aren't.

ALAN BARTHOLEMEW
Australian penologist
The Bulletin 1970
Prisons as they are do not teach a person to live in society – they teach him to live in prison.

'BONNIE AND CLYDE'
Warner Bros 1967 screenplay by David Newman and Robert Benton
Warren Beatty: We rob banks.

JIMMY BRESLIN
American writer
quoted in Sunday Times 1970
The first requisite a gangster must bring to his work is an unwillingness to work. If they weren't being gangsters they'd be out digging ditches. They'd rather shoot someone than punch a time clock.

ANTHONY COLLINGWOOD
British butler
to the judge who had just sentenced him to six
years jail for theft, 1973
I am much obliged, my lord.

'COOLHAND LUKE'
Warner Bros 1967 screenplay by Donn Pearce
and Frank Pierson, from novel by Donn Pearce
Strother Martin: What we've got here is
a failure to communicate.

QUENTIN CRISP
British author
'The Naked Civil Servant' 1968
Mass murderers are simply people who
have had *enough*.

TONY CURTIS
American film star
after portraying him on film, 1967
There's a bit of the Boston Strangler in
everyone.

ROBERT LINDNER
American psychoanalyst
in 'Close-Up' by John Gruen 1967
We are all criminals – it's a matter of
degree. Crime is as human as being
charitable. Of course we must have
tribal laws. But crime, crime is like art
and the artist has always understood the
criminal. The fear of the criminal is the
same as the fear of the artist: both are
terrified of exposure.

JOHN McVICAR
British criminal
The Observer 1979
Being a thief is a terrific life, but the
trouble is they do put you in the nick for
it.

MALCOLM X
American radical
'Autobiography' 1965
There shouldn't be bars. Behind bars, a
man never reforms. He will never forget.
He will never get completely over the
memory of the bars.

HENRY MILLER
American writer
'The Air-Conditioned Nightmare' 1945
The study of crime begins with oneself.

A prisoner has no sex. He is God's own
eunuch.

JESSICA MITFORD
British writer
'The American Prison Business' 1971
When is conduct a crime and when is a
crime not a crime? When Somebody Up
There – a monarch, a dictator, a Pope,
a legislator – so decrees.

HUEY P. NEWTON
American radical
The prison cannot be victorious, because
walls, bars and guards cannot conquer
or hold down an idea.

ENOCH POWELL
British politician 1961
It may not be a popular view, but I
would dare to say that prisons are our
most important and also our most defi-
cient social service.

L. A. J. QUETELET
Belgian statistican
Society . . . prepares crimes, criminals
are only the instruments necessary for
executing them.

MAX STIRNER
The state calls its own violence law, but
that of the individual, crime.

WILLIE 'THE ACTOR' SUTTON
American criminal
in 'I, Willie Sutton' 1953
It is a rather pleasant experience to be
alone in a bank at night.

J. D. TANGEY
Australian penologist
Nine out of ten juvenile delinquents are
just inferior.

VINCENT 'BIG VINNIE' TERESA
American criminal 1977
I know what the Mafia can do to a man
who has crossed them. One day you
wake up with your head in one room
and your legs in another.

'TOM JONES'
United Artists 1963 screenplay by John Os-
borne, based on Henry Fielding novel
Michael Macliammoir: A generous man
is merely a fool in the eyes of a thief.

JOE VALACHI
American criminal 1963
You live by the gun and knife and die by the gun and knife.

Advertising

CRISTOBAL BALENCIAGA
Spanish couturier
in Sunday Telegraph 1968
If you want publicity – add a touch of vulgarity.

BRUCE BARTON
American advertising man
Reader's Digest 1955
Advertising is the very essence of democracy.

If advertising encourages people to live beyond their means, so does matrimony.

Town & Country 1955
Good times, bad times, there will always be advertising. In good times people want to advertise, in bad times they have to.

JOHN BERGER
British art critic
'Ways of Seeing'
Oil painting, before it was anything else, was a celebration of private property. As an art-form it derived from the principle that you are what you have. It is a mistake to think of advertising publicity supplanting the visual art of post-Renaissance Europe; it is the last moribund form of that art.

BILL BERNBACH
American advertising man
quoted in 'Madison Avenue, USA' by Martin Mayer, 1958
Advertising isn't a science. It's persuasion. And persuasion is an art.

HUGH M. BEVILLE JR.
American TV executive 1954
In advertising there is a saying that if you can keep your head while all those around you are losing theirs – then you just don't understand the problem.

DANIEL J. BOORSTIN
American writer
'The Image' 1962
The deeper problems connected with advertising come less from the unscrupulousness of our 'deceivers' than from our pleasure in being deceived; less from the desire to seduce than from the desire to be seduced.

STEWART H. BRITT
American advertising consultant
New York Herald Tribune 1956
Doing business without advertising is like winking at a girl in the dark. You know what you're doing but no one else does.

KENNETH BROMFIELD
American advertising artist
'Advertiser's Weekly' 1962
From any cross section of ads, the general advertiser's attitude would seem to be: If you are a lousy, smelly, idle, underprivileged and over-sexed status-seeking neurotic moron, give me your money.

CHARLES BROWER
American advertising executive 1958
There is no such thing as 'soft sell' and 'hard sell'. There is only 'smart sell' and 'stupid sell'.

TRUMAN CAPOTE
American writer
quoted in Esquire 1971
A boy's gotta hustle his book.

FAIRFAX CONE
American advertising executive
Christian Science Monitor 1963
Advertising is what you do when you can't go to see somebody. That's all it is.

JERRY DELLA FEMINA
American advertising executive
'From Those Wonderful Folks Who Gave You Pearl Harbor' 1970
Advertising is the most fun you can have with your clothes on.

Oui 1981
Everyone has a button. If enough people have the same button you have a successful ad and a successful product.

NORMAN DOUGLAS
British author
'South Wind'
You can tell the ideals of a nation by its advertisements,

WILLIAM FEATHER
American businessman
'The Business of Life' 1949
The philosophy behind much advertising is based on the old observation that every man is really two men – the man he is and the man he wants to be.

BERNICE FITZGIBBON
American businesswoman
'Macy's, Gimbels & Me' 1967
A good ad should be like a good sermon; it must not only comfort the afflicted, it also must afflict the comfortable.

MARION HARPER JR.
American advertising executive
New York Herald Tribune 1960
Advertising is found in societies which have passed the point of satisfying the basic animal needs.

ALAN HARRINGTON
American writer
'Life in the Crystal Palace' 1960
There are a million definitions of public relations. I have found it to be the craft of arranging the truth so that people will like you.

HARRY HENRY
'Motivation Research' 1958
In the fields of marketing and advertising, statistics are like bikinis: they reveal a good deal that is both interesting and instructive, but they usually conceal what is really vital.

ALDOUS HUXLEY
British writer
quoted in Jeremy Tunstall 'The Advertising Man' 1964
It is far easier to write ten passably effective sonnets, good enough to take in the not too enquiring critic, than to write one effective advertisement that will take in a few thousand of the uncritical buying public.

MICK JAGGER &
KEITH RICHARD
British rock composers
'Satisfaction'
When I'm watching my TV / and that man comes on and tells me / how white my shirts can be. / Well, he can't be a man / 'Cos he doesn't smoke / The same cigarettes as me. (Essex Music)

LUDOVIC KENNEDY
British journalist
'Advertiser's Weekly' 1958
Research men in advertising are really blind men groping in a dark room for a black cat that isn't there.

STEPHEN LEACOCK
British humorist
Advertising may be described as the science of arresting the human intelligence long enough to get money from it.

JOSEPH E. LEVINE
American film producer
You can fool all the people all of the time if the advertising is right and the budget is big enough.

GEORGE LOIS
American art director
quoted in 'The Dictionary of Visual Language' Philip Thompson and Peter Davenport 1980
Without the visual cliché, there would be virtually no communication on the printed page or on TV.

'The Art of Advertising' 1977
Most advertising is absolutely awful, easily forgotten, invisible garbage. *That's* why most advertising is ignored.

MARSHALL McLUHAN
Canadian academic
Advertising Age 1968
Advertising is the greatest art form of the twentieth century.

'The Mechanical Bride' 1962
The world in which Advertisement dwells is a one-day world . . . the average man is invited to slice his life into a series of one-day lives, regulated by the clock of fashion.

ALAN H. MEYER
Marketing/Communications 1970
The best ad is a good product.

ROBERT MORLEY
British actor and wit
Time 1978
Commercials are the last things in life you can count on for a happy ending.

MALCOLM MUGGERIDGE
British journalist
Esquire 1968
In love . . . there is always one who embraces and one who extends the cheek. So also with publicity. In this field there is but a single shore against which all minds – acute and obtuse, sophisticated and un-sophisticated – must beat. It is called cupidity.

'Newsweek' 1967
In the ad biz, sincerity is a commodity bought and paid for like everything else.

DAVID OGILVY
British advertising executive
quoted in 'Madison Avenue, USA', by Martin Mayer 1958
Advertising is the place where the selfish interests of the manufacturer coincide with the interests of society.

indoctrination booklet for employees:
Content is more important than form. What you say in advertising is more important than how you say it.

New York Herald Tribune 1956
The consumer is not a moron. She is *your* *wife*. And she is grown up.

1978
I don't think politicians should be sold like tubes of toothpaste . . . political advertising is the most dishonest in the world.

You cannot bore people into buying your product. You must interest them into buying it. You cannot save souls in an empty church.

GEORGE ORWELL
British essayist
Advertising is the rattling of a stick inside a swill bucket.

SHELBY PAGE
New York Times 1968
The number of agency people required to shoot a commercial on location is in direct proportion to the mean temperature of the location.

ENOCH POWELL
British politician 1965
The professional politician can sympathise with the professional advertiser. Both must resign themselves to a low public estimation of their veracity and sincerity.

ROSSER REEVES
American advertising executive
Reality in Advertising 1961
The true role of advertising is exactly that of the first salesman hired by the first manufacturer – to get business away from his competitors.

EDGAR A. SHOAFF
quoted in 'Peter's Quotations' by Laurence J. Peter 1977
Advertising is the art of making whole lies out of half truths.

ARNOLD TOYNBEE
British historian
Playboy 1967
Pushing sales by advertising is propagating what Plato called 'the lie in the soul'. It is substituting the 'image' of things for the truth about them – in fact a campaign of subversion against intellectual honesty and moral integrity.

JEREMY TUNSTALL
British writer
'The Advertising Man' 1964
It has been said that Public Relations is the art of winning friends and getting people under the influence.

Advertising can't sell any product; it can only help to sell a product the people want to buy.

E. S. TURNER
British writer
'The Shocking History of Advertising' 1952
Advertising, after all, is the mirror of man, and man has never been in serious danger of becoming bogged down in grace.

Advertising is the whip which hustles humanity up the road to the Better Mousetrap. It is the vision which reproaches man for the paucity of his desires.

ARNA-MARIA WINCHESTER
Australian actress 1972
In advertising terms, an intellectual is anybody who reads a morning newspaper.

JACK WYNNE-WILLIAMS
British advertising executive 1969
There is a tendency in advertising people to fall in love with their own advertising.

Architects

MAX ABRANOVITZ
American architect
'Contemporary Architects' 1980
A building or a space should make one feel that a thought is within it, that it is more than a shelter, as a good book is more than words put together, as music is more than an arrangement of notes.

SIR OVE ARUP
British structural engineer/designer
'Contemporary Architects' 1980
When engineers and quantity surveyors discuss aesthetics, and architects study what cranes can do, we are on the right road.

in The Architects Journal 1966
Architecture has been defined as 'building plus delight'.

YOSHINOBU ASHIHARA
Japanese architect
'Contemporary Architects' 1980
Architecture is the art of creating a space.

NANCY BANKS SMITH
British journalist
The Guardian 1979
In my experience, if you have to keep the lavatory door shut by extending your left leg, it's modern architecture.

MARCEL BREUER
Hungarian architect
'Contemporary Architects' 1980
Shall we attempt to condense the central issue facing architecture today into one

sentence? Colours which you can see with ears; sounds to see with eyes; the void you touch with your elbows; the taste of space on your tongue; the fragrance of dimensions; the juice of stone.

HENRYK BUSZKO &
ALEKSANDER FRANTA
Polish architects
'Contemporary Architecture' 1980
The architect is a specialist, designing space for man in accordance with nature.

Architecture is planned environmental conditioning and the architect's task is to design space for human needs – biological, functional and psychological.

SIR WINSTON CHURCHILL
British statesman
Time 1960
We shape our buildings, thereafter they shape us.

CYRIL CONNOLLY
British critic
'The Unquiet Grave' 1945
Slums may well be breeding grounds of crime, but middle class suburbs are incubators of apathy and delirium.

JAMES CUBITT
British architect
'Contemporary Architects' 1980
Architecture is significant only in its response to specific needs.

FATHER JOHN CULKIN S. J.
American priest
'A Handful of Postulates' 1966
We shape our tools and thereafter they shape us. (cf. Winston Churchill)

HARALD DEILMANN
German architect
'Contemporary Architects' 1980
Architecture is mainly a question of overcoming certain practical problems.

ERNEST DIMNET
French writer
'What We Live By'
Architecture, of all the arts, is the one which acts the most slowly, but the most surely, on the soul.

PHILIP DOWSON
British architect
'Contemporary Architects' 1980
Architecture requires us continually to reinterpret and revalue technology in human and social terms.

WERNER DUTTMANN
German architect
'Contemporary Architects' 1980
If interpretation becomes necessary, architecture may have failed.

CRAIG ELLWOOD
American architect
'Contemporary Architects' 1980
The essence of architecture is the inner-relation and intercation of mass, space, place and line. The purpose of architecture is to enrich the joy and drama of living. The spirit of architecture is its truthfulness to itself.

RICHARD ENGLAND
Maltese architect
'Contemporary Architects' 1980
Modern man is born in a clinic and dies in a clinic. Is it therefore not surprising that he should spend the intermediate period between these two paramount events of his life in utterly soulless clinical environments?

ARTHUR ERICKSON
Canadian architect
'Contemporary Architects' 1980
Life is rich, always changing, always challenging, and we architects have the task of transmitting into wood, concrete, glass and steel, of transforming human aspirations into habitable and meaningful space.

CHRIS FAWCETT
British architecture critic
'Contemporary Architects' 1980
A building is a string of events belonging together.

ROBERT GEDDES
American architect
'Contemporary Architects' 1980
Architecture arises out of our need to shelter the human animal in a spatial environment and to enclose the social animal in a group space. In this sense architecture serves our institutions and expresses the values of our culture.

ERNO GOLDFINGER
British architect
'Contemporary Architects' 1980
A particle is snatched from space, rhythmically modulated by membranes dividing it from surrounding chaos: that is Architecture.

WALTER GROPIUS
German architect
Sunday Times 1960
The car is the greatest problem for architecture.

CHARLES GWATHMEY
American architect
'Contemporary Architects' 1980
The transcendence of accommodation is the difference between the art of architecture and building.

HIROSHI HARA
Japanese architect
'Contemporary Architects' 1980
The basic nature of architecture is in its holes.

RON HERRON
British architect
'Contemporary Architects' 1980
When you are looking for a solution to what you are told in an architectural problem – remember, it may not be a building.

TAO HO
Chinese architect
'Contemporary Architects' 1980
Good architecture is like a piece of beautifully composed music crystallized in space that elevates our spirits beyond the limitation of time.

ARATA ISOZAKI
Japanese architect
'Contemporary Architects' 1980
Architecture is a machine for the production of meaning.

PHILIP JOHNSON
American architect
Esquire 1974
When things are built they should be put in mothballs.

The architect is the servant of society, of the style and of the mores, of the baits, of the customs, of the demands of the time in which he works.

I don't believe that architecture is ennobling . . . to me, it's merely a matter of kicks.

New York Times 1964
Architecture is the art of how to waste space.

REM KOOLHAAS
Dutch architect
'Delirious New York' 1978
Postwar architecture is the accountants' revenge on the prewar businessmen's dreams.

KISHO KUROKAWA
Japanese architect
'Contemporary Architects' 1980
Architecture (is) a theatre stage setting where the leading actors are the people, and to dramatically direct the dialogue between these people and space is the techique of designing.

SIR DENYS LASDUN
British architect
'Contemporary Architects' 1980
Architecture is a social art and only makes sense as the promoter and extender of human relations.

LE CORBUSIER
(Charles Edouard Jeanneret)
French architect
quoted in The Times 1965
The materials of city planning are sky, space, trees, steel and cement in that order and in that hierarchy.

The house . . . a machine for living.

ADOLF LOOS
American architect
Architecture provokes spiritual reactions in man . . . the mission of architects is to make these explicit.

WILLIAM O. MEYER
South African architect
'Contemporary Architects' 1980
Architecture means the thoughtful housing of the human spirit in the physical world.

COLIN NAYLOR
American architect
'Contemporary Architects' 1980
Architecture is more than a reflective act of civilisation. It is a regenerative force.

CLAES OLDENBERG
Danish artist
I saw the bathroom fixtures as a kind of American Trinity.

YOKO ONO
Japanese artist
Esquire 1969
They should turn everywhere into a museum. It is a museum, they just need to put a label on it all.

CEDRIC PRICE
British architect 1975
The reason for architecture is to encourage people . . . to behave, mentally and physically, in ways they had previously thought impossible.

RALPH RAPSON
American architect
'Contemporary Architects' 1980
Develop an infallible technique and then place yourself at the mercy of inspiration.

MIES VAN DER ROHE
American architect
quoted in Sunday Times 1971
I see no reason to invent a new architecture every Monday morning. I don't want to be interesting – I want to be good.

quoted in New York Herald Tribune obituary, 1969
Architecture is the will of an epoch translated into space.

in 'Mies van der Rohe' by Werner Blaser 1965
Architecture has little or nothing to do with the invention of interesting forms or of personal inclinations. True architecture is always objective and is the expression of the inner structure of our time from which it stems.

GUSTAVO DE ROZA
Canadian architect
'Contemporary Architects' 1980
Architecture is the art of resolving our needs for physical shelter harmoniously with the environment, while responding to visual aspirations, thus contributing to our cultural heritage.

EERO SAARINEN
Finnish architect
Time 1956
Always design a thing by considering it in its larger context: a chair in a room, a room in a house, a house in an environment, an environment in a city plan.

Architecture is the total of man's manmade physical surroundings. The only thing I leave out is nature. You might say it is manmade nature. It is the total of everything we have around us. . . It is man's total physical surroundings, outdoors and indoors.

RICHARD SEIFERT
British architect 1974
There aren't in fact many individual buildings which need to be preserved.

SIR BASIL SPENCE
British architect 1966
Slums have their good points, they at least have a community spirit and solve the problem of loneliness.

PAUL THIRY
American architect
'Contemporary Architects' 1980
Buildings should be good neighbours.

ALDO VAN EYCK
Dutch architect
What we need is to be at home – wherever we are. As long as home is somewhere else, there will be no question of real participation. Architecture must extend these narrow borderlines; persuade them to loop into realms, articulated *in-between* realms.

Architecture need do no more than assist man's 'home-coming'. Since I like to identify architecture with whatever it can effect in human terms, I like to think of it as the constructed counter-form of perpetual homecoming. When I speak of house or city as a bunch of places, I imply that you cannot leave a real place without entering another, if it is a real 'bunch'. Departure must mean entry.

Places remembered and places anticipated dovetail in the temporal span of the present. They constitute the real perspective of space.

FRANK LLOYD WRIGHT
American architect
quoted in Manchester Guardian 1959
We should learn from the snail: it has devised a home that is both exquisite and functional.

We are all victims of the rectangle and the slab. We go on living in boxes of stone and brick while the modern world is dying to be born in the discovery that concrete and steel can sleep together.

quoted in Daily Express 1959
Very few architects know anything about architecture. For 500 years architecture has been a phoney.

Sunday Times 1957
Architecture is the frame of human existence. Architecture is the only record you can read now of those civilisations which have passed into the distance.

A doctor can bury his mistakes, but an architect can only advise his client to plant vines.

Publishing

IMAMU AMIRI BARAKA
(LeRoi Jones)
American playwright
'Home' 1966
Publishers are usually not very intelligent, or they might be intelligent, but it's usually hard to tell. Publishers don't publish a lot of fine books they should publish.

CASS CANFIELD
American publisher
Esquire 1969
The good editor or publisher is . . . part chameleon, part humming-bird, tasting every literary flower, and part warrior ant.

JOHN FARRAR
American editor
'What Happens in Book Publishing' 1957
Great editors do not discover nor produce great authors; great authors create and produce great publishers.

PAUL HAMLYN
British publisher 1968
Fiction is the most uncreative form of publishing.

MICHAEL JOSEPH
British publisher
The Observer 1949
Authors are easy to get on with – if you are fond of children.

ARTHUR KOESTLER
British philosopher
A publisher who writes is like a cow in a milkbar.

FAIR COMMENT

JAMES AGATE
British critic
on Lord Olivier
A comedian by instinct and a tragedian by art.

ANONYMOUS
Fleet Street journalist on Pierre Trudeau, Canadian Prime Minister, 1969
The greatest thing in political circles since Christine Keeler.

ANONYMOUS
member of audience at Bob Dylan concert 1966
Dylan makes a person think, even if that person doesn't know what he's thinking about.

ANONYMOUS
Hollywood Wit on Bette Davis
Nobody's as good as Bette when she's bad.

ANONYMOUS
Sociologist quoted in 'Bootleggers' by K. Allsop
Gangsters . . . did more advertising of the Cadillac as a fundamental part of the American way of life than General Motors ever did.

ANDRE BAZIN
French critic
Cahiers du Cinéma 1957
Bogart is the man with a past. When he comes into a film it is already the morning after.

CONSTANCE BENNETT
American film actress
on Marilyn Monroe
There's a broad with her future behind her.

RONALD BLYTHE
British writer
The Listener 1979 on Groucho Marx . . .
What Groucho preached was a life without a script.

JACOB BRONOWSKI
British scientist
'The Ascent of Man' 1975
Einstein was a man who could ask immensely simple questions. And what his work showed is that when the answers are simple too, then you can hear God thinking.

BILLY CARTER
brother of President Jimmy Carter
on his Presidential brother 1976
There's not much difference between Jimmy and George Wallace on basic things.

DAVE CHASEN
Hollywood restaurateur
on Humphrey Bogart
Bogey's a hell of a nice guy until 11.30 pm. After that he thinks he's Bogart.

JEAN COCTEAU
French writer and film director
on Marlene Dietrich
A frigate, a figurehead, a Chinese fish, a lyrebird, a legend and a wonder.

on Orson Welles
A kind of giant with a child-like face, a tree filled with birds and shadows, a dog who has snapped his chain and lies in the flowerbeds, an active idler, a wise fool, isolation surrounded by humanity, a student who dozes in class, a strategist who pretends to be drunk when he wants to be left in peace.

CYRIL CONNOLLY
British critic
'The Evening Colonnade' On George Orwell
. . .
He would not blow his nose without moralising on conditions in the handkerchief industry.

CONSTANCE CUMMINGS
on Aneurin Bevan, quoted in Michael Foot's 'Aneurin Bevan' . . .
He was like a fire in a room on a cold winter's day.

SALVADOR DALI
Spanish artist
on Lord Olivier
I see him as a rhinoceros.

BRIAN EPSTEIN
British rock manager
on The Beatles 1963
We are the antidote, the medicine men dispensing the balm for a very sick society. We are selling a kind of canned amnesia. But don't be taken in – the Beatles' music is really saccharined anarchy. They're saying 'Go to hell' tunefully. I have an uneasy feeling that every time they get a big hand they return the compliment with two fingers.

LESLIE FIEDLER
American critic
proposing his own epitaph Time 1978
He was nothing if not ambivalent.

GERALD GARDNER
American writer
'Robert Kennedy in New York'
That was the Kennedy way: you bit off more than you could chew and then you chewed it.

SAM GOLDWYN
American film producer
on Charlie Chaplin
Chaplin is no businessman – all he knows is that he can't take anything less.

on Freud
The greatest love specialist in the world.

ROBERT GOODMAN
American political planner
on Spiro Agnew 1966
He was a beautiful, beautiful body, and we were selling sex.

DICK GREGORY
American radical comedian
On Malcolm X . . .
He spoke like a poor man and walked like a king.

TOM HAYDEN
American radical
'Trial' 1971
The Weathermen . . . were not the conscience of their generation, but more like its id.

MOHAMMAD HEIKAL
Arab journalist
Nasser knew what he did not want, but not quite what he wanted.

PAULINE KAEL
American critic
quoted in Esquire 1969
Godard is making documentaries of the future in the present.

GENE KELLY
American film star
on Fred Astaire quoted in Esquire 1976
I'm the truck driver, he's the aristocrat.

JACQUELINE KENNEDY
on her late husband John Kennedy 1963
Now he is a legend when he would have preferred to be a man.

JOHN LENNON
British rock star
on Yoko Ono
As usual there's a great woman behind every idiot.

CLARE BOOTHE LUCE
American diplomat
on Greta Garbo
A deer in the body of a woman, living resentfully in the Hollywood zoo.

EDGAR LUSTGARTEN
British journalist
on Robert Boothby
He could make the most ridiculous statements sound as if they'd been inscribed on tablets brought down from the mountain.

LOUIS B. MAYER
American film producer
on John Wayne
Wayne has an endless face and he can go on forever.

KERRY PACKER
Australian entrepreneur 1979
Ghengis Khan was not exactly lovable, but I suppose he is my favourite historical character because he was damned efficient.

LESTER PEARSON
Canadian politician
Time 1971 on Dean Acheson
Not only did he not suffer fools gladly, he did not suffer them at all.

PRINCE PHILIP
1966
I don't know whether Churchill enjoyed making speeches, but he looked as if he did.

REX REED
American journalist 1972
If a swamp alligator could talk, it would sound like Tennessee Williams.

WILLIAM REES MOGG
British editor
The Times 1980
To have published an obituary of Tom Driberg without mentioning homosexuality would have been like publishing an obituary of Maria Callas without mentioning opera.

A.L. ROWSE
British academic
The Observer 1971
Shakespeare is the sexiest great writer in the language.

STEPHEN SPENDER
British poet
on W. H. Auden's face
A wedding cake left out in the rain.

KENNETH TYNAN
British critic
on Noel Coward, The Observer 1973
Coward invented the concept of cool. And if his face suggested an old boot, it was unquestionably hand-made.

on Greta Garbo
What, when drunk one sees in other women, one sees in Garbo sober.

RAOUL WALSH
American film director
on seeing the young John Wayne
Dammit, the sonofabitch looked like a man.

NATIONS

United Kingdom

DEAN ACHESON
American Secretary of State 1962
Britain has lost an empire and not yet found a role.

CLEMENT ATTLEE
British Prime Minister
Time 1950
I think the British have the distinction above all other nations of being able to put new wine into old bottles without bursting them.

SIR THOMAS BEECHAM
British conductor 1961
The British do not care much for music, but they do like the noise it makes.

ALAN BENNETT
British playwright
'The Old Country'
They are the most embarrassed people in the world, the English. You cannot look each other in the face. . . Is there anyone not embarrassed in England? The Queen perhaps. With the rest it's 'I won't make you feel bad as long as you don't make me feel bad'. That is the social contract. Society is making each other feel better.

QUENTIN CRISP
British writer
'How To Become A Virgin' 1981
Britain cherishes her eccentrics and wisely holds that the function of government is to build a walled garden in which anarchy can flourish.

New York Times 1977
The English think incompetence is the same thing as sincerity.

RALF DAHRENDORF
British academic 1976
I have a feeling that (Britain) is uninhabitable, and therefore people have tried to make it habitable by being reasonable with each other.

GEORGES DUHAMEL
French writer
The Observer 1953
Courtesy is not dead – it has merely taken refuge in Great Britain.

J. K. GALBRAITH
American economist
New York Times 1966
The problem of economics in Britain is very much like that of sex in the United States. Both countries have enormous difficulties in keeping it in perspective.

LORD GOODMAN
British lawyer
in 'Quote and Unquote' 1970
One of the freedoms of the English is freedom from culture.

SIR HUGH GREENE
British TV executive 1968
We British still recognise ourselves in Falstaff – a man who lied, drank, wenched, belched his way through the mean streets and rowdy pubs of his time.

JO GRIMOND
British politician 1966
The attendance at Ascot of the Queen driven up the main course, does nothing to remind the people of Britain just how serious a plight their country is in.

LORD HAILSHAM
British lawyer
Now! 1981
The English regard brains either as a sign of wickedness or of impracticality. Irresponsible, unpredictable, unsafe – these are the words that rise naturally to their lips about people who are cleverer than they are. I am in favour of brains. I think people need them!

1972
The English will never forgive a man for being clever.

MARGARET HALSEY
American writer
'With Malice Toward Some'
The attitude of the English towards English history reminds one a good deal of the attitude of a Hollywood director towards love.

The English never smash in a face. They merely refrain from asking it to dinner.

SIR WILFRID HUGHES
British aristocrat 1967
Communists have taken over England, though nobody knows it. England is lost in a Sargasso Sea of sex, sadism and psychedelics.

JOHN HURT
British actor
Now! 1981
You're allowed to be boring in Britain . . . abroad people expect one to be entertaining.

EDWARD KENNEDY
American politician 1971
It is fair to say that Britain stands towards peace in Northern Ireland today where America stood in SE Asia during the early 1960s.

ROBERT McCRUM
British writer
'In The Secret State'
We are conditioned to spy on other people. The English *are* a secret society – we are programmed for it, for arcane and historical reasons.

MARSHALL McLUHAN
Canadian academic
'The Mechanical Bride' 1951
One matter Englishmen don't think in the least funny is their happy consciousness of possessing a deep sense of humour.

LORD MANCROFT
British politician 1963
The British have never been a spiritually minded people, so they invented cricket to give them some notion of eternity.

GEORGE MIKES
Czech humorist
'How To Be An Alien'
Continental people have sex-lives. The English have hot water bottles.

ROBERT MORLEY
British actor and wit
The Observer 1975
The reason nobody talks in England is because children are taught manners instead of conversation.

MALCOLM MUGGERIDGE
British journalist
Esquire 1961
A ready means of being cherished by the English is to adopt the simple expedient of living a long time.

DAVID ORMSBY-GORE
British diplomat 1962
In the end it may well be that Britain will be honoured by the historians more for the way she disposed of an empire than for the way in which she acquired it.

S. J. PERELMAN
American humorist
on England, 1972
There is such a thing as too much couth.

HARRY SECOMBE
British comedian
on UK crisis 1974
There's always the cloud with the silver lining, though we may well have to sell the silver lining.

DUNCAN SPAETH
quoted in 'The Book of Insults' by Nancy McPhee 1978
I know why the sun never sets on the British Empire – God wouldn't trust an Englishman in the dark.

R. H. TAWNEY
British historian
quoted in The Guardian 1960
It is a commonplace that the characteristic virtue of Englishmen is power of sustained practical activity and their characteristic vice a reluctance to test the quality of that activity by reference to principles. They are incurious as to

theory, take fundamentals for granted, and are more interested in the state of the roads than in their place on the map.

E. P. THOMPSON
British historian
The Observer 1981
We are now approaching a point of crisis which is not fascism but a particularly British form of authoritarianism. For two decades the state has been taking liberties, and these liberties were once ours.

PETER TOWNSEND
Former British diplomat
'Time & Chance' 1978
Most Englishmen have the soul of a but-

ler in them – it is after all only a chance to serve.

HEATHCOTE WILLIAMS
British playwright
'The Speakers' 1964
The English people are the most obscene and indecent people ever allowed to live on the earth's surface by a god in his interests . . . the English are *nice*, *nice* . . . now *Niceness* is the Englishman in a state of suspended animation.

TOM WOLFE
American journalist
Friends 1970
England is a museum of style.

America

COL. EDWIN ALDRIN
Father of astronaut Buzz 1969
Once the American flag is embedded in lunar soil, then we shall see that the dollars were well spent.

JOAN ARMATRADING
British singer
In America you watch TV and think that's totally unreal, then you step outside and it's just the same.

BROOKS ATKINSON
American essayist
'Once Around the Sun' 1951
Americans . . . cheefully assume that in some mystic way love conquers all, that good outweighs evil in the just balance of the universe and that at the eleventh hour something gloriously triumphant will prevent the worst before it happens.

JACQUES BARZUN
American academic
Whoever wants to know the hearts and minds of America had better learn baseball.

ELDRIDGE CLEAVER
American radical
'Soul On Ice' 1968
Americans think of themselves collec-

tively as a huge rescue squad on twenty-four hour call to any spot on the globe where dispute and conflict may erupt.

MARLENE DIETRICH
German film star
In America sex is an obsession, in other parts of the world it is a fact.

GENERAL JAMES DOOLITTLE
American soldier
quoted in Guideposts 1969
One trouble with Americans is that we're fixers rather than preventers.

ALBERT EINSTEIN
German physicist
'Ideas & Opinions' 1954
Life for (the American) is always becoming, never being.

EDGAR Z. FREIDENBERG
American sociologist
'The Vanishing Adolescent' 1951
So much of learning to be an American is learning not to let your individuality become a nuisance.

The growing American characteristically defends himself against anxiety by learning not to become too involved.

ROBERT FROST
American poet
Americans are like a rich father who wishes he knew how to give his son the hardships that made him rich.

PAUL GOODMAN
American writer
'The Community of Scholars' 1962
The organisation of American society is an interlocking system of semi-monopolies notoriously venal, an electorate notoriously unenlightened, misled by a mass media notoriously phoney.

PHILIP GUEDALLA
British writer
attributed
The 20th Century is only the 19th speaking with a slight American accent.

MONTY HALL
American TV game-show compere
You can learn more about America watching one half-hour of 'Let's Make A Deal' than by watching Walter Cronkite for an entire month.

HUGH HEFNER
American publisher 1973
I wanted to put the play and pleasure back into the concept of American living. Americans knew very well how to earn money, but not how to spend it.

CLIVE JAMES
Australian critic
The Observer 1981
It is an American characteristic not to stop running even after you have arrived.

LYNDON B. JOHNSON
American President 1968
America never stands taller than when her people go down on their knees.

JIM KEEHNER
CIA psychologist
New Times 1976
No American who works for the CIA is a spy. A spy is a foreign agent who commits treason.

MURRAY KEMPTON
American journalist
New York Times 1977
America ... An economic system prouder of the distribution of its products than of the products themselves.

HENRY KISSINGER
American diplomat
New York Times 1973
Nothing is more difficult for Americans to understand than the possibility of tragedy.

LOUIS KRONENBERGER
American critic
'Company Manners' 1951
The moving van is a symbol of more than our restlessness, it is the most conclusive possible evidence of our progress.

The American Way is so restlessly creative as to be essentially destructive; the American way is to carry common sense almost to the point of madness.

JOSEPH WOOD KRUTCH
American essayist
'If You Don't Mind My Saying So' 1964
The typical American believes that no necessity of the soul is free, and that there are precious few, if any, which cannot be bought.

LE CORBUSIER
(Charles Edouard Jeanneret)
French architect
'When Cathedrals Were White'
America is full of a violent desire to learn.

WALTER LIPPMANN
American journalist 1966
Because we are neither omniscient nor omnipotent, we, even we Americans, cannot always win.

MARY McCARTHY
American writer
'On The Contrary' 1962
The immense popularity of American movies abroad demonstrates that Europe is the unfinished negative of which America is the proof.

We are a nation of twenty-million bathrooms with a humanist in every tub.

The happy ending is our national belief.

GREIL MARCUS
American critic
'Mystery Train' 1977
Like a good American Robert Johnson lived for the moment and died for the past.

MALCOLM MUGGERIDGE
British journalist
'The Most of Malcolm Muggeridge' 1966
The pursuit of happiness, which American citizens are obliged to undertake, tends to involve them in trying to perpetuate the moods, tastes and attitudes of youth.

The Observer 1969
The ... American tragedy: trying to nourish the imagination on the will's food, of turning art into dollars, love into orgasms, the pursuit of truth into curiosity.

RICHARD NIXON
American politician 1970
America has never been defeated in the proud one hundred and ninety year history of this country and we shall not be defeated in Vietnam.

If you think the US has stood still, who built the largest shopping centre in the world?

LAURENCE J. PETER
Canadian educator
'Peter's Quotations' 1977
America is a country that doesn't know where it is going, but is determined to set a speed record getting there.

J. B. PRIESTLEY
British writer
New Statesman 1971
American civilisation is ... a bloodless extrapolation of a satisfying life.

R. D. ROSEN
American writer
'Psychobabble' New Times 1975
In America, where movements spring up overnight like fastfood outlets, all God's children gotta have ideology.

DORE SCHARY
American film producer
America is a 'happy ending' nation.

KARL SHAPIRO
American writer
'To Abolish Children & Other Essays'
America is the child society *par excellence*, and possibly the only one ever politically arrived at. It is the society of all rights and no obligations, the society of deliberate wreckage and waste, the only society that ever raised gangsterism to the status of myth and murder to the status of tragedy or politics.

GLORIA STEINEM
American feminist
New York Times 1964
Every country has peasants – ours have money.

ADLAI STEVENSON
American politician 1952
In America any boy may become President and I suppose that's just the risk he takes.

Wall Street Journal 1960
With the supermarket as our temple and the singing commercial as our litany, are we likely to fire the world with an irresistible vision of America's exalted purpose and inspiring way of life?

ARNOLD TOYNBEE
British historian 1970
In the number of lives taken and lands laid waste America's score is unhappily far higher than any other country's since the end of World War Two.

HARRY S. TRUMAN
American President 1949
The White House is the finest jail in the world.

JOHN TUNIS
New York Times 1977
Losing is the great American sin.

PETER USTINOV
British actor and wit
Illustrated London News 1968
America is somewhat like Palestine before Christ appeared – a country full of minor prophets.

Time & Tide
In America, through pressure of conformity, there is freedom of choice, but nothing to choose from.

GORE VIDAL
American writer
The more money an American accumulates, the less interesting he becomes.

PHIL WALDEN
American record business executive
That's the old American way – if you've got a good thing, then overdo it.

KATHARINE WHITEHORN
British journalist
'Observations'
Americans, indeed, often seem to be so overwhelmed by their children that they'll do anything for them except stay married to the coproducer.

Travel

NELSON ALGREN
American author
'Chicago: City On The Make'
Chicago . . . it's a joint where the bulls and the foxes live well and the lambs wind up head-down from the hook.

MUHAMMAD ALI
World heavyweight boxing champion 1978
Russia scares me – the people on the buses are so serious they look like they're going to the electric chair.

ANONYMOUS
Israel – Hitler's revenge on the world.

ANONYMOUS SPOKESMAN
for the Australian Toy Trade 1969
Australians are still too conservative for anatomically correct dolls.

ANONYMOUS
quoted in 'Times & Tendencies' by Agnes Repplier
The city is the flower of civilisation. It gives to men the means to make their lives expressive. It offers a field of battle, and it could be made a livable place if its sons would stay and fight for it instead of running away.

JEAN ANOUILH
French playwright
'Cecile' 1949
Everything in France is a pretext for a good dinner.

HANNAH ARENDT
American writer
'On Violence'
The Third World is not a reality, but an ideology.

EDMUND N. BACON
American architect
'Contemporary Architects' 1980
The building of cities is one of man's greatest achievements. The form of his city always has been and always will be a pitiless indicator of the state of his civilisation.

GEORGE BALL
American statesman
Newsweek 1975
The Japanese are a people with a genius for doing anything they set out to do as a matter of national decision.

SAMUEL BECKETT
Irish author
quoted in The Listener 1979
It is suicide to be abroad.

SYBILLE BEDFORD
British writer
Esquire 1964
A part, a large part of travelling is an engagement of the ego against the world. The world is hydra-headed, as old as the rocks and as changing as the sea . . . the ego wants to arrive at places safely and on time.

CHARLES BUKOWSKI
American writer
'Notes of a Dirty Old Man' 1969
Cities are built to kill people, and there are lucky towns and the other kind, mostly the other kind.

TRUMAN CAPOTE
American writer 1961
Venice is like eating an entire box of chocolate liqueurs in one go.

FIDEL CASTRO
Cuban leader
The city is the graveyard of the guerilla.

SIR WINSTON CHURCHILL
British statesman
India is an abstraction. India is no more a political personality than Europe. India is a geographical term. It is no more a united nation than the Equator.

CYRIL CONNOLLY
British critic
'The Unquiet Grave' 1945
No city should be too large for a man to walk out of it in a morning.

EDWARD DAHLBERG
American writer
There is no place to go, and so we travel. You and I; and what for, just to imagine we could go somewhere else.

ELAINE DUNDY
American writer
'The Dud Avocado' 1958
Make voyages. Attempt them. That's all there is.

AVA GARDNER
American film star
talking to Australian pressmen about her film 'On the Beach'. . .
Well, it's about the end of the world and God knows, this place is the absolute end.

CHARLES DE GAULLE
French statesman
How can anyone govern a nation that has 240 different kinds of cheese?

LORD GEDDES
British politician 1966
Tourism is the nearest thing we have in the world today to free trade.

JOHN GUNTHER
American journalist
'Inside Russia Today' 1962
Moscow is the only city where, if Marilyn Monroe walked down the street with nothing on but a pair of shoes, people would stare at her feet first.

SIR PAUL HASLUCK
Australian politician 1969
The Prime Minister won the affection of the African leaders with his grin. The Africans like a grin and a laugh.
during Australia's National Bible Society Week . . . 1971
For nearly two centuries the Bible has had a strong and continuing influence on the life of Australia. It has set the standards for both personal and national behaviour and outlook.

LILLIAN HELLMAN
American playwright
'An Unfinished Woman'
France . . . may be the only country in the world where the rich are sometimes brilliant.

ERNEST HEMINGWAY
American writer
'A Moveable Feast' 1964
If you are lucky enough to have lived in Paris as a young man, then wherever you go for the rest of your life it stays with you, for Paris is a moveable feast.

BARRY HUMPHRIES
Australian comedian 1976
To live in Australia permanently is rather like going to a party and dancing all night with one's mother.

ROBERT INDIANA (Robert Clark)
American artist
inscription on a picture of Selma, Alabama 1966
Just as in the anatomy of man, every nation must have its hind part.

LE CORBUSIER (Charles Edouard Jeanneret)
French architect
quoted beneath his picture in Charlie O's bar, New York City
New York is a catastrophe – but a magnificent catastrophe.

ALISON LURIE
American novelist
As one went to Europe to see the living past, so one must visit Southern California to observe the future.

JONATHAN MILLER
British doctor and writer
Daily Herald 1962
Holidays are an expensive trial of strength. The only satisfaction comes from survival.

LORD MONTGOMERY
British soldier 1966
I have said many times in private conversation that the real danger in Europe is Germany.

JOHN MORGAN
British TV journalist
reporting on California for BBC-TV 1978
I have seen the future and it plays.

ROBERT MORLEY
British actor and wit
on Sydney, Australia 1968
Manchester with a harbour backdrop.

GEORGE MOSCONE
Mayor of San Francisco
Newsweek 1976
I hate to say it, but crime is an overhead you have to pay if you want to live in the city.

LEWIS MUMFORD
American critic
In the city, time becomes visible.

JOSE ORTEGA Y GASSET
Spanish philosopher
in 'The Faber Book of Aphorisms' 1964
What makes a nation great is not primarily its great men, but the stature of its innumerable mediocre ones.

DOROTHY PARKER
American writer
Paris Review 1958
Hollywood money isn't money. It's congealed snow.

The only 'ism' Hollywood believes in is plagiarism.

SHIMON PERES
Israeli politician
Newsweek 1973
Israel is moving from the realm of poetry to the realm of prose.

V. S. PRITCHETT
British critic
'Midnight Oil'
Ireland is really a collection of secret societies.

JONATHAN RABAN
British writer
'Soft City' 1974
The city . . . a natural territory for the psychopath with histrionic gifts.

'Readers' Digest' 1976
In an underdeveloped country don't drink the water, in a developed country, don't breathe the air.

LOU REED
American rock star
'Coney Island Baby'
Remember that the city is a funny place / Something like a circus or a sewer. (Sunbury Music)

JEAN-PAUL SARTRE
French philosopher 1967
Israel is the only country where one can say of someone that he is a Jew without being an anti-semite.

GENE SIMMONS
American rock star
Living in New York is like coming all the time.

MARK STEVENS
Newsweek 1977
In France art is often politics conducted by other means.

IGOR STRAVINSKY
Russian composer
New York Review of Books 1971
The street is the city's parade ground.

SAMUEL TENENBAUM
American academic
New York Times 1971
A city is like a magnet – the bigger it is, the greater the drawing power.

H. B. TURNER
Australian politician 1970
Australia is governed by a hierarchy of hicks.

GOUGH WHITLAM
Australian politician 1971
China is one of the few countries an American President can visit without having to face demonstrations.

EARL WILSON
American columnist
Ladies' Home Journal 1961
If you look like your passport photo, in all probability you need the journey.

Hollywood

FRED ALLEN
American wit
Hollywood is a place where people from Iowa mistake each other for stars.

Hollywood is a great place if you're an orange.

MICHELANGELO ANTONIONI
Italian film director
Sunday Times 1971
Hollywood is like being nowhere and talking to nobody about nothing.

CANDICE BERGEN
American actress
New York Post 1967
Hollywood is like Picasso's bathroom.

BERTOLT BRECHT
German playwright
'Hollywood'
Every day, to earn my daily bread / I go to the market where lies are bought / Hopefully / I take up my place among the sellers.

RAYMOND CHANDLER
American novelist
quoted in 'Raymond Chandler Speaking' ed. Dorothy Gardiner & Katherine S. Walker 1962
If my books had been any worse I would not have been invited to Hollywood, and if they had been any better I would not have come.

PHYLLIS DILLER
American comedienne 1970
Living in Hollywood is like living in a lit cigar butt.

KIRK DOUGLAS
American film star
Esquire 1970
I'm plenty proud of Hollywood . . . I say if you want to grow a plant, put it where there's some good horseshit around to grow it in.

WILLIAM GOLDMAN
American screenwriter 1975
Hollywood pays for silence. If you argue too much you have too much to lose.

JOHN HUSTON
American film director
Hollywood has always been a cage – a cage to catch our dreams.

ALVA JOHNSTON
American journalist
The title 'little Napoleon' in Hollywood is equivalent to the title 'Mister' in any other community.

ANITA LOOS
American writer
A leader of public thought in Hollywood wouldn't have sufficient mental acumen anywhere else to hold down a place in the bread line.

REX REED
American journalist
In Hollywood, if you don't have happiness, you send out for it.

JOHN SCHLESINGER
British film director
New York Times 1975
Hollywood is an extraordinary kind of temporary place.

PETER USTINOV
British actor and wit
Everybody's 1957
Hollywood is like death – the great leveller.

ORSON WELLES
American film director
Hollywood's all right, it's the pictures that are bad.

The Observer 1969
Hollywood is a golden suburb for golf addicts, gardeners, men of mediocrity and satisfied stars. I belong to none of these categories.

WALTER WINCHELL
American columnist
Hollywood is a place where they place you under contract instead of under observation.

Isms

ANDREI AMALRIK
Soviet dissident 1977
Marxism has placed its stake on force – which Marx called the midwife of history. And though the midwife perpetually delivers monsters . . . Marxists never tire of promising that the next child will be a splendid one.

RAYMOND ARON
French academic
'The Opium of the Intellectuals' 1957
Reality is always more conservative than ideology.

BROOKS ATKINSON
American essayist
'Once Around the Sun' 1951
There is a good deal of solemn cant about the common interests of capital and labour. As matters stand, their only common interest is that of cutting each other's throat.

W. H. AUDEN
British poet
Newsweek 1972
Antisemitism is unfortunately not only a feeling which all gentiles at times feel, but also, and this is what matters, a feeling of which the majority of them are not ashamed.

WAYNE R. BARTZ
American writer
in Human Behaviour 1975
The more ridiculous a belief system, the higher the probability of its success.

BRENDAN BEHAN
Irish playwright
The Guardian 1960
An author's first duty is to let down his country.

CHRISTOPHER BOOKER
British journalist
'The Games War' 1981
The real tragedy of Communism is that it so desperately tries to pretend through its glorification of power and organisation and the collective that it can inspire the loftiest feelings, can speak of human dignity, can breathe the language of the soul. And it cannot do this because it denies those very parts of the human personality from which such things derive.

GERALD BRENAN
British writer
'Thoughts in a Dry Season' 1978
The new ideas of one age become the ideologies of the next, by which time they will in all probability be out of date and inapplicable.

LENNY BRUCE
American comedian
'The Essential Lenny Bruce' ed. Cohen 1967
Now a Jew, in the dictionary, is one who is descended from the ancient tribes of Judea . . . but you and I know what a Jew is – One Who Killed Our Lord . . . a lot of people say to me 'Why did you kill Christ?' 'I dunno, it was one of those parties, got out of hand, you know'. We killed him because he didn't want to become a doctor, that's why we killed him.

JOHN CAGE
American musician
Ideas are one thing, and what happens is another.

ALBERT CAMUS
French writer
'The Rebel' 1951
Fascism . . . represents the exaltation of the executioner by the executioner . . . Russian Communism . . . represents the exaltation of the executioner by the victim. The former never dreamed of liberating all men, but only of liberating the few by subjugating the rest. The latter, in its most profound principle, aims at liberating all men by provisionally enslaving them all.

I should like to love my country and still love justice.

CHINESE CHILDREN'S SONG
during the Cultural Revolution
When I Grow Up I Am Determined To Become A Peasant.

SIR WINSTON CHURCHILL
British statesman
Trying to maintain good relations with the Communists is like wooing a crocodile. You do not know whether to tickle it under the chin or to beat it over the head. When it opens its mouth you cannot tell whether it is trying to smile or preparing to eat you up.

The inherent vice of capitalism is the unequal sharing of blessings; the inherent virtue of socialism is the equal sharing of miseries.

E. M. CIORAN
French philosopher
'The Temptation to Exist' 1956
Only at the price of great abdications does a nation become *normal*.

GARY COOPER
American film star 1947
I could never take any of this pinko mouthing very seriously, because I didn't feel it was on the level.

From what I hear about Communism I don't like it because it isn't on the level.

JOAN DIDION
American writer
'The White Album' 1979
To believe in 'the greater good' is to operate, necessarily, in a certain ethical suspension. Ask anyone committed to a marxist analysis how many angels on the head of a pin, and you will be asked in return to never mind the angels, tell me who controls the production of pins.

'DR. STRANGELOVE'
1964 screenplay Stanley Kubrick, Terry Southern and Peter George, based on novel by Peter George
Sterling Hayden: I can no longer sit back and allow Communist infiltration, Communist indoctrination, Communist subversion and the international Communist conspiracy to sap and impurify all of our precious bodily fluids.

JOHN GREGORY DUNNE
American scriptwriter
Atlantic 1971
The territory behind rhetoric is too often mined with equivocation.

WILL & ARIEL DURANT
American historians
The fear of capitalism has compelled socialism to widen freedom, and the fear of socialism has compelled capitalism to increase equality.

PAUL ELDRIDGE
American writer
'Horns of Glass'
Man is ready to die for an idea, provided that idea is not quite clear to him.

E. M. FORSTER
British novelist
'Two Cheers for Democracy' 1951
There lies at the back of every creed something terrible and hard for which the worshipper may one day be required to suffer.

'What I Believe' 1951
Faith, to my mind, is a stiffening process, a sort of mental starch, which ought to be applied as sparingly as possible.

'Two Cheers for Democracy' 1951
If I had to choose between betraying my country and betraying my friend, I hope I should have the guts to betray my country.

R. BUCKMINSTER FULLER
American engineer
Playboy 1972
Faith is much better than belief. Belief is when someone *else* does the thinking.

J. K. GALBRAITH
American economist
'The Affluent Society' 1958
Few things are as immutable as the addiction of political groups to the ideas by which they have once won office.

ANDRE GIDE
French writer
'Journal'
Faith moves mountains. Yes. Mountains of absurdity.

JAMES M. GILLIS
'In This Our Day'
Fanatics seldom laugh. They never laugh at themselves.

GUNTER GRASS
German novelist
The Observer 1962
It is possible, and better, to live without ideals.

HENRY S. HASKINS
American writer
'Meditations in Wall Street'
Known principles are the barbed wire entanglements around the detention camps where our intuitions are restrained from going into warfare.

ROLF HOCHHUTH
German playwright
'The Soldiers' 1967
Men may be linked in friendship. Nations are linked only by interests.

ERIC HOFFER
American philosopher
'The True Believer' 1951
Faith in a holy cause is to a considerable extent a substitute for the lost faith in ourselves.

Mass movements can rise and spread without belief in God, but never without belief in a devil.

ALDOUS HUXLEY
British writer
'Letters of Aldous Huxley' 1971
Either you choose . . . to be a totalitarian fascist . . . and you find yourself involved in the most atrocious military tyranny. Or you choose socialism or communism, and call the resulting totalitarianism by the name of 'democracy' and end up, if you are sensitive and honest, by finding yourself horribly disillusioned. Or finally, you cling to democratic capitalism, and find yourself forced, by the logic of advanced technology, to embrace some form of totalitarianism.

EUGENE IONESCO
French playwright
'Present Past Past Present' 1971
Every ideology is a mythology, a system of conventions. Marxism has been adopted, because force has made it fashionable, because it allows hate.

'Notes and Counter-Notes'
An established form of expression is also a form of oppression.

WILLIAM NORTH JAYME
Newsweek 1973
Scratch a fanatic and you find a wound that never healed.

LYNDON B. JOHNSON
American President 1966
Patriotism too often means concealing a world of error and wrong judgement beneath the flag.

JOHN F. KENNEDY
American president
Inaugural address, 1960
Ask not what your country can do for you, but what you can do for your country.

ARTHUR KOESTLER
British philosopher
The Observer 1963
When all is said and done, one loves one's country not *because* of this or that, but rather, in spite of it all.

STANLEY KUBRICK
American film director 1963
The great nations have always acted like gangsters and the small nations like prostitutes.

PAUL LEAUTAUD
French writer
'Passe-Temps'
Love makes fools, marriage cuckolds and patriotism malevolent imbeciles.

GILBERT LONGDEN
British politician 1967
Since excellence is the first casualty of equality, Socialism is the standard bearer of the second rate.

JOSEPH McCARTHY
American politician
speech 1952
McCarthyism is Americanism with its sleeves rolled.

NORMAN MAILER
American writer
Totalitarianism is the interruption of mood.

The function of socialism is to raise suffering to a higher level.

H. L. MENCKEN
American essayist
'Minority Report' 1956
The objection to a Communist always resolves itself into the fact that he is not a gentleman.

MICHAEL MILES
American writer
'The Radical Probe' 1971
Left politics abhors an ideological vacuum.

'MIRACLE ON 34TH STREET'
20th Century Fox 1947 screenplay by George Seaton, based on story by Valentine Davis
Maureen O'Hara: Faith is believing things when common sense tells you not to.

VICTOR S. NAVASKY
American radical
New York Times 1968
It is better to be attacked by an establishment comrade than to be praised by an outsider.

ANAIS NIN
French novelist
'Diaries' vol.IV 1971
When we blindly adopt a religion, a political system, a literary dogma, we become automatons. We cease to grow.

GEORGE ORWELL
British essayist
'Notes On Nationalism' 1945
Nationalism is power hunger tempered by self-deception.

ALAN L. OTTEN
in 'The Book of Laws' by Henry Faber 1980
The length of a country's national anthem is inversely proportional to the importance of that country.

CESARE PAVESE
Italian novelist
in 'The Faber Book of Aphorisms' 1964
Every zeal or passion brings with it a superstitious conviction of having to face a day of reckoning: even the zeal of a disbeliever.

EVITA PERON
Argentine politician
Time 1951
Without fanaticism we cannot accomplish anything.

JOHN QUAIL
British writer
'The Slow Burning Fuse' 1978
It is an unfortunate fact that political theory, no matter how worthy or perceptive, is curiously disembodied; it gives no clues to the passions, the heroisms or the squalid conflicts that it inspired.

JAMES RESTON
American journalist
'Sketches in the Sand' 1967
Nations, like individuals, have to limit
their objectives or take the cons-
equences.

WILL ROGERS
American humorist
'A Rogers Thesaurus' 1962
Any nation is heathen that ain't strong
enough to punch you in the jaw.

BERTRAND RUSSELL
British philosopher
quoted in 'The Faber Book of Aphorisms' 1964
A fanatical belief in democracy makes
democratic institutions impossible.

'Unpopular Essays' 1950
Man is a credulous animal and must
believe *something*. In the absence of good
grounds for belief, he will be satisfied
with bad ones.

GILBERT RYLE
British philosopher
The Listener 1971
Blast any words that end in 'ist' or 'ism'.
They always interfere with any serious
discussion of any subject.

PETER SHAFFER
British playwright
quoted in 'Contemporary Dramatists' 1977
The greatest tragic factor in history is
man's apparent need to mark the intensity of his reaction to life by joining a
band; for a band, to give itself definition
must find a rival or an enemy.

LORD SNOW
British novelist
interviewed on Radio Moscow 1971
Writers are much more esteemed in Russia, they play a much larger part in society than they do in the West. The
advantage of not being free is that people
listen to you.

ALEXANDER SOLZHENITSYN
Russian novelist
The Listener 1979
For us in Russia Communism is a dead
dog, while for many people in the West
it is still a living lion.

I. F. STONE
American journalist 1967
If God, as some now say, is dead, He no
doubt died of trying to find an equitable
solution to the Arab-Jewish problem.

Those who set out nobly to be their
brother's keeper sometimes end up by
becoming his jailer. Every emancipation
has in it the seeds of a new slavery, and
every truth easily becomes a lie.

JOHN SUTRO
British writer
in 'Quote and Unquote' 1970
You can do very little with faith. But
you can do nothing without it.

ARNOLD TOYNBEE
British historian
Playboy 1967
Nationalism is the big enemy of the human race. Technology has made the
world one, and nationalism tries to keep
it apart.

GORE VIDAL
American writer
New York Review of Books 1973
Loyalty and obedience . . . two qualities
that flourish most luxuriantly in the ig-
norant, most dangerously in the fanatic.

LECH WALESA
Polish trade unionist
interviewed by Oriana Fallaci 1981
The hungry hare has no frontiers and
doesn't follow ideologies. The hungry
hare goes where it finds the food. And
the other hares don't block its passage
with the tanks.

ALFRED NORTH WHITEHEAD
British philosopher
A clash of doctrines is not a disaster – it
is an opportunity.

HEATHCOTE WILLIAMS
British playwright
'The Speakers' 1964
Nothing makes sense . . . we're all nut
cases up here talking whether it's rheu-
matism, communism, unimultilateral-
ism, labourism, fascism or any otherism.
There's only one ism today, and that's
moneyism.

SIR WILLIAM YEO
Australian politician
The bloke I hate worse than a Communist is the one who's as near as damn to a Commo but doesn't have the guts to admit it.

THEODORE ZELDIN
British historian
The Listener 1978
The paradox of nationalism is that nations are, first of all, geographical units, but they try to give themselves a spiritual significance, or to distill some kind of unique essence from their history and culture. The image they form of themselves is not always completely in accord with the kind of life they lead in practice.

Race

MUHAMMAD ALI
World heavyweight boxing champion
refusing to serve in Vietnam, 1966...
No Viet Cong ever called me nigger.

SAUL ALINSKY
American radical
A racially integrated community is a chronological term timed from the entrance of the first black family to the exit of the last white family.

RAYMOND ARON
French academic
Racism is the snobbery of the poor.

CLAUDE AVELINE
French writer
'Avec Toi-même'
White, black and yellow men – they all cry salt tears.

JAMES BALDWIN
American writer
Who needs to be integrated into a burning house?

Playboy 1973
The white man . . . is trapped in his own history, a history that he cannot comprehend, and therefore what can I do but love him?

1979
You can't tell a black man by the colour of his skin.

BLACK POWER SLOGAN
Say it out loud, I'm black and I'm proud!

Black is beautiful!

ARTHUR CALWELL
Australian politician
Expounding his anti-immigrant stand...
Two Wongs don't make a white.

GODFREY CAMBRIDGE
American comedian
Esquire 1964
With the Negro's sexual image, how do they have time to write spirituals?

STOKELY CARMICHAEL
American radical
New York Times 1966
I'm *for* the Negro. I'm not *anti* anything.

MARY FRANCIS
Wife of crime writer Dick Francis 1972
You know the phrase 'Black is beautiful' was invented by the whites in South Africa to raise the morale of the black people.

LINTON KWESI JOHNSON
British poet
The S.W.P. are racists, the worst kind of racists – liberal racists. They're the ones who believe they have to *help* blacks. They don't believe blacks can help themselves, can make an indepen-

dant intervention in the political life of this country.

MARTIN LUTHER KING JR.
American activist 1963
I want to be the white man's brother, not his brother-in-law.

DR. PIET KOORNHOF
South African immigration minister 1972
Regardless of how much South Africa may need expertise and skills I will not allow in any person who professes to being an atheist. Tolerance and mutual respect are basic needs if people of different societies are to live in harmony.

ALEXEI KOSYGIN
Russian leader 1971
Some of my best friends are Jews.

WALTER LAQUEUR
American writer
'The History of Zionism' 1972
It was the historical tragedy of Zionism that it appeared on the international scene when there were no longer any empty spaces on the world map.

ARNOLD LEESE
British fascist
slogan 1952
Keep Britain White.

JULIUS LESTER
American writer
Black people have never rioted. A riot is what white people think blacks are involved in when they burn stores.

ADAM CLAYTON POWELL
American politician
Beware of Greeks bearing gifts, coloured men looking for loans and whites who understand the Negro.

ENOCH POWELL
British politician
on immigration, 1968
As I look ahead I am filled with foreboding. Like the Roman, I seem to see the River Tiber foaming with much blood.

after the Brixton riots, 1981
We have seen nothing yet.

PROFESSOR WILLIAM B. SHOCKLEY
American inventor and eugenics theorist
Esquire 1973
Nature has colourcoded groups of individuals so that statistically reliable predictions of their adaptability to intellectually rewarding and effective lives may be made and profitably used by the pragmatic man in the street.

SUSAN SONTAG
American essayist
Partisan Review
The white race is the cancer of human history. It is the white race, and it alone, its ideologies and inventions, which eradicate autonomous civilisations wherever it spreads. It has upset the ecological balance of the planet which now threatens the very existence of life itself.

PROF. C. F. VAN DER MERWE
South African politician
Hate, destruction and Communism, these are the consequences of the black man's nature.

GORE VIDAL
American writer
Esquire 1970
It is not possible to regard our race with anything but alarm. . . From primeval ooze to the stars, we killed anything that stood in our way, including each other.

GRAFFITI

Graffito 1968
Hey, hey, LBJ, how many kids did you
kill today.

Paris 1968
Any view of things that is not strange is
false.

during Paris 'Evenements' 1968
The barricade closes the street but opens
the way.

1969
What do we want? Everything. When do
we want it? Now!

on London's (defunct) 'Revolution' Club
If this is the revolution, why are the
drinks so fucking expensive?

London 1975
God is not dead. He is alive and working
on a much less ambitious project.

during student revolts in France, 1968
Socialism without liberty is the barracks.

in London 1979
If voting changed anything, they'd make
it illegal.

on GI helmets during Vietnam War. . .
We are the unwilling, led by the un-
qualified, doing the unnecessary for the
ungrateful.

You're never alone with schizophrenia.

Death is life's answer to the question
'Why?'

Death is Nature's way of telling you to
slow down.

Death is the greatest kick of all. That's
why they save it till last.

Give me librium or give me meth!

Nanterre University 1968
Je suis Marxiste – tendence Groucho.
(I'm a Marxist – Groucho-style)

Paris 1968
Culture is like jam. The less you have
the more you spread it around.

Nanterre University 1968
The prospect of tomorrow's joy will
never console me for today's boredom.

Paris 1968
A cop sleeps within all of us. He must
be killed.

The only difference between graffiti and
philosophy is the word fuck.

More deviation, less population.

Life is a hereditary disease.

The truth is the safest lie.

Reality is sometimes good for kicks, but
don't let it get you down.

We didn't invent sin. We're just trying
to perfect it.

God is alive. He just doesn't want to get
involved.

Revolution allows the revolutionary to
sublimate his sado-masochistic, neurotic, anal tendencies into a concern for
the working class.

Nostalgia isn't what it used to be.

If you can keep your head when all
about you are losing theirs, perhaps you
have misunderstood the situation.

INDEX

As within the text of the Dictionary I have attempted to offer a 'job description' for as many as possible of those quoted, I have tried here in the Index to provide dates for the majority of the three thousand odd people who have provided the material. Unfortunately, just as some of those I have quoted are unknown to me over and above their 'line', so are the dates of a number of those listed here. I have scoured the *Who's Who* volumes of the world, as well as many additional works of reference to amass as large a number of dates as possible. Some names, inevitably, have no record; others, more irritatingly, are sufficiently long dead to have vanished from contemporary reference lists. As to those included, I have only those same lists as proof of accuracy and I have trusted them accordingly. I hope that here, as with any other vagaries to be found in the Dictionary, the reader will bear with me.

440 Index